Long Island's

Prominent South Shore Families:

Their Estates and Their Country Homes

in the Towns of Babylon and Islip

Raymond E. and Judith A. Spinzia

VirtualBookworm

College Station, Texas

Revised Edition

2021

"Long Island's Prominent South Shore Families: Their Estates and Their Country Homes in the Towns of Babylon and Islip" by Raymond E. and Judith A. Spinzia. ISBN 978-1-63868-032-1.

Library of Congress Control Number on file with publisher.

Published 2007; revised 2021 by Virtualbookworm.com Publishing Inc., P.O. Box 9949, College Station, TX 77842, US. © 2007, 2021, Raymond E. and Judith A. Spinzia. All rights reserved. No part of this publication may be reproduced, stored in a retrieval system, or transmitted in any form or by any means, electronic, mechanical, recording or otherwise, without the prior written permission of Raymond E. and Judith A. Spinzia

Also by Raymond E. and Judith A. Spinzia

Long Island: A Guide to New York's Suffolk and Nassau Counties
(*with* Kathryn Spinzia Rayne)

Long Island's Prominent North Shore Families:
Their Estates and Their Country Homes, Volumes *I* and *II*

Long Island's Prominent Families
in the Town of Hempstead:
Their Estates and Their Country Homes

Long Island's Prominent Families
in the Town of Southampton:
Their Estates and Their Country Homes

Long Island's Prominent Families
in the Town of East Hampton:
Their Estates and Their Country Homes

offered as tribute to our Island
which grows and is nurtured by its people

Table of Contents

Acknowledgments	vi
Factors Applicable to Usage	viii
Introduction	ix
Maps of Long Island Estate Areas	xi
Surname Entries A – Z	1

Appendices:

Architects	395
Civic Activism	403
Estate Names	409
Golf Courses on Former South Shore Estates	417
Landscape Architects	419
Maiden Names	423
Occupations	443
Rehabilitative Secondary Uses of Surviving Estate Houses	457
Statesmen and Diplomats Who Resided on Long Island's South Shore	459
Village Locations of Estates	461
America's First Age of Fortune: A Selected Bibliography	471
Selected Bibliographic References to Individual South Shore Estate Owners	479

Biographical Sources Consulted	501
Maps Consulted for Estate Locations	503
Illustration Credits	505
About the Authors	507

The authors are sincerely indebted to the following for their assistance:

Ruth Albin, Curator, Babylon Village Museum, Village of Babylon Historical and Preservation Society

Maryann Almes, President, Oakdale Historical Society

Victoria Aspinwall, Long Island Studies Institute, Hofstra University, Hempstead, NY

Cathy Ball, Librarian, Long Island Room, Smithtown Library

Wallace W. Broege, former Director, Suffolk County Historical Society Museum, Riverhead, NY

Mary Cascone, Historian, Town of Babylon

Perry Colmore for information on the Vander Ver family.

Christopher M. Collora

James Connell, President, Bayport Heritage Association

Constance Gibson Currie, former President, Sayville Historical Society

Carey Davis, Babylon Village Museum, Village of Babylon Historical and Preservation Society,

Barry Dlouhy, President, Bay Shore Historical Society

Louise Dougher, former Director, Greenlawn–Centerport Historical Association

Frank Giebfried, Director at Large, Bayport–Blue Point Heritage Association

Carl Ilardi, Historian/Archivist, The Admiralty, West Bay Shore, NY

David Kerkhof, Reference Librarian, Suffolk County Historical Society, Riverhead, NY

Thomas A. Kuehhas, former Director, Oyster Bay Historical Society

Gary Lawrance, AIA, Architect

Raymond Lembo, President and Archivist, East Islip Historical Society

Lynn Luttenberger, President, West Islip Historical Society

Richard Martin, Suffolk County Historian, Great River, NY

Rodney G. Marve, Assistant Director, Bay Shore–Brightwaters Public Library

Gasper Merced, Sayville, NY

George J. Munkenbeck, Historian, Town of Islip

Dr. Natalie A. Naylor, Director Emerita, Long Island Studies Institute, Hofstra University, Hempstead, NY

E. Lee North, Historian, Village of Brightwaters

Florence Olsson, Director, Bayport Heritage Association

Eric Gordon Ramsay III, President, Eric Gordon Ramsay, Jr. Associates, LLC, Bay Shore, NY

John S. Rienzo, Jr., Librarian/Archivist, Dowling College, Oakdale, NY

Mark H. Rothenberg, former Senior Reference Specialist and Historian, Suffolk Cooperative Library System and Patchogue – Medford Library

Coleen A. Smisek, Head Librarian, Adult Reference Services, Bay Shore–Brightwaters Public Library

Thomas B. Smith, former Historian, Town of Babylon

Walker Anne, Author and Architectural Historian

Debra Willett, Associate Director, Long Island Studies Institute, Hofstra University, Hempstead, NY

William Zantz for information on the Hawley estate

Alice Zaruka, former President, Babylon Village Museum, Village of Babylon Historical and Preservation Society; current Historian, Village of Babylon

We would especially like to thank:

Frederic Lawrence Atwood, Barbara Gulden Black, Marjorie Wilson Candiano, Elena de Murias, John Vanderveer Gibson, William Greve, Frank Gulden III, Harry W. Havemeyer, Louise Gulden Henriksen, William R. Hulse, Peter G. Johnston, Jr., Matthew Morgan, Helena Parsons Hallock Pless, Eric Gordon Ramsay III, John C. Snedeker, Raymond Joseph Terry, Peter Titus, and Douglas Thomas Yates, Sr. for reviewing entries pertaining to their families and for providing invaluable genealogical information.

Raymond E. and Judith A. Spinzia

Even though an individual may not have used Sr., Jr., I, II, etc., they have been added to the surnames in an attempt to designate relationships and alleviate confusion. In some instances, birth dates have been calculated using the age at the time of death as given in *The New York Times* obituary.

Current street and village designations are given with the exception of Montauk Highway (Route 27A), which changes names several times from West Main Street, Main Street, East Main Street, and South Country Road as it passes through the various villages. To alleviate confusion, we have chosen to use South Country Road, its original name, as the sole designation for the street.

The exact street address of some houses could not be determined due to the diminution of the estates by subdivision. In these cases, the road on which a major portion of the estate bordered has been recorded as the address. It should also be noted that some of the subsequent owners may not have lived in the estate's main house but rather in a service building that had been converted into a residence. To aid in tracing the estate properties, these owners have been included in the hope that this will prove useful to future researchers.

The Spinzias

Introduction

Previously studded with estates and grand hotels, the quiet, year-round villages in the Towns of Babylon and Islip today suggest little of the past and the seasonal frenzy of social activity that was the "Hidden Gold Coast" on the South Shore of Long Island. To many who pick up this volume, the concept of an estate area, a "Gold Coast," in this section of the South Shore of Long Island will be a new concept. In truth it is an old reality; preceding the development of Long Island's North Shore Gold Coast by some forty years. Spending the Spring and Autumn months in this area of western Suffolk County on the land that slopes down to the Great South Bay with the Atlantic Ocean visible on the horizon beyond Fire Island was such a social phenomenon that the *Brooklyn Daily Eagle* and local newspapers announced the rental intentions and seasonal arrivals of families. When houses were sold; when houses were renovated; when new houses were built, that was news.

The South Shore estate owners built their homes, generally more modest than those that would be built in the estate area of the North Shore, conveniently close to the main roads and actually financed railroad spurs to serve the South Shore communities where their homes were located. The plank roads gave way to gravel roads which eventually gave way to paved roads. Families who had moved their households in wagons and carriages and boats soon had automobiles. The arrival of fleets of moving vans heralded the summer season. The seasonal visitors enjoyed the congenial socialization of the seaside environment so much that families who rented soon became families that owned homes to which they escaped from the very different world of the city. Coming out to the Island primarily from Brooklyn and Manhattan, they tended to build near their friends thus establishing streets of country homes that could almost be labeled as "Manhattan streets" and "Brooklyn streets."

The North Shore Gold Coast extended eastward along the Island's North Shore from the Queens / Nassau boundary for approximately twenty-five miles to the Village of Centerport in Suffolk County and some fifteen miles southward from the shoreline of the Long Island Sound, an area of approximately three hundred and seventy-five square miles. The South Shore Gold Coast began at the Nassau / Suffolk border and extended eastward about sixteen miles to the Bayport / Blue Point village boundary and about one mile southward from South Country Road to the shore of the Great South Bay, an area of approximately sixteen square miles. The expanse of the North Shore area and the relative exclusivity of its residents created a significantly different social structure from that of the South Shore.

A closely knit, but ethnically and religiously diverse and tolerant, social and business community evolved on the South Shore as families settled in for the season. They were predominately sugar plantation owners and sugar refiners, merchants, shipping magnets, attorneys, capitalists, and investment bankers. Curtiss–Wright aeroplanes, the New York Central Railroad, Gulden mustard, Domino sugar, Entenmann bakery, Moran tugboats, Adams and Chicle chewing gum, Doxsee clams, Lorillard and American Tobacco, deMurias and Bachia cigars, Abraham and Straus, Arnold and Constable, Singer sewing machines, Bon Ami cleanser, Republic Pictures, and Pinkerton National Detective Agency are names still recognizable today; they were the businesses of South Shore families.

With the notable exceptions of William Collins Whitney, Benjamin Sumner Welles III, August Belmont, Sr., Perry Belmont, George Scott Graham, Meyer Robert Guggenheim, Sr., Walter Hines Page, Sr., Regis Henri Post, Sr., Robert Barnwell Roosevelt, Sr., George Campbell Taylor, and Landon Ketchum Thorne, Jr., few South Shore Gold Coast residents served in national politics. Unlike their counterparts who lived in the North Shore's Gold Coast area, those living on the South Shore were more likely to serve at the local level.

Their sons and daughters grew up along the shore, socialized, and married. They, in turn, brought their families to the South Shore. Today, many of their descendents still live on the South Shore, having chosen to live on Long Island year-round; the island so aptly described in Hal B. Fullerton's promotional campaign for the Long Island Rail Road as the "Blessed Isle."[1]

Raymond E. and Judith A. Spinzia

Endnotes

1. For additional information on the prominent families of Long Island's South Shores and the social history of Long Island's South Shore see Harry W. Havemeyer, *Along the Great South Bay from Oakdale to Babylon: The Story of a Summer Spa 1840-1940* (Mattituck, NY: Amereon House, 1996); Harry W. Havemeyer, *East on the Great South Bay: Sayville and Bellport 1860-1960* (Mattituck, NY: Amereon House, 2001); Harry W. Havemeyer, *Fire Island's Surf Hotel and Other Hostelries on Fire Island Beaches in the Nineteenth Century* (Mattituck, NY: Amereon House, 2006); and Harry W. Havemeyer, "The Story of Saxton Avenue," *Long Island Forum* (Winter, February 1, 1990 and Spring, May 1, 1990). For information on Long Island's North Shore estates see Edward A. T. Carr, Michael W. Carr, and Kari-Ann R. Carr, *Faded Laurels: The History of Eaton's Neck and Asharoken* (Interlaken, NY: Heart of the Lakes Publishing, 1994); Robert B. Mackay, Anthony K. Baker, and Carol A. Traynor, eds., *Long Island Country Houses and Their Architects, 1860-1940* (New York: W. W. Norton & Co., 1997); Liisa and Donald Sclare, *Beaux-Arts Estates: A Guide to the Architecture of Long Island* (New York: The Viking Press, 1980); Raymond E. and Judith A. Spinzia, *Long Island's Prominent North Shore Families: Their Estates and Their Country Homes*, vols. I, II (College Station, TX: VirtualBookworm, 2006; revised 2019); Raymond E. and Judith A. Spinzia, *Long Island's Prominent Families in the Town of Hempstead: Their Estates and Their Country Homes* (College Station, TX: VirtualBookworm, 2010); Raymond E. and Judith A. Spinzia, *Long Island's Prominent Families in the Town of Southampton: Their Estates and Their Country Homes*. (College Station, TX: VirtualBookworm, 2010); and Raymond E. and Judith A. Spinzia, *Long Island's Prominent Families in the Town of East Hampton: Their Estates and Their Country Homes* (College Station, TX: VirtualBookworm, 2020).

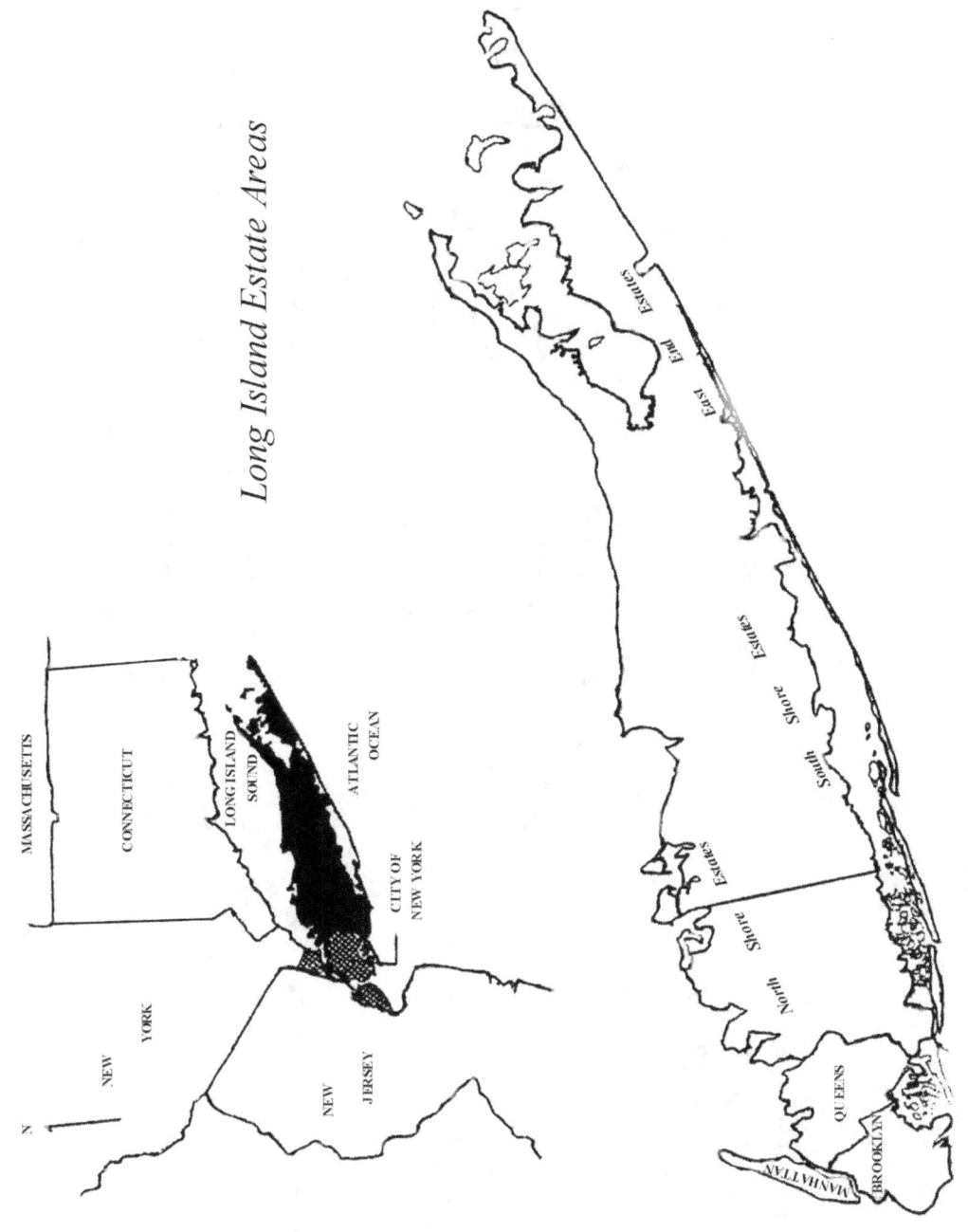

Long Island Estate Areas

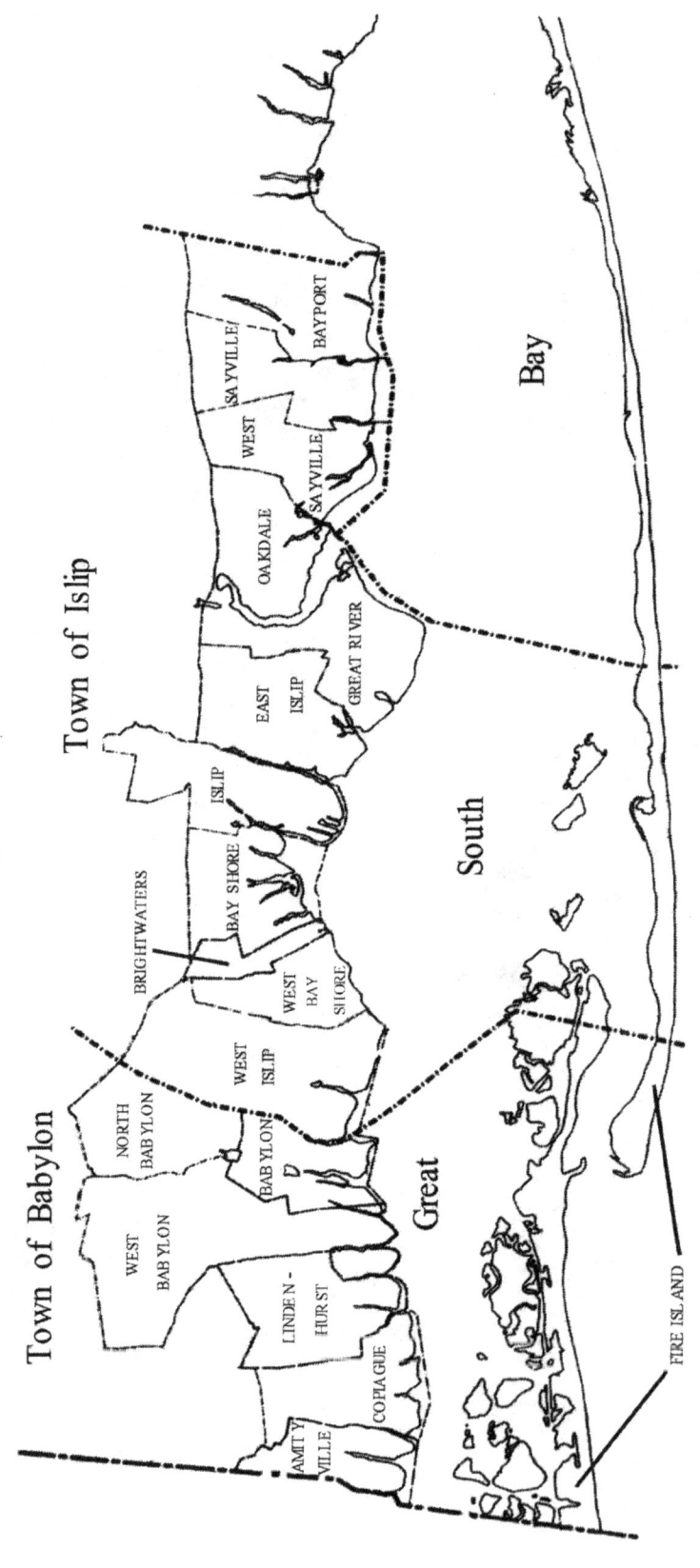

Adams, John Dunbar (1849-1934)

Occupation(s):	industrialist - president and chairman of board, American Chicle Co. (chewing gum manufacturer) (a merger of Adams & Sons; Beeman Chemical Co.; W. J. White & Sons of Cleveland, OH; S. T. Britten of Toronto, Canada; Kisme Gum Co. of Louisville, KY; and J. P. Primley of Chicago, IL)
Marriage(s):	Susan Burchell (1868-1937)
Address:	South Country Road, Bay Shore
Name of estate:	*Woodlea*
Year of construction:	c. 1902
Style of architecture:	Modified Neo-Tudor
Architect(s):	
Landscape architect(s):	
House extant: no; destroyed by fire, c. 1955*	
Historical notes:	

The house was built by Dr. Alfred Ludlow Carroll. It was purchased from Mrs. Carroll by Adams, who called it *Woodlea*.

The *Brooklyn Blue Book and Long Island Society Register, 1918* lists Mr. and Mrs. John Dunbar Adams as residing at *Woodlea* in Bay Shore.

He was the son of Thomas and Martha Dunbar Adams, Sr. His brother Thomas Adams, Jr., who married Emma Mills and, subsequently, Elizabeth Flood, resided at *Ardmore* in West Bay Shore. His brother Horatio married Mary Hartwell Carter and resided at *Appledale* in Glen Cove.

Susan Burchell Adams was the daughter of Thomas Burchell.

In 1917, John Dunbar and Susan Burchell Adams' son Dunbar married Edith Temple Gracie, the daughter of Archibald and Constance Elise Schack Gracie of Manhattan. Archibald, who was the last man rescued when the *Titanic* sunk, died several months later due to the effects of exposure caused by the accident. Archibald's will stipulated that his estate was to be divided equally between his daughter Edith and his wife. Edith died during World War I while Dunbar was serving in the army. Mrs. Gracie accused Mr. and Mrs. John Dunbar Adams of entering her daughter's house and stealing Edith's will which left Edith's estate entirely to her mother. After a lengthy court trial, which finally ended in 1922, the Adamses were exonerated but agreed to pay Mrs. Gracie $75 per week as her share of the estate. In 1925, Mrs. Gracie married Count Humbert Aguirre de Urbino who, it turned out, was not a count but instead a dishwasher who absconded with Mrs. Gracie's jewelry which was valued at $5,000. [*The New York Times* January 7, 1929, p. 26.]

[See following entry for additional family information.]

In 1929, Mr. and Mrs. John Dunbar Adams donated their son Dunbar's 1912 Simplex racing car to the Smithsonian Institution.

*In the 1950s, the house became Mimi's Awixa Pond Restaurant. The estate is now the site of Windemere Condominiums.

rear facade

Adams, Thomas, Jr. (1846-1926)

Occupation(s):	industrialist - president, Adams & Sons (chewing gum manufacturer) (which merged with Beeman Chemical Co.; W. J. White & Sons of Cleveland, OH; S. T. Britten of Toronto, Canada; Kisme Gum Co. of Louisville, KY; and J. P. Primley of Chicago, IL, to form American Chicle Co.); president, American Chicle Co.
Marriage(s):	M/1 – 1871-1925 – Emma Mills (d. 1925) M/2 – 1925-1926 – Elizabeth Flood (b. 1884)
Address:	South Country Road, West Bay Shore
Name of estate:	*Ardmore*
Year of construction:	c. 1905
Style of architecture:	Mediterranean Villa
Architect(s):	
Landscape architect(s):	
House extant: yes	
Historical notes:	

The house, originally named *Ardmore*, was built by Thomas Adams, Jr.

The *Brooklyn Blue Book and Long Island Society Register, 1918* lists Mr. and Mrs. Thomas Adams [Jr.] as residing in Bay Shore [West Bay Shore].

Known locally as "Tutti Frutti Adams," he was the son of Thomas and Martha Dunbar Adams, Sr. of Brooklyn. His brother Horatio resided at *Appledale* in Glen Cove. [*See* Spinzia, *Long Island's Prominent North Shore Families*, vol. I – Adams entries – and Harry W. Havemeyer, *Along the Great South Bay From Oakdale to Babylon: The Story of a Summer Spa 1840 to 1940* (Mattituck, NY: Amereon House, 1996), p. 291.]

In 1896, an actress by the name of Myrtle Thurlow sued Adams for breach-of-promise. She claimed to have over one hundred letters in her possession that Adams had written to her in which he referred to her as "Dear Little Chick," "Darling Little Rosebud," and "My Dear Little Bluebird." [*The New York Times* August 18, 1896, p. 2.]

Elizabeth Flood Adams was the daughter of Thomas Flood of Manhattan.

[See previous entry of additional family information.]

Thomas and Emma Mills Adams, Jr.'s son George J. Adams, Sr. resided in Hempstead. Their daughter Florence, who married George Augustus Ellis, Jr., subsequently owned *Ardmore*.

The house is currently part of Southward Ho Country Club.

front facade, 2005

Aldrich, Spencer (1854-1936)

Occupation(s):	attorney - member. Blatchford, Steward, Griswold, and DaCosta; member, DeWitt, Lockman, and DeWitt
	capitalist*
Civic Activism:	trustee, St. Luke's Home for Aged Women, NYC; president, South Shore Field Club, Bay Shore; member, executive committee, Bay Shore Protective Association, 1911
Marriage(s):	1878-1936 – Hariette Holley Dall (1855-1937)
Address:	Bay Shore Avenue, Bay Shore
Name of estate:	*Windermere*
Year of construction:	
Style of architecture:	
Architect(s):	
Landscape architect(s):	
House extant: unconfirmed	
Historical notes:	

   The *Long Island Society Register, 1929* lists Spencer and Hariette Holly Dall Aldrich as residing at *Windermere* on Bay Shore Avenue in Bay Shore.
   He was the son of Herman Daggett and Elizabeth Wyman Aldrich. Spencer's brother James married Gertrude Edson and resided at *Maycroft* in North Haven. Their sister Helen married The Reverend James Nevett Steele, Sr. and resided at *Dunemere* in East Hampton. [*See* Spinzia, *Long Island's Prominent Families in the Town of Southampton* – Aldrich entry – and *Long Island's Prominent Families in the Town of East Hampton* – Steele entry.]
   Hariette Holley Dall Aldrich was the daughter of Austin Dall of Baltimore, MD.
   Spencer and Hariette Holley Dall Aldrich's daughter Louise married William Christen Meissner and resided in Garden City. [*See* Spinzia, *Long Island's Prominent Families in the Town of Hempstead* – Meissner entry.] Their daughter Mary married Charles Malcolm Fraser. Their daughter Helen married Talcott Hunt Clark. Their daughter Maude married Stanley Matthews. Their son Spencer Wyman Aldrich, who resided in East Hampton, married Imogen Gaither, the daughter of George Riggs and Frances Imogen Gaither, Sr. of Baltimore, MD, and, later, Lillian B. Turk, the daughter of Charles and Harriet Nelson Turk. [*See* Spinzia, *Long Island's Prominent Families in the Town of East Hampton* – Aldrich entry.]
   *Upon the death of his father Herman, Spencer Aldrich retired from the practice of law to administer his father's extensive real estate holdings, which included twenty-eight different trusts and legacies of Manhattan property.

Allen, Theodore (1838-1908)

Occupation(s):	politician - Republican Ward Boss, Eighth Ward, Manhattan
	gambler*
Marriage(s):	*[unable to determine first name]* Smith (d. 1903)
Address:	Fairview Avenue, Bayport
Name of estate:	
Year of construction:	c. 1880s
Style of architecture:	Victorian
Architect(s):	Isaac Henry Green II designed alterations (for Allen)
Landscape architect(s):	
House extant: no; destroyed by fire, 1911	
Historical notes:	

front facade

   In 1883, Allen purchased the Daniel Coger house.
   *The son of an Episcopalian clergyman, Allen's unsavory lifestyle was accented by his ownership of several illegal gambling establishments, a thriving bookie operation, and taverns that were patronized by criminals and prostitutes. In 1871, he was critically injured and permanently disfigured when a disgruntled gambler stabbed him several times with an ice pick and bit off a portion of his nose. [Harry W. Havemeyer, *East on the Great South Bay: Sayville and Bayport 1860-1960* (Mattituck, NY: Amereon House, 2001), pp. 71-73.]
   The house was subsequently owned by Allen's granddaughter Mrs. Clarence Owens.

Allgood, Andrew Perry de Forest (1885-1956)

Occupation(s): engineer - Lockwood and Green Engineers, Inc., NYC

Marriage(s): 1920-1956 – Laurie Elward Smith (1893-1959)

Address: Handsome Avenue, Sayville
Name of estate:
Year of construction:
Style of architecture:
Architect(s):
Landscape architect(s):
House extant: unconfirmed
Historical notes:

   Andrew Perry de Forest Allgood was the son of de Forest and Susan M. Wright Allgood.
   Laurie Smith Allgood was the daughter of Elward and Frances Cairns Smith, Sr., who resided in Sayville. Her sister Frances married Admiral Harry Alexander Baldridge, Sr. and also resided in Sayville, as did their brother Jewett, who married Virginia Woodhull Otto, and their brother Elward Smith, Jr., who married Ella Bailey. Their brother Irving was killed in World War I.
   In 1925, Andrew inherited $100,000 from a prominent Syracuse, NY, woman, who jumped or fell from the window of her Manhattan hotel room after having dinner with Allgood. Her will was contested by her two nieces, whose bequest amounted to only $100 each. Allgood agreed to a settlement of $10,000 to cover his legal fees. The nieces divided $25,000 between them and the balance of $65,000 went to a Syracuse hospital.
   Allgood was killed when he was struck by a Manhattan bus as he was crossing Third Avenue at Thirty-second Street.
[*The New York Times* January 25, 1956, p. 16.]

Allison, William Manwaring, Sr. (1869-1946)

Occupation(s): capitalist - president, William M. Allison & Co. (wholesale
                                        importer and exporter of drugs and spices)
Civic activism: trustee, Southward Ho Country Club, West Bay Shore

Marriage(s): 1901-1946 – Alice Crosby (1876-1952)

Address: 29 South Clinton Avenue, Bay Shore
Name of estate:
Year of construction:
Style of architecture: Victorian
Architect(s):
Landscape architect(s):
House extant: yes
Historical notes:

   The *Long Island Society Register, 1929* lists Mr. and Mrs. William Manwaring Allison [Sr.] as residing at 29 South Clinton Avenue in Bay Shore.
   He was the son of William Gentil and Hester Julia Manwaring Allison.
   Alice Crosby Allison was the daughter of George L. and Fannie Edwards Crosby of Brooklyn.
   In 1926, their son William Manwaring Allison, Jr. died at the age of twenty-one.
   Their daughter Frances married Wilbur Kyle McAneny, the son of Samuel Wright McAneny of Fanwood, NJ.
   Their son Crosby married Shirley Ritchie and resided in Bay Shore.

front facade, 2005

Andrews, William Loring (1837-1920)

Occupation(s):	financier - trustee, Bank for Savings, NYC;
	director, Continental Insurance Co.
	industrialist - partner, Loring Andrews and Co. (later, Loring Andrews
	and Sons (hide and leather firm);
	partner, Loring Andrews and Sons
	writer - *New Amsterdam, New Orange, New York*, 1898;
	Fragments of American History, 1898;
	Old Book Sellers of New York; A Trio of French Engravers, 1899;
	Portraiture of American Revolutionary War; James Lyne's Survey, 1900;
	Gossip About Book Collecting, 1900;
	Paul Revere and His Engravings;
	Iconography of Battery and Castle;
	Treatyse of Fysshynge Wyth An Angle, 1903;
	New York as Washington Knew It After the Revolution, 1906;
	Sportsmen and Binder of Angling Books, 1907;
	The Heavenly Jerusalem;
	Catalogue of Early Printed Books Given to Yale University, 1912
Civic Activism:	manager, House of Refuge, Randall's Island;
	trustee, School District #1, Town of Islip;
	member, executive board, Metropolitan Museum of Art, NYC;
	a founder, Grolier Club, NYC;
	a founder and president, Society of Iconophiles of New York;
	a founder and director, South Shore Country Club, West Islip, 1895
Marriage(s):	1860-1920 – Jane Elizabeth Crane (1840-1930)
	- Civic Activism: trustee, Women's Hospital;
	trustee, National Society of Colonial Dames
Address:	Oak Neck Lane, West Islip
Name of estate:	*Pepperidges*
Year of construction:	before 1873
Style of architecture:	Colonial Revival
Architect(s):	
Landscape architect(s):	
House extant: yes	
Historical notes:	

    William Loring Andrews was the son of Loring and Caroline Catherine Delamater Andrews.
    Jane Elizabeth Crane Andrews was the daughter of Theodore and Margaret B. Crane of New York.
    [*See* Spinzia, *Long Island's Prominent Families in the Town of East Hampton* – Andrews entry – for information about his Montauk residence.]
    In 1951, Hans Grosser purchased the house. It was still owned by Grosser in 1976.

front facade, 1903

Arnold, Alexander Duncan Cameron (1891-1981)

Occupation(s):

Marriage(s): M/1 – 1911-div. 1919* – Evelyn Hollins Nicholas (1895-1930)
M/2 – 1918 – Katharine Weeks (d. 1969)

Address: South Country Road, West Islip
Name of estate:
Year of construction:
Style of architecture:
Architect(s):
Landscape architect(s):
House extant: unconfirmed
Historical notes:

Alexander Duncan Cameron Arnold was the son of Edward Miller and Annie Snedecor Carll Cameron of West Islip. After the death of their parents, Alexander and his brother Edward William Cameron were adopted by their aunt Annie Cameron Arnold and assumed the Arnold surname. Edward married Edith Isabelle Trenchard and resided at *Oknoke* in West Islip. [Harry W. Havemeyer, *Along the Great South Bay From Oakdale to Babylon: The Story of a Summer Spa 1840 to 1940* (Mattituck, NY: Amereon House, 1996), pp. 253-54.]

Evelyn Hollins Nicholas Arnold was the daughter of Harry Ingersoll and Alice McKim Hollins Nicholas, Sr. of *Virginia Farm* in Babylon. Evelyn subsequently married Joseph Hutchinson Stevenson of *The Farm* in Hewlett Bay Park. Her brother Harry Ingersoll Nicholas II married Dorothy Snow and resided at *Rolling Hill Farm* in Muttontown. Her sister Beatrice married Edward Nicholl Townsend, Jr. of Garden City. Her sister Rita married Uriel Atwood Murdock II and resided in Babylon. Her sister Daisy married Grosvenor Nicholas and resided in Old Westbury. Her sister Elsie married Alonzo Potter and resided at *Harbor House* in St. James and *Westmoor* in Southampton.

Alexander Duncan Cameron and Evelyn Hollins Nicholas Arnold's son Duncan Cameron Arnold (aka Duncan Stevenson) married Ruth Gilmore, the daughter of Robert and Mildred Sybil Koch Gilmore of Babylon. Their daughter Evelyn married Charles Franklyn Green. Evelyn's sister Maud married George Casper Niles and resided at *Cross Cottage* in Bridgehampton. [*See* Spinzia, *Long Island's Prominent North Shore Families, vol. II*– Nicholas entry; *Long Island's Prominent Families in the Town of Hempstead* – Stevenson and Townsend entries; and *Long Island's Prominent Families in the Town of Southampton* – Niles and Potter entries.]

*In 1919, Evelyn filed for divorce. The court ruled that the 1918 Nevada divorce, secretly obtained by Alexander, was invalid and gave Evelyn custody of their two children. [*The New York Times* October 7, 1919, p. 19.] Presumably, Alexander had legal problems with his 1918 marriage to Katharine Weeks.

Katharine Weeks Arnold was the daughter of Edwin Carnes and Emily Smedberg Weeks of Babylon.

[See other Arnold entries for additional family information.]

*Annie Stuart Cameron Arnold estate, Clovelly,
rear facade, 2006*

Arnold, Annie Stuart Cameron (1861-1945)

Civic Activism:	bequeathed $50,000 and one-quarter of her estate residuary and a contingent interest in the remainder to St. Rose's Settlement of the Catholic Social Union, NYC; bequeathed *Clovelly* to the Dominican Fathers of the Provence of St. Joseph*
Marriage(s):	1886 - William Arnold (1863-1891) - merchant - partner, Arnold, Constable & Co. (department store chain)
Address:	South Country Road, West Islip
Name of estate:	*Clovelly*
Year of construction:	1906
Style of architecture:	Georgian Revival
Architect(s):	
Landscape architect(s):	
House extant:	yes**
Historical notes:	

Annie Stuart Cameron Arnold demolished her father-in-law's house and built a new house, which she called *Clovelly*.

She was the daughter of Annanias Miller and Margaret Mott Cameron of Manhattan. Her brother Edward, who resided in West Islip, married Marie Louise Arnold and, later, Annie Snedecor Carll.

William Arnold was the son of Richard and Pauline Bicar Arnold.

[See other Arnold entries for additional family information.]

*In 1948, the religious order sold *Clovelly* to Cadman H. Frederick, who subdivided its property for a housing development. [*The New York Times* September 18, 1948, p. 25.]

**The house and the estate's greenhouse survive. The house is currently the Fairfield Arnold Manor apartment complex. The greenhouse is located on the SUNY Farmingdale campus.

front facade, nd

front facade, 2005

Arnold, Edward William Cameron (1887-1954)

Occupation(s):	
Civic Activism:	donated twenty-one ship models, dating from 1776-1875, to the Museum of the City of New York
Marriage(s):	M/1 – 1909-div. c. 1921 – Dorothy Whiting Frothingham (1895-1986)
	M/2 – 1921-div. 1935 – Edith Isabelle Trenchard (1883-1967)
	M/3 – Mary Knight (b. 1898)
	- Civic Activism: donated works of art to the Metropolitan Museum of Art, NYC
Address:	South Country Road, West Islip
Name of estate:	*Oknoke*
Year of construction:	
Style of architecture:	
Architect(s):	Prentice Sanger designed the house (for E. W. C. Arnold)
Landscape architect(s):	Lewis and Valentine supplied the plantings (for E. W. C. Arnold)

House extant: unconfirmed
Historical notes:

The house, originally named *Oknoke*, was built by Edward William Cameron Arnold.

Dorothy Whiting Frothingham Arnold was the daughter of Charles Frederick and Mary MacDonald Frothingham, Sr. She later married George Barnard Wagstaff of Bay Shore.

Edward William Cameron and Dorothy Whiting Frothingham Arnold's thirty-three-year-old son Richard died in a fire while asleep in his three-room tenement apartment at 826 Ninth Avenue, Manhattan. [*The New York Times* April 23, 1945, p. 18.] Their son Frederick married Katherine L. Carney and resided in Babylon.

The *Long Island Society Register, 1929* lists Edward William Cameron and E. Isabelle Trenchard Arnold as residing at *Oknoke* on South Country Road in West Islip.

She was the daughter of Edward and Mary Cornelia Stafford Trenchard II of Babylon. Edith had previously been married to John Anthony Power, with whom she resided in Manhattan. She subsequently married Storer Goodwin Decatur, the son of Stephan and Mabel Storer Decatur, with whom she resided in Kittery Point, ME.

[See other Arnold entries for additional family information.]

Arnold, Richard (1825-1886)

Occupation(s):	merchant - partner, Arnold, Constable & Co. (department store chain)
Marriage(s):	M/1 – Pauline Bicar (d. 1875)
	M/2 – 1882-1886 – Georgiana Eleanor Bolmer (1856-1903)
Address:	South Country Road, West Islip
Name of estate:	*The Crescent*
Year of construction:	1873
Style of architecture:	
Architect(s):	
Landscape architect(s):	

House extant: no
Historical notes:

The house, originally named *The Crescent*, was built by Richard Arnold.

His father Aaron was a founder of Arnold, Constable & Co.

The Crescent

Pauline Bicar Arnold was the daughter of Noel J. Bicar of Manhattan.

Richard and Pauline Bicar Arnold's daughter Marie married Edward Miller Cameron and resided in West Islip. Their son William inherited the house. Upon William's death, his wife Annie Stuart Cameron Arnold demolished *The Crescent* and built a new house, which she called *Clovelly*.

Georgiana Eleanor Bolmer Arnold was the daughter of Manuel Texido and Georgiana Elenora Buckmaster Bolmer of Manhattan. Georgiana subsequently married The Reverend Charles Harvey Hartman. Her sister Louise married Frederick Augustus Constable and resided in Manhattan.

[See other Arnold entries for additional family information.]

Ash, Dr. Charles F. (1848-1938)

Occupation(s):	physician - dentist
Civic Activism:	president, First Dental Society of New York State; president, Second Dental Society of New York State; member, fund raising committee, Beekman Street Hospital, NYC (which became Beekman–Downtown Hospital after its merger with Downtown Hospital)
Marriage(s):	Lucretia Durfey (1869-1952)
Address:	122 South Penataquit Avenue, Bay Shore
Name of estate:	
Year of construction:	c. 1912
Style of architecture:	Contemporary
Architect(s):	
Landscape architect(s):	
House extant:	yes
Historical notes:	

The house was built by Dr. Charles F. Ash on property he purchased from John Adolph Mollenhauer. [Harry W. Havemeyer, *Along the Great South Bay from Oakdale to Babylon: The Story of a Summer Spa 1840-1940* (Mattituck, NY: Amereon House, 1996), p. 371.]

Lucretia Durfey Ash was the daughter of Joseph P. and Lucretia Miller Durfey of Brooklyn. The Ashes resided in the Durfey mansion until 1906.

Dr. Charles F. and Mrs. Lucretia Durfey Ash's son Prentice married Olive Louise Snow, the daughter of Elmer J. Snow, and resided in Mahwah, NJ. Their daughter Kathryn married Harry Carlson, and resided in Englewood, NJ.

In 2018, the 5,900-square-foot house with seven bedrooms and six-and-a-half bathrooms sold for $990,000.

2018

Asher, John J. (d. 1925)

Occupation(s):	Brooklyn police detective capitalist - founder and president, Asher Detective Agency, NYC
Marriage(s):	
Address:	Middle Road, Bayport
Name of estate:	
Year of construction:	
Style of architecture:	Colonial Revival
Architect(s):	
Landscape architect(s):	
House extant:	yes
Historical notes:	

In 1909, Asher purchased the Henry Richmond house *Maplewood* for $18,000 and changed its architectural style from Victorian Italianate to Colonial Revival. [*The Brooklyn Daily Eagle* June 4, 1909, p. 7.]

In 1923, Asher was indicted for padding his payrolls while furnishing guards during the 1921 New York Central Railroad strike. [*The Buffalo Commercial* May 2, 1923, p. 1, and *The Buffalo Enquirer* August 30, 1924, p. 2.]

*John J. Asher's residence,
front facade*

Astaire, Phyllis Livingston Baker (1908-1954)

Marriage(s):	M/1 – 1927-div. 1932 – Eliphalet Nott Potter III (1906-1981)
	  - financier - partner, Potter and Co. (stock brokerage firm);
	                     partner, Combs, Maxwell, and Potter (stock
	                        brokerage firm);
	                     a founder and partner, E. N. Potter and Co.
	                        (stock brokerage firm)
	M/2 – 1933-1954 – Fred Astaire, Sr. (aka Frederick Austerlitz) (1899-1987)
	  - entertainers and associated professions - dancer;
	                                              choreographer;
	                                              actor

Address:	St. Mark's Lane, Islip*
Name of estate:	
Year of construction:	
Style of architecture:	Victorian Gothic
Architect(s):	
Landscape architect(s):	
House extant: yes	
Historical notes:	

    The house was built by Parmenus Johnson, Sr. In January 1880, the twenty-one-acre estate was purchased by C. A. Backett of New York. By June 1880 it was owned by E. B. Spaulding who enlarged and modernized the house [*The Brooklyn Daily Eagle* January 27, 1880, p. 4, and June 7, 1880, p. 1.] In 1886, the estate was purchased by Robert Cambridge Livingston III who called it *Lakeside*. The estate was then owned by the Livingstons' daughter Maud who married Henry Worthington Bull. By the early 1940s it was owned by the Bulls' niece Phyllis Livingston Baker Astaire, the daughter of Boston gynecologist Dr. Harold Woods and Mrs. Caroline E. Livingston Baker.

    Eliphalet Nott Potter III was the son of Eliphalet Nott and Josephine T. Atterbury Potter II of Mount Kisco, NY, and NYC. His sister Nancy married George Galt Bourne of Lattingtown and, later, Robert Vandenburgh McKim of Old Westbury. [*See* Spinzia, *Long Island's Prominent North Shore Families, vol. I* – Bourne entry.]

    [For the Potter's Muttontown house, *see* Spinzia, *Long Island's Prominent North Shore Families, vol. II*– Potter entry.]

    Eliphalet Nott and Phyllis Livingston Baker Potter III's son Eliphalet Nott Potter IV [aka Peter] married Sally FitzGibbons, the daughter of Leslie FitzGibbons of Garden City.

    Fred Astaire Sr. was the son of Friedrich Emanuel and Johanna Geilus Austerlitz.

    Fred and Phyllis Livingston Baker Astaire, Sr.'s daughter Ava married Richard MacKenzie. Their son Fred Astaire, Jr. married Gale ____.

    In 1980, Fred Astaire, Sr. married the noted jockey Robyn Smith.

    In 2006, the house was owned by ____ Dowden.

    In 2008, the seven thousand-square-foot, twenty-room house with seven bedrooms was for sale. The asking price was $1,499,990; the taxes were $16,089.

    *The estate originally bordered on St. Marks Lane. With its subdivision, the house is currently located on Suellen Road.

Asten, Thomas B. (1825-1895)

Occupation(s):	politician - president, NYC Board of Taxes and Assessments;*
Civic Activism:	president, Olympic Club
Marriage(s):	Elizabeth Smith (d. 1923)
Address:	Saxon Avenue, Bay Shore
Name of estate:	
Year of construction:	
Style of architecture:	
Architect(s):	
Landscape architect(s):	
House extant:	unconfirmed
Historical notes:	

The house was built by Thomas B. Asten.
*He was a delegate to the 1864 Republican National Convention that nominated Abraham Lincoln.
Asten's daughter Louise married Frank Curtis.

Aston, William K. (d. 1919)

Occupation(s):	attorney
	capitalist - extensive holdings in NYC and on Long Island; director, South Bay Hotel
Marriage(s):	1874-1909 – Mary Lorena Kronkright (1839-1909)
Address:	south of Montauk Highway, Oakdale
Name of estate:	*Peperidge Hall*
Year of construction:	c. 1880
Style of architecture:	French Chateau
Architect(s):	H. Edward Ficken designed and reassembled the house (for C. R. Robert, Jr.)*
Landscape architect(s):	
House extant:	no; demolished in 1940
Historical notes:	

The house, originally named *Peperidge Hall*, was built by Christopher Rhinelander Robert, Jr.
*Its interior had been removed from a chateau in Normandy, France. Robert brought the crated interior to Long Island and had it reassembled in his country house.
In 1896, Robert sold the estate to Aston, who unsuccessfully attempted to subdivide its property for a housing development in 1907.
Mary Lorena Kronkright Aston was the daughter of James Kronkright.

Peperidge Hall

Atwood, Frederic Lawrence, Sr. (1930-2012)

Occupation(s):	attorney - partner, Pelletreau and Pelletreau; partner, Fisher, Egan, and Golden, LLP, Patchogue
	judge - U. S. Magistrate, Federal Court, Nassau and Suffolk Counties
Civic Activism:	trustee, Long Island Maritime Museum, West Sayville;
	member, advisory committee, Long Island Community Foundation;
	a founder and president, Seatuck Environmental Association, Islip;
	trustee, Bayard Cutting Arboretum, Great River;
	member of board, Southside Hospital, Bay Shore (now, South Shore University Hospital);
	president, Society for the Preservation of Long Island Antiquities;
	president, Nassau–Suffolk Hospital Council;
	president, U. S. Magistrate Judges Association;
	commodore, Bayberry Yacht Club
Marriage(s):	1955-2012 – Elizabeth Morse
Address:	272 Ocean Avenue, Islip
Name of estate:	
Year of construction:	1961
Style of architecture:	Ranch
Architect(s):	
Landscape architect(s):	
House extant:	yes

front facade

Historical notes:
   The five-bedroom house was built by Frederic Lawrence Atwood, Sr. on a portion of his parents' estate.
   Elizabeth Morse Atwood was the daughter of George Perley and Ruth Sterling Morse of Brookhaven.
   Frederic Lawrence and Elizabeth Morse Atwood, Sr.'s daughter Julia married ____ Berman and resides in Deep River, CT. Their son George resides in Killingworth, CT. Their son James lives in Arundel, ME. Their son Frederic Lawrence Atwood, Jr. resides in Bethesda, MD.

[See following entry for family information.]

Atwood, Kimball Chase, Jr. (1892-1969)

Occupation(s):	attorney
	financier - secretary, president, and chairman of board, Preferred Accident Insurance Co.
Civic Activism:	director, New York State Chamber of Commerce
Marriage(s):	M/1 – 1919-1923 – Mary Evelyn Girdner (d. 1923)
	M/2 – 1925-1969 – Adela Overton Girdner (1891-1976)
Address:	Ocean Avenue, Islip
Name of estate:	*Mapleton*
Year of construction:	c. 1890
Style of architecture:	Shingle
Architect(s):	Isaac Henry Green II designed the house (for Schieren)
Landscape architect(s):	Olmsted
House extant:	no; demolished in 1979*

west facade, c. 1908

Historical notes:
   The house, originally named *Mapleton*, was built by Charles Adolph Schieren, Sr. In 1926, it was purchased by Atwood, who continued to call it *Mapleton*.
   He was the son of Kimball Chase and Caroline B. Hutchins Atwood, Sr.
   Mary Evelyn and Adela Overton Girdner Atwood were the daughters of Dr. John Harvey and Mrs. Adela Overton Pratt Girdner. Dr. Girdner was one of the attending physicians at President Garfield's deathbed.
   Kimball's son John married Judith Avery King, the daughter of A. Lincoln King of Portland, ME, and resided in West Redding, CT. His son Frederic married Elizabeth Morse, the daughter of George Perley and Ruth Sterling Morse of Brookhaven. His son Roger married Nancy Coke Smith, the daughter of Perry Coke Smith of NYC. His son Kimball Chase Atwood III, a noted geneticist, married Barbara Frances Drew.
   *The garage, stable, and caretaker's apartment are extant and are currently private residences. The estate's carriage house is also extant. It was moved to Frederic Lawrence Atwood's property.
   [For other Long Island residents associated with Garfield's assassination, *see* Spinzia, *Long Island's Prominent Families in the Town of Southampton* – Francklyn entry.]

Bachia, Richard Augustus, Jr. (1857-1930)

Occupation(s):	industrialist - founder and president, R. A. Bachia & Co., Long Island City (manufacturer of "fine" Havana cigars)
	financier - trustee, Citizens Savings Bank, NYC
Civic Activism:	treasurer, Penataquit Corinthian Yacht Club; a founder and director, Bay Shore Protective Association
Marriage(s):	M/1 – Mary Teresa Rieliey (1860-1885)
	M/2 – 1890-1930 – Emily F. Reilly (d. 1945)
Address:	Montgomery Avenue and Montauk Highway, Bay Shore
Name of estate:	
Year of construction:	
Style of architecture:	Mediterranean Villa
Architect(s):	
Landscape architect(s):	
House extant: no	
Historical notes:	

The Long Island Society Register, 1929 lists Mr. and Mrs. Richard A. Bachia [Jr.] as residing on South Country Road in Bay Shore.

He was the son of Richard Augustus and Mary E. Bachia, Sr. of Brooklyn.

Mary Teresa Rieliey Bachia was the daughter of James and Teresa Rieliey of Brooklyn.

side facade

Baker, George William, Sr. (1863-1928)

Occupation(s):	industrialist - partner, George Baker and Sons; founder and president, George W. Baker Shoe Co., Brooklyn (manufacturer of men's shoes)
	financier - director, First National Bank, Brooklyn; director, People's National Bank
	merchant - president, Frank H. Tuttle Co., Omaha, NB (shoe retailers); president, Tuttle & Co., Sioux City, IA (shoe retailers)
	politician*
Civic Activism:	a founder, Shoe Manufacturers Board of Trade, Brooklyn;
	member, board of management, YMCA, Bedford, Brooklyn branch;
	member, board of management, Brooklyn Association for Improving the Condition of the Poor;
	president, Rotary Club, Brooklyn;
	governor, Union League Club, NYC;
	governor, Brooklyn Club;
	chairman, industrial committee, United War Drive during World War I;
	member, Shoe Manufacturers War Service Board during World War I;
	chairman, all shoe manufacturers' Liberty Loan committees in Brooklyn during World War I;
	member, Liberty Loan Drive during World War I;
	chairman of board, Shoe Manufacturers' Red Cross Committee, Brooklyn
Marriage(s):	1884-1928 – Isabelle Caroline Huggins (d. 1936)
Address:	Saxon Avenue, Bay Shore
Name of estate:	*Fairlawn*
Year of construction:	
Style of architecture:	Shingle
Architect(s):	
Landscape architect(s):	
House extant: no	
Historical notes:	

The *Long Island Society Register, 1929* lists George William and Isabelle Caroline Huggins Baker [Sr.] as residing at *Fairlawn* on Saxon Avenue in Bay Shore.

He was the son of George and Sarah Randell Baker of Philadelphia, PA.

George William and Isabelle Huggins Baker, Sr.'s son George William Baker, Jr. married Marion Adele Souville, the daughter of Lloyd A. Souville, Jr. of Brooklyn. Their daughter Florence married Charles Morton Stafford, the son of Willis E. Stafford of Brooklyn. Their daughter Evelyn married Frank Frederick Koehler, Jr. and resided in Brooklyn.

*In 1921, Baker was the unsuccessful Republican candidate for Brooklyn Borough president.

At the time of her death, Mrs. Baker was residing at 19 Montgomery Avenue, Bay Shore.

front facade

Baker, William Dunham (1878-1951)

Occupation(s):

Marriage(s): Louise Ethel Thompson (1880-1966)

Address: 146 East Bayberry Road, Islip
Name of estate:
Year of construction: 1899-1900
Style of architecture: Moorish
Architect(s): Grosvenor Atterbury designed the house
    (for H. O. Havemeyer)*
Landscape architect(s): Nathan F. Barrett
    (for H. O. Havemeyer)**
Builder: [*See* Jabez Ephraim Van Order entry.]
House extant: yes
Historical notes:

    The house was built by Henry Osborne Havemeyer as part of his "Modern Venice" development. It was subsequently purchased by Baker.
    He was the son of John Henry and Elizabeth Sarah Edmans Baker.
    William Dunham and Louise Thompson Baker's daughter Elizabeth married Temple Eppes Dalrymple, the son of Matthew Dalrymple of Carthage, NC. Their son William Thompson Baker, Sr. married Elizabeth Baird, the daughter of William Parfitt Baird of Bay Shore, and, later, Elise Durrin, the daughter of Dr. William Durrin of Brooklyn.
    The house was later owned by Joseph Francis Dempsey, Jr.
    *The sales brochure for "Modern Venice" states that the Moorish-style architecture was suggested by Louis Comfort Tiffany.
    **The sales brochure also states that "Modern Venice" would be devoid of trees and vegetation and that Nathan F. Barrett was the landscape architect.

front facade, 2006

Baldridge, Harry Alexander, Sr. (1880-1952)

Occupation(s):	military -	admiral, United States Navy;
		fleet ordinance officer, Pacific Fleet, 1913;
		commander, Destroyer Division 20, World War I;
		instructor, Naval War College, Newport, RI, 1921-1923;
		director, Department of Seamanship and Flight Tactics, 1924-1928;
		director, aviation, United States Naval Academy, 1937-1952;
		director, Military Museum, United States Naval Academy, 1937-1952
	intelligence agent -	director, Naval Intelligence Department, 1930-1932

Marriage(s): M/1 – 1910-1911 – Rosalie Thurston McDermont (1883-1911)
M/2 – 1914-1952 – Frances Elward Smith (1885-1959)

Address: Handsome Avenue, Sayville
Name of estate:
Year of construction:
Style of architecture:
Architect(s):
Landscape architect(s):
House extant: unconfirmed
Historical notes:

    Harry Alexander Baldridge, Sr. was the son of William and Anna Reynolds Baldridge of Albany, NY.
    Harry Alexander and Rosalie Thurston McDermont Baldridge, Sr.'s son Harry Alexander Baldridge, Jr. married Louise Brown Simmons.
    Frances Elward Smith Baldridge was the daughter of Elward and Frances Cairns Smith, Sr., who resided in Bayport. Her sister Laurie married Andrew Perry de Forest Allgood and resided in Sayville. Her brother Jewett married Virginia Woodhull Otto of Patchogue. Her brother Elward Smith, Jr. married Ella Bailey and resided in Sayville. Her brother Irving was killed in World War I.
    Harry Alexander and Frances Elward Smith Baldridge, Sr.'s son Jewett married Gabriella Harrison Parker, the daughter of William LeRoy Parker, and, later, Julia Sands of Newport, RI.

Ballard, Frederick Edward, Sr. (1854-1915)

Occupation(s): financier - member, Cyril de Cordova (stock brokerage firm)

Marriage(s): 1877-1915 – Elizabeth B. Keeler (1856-1945)

Address: Awixa Avenue, Bay Shore
Name of estate:
Year of construction:
Style of architecture:
Architect(s):
Landscape architect(s):
House extant: unconfirmed
Historical notes:

    Frederick Edward Ballard was the son of Loomis Ballard.
    Elizabeth B. Keeler Ballard was the daughter of James Rufus and Mary Louise Davidson Keeler. Elizabeth's sister Emma married Frederick Gilbert Bourne and resided at *Indian Neck Hall* in Oakdale.
    Frederick Edward and Elizabeth B. Keeler Ballard, Sr.'s daughter Helen married Walter Hayward Powers, Jr. Their daughter Grace married Philip Barnard Philipp.

Baruch, Bernard Mannes, Sr. (1870-1965)

Occupation(s):	financier - member, A. A. Housman and Co. (stock brokerage firm)
Civic Activism:	member, Council of National Defense, Wilson administration; commissioner, raw materials, minerals, and metals, 1916; chairman, Allied Purchasing Commission (later, War Industries Board) during World War I; member, U. S. delegation to Peace Conference, 1919; trustee and major benefactor, College of the City of New York; a founder, Camden Hospital, Camden, SC
Marriage(s):	1897 – Annie Griffen
Address:	Ocean Avenue, Bayport
Name of estate:	*Strandhome*
Year of construction:	1890
Style of architecture:	Shingle
Architect(s):	Isaac Henry Green II designed the house (for W. R. Foster, Jr.) George Browne Post designed the alterations (for Charles Alfred Post)
Landscape architect(s):	
House extant: no; demolished in the 1950s	

Strandhome

Historical notes:

The house, originally named *Strandhome*, was built by William Riley Foster, Jr. In 1888, it was purchased at public auction by the Produce Exchange Gratuity Fund. In 1890, the Fund sold the house to Charles Alfred Post, who also called in *Strandhome*. It was subsequently owned by his son Waldron Kintzing Post, who continued to call it *Strandhome*.

Baruch rented the house during the summers of 1915 and 1916.

He was the son of Simon and Belle Wolfe Baruch of Camden, SC. His brother Dr. Herman Benjamin Baruch, who resided in Dix Hills, married Rosemary Emetaz and, subsequently, Baroness Anna Marie Mackay of The Hague. [*See* Spinzia, *Long Island's Prominent North Shore Families, vol. I* – Baruch entry.]

Annie Griffen Baruch was the daughter of Benjamin Griffen of New York.

Bernard Mannes and Annie Griffen Baruch, Sr. had three children, Isabelle (aka Belle), Renee, and Bernard Mannes Baruch, Jr. Isabelle, who did not marry, was a noted suffragist.

Bates, William Graves (1860-1944)

Occupation(s):	military - general, United States Army attorney
Civic Activism:	trustee, Grant Monument Association; treasurer, New York State Society of Colonial Wars; member, Citizen's Visiting Committee, Bay Shore High School; a founder and director, Bay Shore Protective Association
Marriage(s):	1899-1944 – Amy Rowan Scott (1866-1953)
Address:	South Country Road and Penataquit Avenue, Bay Shore
Name of estate:	*The Evergreens*
Year of construction:	
Style of architecture:	Shingle
Architect(s):	
Landscape architect(s):	
House extant: no	

Historical notes:

William Graves Bates was the son of Levi Miles and Martha Arnold Tucker Bates.

Amy Rowan Scott Bates was the daughter of James Rowan and Sarah Antoinette Tams Scott. She had previously been married to Effingham Lawrence Johnson with whom she resided at *The Evergreens*.

Effingham Lawrence and Amy Rowan Scott Johnson's daughter Amy married Herbert Groesbeck and resided in Manhattan.

front facade, 1903

Baxter, John Edward (1878-1958)

Occupation(s):	industrialist - president, Baxter, Kelly, & Faust, Inc. (textile manufacturers)
	financer - trustee, Dime Savings Bank of Brooklyn
Civic Activism -	director, Brooklyn Society for Prevention of Cruelty to Children; *
Marriage(s):	1902-1953 – Katherine Byrne (1879-1953)
	- Civic Activism: regent, Brooklyn Circle of International Federation of Catholic Alumnae;
	a founder, Catholic Thrift Shop of Brooklyn;
	a founder, Villa de Sales Convalescent Home;
	director, Dr. White Memorial Catholic Settlement;
	chairman, Brooklyn Red Cross, home nursing chapter, during World War II;
	trustee, Brooklyn Girl Scout Council

Address: Clinton Avenue, Bay Shore
Name of estate:
Year of construction:
Style of architecture:
Architect(s):
Landscape architect(s):
House extant: unconfirmed
Historical notes:

  The *Long Island Society Register, 1929* lists the Baxters' residence as Clinton Avenue in Bay Shore.
  Their daughter Claire married Norman C. Hilborn, the son of Hedley H. Hilborn of Brooklyn and Belle Terre. Their daughter Ann married John de Lacey Regan, the son of John F. Regan of Brooklyn.
  *Because of his extensive civic activities, Baxter was made a Knight of St. Gregory in 1919 by Pope Pius X and a Knight of Malta in 1945 by Pope Pius XII.

*Anson Mc Cook Beard, Jr. residence,
front facade, c. 2006*

Beard, Anson Mc Cook, Jr. (1909-1997)

Occupation(s):   financier -   investment banker

Marriage(s):   1934-1993 – Roseanne Hoar (1914-1993)

Address: 126 East Bayberry Road, Islip
Name of estate:
Year of construction: 1899-1900
Style of architecture: Moorish
Architect(s):   Grosvenor Atterbury designed the house
                            (for H. O. Havemeyer)*
Landscape architect(s): Nathan F. Barrett
                            (for H. O. Havemeyer)**
Builder: [See Jabez Ephraim Van Order entry.]
House extant: yes
Historical notes:

 The house was built by Henry Osborne Havemeyer as part of his "Modern Venice" development. It was owned by Richard Sturgis Perkins, Sr. and, subsequently, by Beard.
 The *Social Register, 1945* lists Captain Anson Mc Cook and Mrs. Roseanne Hoar Beard [Jr.] as residing at 152 South Main Street, Southampton. The *Social Register, 1946* lists the Beards as residing in Islip. They later relocated to the West Hills section of Huntington and, subsequently, to 111 High Farms Road, Glen Head.
 He was the son of Anson Mc Cook and Ruth Hill Beard, Sr., who resided on Gin Lane in Southampton. Ruth Hill Beard was the daughter of James Jerome Hill, a founder of the Great Northern Railroad. After her husband's death she married Pierre Lorillard V and resided in Tuxedo Park, NY, and Southampton. [*See* Spinzia, *Long Island's Prominent Families in the Town of Southampton* – Beard and Lorillard entries.]. Ruth's brother James Norman Hill married Marguerite Sawyer and resided at *Big Tree Farm* in Brookville. [*See* Spinzia, *Long Island's Prominent North Shore Families, vol. I* – Hill entry.] Her daughter Mary married Frederick C. Havemeyer II and resided in Tuxedo Park, NY.
 Roseanne Hoar Beard was the daughter of Friend and Virginia Goffe Hoar, who resided at *Little Orchard* in Southampton. [*See* Spinzia, *Long Island's Prominent Families in the Town of Southampton* – Hoar entry.]
 Anson Mc Cook and Roseanne Hoar Beard, Jr.'s son Samuel married Patricia Dranow, the daughter of Harry Dranow of Manhattan and resided in Manhattan, Delaware, and Clinton Corners, NY. Their son Peter, who resided in Montauk, married Mary Olivia Cochran Cushing, the daughter of Howard Gardiner Cushing, Sr. of Newport, RI, Cheryl Rae Tiegs, and, subsequently, Nejma Khanum. [*See* Spinzia, *Long Island's Prominent Families in the Town of East Hampton* – Beard entry.] Their son Anson Mc Cook Beard, Jr. [III] married Jean Jones, the daughter of Gilbert E. Jones of Greenwich, CT, and resided in Greenwich, CT.
 *The sales brochure for "Modern Venice" states that the Moorish–style architecture was suggested by Louis Comfort Tiffany.
 **The sale brochure also states that "Modern Venice" would be devoid of trees and vegetation and that Nathan F. Barrett was the landscape architect.
 In 2005, the house sold for $1.85 million.

Bedell, Walter Ellwood

Occupation(s): financier - partner, Woodworth, Lounsbery and Co. (stock brokerage firm);
partner, Morris and Smith (stock brokerage firm);
trustee, Kings County Trust Co., Brooklyn
capitalist - director, Francis Realty Co., Brooklyn

Marriage(s):

Address: Saxon Avenue, Bay Shore
Name of estate:
Year of construction:
Style of architecture: Shingle
Architect(s):
Landscape architect(s):
House extant: unconfirmed
Historical notes:

In 1915, Bedell purchased the house from Robert Law Pierrepont. [*The Suffolk County News* February 26, 1915, p. 2.]

The *Long Island Society Register, 1928* lists Mr. and Mrs. Walter Ellwood Bedell as residing on Saxon Avenue in Bay Shore.

The house was purchased from Bedell in 1927 by Beverley Montagu Eyre. [*The New York Times* June 17, 1927, p. 41.]

side / front facade

Behman, Louis C., Sr. (1855-1902)

Occupation(s): capitalist - partner, with Richard Hyde, Hyde and Behman Amusement Co., which owned and operated Volks Garden, Brooklyn; Park Bijou, Brooklyn; Amphion Theatre, Brooklyn; Folly Theatre, Brooklyn; Grand Opera House, Brooklyn; Gaiety Theatre, Brooklyn; and Newark Theatre, Newark, NJ

Marriage(s): M/1 – Margaret Scott (1845-1899)
 - entertainers and associated professions - stage singer
M/2 – 1900-1902 – Evelyn Phoebe Scott (1871-1942)

Address: 80 Seaman's Avenue, Bayport
Name of estate: *Lindenwalt*
Year of construction: 1883
Style of architecture: Shingle
Architect(s): Clarence K. Birdsall, 1898 alterations (for Behman)
Landscape architect(s):
House extant: yes
Historical notes:

Lindenwalt

The house was built by Albert Payne. In c. 1893, it was purchased by Behman who made extensive alterations to the house and property.

Louis C. and Margaret Scott Behman, Sr.'s daughter Marguerite, who did not marry, resided in Bayport. She was the author of a children's book entitled *Lindenwood Tales*. Their son August married Marjorie Downey and resided in *Lindenwalt*'s gatehouse. Their daughter Consuelo married Dr. Henry T. Hagstrom of Brooklyn.

Louis subsequently married his sister-in-law Evelyn Phoebe Scott. Louis C. and Evelyn Phoebe Scott Behman, Sr.'s son Louis C. Behman, Jr. did not attain adulthood.

Belmont, August, Jr. (1853-1924)

Occupation(s):	financier -	partner, Belmont and Co. (investment banking firm); trustee, Bank for Savings, NYC
	capitalist -	chairman of board, Interborough Rapid Transit Co.; chairman of board, Rapid Transit Subway Construction Co.; president, Boston, Cape Cod, and New York Canal Co.

Civic Activism: first president, The Jockey Club;
chairman, New York State Racing Commission;
a founder, National Steeplechase Association

Marriage(s): M/1 – 1881-1898 – Elizabeth Hamilton Morgan (1862-1898)*
M/2 – 1910-1924 – Eleanor Robson (1879-1979)
- entertainers and associated professions -   actress
writer - *The Fabric of Memory,* 1957
Civic Activism:
a founder, Working Girls Vacation Association;
founder, SPUGS, Society for the Prevention of Useless Giving;
assistant to Red Cross War Council during World War I;
chair, National Council for Home Nursing Courses;
chair, Women's Division of the Emergency Unemployment Relief;
a founder and chairman, Adopt–a–Family Committee;
chair, Nurses' House Committee for the Association for Improving
    the Condition of the Poor;
founder and president, Metropolitan Opera Guild, NYC;
president, Motion Picture Research Council;
a founder and chairman of board, Northeast Harbor Library, Northeast,
MA

Address: Southern State Parkway, North Babylon
Name of estate: *Nursery Stud Farm*
Year of construction: c. 1868
Style of architecture: Modified Second Empire
    with Colonial Revival elements
Architect(s): Detlef Lienau designed the
    house (for A. Belmont, Sr.)
Landscape architect(s):
House extant: no; demolished in 1935
Historical notes:

August Belmont Jr. purchased his parent's 1,300-acre estate.

Elizabeth Hamilton Morgan was the daughter of Edward Morgan.

August and Elizabeth Hamilton Morgan Belmont, Jr.'s son Morgan married Margaret F. Andrews. Their son Raymond Rogers Belmont II married Ethel Helen Linda, whose stage name was Ethel Loraine; Caroline Hubbard of Virginia; and, subsequently, Marie Muurling, the daughter of I. J. R. Muurling, and resided with her at *Belray Farms* in Middleburg, VA. Raymond's daughter Bettina married Newell Jube Ward, Jr., the son of Newell Jube and Ethel L. Conderman Ward, Sr. of East Hampton. [*See* Spinzia, *Long Island's Prominent Families in the Town of East Hampton* – Ward entry.] Their son August Belmont III married Alice Wall de Goicouria, the daughter of Albert Valentine and Mary Cecelia Wall de Goicouria of Islip, and resided in Bay Shore. Alice subsequently married John Daniel Wing of Southampton. [*See* Spinzia, *Long Island's Prominent Families in the Town of Southampton* – Wing entry.]

For Belmont's Hempstead estate *Blemton Manor,* see Spinzia, *Long Island's Prominent Families in the Town of Hempstead* – Belmont entry.]

*A memorial window in St. George's Episcopal Church, Hempstead, honors Elizabeth Morgan Belmont.

Belmont estate, Nursery Stud Farm, rear facade, 1935, during demolition; servants' quarters on left

Belmont, August, Sr. (1816-1890)

Occupation(s):	financier -	president, August Belmont and Co. (investment banking firm); agent for Rothschild banking interest in United States
	diplomat -	United States *Charge d' affaires* and, later, Minister to The Netherlands; Austrian Council General to the United States
	politician -	delegate, Democratic Convention, 1860*; chairman, National Democratic Committee, 1864-1868
	capitalist -	co-owner, with Electus Backus Litchfield, Argyle Hotel, Babylon, NY
Civic Activism:		helped raise and equip the first German regiment for the Union during the Civil War
Marriage(s):		1849-1890 – Caroline Slidell Perry (1829-1892)
Address:		Southern State Parkway, North Babylon
Name of estate:		*Nursery Stud Farm*
Year of construction:		c. 1868
Style of architecture:		Modified Second Empire with Colonial Revival elements
Architect(s):		Detlef Lienau designed the house (for A. Belmont, Sr.)

Landscape architect(s):
House extant: no; demolished in 1935**
Historical notes:

The twenty-four-room house, originally names *Nursery Stud Farm*, was built by August Belmont, Sr.

He was the son of Simon and Frederika Elsaas Belmont of Alzei, Rhenish Palatinate, Prussia.

An avid breeder of thoroughbred horses, Belmont purchased 1,300 acres in North Babylon in 1864 to be used as a stud farm. Eventually there were thirty outbuildings, a one-mile racetrack with a grandstand, and five hundred acres of the farm property under cultivation.

Caroline Slidell Perry Belmont was the daughter of Commodore Matthew Calbraith and Mrs. Jane Slidell Perry and a niece of Commodore Oliver Hazard Perry.

The Belmonts' son Perry, who married Jessie Robbins, did not own the estate but listed *Nursery Stud Farm* as his legal address. Their son Oliver, who resided at *Belcourt* in Newport, RI, and at *Brookholt* in East Meadow, married Sallie Whiting and, subsequently, Alva Erskine Smith Vanderbilt, the wife of his close friend William Kissam Vanderbilt, Sr., who resided at *Idlehour* in Oakdale. Their son August Belmont, Jr., who purchased *Nursery Stud Farm*, married Elizabeth Hamilton Morgan and, subsequently, Eleanor Robson. After August's death, Eleanor resided in Syosset. [*See* Spinzia, *Long Island's Prominent Families in the Town of Hempstead* and *Long Island's Prominent North Shore Families, vol. I* – Belmont entries.] Their son Raymond Rogers Belmont I, who was a bachelor, committed suicide in 1887 at the age of twenty-four. Their daughter Jane died at the age of twenty-one.

[See other Belmont entries for additional family information.]

*During the 1860 Democratic Convention, Belmont supported Stephen A. Douglas as a compromise candidate.

During World War I a portion of the estate became the United States Army Air Corps' Camp Damm (aka Camp Henry J. Damm).

**In 1935, the house was demolished by the Long Island State Park Commission. Part of the estate's property is now Belmont Lake State Park. The two cannons in front of the commission's headquarters in the park are from a British ship sunk at the Battle of Lake Erie by Commodore Oliver Hazard Perry during the War of 1812. They were recovered by Belmont from a Pittsburgh junkyard.

Nursery Stud Farm, side / front facade

Belmont, August, III (1882-1919)

Occupation(s):	financier -	partner, August Belmont and Co. (investment banking firm); director, Windsor Trust Co.; director, First National Bank of Hempstead
	capitalist -	treasurer, August Belmont Hotel Co.; director, Interborough–Metropolitan Co.; director, Cape Cod Construction Co.; treasurer, Park Row Realty Co.; director, Degon Realty & Terminal Improvement Co.; director, Degon Terminal Railroad Corp.

Marriage(s): 1906-1919 – Alice Wall de Goicouria (1885-1926)
- Civic Activism: suffragist, member, Islip Woman's Suffrage Club

Address: 52 South Saxon Avenue, Bay Shore
Name of estate:
Year of construction: 1880
Style of architecture: Colonial Revival
Architect(s): Isaac Henry Green II designed the 1889 southwestern wing addition of a living room and four bedrooms (for E. S. Knapp, Sr.)
Landscape architect(s):
House extant: yes
Historical notes:

The house, originally named *Awixa Lawn*, was built by Edward Spring Knapp, Sr. In 1915, it was purchased by Belmont.

The *Brooklyn Blue Book and Long Island Society Register, 1921* incorrectly lists August and Alice W. de Goicouria Belmont, Jr. [III], as residing on Saxon Avenue in Bay Shore.

He was the son of August and Elizabeth Hamilton Morgan Belmont, Jr. of *Nursery Stud Farm* in North Babylon and *Blemton Manor* in Hempstead. [*See* Spinzia, *Long Island's Prominent Families in the Town of Hempstead* – Belmont entry.]

Alice Wall de Goicouria Belmont was the daughter of Cuban-born Albert Valentine and Mary Cecelia Wall de Goicouria of Islip. Alice subsequently married John Daniel Wing, who resided in Southampton. [*See* Spinzia, *Long Island's Prominent Families in the Town of Southampton* – Wing entry.] Alice's sister Rosalie married Walter Scott Cameron, with whom she resided at *Wee Home* on Gin Lane in Southampton, and, subsequently, Benjamin Curtis Allen of Philadelphia, PA. [*See* Spinzia, *Long Island's Prominent Families in the Town of Southampton* – Cameron entry.]

August and Alice Wall de Goicouria Belmont III's daughter Bessie married Louis Felix Timmerman, Jr. and resided in Manhattan and on Shelter Island. Their daughter Cecelia married Gardiner Lothrop Lewis of Swampscott, MA. Their daughter Barbara married Robert Livermore, Jr. In 1955 the Belmont's forty-five-year-old daughter Alice, who did not marry, committed suicide in her apartment on 113th Street in Manhattan. Their son August Belmont IV married Elizabeth Lee Saltonstall, the daughter of John L. Saltonstall of Topsfield, MA, and, subsequently, Louise Vietor, the daughter of George F. Vietor of Manhattan. Louise had previously been married to Francis L. Winston. August and Louise Belmont IV resided on Burtis Lane in Syosset.

[See other Belmont entries for additional family information.]

In 1923, Mrs. Belmont sold the estate, which consisted of a twenty-five-room main residence on nine acres with six hundred feet of shoreline on Awixa Creek, stables, and a five-car garage to John Allen Dillon, Sr.

It was later owned by Julius Oppenheimer.

front facade, 2006

Belmont, Perry (1851-1947)

Occupation(s):	attorney
	politician - member, 47th through 50th Congresses, 1881-1887
	diplomat - United States Minister to Spain, 1887-1888
	writer - *National Isolation: An Illusion*, 1924;
	Survival of Democratic Principle, 1926;
	Return to the Secret Party Funds, 1927;
	Political Equality, Religious Toleration, 1928;
	An American Democrat, 1940;
Civic Activism:	member, advisory board, American Defense Society
Marriage(s):	1899-1935 – Jessie A. Robbins (d. 1935)
Address:	Southern State Parkway, North Babylon
Name of estate:	*Nursery Stud Farm*
Year of construction:	c. 1868
Style of architecture:	Modified Second Empire with Colonial Revival elements
Architect(s):	Detlef Lienau designed the house (for A. Belmont, Sr.)
Landscape architect(s):	
House extant: no; demolished in 1935	
Historical notes:	

Nursery Stud Farm

Perry Belmont did not own the estate but listed *Nursery Stud Farm Farm* as his legal address. He was the eldest son of August and Caroline Slidell Perry Belmont, Sr.

Jessie A. Robbins Belmont was the daughter of Daniel C. and Matilda L. Robbins of Brooklyn. She had previously been married to Henry T. Sloane.

Henry T. and Jessie Robbins Sloane's daughter Jessie married William Earle Dodge of Manhattan and, subsequently, George Dunton Widner, Jr., with whom she resided in Old Westbury. [*See* Spinzia, *Long Island's Prominent North Shore Families*, *vol. II* – Widner entry.] The Sloanes' daughter Emily married Baron Amaury de la Grange and resided in Paris, France.

[See previous Belmont entries for additional family information.]

Benkard, James Gerald (1875-1941)

Occupation(s):	financier - partner, J. P. Benkard and Co. (stock brokerage firm)
Civic Activism:	secretary and master, Holland Lodge of Masons;
	Grand Swordbearer, Grand Masonic Lodge of New York State;
	vice-chairman, American Legion Posts, Suffolk County;
	founder and president, Babylon American Legion Post;
	suffragist - member, Babylon Suffrage Club, 1914
Marriage(s):	1911 – Edith Lake (1886-1938)
Address:	57 Prospect Street, Babylon
Name of estate:	
Year of construction:	
Style of architecture:	Victorian
Architect(s):	
Landscape architect(s):	
House extant: yes	
Historical notes:	

In 1915, Benkard purchased the house from H. Van Hemert and immediately remodeled it. [*South Side Signal* (Babylon), November 5, 1915, p. 5.]

The *Long Island Society Register, 1928* lists J. Gerald and Edith Lake Benkard as residing at 57 Prospect Street, Babylon.

He was the son of James Julius and Fanny Gage Horton Benkard. His brother Henry married Bertha King Bartlett, the daughter of Franklin and Bertha King Post Bartlett, and resided in Garden City. After Henry's death, Mrs. Benkard relocated from Garden City to Upper Brookville. [*See* Spinzia, *Long Island's Prominent Families in the Town of Hempstead* and *Long Island's Prominent North Shore Families*, *vol. I* – Benkard entries.]

Edith Lake Benkard was the daughter of Louis N. Lake of NYC.

James Gerald and Edith Lake Benkard's daughter Jane married Patrick Cusack.

Bergen, Charles M. (1853-1930)

Occupation(s):	
Civic Activism:	treasurer, First Presbyterian Church, Babylon; bequeathed $1,000 to foreign missions of the Presbyterian Church of America; bequeathed $1,000 to the First Presbyterian Church, Babylon
Marriage(s):	Ellen Cowenhoven (1853-1940)
Address:	West Main Street, West Babylon
Name of estate:	
Year of construction:	1902
Style of architecture:	Queen Anne
Architect(s):	
Landscape architect(s):	
House extant:	yes
Historical notes:	

The house was built by Charles M. Bergen.

He was the son of Michael and Rebecca Bergen of Brooklyn. Charles' brother Jacob married Joanna N. Beekman and resided in West Babylon.

Ellen Cowenhoven Bergen was the daughter of Garret and Madaline Cowenhoven of Brooklyn.

Charles M. and Ellen Cowenhoven Bergen's son Harold married Lina Van Weeldon, the daughter of Henry Van Weeldon, and resided in West Hartford, CT.

In 1990, the house was moved to just south of Thompson Avenue onto the site of Robert Moses' former house.

side facade

Bergen, Cornelius J., Sr. (1814-1884)

Occupation(s):	merchant - partner, with his brother Alexander, wholesale grocery firm
	capitalist - partner, with his brother Alexander, Brooklyn and Babylon land speculation
Marriage(s):	1838-1884 – Helen M. Clark (1818-1912)
Address:	South Country Road, West Babylon
Name of estate:	
Year of construction:	c. 1880
Style of architecture:	
Architect(s):	
Landscape architect(s):	
House extant:	unconfirmed
Historical notes:	

Cornelius J. Bergen was the son of John Tunis and Margaret Donald McLeod Bergen of Brooklyn.

Helen M. Clark Bergen was the daughter of Daniel Clark of Brooklyn.

The Bergen's foster son James Cornelius Bergen, who resided in Babylon, married Jennie Adele McCue, the daughter of Alexander McCue of Babylon. Their son Victor married Cornelia J. Udall, the daughter of General Richard Udall of Islip, and resided in Bay Shore. Their son Cornelius J. Bergen, Jr. died at an early age in China.

In 1882, a barn and a carriage house were built. [*South Side Signal* March 11, 1882, p. 2.]

The house was later owned by Cornelia J. Udall Bergen.

Bergen, Jacob M. (1837-1913)

Occupation(s):

Marriage(s): Joanna N. Beekman (1839-1909)

Address: Little East Neck Road, Babylon
Name of estate:
Year of construction:
Style of architecture: c. 1890
Architect(s):
Landscape architect(s):
Builder: E. W. Howell, 1912 alterations
(for L. W. T. Coleman)
House extant: unconfirmed
Historical notes:

    Jacob M. Bergen was the son of Michael and Rebecca Bergen of Brooklyn. Jacob's brother Charles married Ellen Cowenhoven and resided in West Babylon.
    Joanna N. Beekman Bergen was the daughter of Abraham John and Catharine Schoonmaker Beekman.
    The Bergens' son Abraham married Linda Elizabeth Robbins, the daughter of John and Selinda E. Smith Robbins of Babylon.
    In 1912, the house was sold to Leander Walter Townsend Coleman who had previously resided on The Crescent in Babylon. [*South Side Signal* October 25, 1912, p. 5.]

Bergen, James Cornelius (1852-1906)

Occupation(s): attorney - partner, Bergen and Dykman;
partner, partner, Crook, Bergen, and Platt;
partner, Irvine and Bergen;
partner, Bergen and Prentergast

Civic Activism: director, South Shore Country Club, West Islip

Marriage(s): 1878-1906 – Jennie Adele McCue (d. 1921)

Address: South Country Road, West Babylon
Name of estate: *Suanne*
Year of construction:
Style of architecture:
Architect(s):
Landscape architect(s):
House extant: unconfirmed
Historical notes:

    James Cornelius Bergen was the son of Dr. Andrew Otterson of Brooklyn and the foster son of his mother's brother Cornelius James Bergen, Sr. whose surname he adopted.
    Jennie Adele McCue Bergen was the daughter of Alexander McCue of Babylon. Her sister Heloise married Francis Blair Sands and resided in Babylon.
    The Bergens did not have children.

side facade, 1916

Betts, Roland Whitney (1877-1954)

Occupation(s):	financier - partner, Betts, Power, and King (produce exchange brokerage firm)
Marriage(s):	1905-div. 1929 – Mabel Granbery (d. 1958) - Civic Activism: major, Motor Ambulance Corp of New York during World War I; president, auxiliary, Southside Hospital, Bay Shore (now, South Shore University Hospital)
Address:	Handsome Avenue, Sayville
Name of estate:	*Sunneholm*

Year of construction:
Style of architecture:
Architect(s):
Landscape architect(s):
House extant: unconfirmed
Historical notes:

    The *Brooklyn Blue Book and Long Island Society Register, 1918* and *1921* lists Roland Whitney and Mabel Granbery Betts as residing at *Sunneholm* in Sayville.

    The *Long Island Society Register, 1929* lists Mabel Granbery Betts as residing on Handsome Avenue in Bayport [Sayville] and Roland as residing in Manhattan.

    He was the son of Edward and Emma Whitney Betts of Brooklyn. His brother Herbert married Jessica Watkins, the daughter of Albert Watkins.

    Mabel Granbery Betts was the daughter of Henry Augustus Thaddeus and Prudence Nimmo Granbery of Norfolk, VA. In 1929, Mabel married Charles Edward Spratt. Her sister Mary married Frank Smith Jones and resided at *Beechwold* in Sayville. Mabel's sister Mrs. Paul Strayer resided in Rochester, NY.

    Roland Whitney and Mabel Granbery Betts' son Allan married Evelyn Ohman and reside in Laurel Hollow. Their daughter Louise married Frederick David Anderson, the son of Frederick and Florence Sweetland Anderson of Ottawa, Canada.

Bigelow, Edwin Hicks (1886-1970)

Occupation(s):	financier - partner, Dillon, Read, and Co. (investment banking firm)
Civic Activism:	president, East Side Draft Board, NYC, during World War I; member, building fund committee, Beekman–Downtown Hospital, NYC
Marriage(s):	1920-div. – Alice Isabel Blum (1895-1988)
Address:	*[unable to determine street address]*, East Islip

Name of estate:
Year of construction:
Style of architecture:
Architect(s):
Landscape architect(s):
House extant: unconfirmed
Historical notes:

    The *Long Island Society Register, 1929* lists the Bigelows as residing in East Islip.

    He was the son of Elliot and Edwina Richards Bigelow.

    Alice Isabel Blum Bigelow was the daughter of Edward Charles and Florence May Abraham Blum, who resided at *Shore Acres* in Bay Shore. After her divorce from Bigelow, Alice married Eugene Sinclair Taliaferro and resided at *The Wilderness* in Cove Neck. [*See* Spinzia, *Long Island's Prominent North Shore Families, vol. II* – Taliaferro entry.] She subsequently married Ethelbert Warfield, with whom she resided in Oyster Bay. Her brother Robert married Ethel Halsey and resided in Bay Shore.

    Edwin Hicks and Alice Isabel Blum Bigelow's son Edwin Richards Bigelow married Melissa Weston, the daughter of Herbert Weston of Southampton, and, subsequently, Joan Evelyn Turnburke, the daughter of Harry Milton Turnburke of Clearwater, FL, and resided in Denver, CO. [*See* Spinzia, *Long Island's Prominent Families in the Town of Southampton,* – Weston entry.] Their daughter Florence married Norman Schaff, Jr. and resided in Westport, CT.

Birdsall, Clarence K. (1871-1936)

Occupation(s): architect
[See architect appendix for a list of Birdsall's South Shore commissions.]

Marriage(s): 1895 – Mary Abby Maynard (b. 1870)

Address: Oakland Avenue, Bay Shore
Name of estate:
Year of construction:
Style of architecture:
Architect(s):
Landscape architect(s):
House extant: unconfirmed
Historical notes:

In 1904 Clarence K. Birdsall leased the Sands residence on Oakland Avenue. [*The Suffolk County News* April 1, 1904, p. 2.]

He was the son of Thomas H. and Sarah Frances Stice Birdsall of Brooklyn.

Mary Abby Maynard Birdsall was the daughter of Edgar Augustus and Mary Abby Kellogg Maynard of Brockport, NY.

Clarence K. and Mary Abby Maynard Birdsall's son Edgar resided in Los Angeles, CA.

Blagden, Crawford, Sr. (1882-1937)

Occupation(s): financier - member, Clark, Dodge, and Co. (private investment firm); member, Walker and Sons (stock brokerage firm)

Civic Activism: *

Marriage(s): M/1 – 1911-1912 – Mary Hopkins (d. 1912)
M/2 – 1918-1937 – Mina E. MacLeond

Address: 109 Fire Island Avenue, Babylon
Name of estate:
Year of construction: 1874
Style of architecture: Second Empire
Architect(s): Hallock & Hait designed the house (for S. C. Smith)
Landscape architect(s):
Builder: under the direction of William L. Hallock of Hallock & Hait

House extant: yes
Historical notes:

The house, known as *Smith Cottage*, was built by Selah Carll Smith. It was later owned by Blagden.

He was the son of Samuel P. and Julia G. Blagden of Manhattan.

Mary Hopkins Blagden was the daughter of Archibald and Charlotte Everett Hopkins.

The *Long Island Society Register, 1929* lists Crawford and Mina E. MacLeond Blagden, [Sr.] as residing at 109 Fire Island Avenue, Babylon.

Blagden's son Crawford Blagden, Jr. married Mary Kernochan, the daughter of Justice Frederic Kernochan of Tuxedo Park, NY.

*Crawford Blagden, Sr. and Grenville Clark, Sr. of Albertson are credited with being major supporters for the establishment of the Plattsburg, NY, training camps, which, during World War I, trained over 16,000 men to become army officers. [*The New York Times* January 13, 1937, p. 23.]

front / side facade, 2005

Blum, Edward Charles (1863-1946)

Occupation(s):	merchant - chairman of board, Abraham & Straus (department store chain) (which merged into Federated Department Stores Inc.)
	financer - trustee, Dime Savings Bank of Brooklyn; trustee, Kings County Trust Co.; trustee, Security Safe Deposit Co.
	capitalist - vice-president, Abrast Realty Co.; treasurer, Flatbush Avenue Realty Co.
Civic Activism:	chairman of board, Brooklyn Institute of Arts and Sciences; board member, French Hospital; board member, Brooklyn Chamber of Commerce; board member, National Council Economic League; member, Red Cross Auxiliary during World War I; president, Jewish Hospital of Brooklyn; director, Brooklyn Federation of Jewish Charities; director, Brooklyn League; director, Juvenile Probation Association; director, Bay Shore Horse Show, 1903; a founder and director, Great River Club, 1920 (later, Timber Point Club); a founder and director, Bay Shore Protective Association; governor, Penataquit Corinthian Yacht Club
Marriage(s):	1894-1946 – Florence May Abraham (1872-1959)
	- Civic Activism: member of board, American Women's Voluntary Services during World War I; member, advisory committee, New York's World Fair, 1939; president, Hebrew Educational Society Auxiliary; vice-chairman, women's committee, Boston Symphony concerts in Brooklyn; suffragist
Address:	Penataquit Avenue, Bay Shore
Name of estate:	*Shore Acres*
Year of construction:	1902
Style of architecture:	Queen Anne
Architect(s):	Walker and Gillette, alterations (for Blum)
Landscape architect(s):	
House extant:	no
Historical notes:	

The house, originally named *Shore Acres*, was built by Edward Charles Blum. [*The Brooklyn Daily Eagle* October 13, 1901, p. 11.]

The *Long Island Society Register, 1929* lists Edward Charles and Florence May Abraham Blum as residing at *Shore Acres* in Bay Shore.

He was the son of Adolph and Ida Deutsch Blum of Manhattan.

Florence May Abraham Blum was the daughter of the co-founder of Abraham and Straus Department Store, Abraham Abraham. Her sister Lillian married Simon Frank Rothschild and resided in Bay Shore. Her sister Edith married Percy S. Straus and resided in Manhattan and Red Bank, NJ.

Edward Charles and Florence May Abraham Blum's daughter Alice married Edwin Hicks Bigelow and resided in East Islip. She later married Eugene Sinclair Taliaferro and resided at *The Wilderness* in Cove Neck. [*See* Spinzia, *Long Island's Prominent North Shore Families, vol. II* – Taliaferro entry.] Alice subsequently married Ethelbert Warfield and resided in Oyster Bay. The Blums' son Robert married Ethel Mildred Halsey and resided in Bay Shore.

[*See following entry for additional family information.*]

Italian garden, 1903

Blum, Robert Edward (1899-1999)

Occupation(s):	merchant - vice president and secretary, Abraham & Straus (department store chain) (which merged with F. R. Lazarus, Shillito's, and Filene's of Boston in 1929 to form the holding company Federated Department Stores Inc.*);
	director, Federated Department Stores Inc.
	financer - director, Equitable Life Assurance Society of the United States; trustee, Dime Savings Bank of Brooklyn; trustee, Kings County Trust Co.
Civic Activism:	president of board, Brooklyn Institute of Arts and Sciences; member, New York State Board of Social Welfare (Dewey administration); treasurer, Lincoln Center for the Performing Arts, NYC; trustee, The Wildlife Conservation; member, New York City Municipal Art Commission (Lindsay administration); director, Better Business Bureau; trustee, Foundation for Youth and Student Affairs**
Marriage(s):	1928-1991 – Ethel Mildred Halsey (1901-1991)
	- journalist
	artist - watercolorist
	Civic Activism: a founder, Brooklyn Committee for Planned Parenthood; president, Brooklyn Juvenile Guidance Center; trustee, Mount Desert Hospital, Bar Harbor, ME; a founder and president, Mount Desert Island Highway Safety Council, Bar Harbor, ME; trustee, Mount Desert Biological Laboratory, Bar Harbor, ME
Address:	Penataquit Avenue, Bay Shore
Name of estate:	
Year of construction:	
Style of architecture:	
Architect(s):	
Landscape architect(s):	
House extant: unconfirmed	
Historical notes:	

The *Long Island Society Register, 1929* lists Robert Edward and Ethel Mildred Halsey Blum as residing in Bay Shore. They subsequently resided at *Slope Oaks* in the Roslyn area of Long Island's North Shore.

He was the son of Edward Charles and Florence May Abraham Blum of *Shore Acres* in Bay Shore.

Ethel Mildred Halsey Blum was the daughter of Dr. and Mrs. John T. Halsey.

Robert Edward and Ethel Mildred Halsey Blum's son John married Susanne Holcomb Jousseam Delatour, the daughter of Dr. Beeckman J. Delatour of South Worcester, NY. Their daughter Alice married Robert H. Yoakum and resided in Lakefield, CT.

[See previous entry for additional family information.]

*Federated Department Stores, Inc. owned and operated 992 stores in forty-five states, the District of Columbia, Guam, and Puerto Rico under the names Bloomingdale's, Famous – Barr, Filene's, Foley's, Hecht's, Kaufmann's, Lord & Taylor, L. S. Ayres, Macy's, Marshall Field's, Meier & Frank, Robinsons – May, Strawbridge's, and The Jones Store. It also owned and operated 721 bridal and formalwear stores in forty-seven states and Puerto Rico under the names of David's Bridal, After Hours Formalwear, and Priscilla of Boston.

**Founded in 1952, the Foundation for Youth and Student Affairs received financial support from the Central Intelligence Agency.

Bohack, Henry Christian (1865-1931)
aka Hinrich Christian Bohack

Occupation(s):	merchant - president, H. C. Bohack & Co. (grocery store chain of 740 stores)
	capitalist - president, Bohack Realty Corp.
	financier - director, People's National Bank of Brooklyn; director, Guarantee Title and Mortgage Co.; director, East New York Securities Co.; trustee, Hamburg Savings Bank of Brooklyn
Civic Activism:	trustee, Wartburg Orphan Training School, Mount Vernon, NY; director, Queensborough Chamber of Commerce
Marriage(s):	1889-1931 – Emma Augusta Steffens (1870-1961)
Address:	South Country Road and Greeley Avenue, Sayville
Name of estate:	
Year of construction:	
Style of architecture:	
Architect(s):	
Landscape architect(s):	
House extant: yes	
Historical notes:	

The Bohacks spent one summer in Sayville.
He was the son of Christian and Dorothea Postel Bohack.
Emma Augusta Steffens Bohack was the daughter of Jacob Jurgen and Anna Heuck Steffens. She, subsequently, married Frank Schindl.

Bossert, Charles Volunteer (1888-1953)

Occupation(s):	industrialist - partner, with his half-brother John, Bossert Lumber Co., Brooklyn*
	capitalist - partner, with his mother Philippine and half-brother John, Hotel Bossert, Brooklyn Heights; president, Bossert Building Corp., Trenton, NJ
Marriage(s):	1913-1953 – Natalie L. Taylor (1891-1977)
Address:	*[unable to determine street address]*, Sayville
Name of estate:	
Year of construction:	
Style of architecture:	
Architect(s):	
Landscape architect(s):	
House extant: unconfirmed	
Historical notes:	

Charles Volunteer Bossert was named after the America Cup winner *Volunteer*.
He was the son of Louis and Philippine Louise Krippendorf Bossert who resided at *The Oaks* in West Islip.
Natalie L. Taylor Bossert was the daughter of Peter G. and Emma Jane Taylor of Brooklyn.
Charles Volunteer and Natalie L. Taylor Bossert's daughter Isabelle married Edward Peter Ruddy of Forest Hills, Queens. Their daughter Natalie married John Gildersleeve Heemans, Jr. of Brooklyn.
[See following entry for additional family information.]
*The Bossert Lumber Company, which was one of the largest lumber companies in the country, filed for bankruptcy during the Depression. [Liz Howell, *Continuity: Biography 1819-1934* (Sister Bay, WI: The Dragonsbreath Press, 1993), pp. 364-65.]

Bossert, Louis (1843-1913)

Occupation(s):	capitalist - builder and owner, Hotel Bossert, Brooklyn Heights; director, Estates of Long Island (real estate developer)
	industrialist - president, Bossert Lumber Co., Brooklyn; president, Louis Bossert & Sons, Brooklyn (sash manufacturer)
	financier - president, Broadway Bank of Brooklyn; trustee, Germania Savings Bank
Civic Activism:	trustee, Brooklyn Academy of Music
Marriage(s):	M/1 – 1869-1884 – Elizabeth Neger (d. 1884)
	M/2 – 1885-1913 – Philippine Louise Krippendorf (1858-1945)
Address:	South Country Road, West Bay Shore
Name of estate:	*The Oaks*
Year of construction:	c. 1874-1876
Style of architecture:	Stick Style
Architect(s):	Calvert Vaux designed the house (for H. B. Hyde, Sr.)
Landscape architect(s):	Olmsted, with Jacob Weidenman (for H. B. Hyde, Sr.)*

House extant: yes**
Historical notes:

The forty-room house, situated on 365 acres, was originally named *Masquetux* before being renamed *The Oaks*. It was built by Henry Baldwin Hyde, Sr. The estate was inherited by his son James, who continued to call it *The Oaks*. In 1901, the estate and most of James Hazen Hyde's furniture were purchased by Bossert. [Liz Howell, *Continuity: Biography 1819-1934* (Sister Bay, WI: The Dragonsbreath Press, 1993), p. 221.]

Louis Bossert was the son of Alois and Mary Bossert of Brooklyn.

Elizabeth Neger Bossert was the daughter of Mathias Neger, a successful Brooklyn wine merchant.

Louis and Elizabeth Neger Bossert's son John married Mary A. James and resided in Garden City and, later, in Jamaica, Queens. [*See* Spinzia, *Long Island's Prominent Families in the Town of Hempstead* – Bossert entry.] Their daughter Harriet married Frederick Max Huber, Sr. and resided in Bay Shore. Their daughter Josephine married Dr. Henry Moser of Brooklyn.

Philippine Louise Krippendorf was originally the Bossert children's piano teacher.

Louis and Philippine Louise Krippendorf Bossert's son Charles married Natalie L. Taylor and resided in Sayville. Their daughter Bienie married Carroll Trowbridge Cooney, the son of John J. Cooney of Brooklyn, and resided in Plandome.

Louis Bossert died of a ruptured appendix half way between Honolulu and San Francisco, while returning from a round-the-world tour.

[See previous entry for additional family information.]

*Weidenman's landscape plans were awarded special honor at the 1876 Centennial Exhibition in Philadelphia, PA.

**The house, which has been extensively modified over the years, is currently the clubhouse of the Southward Ho Country Club.

The Oaks

*Louis Bossert estate, The Oaks
service building, front facade, 2005*

Bourne, Alfred Severin, Sr. (1883-1956)

Occupation(s):
Civic Activism: donated Barnes Memorial Field, in memory of his wife, to Gunnery School, Washington, CT*;
    donated Bourne Field to Berkshire School, Sheffield, MA;
    a founder and director, Great River Club (later, Timber Point Club)

Marriage(s):   1905-1955 – Hattie Louise Barnes (1885-1955)
     - Civic Activism: president, Garden Club, Washington, CT;
            president, Sands Hill Garden Club, Augusta, GA

Address: South Country Road, Oakdale
Name of estate:
Year of construction:
Style of architecture:
Architect(s):
Landscape architect(s):
House extant: unconfirmed
Historical notes:

    The *Brooklyn Blue Book and Long Island Society Register, 1918* lists Alfred S. and Hattie Louise Barnes Bourne [Sr.] as residing in Oakdale. The *Brooklyn Blue Book and Long Island Society Register 1921* lists their address as South Country Road, Oakdale.
    He was the son of Frederick Gilbert and Emma Sparks Keeler Bourne, who resided at *Indian Neck Hall* in Oakdale.
    Hattie Louise Barnes Bourne was the daughter of Richard Storrs and Hattie Day Barbour Barnes.
    Alfred Severin and Hattie Louise Barnes Bourne, Sr.'s son Alfred Severin Bourne, Jr. married Nancy H. Work, the daughter of James Henry and Mary Laying Davies Work, Jr. of *Engleside* in Lawrence, and resided at *The Woodlands* on Oakwood Lane in Greenwich, CT. [*See* Spinzia, *Long Island's Prominent Families in the Town of Hempstead* – Work entry.] Their son Kenneth married Ann E. Clark, the daughter of Raymond P. Clark of Rochester, NY, and resided in Rochester. Their daughter Barbara married John B. Von Schiegell and resided in Pinehurst, NC. Their son Frederick Gilbert Bourne II died in infancy.
[See other Bourne entries for additional family information.]
*In 1958, the Gunnery School purchased Bourne's 140-acre Washington, CT, estate.

Bourne, Arthur Keeler, Sr. (1877-1967)

Occupation(s):	industrialist - director, Singer Sewing Machine Co.
	capitalist - president, Round Hill Resort, Lake Tahoe, CA
Civic Activism:	established Claire Louise Progressive Elementary School, San Gabriel, CA (now, Clairbourn School)
Marriage(s):	M/1 – 1903-div. – Ethel L. Hollins (1879-1970)
	M/2 – Emily Boxley Miller
	M/3 – Jean *[unable to determine maiden name]*
Address:	South Country Road, Oakdale
Name of estate:	*Lake House*
Year of construction:	c. 1904
Style of architecture:	Colonial Revival
Architect(s):	Isaac Henry Green II designed the house (for A. K. Bourne, Sr.)

Landscape architect(s):
House extant: yes
Historical notes:

The house, originally named *Lake House*, was built by Arthur Keeler Bourne, Sr.

He was the son of Frederick Gilbert and Emma Sparks Keeler Bourne of *Indian Neck Hall* in Oakdale.

Ethel L. Hollins Bourne was the daughter of Frank C. Hollins, a stockbroker who committed suicide in 1909. [*The New York Times* April 10, 1909, p. 9.] Her sister Daisy married Willard F. Smith and resided at *Ledgeland* in Lee, MA.

In 1922, at the age of eighteen, Arthur Keeler and Ethel L. Hollins Bourne, Sr.'s son Arthur Keeler Bourne, Jr. eloped with Beatrice Clancy, the daughter of John F. Clancy, an Astoria, Queens, general building contractor. Their marriage was shaky almost from the start. In 1924, Beatrice sued Arthur for separation on the charge of desertion and sued her mother-in-law for alienation of affections. In 1925, Beatrice had Arthur arrested and jailed for disorderly conduct, claiming that he had struck her. The arresting officer had to pursue Bourne for three city blocks before apprehending him. In spite of his having jumped bail on the desertion charge, Arthur's bail for the disorderly conduct charge was set at only $1,000. In 1926, after two years of legal battles, Arthur and Beatrice were reunited, but the reunion didn't end Arthur's legal problems. In 1927, he was involved in a fatal head-on automobile accident on Motor Parkway in the Village of Lake Success in which Frank A. Cotton of Indianapolis was killed. Bourne and the other driver Frank G. Brown, a cotton broker, accused each other of being drunk. [*The New York Times* June 25, 1925, p. 3; August 19, 1927, p. 19; August 20, 1927, p. 3; August 21, 1927, p. 27; and August 30, 1927, p. 10.]

In the midst of his son's problems, Arthur Keeler Bourne, Sr. had his own legal battles which involved suits and counter-suits with his brothers and sisters over the distribution of their father's inheritance.

[See other Bourne entries for additional family information.]

The house was purchased by LaSalle Military Academy. In 1999 it was sold to St. John's University. In 2016, it was purchased by Amity Education Group.

front facade, 2005

Bourne, Frederick Gilbert (1851-1919)

Occupation(s):	industrialist - president, Singer Sewing Machine Co;
	director, Diehl Manufacturing Co.;
	director, Babcock & Wilcock Co.;
	director, Atlas Portland Cement Co.;
	director, Aeolian Piano & Pianola Co.;
	trustee, New York Phonograph Co.
	financier - director, Knickerbocker Safe Deposit Co.;
	director, Bank of Manhattan Co.; Liberty National Bank;
	Knickerbocker Trust Co.; Albany Trust Co.; and
	Commercial Trust Co. of New Jersey
	capitalist - director, Long Island Rail Road;
	director, Bourne & Co., Ltd. of New Jersey;
	director, Long Island Motor Parkway;
	director, Long Branch Rail Road Co.
Marriage(s):	1875-1916 – Emma Sparks Keeler (1855-1916)
Address:	South Country Road, Oakdale
Name of estate:	*Indian Neck Hall*
Year of construction:	1897-1900
Style of architecture:	Modified Neo-Federal
Architect(s):	Ernest Flagg designed the house, 1907 and 1912 alterations,
	c. 1909 garage, and the original boathouse (for F. G. Bourne)
	Alfred Hopkins designed the c. 1910 farm complex (for F. G. Bourne)
	Isaac Henry Green II designed the c. 1904 gatehouse, c. 1905 boathouse,
	c. 1913 pump house, groundsman's house, superintendent's house, and
	barn (for F. G. Bourne)
Landscape architect(s):	Olmsted (for F. G. Bourne)*
House extant: yes	
Historical notes:	

The house, originally named *Indian Neck Hall*, was built by Frederick Gilbert Bourne.

He was the son of The Reverend George Washington and Mrs. Harriet Gilbert Bourne of Boston, MA.

Emma Sparks Keeler Bourne was the daughter of James Rufus and Mary Louise Davidson Keeler. Emma's sister Elizabeth married Frederick E. Ballard, Sr. and resided in Bay Shore.

Frederick Gilbert and Emma Sparks Keeler Bourne's son Arthur Keeler Bourne, Sr., who resided at *Lake House* in Oakdale, married Ethel L. Hollins, Emily Boxley Miller, and, subsequently, Jean ____. Their son Alfred Severin Bourne, Sr. married Hattie Louise Barnes and resided in Oakdale. Their son George Galt Bourne, who resided in Lattingtown, married Helen Cole Whitney and, subsequently, Nancy Atterbury Potter, the daughter of Eliphalet N. Potter. Their daughter Florence married Anson Wales Hard, Jr., with whom she resided at *Meadowedge* in West Sayville; Robert Barr Deans, Sr., with whom she resided at *Yeadon* on Centre Island; and, subsequently, Alexander Dallas Thayer of Philadelphia, PA. The Bournes' daughter Marjorie also was married to Alexander Dallas Thayer. Their daughter Marion married Robert George Elbert, the son of George Cleveland and Emma Breuer Elbert of Frederick, MD, and resided at *Elbourne* in North Hills. Their daughter May married Ralph Beaver Strassburger and resided at *Normandy Farm* in Gwynedd Valley, PA. Their son Howard died at age twenty-five. He was a bachelor. Their son Kenneth did not attain adulthood. [*See* Spinzia, *Long Island's Prominent North Shore Families, vol. I* – Bourne, Deans, and Elbert entries.]

[See other Bourne entries for additional family information.]

*The landscaping on the approximately two-thousand-acre estate included the planting of 10,000 trees and shrubs, the creation of two artificial fresh water lakes, and the dredging of a three-mile canal system.

In 1925, the Bourne family sold the estate to a land development syndicate headed by Joseph P. Day.

In 1926, Clason Point Military Academy of The Bronx purchased the main house, the boathouse, the garage complex, the gatehouse, and the surrounding 154 acres and renamed the academy LaSalle Military Academy. [James Fordyce, "Frederick Bourne and Indian Neck Hall" *Long Island Forum* April 1987, p. 88.]

In 2001, the academy, then named LaSalle Center, sold it to St. John's University. In 2016, it was purchased by Amity Education Group.

Frederick Gilbert Bourne estate, *Indian Neck Hall*

library, 1910

front facade, c. 1905

rear facade, 1955

gatehouse, 1991

boathouse, 1991

Frederick Gilbert Bourne estate, *Indian Neck Hall*

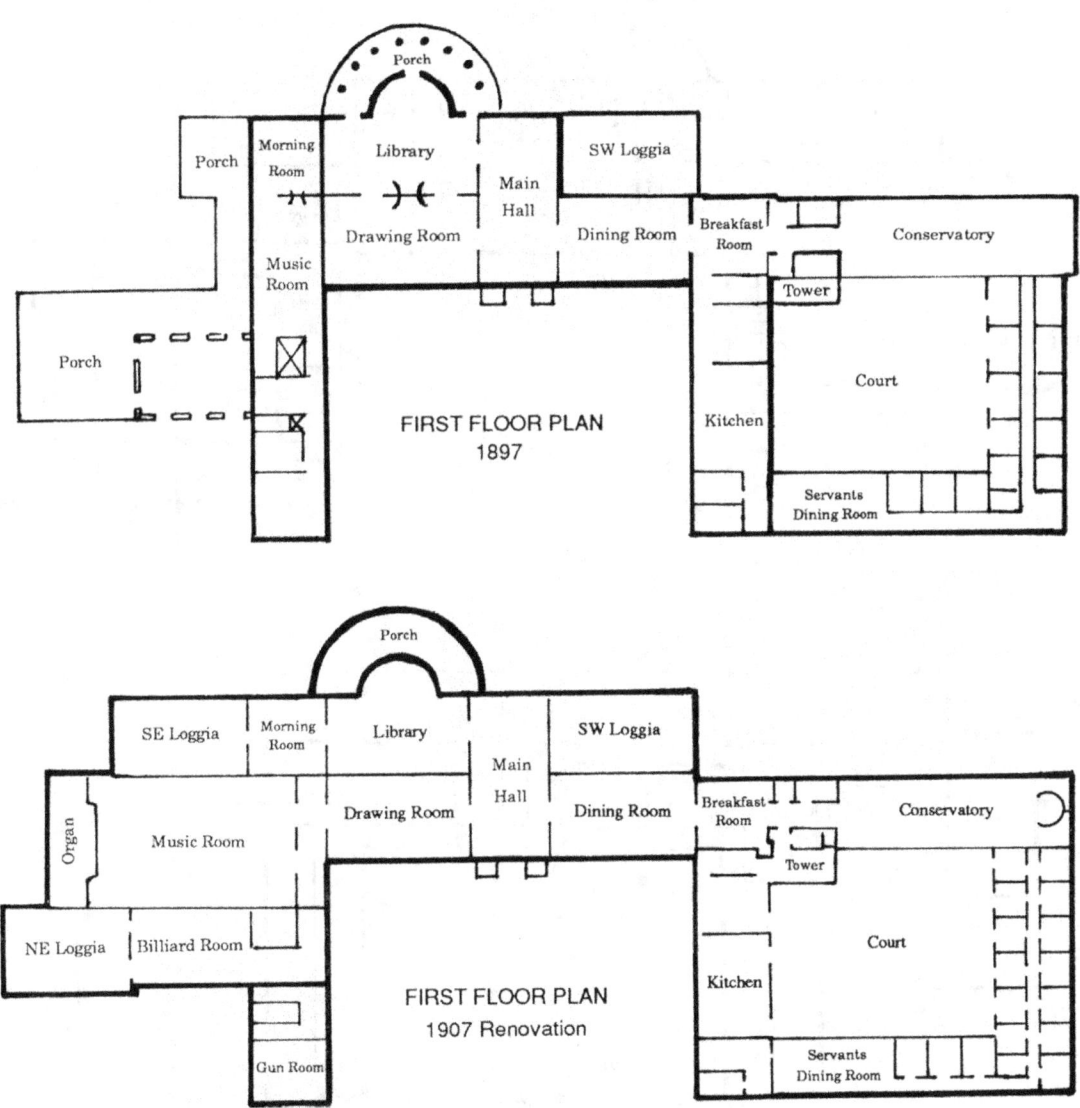

Frederick Gilbert Bourne estate, *Indian Neck Hall*

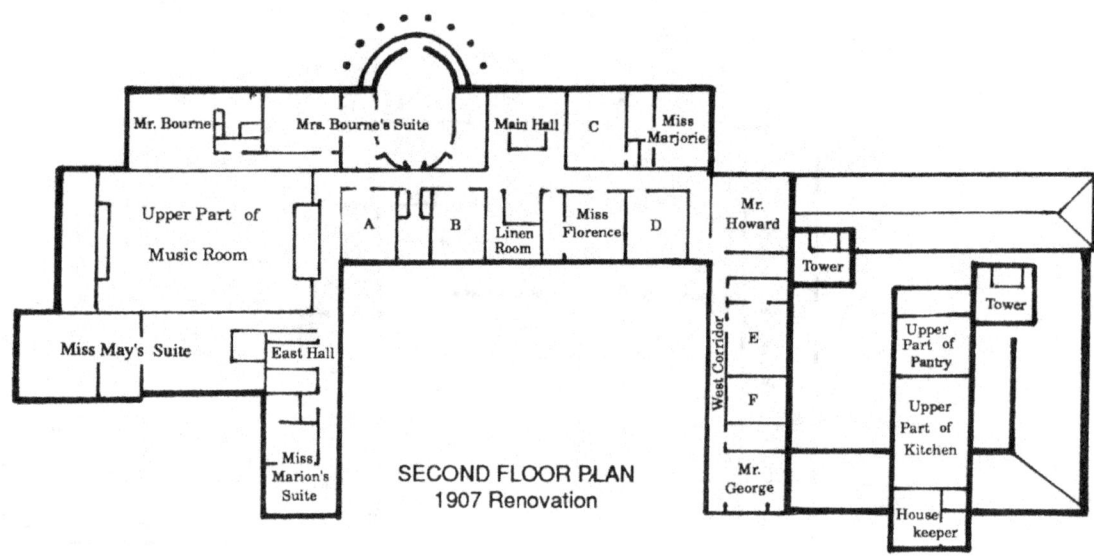

SECOND FLOOR PLAN
1907 Renovation

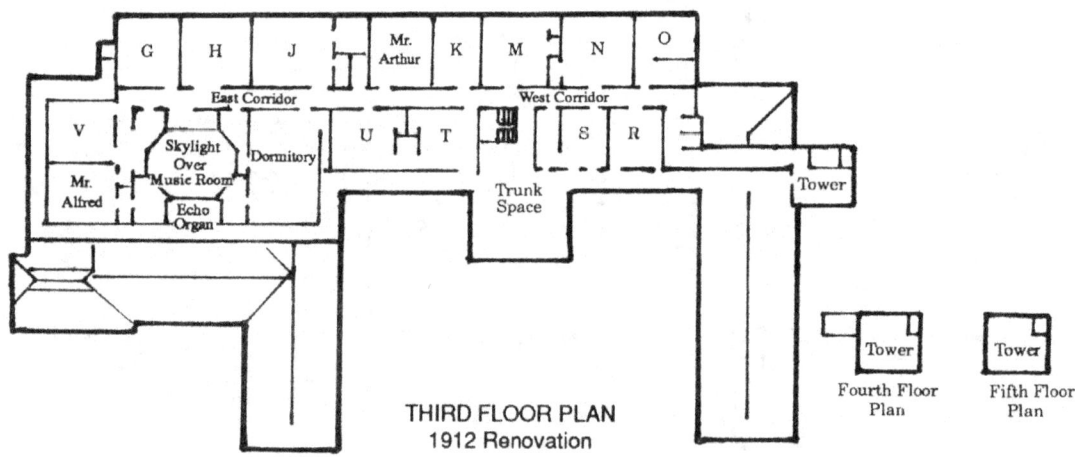

THIRD FLOOR PLAN
1912 Renovation

Fourth Floor Plan

Fifth Floor Plan

**Breese, William Laurence, Sr. (1856-1888)
aka William Lawrence Breese, Sr.***

Occupation(s):	financier - partner, Breese and Smith (stock brokerage firm)
Marriage(s):	1880-1888 – Marie Louise Parsons (b. 1857)
Address:	Great River Road, Great River
Name of estate:	*Timber Point*
Year of construction:	1882
Style of architecture:	Shingle
Architect(s):	Hart and Shape designed the alterations, converting the house to Colonial Revival (for Timber Point Club)
Landscape architect(s):	Martha Brooks Brown Hutcheson (for Breese)
Builder:	E. W. Howell

House extant: yes
Historical notes:

The house, originally named *Timber Point*, was built by William Laurence Breese, Sr.

He was the son of Joshua Salisbury and Augusta Eloise Lawrence Breese of Manhattan. William's brother James, who married Frances Tileston Potter and, later, Grace Lucille Momand, resided at *The Orchard* in Southampton. [*See* Spinzia, *Long Island's Prominent Families in the Town of Southampton* – Breese entry.]

Marie Louise Parsons Breese was the daughter of George McClellan and Jane Swan Parsons of Columbia, OH. Marie subsequently married Henry Vincent Higgins with whom she resided in London, England.

William Laurence and Marie Louise Parsons Breese, Sr.'s daughter Eloise married Gilbert Heathcote Drummond–Willoughby, the Second Earl of Ancaster. Their daughter Anne married Lord Alastair Robert Innes–Kerr. Both daughters resided in Great Britain. [Harry W. Havemeyer, *Along the Great South Bay From Oakdale to Babylon: The Story of a Summer Spa 1840 to 1940* (Mattituck, NY: Amereon House, 1996), pp. 130, 355, and 418.] Their son William Laurence [Lawrence] Breese, Jr. married Julia Kean Fish, the daughter of Secretary of State in the Grant administration Hamilton Fish.

*The spelling of William's middle name in genealogical records can be found as both Laurence and Lawrence.

In 1905, the estate was purchased by Julian Tappan Davies, who continued to call it *Timber Point*. In 1923, his heirs sold the estate to the Great River Club, which changed its name to the Timber Point Club in 1925.

It was owned for a period of time by the Republican Party of Suffolk County before being purchased by Suffolk County. The house is currently the clubhouse of the county's Timber Point Country Club.

Timber Point, c. 1925

Bromell, Alfred Henry (1862-1925)

Occupation(s):	shipping - vice-president, Munson Steamship Line
Marriage(s):	M/1 – 1883-1917 – Josephine Brumley (1864-1917) M/2 – Estelle M. Knowles (1896-1969)
Address:	South Country Road, Babylon
Name of estate:	
Year of construction:	
Style of architecture:	Shingle
Architect(s):	
Landscape architect(s):	
House extant:	unconfirmed
Historical notes:	

front facade, 1916

Alfred Henry Bromell was the son of William Brunswick and Sarah Hamilton Bromell.
Estelle M. Knowles Bromell subsequently married Charles Arthur Smith of Centre Island.
In 1923, Alfred Henry and Estelle M. Knowles Bromell's infant daughter Mary died.
At the time of his death the Bromells were residing on Centre Island. [For Bromell's Centre Island residence, *see* Spinzia, *Long Island's Prominent North Shore Families, vol. I* – Bromell entry.]

Brownlie, George

Occupation(s):	capitalist - Manhattan real estate politician - mayor, Dearing Harbor, Shelter Island
Marriage(s):	
Address:	307 Little East Neck Road, Babylon
Name of estate:	*Willow Close*
Year of construction:	1910
Style of architecture:	Georgian Revival
Architect(s):	Nelson and Van Wagenen designed the house (for Trenchard)
Landscape architect(s):	
Builder:	E. W. Howell
House extant:	yes
Historical notes:	

The house was built by Edward Trenchard II. It was later owned by David P. Stewart and then by Brownlie, who called it *Willow Close*.
It is currently the clubhouse of the Long Island Yacht Club.

rear facade, 2005

Bruce–Brown, Ruth Arabella Loney (1853-1927)

Civic Activism:	bequeathed $1,537,654 each to the New York Post Graduate Medical School and Hospital and to the Home for Incurables*
Marriage(s):	George Bruce–Brown (1844-1892)
Address:	Main Street and Route 111, Islip
Name of estate:	*Bronhurst*
Year of construction:	1912
Style of architecture:	Modified Neo-Federal
Architect(s):	
Landscape architect(s):	
House extant: yes	
Historical notes:	

   The house, originally named *Bronhurst*, was built by Ruth Arabella Loney Bruce–Brown.
   She was the daughter of William Amos and Ruth Ann Barker Loney of Baltimore, MD. Her sister Mary married Frederick Roosevelt and resided in Manhattan. Her sister Alice married Harry S. Abbot and resided in Pelham Manor, NY. Her brother Henry resided in Mountain Lake, NJ.
   George Bruce–Brown was the son of George and Janet Bruce Brown. He had previously been married to Virginia Greenway McKesson.
   George and Virginia Greenway McKesson Bruce–Brown's daughter Catherine Wolf Brown married Ruth's half-brother Allen Loney. Their son George McKesson Brown resided at *West Neck Farm* in Lloyd Harbor. George eliminated the hyphenated Bruce–Brown. [S*ee* Spinzia, *Long Island's Prominent North Shore Families, vol. I* – Brown entry.]
   George and Ruth Arabella Loney Bruce–Brown's son William Bruce–Brown died in 1919 at the age of thirty-two. At the time of his death he was residing with his mother. Their son David Loney Bruce–Brown, a famous race car driver died in 1912 when his car crashed during a race in Milwaukee, WI. [*The New York Times* November 21, 1928, p. 2.]
   *Ruth established the Bruce–Brown Memorial Fund in memory of her husband George and her sons William and David.

front facade

Bull, Henry Worthington (1874-1958)

Occupation(s):	financier - partner, Harriman and Keech (stock brokerage firm); partner, Harriman and Co. (investment banking firm); partner, Winthrop, Whitehouse and Co. (stock brokerage firm); partner, Edward Sweet and Co. (investment banking firm); partner, Bull, Holden, and Co. (stock brokerage firm); director, Fulton Trust Co., NYC
Civic Activism:	president, National Steeplechase and Hunt Association; president, Turf and Field Club, Belmont Park, Elmont, NY
Marriage(s):	1904-1958 – Maud Livingston (1873-1962)
Address:	St. Mark's Lane, Islip*
Name of estate:	
Year of construction:	
Style of architecture:	Victorian Gothic
Architect(s):	
Landscape architect(s):	
House extant: yes	
Historical notes:	

    The house was built by Parmenus Johnson, Sr. In January 1880, the twenty-one-acre estate was purchased by C. A. Backett of New York. By June 1880 it was owned by E. B. Spaulding who enlarged and modernized the house [*The Brooklyn Daily Eagle* January 27, 1880, p. 4 and June 7, 1880, p. 1.] In 1886, the estate was purchased by Robert Cambridge Livingston III, who called it *Lakeside*. It was later owned by Livingston's daughter Maud, who married Henry Worthington Bull.

    Maud's brother John married Clara M. Dudley, the daughter of B. William and Maria Hunt Dudley and resided in Lawrence. Her brother Johnston, who resided at *Still Pond* in Huntington, married Natalie Havemeyer, Natalie F. Moss, and, subsequently, Ruth H. Moller. Her brother Louis married Charlotte Atlee Black, the daughter of C. Irving Cunard Black of Chicago, IL, and, later, Catherine Murphy with whom he resided in Manhattan. Her brother Henry, who resided in Islip, remained a bachelor. Her sister Caroline married Maxwell Stevenson, the son of A. L. Stevenson, with whom she resided at *The Lodge* in Hempstead, and, later, ____ Male of Paris, France. [*See* Spinzia, *Long Island's Prominent Families in the Town of Hempstead* – Livingston and Stevenson entries – and *Long Island's Prominent North Shore Families, vol. I* – Livingston entry.]

    Henry Worthington Bull was the son of William Lanman and Sara Newton Worthington Bull. A sergeant in the Rough Riders, Henry participated in the engagements at Las Guasimas, San Juan Hill, and the siege of Santiago.

    The Bulls did not have children.

    In 1945, Maud Livingston Bull purchased *Enderby*, the North Hills estate of Edward Jordan Dimock. [*The New York Times* September 23, 1945, p. 131, and Spinzia, *Long Island's Prominent North Shore Families, vol. I* – Bull entry.]

    By the early 1940s the Islip estate was owned by the Bulls' niece Phyllis Livingston Baker Astaire who was married to the noted actor/choreographer/actor Fred Astaire, Sr. (aka Frederick Austerlitz).

    In 2006, the house was owned by ____ Dowden.

    In 2008, the seven thousand-square-foot, twenty-room house with seven bedrooms was for sale. The asking price was $1,499,990; the taxes were $16,089.

*The estate originally bordered on St. Marks Lane. With its subdivision, the house is currently located on Suellen Road.

Bunce, Frederick Sidney, Sr. (1856-1918)

Occupation(s):	capitalist - director, Deer Park and Babylon Railroad Co.; director, Babylon and Oak Island Ferry
	merchant - partner, Wood Lumber Co., Amityville; partner, Suffolk Lumber Co., Lindenhurst; owned lumber company in Babylon
Civic Activism:	a founder, Babylon Yacht Club
Marriage(s):	M/1 – Annie M. Towne (1861-1886)
	M/2 – Emma Lux (1869-1932)
Address:	35 George Street, Babylon
Name of estate:	
Year of construction:	
Style of architecture:	
Architect(s):	
Landscape architect(s):	
House extant: yes	
Historical notes:	

Frederick Sidney Bunce was the son of Sidney and Sarah Lucinda Wicks Bunce.

Frederick Sidney and Annie M. Towne Bunce, Sr.'s daughter Virginia married Fernando Enrique de Murias, the son of Ramon and Clara Garden de Murias of Manhattan, and Havana, Cuba, and resided in Babylon.

Frederick Sidney and Emma Lux Bunce, Sr.'s son Frederick Sidney Bunce, Jr. was residing at the house at the time of his death in 1967. The house was inherited by Ramon de Murias II.

Burchell, George W. (1850-1926)

Occupation(s):	financier - vice president, Queens Insurance Co. of America
Civic Activism:	president, National Board of Fire Underwriters of New York; vice-president, New York Board of Fire Underwriters; a founder and director, Bay Shore Protective Association; governor, Penataquit Corinthian Yacht Club
Marriage(s):	1870-1924 – Ellen Rushton Haviland (1851-1924)
Address:	46 Penataquit Avenue, Bay Shore
Name of estate:	
Year of construction:	1897
Style of architecture:	Shingle
Architect(s):	Clarence K. Birdsall designed the house (for Burchell)
Landscape architect(s):	
House extant: yes	
Historical notes:	

The house was built by George W. Burchell.

He was the son of George and Sarah M. Burchell.

Ellen Rushton Haviland Burchell was the daughter of Samuel Carpenter and Mary Ann Ruston Haviland.

George W. and Ellen Rushton Haviland Burchell's daughter Sarah married Harry Townsend Rounds. Their daughter Florence married Irving G. Day of Newark, NJ.

front facade, 2006

Burke, Charles Felix (1881-1937)

Occupation(s):	capitalist - advertising manager, William E. Harmon & Co. (Cincinnati, Detroit, and New York real estate developer); vice-president, Edmund G. and Charles F. Burke, Inc. (New York and Pittsburgh, PA, real estate development company)*
Civic Activism:	trustee, Denison University, Granville, OH; chairman, Gifts and Bequests Committee, Denison University; trustee, First Baptist Church of Pittsburgh; deacon, Riverside Church, NYC; director, Brooklyn Real Estate Board
Marriage(s):	Lorena M. Woodrow (1877-1967)
Address:	island in Connetquot River, Oakdale
Name of estate:	
Year of construction:	
Style of architecture:	
Architect(s):	
Landscape architect(s):	
House extant:	unconfirmed
Historical notes:	

Burke residence

Born in Bethel, OH, Charles Felix Burke was the son of Orville and Jennie Glenn Burke. His father Orville was associated with President Ulysses S. Grant in the tannery and leather firm of Grant–Burke–Medary. [*The New York Times* January 23, 1937, p. 17.]

Lorena M. Woodrow Burke had previously resided in Emporia, Kansas.

*Edmund G. and Charles F. Burke, Inc. were developers of major subdivisions in Manhattan, Howard Beach, Queens, Bergen Beach, Brooklyn, and on the site of Camp Upton in Yaphank. The Burkes purchased the William Kissam Vanderbilt, Sr. estate *Idlehour* and subdivided its property for a residential development. The furnishings from the main residence were sold by the firm through the American Art Galleries in New York City. In 1943, Charles' brother Edmund acquired *Beacon Towers*, the Sands Point estate of Vanderbilt's first wife Alva, demolished it, and created a housing subdivision on the estate's property. [*The New York Times* May 10, 1966, p. 45, and Spinzia, *Long Island's Prominent North Shore Families*, vol. I – Belmont and Hearst entries.]

Busby, John (1902-1980)

Occupation(s):	merchant - president, Busby Metals, Long Island City (metal distributing firm)
Civic Activism:	president, Bay Shore Draft Board
Marriage(s):	Alice Larsen (1909-1991)
Address:	120 South Gillette Avenue, Bayport
Name of estate:	
Year of construction:	1909
Style of architecture:	Dutch Colonial Revival
Architect(s):	Isaac Henry Green II designed the house (for Pollock)
Landscape architect(s):	
Builder:	Frederick D. Smith, 1909 house and garage (for Pollock) Clifford Munsell, 1928 alterations to main residence (for Major)
House extant:	yes
Historical notes:	

front facade

The fourteen-room house, with six bedrooms and three full and two half bathrooms, was built by Walter B. Pollock. [*The Brooklyn Daily Eagle* April 4, 1909, p. 16, and *The Suffolk County News* February 12, 1909, p. 2.] In 1926, it was purchased by Alfred Sarony Major. [*The Suffolk County News* June 4, 1926, p. 2.] In 1935, Mrs. Major sold the house to James McClung of Brooklyn. [*The Suffolk County News* August 16, 1935, p. 8.] In 1955, it was purchased by Busby. [*The Suffolk County News* September 2, 1955, p. 5.]

John and Alice Larsen Busby's daughter Barbara married Donald Buskirk and resided in Blue Point. Their daughter Linda married Eugene LaColla and resided in Bayport.

In 1966, their son Alan lost three of his children when a fire erupted in their Port Washington residence.

In 2017, the Bayport house sold for $1.35 million.

Cameron, Edward Miller (1863-1895)

Occupation(s):	industrialist - president, Hygeia Distilled Water Co.
	financier - member, Kerr and Co. (stock brokerage firm)
Marriage(s):	M/1 – 1886 – Marie Louise Arnold
	M/2 – 1891-1895 – Annie Snedecor Carll (1869-1939)
Address:	South Country Road, West Islip

Name of estate:
Year of construction:
Style of architecture:
Architect(s):
Landscape architect(s):
House extant: unconfirmed
Historical notes:

In 1891, Cameron purchased the house of Annie's grandfather Obadiah Snedecor. [*The Brooklyn Daily Eagle* March 4, 1891, p. 1.]

Edward Miller Cameron died of a self-inflicted pistol wound to the heart. He was the son of Ananias Miller and Margaret Mott Cameron of Manhattan. Edward's sister Annie, who resided at *Clovelly* in West Islip, married William Arnold.

Marie Louise Arnold Cameron was the daughter of Richard and Pauline Bicar Arnold of *The Crescent* in West Islip.

Annie Snedecor Carll Arnold was the daughter of James Harvey and Deborah Ann Carll, who resided at *The Red Cottage* in West Islip.

Edward and Annie Snedecor Carll Cameron's sons Alexander Duncan Cameron and Edward William Cameron were adopted by their aunt Annie Arnold and assumed the surname of Arnold. Their daughter Margaret married Thomas M. Galbreath.

Cameron, Miss Emma Cornelia (1875-1926)
aka Miss Emma Cornelia Sturges

Marriage(s):	
Address:	Parkwood and George Street, West Islip
Name of estate:	*Effingham Towers*
Year of construction:	1898
Style of architecture:	Colonial Revival
Architect(s):	Charles Pierrepont Henry Gilbert
	designed the house (for Hawley)
Landscape architect(s):	William Roe Jones designed the 1910
	waterfall dam complex (for Hawley)*
Builder:	Harvey Murdock

House extant: no; destroyed by arson, 1958
Historical notes:

The fourteen-bedroom, seven-bath house, originally named *Effingham Towers*, was built by Edwin Hawley. [information confirmed from the research of Bill Jantz, November 2012]

It was later owned by his ward Emma Cornelia Cameron who received it as part of a settlement with his heirs. She also received $50,000, Hawley's Manhattan residence, and an annual income from a trust fund of $25,000. [*The Beacon* July 19, 2012, p. 2.]

Emma was the daughter of Cornelius and Emma Ackerman Sturges.

The house was purchased by the Haarman family who operated it as the Parkwood Lake Mansion and Inn from 1926 to 1938. It then was the site of the Parkwood Lake Private School until 1949. In 1951, the West Islip School District used the house for its grades five and six.

*The estate's waterfall/dam complex was demolished in the 1960s when Montauk Highway and Route 231 were widened.

front facade

Cameron, Miss Emma Cornelia (1875-1926)
aka Miss Emma Cornelia Sturges

Marriage(s):

Address: Deer Park Avenue, North Babylon
Name of estate:
Year of construction: c. 1925
Style of architecture:
Architect(s):
Landscape architect(s):
House extant: yes
Historical notes:

The house was built by Emma Cornelia Cameron.
[See previous entry for family information.]

front facade, 2013

Carlisle, Jay Freeborn, Sr. (1868-1937)

Occupation(s): financier - partner, Mellick and Co. (stock brokerage firm);
    member, board of governors, New York Stock Exchange
Civic Activism: trustee, Southside Hospital, Bay Shore (now, South Shore University Hospital);
a founder and director, Great River Club (later, Timber Point Club)

Marriage(s): 1906-1937 – Mary Pinkerton (1886-1937)
  - Civic Activism: member, fund raising committee, Southside Hospital,
    Bay Shore (now, South Shore University Hospital);
    suffragist - member, Islip Woman's Suffrage Club

Address: Suffolk Lane, East Islip
Name of estate: *Rosemary*
Year of construction: 1917
Style of architecture: Mediterranean Villa
Architect(s): Trowbridge and Ackerman designed the house (for Carlisle)
Landscape architect(s): Vitale, Brinkerhoff, and Geiffert (for Carlisle)
House extant: no; demolished c. 1940
Historical notes:

The house, originally named *Rosemary*, was built by Jay Freeborn Carlisle, Sr.

Mary Pinkerton Carlisle was the daughter of Robert Allan and Anna Elizabeth Hughes Pinkerton, who resided at *Dearwood* in Bay Shore. Her sister Anna married Lewis Mills Gibb, Sr. and resided at *Cedarholme* in Bay Shore. Her brother Allan Pinkerton II married Franc Woolworth and resided in Bay Shore.

Jay Freeborn and Mary Pinkerton Carlisle, Sr.'s son Jay Freeborn Carlisle, Jr. married Margaret Moffett, the daughter of James Andrew and Adelaide Taft McMichael Moffett, Jr. of *Inadune* in East Hampton, and resided in Brookville. [*See* Spinzia, *Long Island's Prominent Families in the Town of East Hampton* – Moffett entry.] In 1932, prior to the younger Carlisle's marriage to Margaret, his father foiled a plot to kidnap the young couple and hold them for $30,000 ransom. [*The New York Times* November 13, 1937, p. 5.]

Mrs. Carlisle's sitting room

Jay Freeborn Carlisle, Sr. estate, *Rosemary*

courtyard

front facade

garden stairs

rear facade

Carroll, Dr. Alfred Ludlow (1833-1893)

Occupation(s):	physician
	writer - *Memoir of the Late Alfred Ludlow Carroll, M.D.*, 1894; articles in numerous medical journals
Civic Activism:	a founder, New York State Medical Association;
	a founder, New York State Board of Health, 1872;
	secretary and president, New York State Board of Health;
	a founder, Society of Letters, Arts & Sciences
Marriage(s):	1862-1893 – Lucy Ann Johnson (1838-1909)
Address:	South Country Road, Bay Shore
Name of estate:	
Year of construction:	c. 1902
Style of architecture:	Modified Neo-Tudor
Architect(s):	
Landscape architect(s):	

House extant: no; destroyed by fire, c. 1955*
Historical notes:

The house was built by Dr. Alfred Ludlow Carroll.

He was the son of Anthony and Frances Ludlow Carroll. His parents were first cousins.

Lucy Ann Johnson Carroll was the daughter of Bradish and Louisa Anna Lawrence Johnson, Sr., who resided at *Sans Souci* in Bay Shore. Her brother Bradish Johnson Jr. married Amiee Elizabeth Gaillard and resided at *Woodland* in East Islip. Her brother Effingham married Amy Rowan Scott and resided at *The Evergreens* in Bay Shore. Her sister Helena married Schuyler Livingston Parsons, Sr. and resided at *Whileaway* in Islip.

Dr. Alfred Ludlow and Mrs. Lucy Ann Johnson Carroll's son Bradish married Marion Bowers, the daughter of Henry and Louise Grant Bowers of Manhattan. Marion's sister Louise, who resided in East Hampton, married Arthur Aymar Cater. [*See* Spinzia, *Long Island's Prominent Families in the Town of East Hampton*– Cater entry.] Their son Anson, who died in 1903, married Mabel Wilmot Merritt, the daughter of Joseph King and Julie Therese Rowe Merritt.

The house was purchased from Lucy Johnson Carroll by John Dunbar Adams.

*In the 1950s, the house became Mimi's Awixa Pond Restaurant. The estate is now the site of the Windemere Condominiums.

front facade

Catlin, Dr. Daniel, Sr. (1908-2001)

Occupation(s):	physician - surgeon
Marriage(s):	1937-1975 – Doris Havemeyer (1912-1975)
Address:	South Saxon Avenue, Bay Shore
Name of estate:	*Orowoc Point*
Year of construction:	1949
Style of architecture:	Contemporary Ranch
Architect(s):	
Landscape architect(s):	
House extant:	no; demolished in 2004
Historical notes:	

The *Social Register Summer, 1950* lists the name of the Catlin residence as *Orowoc Point*.

Dr. Daniel Catlin, Sr. was the son of Daniel K. Catlin of Dublin, NH.

Doris Havemeyer Catlin was the daughter of Horace and Doris Anna Dick Havemeyer of *Olympic Point* in Bay Shore. Her sister Adaline married Richard Sturgis Perkins, Sr. and, subsequently, Laurance B. Rand of Southport, CT. Her brother Horace Havemeyer, Jr. married Rosalind Everdell and resided in Islip and, later, Dix Hills. [*See* Spinzia, *Long Island's Prominent North Shore Families, vol. I* – Havemeyer entry.] Her brother Harry married Eugenie Aiguier and resides on the *Olympic Point* property in Bay Shore.

Dr. Daniel and Mrs. Doris Havemeyer Catlin, Sr.'s son Daniel Catlin, Jr. married Dundeen Bostwick, the daughter of Dunbar Wright Bostwick of Shelburne, VT. Their son Loring married Susan Carol Johnson, the daughter of Charles Raymond Johnson of Litchfield, CT. Their daughter Doris, who married Douglas Thomas Yates, Jr., the son of Douglas Thomas and Margaret Louise Titus Yates, Sr. of Islip, resides in Vermont. Their daughter Leigh married Wayne Grant Quasha, the son of William H. Quasha of Glen Cove. Leigh subsequently married John R. French and resides in Greenwich, CT, and at *Windswept* in Bridgehampton. The Catlins' son Brian married Rosalie Hornblower, the daughter of Ralph Hornblower, Jr. Rosalie subsequently married Willits H. Sawyer III and resides in Cambridge, MA.

Catlin, John Bernsee, Sr. (1888-1952)

Occupation(s):	financier - oil industry analyst, Guaranty Trust Co.; member, H. T. Carey and Co. (stock brokerage firm.)
Marriage(s):	1920-1952 – Helen Gordon Robb (1898-1993)
Address:	127 Gillette Avenue, Sayville
Name of estate:	
Year of construction:	
Style of architecture:	shingle
Architect(s):	
Landscape architect(s):	
House extant:	yes
Historical notes:	

front facade

The *Long Island Society Register, 1929* lists John Bernsee and Helen Robb Catlin as residing at 127 Gillette Avenue in Sayville.

He was the son of Rufus Olmsted and Caroline Bernsee Catlin of Brooklyn.

Helen Gordon Robb Catlin was the daughter of James and Elizabeth Donovan Robb of Sayville and Brooklyn.

John Bernsee and Helen Gordon Robb Catlin, Sr.'s daughter Elizabeth married John Whitehouse. Their son John Bernsee Catlin, Jr. married Patricia Ruth Hunt, the daughter of William A. Hunt of New Rochelle, NY, and resided in Sayville.

At the time of his death, Catlin was residing on Sunset Drive, Sayville.

Ceballos, Juan Manuel, Sr. (1859-1913)

Occupation(s):	financier -	partner, Czarikow–Rionda (sugar brokerage firm);
		president, J. M. Ceballos and Co. (investment banking firm)*;
		a founder and president, Sollabec [Ceballos spelled in reverse] (investment banking firm);
		director, International Banking Corp.
	capitalist -	president, Brighton Pier and Navigation Co.;
		vice-president, Development Company of Cuba;
		vice-president, Edgewater Basin Co.;
		vice-president and director, New York and Coney Island Railroad Co.;
		director, Prospect Park and Southern Brooklyn Railroad Co.
	shipping -	vice president, Iron Steamboat Co.;
		director, New York & Porto [Puerto] Rico Steamship Co.;
		vice-president and director, New Jersey Navigation Co.
	industrialist -	president and director, Posario Sugar Co.
Civic Activism:		director, International Banking Association;
		director, South Shore Country Club, West Islip

Marriage(s): 1886-1913 – Louisa Washington (1859-1934)
 - Civic Activism: treasurer, International Association for Southern Mountaineers

Address: South Country Road, Bay Shore
Name of estate: *Brookhurst Farm*
Year of construction:
Style of architecture: Modified Colonial Revival
Architect(s):
Landscape architect(s):
House extant: unconfirmed
Historical notes:

In about 1894, Ceballos purchased the ancestral home of John Mowbray.

The *Brooklyn Blue Book and Long Island Society Register, 1921* lists Mr. and Mrs. Juan M. Ceballos as residing on Main Road [South Country Road] in Bay Shore.

One month after the sinking of the battleship USS *Maine*, Ceballos was appointed by the Spanish government to a commission that was seeking a *rapprochement* between the governments of the United States and Spain. War broke out between the two nations when the commission's recommendations were rejected by both the Cuban dissidents and President McKinley. [Harry W. Havemeyer, *Along the Great South Bay From Oakdale to Babylon: The Story of a Summer Spa 1840 to 1940* (Mattituck, NY: Amereon House, 1996), pp. 261-62.]

Louisa Washington Ceballos was the daughter of Allan C. and Catherine L. Washington.

Juan Manuel and Louisa Washington Ceballos, Sr.'s son Juan Manuel Ceballos, Jr., who resided at *Three Winds* in Old Westbury, married Maude Elizabeth Hammill and, subsequently, Evalyn Dun Douglas, the daughter of Benjamin Dun Douglas. [*See* Spinzia, *Long Island's Prominent North Shore Families, vol. I* – Ceballos entry.] Their daughter Louisa married the Austro-Hungarian Council General to Canada, Dr. Charles Winter.

*The firm of J. M. Ceballos and Co. was forced to declare bankruptcy in 1906 when Manuel Silvelras, a trusted employee of the firm, absconded with $1 million of the firm's funds.

front facade, c. 1903

Chase, Edna Woolman Alloway (1877-1957)

Occupation(s):	journalist - editor-in-chief, *Vogue*, 1929; chairman of editorial board, *Vogue*, 1952 writer - *Always in Vogue*, 1954 (co-authored with her daughter Ilka Chase)

Marriage(s):	M/1 – 1904-div. – Francis Dane Chase (1874-1949)
	   - manager, Park Chambers Hotel, NYC
	M/2 – 1921-1950 – Richard T. Newton (1874-1950)
	   - inventor - developed automobile engines

Address:	4 Argyle Avenue, Babylon
Name of estate:	
Year of construction:	1927
Style of architecture:	Contemporary
Architect(s):	
Landscape architect(s):	
House extant: yes	
Historical notes:	

   Edna Woolman Alloway Chase was the daughter of Franklyn and Laura Woolman Alloway.
   Francis Dane and Edna Woolman Alloway Chase's daughter Ilka married Louis Calhern, William B. Murray, and, subsequently, Dr. Norton Sager Brown.
   At the time of his death, Francis Dane Chase was residing at 4 Argyle Avenue, Babylon. [*The New York Times* November 10, 1949, p. 31.]
   [For Edna's Upper Brookville residence, *see* Spinzia, *Long Island's Prominent North Shore Families, vol. I* – Chase entry.]
   In 2003, the house, which has been extensively remodeled, sold for $445,000.

front facade

Childs, Eversley, Sr. (1867-1953)

Occupation(s):	capitalist - director, Technicolor Motion Picture Corp.;
	director, Technicolor, Inc.;
	director, Long Island Lighting Co.;
	director, Queens County Gas and Electric;
	director, Kings County Gas Co.;
	industrialist - president, Mica Roofing Co. (which merged with Barrett Manufacturing Co.; later, with United Coke and Gas Co.; and, subsequently, with American Coal, becoming Barrett Co.);
	vice president, Barrett Manufacturing Co.;
	president and chairman of board, Bon Ami Co., Inc.;
	chairman of board, Barrett Co.;
	director, Boorum and Pease Co.;
	director, Congoleum Nairn Inc.
Civic Activism:	a founder, with General Leonard Wood, Childs Leprosarium in Cebu, The Philippines, 1930;
	donated, with his son Eversley Childs, Jr., thirty-four acres and buildings in Setauket to the Salvation Army to establish a children's home, 1942;
	chairman of board, Leonard Wood Memorial
Marriage(s):	M/1 – 1889-1944 – Mary Shubrick Lockwood (1867-1944)
	M/2 – 1947-1953 – Alice Barnard
Address:	Edwards Avenue, Sayville
Name of estate:	
Year of construction:	1895
Style of architecture:	Colonial Revival
Architect(s):	Isaac Henry Green II designed the house (for Childs)
Landscape architect(s):	
House extant: yes	
Historical notes:	

The house was built by Eversley Childs, Sr.

In 1902, Childs moved to Long Island's North Shore.

The *Brooklyn Blue Book and Long Island Society Register, 1918* lists Eversley and Mary Shubrick Lockwood Childs [Sr.] as residing at *Crane Neck Farm* in Setauket.

He was the son of William Henry Harrison and Maria Eversley Childs, Sr. of Brooklyn.

Mary Shubrick Lockwood Childs was the daughter of Dr. Charles Edward Lockwood of Manhattan.

Eversley and Mary Shubrick Lockwood Childs, Sr.'s daughter Dorothy married Archibald McLaren. Their son William Henry Harrison Childs II married Catharine Stuart Orland and resided in Kensington in the Great Neck area of Long Island. Their son Eversley Childs, Jr. married Margherita Abbey and resided in Garden City, and, subsequently, Georgiana A. Van Epps, with whom he resided at *Crane Neck Farm* in Setauket.

Alice Barnard Childs was the daughter of Arthur Barnard of Cheltenham, England.

Childs, William Hamlin (1857-1928)

Occupation(s):	industrialist - a founder and chairman of board, Bon Ami Co., Inc.; director, Congoleum Co.; director, Crucible Steel Co., of America; vice-president, American Coal Products Co.; vice-president, Barrett Manufacturing Co.; vice-president, United States Wood Preserving Co.; president, United Coke and Gas Co.
	capitalist - director, Loew's Inc. (motional picture studio and theaters); director, Technicolor Motion Picture Corp.
Civic Activism:	donated $250,000 for the improvement of the Downtown Community House, NYC; chairman, Brooklyn Bureau of Charities; president, Battery Park Association; vice-president, Park Association of NYC; chairman, subcommittee on Coal Tar Products and Raw Materials, Council of National Defense, during World War I; president, Friendly House Association
Marriage(s):	1881-1928 – Nellie White Spencer (1859-1946) - Civic Activism: donated 800 trees to be planted between Flatbush Avenue and Bay Ridge Parkway, Brooklyn; donated fountain, Brooklyn Botanic Garden
Address:	Edwards Avenue, Sayville
Name of estate:	
Year of construction:	c. 1894
Style of architecture:	Colonial Revival
Architect(s):	Isaac Henry Green II designed the house (for W. H. Childs)

Landscape architect(s):
House extant: no; destroyed by fire, c. 1995
Historical notes:

The *Brooklyn Blue Book and Long Island Society Register, 1918* lists William Hamlin and Nellie Spencer Childs as residing at *Belle Haven* in Greenwich, CT.

He was the son of Gordon H. and Julia Richards Childs of Hartford, CT.

William Hamlin and Nellie White Spencer Childs' daughter Mary married Ernest G. Draper and resided in Greenwich, CT. Their son Richard, the noted political reformer, married Grace P. Hatch and resided at *Chimney Lot* in Stamford, CT.

William Kemble Clarkson, Jr. residence, side / front facade, 2005

Clarkson, William Kemble, Jr. (1849-1933)

Occupation(s):	capitalist - treasurer, Kemble Realty, Co.; industrialist - executive, Nassau Brewing Co.
Civic Activism:	vice-president, Brewer's Association
Marriage(s):	1889-1923 – Mary Augusta Brown (1852-1923)
Address:	32 Awixa Avenue, Bay Shore
Name of estate:	
Year of construction:	c. 1899
Style of architecture:	Shingle
Architect(s):	Ernest George Washington Dietrich designed the house (for Wray)
Landscape architect(s):	
House extant: yes	
Historical notes:	

front facade, c. 1902

The house, originally named *Whileaway*, was built by William Henry Wray, Sr. It was later owned by Frederick C. Lemmerman and, then, by Clarkson.

He was the son of William Kemble and Ann Elizabeth Van Tuyl Clarkson, Sr.

Mary Augusta Brown Clarkson was the daughter of William and Jessie Dunsmore Brown.

The *Brooklyn Blue Book and Long Island Society Register, 1921* lists William Kemble and Mary Augusta Brown Clarkson [Jr.] as residing in Bay Shore.

William Kemble and Mary Augusta Brown Clarkson, Jr.'s son Jesse, who was a professor of history at Brooklyn College, married Mary Rose Griffits and resided in Bay Shore. Their son Thomas was one year old at the time of his death in 1901. Their son Van Tuly was twenty-eight at the time of his death in 1922. Their son William Brown Clarkson married Harriet Colony Perkins.

In 2003, the house was purchased by Dr. Mark Foehr.

Clyde, William Pancoast, Sr. (1839-1923)

Occupation(s):	shipping - a founder and president, Clyde Steamboat Co., Wilmington, DE (Atlantic coast shipbuilding and shipping firm); president, Pacific Mail Steamship Co. (Pacific coast shipbuilding and shipping firm)
	capitalist - president, Richmond & Danville Railroad; president, Richmond & West Point Terminal & Warehouse Co.*;
	capitalist - a founder, South Side Improvement Co., 1885 (accumulation of water to sprinkle roads)
Marriage(s):	1865-1923 – Emeline Field Hill (1841-1931)
Address:	South Country Road, West Islip
Name of estate:	
Year of construction:	
Style of architecture:	Modified French Empire
Architect(s):	
Landscape architect(s):	
House extant: no; demolished c. 1937	
Historical notes:	

front facade

In the 1880s, Clyde purchased the Minor Cooper Keith house. [Harry W. Havemeyer, *Along the Great South Bay From Oakdale to Babylon: The Story of a Summer Spa 1840 to 1940* (Mattituck, NY: Amereon House, 1996), p. 179.] The house was built over an old Native American burying ground. [*South Side Signal* August 25, 1888, p. 2.]

The *Brooklyn Blue Book and Long Island Society Register, 1918* lists William P. and Emeline F. Hill Clyde [Sr.] as residing at *Uplands* in New Hamburg, NY.

He was the son of Thomas and Rebecca Pancoast Clyde of Delaware.

Emeline Field Hill Clyde was the daughter of Marshall and Harriet Smallwood Field Hill of Philadelphia, PA.

William Pancoast and Emeline Field Hill Clyde, Sr.'s son William Pancoast Clyde, Jr. married Dora Jesslyn Taylor, the daughter of Joshua Taylor of England. Their daughter Mabel married Metropolitan Opera singer William Wade Henshaw. Their son Marshall married Margery L. Bucklin.

*As a result of the Panic of 1893, Clyde sold his interest in the Richmond & West Point Terminal and Warehouse Co. to J. P. Morgan. [Jean Strouse, *Morgan: American Financier* (New York: Random House, 1999), p. 321.]

Coffey, John Edward Develin, Sr. (b. 1890)

Occupation(s):	advertising executive
	journalist - *Philadelphia Public Ledger*
Marriage(s):	Clara Sebring (aka Elizabeth Troy) (1892-1969)
	- journalist - *Grit*, Williamsport, PA;
	Philadelphia Public Ledger
	writer - articles for various magazine;
	fiction;
	short stories
Address:	Sequams Lane, West Islip
Name of estate:	
Year of construction:	
Style of architecture:	
Architect(s):	
Landscape architect(s):	
House extant: unconfirmed	
Historical notes:	

  John Edward Develin Coffey, Sr. was the son of Edward Hope and Annie Stetson Coffey, Sr. of Manhattan.
  Clara Sebring Coffey was born in Williamsport, PA.
  John Edward Develin and Clara Sebring Coffey, Sr.'s daughter Hope married John Harrison Tompkins, the son of Howard Campbell Tompkins of Babylon. Their daughter Ann married Robert Newton Gilmore, Jr. of Brooklyn and Babylon. Their son John Edward Develin, Jr. married Marcia Clark Catlin, the daughter of John Blanchard Catlin of Neenah, WI.

Coleman, Leander Walter Townsend (1868-1954)

Occupation(s):	financier - de Coppet and Doremus (stock brokerage firm)
Civic Activism:	rear admiral, Babylon Yacht Club, 1906
Marriage(s):	1899-1953 – Harriet Sheldon Putnam (1873-1953)
Address:	Little East Neck Road, Babylon
Name of estate:	
Year of construction:	c. 1890
Style of architecture:	
Architect(s):	
Landscape architect(s):	
Builder:	E. W. Howell, alterations
	(for L. W. T. Coleman)
House extant:	
Historical notes:	

  In 1912, Coleman, who previously resided on *The Crescent* in Babylon, purchased the Jacob M. Bergen residence. [*South Side Signal* October 25, 1912, p. 5.]
  The Brooklyn Blue Book and Long Island Society Register, 1921 lists Leander W. T. and Harriet Sheldon Putnam Coleman as residing on Little East Neck Road, Babylon.
  He was the son of James Macy and Mary Elma Townsend Coleman.
  Harriet Sheldon Putnam Coleman was the daughter of Charles Calvin and Eliza Sheldon Bull Putnam of Brooklyn.
  Leander Walter Townsend and Harriet Sheldon Putnam Coleman's son Sheldon married Harriet Comstock Simmons. Their son Townsend married Carlys Peabody, the daughter of Charles Samuel Peabody. Their son Eliot married Dorothy Palmer Morrell, the daughter of Clarence Pitman and Isabell Halstead Palmer.

Colt, Robert Oliver (1812-1885)

Occupation(s):	capitalist - a founder, president, and director, South Side Railroad Co., Long Island (which merged with other small lines to form the Long Island Rail Road)
Civic Activism:	director, Suffolk County Agricultural Society; president, Babylon Rural Cemetery, Babylon, NY
Marriage(s):	1852-1865 – Adelaide Heideberg (d. 1865)
Address:	South Country Road, West Bay Shore
Name of estate:	*The Poplars*
Year of construction:	
Style of architecture:	
Architect(s):	
Landscape architect(s):	
House extant:	unconfirmed
Historical notes:	

Robert Oliver Colt was the son of Roswell Lyman and Margaret Oliver Colt.

Robert Oliver and Adelaide Heideberg Colt's daughter Amy married Cornelius DuBois Wagstaff and resided at *Church Lawn* in West Islip. Their son Charles married Margaret MacDonald, the daughter of Francis MacDonald of Halifax, Nova Scotia. Their daughter Adelaide married E. Calvin Williams, the son of The Reverend J. W. M. Williams.

Conover, Augustus Whitlock, Sr. (1848-1901)

Occupation(s):	merchant - partner, with H. Schaus, William Schaus (art dealers)
Marriage(s):	1878-1901 – Mary Henrietta Robinson (1849-1911)
Address:	80 South Saxon Avenue, Bay Shore
Name of estate:	
Year of construction:	c. 1880
Style of architecture:	Victorian
Architect(s):	
Landscape architect(s):	
House extant:	no; demolished in 1932
Historical notes:	

The house was built by Daniel Denice Conover. It was later owned by his son Augustus Whitlock Conover, Sr.

Augustus Whitlock and Ettie Conover, Sr.'s son Augustus Whitlock Conover, Jr. died before attaining adulthood. Their daughter Lillian married William Phelps Jones.

[See following entry for additional family and estate information.]

stables, front facade, 2020

Conover, Daniel Denice (1822-1896)

Occupation(s):	capitalist - president, Forty-Second Street Railroad, NYC; vice-president, Metropolitan Surface Railroad Co., NYC; land developer and builder, Town of Islip; secretary, South Ferry Railway Co.; director, Rockaway Railroad Co.; director, New York, Woodhaven, and Rockaway Beach Railroad; president, Twenty-Eighth Street and Twenty-Ninth Street Crosstown Railroad; director, Thirty-Fourth Street Railroad; president, Fulton Street, Wall Street, and Cortlandt Street Ferries Railroad Co. politician - New York City Street Commissioner, 1857; member, New York City Common Council
Civic Activism:	president, Olympic Club, Bay Shore; manager, The Woman's Hospital Association
Marriage(s):	1846-1896 – Catharine Eliza Whitlock (1821-1900)
Address:	80 South Saxon Avenue, Bay Shore
Name of estate:	
Year of construction:	c. 1880
Style of architecture:	Victorian
Architect(s):	
Landscape architect(s):	
House extant:	no; demolished in 1932*
Historical notes:	

The house was built by Daniel Denice Conover.

Catharine Eliza Whitlock Conover was the daughter of Samuel M. and Phebe Ludlow Whitlock.

Daniel Denice and Catharine Eliza Whitlock Conover's daughter Catharine married Morris B. Place and resided in Manhattan. Their son Augustus later owned the house.

[See previous entry for additional family information.]

In 1902, the house was purchased by John Lorimer Worden III. [*The Brooklyn Daily Eagle* May 3, p. 10, 1902.]

In 1912, it was purchased by Franklyn Laws Hutton, who called it *Win Sum Lodge*. He later sold it to his brother Edward Francis Hutton.

In 1921, it was purchased from E. F. Hutton by Philip Balch Weld.

In 1930, the house was purchased from Weld by Hamlet Cecil Sharp, who demolished it and built a new house on the site.

*The estate's barn complex, stables, and windmill are extant.

front facade, c. 1903

Cooper, James Brown, Sr. (1825-1907)

Occupation(s):	attorney -	Justice of the Peace, Babylon
	politician -	Suffolk County Clerk;
		Inspector of Customs, NY;
		assistant assessor, Internal Revenue;
		a founder, New York State Republican Party
	financier -	assistant secretary, Lafayette Fire Insurance Co.
	publisher -	owner, *Inquirer* (Hempstead newspaper)
Civic Activism:		president, Captain Cook Monument Association;
		abolitionist

Marriage(s): 1863-1907 – Gloriana S. Rice (1836-1912)
- educator - teacher, Commack School District;
principal, Bellport Academy;
teacher, Babylon School District, 1858;
principal, her own private school, Babylon
Civic Activism: treasurer, Babylon Women's Exchange;
member, Babylon Board of Education

Address: Cooper and George Streets, Babylon
Name of estate:
Year of construction: c. 1873
Style of architecture: Victorian
Architect(s):
Landscape architect(s):
House extant: no; demolished c. 1931
Historical notes:

James Brown Cooper, Sr. was the son of Simon Wheeler and Grace Dibble Cooper.

Gloriana S. Rice Cooper was the daughter of David and Gloriana Hartt Rice of Commack.

James Brown and Gloriana S. Rice Cooper, Sr.'s son Simon married Coralie Eugenie Chasmar, the daughter of James H. and Louisa A. Chasmar and resided in Darien, CT. Their son James Brown Cooper, Jr. married Jean Elizabeth Campbell of Babylon and resided in Babylon.

The house was utilized as a boarding school and day school before becoming the twenty-one bed Southside Hospital in 1911. Chartered in 1913, it was relocated to a new site in Bay Shore in 1923 and is currently called South Shore University Hospital. The original Babylon site of the hospital is occupied by the Babylon Post Office.

front facade

Corbin, Austin, Jr. (1827-1896)

Occupation(s):	attorney
	financier - a founder, Maklot and Corbin (banking firm);
	a founder, First National Bank of Davenport
	capitalist - president, Long Island Rail Road;
	president, Philadelphia & Reading Rail Road;
	president, Chicago Railroad;
	president, Bay Ridge & Coney Island Rail Road;
	director, Lehigh Railroad;
	president, Manhattan Beach Hotel, Coney Island;
	president, Long Island Improvement Co.;
	president, Argyle Hotel, Babylon;
	president, Oriental Hotel;
	director, Western Union Telegraph Co.;
	director, Marine Railway Co.;
	director, Long Island Elevated Railroad
	industrialist - director, Reading Coal & Iron Co.
Marriage(s):	1853-1896 – Hannah Maria Wheeler (1832-1908)
Address:	off Deer Park Avenue, North Babylon
Name of estate:	*Deer Park Farm*
Year of construction:	c. 1875
Style of architecture:	Modified Neo-Tudor
Architect(s):	
Landscape architect(s):	
House extant:	no
Historical notes:	

Deer Park Farm, c. 1893

The house, originally named *Deer Park Farm*, was built by Austin Corbin, Jr. on his 1,000-acre estate. In *The Old Oakdale History*, vol. 1, p. 28, the estate's name is incorrectly referred to as *Deer Park* instead of *Deer Park Farm*.

He was the son of Austin and Mary Chase Corbin, Sr.

Hannah Maria Wheeler Corbin was the daughter of Simeon and Hannah Haven Wheeler of Newport, RI.

Austin and Hannah Maria Wheeler Corbin, Jr.'s daughter Mary married René C. Champollion. Their daughter Isabella married George Stephen Edgell. Their daughter Anna married Hallett Alsop Borrowe and resided at *The Downs* in Shinnecock Hills. [*See* Spinzia, *Long Island's Prominent Families in the Town of Southampton*– Borrowe entry.] Their son William died in 1870 at the age of three.

Corbin maintained a private zoo on the estate grounds.

Corbin and his coachman died of injuries sustained in a coach accident in the driveway of his Newport, RI, estate.

In 1902, the estate was purchased by Arthur Albert Housman from Mrs. Corbin for use as a stock farm. [*The Brooklyn Daily Eagle* August 15, 1902, p. 1.]

Corse, Israel, Jr. (1819-1885)

Occupation(s):	merchant - partner, with his father, Israel Corse & Son (leather merchants);
	partner, Jonathan Thorne & Co. (leather merchants);
	a founder and partner, Corse & Thompson (leather merchants);
	partner, Corse & Pratt (leather merchants)
Marriage(s):	Catherine Ketchum (1828-1906)
Address:	South Country Road, Sayville
Name of estate:	*The Swamp*
Year of construction:	
Style of architecture:	
Architect(s):	
Landscape architect(s):	
House extant:	no
Historical notes:	

Israel Corse, Jr. was the son of Israel and Abigail Doughty Corse, Sr.

Catherine Ketchum Corse was the daughter of Morris and Angeline Burr Ketchum.

Israel and Catherine Ketchum Corse, Jr.'s daughter Katherine married Charles Lyman, the son of G. T. Lyman of Bellport. Their daughter Angelina married Cadwalader Evans. Their daughter Abigail married Pedro Ramon De Florez. Their daughter Margaret married Joseph Beale.

Covell, Charles Heber, Sr. (1833-1915)

Occupation(s):	merchant - specialty foods store
Marriage(s):	Ximena Estelle Simpson (1848-1925)
Address:	Clinton Avenue, Bay Shore
Name of estate:	*Villa Avalon*
Year of construction:	1897
Style of architecture:	Neo-Tudor
Architect(s):	Clarence K. Birdsall designed the house (for Covell)
Landscape architect(s):	
Builder:	Jabez Ephraim Van Orden built the house
House extant: yes	
Historical notes:	

The house, originally named *Villa Avalon*, was built by Charles Heber Covell, Sr.
He was the son of The Reverend Joseph Smith and Mrs. Laura Smith Covell.
Ximena Estelle Simpson Covell was the daughter of William and Ann Ximena Hains Simpson.
Charles Heber and Ximena Simpson Covell, Sr.'s son Charles Heber Covell, Jr. married Florence Allison. Their son William married Harriet Madeline Van Orden, the daughter of Edward and Margaret Ingraham Van Orden.
The house was later owned by Henry Scott Rokenbaugh who continued to call it *Villa Avalon*.

front / side facade, c. 1903

Cox, George, Jr. (1857-1933)

Occupation(s):	financier - partner, with Thomas Calender, Cox and Calender (foreign exchange stock brokerage firm); vice-president, Dime Savings Bank of Brooklyn (later, Dime Savings Bank of New York; now, The Dime); president, Security Safe Deposit Co., Brooklyn
Marriage(s):	Edna Louise Johnson (1859-1950)
Address:	19 Argyle Avenue, Babylon
Name of estate:	
Year of construction:	c. 1884
Style of architecture:	Modernized Victorian
Architect(s):	
Landscape architect(s):	
House extant: yes	
Historical notes:	

The *Long Island Society Register, 1929* lists Mr. and Mrs. George Cox [Jr.] as residing in Argyle Park, Babylon.
He was the son of George and Eliza Van Sant Cox, Sr. His brother Thomas resided in Center Moriches.
George and Edna Louise Johnson Cox, Jr.'s daughter Maybelle married Lawrence Marcellus Bainbridge and resided in Montclair, NJ, and Nassau Point, NY.
In 2017, the six-bedroom, seven-bath, 5,400-square-foot house sold for $1.395.

Cox, Stephen Perry

Occupation(s):

Marriage(s): 1889 – Eliza Jane Stoppani (1860-1938)

Address: Fairview Avenue, Bayport
Name of estate: *Arcadia*
Year of construction: 1888
Style of architecture:
Architect(s): Isaac Henry Green II designed the house (for C. F. Stoppani, Sr.)
Landscape architect(s):
House extant: no*
Historical notes:

Arcadia

The house, originally named *Arcadia*, was built by Charles Francis Stoppani, Sr.

It was later owned by his daughter Eliza, who married Stephen Perry Cox. The Coxes continued to call it *Arcadia*.

The *Brooklyn Blue Book and Long Island Society Register, 1918* lists Stephen Perry and E. Jennie [Jane] Stoppani Cox as residing at *Arcadia* in Bayport.

She had previously been married to ____ Harris. The Harrises' daughter May married Louis R. Hamersley Jr., who was the brother-in-law of John Ellis Roosevelt and Robert Barnwell Roosevelt, Jr. *[See Roosevelt entries for additional Hamersley family information.]* Mrs. Cox' brother Charles Francis Stoppani, Jr. married Evalyn Henry and resided in Bayport. Her brother Joseph married Ida Maloney and resided at *Liberty Hall* in Bayport.

In 1919, Cox sold the house to John J. O'Connor, who defaulted on its property taxes.

The house was purchased by Martin Thomas Manton. In 1939, Manton lost the house for failure to pay its property taxes.

*The gardener's house and carriage house are extant.

**Creamer, Francis D., Sr. (1862-1913)
aka Frank D. Creamer**

Occupation(s): politician - sheriff, Kings County, NY, 1898
capitalist - treasurer, Boston Development and Borough Construction Co.;
treasurer, Sanitary Co.;
trustee, New York Building Exchange
merchant - president Frank D. Creamer & Co. (brick and building supplies)

Marriage(s): 1883-1912 – Louisa Murray (1862-1912)

Address: 712 South Country Road, Islip
Name of estate:
Year of construction:
Style of architecture: Queen Anne
Architect(s):
Landscape architect(s):
House extant: yes
Historical notes:

front facade, c. 1900

Francis D. Creamer, Sr. was the son of Dr. Joseph M. and Mrs. Helen M. Tuttle Creamer of Brooklyn.

Louisa Murray Creamer was the daughter of Peter and Helen Murray of New York.

In 1921, the Creamers' son Francis D. Creamer, Jr., who married Laura Calderwood, was indicted for allegedly restraining trade by exchanging bids and prices with other building material suppliers, thereby creating a fixed price for building supplies within the industry. [*The New York Times* February 1, 1921, p. 27.] Their son Joseph Byron Creamer, Sr. married Ellen Juliette Moffitt, the daughter of William Henry and Ellie F. Moffitt of *Beautiful Shore* in Islip, and resided in Islip.

[See following entry for additional family information.]

The house later became The Gatsby Restaurant. It is currently the office of South Shore Neurologic Associates.

Francis D. Creamer, Sr.'s house, 2006

Creamer, Joseph Byron, Sr. (1885-1930)

Occupation(s):	merchant -	director, Frank D. Creamer & Co. (brick and building supplies); president, Frank Byron Co.
	capitalist -	director Phoenix Reclamation Co.; director, Brooklyn Ash Removal Co.

Marriage(s): 1913-1930 – Ellen Juliette Moffit (d. 1941)

Address: South Country Road, Islip
Name of estate:
Year of construction:
Style of architecture:
Architect(s):
Landscape architect(s):
House extant: unconfirmed
Historical notes:

    The *Long Island Society Register, 1929* lists J. Byron and Ellen Juliette Moffit Creamer [Sr.] as residing on Main Street [South Country Road], Islip.
    He was the son of Francis D. and Louisa Murray Creamer, Sr. of Islip.
    Ellen Juliette Moffit Creamer was the daughter of William Henry and Ellie F. Moffitt of *Beautiful Shore* in Islip.
    Joseph Byron and Ellen Juliette Moffit Creamer, Sr.'s daughter Louellen married Eugene Conway Cohalan, the son of New York State Supreme Court Justice Denis O'Leary Cohalan, Sr.
    [See previous entry for additional family information.]
    In 1924, Mrs. Creamer sold the house and twelve acres to Andrew Lazare of Woodmere. [*The New York Times* October 3, 1924, p. 36.]

Crothers, Gordon (1902-1979)

Occupation(s):	industrialist - member, Dennison Manufacturing Co., Framingham, MA (now, a subsidiary of Avery–Dennison paper products manufacturer)
Marriage(s):	Marie Gaillard Johnson (1896-1977)
Address:	Ocean Avenue, Islip
Name of estate:	*La Casetta*
Year of construction:	
Style of architecture:	
Architect(s):	
Landscape architect(s):	
House extant:	unconfirmed
Historical notes:	

The *Social Register, Summer 1946* lists Gordon and Marie G. Johnson Crothers as residing at *La Casetta* in Islip. The *Social Register, Summer 1950* lists their address as Ocean Avenue, Islip.

He was the son of The Reverend Dr. Samuel McChord and Mrs. Louise M. Bronson Crothers of Cambridge, MA. His sister Helen did not marry.

Marie Gaillard Johnson Crothers was the daughter of Bradish and Aimiee Elizabeth Gaillard Johnson, Jr. of *Woodland* in East Islip. Her brother Aymar, who inherited *Woodland*, married Marion Krumbhaar Hoffman. Her brother Bradish Gaillard Johnson III married Emma Marie Grima and resided at *Enfin* in Islip. Marie had previously been married to William Hamilton Russell, Jr., with whom she resided at *Le Rozel* in Islip. William Hamilton and Marie Gaillard Johnson Russell, Jr.'s daughter Amie married Don Cino Tomaso Corsini, the eldest son of Don Emmanuele and Donna Maria Carolina Corsini of Florence, Italy. Their daughter Joan married Malcolm Scollay Low, the son of Benjamin R. C. Low of Manhattan. Their son The Reverend William Hamilton Russell III married Joan Schildhauer, the daughter of Clarence Henry Schildhauer of *White Oak* in Owings Mills, MD; Diane Sawyer Fenton; and, subsequently, Elizabeth Buck Truslow, the daughter of Francis Adams and Elizabeth Auchincloss Jennings Truslow of *The Point* in Laurel Hollow. [*See* Spinzia, *Long Island's Prominent North Shore Families, vol. II* – Truslow entry.]

Cusachs, Philip Alain (1887-1931)

Occupation(s):	architect - partner, with his brother-in-law Raymond Francis Amirall, Amirall and Cusachs*
Civic Activism:	chairman, Prize Committee of the Beaux Arts Institute, 1926
Marriage(s):	1928-1931 – Helen Margaret Krech (1899-1967)
Address:	*[unable to determine street address]*, East Islip
Name of estate:	
Year of construction:	
Style of architecture:	
Architect(s):	
Landscape architect(s):	
House extant:	unconfirmed
Historical notes:	

The *New York Social Blue Book, 1930* lists Mr. and Mrs. Philip A. Cusachs as residing in East Islip.

He was the son of Pierre Leon Cusachs of New Orleans, LA. Philip's sister Marguerite married Raymond Francis Amirall and resided at *Ma Chaumiere* in Hempstead. [*See* Spinzia, *Long Island's Prominent Families in the Town of Hempstead* – Amirall entry.]

Helen Margaret Krech Cusachs was the daughter of Alvin William and Angeline Sherwood Jackson Krech of *Hedgerow* in Southampton. [*See* Spinzia, *Long Island's Prominent Families in the Town of Southampton*– Krech entry.] Helen's sister Angeline married Oliver Burr James, Sr. of *Rocky Point* in Laurel and, later, the noted architect Harrie Thomas Lindeberg of *West Gate Lodge* in Matinecock. [*See* Spinzia, *Long Island's Prominent North Shore Families, vol. I* – James and Lindeberg entries.] Helen had previously been married to Louis Stuart Wing, Jr. After Philip's death she married Duncan Argle Holmes of Brookville. [*See* Spinzia, *Long Island's Prominent North Shore Families, vol. I* – Holmes entry.]

*Almirall and Cusachs designed Notre Dame Home for the Aged, The Bronx; Brooklyn Public Library, Brooklyn; Roman Catholic Church of the Nativity (addition), Brooklyn; and 386 Park Avenue, NYC.

Cutting, Robert Fulton (1852-1934)

Occupation(s):	capitalist -	director, St. Louis, Alton & Terre Haute Railroad;
		director, Cairo Short Line (which merged into Illinois Central Railroad;
		director, Florida Central & Peninsular Railroad (which merged into Seaboard Air Railway Co.);
		director, International Telephone & Telegraph;
		director, All America Cables, Inc.;
		director, Manhattan Storage & Warehouse Co.
	financier -	director, American Exchange Securities Co.;
		director, American Exchange National Bank;
		director, Manhattan Safe Deposit Co.;
		director, Church Properties Fire Insurance Corp.;
		director, Church Pension Corp.

Civic Activism: president, Metropolitan Opera & Real Estate Co.;
president, board of trustees, Cooper Union, NYC;
president, Association for Improving the Condition of the Poor;
a founder and chairman of board, Suburban Homes (provided low income housing);
president, board of trustees, New York Trade School;
member, executive committee, Relief of Belgium, in NYC, during World War I;
a founder and president, Citizens Union (civic reform);
a founder and chairman, Bureau of Municipal Research

Marriage(s): M/1 – 1874-1875 – Natalie Schenck (1852-1875)
M/2 – 1883-1919 – Helen Suydam (1858-1919)

Address: South Country Road, Great River
Name of estate:
Year of construction: c. 1860s
Style of architecture: Neo-Tudor
Architect(s):
Landscape architect(s):
House extant: no; demolished in c. 1900*
Historical notes:

The house, originally named *Westbrook Farm*, was built by Robert Lenox Maitland. In 1873, Mr. Maitland sold it to George Lyndes Lorillard. It was later owned by Robert Fulton Cutting and, subsequently, by his brother William Bayard Cutting, Sr. They were the sons of Fulton and Elise Justine Bayard Cutting of Manhattan.

Natalie Schenck Cutting was the daughter of Noah H. Schenck of Brooklyn.

Helen Suydam Cutting was the daughter of Charles and Ann White Schermerhorn Suydam of Bayport. Helen's brother Walter married Jane Meiser Suydam and resided at *Manowtasquott Lodge* in Blue Point.

Robert Fulton and Helen Suydam Cutting's daughter Helen married Lucius Kellogg Wilmerding, Jr., the son of Lucius Kellogg and Caroline Murray Wilmerding, Sr. of *White Lodge* in East Islip, and resided in Far Hills, NJ. Their daughter Elizabeth married Stafford McLean. Their daughter Ruth married Reginald L. G. Auchincloss, the son of Edgar Sloan Auchincloss of Manhattan. Their son Fulton married Mary Josephine Amory, the daughter of Francis Inman and Grace Minot Amory of Boston, MA, and resided in North Hills, Brookville, and at *A-Weely-y-Moor* in Southampton. [*See* Spinzia, *Long Island's Prominent North Shore Families, vol. I* and *Long Island's Prominent Families in the Town of Southampton*– Cutting entries.] Their son Charles married Helen McMahon, the daughter of John T. McMahon of Flushing.

*After the Spanish American War, the house was used by the federal government as a convalescent home for returning servicemen and, then, demolished. [Harry W. Havemeyer, *Along the Great South Bay From Oakdale to Babylon: The Story of a Summer Spa 1840 to 1940* (Mattituck, NY: Amereon House, 1996), p. 148.]

Westbrook Farm

Cutting, William Bayard, Sr. (1850-1912)

Occupation(s):	attorney
	capitalist - president, St. Louis, Alton & Terre Haute Railroad;
	director, Illinois Central Railroad;
	director, Southern Pacific Railroad Co.;
	director, Norfolk & Southern Railway Co.;
	director, Oxnard Sugar Co. (later, American Beet Co.)
	financier - trustee, United States Trust Co.;
	director, American Exchange National Bank;
	director, Commercial Union Assurance Co.;
	director, Commercial Union Fire Insurance Co.
Civic Activism:	president, Improved Dwellings Association (provided low income housing);
	president, New York Chamber of Commerce;
	director, Suburban Homes Co. (provided low income housing);
	director, Metropolitan Opera, NYC;
	director, American Museum of Natural History, NYC;
	director, Metropolitan Museum of Art, NYC;
	trustee, Columbia University, NYC;
	trustee, General Theological Seminary, NYC;
	trustee, Episcopal Church Board of Domestic and Foreign Missions;
	a founder and trustee, Waverly Gun Club, Islip, 1890
Marriage(s):	1877-1912 – Olivia Peyton Murray (1855-1949)
	- Civic Activism: established traveling fellowships, Columbia Univ., NYC; established memorial scholarship in her son Bronson's name, Harvard University, Cambridge, MA; trustee, East Islip Public School District; a founder, woman's auxiliary, Episcopal Diocese of New York's Board of Missions
Address:	South Country Road, Great River
Name of estate:	*Westbrook Farm*
Year of construction:	1886
Style of architecture:	Modified Neo-Tudor
Architect(s):	Charles Coolidge Haight designed the house and 1884 east gatehouse (for W. B. Cutting, Sr.)
	Isaac Henry Green II designed the 1911 barns, staff houses, sheds *[unconfirmed]* and gatehouse *[confirmed]* (for W. B. Cutting, Sr.)
Landscape architect(s):	Olmsted, 1887-1894 (for W. B. Cutting, Sr.)
	Beatrice Jones Farrand designed the animal cemetery (for W. B. Cutting, Sr.)
	Ferruccio Vitale designed entrance drive (for W. B. Cutting, Sr.)

House extant: yes
Historical notes:

rear facade, 2005

William Bayard Cutting, Sr. purchased the Robert Lenox Maitland, Sr. / George Lyndes Lorillard estate. After residing in the former Lorillard house for approximately a year, Cutting built a new house on the property, which he called *Westbrook Farm*.

He was the son of Fulton and Elise Justine Bayard Cutting of Manhattan.

Olivia Peyton Murray Cutting was the daughter of Bronson and Ann Ann Eliza Peyton Murray of Manhattan.

William Bayard and Olivia Peyton Murray Cutting, Sr.'s son William Bayard Cutting, Jr. married Lady Sybil Marjorie Cuffe. Their daughter Justine, who was an anti-suffragist, married George Cabot Ward. Their daughter Olivia married Henry James, who resided at *Greenleaves* in Cold Spring Harbor. [*See* Spinzia, *Long Island's Prominent North Shore Families, vol. I* – James entry.] Their son Bronson, a bachelor, was killed in an airplane crash. He was an United States Senator from New Mexico.

The estate is now the Bayard Cutting Arboretum. The house is open to the public.

Dahl, George Washington (1874-1958)

Occupation(s):	industrialist - president, H. A. C. Dahl & Co., Brooklyn (manufacturer of health foods)
Civic Activism:	director, Bayport Republican Club; vice-president, St. Ann's Men's Club, Sayville
Marriage(s):	1901-1958 – Annabel Bancker Cox (1882-1969)
Address:	22 South Ocean Avenue, Bayport
Name of estate:	*The Maples*
Year of construction:	1881
Style of architecture:	Neo-Italianate
Architect(s):	
Landscape architect(s):	
House extant: yes	
Historical notes:	

front facade

The house was built by Joseph William Meeks, Jr. In 1916, Mrs. Meeks sold it to Dahl.

The *Long Island Society Register, 1929* lists George W. and Amabel [sic] Bancker Cox Dahl as residing on Ocean Avenue in Bayport. They had previously resided on Main Street.

He was the son of Harold Alfred Casmir and Gustava Karolina Elisbet Thomsson Dahl.

Annabel Bancker Cox Dahl's brother Harold Newton Cox of Southold invented the Cox method of taking colored motion pictures. [*The New York Times* March 16, 1936, p. 17.] They were the children of Benoit J. and Francella A. Cox of Brooklyn.

George Washington and Annabel Bancker Cox Dahl's daughter Elizabeth married Henry Ware, Jr., the son of Henry and Louise Fuller Wilson Ware, Sr. Their daughter Florence married Moses Edward Cheny with whom she resided on Ocean Avenue, Bayport, and, later, Seth W. Warner of Vermont. Their son Harold married Elizabeth King Tuthill, the daughter of Charles Arthur Wilson and Edith Elizabeth King Tuthill, Jr.

Dana, Richard Turner (1876-1928)

Occupation(s):	civil engineer - assistant engineer, Erie Railroad; chief engineer, Construction Service Co.
Marriage(s):	1902-1928 – Mary Rattoone Meredith (1876-1943)
Address:	Suffolk Lane and South Country Road, East Islip
Name of estate:	*Azimuth*
Year of construction:	
Style of architecture:	Colonial Revival
Architect(s):	
Landscape architect(s):	
Builder:	Jabez Ephraim Van Orden
House extant: yes	
Historical notes:	

The *Long Island Society Register, 1929* lists Richard T. and Mary R. Meredith Dana as residing in East Islip. The *Social Register Summer, 1932* lists Mary R. Meredith Dana as residing at *Azimuth* in East Islip.

He was the son of Richard Starr and Florine Enders Turner Dana.

Mary Rattoone Meredith Dana was the daughter of William Tuckey and Mary R. Watson Meredith. Her sister Gertrude married J. Osgood Nichols.

Richard Turner and Mary Rattoone Meredith Dana's daughter Mary married William C. Kopper, the son of Philip W. Kopper of Manhattan.

front facade

Davies, Julien Tappan (1845-1920)

Occupation(s):	attorney - partner, Davies, Stone, and Auerbach; partner, Davies, Auerbach, Cornell, and Barry; partner, Davies, Short, and Townsend*
	financier - vice-president, New York Title Guarantee & Trust Co.; trustee, Mutual Life Insurance Co. of New York; director, Bond and Mortgage Trust Co.
Civic Activism:	vice-president, Bar Association of the City of New York; president, Saint David's Society, 1900-1903; a founder, Young Men's Municipal Association, 1871; member, board of managers, Foreign and Domestic Mission Society, Protestant Episcopal Church in the United Sates of America; trustee, St. George's School, Newport, RI
Marriage(s):	1869-1904 – Alice Martin (1848-1904)
Address:	Great River Road, Great River
Name of estate:	*Timber Point*
Year of construction:	1882
Style of architecture:	Shingle
Architect(s):	Hart and Shape designed the alterations, converting the house to Colonial Revival (for Timber Point Club)
Landscape architect(s):	Martha Brooks Brown Hutcheson (for Breese)
Builder:	E. W. Howell
House extant: yes	
Historical notes:	

The house, originally named *Timber Point*, was built by William Laurence Breese, Sr. In 1905, the estate was purchased by Davies, who continued to call it *Timber Point*.

He was the son of Judge Henry Ebenezer and Mrs. Rebecca Waldo Tappan Davies of New York. Julien's brother Francis married Cornelia Scott Rokenbaugh and resided at *Tidelands* in East Hampton. [*See* Spinzia, *Long Island's Prominent Families in the Town of East Hampton*– Davies entry.]

Alice Martin Davies was the daughter of Henry Hull and Anna Townsend Martin of Albany, NY. Her brother Henry married Justine de Peyster, the daughter of Johnston de Peyster. Her brother Frederick Townsend Martin was a bachelor. Her brother Bradley Martin, Sr. married Cornelia Sherman. Her sister Anna married General William B. Rochester.

Julien Tappan and Alice Martin Davies' daughter Ethel married Archibald d'Gourlay Thatcher and resided at *Pondcroft* in Old Westbury. Their son Julien Townsend Davies, Sr. married Marie Rose de Garmendia and resided at *Casa Rosa* in West Islip. Their son Frederick married Emily Martha O'Neill, the daughter of Eugene M. O'Neill of Pittsburgh, PA, and resided at *Dune Ward* in Southampton. [*See* Spinzia, *Long Island's Prominent Families in the Town of Southampton*– Davies entry.]

[See following entry for additional family information.]

In 1923, the Davieses' heirs sold the estate to the Great River Club, which, in 1925, changed its name to the Timber Point Club. It was owned for a period of time by the Republican Party of Suffolk County. The house is currently the clubhouse of the county's Timber Point Country Club.

*Davies' law partner Howard Townsend, Jr. resided at *Hopeland* in Southampton. [*See* Spinzia, *Long Island's Prominent Families in the Town of Southampton*– Townsend entry.]

Timber Point, c. 1900

Davies, Julien Townsend, Jr. (1895-1978)

Occupation(s):	attorney - partner, Davies, Ives, and Lawther
Civic Activism:	trustee, Village of Flower Hill;
	mayor, Village of Flower Hill, 1940-1944;
	vice-president, board of managers, Southside Hospital, Bay Shore (now, South Shore University Hospital);
	director, Suffolk County Taxpayers Good Roads Association
Marriage(s):	M/1 – 1920-div. 1933 – Faith de Moss Robinson (d. 1967)
	- Civic Activism: trustee, Southside Hospital Auxiliaries, Bay Shore (now, South Shore University Hospital)
	M/2 – 1933-div. 1960 – Marie O'Connor (d. 1969)
	M/3 – 1960 – Ida Pasquali
Address:	*[unable to determine street address]*, West Islip
Name of estate:	*Cherry Pool*
Year of construction:	
Style of architecture:	
Architect(s):	
Landscape architect(s):	

House extant: unconfirmed
Historical notes:

The *Social Register New York, 1933* lists Julien T. and Faith de M. Robinson Davies [Jr.] as residing at *Cherry Pool* in West Islip.

He was the son of Julien Townsend and Marie Rose de Garmendia Davies, Sr. of *Casa Rosa* in West Islip.

Julien Townsend and Faith de Moss Robinson Davies, Jr.'s son John was fourteen when he was killed in an automobile accident. Their daughter Faith married George Ross Le Sauvage, Jr. and resided in West Islip and, later, Manhasset Bay Estates. Their son Julien Townsend Davies III married Janet Elizabeth Harnell, the daughter of James H. Harnell of Babylon.

Marie O'Connor Davies had previously been married to ____ Quinn.

By 1940 Davies had relocated to the North Shore community of Flower Hill. [For Davies' North Shore residence, *see* Spinzia, *Long Island's Prominent North Shore Families, vol. I* – Davies entry.]

[See following entry for additional family information.]
[For information on the Southside Hospital, see Cooper entry.]

Davies, Julien Townsend, Sr. (1870-1917)

Occupation(s):	attorney - partner, Davies, Auerbach and Cornell
	capitalist - president and director, Bancroft Realty Co.;
	director, Maplewood Hotel Co.
Civic Activism:	vice-president of board, Southside Hospital, Bay Shore (now, South Shore University Hospital);
	member, executive committee, Suffolk County Taxpayers' Good Roads Association
Marriage(s):	1891-1917 – Marie Rose de Garmendia (1872-1951)
Address:	South Country Road, West Islip
Name of estate:	*Casa Rosa*
Year of construction:	c. 1880s
Style of architecture:	Neo-Federal
Architect(s):	
Landscape architect(s):	
Builder:	Rogers and Blydenburgh, 1896 alterations to house

House extant: yes
Historical notes:

rear facade

In 1901, Julien Townsend Davies, Sr. purchased the Francis Peabody Magoun, Sr.'s house and called it *Casa Rosa*.

He was the son of Julien Tappan and Alice Martin Davies of *Timber Point* in Great River.

Marie Rose de Garmendia Davies was the daughter of Carlos G. de Garmendia.

Julien Townsend and Marie Rose de Garmendia Davies, Sr.'s daughter Alice married Henry Sellers McKee II, the son of Thomas M. and Nellie Wood McKee of Woodmere, and resided in Babylon. Their daughter Phebe married Walter J. Sutherland, Jr. Their son Julien Townsend Davies, Jr. resided West Islip. Their daughter Marie died at the age of fifteen.

[See previous entry for additional family information.]

deCoppet, Andre H. (1892-1953)

Occupation(s):	financier - president, deCoppet and Doremus (stock brokerage firm)
	industrialist - president, Haitian–American Development Co.*
	capitalist - owner, Dauphin, a sugar plantation in Haiti
Marriage(s):	M/1 – 1920-div. – Clara Wright Barclay (1890-1959)
	M/2 – 1931-div. 1943 – Muriel Johnson
	M/3 – 1943-1953 – Eileen Johnston (1922-1985)
Address:	South Country Road, Islip
Name of estate:	*The Willows*
Year of construction:	c. 1925
Style of architecture:	
Architect(s):	
Landscape architect(s):	
House extant: no	

Historical notes:

  The house was built by William Henry Moffitt. In 1925, it was purchased by deCoppet, who called it *The Willows*.

  The *Long Island Society Register, 1929* lists Andre H. and Clara W. Barclay deCoppet as residing at *The Willows* on South Country Road, Islip.

  He was the son of Edward J. and Pauline deCoppet of New York.

  Clara Wright Barclay deCoppet was the daughter of Henry Anthony and Clara Oldfield Wright Barclay. She had previously been married to Jose Victor Onativia, Jr. of Southampton and, subsequently, John Lord Boatwright of Richmond, VA. [*See* Spinzia, *Long Island's Prominent Families in the Town of Southampton*– Onativia, Jr. entry.] Jose and Clara Onativia, Jr.'s daughter Clara married Francis Bacon Gilbert, the son of Clinton Gilbert of Manhattan. Their daughter Jacqueline married Philippe Joseph Berthet of Paris, France. Jose Victor Onativia, Jr. subsequently married Clarisse Coudert Nast, the former wife of Conde Nast, who resided at *Sandy Cay* in Sands Point. [*See* Spinzia, *Long Island's Prominent North Shore Families, vol. II* – Nast entry.]

  Muriel Johnson was the daughter of Goodwin Johnson of San Francisco, CA. She had previously been married to Raymond Belasco. She subsequently married George Hopper Fitch of Manhattan.

  Andre H. and Muriel Johnson deCoppet's daughter Diane married George Simpson, the son of William Simpson of London, England, and resided in London. She subsequently married Richard Russell and resided in Manhattan and South Carolina. Their daughter Laura did not marry.

  Eileen Johnston deCoppet was the daughter of George Johnston of Islip. She subsequently married Prince Karl Viktor Zu Wied of Albania.

  *During World War II, the Haitian–American Development Co. played a major role in developing substitute fibers to be used in the manufacture of rope to eliminate the dependence on hemp.

de Forest, James Goodrich, Sr. (1822-1903)

Occupation(s):	financier - trustee, Atlantic Mutual Insurance;
	partner, W. W. de Forest and Co.;
	director, Gallatin National Bank;
	director, Phoenix Insurance Co.
Marriage(s):	1852-1875 – Julia T. Hallett (1826-1875)
Address:	South Country Road and de Forest Avenue, West Islip
Name of estate:	
Year of construction:	
Style of architecture:	
Architect(s):	
Landscape architect(s):	
House extant: unconfirmed	

Historical notes:

  James Goodrich de Forest, Sr. purchased the Haddock residence. [*South Side Signal* August 25, 1888, p. 2.]

  He was the son of Lockwood and Mehetabel Wheeler de Forest.

  James Goodrich and Julia T. Hallett de Forest, Sr.'s son Stephen married Leila B. Dean, the daughter of William B. Dean of Babylon and resided in West Islip. Their son William was secretly married to Mabel Menzies. Their son Frederick married Lydia Krug and resided in Newark, NJ. Their daughter Louise married Maynard Hollister. Their daughter Eliza eloped with Charles M. Russell. Their son James Goodrich de Forest, Jr. was residing in Babylon at the time of his death.

  In 1913, the estate was purchased by Harford Pinckney Walker, Sr. (aka Frederick Harford Pinckney Walker, Sr.) who subdivided its property into an area he called "The Venice of Babylon," and built a new house as a residence.

de Goicouria, Albert Valentine (1848-1930)

Occupation(s):	financier - stockbroker; trustee, New York Stock Exchange
Civic Activism:	president, New York Athletic Club, NYC; a founder, South Side Field Club, Bay Shore, 1886
Marriage(s):	M/1 – 1877 – Mary Cecelia Wall (1850-1904) M/2 – 1910 – Beatrice Frances Tinley (1872-1935)
Address:	South Country Road, Islip
Name of estate:	
Year of construction:	
Style of architecture:	
Architect(s):	
Landscape architect(s):	
House extant:	unconfirmed
Historical notes:	

Albert Valentine and Mary Cecelia Wall de Goicouria's daughter Rosalie married Walter Scott Cameron, the son of A. Scott Cameron of Hempstead and Southampton, and, subsequently, Benjamin Curtis Allen of Philadelphia, PA. Their daughter Alice, who was a suffragist, married August Belmont III with whom she resided in Bay Shore. Alice subsequently married John Daniel Wing, who resided in Southampton. [*See* Spinzia, *Long Island's Prominent Families in the Town of Hempstead* and *Long Island's Prominent Families in the Town of Southampton* – Cameron and Wing entries.]

Beatrice Frances Tinley de Goicouria was the daughter of Emmet Tinley.

Delaney, John Hanlon (1871-1952)

Occupation(s):	publisher - owner, weekly printing trade journal; manager, *The Morning Telegraph*, NYC* industrialist owner, commercial printing plant; treasurer, bottle manufacturer politician - commissioner, Department of Plant and Structure, NYC, 1918-1919; commissioner, Rapid Transit, NYC, 1919-1921; commissioner, New York City Docks, 1921-1924; commissioner, Board of Transportation, NYC, 1924-1941**
Civic Activism:	trustee, St. John's University, Brooklyn
Marriage(s):	1903-1944 – Eleanor Gertrude Leary (d. 1944) - Civic Activism: president, St. Mary's Hospital Aid Association, Brooklyn
Address:	Fairview Avenue, Bayport
Name of estate:	
Year of construction:	c. 1912
Style of architecture:	
Architect(s):	
Landscape architect(s):	
House extant:	unconfirmed
Historical notes:	

The house was built by John Hanlon Delaney.

He was the son of John and Mary Curran Delaney of Manchester, VT.

*According to Harry Popik, a 2005 candidate for Manhattan Borough President, the use of the name "Big Apple" for New York City first appeared in *The Morning Telegraph* in which an apple graphic was featured in the column head for "Around the Big Apple" with John J. Fitz Gerald. Fitz Gerald refers to the city as "the apple" in his column of February 18, 1924. [electronic source, November 8, 2005.]

**As commissioner of the Board of Transportation Delaney, was the chief architect of New York City's unified transit system, earning him the nickname "Mr. Transit."

del Garcia, Lester Mullen (1866-1944*)

Occupation(s):	financier - stockbroker writer – *The Washington Bells*, 1898 (novel)
Marriage(s):	1899-1944 – Helen Margaret S. Graham (1867-1944*) - Civic Activism: donated 1,000-pound bell to St. Mary's Roman Catholic Church, East Islip, 1903**
Address:	*[unable to determine street address]*, East Islip
Name of estate:	*La Granja*
Year of construction:	
Style of architecture:	
Architect(s):	
Landscape architect(s):	
House extant: yes	
Historical notes:	

    The *Social Register Summer, 1904* lists Lester M. and Helen M. S. Graham del Garcia as residing at *La Granja* in East Islip.
    She was the daughter of William Irving and Helen Schieffelin Graham of New York and a descendant of Washington Irving.
    *The del Garcias died within ten days of each other.
    **The inscription on the bell is "My name is St. Helen. The munificence of Helen Del Garcia caused me to be made in A. D. 1903 and placed here in St. Mary's tower. "*Vox ego sum vitae – Voco vos orate venite*," "I am the voice of life – I call you to come and pray." The inscription repeats the message on the largest of the three famous 1735 Arcadian bells from the Fortress of Louisbourg, on Cape Breton Island, Nova Scotia, Canada. It was known as the Bell of St. Louis. In 1745 the Bell of St. Louis was taken from the fortress by troops from New England and given to the Queen Chapel in Portsmouth, New Hampshire, which then changed its name to St. John's Church. In 1806, the church burned after which Paul Revere recast the damaged bell; the Bell of St. Louis had to be recast again in 1905 at which time the inscription, an inscription on a bell seized during the French Revolution from a parish church in France, was added.

Dempsey, Joseph Francis, Jr.

Occupation(s):	attorney - member, Shearman, Sterling and Wright, NYC
Marriage(s):	1941 – Phebe Thorne (d. 1981)*
Address:	146 East Bayberry Road, Islip
Name of estate:	
Year of construction:	1899-1900
Style of architecture:	Moorish
Architect(s):	Grosvenor Atterbury designed the house (for H. O. Havemeyer)**
Landscape architect(s):	Nathan F. Barrett (for H. O. Havemeyer)***
Builder:	[*See* Jabez Ephraim Van Orden entry.]
House extant: yes	
Historical notes:	

front facade, 2006

    The house was built by Henry Osborne Havemeyer as part of his "Modern Venice" development. It was owned by William Dunham Baker and, subsequently, by Dempsey.
    He was the son of Joseph Francis and May E. Dempsey, Sr. of Great River.
    Phebe Thorne Dempsey was the daughter of Francis Burritt and Hildegarde Kobbe Thorne, Sr. of *Brookwood* in East Islip. Phebe's sister Julia married Dennis McCarty. Her brother Oakleigh Thorne II, who resided at *Valley Ranch* in Cody, WY, married Peggy N. Schroll and, subsequently, Lisa L. Bellows. Her brother Francis Burritt Thorne, Jr. married Ann C. Cobb, the daughter of Boughton Cobb of Manhattan, and resided in Bay Shore.
    *Long Island's Phebe Dempsey Golf Tournament is held in Phebe's honor.
    Joseph Francis and Phebe Thorne Dempsey, Jr.'s daughter Elizabeth married C. F. Lindsay Hewitt and resided in Cold Spring Harbor.
    After the Dempseys' separation, Joseph relocated to Great River and Phebe moved to Stony Brook.
    [See following entry for additional family information.]
    **The sales brochure for "Modern Venice" states that the Moorish-style architecture was suggested by Louis Comfort Tiffany.
    ***The sales brochure also states that "Modern Venice" would be devoid of trees and vegetation and that Nathan F. Barrett was the landscape architect.

Dempsey, Joseph Francis, Sr. (1886-1950)

Occupation(s):	attorney -	partner, Cary and Caroll (which merged with Shearman, Sterling and Wright);
		partner, Shearman, Sterling and Wright, NYC
	capitalist -	president, National Hotel Corporation of Cuba;
		president, Rye Ridge Realty Corp.;
		director, Fifth Avenue Building Co.;
		director, Holmens Newsprint Corporation;
		director, R. W. Goelet Estates, Inc.;
		director, Goelet Realty Co.;
		director, Rhode Island Corporation;
		director, Uddeholm Company of America;
		director, National City Realty Corp.;
		director, Classical Cinematograph Corp.;
		director, Telfair Stockton & Co., Inc.;
		director, Ritz–Carlton Hotel Corp.;
		director, Mark Cross Company;
		director, Mortbon Corporation of New York;
		director, Manchester Land Co.
	industrialist -	director, Pacific Molasses Company, Ltd.;
		director, Commercial Molasses Corp.
	financier -	director, Lawyers Mortgage Guarantee Corp.

Marriage(s):   May E. *[unable to determine maiden name]*
  - Civic Activism: director, Brooklyn Free Kindergarten Society, Inc.

Address: Great River Road, Great River
Name of estate: *Estancia*
Year of construction: 1899
Style of architecture: Neo-Tudor
Architect(s): Charles C. Thain designed the house (for R. S. White)

Landscape architect(s):
House extant: unconfirmed
Historical notes:

The house was built by Raymond S. White. It was later owned by his wife Sarah who married Francis Sessions Hutchins and called the house *Saramond*. It was then owned by Dr. George David Stewart who called it *Appin House* and, subsequently, by Dempsey who renamed in *Estancia*.

Joseph Francis and May E. Dempsey, Sr.'s daughter Susan married Anthony Hugh Barnes, the son of Sir George and Lady Barnes of Prawls, Stone Tenterden, Kent, England. Their son John married Margaret Leighton Moore, the daughter of Dr. David Dodge and Mrs. Margaret Leighton Hatch Moore of Islip. Their son Joseph Francis Dempsey, Jr. married Phebe Thorne and resided in Islip.

[See previous entry for additional family information.]

front facade

de Murias, Fernando Enrique (1884-1926)

Occupation(s):

Marriage(s): 1905-1926 – Virginia Cornwall Bunce (1882-1953)
- Civic Activism: headed Red Cross facilities at Aviation Fields on Long Island

Address: 74 Douglas Avenue, Babylon
Name of estate:
Year of construction:
Style of architecture: Shingle*
Architect(s):
Landscape architect(s):
Builder: E. W. Howell, 1917 alterations
House extant: yes
Historical notes:

The house was originally one of the cottages of the Argyle Hotel. It was purchased in 1908 by Virginia Cornwall Bunce de Murias.

She was the daughter of Frederick Sidney and Annie M. Towne Bunce, Sr. of Babylon.

Fernando Enrique de Murias was the son of Ramon and Clara Garden de Murias of Manhattan and Havana, Cuba. Fernando's sister Sylvia married Dr. Albert Vander Veer, Jr. and resided at *Gray Cottage* in Point O'Woods on Fire Island.

Fernando Enrique and Virginia Cornwall Bunce de Murias' son Ramon de Murias II, who inherited the house, married Ann Carlin Borden, the daughter of General William Ayres Borden.

*The house was remodeled in 1917, in the 1950s, and again in 1960. The present Colonial Revival style house is the result of those alterations.

The house was purchased in 2011 from the de Murias family by Kenneth Rogers.

prior to remodeling

after remodeling

Denby, Thomas Garvin (1877-1933)
aka Garvin Denby

Occupation(s):	industrialist - a founder and president, Denby Motor Truck Co., Detroit, MI; secretary and treasurer, Federal Motor Truck Co., Detroit, MI; president, Fulton Motor Works, Farmingdale
	financier - member, Harrison–Wheaton, Inc., Farmingdale (real estate and industrial financiers)
Civic Activism:	president, Long Island Kennel Club; director, American Kennel Club; anti-suffragist - a founder and treasurer, Men's Association Opposed to Woman Suffrage, Michigan, 1913
Marriage(s):	1903-1933 – Esther Jewell Strong (1878-1941) - restaurateur - established Tea Room, Montauk Highway, Amityville, 1924* Civic Activism: anti-suffragist - director, Michigan Association Opposed to Woman Suffrage; treasurer, Michigan State National League for Woman's Service during World War I; chair, Amityville branch, Southside Hospital Woman's Auxiliary (now, South Shore University Hospital)
Address:	99 Bennett Place, Amityville
Name of estate:	
Year of construction:	1850
Style of architecture:	Colonial Revival
Architect(s):	
Landscape architect(s):	

House extant: yes
Historical notes:

In 1921, the Denbys relocated to Amityville. [*The Brooklyn Daily Eagle* March 16, 1921, p. 12.]

front facade

The *Long Island Society Register, 1928* and *1929* list Garvin and Esther Jewell Strong Denby as residing on Burnett [sic] Place, Amityville. The 1930 Census lists the Denbys as residing at 99 Bennet Place.

He was the son of United States Minister to China Charles Harvey Denby and his wife Martha Fitch Denby. Garvin's brother Edwin resigned his position as Secretary of the Navy due to the Tea Pot Dome Scandal. Harry Ford Sinclair, Sr. of Kings Point and his brother Earle Westwood Sinclair of *Fairlawn* in East Hampton were also implicated in the Teapot Dome Scandal. The Sinclairs' lawyer James William Zevely resided in East Hampton. [*See* Spinzia, *Long Island's Prominent North Shore Families, vol. II* – Sinclair entry – and *Long Island's Prominent Families in the Town of East Hampton* – Sinclair and Zevely entries.]

Esther Jewell Strong Denby was the daughter of William Howard and Florence Walworth Jewell Strong of Michigan.

*The Tea Room was appointed with the Denby family's rare Chinese silks, pottery, and enamels. [*The Brooklyn Daily Eagle* September 19, 1924.]

[For information on the Southside Hospital, see Cooper entry.]

Dick, Adolph Mollenhauer (1894-1956)

Occupation(s):	architect - partner, Fuller and Dick*
Civic Activism	trustee, Southside Hospital, Bay Shore (now, South Shore University Hospital)
Marriage(s):	bachelor
Address:	Ocean Avenue, Islip
Name of estate:	
Year of construction:	1931
Style of architecture:	Georgian Revival
Architect(s):	Adolph Mollenhauer Dick designed his own house
Landscape architect(s):	

House extant: no; demolished in 1960s
Historical notes:

The house was built by Adolph Mollenhauer Dick.

The *Long Island Society Register, 1929* lists Adolph M. Dick as residing in Islip.

He was the son of John Henry and Julia Theodora Mollenhauer Dick, who resided at *Allen Winden Farm* in Islip.

[See other Dick family entries for additional family information.]

*Dick designed the original Islip Town Hall; the wings were added at a later date.

Dick, John Henry (1851-1925)

Occupation(s):	industrialist - director, The National Sugar Refining Co.
	financier - vice president, Manufacturers National Bank, Brooklyn
Marriage(s):	1886-1925 – Julia Theodora Mollenhauer (1863-1931)
Address:	Ocean Avenue, Islip
Name of estate:	*Allen Winden Farm**
Year of construction:	c. 1883
Style of architecture:	Victorian
Architect(s):	Isaac Henry Green II designed the c. 1889 alterations (for W. Dick)
	Alfred Hopkins designed the garage and stables (for John Henry Dick)
Landscape architect(s):	
Builder:	P. B. McEntyre (for C. A. Tucker)
	E. W. Howell, alterations (for W. Dick)

House extant: no; demolished in 1960s**
Historical notes:

    The house was built by Charles A. Tucker. It was purchased in 1889 by William Dick. [*The Brooklyn Daily Eagle* March 31, 1889, p. 11.] It was later owned by his son John Henry Dick, and, subsequently, by William Karl Dick, all of whom called in *Allen Winden Farm*.

    *Allen Winden is German for "all winds."

    The *Brooklyn Blue Book and Long Island Society Register, 1918* lists J. Henry and Julia T. Mollenhauer Dick as residing at *Allen Winden Farm* in Islip.

    He was the son of William and Anna Maria Vagts Dick. His sister Anna Margaretha married John Adolph Mollenhauer and resided at *Homeport* in Bay Shore.

    Julia Theodora Mollenhauer Dick was the daughter of John and Doris Siems Mollenhauer of Bay Shore. Her brother John Adolph married Anna Margaretha Dick and resided at *Homeport* in Bay Shore. Her brother Frederick married May Craig. Her brother Henry married Sarah W. Howe.

    John Henry and Julia Theodora Mollenhauer Dick's son William Karl Dick married Madeline Force and, subsequently, Virginia K. Conner. Their daughter Doris married Horace Havemeyer, Sr. and resided at *Olympic Point* in Bay Shore. Their daughter Julia married William Kingsland Macy, Sr. and resided in Islip. Their son Adolph remained a bachelor.

    [See other Dick family entries for additional family information.]

    **Garage and stables are extant.

rear facade

Dick, William (1823-1912)

Occupation(s):	financier - president, Manufacturers National Bank, Brooklyn; vice president, Mechanics Bank of Williamsburg (which merged with Citizen Trust Co.; then became Manufacturers Trust Co; then, Hanover Bank; then, Manufacturers Hanover Bank); vice-president, Nassau Trust Co.; trustee, German Savings Institution
	industrialist - partner, Dick & Meyer Corp. (Brooklyn sugar refiners); director, American Sugar Refining Co.
Marriage(s):	1848-1898 – Anna Maria Vagts (1819-1898)
Address:	Ocean Avenue, Islip
Name of estate:	*Allen Winden Farm**
Year of construction:	c. 1883
Style of architecture:	Victorian
Architect(s):	Isaac Henry Green II designed the c. 1889 alterations (for W. Dick) Alfred Hopkins designed the garage and stables (for John Henry Dick)
Landscape architect(s):	
Builder:	P. B. McEntyre (for C. A. Tucker) E. W. Howell, alterations (for W. Dick)
House extant:	no; demolished in 1960s**
Historical notes:	

   The house was built by Charles A. Tucker. It was purchased in 1889 by William Dick. [*The Brooklyn Daily Eagle* March 31, 1889, p. 11.] It was later owned by his son John Henry Dick, and, subsequently, by William Karl Dick, all of whom called in *Allen Winden Farm*.

   *Allen Winden is German for "all winds."

   [See other Dick family entries for additional family information.]

   **Garage and stables are extant.

rear facade

Dick, William Karl (1888-1953)

Occupation(s):	industrialist - director, Bates International Bag Co.;
	director, Bates Valve Bag Corp.;
	director, Hecker Products Corp.;
	director, The National Sugar Refining Co.;
	director, New Hampshire–Vermont Lumber Co.;
	director, St. Regis Paper Co.;
	director, Regis Kraft Co. of Canada;
	director, Shenandoah Rayon Corp.
	capitalist - director, Citizens Development Inc.;
	director, Citizens Water Supply, Newtown, NY;
	director, Cord Meyer Development Co.;
	director, Eastern State Corp.;
	director, St. Lawrence Railroad
	financier - director, Irving Trust Co.;
	director, Standard Capital Co.;
	vice president, Manufacturers Trust Company of Brooklyn
Civic Activism:	trustee, Boys' Club of New York;
	director, American Red Cross Disaster Committee;
	trustee, Southside Hospital, Bay Shore (now, South Shore University Hospital);
	a founder and director, Great River Club (later, Timber Point Club);
	a founder and governor, Islip Polo Club, 1912
Marriage(s):	M/1 – 1916-div. 1933 – Madeleine Talmadge Force (1893-1940)
	M/2 – 1941-1953 – Virginia Montez Kenniston Conner (1910-1985)
Address:	Ocean Avenue, Islip
Name of estate:	*Allen Winden Farm**
Year of construction:	c. 1883
Style of architecture:	Victorian
Architect(s):	Isaac Henry Green II designed the c. 1889 alterations (for W. Dick)
	Alfred Hopkins designed the garage and stables (for John Henry Dick)
Landscape architect(s):	
Builder:	P. B. McEntyre (for C. A. Tucker)
	E. W. Howell, alterations (for W. Dick)
House extant:	no; demolished in 1960s**
Historical notes:	

Allen Winden Farm

The house was built by Charles A. Tucker. It was purchased in 1889 by William Dick. [*The Brooklyn Daily Eagle* March 31, 1889, p. 11.] It was later owned by his son John Henry Dick, and, subsequently, by William Karl Dick, all of whom called in *Allen Winden Farm*.

*Allen Winden is German for "all winds."

The *Long Island Society Register, 1929* lists William Karl and Madeleine Force Dick as residing in Islip.

He was the son of John Henry and Julia Theodora Mollenhauer Dick.

Madeline Talmadge Force Dick was the daughter of William Hurlbert Force of Brooklyn. She had previously been married to John Jacob Astor IV, who died aboard the *Titanic*. After her divorce from Dick, she married Enzo Fiermonte, a middle-weight prizefighter.

William Karl and Madeleine Talmadge Force Dick's son William married Virginia Middleton French, the daughter of Francis O. French of Newport, RI. Their son John Henry Dick [II] remained a bachelor.

Virginia Montez Kenniston Conner Dick was the daughter of Edwin Solon Connor of Akron, OH. She subsequently married Frederick S. Moseley, Jr.

William Karl and Virginia Montez Kenniston Conner Dick's daughter Direxa married Christopher Farrell Dearie. Their son Will Kenniston Dick married Sandra Freeman Mueller.

[See other Dick family entries for additional family information.]

**Garage and stables are extant.

[For information on the Southside Hospital, see Cooper entry.]

Dillon, John Allen, Sr. (1885-1950)

Occupation(s):	industrialist - sales agent, American Car and Foundry Co.
Marriage(s):	
Address:	52 South Saxon Avenue, Bay Shore
Name of estate:	
Year of construction:	1880
Style of architecture:	Colonial Revival
Architect(s):	Isaac Henry Green II designed the 1889 southwestern wing addition of a living room and four bedrooms (for E. S. Knapp, Sr.)
Landscape architect(s):	
House extant:	yes
Historical notes:	

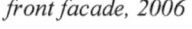

front facade, 2006

The house, originally named *Awixa Lawn*, was built by Edward Spring Knapp, Sr. In 1915, Mrs. Knapp sold the estate to August Belmont III. In 1923, Mrs. Belmont sold the estate, which at that time consisted of a twenty-five-room main residence on nine acres, six hundred feet of shoreline on Awixa Creek, stables, and a five-car garage, to Dillon.

John Allen Dillon, Sr. committed suicide in his Manhattan apartment located at 280 Park Avenue. [*The New York Times* April 12, 1950, p. 31.]

His son John Allen Dillon, Jr. married Mary Stewart Cocken, the daughter of William York Cocken of Pittsburgh, PA.

Dodson, Richard Wolford (1915-2002)

Occupation(s):	scientist -	assistant chemistry division leader, Manhattan Project, Los Alamos, NM;
		technical advisor, United States delegation to International Atoms for Peace Conference, Geneva, Switzerland, 1955;
		founding chairman, chemistry department, Brookhaven National Laboratory, Upton;
		secretary, General Advisory Committee, United States Atomic Energy Commission
	educator -	assistant professor of chemistry, California Institute of Technology, Pasadena, CA;
		professor of chemistry, Columbia University, NYC, 1953-1982
Marriage(s):	Mary Ellen Stout (b. 1915)	
Address:	407 Middle Road, Bayport	
Name of estate:		
Year of construction:	1915	
Style of architecture:	Colonial Revival	
Architect(s):	Isaac Henry Green II, 1915 alterations (for Rice) *[unconfirmed]*	
Landscape architect(s):		
Builder:	Ashby & Breckenridge, garage, greenhouse, and alterations to main residence, 1915 (for Rice)	
House extant:	yes	
Historical notes:		

front facade

Dr. George Edwin Rice remodeled Mrs. Henry M. Waterman's (Amelia E. Needham) residence into a six-bedroom, four-bath, 6,000-square-foot Colonial Revival residence he called *Maywood*. [*The Suffolk County News* May 5, 1916, p. 4.] In 1943, Frederick Merle Johnson, Sr. purchased the house. [*The Suffolk County News* April 30, 1943, p. 5.] In 1955, Mrs. Johnson sold the house to Dodson. [*The Suffolk County News* August 5, 1955, p. 2.]

Mary Ellen Stout Dodson was the daughter of Barrett Stout of Baton Rouge, LA.

Richard Wolford and Mary Ellen Stout Dodson's son Robert married Alberta Jane Fox, the daughter of Albert S. Fox of Olive Bridge, NY, and resided in Bloomington, IN.

In 1986, Dodson sold the house to Mark Kleine. [*The Suffolk County News* June 11, 1998, p. 6.]

Dodson, Robert Bowman (1849-1938)

Occupation(s):	financier - director, National City Bank; partner, Fahnestock and Co. (stock brokerage firm)
Civic Activism:	established the Robert B. and Mary W. Dodson Fund (to improve the condition of the poor)
Marriage(s):	Mary Wells (1848-1942) - Civic Activism: donated Victorian era clothes and a fan to the Metropolitan Museum of Art, NYC
Address:	Oak Neck and South Country Roads, West Islip
Name of estate:	*Kanonsioni**
Year of construction:	c. 1903
Style of architecture:	Queen Anne
Architect(s):	Kirby, Petit, & Green designed the house (for Dodson)
Landscape architect(s):	Harold Truesdel Patterson (for Dodson)**

House extant: no; demolished in c. 1950
Historical notes:

Kanonsioni, c. 1906

The house, originally named *Kanonsioni*, was built by Robert Bowman Dodson.

He was the son of Christian Bowman and Harriet Newell Warren Dodson of Geneva, IL.

Mary Wells Dodson was the daughter of John Augustus and Elizabeth Tobias Wells.

**Kanonsioni* is an Algonquian word for "longhouse."
**Babylon Historical Society has Patterson's landscape plans.

Doxsee, James Harvey, Sr. (1825-1907)

Occupation(s):	industrialist - a founder, James H. Doxsee and Sons (processors of canned clams, clam broth, and clam chowder)*
Marriage(s):	M/1 – Almira Smith (1824-1866) M/2 – 1868-1907 – Almira Smith Jennings (1848-1910) - Civic Activism: treasurer, Woman's Christian Temperance Union, Islip
Address:	Ocean Avenue, Islip
Name of estate:	
Year of construction:	
Style of architecture:	
Architect(s):	
Landscape architect(s):	

House extant: unconfirmed
Historical notes:

James Harvey Doxee was the son of Archelaus and Sarah Smith Doxee.

Almira Smith Doxee was the daughter of Josiah Rogers and Mary Mowbray Willets Smith.

James Harvey and Almira Smith Doxee, Sr.'s son Henry married Caroline Peters.

Almira Smith Jennings Doxsee was the daughter of Henry Smith and Eliza A. Jennings.

James Harvey and Almira Smith Jennings Doxsee, Sr.'s son John married Mabel Blair. Their son Robert married Susan Piepenbrink, the daughter of Charles Piepenbrink. Their daughter Almira died in 1909 at the age of twenty-four. Their son Henry died in 1907 at the age of two.

*Doxsee started the clam business in Islip in 1865, incorporating it into James H. Doxsee and Sons in 1897. Its directors, at the time of incorporation, were James Harvey Doxsee, Sr., John C. Doxsee, and Henry Smith Doxsee. [*The New York Times* January 10, 1897, p. 8.] In 1901, the Islip facility was closed and a new factory was established in Oracoke, NC, by Henry Smith Doxsee. In 1919, Robert Doxsee, Sr. opened a factory on Meadow Island near Point Lookout. In 1933, operations were moved to Point Lookout, where they remain today. Operating under the corporate name of Doxsee Sea Clam Company, Inc., the Point Lookout facility produces clam products for restaurants and retail stores under the brand name Offshore Seafood.

The house was rented by Roland Redmond. [Harry W. Havemeyer, *Along the Great South Bay From Oakdale to Babylon: The Story of a Summer Spa 1840 to 1940* (Mattituck, NY: Amereon House, 1996), p. 173.]

Dresser, Emma Louise Burnham (1869-1933)

Marriage(s):	1889-div.1908 – Daniel LeRoy Dresser, Sr. (1862-1915)

    - merchant - founder, Dresser & Co. (silk commission firm)
    financier - president, Trust Company of the Republic (cotton bank)
    industrialist - director, Benedict & Burnham Manufacturing Co.;
        director, Waterbury Watch Co.;
        director, Waterbury Brass Co.;
        director, American Tubing and Webbing Co.;
        director, Reading Hosiery Co.;
        director, American Brass Co.
    inventor - steam engine
    Civic Activism: president, Merchant Association, NYC

Address: Argyle Park, Babylon
Name of estate:
Year of construction:
Style of architecture:
Architect(s):
Landscape architect(s):
House extant: unconfirmed
Historical notes:

The *Social Register Summer, 1915* lists Emma L. Burnham Dresser as residing in Babylon.

She was the daughter of Douglass Williams and Hannah Elizabeth Blodgett Burnham. Emma was a big game hunter. In 1931, she travelled to within 500 miles of the North Pole to shoot polar bears.

Daniel LeRoy Dresser, Sr. was the son of George Warren and Elizabeth Stuyvesant LeRoy Dresser. Daniel's sister Edith married George Washington Vanderbilt II.

Daniel LeRoy and Emma Louise Burnham Dresser, Sr.'s daughter Susan married Frederick Bull, the son of William Lanman and Sara Newton Worthington Bull. Their son Daniel LeRoy Dresser, Jr. married Olga Teneoff Nairn.

After his divorce from Emma, Daniel married the actress and pianist Marcia Walter Baldwin. Despondent over the failure of the Trust Company of Republic, he committed suicide with a .38 caliber pistol in the Delta Psi fraternity house on Riverside Drive, NYC.

Drummond, Howard (1882-1947)

Occupation(s): financier - partner, Carlisle, Mellick and Co. (stock brokerage firm)

Marriage(s): M/1 – Elizabeth Newall (1880-1916)
              M/2 – 1920-1947 – Lulu Hyde (d. 1958)

Address: South Country Road, Bay Shore
Name of estate: *Little House*
Year of construction:
Style of architecture:
Architect(s):
Landscape architect(s):
House extant: unconfirmed
Historical notes:

Howard Drummond was the son of John L. and Jemima Drummond of Manhattan.

Howard and Elizabeth Newall Drummond's daughters Elizabeth, age nineteen, and Dorothy, age sixteen, were killed when their automobile was struck by the Riverhead Express train of the Long Island Rail Road. The accident occurred at an unprotected crossing at Suffolk Avenue in Bay Shore. [*The New York Times* August 22, 1926, p. 1.]

Lulu Hyde Drummond was the daughter of Richard and Mary Kellar Hyde of West Bay Shore. She had previously been married to Vincent Booth Hubbell, Sr. Her sister Lillian married Quentin Field Feitner, Sr., the son of Thomas L. and Mary C. Moore Feitner of Manhattan, and, subsequently, George Barnard Wagstaff, with whom she resided in Bay Shore. Their brother William married Grace M. Riopelle and resided at *White Cottage* in Bay Shore.

In 1950, Drummond sold the house to David E. Kleinman. [*The New York Times* September 24, 1950, p. R5.]

Durkee, Eugene Return (1825-1902)

Occupation(s):	merchant - founder, E. R. Durkee & Co, Elmhurst, NY (spice, condiments, and grocers' specialties)
Marriage(s):	M/1 – 1849-1889 – Helen Winslow (aka Cynthia Helen Winslow) (1828-1889)
	M/2 – Harriet Carlton (1839-1912)
Address:	Deer Park Avenue, Babylon
Name of estate:	
Year of construction:	c. 1856
Style of architecture:	
Architect(s):	
Landscape architect(s):	
House extant: unconfirmed	

Historical notes:

Eugene Return Durkee was the son of Horatio and Mary Waldo Durkee.

Eugene Return and Helen Winslow Durkee's son Eugene Winslow Durkee married Emma Frances Brigham and resided in Patchogue. Their daughter Jessie married Charles H. Crowe, the son of John and Imallia Hopper Crowe. Their son William resided in Seattle, WA.

The Church of Ascension in West Park, NY, has a bronze tablet dedicated to Eugene Return Durkee and a Tiffany stained-glass window entitled "Hope and St. Agnes" dedicated to Harriet Carleton Durkee and Sarah Carleton Brookman.

In 1880, the house was purchased by Alice McKim Hollins Nicholas who called it *Virginia Farm*.

Duval, Henry Rieman (1843-1924)

Occupation(s):	industrialist - chairman of board, Ornard Sugar Co. (which merged into American Beet Sugar Co.);
	president, American Beet Sugar Co.;
	director, American Car and Foundry Co.
	capitalist - president, Florida Central & Peninsular Railroad (which merged into Seaboard Air Railway Co.);
	director, Atcheson, Topeka & Sante Fe Railroad;
	director, Sonora Rail Road Co.;
	director, Kansas City Southern Railway Co.;
	director, Sante Fe Pacific Railroad;
	president, South Bound Railroad
	financier - trustee, Mutual Life Insurance Co.
Civic Activism:	a founder and director, Great River Club (later, Timber Point Club)
Marriage(s):	1878 – Anne Gordon Thomas (1849-1914)
Address:	Suffolk Lane, East Islip
Name of estate:	*Falmouth*
Year of construction:	
Style of architecture:	Shingle
Architect(s):	
Landscape architect(s):	
House extant: no; demolished in 1952*	

front facade

Historical notes:

The house was built by Lee Johnson. In 1885, it was purchased by Duval, who called it *Falmouth*.

The *Social Register Summer, 1915* lists H. Rieman Duval as residing at *Falmouth* in East Islip.

He was the son of John Rawlings and Elizabeth Warfield Rieman Duval of Baltimore, MD.

Anne Gordon Thomas Duval was the daughter of John Hanson and Annie Campbell Thomas of Baltimore, MD.

Henry Rieman and Anne Gordon Thomas Duval's son Rieman married Elizabeth Williams, the daughter of Charles P. Williams of Stonington, CT, and resided in East Islip. Their daughter Nannie married John Haskins Wilcox and resided at *Mulberry Hill* in Easton, MD. Their son Hanson married Elizabeth Cuzon Hoffman, the daughter of Richard Cuzon Hoffman of Baltimore, MD. After Hanson's death, Elizabeth married John Daniel Wing of *Payne Cottage* in Southampton. [*See* Spinzia, *Long Island's Prominent Families in the Town of Southampton* – Wing entry.]

*The house was severely damaged by fire during World War II.

Two stained glass memorial windows, fabricated by Connick Studio of Boston and dedicated to the Duvals, can be found in the south transept of St. Mark's Episcopal Church in Islip.

Eastwood, John Henry (1853-1921)

Occupation(s):	industrialist - receiver, J. & R. Kingsland Paper Mills, Franklin, NJ; president, Eastwood Wire Manufacturing Co., Belleville, NJ; president, Eastwood Chemical Co., Belleville, NJ
Civic Activism:	president, Belleville Board of Trade; member, executive committee, American Protective Tariff League, 1915; bequeathed over $600,000 to charity
Marriage(s):	Margaret Spence (d. 1946)
Address:	Montgomery Avenue, Bay Shore
Name of estate:	
Year of construction:	1899
Style of architecture:	Neo-Dutch Colonial
Architect(s):	Clarence K. Birdsall designed the house and 1905 farm cottage (for Nathaniel Myers)
Landscape architect(s):	
House extant:	unconfirmed
Historical notes:	

rear facade, 1932

The house was built by Nathaniel Myers. It was subsequently owned by Eastwood.

He was the foster son of John Eastwood of Belleville, NJ, from whom he inherited $700,000 in 1911.

Margaret Spence Eastwood was the daughter of Oscar and Jane Ahearn Spence.

Eaton, James Waterbury, Sr. (1855-1923)

Occupation(s):	publisher - secretary and treasurer, Babylon Publishing Co. industrialist - director, Eaton–Hough Co., NY (manufacturers of computing and adding machines, comptometers, and typewriters); a founder, Kerosene Safety Engine Co., Jersey City, NJ; director, Greenmountain Product Co. of Babylon (manufacturer of carbonated waters and medicines); agent, Parker Plate & Machinery Co. financier - director, Bank of Babylon writer - *Babylon Reminiscences*, 1911; *History of the First Presbyterian Church, Babylon, Long Island*, 1912
Civic Activism:	a founder and president, Babylon Library Association, 1911
Marriage(s):	1901-1923 – Elizabeth Bross (1878-1940)
Address:	Eaton Lane, West Islip
Name of estate:	
Year of construction:	
Style of architecture:	
Architect(s):	
Landscape architect(s):	
House extant:	unconfirmed
Historical notes:	

James Waterbury Eaton, Sr. was the son of William and Adele L. Higbie Eaton.

Elizabeth Bross Eaton was the daughter of Joseph H. Bross of New York.

James Waterbury and Elizabeth Bross Eaton, Sr.'s daughter Elizabeth married Meyer Robert Guggenheim, Sr. of *Firenze Farm* in North Babylon. Their son James Waterbury Eaton, Jr. married Matilda Brown and resided in Cold Spring Harbor.

Ebinger, Walter D. (1885-1945)

Occupation(s):	merchant - president, Ebinger Baking Co., Brooklyn (chain of 43 stores)
Civic Activism:	president, Flatbush Chamber of Commerce;
	president, Flatbush Boys Club;
	director, Brooklyn Association for Improving Conditions of the Poor
Marriage(s):	1908-1945 – Ann Katherine Ottens (1890-1969)
Address:	50 Garner Lane, Bay Shore
Name of estate:	
Year of construction:	1935
Style of architecture:	Colonial Revival
Architect(s):	
Landscape architect(s):	W. C. McCallum & Son, 1937 (for Ebinger)

House extant: yes
Historical notes:

rear facade, 1937

The 5,000-square-foot house was built by Walter D. Ebinger.

He was the son of George and Katherine M. Ebinger. Walter's brother Arthur married Carolyne M. Wingerath and resided in Westhampton Beach. [*See* Spinzia, *Long Island's Prominent Families in the Town of Southampton* – Wing entry.]

Ann Katherine Ottens Ebinger was the daughter of John F. H. and Adeheid Fricks Ottens of Brooklyn.

Walter D. and Ann Katherine Ottens Ebinger's daughter Lorraine married Jack Berner Porter and, later, ____ Rundquiat.

In 2018, the house was listed for sale. It sold for $1.7 million.

[For Ebinger's Garden City residence, *see* Spinzia, *Long Island's Prominent Families in the Town of Hempstead* – Ebinger entry.]

Edwards, Edward (1830-1897)

Occupation(s):	capitalist - Long Island real estate developer (built Edwardsville section of Patchogue)
	merchant - owned general store in Patchogue
	real estate agent
Civic Activism:	funded building of St. Paul's Episcopal Church and 1895 church rectory, Patchogue
Marriage(s):	M/1 – 1852-1868 – Margaret J. Douglass (1837-1868)
	M/2 – c. 1870-1883 – Rebecca A. *[unable to determine maiden name]* (1841-1883)
	M/3 – 1885-1894 – Sophia Ketcham (1842-1894)
Address:	Fairview Avenue, Bayport
Name of estate:	*White House*
Year of construction:	1881
Style of architecture:	Modified Second Empire
Architect(s):	
Landscape architect(s):	

House extant: no; destroyed by fire in 1940s
Historical notes:

The house, originally named *White House*, was built by Edward Edwards.

Born in Barbados, he was the son of Lawrence and Sarah Jane Burgess Edwards of Bayport.

Margaret J. Douglass Edwards was the daughter of Edward N. and Anna Woodhull Douglass.

front facade

Edward and Margaret J. Douglass Edwards' son Lawrence Stewart Edwards married Adaline Jayne Saxton and resided in Patchogue.

Edward and Rebecca A. Edwards' son Edward Stewart Edwards married Mary Augusta Hudson, the daughter of Charles S. and Martha Ann Terry Hudson. Their daughter Margaret married James Osborne Stafford.

Sophia Ketcham Edwards was the daughter of Abel and Sophia Corwin Ketcham.

[See other Edwards entries for additional family information.]

In 1883, the house was purchased by John R. Ely.

Cyrus E. Staples purchased it in 1890.

In 1902, Staples lost the house in foreclosure proceedings. It was then owned by Waldon Kintzing Post and his brother Regis Henri Post, Sr., who, in turn, sold it to James Henry Snedecor in 1925.

Edwards, Lawrence (1793-1860)

Occupation(s):	capitalist - extensive land holdings in Barbados; real estate developer, Bayport
Marriage(s):	1818-1860 – Sarah Jane Burgess (1801-1869)
Address:	429 Middle Road, Bayport
Name of estate:	
Year of construction:	
Style of architecture:	Queen Anne
Architect(s):	Isaac Henry Green II designed alterations
Landscape architect(s):	
House extant:	yes
Historical notes:	

    Sarah Jane Burgess Edwards, like her husband Lawrence, was born in Barbados. She was the daughter of Richard and Dorothy Greaves Burgess.

    Lawrence and Sarah Jane Burgess Edwards' daughter Jane married Silas Smith. Their son Lawrence Barnes Edwards, who was born in Barbados, married Marriette Hawkins and resided in Bayport. Their daughter Sarah, who was born in Barbados, married George William Terry Morris, the son of Jacob and Hannah Terry Morris, and resided in Islip. Their daughter Mary, who was born in Barbados, married Benjamin Franklin Smith, the son of William and Freelove Baldwin Smith, and resided in Bayport. Their son Edward, who was born in Barbados and resided in Bayport, married Margaret J. Douglass, Rebecca A. ____, and Sophia Ketcham. Their daughter Elvira, who was born in Barbados, married George Henry Weeks and resided in Bayport. Their son John, who was born in Bayport, married Emily Josephine Van Orden, the daughter of Andrew and Mary Brown Van Orden and, later, Mary C. Appleget. Their son Albert, who was born in Bayport, died in 1839 at the age of eleven months.

[See other Edwards entries for additional family information.]

front facade

Edwards, Lawrence Barnes (1821-1893)

Occupation(s):

Marriage(s): Marriette Hawkins (1829-1900)

Address: 463 Middle Road, Bayport
Name of estate:
Year of construction: c. 1852
Style of architecture: Greek Revival
Architect(s): Isaac Henry Green II designed alterations, 1886 (for L. B. Lawrence)

Landscape architect(s):
House extant: yes
Historical notes:

front facade

Lawrence Edwards built the house for his son Lawrence Barnes Edwards who, like his father, was born in Barbados.

Marriette Hawkins Edwards was the daughter of John Thomas and Jane Howell Hawkins.

[See other Edwards entries for additional family information.]

Egly, Henry Harris (1893-1958)

Occupation(s): financier - vice-president, Dillon Read and Co. (investment banking firm);
trustee, Lincoln Savings Bank, Brooklyn

Civic Activism: chairman, securities division, Securities and Exchange Commission, 1938-1939;
trustee and chairman, underwriting committee, Beekman–Downtown Hospital, NYC (which was formed by the merger of Beekman Street Hospital and Downtown Hospital);
trustee, Adelphi College (now, Adelphi University, Garden City);
member, executive committee, New York Group of Investment Bankers Association

Marriage(s): 1916-1958 – Matilda Anna Pasfield (1897-1971)

Address: 101 West Bayberry Road, Islip
Name of estate:
Year of construction: 1899-1900
Style of architecture: Moorish
Architect(s): Grosvenor Atterbury designed the house (for H. O. Havemeyer)*

Landscape architect(s): Nathan F. Barrett (for H. O. Havemeyer)**

Builder: *[See Jabez Ephraim Van Order entry.]*
House extant: yes
Historical notes:

front facade, 2006

The house was built by Henry Osborne Havemeyer as part of his "Modern Venice" development. It was later owned by Egly.

He was the son of Louis and Emma Bertha Maturnas Egly of Brooklyn.

Henry Harris and Matilda Anna Pasfield Egly's daughter Jean married Harold Cole, the son of Charles Cole of Cold Spring Harbor. Their daughter Patricia did not marry.

By 1939 the Eglys had relocated to Stewart Avenue in Garden City. [*See* Spinzia, *Long Island's Prominent Families in the Town of Hempstead* – Egly entry.]

*The sales brochure for "Modern Venice" states that the Moorish-style architecture was suggested by Louis Comfort Tiffany.

**The sales brochure also states that "Modern Venice" would be devoid of trees and vegetation and that Nathan F. Barrett was the landscape architect.

Elder, George Waldron, Sr. (1860-1916)

Occupation(s):	industrialist - manager, shipping department, Havemeyers & Elder (sugar refinery, 1862-1891)*
Marriage(s):	1881-div. 1904 – Ellen Therese Cadwell (d. 1939)
Address:	Saxon Avenue and South Country Road, Bay Shore
Name of estate:	
Year of construction:	
Style of architecture:	
Architect(s):	
Landscape architect(s):	
House extant:	no
Historical notes:	

George Waldron Elder, Sr. was the son of George William and Mathilda Adelaide Waldron Elder. His sister Anne married Henry Norcross Munn. His sister Louisine married Henry Osborne Havemeyer and resided at *Bayberry Point* in Islip. His sister Adaline married Samuel Twyford Peters, Jr. and resided at *Windholme* in Islip.

Ellen Therese Cadwell Elder was the daughter of S. W. Cadwell.

George Waldron and Ellen Therese Cadwell Elder, Sr.'s son George Waldron Elder, Jr., who resided in Bellport, married Ganie Felicite Lucile Belynde; Mary Rose D'Auxy, the daughter of Duke Arthur Charles Eugene Edoard D'Auxy and his wife Charlotte Antoinette Lucille Lamar; and, later, Juanita Stewart.

*In 1891 the sugar refining division of Havemeyers & Elder was merged into the American Sugar Refining Company. The remaining property, not used in the sugar refining business, was retained by Havemeyers & Elder as a Brooklyn real estate holding company until the 1950s.

Ellis, George Augustus, Jr. (1875-1942)

Occupation(s):	financier - a founder and partner, E. F. Hutton (investment banking firm)
Civic Activism:	trustee, Southside Hospital, Bay Shore (now, South Shore University Hospital); a founder and director, Great River Club, 1920 (later, Timber Point Club); president, Islip Kennel Club, 1913; president, South Shore Field Club, 1910; secretary, Bay Shore Horse Show Association
Marriage(s):	1900-1942 – Florence Vance Adams (d. 1957)
Address:	South Country Road, West Bay Shore
Name of estate:	*Ardmore*
Year of construction:	c. 1905
Style of architecture:	Mediterranean Villa
Architect(s):	
Landscape architect(s):	
House extant:	yes
Historical notes:	

side / rear facade, c. 1909

The house, originally named *Ardmore*, was built by Thomas Adams, Jr.

It was subsequently owned by his daughter Florence and son-in-law George Augustus Ellis, Jr., who continued to call it *Ardmore*.

The *Brooklyn Blue Book and Long Island Society Register, 1918* lists George Augustus and Florence V. Adams Ellis, Jr. as residing at *Admoor* [*Ardmore*] in Bay Shore [West Bay Shore].

Florence Vance Adams Ellis' brother George J. Adams, Sr. resided in Hempstead.

George Augustus and Florence Vance Adams Ellis, Jr.'s son George Adams Ellis married Georgia Williams, the daughter of Charles P. Williams of Stonington, CT, and subsequently, Margaret C. Richards. Their daughter Jean married M. F. Summers.

The house is currently part of Southward Ho Country Club.

[For information on the Southside Hospital, see Cooper entry.]

Ely, John R. (c. 1859-1895)

Occupation(s): industrialist - partner, with his brother Henry, Ely Brothers Rectifiers and Distillers, Brooklyn

Marriage(s):

Address: Fairview Avenue, Bayport
Name of estate:
Year of construction: 1881
Style of architecture: Modified Second Empire
Architect(s):
Landscape architect(s):
House extant: no; destroyed by fire in 1940s
Historical notes:

The house, originally named *White House*, was built by Edward Edwards. In 1883, it was purchased by Ely.

He was institutionalized for violence and chronic alcoholic insanity at the Long Island Home in Amityville. His mother, brother Henry, who decapitated John Harden's head with an ax, and their sister were declared insane. In 1895, Ely's son George was also declared insane and institutionalized in an Amityville sanitarium. [*The New York Times* October 19, 1895, p. 9.]

In 1890, the house was purchased by Cyrus E. Staples.

In 1902, Staples lost the house in a foreclosure proceeding. It was then owned by Waldron Kintzing Post and his brother Regis Henri Post, Sr., who, in turn, sold it to James Henry Snedecor in 1925.

White House

Ennis, Thomas A.

Occupation(s): financier - partner, Ennis and Stoppani (odd-lot brokerage firm specializing in grain futures)*

Marriage(s): 1898 – Elizabeth L. Riley

Address: *[unable to determine street address]*, Bayport
Name of estate:
Year of construction:
Style of architecture:
Architect(s):
Landscape architect(s):
House extant: unconfirmed
Historical notes:

Elizabeth L. Riley Ennis was the daughter of John A. Riley.

*Because of alleged irregularities in their 1903, 1909, and 1916 stock transactions, arrest warrants were issued for both Ennis and his partner Charles Francis Stoppani, Jr. As a result, the firm of Ennis and Stoppani declared bankruptcy. [Harry W. Havemeyer, *East on the Great South Bay: Sayville and Bayport 1860-1960* (Mattituck, NY: Amereon House, 2001), p. 82; *The New York Times* November 8, 1903, p. 20; April 14, 1909, p. 1; April 16, 1909, p. 5; April 22, 1909, p. 5; April 28, 1909, p. 18; May 5, 1909, p. 7; and May 22, 1909, p. 1.]

Entenmann, Charles, Sr. (b. 1929)

Occupation(s):	industrialist - secretary, Entenmann's Inc., Bay Shore (bakery)*
Civic Activism:	chairman, Town of Islip Republican campaign, 1969;
	vice-president, Bay Shore School Board;
	secretary, Long Island Association of Commerce and Industry;
	president, Bay Shore Tuna Club
Marriage(s):	1951-2014 – Nancy Lee Drake (1930-2014)
	- Civic Activism: neighborhood chair, Bay Shore-Brightwaters Council of Girl Scouts;
	director, Girl Scout Council of Suffolk County, NY
Address:	69 Lawrence Lane, Bay Shore
Name of estate:	
Year of construction:	1922
Style of architecture:	Neo-Tudor
Architect(s):	Hart and Shape designed the house (for W. H. Robbins, Sr.)
Landscape architect(s):	
House extant: yes	
Historical notes:	

The house was built by William H. Robbins, Sr. It was later owned by Entenmann who by 1971 had relocated from 95 Garner Lane in Bay Shore to Lawrence Lane.

He was the son of William Charles and Martha Clara Schneider Entenmann, Jr. of Bay Shore.

Nancy Lee Drake Entenmann was the daughter of Arthur and Hazel Drake of Bay Shore.

Charles and Nancy Lee Drake Entenmann, Sr.'s daughter Susan married James Cook, the son of George Cook of Fort Wayne, IN. Their daughter Barbara married ____ Thompson.

[For information about the Entenmanns' Montauk residence, *see* Spinzia, *Long Island's Prominent Families in the Town of East Hampton* – Entenmann entry.]

*Entenmann's Inc. was purchased in 1978 by Warner–Lambert Co. In 1982, it was purchased by General Foods Corp. In 1985, General Foods was acquired by Philip Morris and became part of Kraft Foods. In 1995, Entenmann's was acquired by CPC International (Bestfoods). In 2000, Bestfoods was purchased by Unilever which sold Entenmann's to Weston in 2001. In 2008, Entenmann's was acquired by the Mexican conglomerate Grupa Bimbo. In July of 2014, the company ended its baking operation in Bay Shore but continued its store, sales, and distribution at the Bay Shore facility.

The Entenmann's sold the house in the 1980s.

In 2020, the 7,000-squart-foot, five-bedroom, nine-bath house was listed for sale. The asking price was $3.995 million.

rear facade, 2020

Entenmann, Robert William, Sr. (1928-2016)

Occupation(s):	industrialist - vice-president, president, and chairman of board, Entenmann's Inc., Bay Shore (bakery)
	capitalist - a founder and co-owner, with his daughter Jacqueline, Martha Clara Vineyards, Riverhead*
Civic Activism:	chairman, fund raising committee, American Cancer Society of Suffolk County, NY, 1970-1971;
	trustee, Y.M.C.A.;
	member, Board of Fire Commissioners, Bay Shore;
	captain, Bay Shore Fire Department's Hose Company
Marriage(s):	div. – Mary L Bayer
Address:	Meadow Farm Road, East Islip
Name of estate:	
Year of construction:	1927
Style of architecture:	Colonial Revival
Architect(s):	Philip Cusack designed the house (for R. W. Morgan, Sr.)
Landscape architect(s):	
House extant:	yes
Historical notes:	

The house was built by Robert Woodward Morgan, Sr. It was later owned by Robert Allan Pinkerton II and, subsequently, by Entenmann.

He was the son of William Charles and Martha Clara Schneider Entenmann, Jr. of Bay Shore.

Mary L Bayer Entenmann is the daughter of Charles J. and Louise Bayer, Sr. of Central Islip.

Robert William and Mary L. Bayer Entenmann, Sr.'s daughter Jacqueline married John Connolly and, later, Jason Damianos, the son of the founder of Pindar Vineyards Dr. Herodotis Damianos.

*The 200-acre Martha Clara Vineyards, which was named after Robert's mother, was for sale in 2014. The asking price was said to be $29 million.

[See other Entenmann entries for additional family information.]

[For information on the Entenmann's Montauk residence, see Spinzia, *Long Island's Prominent Families in the Town of East Hampton* – Entenmann entry.]

Entenmann, William Charles, Jr. (1903-1951)

Occupation(s):	industrialist - president, Entenmann's Inc., Bay Shore (bakery)
Marriage(s):	1925-1951 – Martha Clara Schneider (1906-1996)
	- industrialist - vice-president, Entenmann's, Inc., Bay Shore
Address:	Shore Lane, Bay Shore
Name of estate:	
Year of construction:	1922
Style of architecture:	Modified Tudor
Architect(s):	
Landscape architect(s):	
House extant:	yes
Historical notes:	

He was the son of William Charles and Bertha Kloepfer (aka Bertha Goepfel) Entenmann, Sr. of Bay Shore.

William Charles and Martha Clara Schneider Entenmann, Jr.'s son Robert, who resided in East Islip and Montauk, married Mary L. Bayer. Their son Charles Entenmann Sr., who married Nancy Lee Drake, had residences in Bay Shore and Montauk. [*See* Spinzia, *Long Island's Prominent Families in the Town of East Hampton* – Entenmann entries.] Their son William Charles Entenmann III married Christine Sutton and resided in Islip and at *Timber Bay Farm* in Old Westbury. [*See* Spinzia, *Long Island's Prominent North Shore Families, vol. I* – Entenmann entry.]

[See other Entenmann entries for additional family information.]

Entenmann, William Charles, Sr. (1878-1973)

Occupation(s): industrialist - founder and president, Entenmann's Inc., Bay Shore (bakery)

Marriage(s): Bertha Kloepher (aka Bertha Goepfel) (c. 1880-1952)

Address: 36 Maple Avenue, Bay Shore
Name of estate:
Year of construction: 1920
Style of architecture: 20th Century
Architect(s):
Landscape architect(s):
House extant: yes
Historical notes:

William Charles and Bertha Kloepfer (aka Bertha Goepfel) Entenmann, Sr.'s daughter Lillian was an infant at the time of her death. Their daughter Bertha married Casper A. Peterson, the son of Gus Peterson of Brooklyn, and resided on Sequams Lane, West Islip. Their son William Charles Entenmann, Jr. married Martha Clara Schneider.
[See other Entenmann entries for additional family information.]

In 2017, the 3,561-square-foot house, with five bedrooms and four-and-a-half bathrooms, sold for $650,000.

front facade, 2017

Entenmann, William Charles, III (1931-2011)

Occupation(s): industrialist - treasurer, president, and chairman of board, Entenmann's Inc., Bay Shore (bakery)
financier - director and partner, First Long Island Investors, Inc., Jericho, NY (wealth management firm)

Marriage(s): 1953-2011 – Christine Sutton (1933-2020)

Address: Beech Road, Islip
Name of estate:
Year of construction:
Style of architecture:
Architect(s):
Landscape architect(s):
House extant: unconfirmed
Historical notes:

William Charles Entenmann III was the son of William Charles and Martha Clara Schneider Entenmann, Jr. of Bay Shore.

Christine Sutton Entenmann was from Great River.

William Charles and Christine Sutton Entenmann III's daughter Denise married Thomas Walsh and resides in South Pines, NC. Their daughter Jamie married John Padden and resides in Islip. Their son William J. Entenmann was a former steeplechase rider and trainer.
[See other Entenmann entries for additional family information.]

[For information about the Entenmann's Old Westbury estate *Timber Bay Farm*, see Spinzia, *Long Island's Prominent North Shore Families, vol. 1* – Entenmann entry.]

Esteva, Manuel A., Sr. (1878-1936)

Occupation(s):	diplomat - Mexican vice-council to United States; Mexican council general to the United States, 1914
Marriage(s):	1909-1936 – Calla Wheaton (1883-1968)
Address:	South Country Road and Windsor Avenue North, Brightwaters
Name of estate:	
Year of construction:	1910
Style of architecture:	Spanish Villa
Architect(s):	
Landscape architect(s):	
House extant: unconfirmed	
Historical notes:	

The house was built by Manuel A. Esteva, Sr.
He was the son of Roberto and Ysabel Ruiz Esteva.
Calla Wheaton Esteva was the daughter of Frank Wheaton of Philadelphia, PA.

Evers, Cecil Calvert (1866-1936)

Occupation(s):	financier - vice-president and secretary, Lawyers Mortgage Co.; director, The Mortgage–Bond Co. of New York
	writer - *The Commercial Problem in Building*, 1914
Civic Activism:	a founder and secretary of board of managers, Southside Hospital, Babylon (now, South Shore University Hospital)
Marriage(s):	1910-1930 – Violet Eleanor Vans Agnew (1872-1930)
	- Civic Activism: president, Babylon chapter, National Special Aid Society (World War I relief organization)
Address:	87 Argyle Avenue, Babylon
Name of estate:	
Year of construction:	c. 1911
Style of architecture:	Eclectic Queen Anne
Architect(s):	
Landscape architect(s):	
House extant: yes	
Historical notes:	

Violet Eleanor Vans Agnew Evers was the daughter of George Vans and Rosa Coppard Wilson Agnew.

Cecil Calvert and Violet Eleanor Vans Agnew Evers' son Vans married Frances Fenton, the daughter of Claude William and Ida Viola Gillean Fenton. Their son Patrick married Pamela Rolston, the daughter of John Mitchell Rolston of Vancouver, Canada. Their daughter Rosemary married A. Bustanoby.

In 1923, the house was purchased by William Tyson Hayward, Jr. [*The Suffolk County News* February 2, 1923, p. 5.]

Cecil Calvert Evers was residing in Elmsford, NY, at the time of his death. [*The New York Times* July 17, 1936, p. 17.]

[For information on the Southside Hospital, see Cooper entry.]

front / side facade, 2006

Eyre, Beverley Montagu (1891-1958)

Occupation(s):	financier - member, Berg, Roesler, and Kerr (later, Berg, Eyre, and Kerr) (stock brokerage firm); partner, Berg, Eyre, and Kerr; partner, Delafield and Delafield (stock brokerage firm); member, Theodore Tsolianos and Co. (stock brokerage firm)
Marriage(s):	1920-1958 – Mary Ludlow Smedberg Weeks (1893-1976)
Address:	Saxon Avenue, Bay Shore
Name of estate:	
Year of construction:	
Style of architecture:	Shingle
Architect(s):	
Landscape architect(s):	
House extant:	unconfirmed
Historical notes:	

The house was previously owned by Robert Low Pierrepont and, then, by Walter Ellwood Bedell. In 1927, Eyre purchased the house from Bedell. [*The New York Times* June 17, 1927, p. 41.]

The *Long Island Society Register, 1929* lists Beverley M. and Mary L. Weeks Eyre as residing on Saxon Avenue, Islip [Bay Shore.]

He was the son of Maynard Campbell and Mary Eloise Clark Eyre of Staten Island, NY.

Mary Ludlow Weeks Eyre was the daughter of Edwin Carnes and Emily Smedberg Weeks of Babylon.

Beverley Montagu and Mary Ludlow Weeks Eyre's son Edwin married Elizabeth de Reeder, the daughter of Edward L. de Reeder of Islip, and resided in Islip. Their son William married Margaret Anne Lerner and resided in Manhattan. Their daughter Emily married George Lockhard Rives, the son of Francis Bayard and Helen Leigh Hunt Rives of *Mapleglades* in Hewlett Bay Park. [*See* Spinzia, *Long Island's Prominent Families in the Town of Hempstead* – Rives entry.]

side / front facade

Fairchild, Julian Douglas (1850-1926)

Occupation(s):	financier -	a founder and president, Kings County Trust Co.;
		president, Capital Surplus;
		vice-president, Mortgage Bond Co.;
		director, Metropolitan Casualty Co.;
		director, Pacific Fire Insurance Co.;
		director, Nassau Fire Insurance Co.;
		vice-president, Mortgage–Bond Co.;
		director, Lawyers Title Insurance & Trust Co.;
		director, National City Bank of Brooklyn;
		director, Metropolitan Plate Glass Insurance Co.;
		director, Bedford Bank;
		trustee, East River Savings Bank
	capitalist -	director, Eagle Warehouse & Storage Co.;
		president, Union Ferry Co.;
		director, Queens Electric Light & Power Co.
	industrialist -	secretary, Quinnipiac Fertilizer Co.
	politician -	treasurer, Democratic Campaign Committee, Kings County, 1923*
Civic Activism:		regent, Long Island College Hospital, Brooklyn;
		trustee, Brooklyn Institute of Arts and Sciences;
		president, Brooklyn Central Dispensary;
		a founder and director, Bay Shore Protective League
Marriage(s):		1879-1926 – Florence Irene Bradley (1856-1937)
Address:		Awixa Avenue, Bay Shore
Name of estate:		
Year of construction:		1894
Style of architecture:		Queen Anne
Architect(s):		
Landscape architect(s):		
House extant: no		
Historical notes:		

The house was built by Emil Henry Frank, Sr. In 1904, it was purchased by Fairchild.

The *Brooklyn Blue Book and Long Island Society Register, 1918* lists Julian D. and Florence I. Bradley Fairchild as residing in Bay Shore.

He was the son of Douglas and Lydia Hawley Fairchild.

Florence Irene Bradley Fairchild was the daughter of Charles Leeman Bradley of New Haven, CT.

Julian Douglas and Florence Irene Bradley Fairchild's son Julian Percy Fairchild, Sr., who resided in Glen Cove, married Helen Louise Fitch, the daughter of Ezra Charles Fitch of Boston, MA, and, subsequently, Ruth Callender. [*See* Spinzia, *Long Island's Prominent North Shore Families, vol. I* – Fairchild entry.] Their daughter Florence married Edward Everett Read and, later, Frank Erdman Simmons.

*In 1894, Fairchild refused the Democratic nomination for mayor of Brooklyn and, in 1896, he also refused the party's nomination for comptroller of New York City.

front facade, c. 1894

Farrell, Frank J. (c. 1866-1926)

Occupation(s):	capitalist - owner, Savoy Theater
	real estate speculator
	co-owner, with Tammany Hall operative and former New York City Deputy Police Commissioner William Stephen Devery, Baltimore Orioles (later, New York Highlanders and, subsequently, New York Yankees) (baseball teams)
	owned thoroughbred racing stable*
	owned approximately 250 off-track betting establishments (legal in New York State until 1908)
	owned pool halls, saloons, and illicit gambling establishments**
Marriage(s):	Anna E. *[unable to determine maiden name]*
Address:	66 Ocean Avenue, Bay Shore
Name of estate:	
Year of construction:	1902
Style of architecture:	Neo-Tudor
Architect(s):	
Landscape architect(s):	
House extant: unconfirmed	
Historical notes:	

front facade, 2017

    The house was built by Frank J. Farrell, who was known as "the Pool Hall King."
    *Julius Fleishmann, Sr. of the Fleishmann Yeast fortune, who resided at *The Lindens* in Sands Point, was Farrell's partner in various racing enterprises. [*See* Spinzia, *Long Island's Prominent North Shore Families, vol. I* – Fleishmann entry.]
    **His illicit operations included being a member of Tammany Hall's protection syndicate which is reputed to have grossed $3 million per year; the Monte Carlo, a midtown gambling casino; and "The House with the Bronze Door," a four-story Manhattan gambling site. A high-stakes gambler, Farrell died virtually destitute.
    In 2017, the seven-bedroom, six-bath, 3,621-square-foot house sold for $675,000.

Feitner, Quentin Field, Sr. (1886-1933)

Occupation(s):	financier - partner, Q. F. Feitner and Co. (stock brokerage firm)
	capitalist - member, Douglas L. Elliman Co. (real estate firm)
Marriage(s):	1916-1933 – Lillian B. Hyde (1888-1974)
Address:	South Country Road, Bay Shore
Name of estate:	
Year of construction:	
Style of architecture:	
Architect(s):	
Landscape architect(s):	
House extant: unconfirmed	
Historical notes:	

    The *Long Island Society Register, 1929* lists Quentin Field and Lillian B. Hyde Feitner [Sr.] as residing on South Country Road, Bay Shore.
    He was the son of Thomas Lowe and Mary C. Moore Feitner of Manhattan.
    Lillian B. Hyde Feitner was the daughter of Richard and Mary Kellar Hyde of West Bay Shore. She subsequently married George Barnard Wagstaff with whom she resided in Bay Shore.
    Quentin Field and Lillian B. Hyde Feitner, Sr.'s daughter Lillian married orchestra leader Aaron Bernard Mussoff (aka Ray Benson) and, later, David Wagstaff, Jr. of *Ledgeland* in Tuxedo Park, NY. Their daughter Mary married George Mitchell Gregory, the son of William Hamilton and Elizabeth Mitchell Gregory, Sr. of Bay Shore, and resided in Bay Shore. Their son Quentin Field Feitner, Jr. married Judith H. Underdown and resided in Sands Point and Old Brookville.

Field, Benjamin Prince, Jr. (1831-1920)

Occupation(s):	inventor
	financier - director, Babylon National Bank
	writer - *Babylon Reminiscences*, 1911;
	Beauties of Life and Other Poems
Civic Activism:	a founder and trustee, Captain Cook Monument Association, 1906;
	member of board, Babylon Union Free School District;
	commissioner, Babylon Fire Department;
	member, Babylon Village Board of Health
Marriage(s):	1852-1916 – Mary Ann Purchase (1835-1916)
Address:	11 The Crescent, Babylon
Name of estate:	
Year of construction:	1891
Style of architecture:	Queen Anne
Architect(s):	
Landscape architect(s):	
Builder:	Elmer W. Howell moved the house further South and added several large wings, 1904 (for Harris)

House extant: yes
Historical notes:

The house was built by Benjamin Prince Field, Jr. [*The Brooklyn Daily Eagle* March 4, 1891, p. 1.]

He was the son of Benjamin Prince and Eliza Post Field, Sr. of Flushing.

Mary Ann Purchase Field was the daughter of John and Susanna Bloodgood Cutter Purchase of Flushing.

Benjamin Prince and Mary Ann Purchase Field, Jr.'s son Mortimer married Emma Armstrong, the daughter of William and Amanda V. Mead Armstrong.

In 1903, Alfred H. Harris purchased the house from Field. [*South Side Signal* December 19, 1903, p. 3.]

In 2006, the house sold for $740,000.

front facade

Fishel, Leopold Henry (1839-1913)

Occupation(s):	capitalist - a founder and president, Babylon Electric Light Co.;
	director, Sumpwams Water Works Co.;
	real estate holdings in Babylon
	financier - director, Babylon National Bank
	merchant - Fishel's, Babylon (dry goods store);
	partner, with Jeremiah Robbins, Fishel & Robbins, Babylon (dry goods store)
Civic Activism:	member, Babylon Board of Education
Marriage(s):	Theresa Schott (1835-1902)
Address:	East Main Street, Babylon
Name of estate:	
Year of construction:	
Style of architecture:	
Architect(s):	
Landscape architect(s):	

House extant: unconfirmed
Historical notes:

Theresa Schott Fishel was the daughter of Leopold Schott.

Leopold Henry and Theresa Schott Fishel's daughter Lillian, who was an ardent suffragist, married Robert T. Oliver and resided on Magoun Road in West Islip. Their son Harry married Eleanor Munroe and resided in Denver, CO. Their daughter Lulu, who didn't marry, resided in Babylon. Their son Leo, who made one major league appearance as a pitcher for the New York Giants against the Phillies in 1899, married Laura Duerstein and resided in Freeport.

front facade

Flint, Sherman (1869-1954)

Occupation(s):	financier - partner, Hetherington and Co. (stock brokerage firm); partner, Lawton, Flint and Co. (stock brokerage firm) capitalist - director, Second Avenue Railway Co.
Marriage(s):	1899-1946 – Margaret Olivia Slocum (1870-1946) - Civic Activism: member, Babylon Hospital Auxiliary committee; member, advisory board, Islip Chapter of Red Cross
Address:	St. Mark's Lane, Islip
Name of estate:	*Evershade*
Year of construction:	
Style of architecture:	
Architect(s):	
Landscape architect(s):	Beatrix Jones Ferrand, designed landscape plan, 1912 (for Flint) [landscape plan not executed]

House extant: unconfirmed
Historical notes:

Sherman Flint was the son of Dr. Austin and Mrs. Elizabeth McMaster Flint, Sr. of Manhattan. His brother Dr. Austin Flint III married Marion Wing and resided at *Kirkside* in Muttontown. [*See* Spinzia, *Long Island's Prominent North Shore Families, vol. 1* – Flint entry.] His sister Ann did not marry.

Margaret Olivia Slocum Flint was the daughter of Joseph Jermain and Sallie S. L'Hommedieu Slocum, Jr. Joseph was Russell Sage's partner and brother-in-law. Russell was married to Margaret Olivia Slocum (1828-1918) of Lawrence and Sag Harbor, whose philanthropy distributed an estimated $80 million. [*See* Spinzia, *Long Island's Prominent Families in the Town of Hempstead* and *Long Island's Prominent Families in the Town of Southampton* – Sage entries.]

Sherman and Margaret Olivia Slocum Flint's daughter Margaret married Thomas Emerson Proctor II, the son of James Howe Proctor of Boston, MA. The Flints' son Austin died in 1919 prior to attaining adulthood.

Malcolm Webster Ford, Sr. residence, My Fancy, front facade

Ford, Malcolm Webster, Sr. (1862-1902)

Occupation(s):	capitalist - Long Island real estate developer
	journalist - editor, *New Centaura* (automotive magazine)*
	financier - director, Babylon National Bank
Civic Activism:	a founder and director, South Shore Country Club, West Islip, 1895
Marriage(s):	1892-div. 1898 – Jeanette Wilhelmina Graves
Address:	South Country Road, West Babylon
Name of estate:	*My Fancy***
Year of construction:	
Style of architecture:	Eclectic
Architect(s):	Clarence K. Birdsall, 1894 alterations (for Ford)
Landscape architect(s):	
Builder:	Brown & Howell, billiard room addition, 1893; enlargement of carriage house, 1893 (for Ford)

House extant: no; demolished in 1950s***
Historical notes:

In 1892, Malcolm Webster Ford, Sr. purchased sixty-five acres and the house where the noted poet Walt Whitman resided from Jeremiah Robbins and named it *My Fancy*. [*The Suffolk County News* October 1, 1892, p. 2.] In 1895, he added to his holdings by purchasing the fourteen-acre adjoining farm of John Clinton Robbins. [*The Suffolk County News* December 13, 1895, p. 1.]

He was the son of Gordon Lester and Emily Ellsworth Webster Ford of Brooklyn. Because of Malcolm's obsession with sports, his father disinherited him. In 1891, on his deathbed suffering from typhoid fever which he had contracted from Malcolm, Gordon is reputed to have had a change of mind and asked his other six children to share their inheritance with Malcolm. Because of the verbal agreement, Malcolm did not contest the will. In 1894, he sued his brothers and sisters for failing to implement the agreement but lost his case for lack of proof. In the end only Malcolm's sister Mabel Mayo–Smith of Bellport shared her portion of the inheritance with Malcolm. In spite of this, Malcolm appears to have reconciled with his siblings. Despondent over his finances, Malcolm began to brood over the loss of his inheritance. In 1902, he murdered his thirty-eight-year-old brother Paul and then committed suicide.

Jeanette Wilhelmina Graves Ford was the daughter of Robert Graves of *Pouch Mansion* in Brooklyn. She subsequently married Joseph Britton Leavy, the heir to Brooklyn's Leavy and Britton Brewing Company. Jeanette's brother Robert Graves II, who became despondent over his finances and committed suicide in 1931, resided at *Treborcliffe* in Lloyd Harbor. Her brother Andrew married Genevieve J. Herne. Her sister Cesarine married Percy Pyne Lewis and, later, Howard C. Kerr. Her sister Marie married Henry Herman Harjes, Sr. of Oyster Bay Cove. Her sister Emma married James J. Faye, Sr. and resided at *Woodlands Farm* in Sands Point and, later, William H. Erhart with whom she resided at *Five Oaks* in Lawrence. Her brother William married Florence C. Eno and resided in NYC. Her sister Lillie died at the age of nineteen. [*See* Spinzia, *Long Island's Prominent North Shore Families, vol. I* – Faye, Graves, and Harjes entries – and *Long Island's Prominent Families in the Town of Hempstead* – Erhart entry.]

Malcolm Webster and Jeanette Wilhelmina Graves Ford, Sr.'s son Malcolm Webster Ford, Jr. married Mary Mace Chestnut, the daughter of Judge William Calvin and Mrs. Florence Elizabeth Carroll Chestnut of Baltimore, MD, and resided in Oyster Bay Cove.

*In 1902, the short-lived *New Centaura* magazine declared bankruptcy.

Because of his mounting financial problems, Ford sold *My Fancy* to William Guy Gilmour, Sr. in 1899 but retained the smaller Robbins house which he eventually lost in foreclosure proceedings.

**The estate was named *My Fancy* after Walt Whitman's poem of the same name.

***The estate's property is currently the site of the Great South Bay Shopping Center.

My Fancy

Fortescue, Granville Roland (1875-1952)

Occupation(s):	military - member, Rough Riders – wounded at San Juan Hill; saw action in Philippines, 1898-1901; served as President Theodore Roosevelt's military attaché in Japan; special agent, Cuban Rural Guard; active duty in France, 314 Field Artillery, during World War I
	journalist - war correspondent, *London Standard*, during Riff War in Spanish Morocco; war correspondent, *London Daily Telegraph* during World War I; editor, *Liberty Magazine* (fiction)
	writer - *At the Front with Three Allies: My Adventures in the Great War*, 1914; *Russia, the Balkans and the Dardanelles*, 1915; *What of the Dardanelles? An Analysis*, 1915; *Forearmed: How to Build a Citizen Army*, 1916; *France Bears the Burden*, 1917; *Delor*, 1915 (a play); *Love and Live*, 1921 (a play); *The Unbeliever*, 1925 (a play); *Frontline and Dead Line: The Experiences of a War Correspondent*, 1937
Marriage(s):	1910-1952 – Grace Hubbard Bell (1883-1979)
Address:	McConnell Avenue, Bayport
Name of estate:	*Wildholme*
Year of construction:	c. 1873
Style of architecture:	Eclectic with Italianate elements
Architect(s):	
Landscape architect(s):	

House extant: no; destroyed by fire in 1958*
Historical notes:

In 1873, Robert Barnwell Roosevelt, Sr. purchased the two-hundred-acre farm of Daniel Lane and remodeled its farm house into his country residence *Lotos Lake*. It was subsequently owned by Granville Roland Fortescue, who called it *Wildholme*.

Granville Roland Fortescue was the only Roosevelt to be buried in Arlington Cemetery. He was the illegitimate son of Robert Barnwell and Marion Theresa O'Shea Roosevelt, Sr., who resided at *Lotos Lake* in Bayport. His brother Kenyon, a bachelor, resided in Sayville. His sister Maude married Ernest W. S. Pickhardt and resided in London, England.

Grace Hubbard Bell was the daughter of Charles John and Roberta Wolcott Hubbard Bell of *Twin Oaks* in Washington, DC. Grace's sister Helen married Julian Ashton Ripley, Sr. and resided at *Three Corners Farm* in Muttontown. [*See* Spinzia, *Long Island's Prominent North Shore Families, vol. II* – Ripley entry.]

Granville Roland and Grace Hubbard Bell Fortescue's daughter Marion married Daulton Gillespie Viskniskki, the son of journalist Guy Thomas and Virginia Gillespie Viskniskki of Montclair, NJ, and resided in Canterbury, OH. Their daughter Helen married Julian Louis Reynolds, the son of Richard Samuel and Julia Louise Parham Reynolds, Sr. of *Slow Tide* and *Winfield Hall* in Glen Cove. Reynolds was heir to the Reynolds aluminum and tobacco fortune. [*See* Spinzia, *Long Island's Prominent North Shore Families, vol. II* – Reynolds entry.] In 1966, the Reynoldses' twenty-nine-year-old son Richard accidentally walked into the moving propeller of a plane that he was inspecting for possible purchase.

The Fortescue's sixteen-year-old daughter Grace (Thalia) married naval lieutenant Thomas Hedges Massie, the son of a Winchester, KY, shoe store proprietor, and, subsequently, Robert Uptigrove.

[For a detailed account of the murder trial of Grace Fortescue and her son-in-law Thomas Hedges Massie *see* Harry W. Havemeyer, *East on the Great South Bay: Sayville and Bellport 1860-1960* (Mattituck, NY: Amereon House, 2001), pp. 37-46, 207-225; *The New York Times* April 30, 1932, pp. 1, 16.]

[For a discussion of the Fortescue family *see* Raymond E. Spinzia, "Those Other Roosevelts: The Fortescues" *The Freeholder,* 11 (Summer 2006), pp. 8-9, 16-22, and www.spinzialongislandestates.com.]

*In 1953, the house and its furnishings were severely vandalized. In 1954, it was sold to real estate developer Maurice Babash. While he was demolishing it, the house was destroyed by fire.

Wildholme

Fortescue, Kenyon (1870-1939)

Occupation(s): attorney - partner, Roosevelt and Kobbe

Marriage(s): bachelor

Address: *[unable to determine street address]*, Sayville
Name of estate:
Year of construction:
Style of architecture:
Architect(s):
Landscape architect(s):
House extant: unconfirmed
Historical notes:

Kenyon Fortescue was the illegitimate son of Robert Barnwell and Marion Theresa O'Shea Roosevelt, Sr.
[See previous entry for additional family information.]

Foster, Andrew D. (1826-1907)
(aka Andrew D. Forsslund)*

Occupation(s): capitalist - owner, Delavan Hotel, Foster Avenue, Sayville;
owner, Foster House Hotel, South Main Street, Sayville

Marriage(s): 1853-1907 – Ann Eliza Brown (1834-1918)

Address: 302 Foster Avenue, Sayville
Name of estate: *Greycote*
Year of construction: c. 1883
Style of architecture: Colonial Revival
Architect(s): Isaac Henry Green II designed
the house (for A. D. Foster)
Landscape architect(s):
House extant: yes
Historical notes:

The house, originally named *Greycote*, was built by Andrew D. Foster.
*He was the son of Peterson Forsslund of Sweden.
Andrew D. and Ann Eliza Brown Foster's daughter Amelia married Dr. George A. Robinson and resided in Bayport. Their daughter Ann married Dr. ____ Haines. Their daughter Amy was a Broadway actress. Their daughter Louise, a writer whose books were set in Sayville, married Carey Waddell and resided in Sayville.

front facade, 2006

Foster, Jay Stanley (1877-1925)

Occupation(s):	attorney
	financier - president and chairman of board, Bowery Bank; vice-president, Bank of Babylon
	capitalist - director, Sumpwams Water Works Co.
Civic Activism:	*
Marriage(s):	1903-div. c. 1910 – Jennie Rice Morgan (1879-1934)
Address:	Little East Neck and South Country Roads, Babylon
Name of estate:	
Year of construction:	1905
Style of architecture:	Mediterranean Villa
Architect(s):	York and Sawyer designed the house (for J. S. Foster)
Landscape architect(s):	
House extant: no**	
Historical notes:	

The house was built by John Strong Foster for his son Jay Stanley Foster. [*The Brooklyn Daily Eagle* April 24, 1906, p. 12.]

He was the son of John Strong and Caroline Oakley Foster of *The Meadows* in Babylon.

In 1915, the actress Lillian Benson sued Jay for $20,000 alleging breach of promise. The case was dismissed when she failed to appear in court. [*The New York Times* August 4, 1915, p. 20; August 6, 1915, p. 18; and August 8, 1915, p. 17.]

Jennie Rice Morgan Foster was the daughter of Richard Jessup Morgan and the granddaughter of Charles Morgan, the founder of the Morgan Steamship Line. She later married her chauffeur Edward Voelker.

*In 1921, Foster donated Argyle Park to the Village of Babylon. In 1927, his sister Caroline donated the park's ornamental stone steps, gates, and waterfalls to the village.

[See following entry for additional family information.]

Over the years the estate has had a succession of owners. In 1927, it became the Sumpwams Country Club. [*Patchogue Advance* May 17, 1927, p. 9.] In 1933, it became the Princeton Alumni Country Club. [*The Suffolk County News* May 12, 1933, p. 9.] In 1947, it was purchased by Babylon Post 94 Inc. of the American Legion. [*Patchogue Advance* August 7, 1947, p. 15.]

**Only the carriage house is extant.

Argyle Park, 2005

Jay Stanley Foster estate

side / front facade, 1945

front facade, 1976

rear facade, 1976

south facade, 1976

front facade, c. 1894

Foster, John Strong (1843-1914)

Occupation(s):	capitalist - president, Forty-Second Street and Boulevard Railway, Co. NY;
	director, American Light and Traction Co.;
	director, Western Gas Co.;
	director, Consolidated Gas Company of New Jersey;
	director, Sumpwams Water Works Co;
	president, Forty-Second Street, Manhattanville, and St. Nicholas Avenue Railroad
	financier - president, Bowery Bank;
	chairman of board, Babylon National Bank
Civic Activism:	governor, Babylon Yacht Club, 1906
Marriage(s):	1872-1914 – Caroline Oakley (d. 1917)
Address:	Little East Neck and South Country Roads, Babylon
Name of estate:	*The Meadows*
Year of construction:	c. 1863
Style of architecture:	
Architect(s):	
Landscape architect(s):	
House extant: unconfirmed	
Historical notes:	

The house, originally named *The Meadows*, was built by William Riley Foster, Sr. It was later owned by his son John who continued to call it *The Meadows*.

Caroline Oakley Foster had previously been married to ____ Thompson
[See other Foster entries for additional family information.]

Foster, William Riley, Jr. (b. 1839)

Occupation(s):	attorney - partner, Foster and Wentworth;
	attorney for New York Produce Exchange
Marriage(s):	Leola Bellotte (common-law wife)
Address:	Ocean Avenue, Bayport
Name of estate:	*Strandhome*
Year of construction:	1880
Style of architecture:	Shingle
Architect(s):	Isaac Henry Green II designed the house (for W. R. Foster, Jr.)
	George Browne Post designed the alterations (for C. A. Post)
Landscape architect(s):	
House extant: no; demolished in 1950s	
Historical notes:	

Strandhome

The house, originally named *Strandhome*, was built by William Riley Foster, Jr.

He was the son of William Riley and Harriet Peers Foster, Sr. of *The Meadows* in Babylon.

Accounts vary as to exactly how much William Riley Foster, Jr. swindled from the Produce Exchange Gratuity Fund with fraudulent mortgages. Reports place the sum as somewhere between $198,000 and $293,000. What is known is that he and his common-law wife Leola Bellotte fled to Europe where they may have been married in Lisbon, Portugal, and that the Pinkerton National Detective Agency posted a $5,000 reward for Foster's arrest. He remained a fugitive from justice for ten years but was finally arrested in Paris, France, in 1898 where he was residing under the name Mr. Ward. At his arrest, his father offered to pay $80,000 in restitution. While out on $20,000 bail, Foster disappeared and is believed to have returned to Europe with Leola where they remained living off his inheritance.

[See other Foster entries entry additional family information.]

In 1888, *Strandhome* was purchased at public auction by the Produce Exchange Gratuity Fund which sold it in 1890 to Charles Alfred Post. It was subsequently owned by Waldron Kintzing Post. Both Charles and Waldron continued to call the estate *Strandhome*.

Bernard Mannes Baruch, Sr. rented the house during the summers of 1915 and 1916.

Foster, William Riley, Sr. (1813-1890)

Occupation(s):	merchant -	wholesale flour
	financier -	member, Produce Exchange;
		a founder and director, Bowery National Bank, NYC;
		director, Tenth Ward National Bank;
		trustee, Citizen's Bank;
		trustee, Dry Dock Savings Bank;
		director, Corn Exchange Insurance Co.;
		president and director, Mechanics and Traders Insurance Co.
		director, Rutgers Insurance Co.;
		director, American Insurance Co.;
		director, Grocers Insurance Co.;
		director, Republic Insurance Co.;
		director, Columbia Insurance Co.;
		director, Ashbury Insurance Co.
	capitalist -	extensive real estate holdings in Manhattan
	politician -	councilman, New York City, 1833

Marriage(s): c. 1839-1883 – Harriet Peers* (1815-1883)

Address: Little East Neck and South Country Roads, Babylon
Name of estate: *The Meadows*
Year of construction: c. 1863
Style of architecture:
Architect(s):
Landscape architect(s):
House extant: unconfirmed
Historical notes:

The house, originally named *The Meadows*, was built by William Riley Foster, Sr. He purchased the property in c. 1863 for use as his summer residence.

He was the son of The Reverend Sylvester and Mrs. Abigail Downs Foster.

Harriet Peers Foster was the daughter of William John and Ann Mary Burnett Peers.

William Riley and Harriet Peers Foster, Sr.'s daughter Elizabeth married Dr. Edward Dodd and resided in Babylon. Their son John, who married Caroline Oakley, later owned *The Meadows*. Their son William Riley Foster, Jr. resided at *Strandhome* in Bayport with his common-law-wife Leola Bellotte. Their son James married Sara Maria Haighs.

*Some sources on the internet incorrectly refer to Foster's wife as Harriet Peet.

[See other Foster entries for additional family information.]

*Emil Henry Frank residence,
front facade*

Frank, Emil Henry, Sr. (1843-1919)

Occupation(s):	financier - president, Frank and DuBois (marine insurance firm)
Civic Activism:	a founder, Brooklyn Riding and Driving Club; director, South Shore Country Club, West Islip
Marriage(s):	Paula Nathalia Glahn (1863-1906)
Address:	Awixa Avenue, Bay Shore
Name of estate:	
Year of construction:	1894
Style of architecture:	Queen Anne
Architect(s):	
Landscape architect(s):	
House extant: no	
Historical notes:	

    The house was built by Emil Henry Frank, Sr.
    His brother was General Paul Frank.
    Paula Nathalia Glahn Frank was the daughter of Carl Sophus and Laura Adelaide A. Strarup Glahn.
    Emil Henry and Paula Nathalia Glahn Frank, Sr.'s son Emil Henry Frank, Jr. remained a bachelor. Their daughter Adele married Hobart Weekes, the son of Bradford G. and Gladys Onderdonk Weekes, Sr. of Oyster Bay. Their daughter Florence did not marry. Their son Harold married Alice Heath and resided in Chicago, IL. Their daughter Grace married Paul Revere Smith and resided in Staten Island. Their son George married Louise Van Anden, the daughter of William M. and Alice Hannah Frost Van Anden, Sr. of Islip.
    In 1904, the house was purchased by Julian Douglas Fairchild.

Franklin, Emlen Pleasants (1866-1927)

Occupation(s):	industrialist - Blood Knitting Co., Amsterdam, NY
Marriage(s):	Harriet W. Johnson (1860-1934)
Address:	South Bay Avenue, Brightwaters
Name of estate:	*The Moorings*
Year of construction:	1910
Style of architecture:	Mexican Bungalow
Architect(s):	
Landscape architect(s):	
House extant: no	
Historical notes:	

    The house, originally named *The Moorings*, was built by Emlen Pleasants Franklin.
    The *Social Register Summer, 1915* lists Emlen P. and Harriet W. Johnson Franklin as residing at *The Moorings* in Brightwaters. He was the son of Joseph and Miriam Leggett Franklin.
    Emlen Pleasants and Harriet W. Johnson Franklin's son Frederick married Bonnie Frost.

Frothingham, John Sewell (1847-1915)

Occupation(s):	capitalist - director, Brooklyn Warehouse & Storage Co. financier - director, Home Life Insurance Co. industrialist - Frothingham, Baylis & Co. (manufacturer of duck cotton)
Civic Activism:	member, board of regents, Long Island College Hospital, Brooklyn; director, Philharmonic Society of Brooklyn; trustee, Brooklyn Institute of Arts and Sciences; trustee, First Unitarian Church of Our Saviour, Brooklyn
Marriage(s):	Katharine Kent (1847-1930) - Civic Activism: president, Schuman Club, Brooklyn
Address:	Penataquit Avenue, Bay Shore
Name of estate:	
Year of construction:	
Style of architecture:	
Architect(s):	
Landscape architect(s):	
House extant: unconfirmed	
Historical notes:	

The *Brooklyn Blue Book and Long Island Society Register, 1918* and *1921* list Katharine Kent Frothingham as residing in Bay Shore.

John Sewell Frothingham was the son of John Whipple and Mary Angeline Thompson Frothingham of Brooklyn. His sister Mary married Chauncey Edward Low, Sr. and resided at *Seaward* in Bay Shore.

Garben, Dr. Louis Francis, Sr. (1889-1964)

Occupation(s):	physician
Civic Activism:	chairman, mediation committee, Suffolk County Medical Society
Marriage(s):	1918-1964 – Sarita Clara Moore (1900-1987)
Address:	89 West Bayberry Road, Islip
Name of estate:	
Year of construction:	1899-1900
Style of architecture:	Moorish
Architect(s):	Grosvenor Atterbury designed the house (for H. O Havemeyer)*
Landscape architect(s):	Nathan F. Barrett (for H. O. Havemeyer)**
Builder:	*[See Jabez Ephraim Van Orden entry.]*
House extant: yes	
Historical notes:	

front / side facade, 2006

The house was built by Henry Osborne Havemeyer as part of his "Modern Venice" development. It was later owned by Garben.

He was the son of Laue Bodeker and Felicita Adele Monefeldt Garben.

Sarita Clara Moore Garben was the daughter of Frederick and Eva Gardner Moore.

Dr. Louis Francis and Mrs. Sarita Clara Moore Garben, Sr.'s son Robert resided in Dix Hills. Their son Dr. Allan C. Garben married Nancy Hendrickson, the daughter of Glenn Hendrickson of Brightwaters. Their son Bruce resided in Islip. Their son Dr. Louis Francis Garben, Jr. resided in Glen Ridge, NJ.

*The sale brochure for "Modern Venice" states that the Moorish-style architecture was suggested by Louis Comfort Tiffany.

**The sales brochure also states that "Modern Venice" would be devoid of trees and vegetation and that Nathan F. Barrett was the landscape architect.

Gardiner, Robert David Lion (1911-2004)

Occupation(s):	financier - member, Empire Trust Co.
	capitalist - extensive commercial real estate holdings
	intelligence agent - Naval intelligence officer during World War II
Marriage(s):	1961-2004 – Eunice Bailey
	- British fashion model

Address: South Country Road, West Bay Shore
Name of estate: *Sagtikos Manor*
Year of construction: 1692
Style of architecture: Colonial
Architect(s):
Landscape architect(s):
House extant: yes
Historical notes:

In 1692, Stephanus Van Cortlandt purchased 1,200 acres of land, extending from the Great South Bay northward to the middle of the Island, from the Secatogue Indians. He received a manorial grant for the land in 1697 and built his manor house the same year, naming it *Sagtikos*, an Algonquian word meaning "snake that hisses." In 1707, Van Cortlandt's heirs sold the manor along with its extensive lands to Timothy Carle [Carll], a wealthy Huntington farmer. In 1758, the manor was purchased for £1,200 by Jonathan Thompson of Setauket, a wealthy farmer and judge. In 1772, Thompson gave the manor house and 1,207 acres as a wedding gift to his son Isaac, who married Mary Gardiner of East Hampton. The last member of the Thompson/Gardiner family to own the house was Robert David Lion Gardiner, the Sixteenth Lord of the Manor.

The house, which is on the National Register of Historic Places, was purchased by Suffolk County in 2002 and is open to the public.

Eunice Baily Gardiner had previously been married to William Pitt Oakes II whose father Sir Harry Oakes was murdered in the Bahamas in 1943 under questionable circumstances.

[For information about Gardiner's East Hampton residences, *see* Spinzia, *Long Island's Prominent Families in the Town of East Hampton* – Gardiner entries.]

front facade, 2006

rear / side facade, 2006

Garner, Thomas, Jr. (1838-1869)

Occupation(s): industrialist - partner, with his brother William, Garner & Co. (cotton mills)

Marriage(s): 1860-1869 – Harriet H. Amory (1837-1907)

Address: South Country Road, Bay Shore
Name of estate:
Year of construction:
Style of architecture:
Architect(s):
Landscape architect(s):
House extant: unconfirmed
Historical notes:

He was the son of Thomas and Frances Mathilda Thorn Garner, Sr.
Harriet H. Amory Garner was the daughter of Jonathan and Letitia A. Austin Amory of Boston, MA.
In 1878, Harriet filed suit against her brother-in-law William Thorn Garner for failure to disburse $1 million she and her daughter Fanny inherited from her father-in-law. [*The New York Times* December 27, 1878, p. 8.]
Thomas and Harriet H. Amory Garner, Jr.'s daughter Francis married Charles Oliver Iselin, the son of Adrian George and Eleanora O'Donnell Iselin and resided at *Wolver Hollow* in Upper Brookville. [*See* Spinzia, *Long Island's Prominent North Shore Families, vol. I* – Iselin entry.]
[See following Garner entries for additional family information.]

Garner, Thomas, Sr. (1806-1867)

Occupation(s): industrialist - president and partner, with his brother William, Garner & Co. (cotton mills)

Marriage(s): Frances Mathilda Thorn (1809-1962)

Address: South Country Road, Bay Shore
Name of estate:
Year of construction:
Style of architecture:
Architect(s):
Landscape architect(s):
House extant: unconfirmed
Historical notes:

Thomas and Frances Mathilda Thorn Garner, Sr.'s son Thomas Garner, Jr. married Harriet H. Amory and also resided in Bay Shore. Their son William Thorn Garner married Mary Macellite Thorn of New Orleans, LA. Their daughter Frances married Francis Cooper Lawrance, Sr. and resided at *Manatuck Farm* in Bay Shore. Their daughter Anna married George Herbert Watson. Their daughter Josephine married James Lorimer Graham, Jr. Their daughter Caroline, who died in childbirth, married Samuel William Johnson of East Hampton. [*See* Spinzia, *Long Island's Prominent Families in the Town of East Hampton* – Johnson entry.]
[See other Garner entries for additional family information.]

Garner, William Thorn (1840-1876)

Occupation(s): industrialist - partner, with his brother Thomas, Garner & Co. (cotton mills);
president, Harmony Mills (cotton mills);
president, W. T. Garner & Co. (cotton mills)

Marriage(s): 1865-1876 – Mary Macellite Thorn (1842-1876)

Address: South Country Road, Bay Shore
Name of estate:
Year of construction:
Style of architecture:
Architect(s):
Landscape architect(s):
House extant: unconfirmed
Historical notes:

    William Thorn Garner was the son of Thomas and Frances Mathilda Thorn Garner, Sr. After the death of their parents, William and his brother Thomas summered at their parents' estate in Bay Shore.
    Mary Macellite Thorn Garner was the daughter of Frost and Susannah Wroe Edwards Thorn of New Orleans, LA.
    William Thorn and Mary Macellite Thorn Garner both perished in a yachting accident off Staten Island, NY, when their yacht the *Mohawk* was caught in a squall with all its sails set. In 1878, the yacht was purchased by the Coast and Geodetic Survey. Renamed the *Eagre*, it saw service in the Atlantic from 1878 to 1903.
    The Garners' daughter Macellite married Henri Charles Joseph le Tonnelie, the Marquis de Breteuil. Their daughter Edith married Count Leon von Molthe–Hvitfield and resided in Paris, France. Their daughter Florence married Sir William Gordon–Cumming, Baronet of Gordonstoun in Scotland. When accused of cheating at cards, William sued for slander. His position in British society was ruined when the jury found him guilty. [*The New York Times* May 21, 1930, p. 22; for further information on the trial and Florence's unhappy marriage to William, *see* Harry W. Havemeyer, *Along the Great South Bay From Oakdale to Babylon: The Story of a Summer Spa 1840 to 1940* (Mattituck, NY: Amereon House, 1996), pp. 209-10.]
    [See, also, preceding Garner entries for additional family information.]

Mohawk

Gibb, Howard, Sr. (1855-1905)

Occupation(s):	merchant - president, Frederick Loeser & Co., Brooklyn (formerly, H. Batterman Department Store)
Marriage(s):	M/1 – 1874-div. – Mary Louise Burr (b. 1848) M/2 – 1897-1905 – Elizabeth Rossiter (1854-1932)
Address:	Ocean Avenue, Islip
Name of estate:	
Year of construction:	c. 1889
Style of architecture:	Colonial Revival with Shingle elements
Architect(s):	
Landscape architect(s):	
House extant:	no
Historical notes:	

The house was built by Leander Waterbury. In 1890, it was purchased by Gibb. [*Brooklyn Times Union* May 10, 1890, p. 2.]

He was the son of John and Harriet Balsdon Gibb, who resided at *Afterglow* in Islip.

Mary Louise Burr Gibb was the daughter of Cornelius A. and Mary Louise Lynon Burr. She subsequently married ____ Vernet and resided in France.

Howard and Mary Louise Gibb, Sr.'s daughter Mary (aka Minnie) married Count Henri de Moy and resided in France.

The *Brooklyn Blue Book and Long Island Society Register, 1918* lists Elizabeth Rossiter Gibb as residing in Manhattan.

She was the daughter of Lucius Tuttle and Mary Wickes Rossiter. Her brother Edward Van Wych Rossiter, who was vice-president of the New York Central & Hudson River Railroad, married Estelle Hewlett, the daughter of J. Lawrence Hewlett of Great Neck, and resided in Flushing, Queens.

Howard and Elizabeth Rossiter Gibb, Sr.'s son Howard Gibb. Jr. married Elsie Graham MacIlwaine.

Gibb's will stipulated that if Elizabeth remarried, she would be disinherited. [*The New York Times* July 8, 1905, p. 14.]

[See following Gibb entries for additional family information.]

In 1898, the house was purchased by Henry Gerhard Timmermann, who enlarged the house in c.1905. It was later owned by Timmermann's daughter Grace, who married Orvill Hurd Tobey. Both the Timmermanns and the Tobeys called the house *Breeze Lawn*.

front / side facade, c. 1903

Gibb, John (1829-1905)

Occupation(s):	capitalist - partner, Mills & Gibb (importers of lace and linen)
	merchant - president, Frederick Loeser & Co., Brooklyn (formerly, H. Batterman Department Store)
	financier - trustee, Brooklyn Trust Co.
Civic Activism:	president, auxiliary, Adelphi College, Brooklyn (later, Adelphi University, Garden City);
	trustee, Adelphi Academy, Brooklyn
Marriage(s):	M/1 – 1852-1878 – Harriet Balsdon (d. 1878)
	M/2 – 1882 – Sarah D. Mackay
Address:	Ocean Avenue, Islip
Name of estate:	*Afterglow*
Year of construction:	c. 1890
Style of architecture:	Shingle
Architect(s):	
Landscape architect(s):	
House extant:	no; demolished in c. 1950
Historical note:	

Afterglow, c. 1901

The house, originally named *Afterglow*, was built by John Gibb.

Born in Scotland, he was the son of James Gibb.

John and Harriet Balsdon Gibb's son Howard, who resided in Islip, married Mary Louise Burr and, later, Elizabeth Rossiter. Their son Lewis married Anna Pinkerton and resided at *Cedarholme* in Bay Shore. Their son Walter married Florence Althea Swan and resided at *Old Orchard* in Glen Cove. Their son Henry married Grace Dwight, the daughter of Frederick and Antoinette R. McMullen Dwight of *Tanglehedge* in Seabright, NJ, and resided in Morristown, NJ. Their son John Richmond Gibb, Sr. married Emily Mathews, who subsequently married John's brother Arthur, with whom she resided at *Gageboro* and at *Iron Action* in Glen Cove. Their daughter Ada married William Van Ander Hester, Sr. and resided at *Willada Point* in Glen Cove. Their daughter Florence married Herbert Lee Pratt, Sr. and resided at *The Braes* in Glen Cove. [*See* Spinzia, *Long Island's Prominent North Shore Families, vol. I* – Gibb and Hester entries – and *Long Island's Prominent North Shore Families, vol. II* – Pratt entry.]

Sarah D. Mackay Gibb's sister Annie married S. Perry Sturges and resided in Brooklyn.

[See other Gibb entries for additional family information.]

In 1909, the house was purchased by John Barry Stanchfield, Sr. It was later owned by Stanchfield's daughter Alice, who married Dr. Arthur Mullen Wright. Both the Stanchfields and the Wrights continued to call the house *Afterglow*.

living room, c. 1903

Gibb, Lewis Mills, Jr. (1902-1971)

Occupation(s):	merchant - president, Frederick Loeser & Co., Brooklyn (formerly, H. Batterman Department Store)
	capitalist - director, Pinkerton National Detective Agency
Marriage(s):	M/1 – 1927-div. – Martha Carroll Pease (aka Patty Carroll Pease) (1905-1997)
	M/2 – 1943-1971 – Jean Regan (1908-1983)
Address:	Dover Court, Bay Shore
Name of estate:	*Cedarholme*
Year of construction:	1904
Style of architecture:	Shingle
Architect(s):	
Landscape architect(s):	
House extant: yes	
Historical notes:	

    The house, originally named *Cedarholme*, was built by Lewis Mills Gibb, Sr. It was subsequently owned by his son Lewis Mills Gibb, Jr., who continued to call it *Cedarholme*.
    The Long Island Society Register, 1929 lists Lewis Mills and Patty [Martha] Carroll Pease Gibb [Jr.] as residing in Islip [Bay Shore].
    She was the daughter of Walter Albert and Martha Chamberi Rodgers Pease, who resided at *Bethpage* in Hempstead and *Fleur-de-lys* in Southampton. Martha subsequently married Richard Franklin Babcock of *Hark Away* in Woodbury.
    Jean Regan Gibb was the daughter of Thomas J. and Aurora Sala Regan, who resided in Old Westbury. She had previously been married to Rigan McKinney of New York and Cleveland, OH.
    Lewis Mills and Jean Regan Gibb, Jr.'s daughter Jean married Philip O'Donnell Lee, the son of Augustus Wilson Lee of Frederick, MD.
    [*See* Spinzia, *Long Island's Prominent Families in the Town of Hempstead*—Pease entry; *Long Island's Prominent Families in the Town of Southampton* – Pease entry; *Long Island's Prominent North Shore Families, vol. I* – Babcock entry; and *Long Island's Prominent North Shore Families, vol. II* – Regan entry.]
    [See other Gibb entries for additional family information.]
    The house was later owned by Charles H. Tenney, Sr.

front facade, 2005

Gibb, Lewis Mills, Sr. (1868-1912)

Occupation(s):	capitalist - partner, Mills & Gibbs (importers of lace and linen); merchant - partner, Frederick Loeser & Co., Brooklyn (formerly, H. Batterman Department Store)
Marriage(s):	1900-1912 – Anna Joan Pinkerton (1874-1942) - Civic Activism: member, fund raising committee for construction of Southside Hospital, Bay Shore (now, South Shore University Hospital)
Address:	Dover Court, Bay Shore
Name of estate:	*Cedarholme*
Year of construction:	1903
Style of architecture:	Shingle
Architect(s):	
Landscape architect(s):	
House extant: yes	
Historical notes:	

The house, originally named *Cedarholme*, was built by Lewis Mills Gibb, Sr.

The *Brooklyn Blue Book and Long Island Society Register, 1918* lists Anna Pinkerton Gibb as residing at *Cedarholme* in Bay Shore.

She was the daughter of Robert Allan and Anna Elizabeth Hughes Pinkerton, who resided at *Dearwood* in Bay Shore. Her brother Allan Pinkerton II married Franc Woolworth and also resided in Bay Shore. Her sister Mary married Jay Freeborn Carlisle, Sr. and resided at *Rosemary* in East Islip.

Lewis Mills Gibb, Sr. was the son of John and Harriet Balsdon Gibb of *Afterglow* in Islip.

Lewis Mills and Anna Joan Pinkerton Gibb, Sr.'s son Robert married Thyrza Flagg, the daughter of Montague and Thyrza Benson Flagg II of *Applewood* in Upper Brookville, and, later, Hannah Willets, the daughter of Samuel Willets, and resided in Oldwick, NJ. [*See* Spinzia, *Long Island's Prominent North Shore Families, vol. I* – Flagg entry.]

[For additional family information see preceding Gibb entries.]

The house was later owned by Lewis Mills Gibb, Jr., who continued to call it *Cedarholme*, and subsequently, by Charles H. Tenney, Sr.

[For information on the Southside Hospital, see Cooper entry.]

Gibson, Frederick E. (1908-1977)

Occupation(s):	capitalist - president, F. E. Gibson Builders, Inc.; partner, Hempstead Park Acres (builders)
Civic Activism:	president and chairman of board, Long Island Home Builders Association; director, Suffolk County American Cancer Society; member, Long Island Hospital Planning and Review Board; member; advisory board, Southside Hospital, Bay Shore (now, South Shore University Hospital)
Marriage(s):	Jean Giusti
Address:	87 South Saxon Avenue, Bay Shore
Name of estate:	
Year of construction:	1907
Style of architecture:	Colonial Revival
Architect(s):	
Landscape architect(s):	
House extant: yes	
Historical notes:	

front facade, 2013

He was the son of William Robert Gibson, Sr., the founder and developer of the Gibson section of Valley Stream.

Frederick E. and Jean Giusti Gibson's son Gregory married Carol Eugenia Epp and resided in Sayville and, later, in Brightwaters. Their son William Robert Gibson III married Lois Ann Bang, the daughter of Henry R. Bang.

In 2013, the 3,508-square-foot house with five bedrooms and three-and-a-half bathrooms was for sale. The asking price was $849,000.

Gibson, Gregory Martin

Occupation(s):	capitalist - vice-president, F. E. Gibson Builders, Inc. politician - mayor, Brightwaters, 1985
Marriage(s):	1959 – Carol Eugenia Epp (b. 1937)
Address:	Concourse West, Brightwaters
Name of estate:	
Year of construction:	
Style of architecture:	
Architect(s):	
Landscape architect(s):	
House extant:	unconfirmed
Historical notes:	

Gregory Martin Gibson was the son of Frederick E. Gibson of Bay Shore.
Carol Eugenia Epp Gibson was the daughter of Harold B. and Claira Moran Epp of Bay Shore.

Gibson, John James (1871-1936)

Occupation(s):	financier - president, South Side Bank, Bay Shore (which merged into Franklin National Bank); director, First National Bank and Trust Co., Bay Shore pharmacist
Civic Activism:	president, Bay Shore Board of Education; president, Bay Shore–Brightwaters Community Association
Marriage(s):	1904-1936 – Lavonne Jeanette Cushman (1868-1944)
Address:	45 Ocean Avenue, Bay Shore
Name of estate:	
Year of construction:	
Style of architecture:	Neo-Colonial Revival
Architect(s):	
Landscape architect(s):	
House extant:	yes
Historical notes:	

John James Gibson, Sr. was the son of Samuel Burr and Rhoda Jane Reybert Gibson. His sister Aletta married Raymond Hallock Terry and resided in Bay Shore. His sister Mary married William Henry Brown and resided in Bay Shore. His sister Anna married Harry Mortimer Brewster and also resided in Bay Shore. His brother Jesse married Addie May Hutton. His brother Earle married Helen Smith, the daughter of Allan and Anna Powell Petit Smith.

John James and Lavonne Jeanette Cushman Gibson's son John Joseph Gibson married Cornelia Lott Vanderveer and resided in West Islip and Bay Shore.

[See following entry for additional family information.]

front facade, 2006

Gibson, John Joseph (1910-1971)

Occupation(s):	attorney - member, Green and Hurd, NYC; member, Hurd, Hamlin, and Hubbell, NYC; general counsel, Johnson & Johnson, New Brunswick, NJ
	industrialist - vice-president, secretary, and treasurer, Johnson & Johnson, New Brunswick, NJ
	financier - chairman of board, South Side Bank, Bay Shore (which merged into Franklin National Bank); director, Franklin National Bank, Franklin Square
Civic Activism:	chairman of board, Islip Town Planning Board; trustee, Southside Hospital, Bay Shore (now, South Shore University Hospital)
Marriage(s):	1934-1971 – Cornelia Lott Vanderveer (1909-1988)
Address:	99 South Awixa Avenue, Bay Shore
Name of estate:	
Year of construction:	1951-1953
Builder:	Louis Bartos
Style of architecture:	Colonial Revival elements
Architect(s):	Herbert W. Korber
Landscape architect(s):	
House extant: yes	
Historical notes:	

The house was built by John Joseph and Cornelia Lott Vanderveer Gibson.

He was the son of John James and Lavonne Jeannette Cushman Gibson of Bay Shore.

Cornelia Lott Vanderveer Gibson was the daughter of John and Gertrude Van Siclen Lott Vanderveer, who resided at *Sunnymead* in West Islip.

[See previous entry for additional family information.]

The John Joseph Gibson family resided in the gardener's cottage on the John Vanderveer estate *Sunnymead* in West Islip from 1935 to 1945. In 1945, they moved into the *Sunnymead's* main residence and resided there until 1953.

The South Awixa Avenue house was subsequently owned by their son John Vanderveer Gibson.

[For information on the Southside Hospital, see Cooper entry.]

Sunnymead, rear facade, 1930s

99 South Awixa Avenue, front facade, 2006

Gilmore, William Guy, Sr. (1847-1921)

Occupation(s):	industrialist - Arbuckle Brothers Co. (sugar refining firm); director, American Sugar Refining Co.
	merchant - vice-president, Charles William Stores
	financier - director, Lawyers' Title and Trust Co.
Marriage(s):	Mary Jane Cochran (1848-1934)
Address:	South Country Road, West Babylon
Name of estate:	*My Fancy*
Year of construction:	
Style of architecture:	Eclectic
Architect(s):	Clarence K. Birdsall, 1894 alterations (for Ford)
Landscape architect(s):	
Builder:	Brown & Howell, billiard room addition, 1893; enlargement of carriage house, 1893 (for Ford)
House extant:	no; demolished in 1950's*

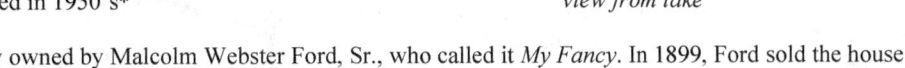
view from lake

Historical notes:

The house was previously owned by Malcolm Webster Ford, Sr., who called it *My Fancy*. In 1899, Ford sold the house to Gilmore who continued to call it *My Fancy*. The estate was named *My Fancy* after Walt Whitman's poem "My Fancy."

The *Brooklyn Blue Book and Long Island Society Register, 1918* lists William G. and Mary Cochran Gilmore [Sr.] as residing on Country Road [South Country Road], Babylon [West Babylon].

William Guy and Mary Jane Cochran Gilmore, Sr.'s son Edward married Edith Ross, the daughter of William G. Ross and, later, Mary Bird Keene, and resided at *My Fancy*. Their son H. Blake Gilmore also resided at *My Fancy*. Their son Robert married Mildred Sybil Koch, the daughter of John Valentine and Elizabeth Fredericka Katrina Sybilla Hufnagel Koch, and resided at *My Fancy*. Their son William Guy Gilmore, Jr. married Olive H. Candee and resided in Brooklyn.

*The estate's property is currently the site of the Great South Bay Shopping Center.

Goodrich, William Winston (1833-1906)

Occupation(s):	attorney - partner, Goodrich and Wheeler; judge, New York State Supreme Court, 1896; chief justice, New York State Appellate Court
	financier - director, Kings County Bank
	capitalist - director, Port Jefferson Co. (real estate developer)
	politician - member, New York State Assembly, 1865, 1870;
	writer - *Early Long Island*, 1904; *The Bench and Bar as Makers of the American Republic*
Civic Activism:	chairman, International Maritime Conference; president of trustees, Brooklyn Homeopathic Hospital; director, Philharmonic Society; member, Brooklyn Board of Education, 1876; a founder, Order of the Founders and Patriots of America
Marriage(s):	1857-1904 – Frances Wickes (1836-1904) - Civic Activism: a founder, New England Kitchen (raised money for Union hospitals during Civil War); manager, Long Island College Hospital, Brooklyn
Address:	Saxon Avenue, Bay Shore
Name of estate:	
Year of construction:	
Style of architecture:	
Architect(s):	
Landscape architect(s):	
House extant: unconfirmed	

Historical notes:

William Winston Goodrich was the son of David and Mary Winston Goodrich.

Frances Wickes Goodrich was the daughter of Henry N. Wickes of Albany, NY.

William Winston and Frances Wickes Goodrich's daughter Jessie married Clinton Lawrence Rossiter and resided at *Old Field Acres* in Setauket. Their daughter Mabel married The Reverend Edward A. George, pastor of the First Congregational Church, Ithaca, NY. Their son Henry married Madeline C. Lloyd and resided at *Windygates* on Sakonnet Point in Rhode Island.

Gordon, Edward

Occupation(s):	financier - president, Edward Gordon and Co.
Marriage(s):	
Address:	80 Montgomery Avenue, Bay Shore
Name of estate:	
Year of construction:	c. 1890
Style of architecture:	Modified Shingle
Architect(s):	
Landscape architect(s):	
House extant: yes	
Historical notes:	

The house was built by Charles Robinson Smith. It was subsequently owned by Gordon.

The fifteen-room house, with nine bedrooms, six fireplaces, and five-and-a-half bathrooms, was for sale in 2006. The asking price was $1,490,000; the annual taxes were $18,055.

front facade, 2006

Graham, George Scott (1850-1931)

Occupation(s):	attorney - partner, Graham and L'Amoreaux; district attorney, Philadelphia, PA, 1880-1899
	capitalist - director, Electric Light Co., Philadelphia, PA; director, Pennsylvania Heat, Light, & Power Co.
	industrialist - Smokeless Powder & Chemical Co.
	financier - director, Columbia Avenue Trust Co.
	politician - member, United States Congress, 1913-1931
	educator - professor of law, University of Pennsylvania, Philadelphia, 1887-1898
Civic Activism:	anti-prohibitionist
Marriage(s):	M/1 – 1870 – Emma M. Ellis
	M/2 – 1898-1931 – Pauline M. Clarke
Address:	South Country Road, Islip
Name of estate:	*Lohgrame*
Year of construction:	1910
Style of architecture:	Modified Mediterranean
Architect(s):	Palmer and Hornbostel designed the house (for Moffitt)
Landscape architect(s):	
House extant: no	
Historical notes:	

The house, originally named *Beautiful Shore*, was built by William Henry Moffitt. In 1915, it was purchased by Walter George Oakman, Sr. In 1918, Mrs. Oakman sold the house to Graham, who called it *Lohgrame*. [*The New York Times* February 3, 1918, p. 32.]

rear facade

He was the son of James Henry and Sarah Jane Scott Graham of Philadelphia, PA.

Emma M. Ellis Graham was the daughter of Charles Ellis.

George Scott and Emma M. Ellis Graham's daughter Ethel married C. Perry Wentz. Their daughter Blanche married Erskine Bains.

George Scott and Pauline M. Clarke Graham's daughter Marion married Graham Williams.

Graham, James Varnum, Jr. (1868-1944)

Occupation(s): real estate agent - NYC broker

Marriage(s): 1897-1944 – Edith Violet Lane (1877-1956)

Address: *[unable to determine street address]*, Sayville
Name of estate: *South Country Lodge*
Year of construction:
Style of architecture:
Architect(s):
Landscape architect(s):
House extant: unconfirmed
Historical notes:

The *Social Register Summer, 1910* lists James Varnum and Edith V. Lane Graham [Jr.] as residing at *South Country Lodge* in Babylon.
He was the son of James Varnum and Kate Acosta Graham of Flushing.
Edith Violet Lane Graham was the daughter of Theodore E. and Isabel A. Gilpin Lane of Flushing.
James Varnum and Edith Violet Lane Graham, Jr.'s daughter Edith married George Dexter Bradford, the son of Kingsland Bradford and, later, William B. Broomall. Their son John married Alice Kristine de la Cour, the daughter of Lauritz Ulrick and Jensine de la Cour.

Green, Isaac Henry, II (1858-1937)

Occupation(s): architect -
[See Architects appendix for selected list of South Shore commissions.]
financier - president, Oysterman's National Bank, Sayville
Civic Activism: member, Board of Education, Sayville Public Schools, Sayville; member, Sayville Fire Department Hose Co.

Marriage(s): 1884-1937 – Emma Louise Hibbard (1866-1945)

Address: Brook Street, Sayville
Name of estate: *Brookside*
Year of construction: 1896-1897
Style of architecture: Neo-Tudor
Architect(s): Isaac Henry Green II designed his own house
Landscape architect(s):
House extant: no; destroyed by fire in 1970*
Historical notes:

The house, originally named *Brookside*, was built by Isaac Henry Green II.
He was the son of Samuel Willet and Henrietta M. Vail Green of Riverhead and Sayville.
Emma Louise Hibbard Green was the daughter of William Frederick and Emma Louise Jacobus Hibbard of Bayport.
Isaac Henry and Emma Louise Hibbard Green II's daughter Henrietta married Isaac Howard Snedecor, the son of Isaac Scudder and Sarah Elizabeth Homan Snedecor of Bayport, and resided in Bayport. Their daughter Beatrice married Edward Halsey Rogers and resided in Westhampton Beach.
A portion of the estate's property was purchased by Suffolk County and is now the county's "water park," Brookside County Park.
*The gatehouse, which is extant, is being used by the Great South Bay Audubon Society.

Brookside

Gregory, George Mitchell (1905-1976)

Occupation(s):	financier - partner, Gregory and Sons (investment banking firm) industrialist - director, Crescent Petroleum Corp.
Marriage(s):	M/1 – 1933-1955 – Marjorie Cooper Waddell (1911-1955) M/2 – 1957-1976 – Mary Louise Feitner (1922-1986)
Address:	40 Lawrence Lane, Bay Shore
Name of estate:	
Year of construction:	
Style of architecture:	Colonial Revival
Architect(s):	
Landscape architect(s):	
House extant: yes	
Historical notes:	

side facade

George Mitchell Gregory was the son of William Hamilton and Elizabeth Mitchell Gregory, Sr. of Bay Shore.

Marjorie Cooper Waddell Gregory was the daughter of Charles Falkiner Morton and Coretta Jean Hagen Waddell of Bay Shore.

George Mitchell and Marjorie Cooper Waddell Gregory's son Robert married Elizabeth Coe Finlayson, the daughter of Daniel Aylesbury and Elizabeth Coe Finlayson, Jr. of Hewlett Bay Park. [*See* Spinzia, *Long Island's Prominent Families in the Town of Hempstead* – Finlayson entry.]

The *Social Register Summer, 1962* lists George M. and Mary L. Feitner Gregory as residing at 40 Lawrence Lane, Bay Shore.

She was the daughter of Quentin Field and Lillian B. Hyde Feitner, Sr. of Bay Shore. Mary's sister Lillian married orchestra leader Aaron Bernard Mussoff (aka Ray Benson) and, later, David Wagstaff, Jr. of *Ledgeland* in Tuxedo Park, NY. Her brother Quentin Field Feitner, Jr. married Judith H. Underdown and resided in Sands Point and Old Brookville.

George Mitchell and Mary Louise Feitner Gregory's son Richard married Renee Estelle Bytner, the daughter of Vincent D. Bytner of Albany, NY.

[See other Gregory entries for additional family information.]

Gregory, William Hamilton, Jr. (1903-1962)

Occupation(s):	financier - partner, Gregory and Sons (investment banking firm)
	capitalist - chairman of board, Susquehanna & Western Railroad
	industrialist - director, Hycon–Caribbean Petroleum;
	    director, Eastern Air Devices;
	    director, Crescent Petroleum Corp.

Civic Activism:	trustee, Hewitt School for Girls, NYC (formerly, Miss Hewitt's Classes); governor, Association of Bond Brokers
Marriage(s):	1929-1962 – Edith A. Crowley (1903-1987)
Address:	Meadow Farm Road, East Islip
Name of estate:	*Creekside*
Year of construction:	1929
Style of architecture:	Neo-Federal
Architect(s):	William Hamilton Russell, Jr. designed the house (for H. K. Knapp II)
Landscape architect(s):	Charles Wellford Leavitt and Sons (for H. K. Knapp II)
House extant: yes	
Historical notes:	

rear facade

The house, originally named *Creekside*, was built by Harry Kearsarge Knapp II. In 1939, it was purchased by Gregory, who continued to call it *Creekside*.

He was the son of William Hamilton and Elizabeth Mitchell Gregory, Sr. of Bay Shore.

Edith A. Crowley Gregory was the daughter of John Augustin Crowley.

William Hamilton and Edith A. Crowley Gregory, Jr.'s son William Hamilton Gregory III, who resided in Glen Cove, married Elsie Bacon Lovering, the daughter of Joseph Sears Lovering, Sr. of Islip, and, later, Elizabeth Coe Finlayson, the daughter of Daniel Aylesbury and Elizabeth Coe Finlayson, Jr. of Hewlett Bay Park. [*See* Spinzia, *Long Island's Prominent North Shore Families, vol. I* – Gregory entry – and *Long Island's Prominent Families in the Town of Hempstead* – Finlayson entry.] Their daughter Anne married Theodore C. Baer, Jr.

Gregory, William Hamilton, Sr. (1876-1948)

Occupation(s): financier - partner, Kountze Brothers (investment banking firm); founder and president, Gregory and Sons (investment banking firm)

Marriage(s): Elizabeth Mitchell (1883-1952)

Address: *[unable to determine street address]*, Bay Shore
Name of estate:
Year of construction:
Style of architecture:
Architect(s):
Landscape architect(s):
House extant: unconfirmed
Historical notes:

    The *Long Island Society Register, 1929* lists William Hamilton and Elizabeth Mitchell Gregory [Sr.] as residing in Bay Shore.
    He was the son of Robert Hamilton and Adria Emma King Gregory.
    William Hamilton and Elizabeth Mitchell Hamilton, Sr.'s son William Hamilton Gregory, Jr. married Edith A. Crowley and resided at *Creekside* in East Islip. Their son George, who resided in Bay Shore, married Marjorie Cooper Waddell and, later, Mary Louise Feitner.
    [See other Gregory entries for additional family information.]

William Marcus Greve, Jr. residence,
Millcreek / Mill Creek Farm,
2020

Greve, William Marcus, Jr. (1884-1962)

Occupation(s):	capitalist -	director, Madison Square Garden Corp.; president, Realty Associates, Brooklyn; director, Brooklyn–Manhattan Transit Corp.; director, Thompson–Starrett Co.; director, Missouri–Kansas–Texas Lines; president, St. Louis Southwestern Railroad; director, Cotton Belt Railway
	financier -	president, Prudence–Bonds Corp.; president, New York Investors; director, Brooklyn Trust Co.
	industrialist -	director, Hupp Motor Car Corp.
Civic Activism:		trustee, Southside Hospital, Bay Shore (now, South Shore University Hospital)
Marriage(s):		M/1 – 1907 – Clara Louise Fergueson (d. c. 1929)
		M/2 – Mary Buford Peirce (d. 1975)
Address:		80 South Saxon Avenue, Bay Shore
Name of estate:		*Millcreek / Mill Creek Farm*
Year of construction:		1933
Style of architecture:		Neo-Tudor
Architect(s):		William Hamilton Russell, Jr. designed the house (for H. C. Sharp)

Landscape architect(s):
House extant: yes
Historical notes:

The earliest mention in local newspapers of William Marcus Greve, Jr. as residing in Bay Shore is in 1922.

The *Long Island Society Register, 1929* lists William M. and Clara Louise Fergueson Greve as residing on Saxon Avenue, Bay Shore. We have not, however, been able to ascertain if he owned the house or was renting. What is clear is that in 1938 Greve was renting the house that Hamlet Cecil Sharp built *Millcreek / Mill Creek Farm*. [*The Suffolk County News* August 18, 1939, p. 12.]

He was the son of William Marcus and Rebecca Greve, Sr.

William Marcus and Clara Louise Fergueson Greve, Jr.'s daughter Lillian married Theodore Grant Caldwell, Jr. and resided on Prospect Park West in Brooklyn. Lillian subsequently married Edward Mark Maclay Carolin. For a period of time the marriage's validity was in question when Carolin was arrested for bigamy. In 1939, Lillian's rejected suitor Lawrence Sprague, the son of society physician Dr. Shirley E. Sprague, shot Lillian twice in the abdomen and then committed suicide in The Village of Branch, Town of Smithtown, house of Mrs. Tracy Higgins.

Greve temporarily gave up his United States citizenship in the 1930s and relocated to Europe. He returned hurriedly from Lichtenstein just ahead of the Nazi advance. [*Time Magazine* June 20, 1955.]

By 1958 Greve and his wife Mary were residing at *The Shallows* on Halsey Neck Lane in Southampton.

Mary Buford Peirce Greve had previously been married to John William Kiser, Jr. of *Sunset Court / Westerly* in Southampton.

[*See* Spinzia, *Long Island's Prominent Families in the Town of Southampton* – Greve and Kiser entries.]

In 1944, the house was purchased from Mrs. Sharp by Frank Riggio who renamed it *Riggio House*.

In 2020, 9.68 acres and the 8,738-square-foot, nineteen-room house, with a seven-car garage, horse stables, guest cottage, and windmill, were for sale. The asking price was $4.999 million.

[For information on the Southside Hospital, see Cooper entry.]

side facade, 2005

Guastavino, Rafael, Jr. (1872-1950)

Occupation(s):	capitalist - president, construction firm that specialized in ecclesiastical timbrel arch tile work
Marriage(s):	1909-div. c. 1941 – Elsie Seidel (1888-1982)
Address:	143 South Awixa Avenue, Bay Shore
Name of estate:	
Year of construction:	1912
Style of architecture:	Mediterranean Villa
Architect(s):	Rafael Guastavino, Jr.
Landscape architect(s):	
House extant: yes	
Historical notes:	

Rafael Guastavino, Jr. designed his own residence.
Elsie Seidel Guastavino subsequently married Randolph Mann and resided in Nyack, NY, and Fort Lauderdale, FL.
The house was subsequently owned by the Guastavinos' daughter Louise, who married Frank Gulden, Jr.
The sixteen-room house on 1.2 acres, with a 230-foot water frontage, was for sale in 2005. The asking price was $1.95 million.
A postcard mailed from Spain and dated April 12, 1912, indicated that the Guastavinos missed the fateful maiden voyage of the *Titanic*, due to travel scheduling, and planned to return to America on its second transatlantic voyage.

front / side facade, 2005

Guggenheim, Meyer Robert, Sr. (1885-1959)

Occupation(s):	industrialist - member, executive committee, American Smelting & Refining Co.; secretary and vice president, U. S. Zinc Co.; director, Guggenheim & Sons; director, Guggenheim Exploration Co.
	diplomat - United States Ambassador to Portugal, 1953-1954*
	financier - director, American Smelting Securities Co.
Civic Activism:	trustee, National Symphony Orchestra, Washington, DC; trustee, Guggenheim Foundation; member, board of managers, Southside Hospital, Bay Shore (now, South Shore University Hospital)
Marriage(s):	M/1 – 1905-div. 1915 – Grace Lilian Bernheimer (1887-1970)
	M/2 – 1915-div. 1928 – Margaret Gibbs Miller Weyher (b. 1893)
	M/3 – 1928-div. 1937 – Elizabeth Bross Eaton (1902-1965)
	M/4 – 1938-1959 – Rebecca Pollard (1903-1994)
Address:	Deer Park Avenue, North Babylon
Name of estate:	*Firenze Farm***
Year of construction:	
Style of architecture:	Colonial Revival
Architect(s):	
Landscape architect(s):	
House extant:	no
Historical notes:	

front facade

The *Long Island Society Register, 1929* lists Colonel and Mrs. M. Robert Guggenheim as residing on Deer Park Avenue in Babylon.

He was the son of Daniel and Florence Shloss Guggenheim, who resided at *Hempstead House* in Sands Point. His brother Harry, who resided at *Falaise* in Sands Point, married Helen Rosenberg, Caroline Morton, and, subsequently, Alicia Patterson. [*See* Spinzia, *Long Island's Prominent North Shore Families, vol. I* – Guggenheim entries.] His sister Gladys married Roger W. Straus and resided in Manhattan.

*Guggenheim's diplomatic career was a disaster; his ambassadorship lasted barely a year. Known within State Department circles for "not having anything above his shoulders," he was also generally known for his indifferent work habits, gambling, habitual womanizing, and social *faux pas*. In his first ambassadorial speech he insulted his Portuguese guests by saying that his preference for an ambassadorial posting would have been for Great Britain but Portugal would do. A few months later, at a state banquet, he began flipping utensils at the dinner table. When a piece of silverware landed in the cleavage of an elderly guest, Guggenheim reached over and retrieved it from the between the dignitary's breasts. [Irwin and Debi Unger, *The Guggenheims* (New York: Harper Collins Publishers, 2005), pp. 186-89.]

Grace Lilian Bernheimer Guggenheim was the daughter of Jacob Bernheimer of Manhattan. She subsequently married Morton E. Snellenberg of Philadelphia, PA.

Meyer Robert and Grace Lilian Bernheimer Guggenheim, Sr.'s son Daniel Guggenheim II suffered from heart disease, as did most of the male line of the Guggenheim family, and died at the age of eighteen while a student at Phillips Exeter Academy. Their son Meyer Robert Guggenheim, Jr. married four times. His first wife Helen Claire Allyn was the daughter of Alfred Warren Allyn of Montreal, Canada. His second wife was his secretary and his fourth wife was Shirlee McMullen.

Guggenheim's conversion to Catholicism and his Roman Catholic ceremony marriage to Margaret Gibbs Miller Weyher, the daughter of Casper F. Weyher of Scranton, PA, stunned the Jewish community as did his subsequent marriage to Elizabeth Bross Eaton, the daughter of James Waterbury and Elizabeth Bross Eaton, Sr. of West Islip. Their Lutheran church wedding was devoid of guests. Elizabeth Guggenheim's brother James Waterbury Eaton, Jr. married Matilda Brown and resided in Cold Spring Harbor.

Rebecca Pollard Guggenheim was the daughter of Andrew W. Pollard. She had previously been married to William Van Lennep, Jr. After Guggenheim's death she married John A. Logan.

**Guggenheim's North Babylon and Washington, DC, houses and his four yachts were all named after his mother, as was his parents' estate in New Jersey.

In 1933, the house, which was located on 531 acres, was damaged by fire.

In 1949, the estate property was acquired by Cadman H. Frederick and became part of his Causeway Acres housing development.

[For information on the Southside Hospital, see Cooper entry.]

Gulden, Charles, Sr. (1843-1916)

Occupation(s): industrialist - a founder, Charles Gulden, Inc. (manufacturer of mustard)*
financier - director, Germania Bank of the City of New York;
    trustee, Citizen Savings Bank

Marriage(s): M/1 – Margaret Williams (1848-1907)
M/2 – Mary Catherine Kellers (d. 1929)
  - Civic Activism: suffragist

Address: 36 Clinton Avenue, Bay Shore
Name of estate: *Netherbay*
Year of construction: c. 1890s
Style of architecture: Queen Anne
Architect(s): Clarence K. Birdsall designed the
    1897 and 1901 alterations
      (for C. Gulden, Sr.)

Landscape architect(s):
House extant: yes
Historical notes:

Charles Gulden, Sr., who was known as "The Father of American Mustard," was the son of Jacob Adam and Albertina Geissen Gulden.

Charles and Margaret Williams Gulden, Sr.'s son Frank Gulden, Sr. married Augusta Henes and resided in Islip. Their daughter Margaret married Walter Livingston Titus, Sr., the son of James Livingston and Harriet Louisa Pratt Titus, and resided in West Islip. Their daughter Emma married Alfred M. Snedeker, the son of Valentine and Susan Ketcham Snedeker, and resided in Manhattan. Their daughter Harriet married Frank Hall. Their daughter Florence married Thomas Francis Mullins. Their son Charles Gulden, Jr. married Genevieve L. Whipple, the daughter of Marcus and Lone Kincaid Whipple, and resided in North Pownal, VT.

[See other Gulden entries for additional family information.]

*Charles Gulden, Inc. was sold to American Home Foods which was a division of American Home Products. In 1996, it was spun off and renamed International Home Foods. In 2000, Con Agra purchased International Home Foods.

The house is currently the Open Gate Association Home for the Aged.

front facade, 1903

front facade, 1997

Gulden, Charles, III (1910-1994)

Occupation(s):	industrialist - president, Charles Gulden, Inc. (manufacturer of mustard)
Marriage(s):	M/1 – 1933-1941 – Samantha Gaynor Isham (1914-1941)
	M/2 – 1942-1949 – Faith Hollins
	M/3 – 1957-1991 – Mary Faran Bulkley (1934-1991)
Address:	88 East Bayberry Road, Islip
Name of estate:	
Year of construction:	1899-1900
Style of architecture:	Moorish*
Architect(s):	Grosvenor Atterbury designed the house (for H. O. Havemeyer)*
Landscape architect(s):	Nathan F. Barrett (for H. O. Havemeyer)**
Builder:	*[See Jabez Ephraim Van Order entry.]*
House extant:	yes
Historical notes:	

The house was built by Henry Osborne Havemeyer as part of his "Modern Venice" development. It was later owned by Charles Gulden III.

He was the son of Frank and Augusta Henes Gulden, Sr. of Islip.

Samantha Gaynor Isham Gulden was the daughter of Ralph Haywood and Marion Gaynor Isham of Glen Head. [*See* Spinzia, *Long Island's Prominent North Shore Families, vol. I* – Isham entry.] Samantha's grandfather New York City Mayor William Jay Gaynor resided at *Deepwells* in St. James. [*See* Spinzia, *Long Island: A Guide to New York's Suffolk and Nassau Counties* – *Deepwells Farm* – Estate of William Jay Gaynor – *Deepwells*, St. James.]

Charles and Samantha Gaynor Isham Gulden III's son Charles Gulden IV married Katherine A. Keogh, the daughter of Thomas Keogh of Larchmont, NY. Their son Michael married Mary Jean Summers, the daughter of Maurice Francis Summers, and resides in Mill Neck.

Faith Hollins Gulden was the daughter of Gerald Vanderbilt and Virginia Kobbe Hollins, Sr. of *The Hawks* in East Islip. She had previously been married to Arthur W. Little. Faith's sister Phyllis married John Grissom. Her brother John remained a bachelor. Her brother Gerald Vanderbilt Hollins, Jr. married Elizabeth Armour, the daughter of Lester Armour of Chicago, IL.

Mary Faran Bulkley Gulden was the daughter of David Tod and Mary F. Boyd Bulkley, who resided at *Rip Wa Leta* in Ridgefield, CT.

*The sales brochure for "Modern Venice" states that the Moorish–style architecture was suggested by Louis Comfort Tiffany.

**The sale brochure also states that "Modern Venice" would be devoid of trees and vegetation and that Nathan F. Barrett was the landscape architect.

The house was subsequently owned by Walter Livingston Titus, Jr.

front facade, 2006

Gulden, Frank, Jr. (1906-1989)

Occupation(s):	industrialist - president and chairman of board, Charles Gulden, Inc. (manufacturer of mustard)
Marriage(s):	1932-1989 – Louise Guastavino (1914-2004)
Address:	143 South Awixa Avenue, Bay Shore
Name of estate:	
Year of construction:	1912
Style of architecture:	Mediterranean Villa
Architect(s):	Rafael Guastavino, Jr. designed his own residence
Landscape architect(s):	
House extant:	yes

rear facade

Historical notes:
   The house was built by Rafael Guastavino, Jr. It was subsequently owned by his daughter Louise, who married Frank Gulden, Jr.
   He was the son of Frank and Augusta Henes Gulden, Sr. of Islip.
   Frank and Louise Guastavino Gulden, Jr.'s daughter Barbara married John Frederick Black, the son of Helen Baxter Black of Bay Shore, and resides in Easton, MD. Their daughter Louise married Rudolph Henriksen, the son of Christian and Jesse Stumme Henriksen of Islip, and resides in Islip. Their son Frank Gulden III married Jennie Giruc, the daughter of Stanley and Mary Korol Giruc of Bay Shore, and resides in Vero Beach, FL, and Point O'Woods, NY.
   [See other Gulden entries for additional family information.]
   The sixteen-room house on 1.2 acres, with a 230-foot water frontage, was for sale in 2005. The asking price was $1.95 million.

Gulden, Frank, Jr. (1906-1989)

Occupation(s):	industrialist - president and chairman of board, Charles Gulden, Inc. (manufacturer of mustard)
Marriage(s):	1932-1989 – Louise Guastavino (1914-2004)
Address:	89 East Bayberry Road, Islip
Name of estate:	
Year of construction:	1934-1935
Style of architecture:	Mediterranean Villa
Architect(s):	Rafael Guastavino, Jr. designed the house (for Gulden)
Landscape architect(s):	
House extant:	yes

Historical notes:
   The house was built by Frank Gulden, Jr.
   He was the son of Frank and Augusta Henes Gulden, Sr. of Islip.
   Louise Guastavino Gulden was the daughter of Rafael and Elsie Seidel Guastavino, Jr. of Bay Shore.
   [See Gulden and Guastavino entries for additional family information.]

front facade, 2006

Gulden, Frank, Sr. (1878-1961)

Occupation(s):	industrialist - chairman of board, Charles Gulden, Inc. (manufacturer of mustard)
Civic Activism:	president, board of trustees, Southside Hospital, Bay Shore (now, South Shore University Hospital);
	trustee, St. John's Hospital, Brooklyn;
	chairman, executive committee, Episcopal Church Charity Foundation;
	trustee, Berkeley Divinity School, New Haven, CT;
	vice-president, Boys Club of New York;
	trustee, Hofstra University, Hempstead;
	chairman, local chapter, New York State Temporary Emergency Relief Committee during the Depression;
	member, Emergency Committee of the Red Cross during World War II
Marriage(s):	1902-1961 – Augusta Henes (1879-1969)
Address:	137 West Bayberry Road, Islip
Name of estate:	
Year of construction:	1899-1900
Style of architecture:	Moorish
Architect(s):	Grosvenor Atterbury designed the house (for H. O. Havemeyer)*
Landscape architect(s):	Nathan F. Barrett (for H. O. Havemeyer)**
Builder:	*[See Jabez Ephraim Van Order entry.]*

House extant: yes; but substantially altered
Historical notes:

    The house, originally named *Bayberry Point*, was built by Henry Osborne Havemeyer as his own residence in his "Modern Venice" development. It was owned by Gulden from the late 1920s to the late 1940s, at which time he relocated to 117 West Bayberry Road.
    He was the son of Charles and Margaret Williams Gulden, Sr., who resided at *Netherbay* in Bay Shore.
    Augusta Henes Gulden was the daughter of William Frederick and Julia Henes.
    Frank and Augusta Henes Gulden, Sr.'s daughter Augusta married Carrick F. Cochran, the son of Dr. Robert W. Cochran of Sarasota, FL. Their son Frank Gulden, Jr. married Louise Guastavino and resided in Islip and Bay Shore. Their daughter Julia married Eric Gordon Ramsay, Sr. and resided in Brightwaters. Their son Charles Gulden III, who married Samantha Gaynor Isham, Faith Hollins, and, subsequently, Mary Faran Bulkley, resided in Islip and, later, in Cold Spring Harbor.
    [See other Gulden entries for additional family information.]
    *The sales brochure for "Modern Venice" states that the Moorish–style architecture was suggested by Louis Comfort Tiffany.
    **The sale brochure also states that "Modern Venice" would be devoid of trees and vegetation and that Nathan F. Barrett was the landscape architect.
    The house was subsequently owned by Dr. David Dodge Moore.
    [For information on the Southside Hospital, see Cooper entry.]

front facade, 2006

Gunther, William Henry, Jr. (1851-1901)

Occupation(s):	merchant - partner, C. G. Gunther's Sons (fur dealer)*
Civic Activism:	a founder, South Side Field Club, Bay Shore, 1886
Marriage(s):	1878-1901 – Marie Louise Hatch (1855-1935)
Address:	Awixa Avenue, Bay Shore
Name of estate:	
Year of construction:	1887
Style of architecture:	
Architect(s):	Isaac Henry Green II designed the greenhouse (for F. E. Ballard)
Landscape architect(s):	

House extant: unconfirmed
Historical notes:

He was the son of William Henby and Mary A. Gunther, Sr.

Marie Louise Hatch Gunther was the daughter of Charles Clarke Hatch.

William Henry and Marie Louise Hatch Gunther, Jr.'s son William Henry Gunther III was killed in Cuba during the Spanish American War. Their daughter Constance married Dr. Carl Anson Clemons and, later, Chester M. McKerr with whom she resided in Babylon.

*C. G. Gunther's Sons, which was founded by William's grandfather Christian G. von Gunther, was one of the largest fur dealers in the country. [*The New York Times* February 16, 1901, p. 7.]

In 1902, the house was owned by F. E. Ballard. [*The Brooklyn Daily Eagle* July 19, 1902, p. 1.]

Haff, Albert Douglas (1869-1954)

Occupation(s):	financier - chairman of board, Bank of Babylon; partner, Haff and Covert, Amityville (mortgage loan and insurance agency)
	attorney - partner, Haff and Farrington, Jamaica, NY
Civic Activism:	president, board of trustees, Babylon Methodist Church; chairman, local YMCA War Fund during World War I
Marriage(s):	1891-1954 – Josephine Farrington (1872-1955)
Address:	Cameron and Montrose Avenues, Babylon
Name of estate:	
Year of construction:	
Style of architecture:	
Architect(s):	
Landscape architect(s):	

House extant: unconfirmed
Historical notes:

Albert Douglas Haff was the son of John Peter and Phoebe Jane Pearsall Haff.

Albert Douglas and Josephine Farrington Haff's daughter Madalene married LeRoy K. Van Nostrand and resided in West Islip.

Albert was residing at 240 Secatogue Lane, West Islip, at the time of his death.

Haight, Gilbert Lawrence, Jr. (b. 1911)

Occupation(s):

Marriage(s):

Address: 183 Ocean Avenue, Amityville
Name of estate:
Year of construction:
Style of architecture: Colonial Revival
Architect(s):
Landscape architect(s):
Builder: E. W. Howell
House extant: unconfirmed
Historical notes:

    Gilbert Lawrence Haight, Jr. was the son of Gilbert Lawrence and Gladys Cook Haight, Sr. of Amityville.
    In 1954, Gilbert Lawrence Haight, Jr.'s three-year-old, adopted son Robert fell off the Haight's schooner into the Amityville River and drowned. [*The New York Times* June 5, 1954, p. 19.]

Gilbert Lawrence Haight, Jr. residence

Haight, Gilbert Lawrence, Sr. (1880-1942)

Occupation(s): entertainers and associated professions -
    horseman, Barnum and Bailey Circus
financier -   member, H. B. Hollins and Co. (stock brokerage firm);
    member, L. A. Norton and Co. (stock brokerage firm)

Marriage(s): 1910-1942 – Gladys Cook (d. 1946)

Address: 191 Merrick Road, Amityville
Name of estate:
Year of construction:
Style of architecture:
Architect(s):
Landscape architect(s):
House extant: no
Historical notes:

    Gilbert Lawrence Haight, Sr. was the son of Louis and Manhattania Elizabeth Cornelia Samuels Haight of Amityville.
    Gladys Cook Haight was severely injured when a monkey, they had just purchased, bit her in the face. [*The Suffolk County News* October 1, 1937, p. 9.]
    Gilbert Lawrence and Gladys Cook Haight, Sr.'s daughter Gloria, who was also a circus horse rider, married Thomas Flynn Young, the son of George Joseph Young of Brightwaters. Their son Gilbert Lawrence, Jr. also resided in Amityville.
    In 1948, Gloria and her brother Gilbert sold the ten-room house with a separate cottage on seven acres to Florence M. Gregory. [*The New York Times* June 4, 1949, p. 41.]

Hallock, Gerard, III (1905-1996)

Occupation(s):	financier - vice-president, Morgan Guaranty Trust Co.; associate, Cross & Brown, NYC
Civic Activism:	president and trustee, Southside Hospital, Bay Shore (now, South Shore University Hospital); president, board of trustees, Hewlett School of East Islip; trustee, Boys' Club of New York City; trustee, Pinkerton Foundation (devoted to helping troubled children)
Marriage(s):	M/1 – 1937-div. 1974 – Marion Wharton (1908-1989) - Civic Activism: member, auxiliary, Southside Hospital, Bay Shore (now, South Shore University Hospital); member, South Shore Garden Club
	M/2 – Virginia Levick (d. 1979)
Address:	St. Mark's Lane, Islip
Name of estate:	
Year of construction:	1924
Style of architecture:	Ranch
Architect(s):	
Landscape architect(s):	
House extant:	no; demolished in 1980s
Historical notes:	

The house, originally named *Pleasure Island*, was built by Schuyler Livingston Parsons, Jr. It was then owned by his niece Marion and her husband Gerard Hallock III, who enlarged the house and moved it to the mainland in the 1970s. [Schuyler Livingston Parsons, Jr. *Untold Friendships* (Boston: Houghton Mifflin Co., 1955), p. 98.]

Gerard Hallock III was the son of Gerard and Mary Adele Harlan Page Hallock, Jr. of Great Barrington, MA. His brother Harlan married Juliet Townshend, the daughter of Raynham and Juliet S. Adee Townshend of New Haven, CT. His brother Richards married Nancy Juelg and resided in Baltimore, MD.

Marion Wharton Hallock was the daughter of Richard and Helena Johnson Parsons Wharton, who resided at *Whileaway* in Islip. Marion's brother Richard T. Wharton, Sr., who married Mara di Zoppola, the daughter of Count Andrea Alexsandro Mario and Countess Edith Mortimer di Zoppola of Mill Neck, inherited *Whileaway*. [*See* Spinzia, *Long Island's Prominent North Shore Families*, vol. I – di Zoppola entry.]

Gerard and Marion Wharton Hallock III's son Gerard Peter Hallock married Joanne Scheerer Babcock, the daughter of John Bodine Babcock, Sr. of Sharon, CT, and, subsequently, Judith Schneider. Their daughter Helena married John Anthony Pless, Jr., the son of John Anthony and Madelaine Sichel Pless, Sr. of Holland and France, and resided in Islip. Their daughter Lisa married Harry Kaye.

[For information on the Southside Hospital, see Cooper entry.]

Pleasure Island

Hallowell, Thomas Jewett, Sr. (1869-1958)

Occupation(s):	financier - clerk, American Surety Co.; manager, fidelity department, Lawyers Security Co.; partner, with Robert E. Henry, Hallowell and Henry (investment banking firm); vice-president and director, Lawyers Incorporation Co. industrialist - treasurer, Associated Industrial Corp, NYC capitalist - treasurer, Montague Realty Co.; treasurer, Kitchawan Telephone Co.; treasurer, Maryland Corp.; treasurer, Associated Indiana Corp.
Marriage(s):	1907 – Marion Ricketson Slocum (b. 1885)
Address:	Main Road, West Babylon
Name of estate:	*On-the-way*
Year of construction:	
Style of architecture:	Long Island Farmhouse
Architect(s):	
Landscape architect(s):	
House extant: unconfirmed	
Historical notes:	

front facade, 1915

In 1910, Hallowell purchased the McCue farmhouse. [*South Side Signal* April 30, 1910, p. 3.]

The *Social Register Summer, 1915* lists Thomas Jewett and Marion R. Slocum Hallowell [Sr.] as residing at *On-the-way* in Babylon [West Babylon].

He was the son of Charles and Nora Belle Jewett Hallowell of Steubenville, OH.

Marion Ricketson Slocum Hallowell was the daughter of Francis Ricketson and Phoebe Hayward Slocum.

Thomas Jewett and Marion Ricketson Slocum Hallowell, Sr.'s son Thomas Jewett Hallowell, Jr. married Marion Lavenia Hewitt.

In 1915, the house was remodeled by Hallowell. [*The Brooklyn Daily Eagle* July 20, 1915, p. 6.]

Harbeck, Charles Thomas (1852-1929)

Occupation(s):	financier - trustee, East St. Louis Terminal Trust writer - *Bibliography of the History of the United States Navy*, c. 1908*
Marriage(s):	M/1 – 1876-1918 – Sophia Child (d. 1918) M/2 – 1919-1929 – Helen Tierney
Address:	Irish Lane, East Islip
Name of estate:	
Year of construction:	
Style of architecture:	
Architect(s):	
Landscape architect(s):	
House extant: unconfirmed	
Historical notes:	

He was the son of Charles Henry and Mary Rebecca Harbeck.

Charles Thomas and Sophia Child Harbeck's son Dr. Charles J. Harbeck married Irene Elizabeth Brouwer, the daughter of Theophilius Anthony and Sophia Frances Rogers Brouwer, Jr. of *Pinewold* in Westhampton. [*See* Spinzia, *Long Island's Prominent Families in the Town of Southampton* – Brouwer entry.]

Their daughters Mildred and Helen did not marry and resided together in a brownstone in Manhattan. In 1932, Mildred, age thirty-five, committed suicide in the Manhattan residence.

*Harbeck's naval history collection consisted of fifteen hundred books and ship logs, forty-six naval medals, numerous historic prints, portraits of virtually all of the nation's prominent naval officers, documents and letters, including one letter written by John Paul Jones. [*The New York Times* August 20, 1916, p. SM6.]

In 1896, Harbeck added to his holdings by purchasing the house of William Gerhardy. [*The Suffolk County News* January 24, 1896, p. 2.]

Harbeck, Charles Thomas (1852-1929)

Occupation(s):	*[See previous entry]*
Marriage(s):	M/1 – 1876-1918 – Sophia Child (d. 1918)
	M/2 – 1919-1929 – Helen Tierney
Address:	Suffolk Lane, East Islip
Name of estate:	*The Pines*
Year of construction:	
Style of architecture:	
Architect(s):	Isaac Henry Green II designed the 1909 house (for Bradish Johnson, Jr.)
Landscape architect(s):	Olmsted, 1915 (for Bradish Johnson, Jr.)
House extant:	first house on the site was destroyed by fire in 1905; second (1909) house was demolished; gatehouse is extant
Historical notes:	

The first house on the site was built by James Boorman Johnston. In 1880, it was purchased from Johnston by Harbeck, who called it *The Pines*.

The *Social Register Summer, 1911* lists Charles T. and Sophia Child Harbeck as residing at *The Pines* in Islip [East Islip.]

[See previous entry for Harbeck family information.]

In 1882, Bradish Johnson, Jr. purchased the house from Harbeck and called it *Woodland*. After it was destroyed by fire, Johnson built a second house on the site, which he also called *Woodland*.

The estate was subsequently inherited by his son Aymar Johnson, who continued to call it *Woodland*.

In 1946, Mrs. Aymar Johnson sold the estate to the Hewlett School of East Islip.

In 2006, the school sold the estate to a developer.

Harbeck, Charles Thomas (1852-1929)

Occupation(s):	*[See previous entry.]*
Marriage(s):	M/1 – 1876-1918 – Sophia Child (d. 1918)
	M/2 – 1919-1929 – Helen Tierney
Address:	South Country Road, West Islip
Name of estate:	
Year of construction:	1880
Style of architecture:	Shingle
Architect(s):	
Landscape architect(s):	
House extant:	no
Historical notes:	

The house, originally named *Sequatogue Farm*, was built by Henry Havemeyer, Sr. It was later owned by Charles Francis Hubbs, who continued call it *Sequatogue Farm*. In 1897, the house was purchased by Harbeck. [*The Brooklyn Daily Eagle* July 2, 1897, p. 5.]

front facade, c. 1903

Hard, Anson Wales, Jr. (1886-1935)

Occupation(s):	financier - stockbroker
Marriage(s):	M/1 – 1908-div. 1932 – Florence Bourne (1886-1969)
	M/2 – 1933-div. – Katherine Potter
Address:	South Country Road, West Sayville
Name of estate:	*Meadow Edge*
Year of construction:	c. 1909
Style of architecture:	Colonial Revival
Architect(s):	Isaac Henry Green II designed the house, barn, gatehouse, and carriage house (for Hard)
Landscape architect(s):	Charles Wellford Leavitt and Sons (for Hard)

House extant: yes
Historical notes:

The house, originally named *Meadow Edge*, was built by Anson Wales Hard, Jr.

He was the son of Anson Wales and Sarah Brown Hard, Sr. of *Driftwood* in Lawrence. His sister Laura married Henry von Lengerke Meyer, Sr. and resided at *Cobblestone Farm* in Suffern, NY. His brother De Courcy married Marjorie Work, the daughter of James Henry and Marie Pierce Warner Work, Sr. of *The Gowans* in Lawrence, and resided at *Briarwood* in Lawrence. His sister Nellie married John Kane Mills and resided at *Ruddington Farm* in Hackettstown, NJ. His sister Sarah married William Reed Taylor, Sr. and resided in Lawrence. His sister Julia married Augustine Jacquelin Smith and resided at *Sunnyside* in Lawrence. [*See* Spinzia, *Long Island's Prominent Families in the Town of Hempstead* – Hard, Smith, Taylor, and Work entries.]

Florence Bourne Hard was the daughter of Frederick Gilbert and Emma Sparks Keeler Bourne, who resided at *Indian Neck Hall* in Oakdale. She later married Robert Barr Deans, Sr., with whom she resided at *Yeadon* on Centre Island, and, subsequently, Alexander Dallas Thayer of Philadelphia, PA. [*See* Spinzia, *Long Island's Prominent North Shore Families, vol. I* – Deans entry.]

[See Bourne entries for additional family information.]

Anson Wales and Florence Bourne Hard, Jr.'s son Frederick married Hildegarde Stevenson, the daughter of Joseph Hutchinson and Hildegarde Kobbe Stevenson. Their daughter Florence married William M. Walthers, Jr. Their son Anson Wales Hard III died before attaining adulthood.

Katherine Potter Hard had previously been married to Joseph W. Hemmersley Avery. After her divorce from Hard, she married Joseph W. Wear of Philadelphia, PA.

In 1966, the estate was sold to Suffolk County. The main residence and its surrounding grounds are the county's West Sayville Golf Course. The carriage house is the headquarters of the Long Island Maritime Museum.

front facade, 1992

Harris, Alfred H. (b. 1852)

Occupation(s):	
Civic Activism:	member, Babylon Draft Exemption Board during World War I; president and director, Babylon Taxpayers Association, 1916
Marriage(s):	1919-1932 – Agnes Ernestine Jacoby (1858-1932)
Address:	11 The Crescent, Babylon
Name of estate:	
Year of construction:	1891
Style of architecture:	Queen Anne
Architect(s):	
Landscape architect(s):	
Builder:	Elmer W. Howell moved the house further south and added several large wings, 1904 (for Harris)

House extant: yes
Historical notes:

The house was built by Benjamin Prince Field, Jr. [*The Brooklyn Daily Eagle* March 4, 1891, p. 1.] In 1903, Harris purchased the house from Field. [*South Side Signal* December 19, 1903, p. 3.]

He was the son of Henry S. and Dora Joel Harris.

Agnes Ernestine Jacoby Harris was the daughter of Samuel and Rosalie Rafelsky Jacoby.

Alfred H. and Agnes Ernestine Jacoby Harris' daughter Rosalie married Stephen Koronski (aka de Koronski), the son of Apolonaire Jacob and Anna Maria Elisa Heidelberger de Koronski. Their son Henry married Margaret Britton and resided in Wyncotte, PA.

In 2006, the house sold for $740,000.

front facade

Havemeyer, Harry Waldron (b. 1929)

Occupation(s):	industrialist - executive vice-president, The National Sugar Refining Co.*
	writer - *Merchants of Williamsburgh*, 1989;
	Along the Great South Bay from Oakdale to Babylon, the Story of a Summer Spa 1840 to 1940, 1996;
	East on the Great South Bay: Sayville and Bayport 1860-1960, 2001;
	Fire Island's Surf Hotel and Other Hostelries on Fire Island Beaches in the Nineteenth Century, 2006
Civic Activism:	trustee, Union Theological Seminary, NYC;
	member, executive council, Episcopal Church of the United States of America;
	treasurer, Episcopal Diocese of New York
Marriage(s):	1951 – Eugenie Aiguier
	- Civic Activism: vice-chairman, board of trustees, Kirkland College**;
	trustee, Vassar College, Poughkeepsie, NY;
	trustee, Hamilton College, Clinton, NY
Address:	South Saxon Avenue, Bay Shore
Name of estate:	
Year of construction:	1960
Style of architecture:	20th century Contemporary
Architect(s):	Francis Day Rogers of Rogers and Butler designed the house (for H. W. Havemeyer)
Landscape architect(s):	
House extant:	yes
Historical notes:	

The house was built by Harry Waldron Havemeyer.

He is the son of Horace and Doris Anna Dick Havemeyer, Sr., who resided at *Olympic Point* in Bay Shore.

Eugenie Aiguier Havemeyer is the daughter of Dr. James Edward and Mrs. Virginia Light Aiguier of Bala–Cynwyd, PA.

Harry Waldron and Eugenie Aiguier Havemeyer's daughter Ann married Tom Richard Strumolo, the son of Richard A. Strumolo of Middlebury, CT, and resides in Norfolk, CT. Their daughter Linden married David Scott Wise, the son of Harry H. Wise, Jr. of Hartsdale, NY, and resides in Manhattan. Their daughter Adaline married Stuart N. Siegel, the son of William Siegel of Mount Vernon, NY, and also resides in Manhattan. Their daughter Eugenie married Julian Pollak, the son of Dr. Victor Pollak, and resides in San Francisco, CA. Their daughter Catherine married Daniel Singer, the son of Jack Singer, and resides in Manhattan. Their daughter Tanya married Dr. Steven Sanford and resides in Greensboro, VT.

[See following Havemeyer entries for additional family information.]

*Claus Doscher, who lived in Sayville and was president of North Side Bank in Brooklyn, was a founder of New York Refining Company, which subsequently merged into The National Sugar Refining as did Mollenhauer Sugar Refining Company, founded by John Mollenhauer, who lived on Awixa Avenue in Bay Shore.

**Kirkland College was a liberal arts college for women which coordinated with Hamilton College in Clinton, NY. It existed for ten years, from 1968 to 1978.

south facade, 2005

Havemeyer, Henry, Sr. (1838-1886)

Occupation(s):	industrialist - president, Havemeyer & Vegelius (tobacco); trustee, Havemeyer Brothers (later, Havemeyer Sugar Refining Co.)
	capitalist - president, Long Island Rail Road; constructed Rockaway Beach Iron Pier; established ferry from Jersey City, NJ, to Hunter's Point, Queens
Marriage(s):	Mary Jane Moller (d. 1889)
Address:	South Country Road, West Islip
Name of estate:	*Sequatogue Farm**
Year of construction:	1880
Style of architecture:	Shingle
Architect(s):	
Landscape architect(s):	
House extant:	no

Historical notes:

The house, originally named *Sequatogue Farm*, was built by Henry Havemeyer.

He was the son of New York City Mayor William Frederick and Mrs. Sarah Agnes Craig Havemeyer, Sr.

Mary Jane Moller Havemeyer was the daughter of Brooklyn sugar refiner William Moller.

Henry and Mary Jane Moller Havemeyer's son William married Clara Stephens, the daughter of Edward and Annie Sutton Stephens. Their daughter Jean married James Adair Campbell.

In 1884, Mary successfully sued Henry, claiming that he was a "habitual drunkard" and unfit to control his finances. [*The New York Times* June 7, 1884, p. 8, and June 3, 1886, p. 5.]

In 1897, the house was purchased by Charles Thomas Harbeck. [*The Brooklyn Daily Eagle* July 2, 1897, p. 5.]

It was subsequently owned by Charles Francis Hubbs, who continued to call it *Sequatogue Farm*.

*The estate was named for the *Sequatogue* [also, *Secatogue*] Indians, who lived in this area of Long Island.

front facade, c. 1903

Havemeyer, Henry, Sr. (1838-1886)

Occupation(s):	*[See previous entry.]*
Marriage(s):	Mary Jane Moller (d. 1889)
Address:	Captree Island Boat Basin, West Islip
Name of estate:	*Armory*
Year of construction:	1880
Style of architecture:	
Architect(s):	
Landscape architect(s):	
House extant:	no

Historical notes:

In 1879, Havemeyer purchased the Whig Inlet House, also known as Stone's Hotel, and converted it into his summer residence.

[See other Havemeyer entries for family information.]

In 1883, Havemeyer leased the house to the Argyle Hotel for use as an adjunct hotel. It was during the first summer as a hotel that President Chester A. Arthur and some of his cabinet member vacationed at the *Armory* for several days. [Harry W. Havemeyer, *Along the Great South Bay From Oakdale to Babylon: The Story of a Summer Spa 1840 to 1940* (Mattituck, NY: Amereon House, 1996), pp. 83-4.]

Havemeyer, Henry Osborne (1847-1907)

Occupation(s):	financier - director, Williamsburgh Trust Co.
	industrialist - managing partner, Havemeyers & Elder (sugar refinery 1862-1891)*;
	founder and president, American Sugar Refining Co.**
	capitalist - developer, "Modern Venice," Islip residential housing development
Civic Activism:	donated 200 feet of shoreline to the Town of Islip for use as a public beach; donated works of art to the Metropolitan Museum of Art, NYC***
Marriage(s):	M/1 – 1870-div.– Mary Louise Elder (1847-1897)
	M/2 – 1883-1907 – Louisine Waldron Elder (1855-1929)
	- writer - "The Suffrage Torch, Memories of a Militant." *Scribner's Magazine*, 1922; "The Prison Special, Memories of a Militant." *Scribner's Magazine*, 1922; "The Waking of Women." (typescript of speech), 1924-1925; *Sixteen to Sixty: Memoirs of a Collector*
	Civic Activism: donated works of art to the Metropolitan Museum of Art, NYC***;
	a founder, Big Sisters, Inc.;
	suffragist - active in Woman's Suffrage Movement
Address:	137 West Bayberry Road, Islip
Name of estate:	*Bayberry Point*
Year of construction:	1899-1900
Style of architecture:	Moorish
Architect(s):	Grosvenor Atterbury designed the house (for H. O. H.)****
Builder:	Sturgis & Hill, NYC
Landscape architect(s):	Nathan F. Barrett (for H. O. H.)*****
Builder:	*[See Jabez Ephraim Van Order entry.]*
House extant:	yes, but substantially altered
Historical notes:	

home of H. O. Havemeyer, left foreground; home of H. Havemeyer, Sr., right background

   The house, originally named *Bayberry Point*, was built by Henry Osborne Havemeyer as his own residence in his "Modern Venice" development.
   He was one of ten children of Frederick Christian and Sarah Louise Henderson Havemeyer.
   Mary Louise Elder Havemeyer was the daughter of George and Hanna Riker Elder.
   Louisine Waldron Elder Havemeyer was the daughter of George William and Mathilda Adelaide Elder. Her sister Anne married Henry Norcross Munn. Her brother George married Therese Cadwell and resided in Bay Shore. Her sister Adaline married Samuel Twyford Peters, Jr. and resided at *Windholme* in Islip.
   Henry Osborne and Louisine Waldron Elder Havemeyer's daughter Adaline married Peter Hood Ballantine Frelinghuysen. Their son Horace married Doris Anna Dick and resided at *Olympic Point* in Bay Shore. Their daughter Electra married James Watson Webb, Sr. and resided at *Woodbury House* in Syosset and in Old Westbury before relocating to Shelburne, VT. [*See* Spinzia, *Long Island's Prominent North Shore Families*, vol. II– Webb entry.]
   [See other Havemeyer entries for additional family information.]
   *In 1891, the sugar refining division of Havemeyers & Elder was merged into the American Sugar Refining Company. The remaining property, not used in the sugar refining business, was retained by Havemeyers & Elder as a Brooklyn real estate holding company until the 1950s.
   **Havemeyer's Sugar Trust was second only to the Standard Oil Trust. The American Sugar Refining Co. controlled more than fifty-percent of the nation's sugar refining. [Frances Westzenhoffer, *The Havemeyers: Impressionism Comes to America* (New York: Harry N. Abrams, Inc. Publishers, 1986), p. 69.]
   ***The Havemeyers donated 1,912 paintings and art objects to the Metropolitan Museum of Art. [Westzenhoffer, p. 11.]
   ****The sales brochure for "Modern Venice" states that the Moorish-style architecture was suggested by Louis Comfort Tiffany.
   *****The sales brochure also states that "Modern Venice" would be devoid of trees and vegetation and that Nathan F. Barrett was the landscape architect.
   The house was later owned by Frank Gulden, Sr. and, subsequently, by Dr. David Dodge Moore.

Havemeyer, Horace, Jr. (1914-1990)

Occupation(s):	industrialist - president, The National Sugar Refining Co.; director, Amalgamated Sugar Co.
	financier - director, The New York Trust Co. (later, Chemical Bank, then, Chase Bank, and now, J. P. Morgan Chase)
Civic Activism:	member of board, Huntington Hospital, Huntington; member of board, Drew University, Madison, NJ; trustee, East Woods School, Oyster Bay Cove; a founder, Bayberry Yacht Club
Marriage(s):	1939-1990 - Rosalind Anne Everdell (1917-2002)
Address:	68 East Bayberry Road, Islip
Name of estate:	
Year of construction:	1899-1900
Style of architecture:	Moorish
Architect(s):	Grosvenor Atterbury designed the house (for H. O. Havemeyer)*
Landscape architect(s):	Nathan F. Barrett (for H. O. Havemeyer)**
Builder:	*[See Jabez Ephraim Van Order entry.]*

House extant: yes; but altered
Historical notes:

   The house was built by Henry Osborne Havemeyer as part of his "Modern Venice" development. It was later owned by his grandson Horace Havemeyer, Jr.
   Rosalind Everdell Havemeyer was the daughter of William K. and Ella Rosalind Romeyn Everdell, Jr. who resided in North Hills. [*See* Spinzia, *Long Island's Prominent North Shore Families, vol. I* – Everdell entry.]
   The Havemeyers' daughter Rosalind married Christopher du Pont Roosevelt, the son of Franklin Delano and Ethel du Pont Roosevelt, Jr. of Woodbury, and resides in Lyme, CT. Their son Horace Havemeyer III married Eugenie C. Cowan and resides in Manhattan. Their son William Everdell Havemeyer married Jane Litzenberg and also resides in Manhattan. Their son Christian Havemeyer, who resides at *The Reward* in Chestertown, MD, is a bachelor.
   [See other Havemeyer entries for additional family information.]
   *The sale brochure for "Modern Venice" states that the Moorish-style architecture was suggested by Louis Comfort Tiffany.
   **The sales brochure also states that "Modern Venice" would be devoid of trees and vegetation and that Nathan F. Barrett was the landscape architect.

front facade, 2006

Havemeyer, Horace, Sr. (1886-1956)

Occupation(s):	industrialist -	president, Havemeyers & Elder (sugar refinery 1862-1891)*;
		director, Remington Arms Co.;
		director, Cuban–American, Cape Cruz, Manati, Great Western, Central Romana, San Domingo, Sante Fe, Warren–Cuba Cane, W. J. McCahan, and South Puerto Rico Sugar Company (sugar cane and sugar beet companies);
		director, Savannah Sugar Refining Co.;
		president, Scranton & Lehigh Coal Co.
	capitalist -	director, Lackawanna & Western Railroad;
		director, Brooklyn Eastern District Terminal
	shipping -	director, American–Hawaiian Steamship Co.
	financier -	director, Bankers Trust Co.;
		director, International Acceptance Bank, Inc;
		director, Lackawanna Securities Co.
Civic Activism:		trustee, Metropolitan Museum of Art, NYC;
		trustee, Frick Museum, NYC;
		sugar and food consultant to federal government during World War I
Marriage(s):		1911-1956 – Doris Anna Dick (1890-1982)
Address:		117 West Bayberry Road, Islip
Name of estate:		
Year of construction:		1899-1900
Style of architecture:		Moorish
Architect(s):		Grosvenor Atterbury designed the house (for H. O. Havemeyer)**
Landscape architect(s):		Nathan F. Barrett (for H. O. Havemeyer)***
Builder:		*[See Jabez Ephraim Van Order entry.]*

House extant: yes, but substantially altered****
Historical notes:

The house was built by Henry Osborne Havemeyer as part of his "Modern Venice" development. After his marriage, Horace Havemeyer, Sr., resided in the house next to his widowed mother. He continued to reside there until 1918, when he built *Olympic Point* in Bay Shore.
[See following entry for family information.]

*In 1891, the sugar refining division of Havemeyers & Elder was merged into the American Sugar Refining Company. The remaining property, not used in the sugar refining business, was retained by Havemeyers & Elder as a Brooklyn real estate holding company until the 1950s.

In the late 1940s, Frank Gulden, Sr. relocated to this house from 137 Bayberry Road.

**The sales brochure for "Modern Venice" states that the Moorish-style architecture was suggested by Louis Comfort Tiffany.

***The sales brochure also states that "Modern Venice" would be devoid of trees and vegetation and that Nathan F. Barrett was the landscape architect.

****The flat roof style was eliminated by a subsequent owner.

front facade, 2006

Havemeyer, Horace, Sr. (1886-1956)

Occupation(s):	*[See previous entry.]*
Civic Activism:	*[See previous entry.]*
Marriage(s):	1911-1956 – Doris Anna Dick (1890-1982)
Address:	South Saxon Avenue, Bay Shore
Name of estate:	*Olympic Point*
Year of construction:	1917-1919
Style of architecture:	Modified Cotswold
Architect(s):	Harrie T. Lindeberg designed the house (for Horace Havemeyer, Sr.)
	Alfred Hopkins designed the farm complex (for Horace Havemeyer, Sr.)
Landscape architect(s):	Olmsted Brothers (for Horace Havemeyer, Sr.)

House extant: no; demolished in 1948*
Historical notes:

The house, originally named *Olympic Point*, was built by Horace Havemeyer, Sr.
He was the son of Henry Osborne and Louisine Waldron Elder Havemeyer, who resided at *Bayberry Point* in Islip.
Doris Anna Dick Havemeyer was the daughter of John Henry and Julia Theodora Mollenhauer Dick, who resided at *Allen Winden Farm* in Islip. Her brother William Karl Dick, who married Madeline Force and, subsequently, Virginia K. Conner, also resided at *Allen Winden Farm* in Islip. Her sister Julia married William Kingsland Macy, Sr. and resided in Islip. Her brother Adolph, a bachelor, resided in Islip.
Horace and Doris Anna Dick Havemeyer, Sr.'s daughter Doris married Dr. Daniel Catlin, Sr. and resided in Bay Shore. Their daughter Adaline married Richard Sturgis Perkins, Sr. and, subsequently, Laurance B. Rand of Southport, CT. Their son Horace Havemeyer, Jr. married Rosalind Everdell and resided in Islip and, later, in Dix Hills. [*See* Spinzia, *Long Island's Prominent North Shore Families, vol. I* – Havemeyer entry.] Their son Harry married Eugenie Aiguier and resides on the *Olympic Point* property in Bay Shore.
[See other Havemeyer entries for additional family information.]
*Horace Havemeyer, Sr. engaged E. W. Howell & Co. to demolish the house in 1948 and build a smaller Colonial-style house on the property for his family.

main staircase

Horace Havemeyer, Sr. estate, *Olympic Point*

south facade

south and west facade

SOUTH

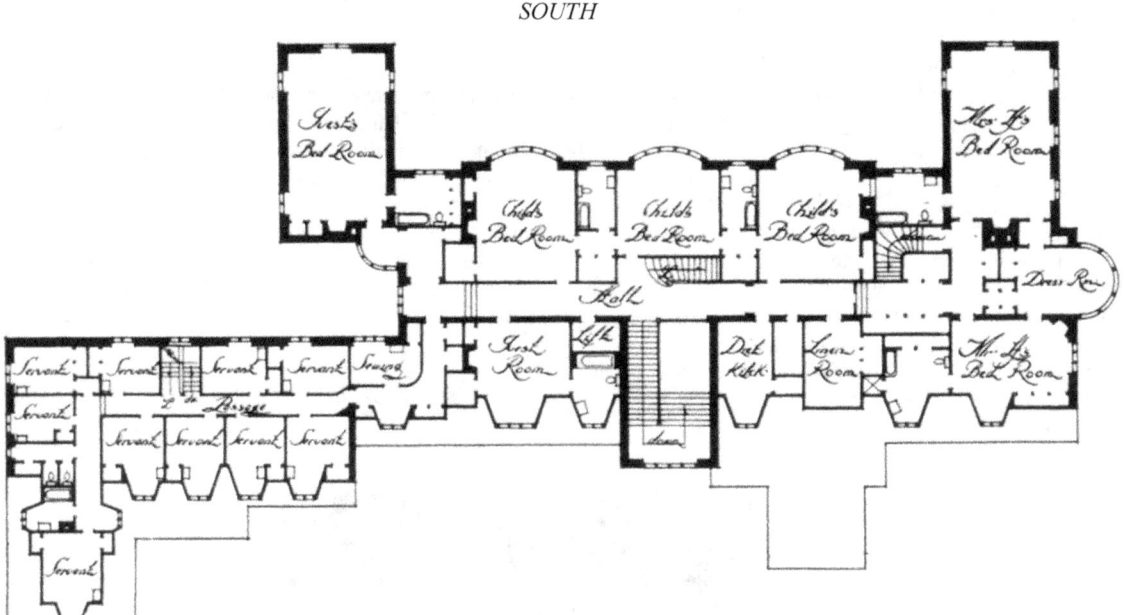

EAST   *second floor plan*   WEST

west facade

north facade

Hawkins, William Elton (1865-1951)

Occupation(s):	industrialist - founder and president, American Brass and Copper Co.; a founder, Donlon and Miller Co., Brooklyn (manufacturer of fixtures)
Marriage(s):	M/1 – 1874-div. 1909 – Nellie C. Jones M/2 – 1914 – Cornelia Udall Bergen (1862-1945)
Address:	South Country Road, Copiague
Name of estate:	*Wild Goose Farm*
Year of construction:	c. 1910
Style of architecture:	Modified Shingle
Architect(s):	
Landscape architect(s):	
House extant:	no
Historical notes:	

Wild Goose Farm

The forty-room house, originally named *Wild Goose Farm*, was built by William Elton Hawkins.

He was the son of William and Theda Elton Hawkins of Derby, CT.

Cornelia Udall Bergen Hawkins was the daughter of Victor B. and Cornelia J. Udall Bergen. She had previously been married to Frederick Schuchardt Stuyvesant.

In 1926, Hawkins sold the estate to Louis G. Gosdorfer, Inc.

In the late 1930's, the house became the Nassau–Suffolk General Hospital. It remained a hospital until the 1970s as the Lakeside Hospital.

A portion of the estate's property is currently the site of Lakeside Manor Apartments.

Hawkins was residing on Saxon Avenue in Bay Shore at the time of his death.

Hawley, Edwin (1850-1912)

Occupation(s):	capitalist* -	director, Southern Pacific Railroad;
		president, Minneapolis & St. Louis Railroad;
		director, Chesapeake & Ohio Railroad;
		director, Iowa Central Railroad;
		director, Missouri, Kansas & Texas Railroad;
		director, Toledo, St. Louis, & Western Railroad;
		director, Chicago & Alton Railroad
	shipping -	director, Pacific Mail Steamship Co.

Marriage(s): bachelor

Address: Parkwood and George Street, West Islip
Name of estate: *Effingham Towers*
Year of construction: 1898
Style of architecture: Colonial Revival
Architect(s): Charles Pierrepont Henry Gilbert designed the house (for Hawley)
Builder: Harvey Murdock
Landscape architect(s): William Roe Jones designed the 1910 waterfall / dam complex (for Hawley)**

House extant: no; destroyed by arson, 1958
Historical notes:

Edwin Hawley purchased the Effingham Brown Sutton, Jr. residence *Effingham Park* and demolished it. He built a fourteen-bedroom, seven-bathroom house on the site and called it *Effingham Towers*. [information confirmed from the research of Bill Jantz, November 2012]

*Hawley was president or director of forty-one companies.

Because he died intestate, his fortune, which was valued at $5,828,322, was divided among relatives who agreed that Hawley's ward Miss Edna Cornelia Cameron (aka Miss Edna Cornelia Sturges) would receive $50,000, his Manhattan residence, and *Effingham Towers* which were valued at $433,100 and an annual income from a trust fund of $25,000. [*South Side Signal* April 10, 1914, p. 1, and *The Beacon* July 19, 2019, p .2.]

The house was purchased by the Haarman family, who operated it as the Parkwood Lake Mansion and Inn from 1926 to 1938. It then was the site of the Parkwood Lake Private School until 1949. In 1951, the West Islip School District used it for grades five and six.

**The estate's waterfall / dam complex was demolished in the 1960s when Montauk Highway and Route 231 were widened.

James Hazen Hyde's private railroad car "Bay Shore" was purchased by Hawley.

front facade

Hayward, Frank Earle, Sr. (1869-1923)

Occupation(s):

Marriage(s): 1905-1923 – Kathleen Gilbert (d. 1960)

Address: Green Avenue, Sayville
Name of estate: *Joy Farm*
Year of construction: c. 1892
Style of architecture: Shingle
Architect(s): Isaac Henry Green II designed the house (for F. E. Hayward, Sr.)
Landscape architect(s):
House extant: yes
Historical notes:

rear facade

The house, originally named *Joy Farm*, was built by Frank Earle Hayward, Sr.

The *Brooklyn Blue Book and Long Island Society Register, 1918* lists Frank Earle and Kathleen Gilbert Hayward [Sr.] as residing at *Joy Farm* in Sayville.

He was the son of New York City Tax Commissioner John Nelson Hayward and his wife Sarah J. Tyson Hayward. His brother William Tyson Hayward, Sr. married Martha Eugenia Wemple. They resided at *The Anchorage*, also on Green Avenue in Sayville.

Kathleen Gilbert Hayward was the daughter of Maurice L. and Kate L. Gilbert of Patchogue. She subsequently married Admiral Richard Philip McCullough and resided in North Plainfield, NJ.

Frank Earle and Kathleen Gilbert Hayward, Sr.'s son Frank Earle Gilbert, Jr. moved to California. Their daughter Kathleen married Owen Atkinson and resided in La Jolla, CA.

[See other Hayward entries for additional family information.]

The house, which was enlarged in 1911, was sold in 1935 to Gustave Adolph Helm. I.

It was purchased in c. 1948 by Curtis Davis of the Davis Brothers Engineering firm and moved by barge to Blue Point where Curtis and his wife Lillian made it their residence. The house is currently located at the corner of Middle Road and Atlantic Avenue. [*Bayport – Blue Point Gazette* April 2011, p. 21.]

Hayward, William Tyson, Jr. (d. 1956)

Occupation(s): industrialist - oil

Marriage(s): 1910 – Jane Louise Baumann (1888-1976)

Address: 87 Argyle Avenue, Babylon
Name of estate:
Year of construction: c. 1907
Style of architecture: Eclectic Queen Anne
Architect(s):
Landscape architect(s):
House extant: yes
Historical notes:

side / front facade, 2006

In 1923, Hayward purchased Cecil Calvert Evers' house. [*The Suffolk County News* February 2, 1923, p. 5.]

By 1929 the Haywards had relocated to Cedar Lane.

The *Long Island Society Register, 1929* lists William Tyson and Jane Louise Baumann Hayward, Jr. as residing on Cedar Lane in Babylon.

He was the son of William Tyson and Martha Eugenia Wemple Hayward, Sr., who resided at *The Anchorage* in Sayville.

Jane Louise Baumann Hayward was the daughter of Dr. Louis and Mrs. Letitia Cadwell Baumann. Jane subsequently married Frank Sutton of *The Cloister* in Babylon and *North East Farm* in North Babylon.

William Tyson and Jane Louise Bauman Hayward, Jr.'s son William Tyson Hayward III married Beverly Marion Frost, the daughter of John Patterson Frost of Winnipeg, Canada. Their daughter Janet married Eugene Kelly of Bermuda.

[See other Hayward entries for additional family information.]

Hayward, William Tyson, Sr. (1857-1921)

Occupation(s):	industrialist - president, Jay C. Wemple Co. (manufacturer of window shades)
Marriage(s):	1885-1921 – Martha Eugenia Wemple (1860-1937) - Civic Activism: chairman, American Red Cross, in Sayville, during World War I
Address:	486 Green Avenue, Sayville
Name of estate:	*The Anchorage*
Year of construction:	1893
Style of architecture:	Shingle
Architect(s):	Isaac Henry Green II designed the house and carriage house (for W. T. Hayward, Sr.)
Landscape architect(s):	
House extant:	no*
Historical notes:	

The house, originally named *The Anchorage*, was built by William Tyson Hayward, Sr.

The *Brooklyn Blue Book and Long Island Society Register, 1918* lists William Tyson and Martha Eugenia Wemple Hayward [Sr.] as residing at *The Anchorage* in Sayville.

front facade, c. 1892

He was the son of New York City Tax Commissioner John Nelson Hayward and his wife Sarah J. Tyson Hayward. His brother Frank Earle Hayward, Sr. married Kathleen Gilbert and resided at *Joy Farm*, also on Green Avenue.

Martha Eugenia Wemple Hayward was the daughter of Jay Cady and Rachel J. Nevins Wemple of Brooklyn.

William Tyson and Martha Eugenia Wemple Hayward, Sr.'s son William Tyson Hayward, Jr. married Jane Louise Baumann and resided in Babylon. Their son Dudley, who also resided in Babylon, married Hannah Matilda Francis, the daughter of Frank and Mary Elizabeth Francis.

[See other Hayward entries for additional family information.]

In 1920, Hayward sold the house to developer Emil Kupler.

*Kupler cut the house in half and sold it as separate residences. He also subdivided the property for a housing development.

Heckscher, Charles Augustus, Jr. (1849-1936)

Occupation(s):	capitalist - Florida fruit grower
Marriage(s):	1894 – Emelia Isabelle Thebaud (1867-1938)
Address:	*[unable to determine street address]*, Islip
Name of estate:	
Year of construction:	
Style of architecture:	
Architect(s):	
Landscape architect(s):	
House extant:	unconfirmed
Historical notes:	

The Long Island Society Register, 1929 lists Charles A. and Emelia I. Thebaud Heckscher, Jr. as residing in Islip.

He was the son of Charles Augustus and Georgiana Louisa Coster Heckscher, Sr. of Quogue. [*See* Spinzia, *Long Island's Prominent Families in the Town of Southampton* – Heckscher entry.]

Emelia Isabelle Thebaud Heckscher was the daughter of Edward B. and Julia Moller Thebaud.

Charles Augustus and Emelia Isabelle Thebaud Heckscher, Jr.'s. daughter Georgiana married John Hancock Tweed and resided in Manhattan.

Heins, John Lewis, Sr. (1844-1929)

Occupation(s):	capitalist - president, Brooklyn City and Newtown Railroad Co.; president and chairman of board, Coney Island and Brooklyn Railroad Co. (which merged into Brooklyn Rapid Transit Co.); director, DeKalb Avenue and North Beach Railroad Co.
	financier - director, National City Bank of Brooklyn; director, Long Island Safe Deposit Co.
Marriage(s):	M/1 – 1871 – Eliza Anna Zundt
	M/2 – 1907-1929 – Margaret Boscher (1875-1934)
Address:	South Country Road, West Islip
Name of estate:	
Year of construction:	
Style of architecture:	Victorian
Architect(s):	
Landscape architect(s):	
House extant:	yes
Historical notes:	

front facade

In 1901, John Lewis Heins, Sr. purchased the residence of Richard Higbie. [*The Suffolk County News* March 15, 1901, p. 1.]

He was the son of Carsten and Anna Evers Heins.

John's daughter Helen married George Walsh, the son of William W. Walsh of Brooklyn, and, subsequently, John Conway of Salem, MA. His daughter Marguerite married R. M. Mansfield. His son John Lewis Heins, Jr. resided in Garden City.

Helm, Gustave Adolph (1860-1926)

Occupation(s):	merchant - partner, Nau and Helm, Brooklyn; manager, furniture, carpet, and upholstery departments, Frederick Loeser and Co.
	financier - director, The Borough Bank of Brooklyn
Marriage(s):	1900-1926 – Evelyn J. Geary (1866-1948)
Address:	Green Avenue, Sayville
Name of estate:	
Year of construction:	1906
Style of architecture:	Shingle
Architect(s):	Isaac Henry Green designed the house (for F. E. Hayward Sr.)
Landscape architect(s):	
House extant:	yes
Historical notes:	

front facade

The house, originally named *Joy Farm*, was built by Frank Earle Hayward, Sr. It was purchased in 1935 by Helm. [*The Patchogue Advance* May 24, 1935, p. 12.]

The *Long Island Society Register, 1929* lists Gustave A. and Evelyn Geary Helm as residing on Green Avenue, Sayville.

He was the son of George A. and Anna M. Helm of Brooklyn.

Mrs. Helm was residing at the estate at the time of her death.

The house, which was enlarged in 1911, was purchased in c. 1948 by Curtis Davis of the Davis Brothers engineering firm and moved by barge to Blue Point where Curtis and his wife Lillian made it their residence. The house is currently located at the corner of Middle Road and Atlantic Avenue. [*Bayport–Blue Point Gazette* April 2011, p. 21.]

Hepburn, Henry Charles, Jr. (1826-1912)

Occupation(s):	financier - stockbroker
Civic Activism:	election inspector, Town of Babylon; trustee, Town of Islip Schools
Marriage(s):	1856-1912 – Elizabeth Sarah Eytinge (1829-1915)
Address:	South Country Road, West Islip
Name of estate:	*The Firs*
Year of construction:	
Style of architecture:	
Architect(s):	
Landscape architect(s):	
House extant:	unconfirmed
Historical notes:	

Henry Charles Hepburn, Jr. was the son of Henry Charles and Maria Chardavoyne Hepburn, Sr.

An intimate friend of Daniel Webster and President Chester A. Arthur, Hepburn was, at the time of his death, reputed to be the oldest telegrapher in the world. [*The New York Times* June 16, 1915, p. 11.]

Elizabeth Sarah Eytinge Hepburn was the daughter of Solomon and Mary Anne Miller Eytinge.

Henry Charles and Elizabeth Sarah Eytinge Hepburn, Jr.'s son Henry Chester Hepburn married Silvie Livingston Strong and resided in Babylon.

[See following entry for additional family information.]

Hepburn, Henry Chester (1859-1921)

Occupation(s):	financier - stockbroker
Civic Activism:	member, board of managers, Southside Hospital, Bay Shore (now, South Shore University Hospital)

Marriage(s):	1911-1921 – Silvie Livingston Strong (1874-1935)
	 - Civic Activism: suffragist –
	  a founder and vice president, Babylon chapter, Equal Suffrage Society, 1912;
	  participated in Manhattan suffrage parades, 1913

Address:	44 Douglas Avenue, Babylon
Name of estate:	*Bide a Wee*
Year of construction:	
Style of architecture:	Modified Dutch Colonial Revival
Architect(s):	
Landscape architect(s):	
House extant:	yes
Historical notes:	

front facade, 2006

The *Social Register Summer, 1915* lists Henry Chester and Silvie L. Strong Hepburn as residing at *Bide a Wee* in Babylon.

He was the son of Henry Charles and Elizabeth Sarah Eytinge Hepburn, Jr., who resided at *The Firs* in West Islip.

Silvie Livingston Strong Hepburn was the daughter of James H. and Georgiana Louisa Berryman Strong of Babylon. She had previously been married to Richard Bayley Post. The Posts' daughter Aletla married John Timothy McMahon and resided in the Manhasset area of Long Island, as did her sister Elizabeth, who did not marry.

The *Long Island Society Register, 1929* lists Silvie Strong Hepburn as residing at 44 Douglas Avenue, Babylon.

[See previous entry for additional family information.]
[For information on the Southside Hospital, see Cooper entry.]

Higbie, Richard (1857-1900)

Occupation(s):	politician - supervisor, Town of Babylon; member, New York State Assembly, 1893, 1894, 1895; member, New York State Senate, 1896-1998; member, New York State Republican Committee financer - vice-president and director, Babylon National Bank; director, Bank of Amityville; director, South Side Bank capitalist - director, Sumpwams Water Works Co.
Civic Activism:	president, Babylon Board of Education
Marriage(s):	1885-1900 – Anna Smith Robbins (1865-1942)
Address:	South Country Road, West Islip
Name of estate:	
Year of construction:	
Style of architecture:	
Architect(s):	
Landscape architect(s):	
House extant: unconfirmed	
Historical notes:	

Anna Smith Robbins Higbie was the daughter of John and Selinda E. Smith Robbins.

Richard and Anna Smith Robbins Higbie's son John married Amy Marguerite Deady, the daughter of Charles and Corinne Louise Hopper Deady. Their son Edwin died in 1901 at the age of twenty-one.

Hobbs, Charles Buxton (1863-1944)

Occupation(s):	attorney - partner, Gifford, Hobbs, and Beard capitalist - a founder, County Light and Power Co.; director, Suffolk, Nassau and Queens Realty Co. industrialist - director, Suffolk Fertilizer Co.
Civic Activism:	member, advisory board, Islip chapter, American Red Cross
Marriage(s):	1893-1944 – Mary E. Minor (1869-1960)
Address:	Great River Road, Great River
Name of estate:	*River Croft*
Year of construction:	c. 1900
Style of architecture:	Shingle
Architect(s):	
Landscape architect(s):	
House extant: no; demolished in 1960	
Historical notes:	

The house, originally named *River Croft*, was built by Charles Buxton Hobbs.

The *Brooklyn Blue Book and Long Island Society Register, 1918* lists Charles Buxton and Mary E. Minor Hobbs as residing at *River Croft* in Great River.

He was the son of Edward Harmon and Julia Ellen Buxton Hobbs.

Mary E. Minor Hobbs was the daughter of Thomas Franklin and Mary Eliza Minor.

Charles Buxton and Mary E. Minor Hobbs' son Edward died in 1902 at the age of seven.

River Croft

Hodges, George Winthrop, Sr. (1869-1935)

Occupation(s):	financier - partner, Remick, Hodges and Co. (investment banking firm)
Civic Activism:	vice-president, Private Bankers Association; president, Investment Bankers' Association; director, New York State Bankers Association; president, Better Business Bureau of New York City; assistant director, Government Loan Organization during World War I
Marriage(s):	1905-1910 – Maita Angus Marvin (1875-1910) - Civic Activism: regent, New Jersey Daughters of the American Revolution
Address:	117 Awixa Avenue, Bay Shore
Name of estate:	
Year of construction:	
Style of architecture:	Shingle
Architect(s):	
Landscape architect(s):	

House extant: no
Historical notes:

The house was built by Rudolph Oelsner, who by 1906 had relocated to Long Island's North Shore. It was later owned by Hodges.

The *Social Register Summer, 1915* lists George W. Hodges as residing in Bay Shore.

He was the son of Joseph Francis and Caroline Elizabeth Andrews Hodges.

Maita Angus Marvin Hodges was the daughter of Charles Matthew and Mary Melanchthon Whelpley Marvin.

In 1923, Hodges sold the house to James P. Kelly, who called it *Awixaway*.

Hollins, Gerald Vanderbilt, Sr. (1886-1955)

Occupation(s):	financier - Charles D. Halsey (investment banking firm)
Civic Activism:	donated a portion of his estate to the Town of Islip for a nature preserve
Marriage(s):	1909-div. 1937 – Virginia Kobbe (1891-1947)
Address:	180 Bay View Avenue, East Islip
Name of estate:	*The Hawks*
Year of construction:	1912
Style of architecture:	Modified-Shingle
Architect(s):	Cross & Cross designed the house (for G. V. Hollins, Sr.)
Landscape architect(s):	

House extant: yes
Historical notes:

The house, originally named *The Hawks*, was built by Gerald Vanderbilt Hollins, Sr.

The *Long Island Society Register, 1929* lists Gerald Vanderbilt and Virginia Kobbe Hollins [Sr.] as residing at *The Hawks* in East Islip.

He was the son of Harry Bowly and Evelina Meserole Knapp Hollins, Sr., who resided at *Meadow Farm* in East Islip.

Virginia Kobbe Hollins was the daughter of Gustav and Carolyn Wheeler Kobbe of Babylon. Virginia subsequently married Henry Morgan, with whom she continued to reside in East Islip. Her sister Hildegarde married Joseph Hutchinson Stevenson and, subsequently, Francis Burritt Thorne, Sr., with whom she resided at *Brookwood* in East Islip. Her sister Carol married Robert Woodward Morgan, Sr. and also resided in East Islip. Carol subsequently married George Palen Snow of Syosset. [*See* Spinzia, *Long Island's Prominent North Shore Families, vol. II*– Snow entry.] Virginia's sister Beatrice married Raymond D. Little. Her brother George married Marjorie W. Goss.

Gerald Vanderbilt and Virginia Kobbe Hollins, Sr.'s son Gerald Vanderbilt Hollins, Jr. married Elizabeth Armour, the daughter of Lester Armour, Sr. of Chicago, IL, and Southampton. [*See* Spinzia, *Long Island's Prominent Families in the Town of Southampton* – Armour entry.] Their daughter Faith married Arthur W. Little and, subsequently, Charles Gulden III and resided in Islip. Their daughter Phyllis married John Grissom. Their son John remained a bachelor.

[See other Hollins entries for additional family information.]

front facade

Hollins, Harry Bowly, Jr. (1882-1956)

Occupation(s):	financier - partner, H. N. Whitney, Goadby and Co. (stock brokerage firm)
	industrialist - director, Perkin Elmer Corp. (optical instrument manufacturer);
	director, Marcaibo Oil Exploration Co.
Civic Activism:	member, Red Cross Auxiliary during World War I;
	a founder and director, Great River Club, 1920 (later, Timber Point Club)
Marriage(s):	1904-1956 – Lilias Livingston (1882-1976)
Address:	18 Crick Holly Lane, East Islip
Name of estate:	*Crickholly*
Year of construction:	1907
Style of architecture:	Georgian Revival
Architect(s):	Cross & Cross designed the house (for H. B. Hollins, Jr.)
Landscape architect(s):	
House extant: yes	
Historical notes:	

rear facade, c. 1912

The house, originally named *Crickholly*, was built by Harry Bowly Hollins, Jr.

The *Long Island Society Register, 1929* lists Harry B. and Lilias Livingston Hollins, Jr. as residing at *Crickholly* in East Islip.

He was the son of Harry Bowly and Evelina Meserole Knapp Hollins, Sr., who resided at *Meadow Farm* in East Islip.

Lilias Livingston Hollins was the daughter of Henry Beekman and Frances Redmond Livingston, Jr. of Bay Shore.

Harry Bowly and Lilias Livingston Hollins, Jr.'s son Harry Bowly Hollins III married Elizabeth Wolcott Elkins, the daughter of William M. Elkins of Elkins Park, PA, and, subsequently, Elizabeth Jay, the daughter of DeLancey Kane and Elizabeth Sarah Morgan Jay of Old Westbury. [*See* Spinzia, *Long Island's Prominent Families, vol. I* – Jay entry.] Their son Robert married Lorraine Young, the daughter of B. Loring Young of Weston, MA. Their daughter Evelina married Henry L. Hoguet and resided in Katonah, NY. Their daughter Hope did not marry.

[See other Hollins entries for additional family information.]

In 2021, the 9,000-square-foot house with seven bedrooms and five-and-a-half bathrooms on 1.38 acres was for sale. The asking price was $1.95 million; the annual taxes were $16,679.

rear facade, 2021

Hollins, Harry Bowly, Sr. (1854-1938)

Occupation(s):	financier - a founder, with H. Duncan Wood, H. B. Hollins and Co. (stock brokerage firm);
	a founder, Knickerbocker Trust Co.;
	president, Central Railroad & Banking Co. of Georgia;
	president, International Bank of Mexico;
	director, Corporation Trust Co. of America;
	director, North American Safe Deposit Co.
	capitalist - director, Central Union Gas Corp.;
	director, Union Gas Co.;
	director, Long Island Motor Parkway, Inc.
	industrialist - director, Havana Tobacco Co.
Civic Activism:	a founder and trustee, Waverly Gun Club, 1890;
	trustee, East Islip School District, 1897
Marriage(s):	1877-1938 – Evelina Meserole Knapp (1854-1938)
Address:	Hollins Lane, East Islip
Name of estate:	*Meadow Farm*
Year of construction:	c. 1880
Style of architecture:	Shingle
Architect(s):	
Landscape architect(s):	Olmsted (for H. B. Hollins, Sr.)

House extant: no; demolished in 2003*
Historical notes:

The house, originally named *Meadow Farm*, was built by Harry Bowly Hollins, Sr.

The *Long Island Society Register, 1929* lists Harry B. and Evelina Knapp Hollins [Sr.] as residing at *Meadow Farm* in East Islip.

He was the son of Francis and Elizabeth Coles Morris Hollins. His sister Alice married Harry Ingersoll Nicholas, Sr. and resided in Babylon.

Evelina Meserole Knapp Hollins was the daughter of William Kumbel and Maria Meserole Knapp, who resided in Islip. Her sister Maria did not marry.

Harry Bowly and Evelina Meserole Knapp Hollins, Sr.'s son Harry Bowly Hollins, Jr. married Lilias Livingston and resided at *Crickholly* in East Islip. Their son Gerald married Virginia Kobbe and resided at *The Hawks* in East Islip.

Harry Bowly and Evelina Meserole Knapp Hollins, Sr.'s Manhattan residence is currently the Argentine Consulate.

[See other Hollins entries for additional family information.] Their daughter Marion was a prominent golfer who designed golf courses. In 1921, she won the U. S. Women's Amateur Golf Championship. She was inducted into the Suffolk Sports Hall of Fame in 2002 and will be inducted into the World Golf Hall of Fame.

In 1940, the estate was sold to Charles Lanier Lawrence.

*The estate's stable and clock tower were purchased by Henry Morgan for use as his residence. In the 1980s, the carriage house was demolished. The farmhouse at 42 Blackmore Lane is also extant.

rear facade

Hollister, Buell, Sr. (1883-1966)

Occupation(s):	financier - partner, Hollister and Babcock (stock brokerage firm); partner, Pyne, Kendall and Hollister (stock brokerage firm)
	capitalist - chairman of board, Cornell–Dublilier Electric Corp.; president, Cayuga & Susquehanna Railroad; director, Stentor Electric
	industrialist - president, Inde Gold Mining Co.; chairman of board, Dubilier Condenser Corp.
Civic Activism:	trustee and treasurer, Southside Hospital, Bay Shore (now, South Shore University Hospital)
Marriage(s):	1912-1963 – Louise R. Knowlton (1886-1963)
Address:	St. Mark's Lane, Islip
Name of estate:	
Year of construction:	
Style of architecture:	
Architect(s):	
Landscape architect(s):	
House extant: unconfirmed	

Historical notes:

The *Brooklyn Blue Book and Long Island Society Register, 1921* lists Mr. and Mrs. Buell Hollister [Sr.] as residing on St. Mark's Lane, Islip.

He was the son of Henry Hutchinson and Sarah Louise Howell Hollister, Sr. of Islip.

Louise R. Knowlton Hollister was the daughter of Danford Henry and Minnie B. Jones Knowlton of Manhattan. Her sister Edith married Allan Appleton Robbins and resided at *Dolancothy Lodge* in Locust Valley. Her sister Natalie married J. Insely Blair and resided in Tuxedo, NY. Her sister Madeleine, who married John E. Cowdin, also resided in Tuxedo, NY.

Buell and Louise R. Knowlton Hollister, Sr.'s son Buell Hollister, Jr. married Eileen Bramwell, the daughter of Gerald A. Bramwell. *[See following entry for additional family information.]*

[For information on the Southside Hospital, see Cooper entry.]

Hollister, Henry Hutchinson, Sr. (1842-1909)

Occupation(s):	financier - partner, Hollister and Babcock (stock brokerage firm)
	capitalist - director, Burlington, Cedar Rapids and Northern Railroad; Durango Central Railroad Co.; Durango Development Co.; Keokuk and Des Moines Railroad Co.; Madison Square Garden Co.; Peoria and Bureau Valley Railroad Co.
	industrialist - director, Mexican Mining and Smelting Co.
Civic Activism:	secretary, Fraunces Tavern, NYC; treasurer and director, National Horse Show of America; director, Bay Shore Horse Show, 1903
Marriage(s):	M/1 – 1871 – Sarah Louise Howell (b. 1851)
	M/2 – 1891-1909 – Anne Willard Stephenson (d. 1918)
Address:	St. Mark's Lane, Islip
Name of estate:	
Year of construction:	
Style of architecture:	
Architect(s):	
Landscape architect(s):	
House extant: unconfirmed	

Historical notes:

The house was built by John Dean Johnson. In 1886, Hollister purchased, remodeled, and expanded the house.

He was the son of Edwin Madison and Gratia Taylor Buell Hollister.

Sarah Louise Howell Hollister was the daughter of William A. and Lucetta B. Gould Howell.

Henry Hutchinson and Sarah Louise Howell Hollister, Sr.'s son Henry Hutchinson Hollister, Jr. married Hope Shepley. His son Buell married Louise R. Knowlton and resided in Islip. His daughter Louise married Richard E. Forest of Lawrence, and, subsequently, Langdon Barrett Valentine, with whom she resided in Islip. *[See Spinzia, Long Island's Prominent Families in the Town of Hempstead – Forest entry.]*

Anne Willard Stephenson Hollister was the daughter of J. H. and Emily Fiske Willard Stephenson of Boston, MA.

[See previous entry for additional family information.]

Hoppin, Bayard Cushing (1884-1956)

Occupation(s):	financier - a founder and partner, Abbott, Hoppin and Co. (stock brokerage firm);
	a founder and partner, Hoppin Brothers and Co. (stock brokerage firm)
	capitalist - director, Beekman Estates (real estate development firm)
Civic Activism:	chairman of board, Southside Hospital, Bay Shore (now, South Shore University Hospital);
	trustee, Seamen's Church Institute of New York;
	a founder and director, Great River Club, 1920 (later, Timber Point Club)
Marriage(s):	M/1 – 1910-div. c. 1936 – Helen Lispenard Alexandre (d. 1953)
	M/2 – Laurette Kennedy (1900-1963)
Address:	Suffolk Lane, East Islip
Name of estate:	
Year of construction:	
Style of architecture:	
Architect(s):	
Landscape architect(s):	
House extant: unconfirmed	
Historical notes:	

The *Long Island Society Register, 1929* lists Bayard Cushing and Helen L. Alexandre Hoppin as residing on Pavilion Lane [Suffolk Lane] in Islip [East Islip].

He was the son of William Warner and Katharine Beekman Hoppin, Sr. of Manhattan. His brother William Warner Hoppin, Jr. married Mary Gallatin, the daughter of Frederic and Almy Goelet Gerry Gallatin of *Breezy Lawn* in East Hampton, and resided at *Friendship Hill* in Old Brookville. His brother Gerard married Rosina Sherman Hoyt, the daughter of Alfred Miller and Rosina Elizabeth Reese Hoyt of Montauk, and resided at *Four Winds* in Oyster Bay Cove. His sister Katharine married A. Wright Post and resided at *White Lodge* in Bernardsville, NJ. His sister Esther married Dr. Eugene Hillhouse Pool and resided in Lattingtown.

[*See* Spinzia, *Long Island's Prominent North Shore Families, vol. I* – Hoppin entry; *Long Island's Prominent North Shore Families, vol. II* – Pool entry; and *Long Island's Prominent Families in the Town of East Hampton* – Gallatin and Hoyt entries.]

Helen Lispenard Alexandre Hoppin was the daughter of John Ernest and Helen Lispenard Webb Alexandre of *Spring Lawn* in Lenox, MA. Her sister Civilise married Frederick Schenck, the son of J. Frederick Schenck of *Valleyhead* in Lenox, MA.

Laurette Kennedy Hoppin had previously been married to ____ Brundage.

[For information on the Southside Hospital, see Cooper entry.]

Housman, Arthur Albert (1856-1907)

Occupation(s):	financier - partner, Burrell and Housman, NYC (stock brokerage firm); a founder and president, A. A. Housman and Co., NYC (stock brokerage firm*
	capitalist - horse, cattle, and swine breeder; director, Northwestern Development Co,
	industrialist - director, Safety Train Order Signal Co.
Marriage(s):	Adelaide Carlotta Rowe (b. 1860)
Address:	South Country Road, West Islip
Name of estate:	
Year of construction:	
Style of architecture:	French Empire
Architect(s):	Clarence K. Birdsall designed addition to main residence; stable and carriage house complex with living quarters for coachmen and grooms, harness rooms, cleaning rooms, and offices; cattle barns and farmer's cottage, 1902 (for Housman)
Landscape architect(s):	
Builder:	Jabez Ephraim Van Orden *[see Architect above]*
House extant:	no
Historical notes:	

front facade, 1905

In c. 1901, Housman purchased the John Busteed Ireland residence and remodeled the house. [*The Brooklyn Daily Eagle* August 20, 1907, p. 1.]

He was the son of Sigmund and Babette Rescher Housman.

Adelaide Carlotta Rowe Housman was the daughter of John W. and Lucy Joan Bigelow Rowe. Adelaide had previously been married to A. C. Hamilton.

The Housmans did not have children.

*Arthur was reputed to be the stock broker for J. P. Morgan.

Housman, Arthur Albert (1856-1907)

Occupation(s):	*[See previous entry.]*
Marriage(s):	Adelaide Carlotta Rowe (b. 1860)
Address:	off Deer Park Avenue, North Babylon
Name of estate:	
Year of construction:	c. 1875
Style of architecture:	Modified Neo-Tudor
Architect(s):	
Landscape architect(s):	
House extant:	no
Historical notes:	

The house, originally named *Deer Park Farm*, was built by Austin Corbin, Jr. In 1902 the 1,000-acre estate was purchased by Housman from Mrs. Corbin for use as a stock farm. [*The Brooklyn Daily Eagle* August 15, 1902, p. 1.]

[See previous entry for family information.]

front facade, c. 1893

Howell, Carlton Bell (b. 1907)

Occupation(s):	capitalist - owner, Horse Happy Farm, Schaefferstown, PA (riding academy)
Civic Activism:	president, Lebanon Valley, PA, Tourist Bureau
Marriage(s):	1934-1977 – Elizabeth Huber
Address:	108 East Bayberry Road, Islip
Name of estate:	
Year of construction:	1899-1900
Style of architecture:	Moorish
Architect(s):	Grosvenor Atterbury designed the house (for H. O. Havemeyer)
Landscape architect(s):	Nathan F. Barrett (for H. O. Havemeyer)
Builder:	*[See Jabez Ephraim Van Order entry.]*
House extant: yes	
Historical notes:	

front facade, 2006

The house was built by Henry Osborne Havemeyer as part of his "Modern Venice" development. It was owned by Edwin Thorne III and, subsequently, by Howell.

He was the son of James Frederick and Adele Cornwell Widdifield Howell, Sr. of Brightwaters.

Elizabeth Huber Howell was the daughter of Frederick Max and Harriet Louise Bossert Huber, Sr. of Bay Shore. *[See Huber entry for additional family information.]*

Carlton Bell and Elizabeth Huber Howell's daughter Daphne married J. T. M. Born, the son of Theodore Born of Bay Shore.

Howell, Elmer Brown, Sr. (1889-1954)

Occupation(s):	capitalist - partner, E. W. Howell & Co. (construction firm)*
	financier - vice-president, Suffolk County Federal Savings & Loan Association;
	director, Babylon National Bank & Trust Co.
Civic Activism:	secretary, Town Economy League Economic Council;
	chairman, Village of Babylon, Board of Appeals;
	member, Babylon School Board;
	a founder and governor, Southward Ho Country Club, West Bay Shore;
	president, Building Trades Employers' Association;
	director, Long Island Chamber of Commerce;
	director, Long Island Association
Marriage(s):	1912-1954 – Frances C. Rogers (1890-1984)
	- Civic Activism: trustee, South Suffolk chapter, American Red Cross; chairperson, finance committee, Suffolk County Young Women's Christian Association; anti-suffragist
Address:	Little East Neck Road, Babylon
Name of estate:	
Year of construction:	
Style of architecture:	
Architect(s):	
Landscape architect(s):	
House extant: unconfirmed	
Historical notes:	

Elmer Brown Howell, Sr. was the son of Elmer Winfield and Kizze A. Brown Howell of Babylon.

Frances C. Rogers Howell was the daughter of Oliver and Minnie Ferguson Rogers.

Elmer Brown and Frances C. Rogers Howell, Sr.'s son John married Mary M. Grover, the daughter of George W. and Margaret Mary O'Connor Grover, Sr. Their son Elmer Brown Howell, Jr married Susan Abbott.

At the time of his death, Howell was residing on Crooked Oak Lane, West Islip.

[See following entry for additional family information.]

*See following entry for a list of E. W. Howell & Co.'s South Shore commissions.

Howell, Elmer Winfield (1861-1954)

Occupation(s):	capitalist - founder and partner, with George S. Brown, Brown & Howell, 1891 (construction firm);
	founder, E. W. Howell & Co. (construction firm)*
	financier - vice-president and director, Babylon National Bank and Trust Co.;
	vice-president, Suffolk County Federal Savings and Loan Assoc.
	publisher - a founder and director, Signal Publishing Co., Babylon
Civic Activism:	member, board of managers, Southside Hospital, Bay Shore (now, South Shore University Hospital);
	trustee, Captain Cook Monument Association, 1906;
	trustee, Village of Babylon;
	member, Babylon Board of Education;
	trustee, First Presbyterian Church, Babylon;
	vice-president, Babylon Cemetery Association, 1916
Marriage(s):	M/1 – 1887-1933 – Kizze A. Brown (1867-1933)
	- trustee, Suffolk County Young Women's Christian Association
	M/2 – 1935-1954 – Florence Elizabeth Sheibeler (1899-1979)
Address:	27 George Street, Babylon
Name of estate:	
Year of construction:	
Style of architecture:	
Architect(s):	
Landscape architect(s):	

House extant: no
Historical notes:

Elmer Winfield Howell was the son of Edmund and Charlotte Ann Petty Howell of Yaphank.

Kizze A. Brown was the daughter of George S. and Mary Howell Brown.

Elmer Winfield and Kizze A. Brown Howell's son Ralph married Jessie Dunseith and resided in Babylon. Their son Elmer Brown Howell, Sr. married Frances C. Rogers and resided in Babylon.

Florence Elizabeth Sheibeler was the daughter of John Henry and Katherine Elizabeth Leidner Sheibeler.

*Among E. W. Howell & Co.'s South Shore commissions were: Jay Freeborn Carlisle, Sr.'s *Rosemary* in East Islip; George T. Turnbull's *The Pines* in West Islip; William Henry Moffitt's *Beautiful Shore* in Islip; Landon Ketchum Thorne, Sr.'s indoor pool at *Thorneham* in West Islip; as well as the house of Adolph Dick in Islip; a New England-style house on Horace Havemeyer, Sr.'s *Olympic Point* estate in Bay Shore; and an addition to William Dick's *Allen Winden Farm* in Islip.

[For information on the Southside Hospital, see Cooper entry.]

Howell, James Frederick, Sr. (1860-1951)

Occupation(s):	politician - Brightwaters Village Clerk, 1924-1954
Marriage(s):	M/1 – 1889-div. 1899 – Greta Hughes (1866-1916)
	- entertainers and associated professions - singer
	M/2 – 1900-1951 – Adele Cornwell Widdifield (1871-1956)
Address:	241 West Main Street, Bay Shore
Name of estate:	
Year of construction:	
Style of architecture:	
Architect(s):	
Landscape architect(s):	

House extant: no*
Historical notes:

James Frederick Howell, Sr., who was a member of Theodore Roosevelt's Rough Riders, was the son of James Bruen and Mary Ann Bowen Howell.

Greta Hughes Howell was the daughter of Felix Turner and Jean Amelia Summerlin Hughes. Greta subsequently married star basso and general manager of the Metropolitan Opera Herbert Witherspoon.

Adele Cornwell Widdifield Howell was the daughter of John and Mary Elizabeth Cornwell Widdifield. Adele's sister Mary married Harry Packer Wilbur of Key West, FL.

James Frederick and Adele Cornwell Widdifield Howell, Sr.'s son Carleton married Elizabeth Huber, the daughter of Frederick Max and Harriet Louise Bossert Huber, Sr. of Bay Shore. Their son James Frederick Howell, Jr. married Velm Veltmann.

The Howells had previously resided in Brightwaters.

*The property is now the site of Fairfield West at Bay Shore, an apartment complex.

Howell, Ralph DeWitt, Sr. (1897-1985)

Occupation(s):	capitalist - partner, E. W. Howell (construction firm)
Civic Activism:	secretary, Babylon Community Association
Marriage(s):	Jessie Dunseith (1894-1943)
	- Civic Activism: president, Babylon Travelers Club
Address:	90 South Carll Avenue, Babylon
Name of estate:	
Year of construction:	1915
Style of architecture:	Colonial Revival
Architect(s):	
Landscape architect(s):	
House extant: yes	
Historical notes:	

Ralph DeWitt Howell, Sr. was the son of Elmer Winfield and Kizze A. Brown Howell of Babylon.

Ralph DeWitt and Jessie Dunseith Howell, Sr.'s daughter Jessica married Herbert Lyon Carpenter, Jr. of Amityville. Their son Ralph DeWitt Howell, Jr. married Natalie Gray and resided in Mill Neck.

front facade

Hubbard, Harmanus Barkulo (1836-1921)

Occupation(s):	attorney - partner, Hubbard and Rushmore, Brooklyn
	capitalist - a founder and trustee, West Brooklyn Water Co.
	financier - director, Kings County Mortgage Co.; director, United States Title Guaranty Co.; director, Long Island Title Guarantee Co.
Civic Activism:	vice-president, Brooklyn Bar Association; president, Olympic Club, Bay Shore; president, Young Men's Democratic Party; vice-president, St. Nicholas Society; a founder and director, Bay Shore Protective Association
Marriage(s):	1859-1915 – Margaret Greenwood McKay (1842-1915)
	- Civic Activism: manager, Home for Aged Men, Brooklyn
Address:	Penataquit Avenue, Bay Shore
Name of estate:	*Oakhurst*
Year of construction:	
Style of architecture:	Queen Anne
Architect(s):	Harry G. Hardenburg designed the house (for Thurber)
Landscape architect(s):	
House extant: no	
Historical notes:	

The house was built by Frederick Charles Thurber. It was subsequently owned by Hubbard, who called it *Oakhurst*.

front facade, c. 1897

The *Brooklyn Blue Book and Long Island Society Register, 1918* lists H. B. Hubbard as residing at *Oakhurst* in Bay Shore.

Margaret Greenwood McKay Hubbard was the daughter of Samuel Moore and Adelaide Elizabeth Evertson McKay.

Harmanus Barkulo and Margaret Greenwood McKay Hubbard's daughter Margaret married William C. Cannon.

Hubbell, Lulu Hyde (1883-1958)

Marriage(s):	M/1 – 1910-div. 1918 – Vincent Booth Hubbell, Sr. (1864-1932)
	M/2 – 1920-1947 – Howard Drummond (1882-1947)
	- financier - partner, Carlisle, Mellick, and Co. (stock brokerage firm)
Address:	South Country Road, Bay Shore
Name of estate:	
Year of construction:	c. 1913
Style of architecture:	
Architect(s):	Cross and Cross designed the house (for Mrs. L. H. Hubbell)
Landscape architect(s):	
Builder:	E. W. Howell
House extant:	unconfirmed

Historical notes:

The house was built by Mrs. Lulu Hyde Hubbell.

She was the daughter of Richard and Mary Kellar Hyde of West Bay Shore.

Vincent Booth Hubbell, Sr. was the son of Gershom Booth and Cornelia Mallory Hubbell.

Vincent Booth and Lulu Hyde Hubbell, Sr.'s son Vincent Booth Hubbell, Jr. married Suzanne Page, the daughter of Cecil Page of Scarborough, NY.

Howard Drummond was the son of John L. and Jemima Drummond of Manhattan.

Hubbs, Charles Francis (1866-1935)

Occupation(s):	industrialist - president, treasurer and chairman of board, Charles F. Hubbs & Co. (paper manufacturer);
	president, Hubbs & Corning Co., Baltimore, MD (paper manufacturer);
	president, Hubbs & Hastings Paper Co., Rochester, NY (paper manufacturer);
	president, Hubbs & Howe Co., Cleveland, OH (paper manufacturer);
	president, Interstate Cordage & Paper Co., Pittsburgh, PA
	financier - director, Dime Savings Bank of Brooklyn (later, Dime Savings Bank of New York; now, The Dime)
Civic Activism:	trustee, Southward Ho Country Club, West Bay Shore;
	director, South Shore Field Club, 1910;
	president and director, Bay Shore Horse Show Association, 1903
Marriage(s):	1889-1934 – Mary Richards Howe (1866-1934)
Address:	South Country Road, West Islip
Name of estate:	*Sequatogue Farm*
Year of construction:	1880
Style of architecture:	Shingle
Architect(s):	
Landscape architect(s):	
House extant:	no

front facade, c. 1903

Historical notes:

The house, originally named *Sequatogue Farm*, was built by Henry Havemeyer, Sr. It was subsequently owned by Hubbs, who continued to call it *Sequatogue Farm*.

The *Brooklyn Blue Book and Long Island Society Register, 1918* lists Charles Francis and Mollie [Mary] R. Howe Hubbs as residing at *Sequatogue Farm* in Babylon [West Islip].

He was the son of Charles and Elizabeth Townsend Pettingell Hubbs of Brooklyn.

Mary Richards Howe Hubbs was the daughter of William Henry and Mary Pitt Angel Howe.

By 1929 the Hubbses had relocated to Hegeman's Lane in Old Brookville.

Charles Francis and Mary Richards Howe Hubbs' daughter Dorothy, who married Richard C. Kettles, inherited her parents' Old Brookville estate. The Kettles called it *Orchard Corners*. The Hubbses' daughter Marjorie, who married George A. Anderson, resided in Old Brookville on adjacent property. [*See* Spinzia, *Long Island's Prominent North Shore Families, vol. I* – Anderson, Hubbs, and Kettles entries.]

In 1897, the house was purchased by Charles Thomas Harbeck. [*The Brooklyn Daily Eagle* July 2, 1897, p. 5.]

Huber, Frederick Max, Sr. (1876-1917)

Occupation(s): industrialist - partner, Otto Huber Brewing, Brooklyn*
restaurateur - owned several taverns

Marriage(s): 1901-1917 – Harriet Louise Bossert (b. 1873)
Civic Activism: chair, Bay Shore / Brightwaters chapter, American Red Cross, 1919

Address: 48 South Clinton Avenue, Bay Shore
Name of estate:
Year of construction:
Style of architecture: Victorian
Architect(s):
Landscape architect(s):
House extant: no; garage complex is extant
Historical notes:

Frederick Max Huber, Sr. was the son of Otto and Emelie Meyer Huber, Jr. of Brooklyn.

Harriet Louise Bossert Huber was the daughter of Louis Bossert of *The Oaks* in West Bay Shore. Her brother John married Mary A. Jones

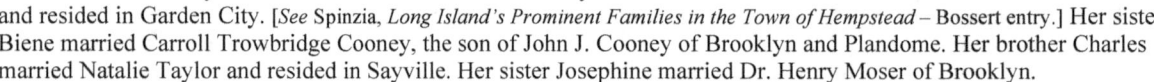

side / front facade

and resided in Garden City. [*See* Spinzia, *Long Island's Prominent Families in the Town of Hempstead* – Bossert entry.] Her sister Biene married Carroll Trowbridge Cooney, the son of John J. Cooney of Brooklyn and Plandome. Her brother Charles married Natalie Taylor and resided in Sayville. Her sister Josephine married Dr. Henry Moser of Brooklyn.

Frederick Max and Harriet Louise Bossert Huber, Sr.'s son Otto was paralyzed in both arms and legs while playing football for St. Paul's School in Garden City. He died a year later at the age of seventeen as a result of his injuries. [Liz Howell, *Continuity: Biography 1819-1934* (Sister Bay, WI: The Dragonsbreath Press, 1993), pp. 320-24.] Their daughter Evelyn married Carl Linn. Their son Frederick Max Huber, Jr. married Louise Draper. Their daughter Elizabeth married Carleton Bell Howell, the son of James F. and Adele Widdifield Howell, Sr.

*During Prohibition, the Huber family sold the brewery to Edward Hittleman. Its name was changed to Hittleman–Goldenrod Brewery, which used illustrations of the Katzenjammer Kids, from a popular comic strip, on its bottle caps. In 1946, the company's name was changed to Edlebrau. The brewery closed in 1951 shortly after Hittleman's death.

Hubert, William Haight (1893-1918)

Occupation(s):
Civic Activism: suffragist*

Marriage(s): 1916-1918 – Dorothy Nicoll (1890-1935)
- Civic Activism: federal director and general secretary, Woman's Land Army of America during World War I;
suffrage -
lecturer and organizer;
treasurer, Woman's Suffragist Movement, Second Assembly District, Suffolk County, NY

Address: Carll Avenue, Babylon
Name of estate:
Year of construction:
Style of architecture:
Architect(s):
Landscape architect(s):
House extant: unconfirmed
Historical notes:

William Haight Hubert was the son of Philip William Gengembre and Anna Haight Holmes Hubert, Jr. of Bellport.

Dorothy Nicoll Hubert was the daughter of William Greenly and Katherine Maurice Cornwell Nicoll of Babylon. Dorothy subsequently married George Strong Baxter, Jr. and resided in Westerly, RI.

*In 1916, William met Dorothy at a suffragist meeting and offered to drive her to her suffrage meetings.

Hulse, The Reverend William Warren (1838-1929)

Occupation(s):	real estate agent
	politician - member, Suffolk County Board of Supervisors; Superintendent of the Poor, Suffolk County; assessor, Town of Islip
	clergy - disciple of Swedenborg, Church of the New Jerusalem
Civic Activism:	trustee, Long Island Chautaqua Assembly (promoted religion, science, art, and "innocent recreation");
	president, Board of Education, Bay Shore
Marriage(s):	1867-1911 – Josephine Worth (1847-1911)
Address:	South Country Road and Clinton Avenue, Bay Shore
Name of estate:	*Elysian Views*
Year of construction:	1897
Style of architecture:	Modified Victorian
Architect(s):	
Landscape architect(s):	
House extant:	no
Historical notes:	

front facade, c. 1903

During the Civil War, Hulse was known as the "Christian Soldier" because of his practice of praying as he entered battle. [*The New York Times* June 24, 1929, p. 16.]

He was the son of David Overton and Sarah Hallock Hulse.

Josephine Worth Hulse was the daughter of The Reverend Justus Overton and Mrs. Martha Bunce Worth.

The Reverend William Warren and Mrs. Josephine Worth Hulse's daughter Marian was an infant when she died in 1868. Their daughter Mary was sixteen when she died in 1880. Their daughter Josephine was an infant when she died in 1892. Their daughter Ethel married Clarence Augustus Hough. Their daughter Laura married Hallett Everett Thurber, the son of Francis Asbury and Carrie L Hendrickson Thurber, and resided in Sayville. Their son Justus married Maud Wicks of Brooklyn. Their daughter Martha married Dr. Charles S. Chase. Their son David married Elizabeth Halton Blydenburgh, the daughter of George W. and Isabel Saxton Blydenburgh, and resided in Bay Shore. Their daughter Bertha married Dean Richardson Quinn.

During World War I, the house was used as a canteen for pilots learning to fly.

Hutchins, Francis Sessions (1877-1924)

Occupation(s):	publisher - director, Berrin & Durstine, Great River (publishing and advertising firm)
	attorney - partner, Baldwin, Hutchins, and Todd
	financier - vice-president, Commonwealth Trust Co.; director, Railway Securities Co.; director, Registration Trust Co.
Marriage(s):	M/1 – 1903-1909 – Margaret Grace Noyes (1882- 1909)
	M/2 – 1914-1924 – Sarah H. Crane
Address:	Great River Road, Great River
Name of estate:	*Saramond*
Year of construction:	1899
Style of architecture:	Neo-Tudor
Architect(s):	Charles C. Thain designed the house (for R. S. White)
Landscape architect(s):	
House extant:	no
Historical notes:	

front facade, c. 1910

The house was built by Raymond S. White. It was later owned by Hutchins.

Margaret Grace Noyes Hutchins was the daughter of Dr. Henry Drury and Mrs. Anna Margaret Grant Noyes.

The *Social Register Summer, 1915* lists Francis S. and Sarah Crane Hutchins as residing at *Saramond* in Great River.

He was the son of The Reverend Robert Grosvenor and Mrs. Harriet Palmer James Hutchins.

Sarah H. Crane Hutchins had previously been married to Raymond S. White.

The house was later owned by Dr. George David Stewart, who called it *Appin House*, and, subsequently, by Joseph Francis Dempsey who renamed in *Estancia*.

Hutton, Edward Francis (1875-1962)

Occupation(s):	financier - founder, E. F. Hutton and Co. (investment banking firm)
	industrialist - chairman of board, General Foods Corp.;
	chairman of board, Zonite Products Corp.;
	director, Chrysler Corp. (now, Daimler–Chrysler Corp.);
	director, The Coca–Cola Co.
Civic Activism:	founder, Freedoms Foundation (dedicated to preserving the "freedoms" in the Constitution and the Bill of Rights)
Marriage(s):	M/1 – 1900-1917 – Blanche Horton (1878-1917)
	M/2 – 1920-div. 1935 – Marjorie Merriweather Post (1887-1973)
	- industrialist - director, General Foods Corp.
	Civic Activism:
	suffragist - member, suffragist delegation that consulted with President Wilson in 1917;
	equipped a 2,000 bed hospital in France during World War I;
	vice-chairman, Emergency Unemployment Drive, NYC;
	vice-president, National Symphony Orchestra, Washington, DC;
	board member, Good Samaritan Hospital, NYC;
	member, arts education committee, National Cultural Center, Washington, DC
	M/3 – 1936-1962 – Dorothy Burgett Dear (1908-2002)
	- nobility
Address:	80 South Saxon Avenue, Bay Shore
Name of estate:	
Year of construction:	c. 1880
Style of architecture:	Victorian
Architect(s):	
Landscape architect(s):	

House extant: no; demolished in 1932*
Historical notes:

   The house was built by Daniel Denice Conover. It was later owned by his son Augustus Whitlock Conover, Sr. In 1902, the house was purchased by John Lorimer Worden III. [*The Brooklyn Daily Eagle* May 3, 1902, p. 10.] In 1912, it was purchased by Franklyn Laws Hutton, who called it *Win Sum Lodge*.

   He later sold it to his brother Edward Francis Hutton. They were the sons of James Laws and Frances Eloise Hulse Hutton of New York.

   In 1920, Edward Francis and Blanch Horton Hutton's eighteen-year-old son Halcourt was killed at the Bay Shore estate when his horse's saddle loosened, throwing Halcourt forward and upside down. Halcourt's head hit the cobblestone pavement resulting in his death a day or two later. [Nancy Rubin, *American Empress: The Life and Times of Marjorie Merriweather Post* (New York: Villard Books, 1995), p. 108.]

   Marjorie Merriweather Post Hutton was the daughter of Charles William and Ella Letitia Merriweather Post of Battle Creek, MI. Marjorie's father Charles was the founder of Postum Cereal Co., which later became General Foods Corp. She had previously been married to Edward Bennett Close. After her divorce from Hutton, she married Joseph Edward Davies and, subsequently, Herbert Arthur May.

   Edward Francis and Marjorie Merriweather Post Hutton's daughter Nedenia (aka Dina Merrill) married Stanley Maddox Rumbough, Jr., the son of Stanley and Elizabeth Morse Colgate Rumbough, Sr. of *Elston Oaks* in Lloyd Harbor, and resided in Old Brookville. Stanley Maddox and Nedenia Marjorie Hutton Rumbough, Jr.'s twenty-three-year-old son David drowned in a boating mishap. Their daughter Nedenia married Charles Stiffer Craig of Birmingham, MI. Ms. Merrill later married actor Cliff Robertson, aka Clifford Parker Robertson III of Water Mill, and, subsequently, Theodore Ringwalt Hartley with whom she resided in East Hampton. [*See* Spinzia, *Long Island's Prominent North Shore Families, vol. II* – Post and Rumbough entries; *Long Island's Prominent Families in the Town of Southampton* – Robertson entry; and *Long Island's Prominent Families in the Town of East Hampton* – Hartley entry.]

   [For information about Hutton's North Shore estate, see Spinzia, *Long Island's Prominent North Shore Families, vol. I* – Hutton entry.]

   [*See following entry for additional family information.*]

   In 1921, the house was purchased from E. F. Hutton by Philip Balch Weld.

   In 1930, it was purchased from Weld by Hamlet Cecil Sharp, who demolished the house and built a new house on the site.

   *The estates barn complex, stables, and windmill are extant.

stables, front facade, 2020

Hutton, Franklyn Laws (1877-1940)

Occupation(s):	financier - partner, E. F. Hutton and Co. (investment banking firm)
Marriage(s):	M/1 – 1907-1917 – Edna Woolworth (1884-1917)*
	M/2 – 1926-1940 – Irene Curley (1891-1965)
Address:	80 South Saxon Avenue, Bay Shore
Name of estate:	*Win Sum Lodge*
Year of construction:	c. 1880
Style of architecture:	Victorian
Architect(s):	
Landscape architect(s):	
House extant:	no; demolished in 1932**
Historical notes:	

The house was built by Daniel Denice Conover. It was later owned by his son Augustus Whitlock Conover, Sr. In 1902, the house was purchased by John Lorimer Worden III. [*The Brooklyn Daily Eagle* May 3, 1902, p. 10.] In 1912, Hutton purchased the house and called it *Win Sum Lodge*.

The *Social Register Summer, 1915* lists Franklyn L. and Edna Woolworth Hutton as residing at *Win Sum Lodge* in Islip [Bay Shore].

He was the son of James Laws and Frances Eloise Hulse Hutton of New York.

Edna Woolworth Hutton was the daughter of Frank Winfield and Jennie Creighton Woolworth, who resided at *Winfield Hall* in Glen Cove. Her sister Helena married Charles Edward Francis McCann and resided at *Sunken Orchard* in Oyster Bay Cove. Her sister Jessie married James Paul Donahue, Sr. and resided at *Wooldron Manor* in Southampton. [*See* Spinzia, *Long Island's Prominent North Shore Families, vol. I* – McCann entry; *Long Island's Prominent North Shore Families, vol. II* – Woolworth entry; and *Long Island's Prominent Families in the Town of Southampton* – Donahue entry.]

Franklyn Laws and Edna Woolworth Hutton's daughter Barbara married Prince Alexis Mdivani, Count Kurt von Haugwitz–Reventlow of Denmark, actor Cary Grant, Prince Igor Troubertzkoy of Lithuania, Porfirio Rubirosa, and, subsequently, Baron Gottfied von Cramm.

*In 1917, Edna, dressed in a white charmeuses evening gown, committed suicide in her room at the Hotel Plaza in Manhattan with an overdose of strychnine crystals. [C. David Heymann, *Poor Little Rich Girl: The Life and Legend of Barbara Hutton* (Secaucus, NJ: Lyle Stuart, Inc., 1984), p. 15.]

Irene Curley Hutton had previously been married to John R. Bodde. She subsequently married James Andrew Moffett, Jr. of *Inadune* in East Hampton. [*See* Spinzia, *Long Island's Prominent Families in the Town of East Hampton* – Moffett entry.] *[See previous entry for additional family information.]*

After Edna's death, Franklyn sold the house to his brother Edward Francis Hutton.

In 1921, the house was purchased from E. F. Hutton by Philip Balch Weld.

In 1930, it was purchased from Weld by Hamlet Cecil Sharp, who demolished the house and built a new house on the site.

**The estate's barn complex, stables, and windmill are extant.

stables, rear facade, 2020

Hyde, Henry Baldwin, II (1915-1997)

Occupation(s):	attorney - partner, Goldstein, Shames, and Hyde
	intelligence agent*
Civic Activism:	director, French Institute Alliance Fund;
	trustee, Hospital for Special Surgery, NYC;
	director, William J. Donovan Foundation
Marriage(s):	M/1 – 1941-div. – Marie de LaGrange (1919-1983)
	- journalist - editor, French division of War Information during World War II
	M/2 – 1961-1997 – Elizabeth Prokoff (d. 2008)
	- fashion model
Address:	Fire Island
Name of estate:	
Year of construction:	
Style of architecture:	
Architect(s):	
Landscape architect(s):	
House extant: unconfirmed	
Historical notes:	

    Henry Baldwin Hyde II was the son of James Hazen and Marthe Leishman Hyde, who resided at *The Oaks* in West Bay Shore.
    Marie de LaGrange Hyde was the daughter of Amcury and Emily Sloane de LaGrange of France.
    Henry Baldwin and Marie de LaGrange Hyde II's daughter Lorna married Baron Hubert de Wangen of Geroldseck. Their daughter Isabel married Jerome J. Jasinowki and resides in Washington, DC.
    Henry Baldwin Hyde II's cousin Annah Ripley, whose parents Sidney Dillon and Mary Hyde Ripley, Sr. resided at *The Crossways* in Uniondale, married Count Pierre de Viel Castel and resided in Normandy, France. During World War II the de Viel Castels' house was occupied by the German army. Because of her impeccable French, the Germans never suspected that Annah was an American. She was able to eavesdrop on the German conversations and pass the information on to the French resistance in a basket of eggs that she took to the local village for sale. [Patricia Beard, *After the Ball: Gilded Age Secrets, Boardroom Betrayals, and the Party That Ignited the Great Wall Street Scandal of 1905* (New York: Harper Collins Publishers, 2003), p. 345, and Spinzia, *Long Island's Prominent Families in the Town of Hempstead* – Ripley entry.]
    *Henry Baldwin Hyde II was the chief of the Office of Strategic Services (OSS) in France and, later, in Switzerland, during World War II. [*See* Raymond E. Spinzia "Socialite Spies: The Grandchildren of Henry Baldwin Hyde, Sr." and "To Look in the Mirror and See Nothing: Long Islanders and the Office of Strategic Services and Its Successor, the Central Intelligence Agency." www.spinzialongislandestates.com]
    Elizabeth Prokoff Hyde had previously been married to Eugene Stanton Piper.
[See entries for Henry Baldwin Hyde, Sr. and James Hazen Hyde for additional family information.]

Henry Baldwin Hyde, Sr.'s, estate, The Oaks

Hyde, Henry Baldwin, Sr. (1834-1899)

Occupation(s):	financier -	president, Equitable Life Assurance Society of the United States;
		director, Mercantile Safe Deposit Co.;
		director, Mercantile Trust Co.
	capitalist -	director, Union Pacific Railway Co.;
		director, Western Union Telegraph Co.;
		director, Westinghouse Electric Co.;
		director, Coney Island and Brooklyn Railroad, Co.;
		director, Brooklyn City and Newtown Railroad Co.;
		a founder, South Side Improvement Co., 1885 (accumulation of water to sprinkle roads)
Civic Activism:		president, Alliance Francaise;
		a founder, Jekyll Island Club
Marriage(s):		1864-1899 – Annie Fitch (aka Annie Truesdell) (1845-1922)
Address:		South Country Road, West Bay Shore
Name of estate:		*The Oaks*
Year of construction:		1874-1876
Style of architecture:		Stick-style
Architect(s):		Calvert Vaux designed the house (for H. B. Hyde, Sr.)
Landscape architect(s):		Olmstead, with Jacob Weidenman (for H. B. Hyde, Sr.)*

House extant: yes**
Historical notes:

The forty-room house, originally named *Marquetux* and later renamed *The Oaks*, was built by Henry Baldwin Hyde, Sr.

He was the son of Henry Hazen and Lucy Baldwin Beach Hyde. His unmarried sister Lucy was institutionalized in Bloomingdale's Insane Asylum. [Patricia Beard, *After the Ball: Gilded Age Secrets, Boardroom Betrayals, and the Party That Ignited the Great Wall Street Scandal of 1905* (New York: Harper Collins Publishers, 2003), p. 31.]

Annie Fitch Hyde was the daughter of Martin Halenbeck and Jane Maria Reed Truesdell. She was adopted by Simeon Fitch.

Henry Baldwin and Annie Fitch Hyde, Sr.'s daughter Mary married Sidney Dillon Ripley, Sr. and resided at *The Crossways* in Uniondale. She subsequently married Charles Robert Scott, with whom she continued to reside at *The Crossways*. [*See* Spinzia, *Long Island's Prominent Families in the Town of Hempstead* – Ripley and Scott entries.] Their son Henry and daughter Annie died before attaining adulthood. Their son James Hazen Hyde, who later owned *The Oaks*, married Marthe Leishman, Helen Walker, and, subsequently, Marthe Dervaux.

[See entries for Henry Baldwin Hyde II and James Hazen Hyde for additional family information.]

In c. 1900, James Hazen Hyde remodeled the house, eliminating some of its High Victorian elements. He also added a bachelor's annex and squash court.

In 1901, Louis Bossert purchased the four-hundred-acre estate and most of its furniture from James Hazen Hyde.

*Weidenman's landscape design was awarded special honor at the 1876 Centennial Exhibition in Philadelphia, PA.

**The house, which has been extensively modified, became the clubhouse of the South Bay Golf Club. It is now the clubhouse of the Southward Ho Country Club.

The Oaks, c. 1923.
after alterations by James Hazen Hyde

Hyde, James Hazen (1876-1959)

Occupation(s):	writer - "Impressions of the Front, the Valiant Army of the Vosges" (articles)
	financier - vice-president, Equitable Life Assurance Society of the United States;
	vice-president, National Bank of Commerce;
	director, International Banking Corp.
	capitalist - vice-president, Coney Island & Brooklyn Railroad Co.
Civic Activism:	director, Alliance Francaise;
	trustee, *Academie de Sciences Morales et Politiques*;
	trustee, Metropolitan Opera Co., NYC;
	chairman of board, French Institute of Washington Aid, American Red Cross in Paris, France, during World War I;
	member, American Committee on Public Information in France during World War I;
	director, Bay Shore Horse Association, 1903
Marriage(s):	M/1 – 1913-div. 1918 – Marthe Leishman (1882-1944)
	M/2 – 1930-div. 1931 – Helen Ella Walker (1875-1959)
	- Civic Activism: donated her villa in Italy and $2 million to the Rockefeller Foundation
	M/3 – Marthe Dervaux (d. 1948)
	- Civic Activism: established a school for Catholic scouts on the grounds of her estate near Paris, France

Address:	South Country Road, West Bay Shore
Name of estate:	*The Oaks*
Year of construction:	1874-1876
Style of architecture:	Stick-style
Architect(s):	Calvert Vaux designed the house (for H. B. Hyde, Sr.)
Landscape architect(s):	Olmstead, with Jacob Weidenman (for H. B. Hyde, Sr.)*
House extant:	yes**
Historical notes:	

stables interior, 1903

    The forty-room house, originally named *Marquetux* and later renamed *The Oaks*, was built by Henry Baldwin Hyde, Sr. It was later owned by his son James Hazen Hyde, who continued to call it *The Oaks*.

    Marthe Leishman Hyde was the daughter of John George Alexander Leishman, who foiled the plot to kill Henry Clay Frick and later became president of Carnegie Steel. Marthe had previously been married to Count Louis de Gontaut–Biron of France, who died of syphilis. As a condition to their marriage, Hyde insisted that she had to be examined by a doctor. Her sister Nancy married Duke de Croy of Germany. Marthe's intense and vocal pro-German position during World War I was one of the primary causes of the Hydes' divorce. [Patricia Beard, *After the Ball: Gilded Age Secrets, Boardroom Betrayals, and the Party That Ignited the Great Wall Street Scandal of 1905* (New York: Harper Collins Publishers, 2003), pp. 314-15.]

    James Hazen and Marthe Leishman Hyde's son Henry Baldwin Hyde II, who married Marie de LaGrange and, subsequently, Elizabeth Prokoff, resided on Fire Island.

    Helen Ella Walker was the daughter of Franklin H. Walker of Detroit, MI. Her grandfather owned Hiram Walker Distilling Co., of Canada [Canadian Club whiskey]. Helen had previously been married to Manfred Matuschka, the Baron of von Toppolczan and Apaaetgen, who was an officer in Kaiser Wilhelm's Bodyguard Regiment. She later married Prince Alexander von Thur and Taxis, the First Prince Della Torre E. Tasso of Italy. During World War II, *Serbelloni*, her Italian villa, was requisitioned by the German army.

    Marthe Dervaux Hyde had previously been married to ____ Thom.

[See previous Hyde entries for additional family information.]

    The Long Island Museum of American Art, History and Carriages in Stony Brook has James Hazen Hyde's coach on display.

    Edwin Hawley of Babylon purchased James Hazen Hyde's private railroad car *Bay Shore*.

    In c. 1900, James Hazen Hyde remodeled the house, eliminating some of its High Victorian elements. He also added a bachelor's annex and squash court.

    In 1901, Louis Bossert purchased the 400-acre estate and most of its furniture from James Hazen Hyde.

    *Weidenman's landscape design was awarded special honor at the 1876 Centennial Exhibition in Philadelphia, PA.

    **The house, extensively modified, became the clubhouse of the South Bay Golf Club. It is now the clubhouse of the Southward Ho Country Club.

Hyde, James Richard (1885-1950)

Occupation(s):	capitalist - director and manager, Madison Square Garden Co.
Civic Activism:	a founder and director, Great River Club, 1920 (later, Timber Point Club); president, Queens County Jockey Club; suffrage - member, Babylon Suffragist Club, 1914 treasurer and secretary, South Shore Field Club, 1910
Marriage(s):	
Address:	South Country Road, West Bay Shore
Name of estate:	
Year of construction:	1895
Style of architecture:	Queen Anne
Architect(s):	Clarence K. Birdsall designed the house, 1899, barn, and 1899 golf course's clubhouse (for Richard Hyde)*
Landscape architect(s):	
Builder:	Brown and Howell
House extant:	no
Historical notes:	

clubhouse

The house was built by Richard Hyde. It was later owned by his son James Richard Hyde.
The *Long Island Society Register, 1929* lists James R. Hyde as residing on South Country Road in Bay Shore.
[See following Hyde entries for family and estate information.]
In 1941, the 311-acre estate was purchased by Hans Jeppesen Isbrandtsen. [*The Suffolk County News* March 14, 1941, p. 9.]
*The clubhouse for the estate's nine-hole golf course survives as a private residence.

Hyde, Richard (1847-1913)

Occupation(s):	entertainers and associate professions - vaudeville entertainer capitalist - partner, with Louis C. Behman, Sr., Hyde and Behman Amusement Co., which owned and operated Volks Garden, Brooklyn; Park Bijou, Brooklyn; Amphion Theatre, Brooklyn; Folly Theatre, Brooklyn; Grand Opera House, Brooklyn; Gaiety Theatre, Brooklyn; and Newark Theatre, Newark, NJ
Civic Activism:	director, South Shore Field Club, 1910
Marriage(s):	Mary Kellar (1855-1917)
Address:	South Country Road, West Bay Shore
Name of estate:	
Year of construction:	1895
Style of architecture:	Queen Anne
Architect(s):	Clarence K. Birdsall designed, the house 1899, barn, and 1899 golf course's clubhouse (for Richard Hyde)*
Landscape architect(s):	
Builder:	Brown and Howell
Landscape architect(s):	
House extant:	no
Historical notes:	

front facade, c. 1903

The house was built by Richard Hyde.
Richard and Mary Kellar Hyde's daughter Lillian married Quentin Field Feitner, Sr., the son of Thomas L. and Mary C. Moore Feitner of Manhattan, and resided in Bay Shore. Lillian, subsequently, married George Barnard Wagstaff, with whom she continued to reside in Bay Shore. Their daughter Lulu married Vincent Booth Hubbell, Sr. and, subsequently, Howard Drummond, with whom she resided at *Little House* in Bay Shore. Both Lillian and Lulu died when their car was struck by a Long Island Railroad train at a Brentwood crossing. Their son William married Grace M. Riopelle and resided at *White Cottage* in Bay Shore. Their son James Richard Hyde later owned the house.
In 1941, the 311-acre estate was purchased by Hans Jeppesen Isbrandtsen. [*The Suffolk County News* March 14, 1941, p. 9.]
*The clubhouse for the estate's nine-hole golf course survives as a private residence.

Hyde, William James (1877-1951)

Occupation(s):	capitalist - president, Hyde and Behman Amusement Co., which owned and operated Volks Garden, Brooklyn; Park Bijou, Brooklyn; Amphion Theatre, Brooklyn; Folly Theatre, Brooklyn; Grand Opera House, Brooklyn; Gaiety Theatre, Brooklyn; and Newark Theatre, Newark, NJ
Marriage(s):	1916-div. 1930 – Grace M. Riopelle (1895-1971) - entertainers and related professions - motion picture actress, star of Vitagraph Pictures
Address:	South Country Road and Higbie Lane, West Islip
Name of estate:	*White Cottage*
Year of construction:	1910
Style of architecture:	Colonial Revival
Architect(s):	
Landscape architect(s):	
Builder:	E. W. Howell, garage, 1910 (for S. J. Wagstaff, Sr.)
House extant:	no
Historical notes:	

In 1923, William James Hyde purchased Samuel Jones Wagstaff, Sr.'s residence *Driftwood*. [*The County Review* May 18, 1923, p. 9, and *The Brooklyn Daily Eagle* June 21, 1923, p. 3]

He was the son of Richard and Mary Kellar Hyde of Bay Shore.

Grace M. Riopelle Hyde had previously been married to James M. Blakeley, an English comedian, who was killed in 1915 during a German zeppelin attack on England. She subsequently married John William Kiser, Jr. of *Sunset Court / Westerly* in Southampton. [*See* Spinzia, *Long Island's Prominent Families in the Town of Southampton* – Kiser entry.]

[See Richard Hyde entry for additional family information.]

front facade

William James Hyde residence, White Cottage, 1915

Ireland, John Busteed (1823-1913)

Occupation(s):	attorney capitalist - building contractor*; owned Manhattan real estate writer - *Wall Street to Cashmere*
Marriage(s):	1863-1913 – Adelia Duane Pell (1838-1915)
Address:	South Country Road, West Islip
Name of estate:	
Year of construction:	1881
Style of architecture:	
Architect(s):	Clarence K. Birdsall designed addition to main residence; stable and carriage house complex with living quarters for coachmen and grooms, harness rooms, cleaning rooms, and offices; cattle barns and farmer's cottage, 1902 (for Housman)
Landscape architect(s):	
Builder:	Jabez Ephraim Van Orden *[see Architect above]*
House extant:	no
Historical notes:	

    The house was built by John Busteed Ireland.
    He was the son of John Lawrence and Mary Gelston Floyd Ireland and the great grandson of William Floyd, who was one of the signers of the Declaration of Independence.
    Adelia Duane Pell Ireland was the daughter of Robert Livingston and Maria Louise Brinckerhoff Pell.
    John Busteed and Adelia Duane Pell Ireland's son John married Elizabeth Gallatin, the daughter of James Gallatin of Manhattan. Their daughter Adelia married Dr. Montgomery Hunt Sicard, the son of Rear Admiral Montgomery Sicard. Their son Robert married Kate Benedict Hanna, the daughter of Howard Melville Hanna, and resided at *Pebble Hill Plantation* in Thomasville, GA. Their daughter Maria married The Reverend Easton Earl Maderia, the rector of Christ Church, Waterloo, IA. Their daughter Laura married the Council General of Switzerland to the United States Louis Henri Junod. Their son James married Elizabeth Clark Ring, the daughter of Clark Lombard Ring of Saginaw, MI.
    In 1881, Ireland's first house on the property was destroyed by fire.
    In c. 1901, Arthur Albert Housman purchased the second house that Ireland had built and remodeled it. [The Brooklyn Daily Eagle August 20, 1907, p. 1.]
    *In 1895, Ireland was censured by a Grand Jury for delinquency in the collapse of the Ireland Building at Third Street and West Broadway in Manhattan. Fifteen construction workers were killed in the accident. [*The New York Times* August 22, 1895, p. 12; August 28, 1895, p. 14; August 30, 1895, p. 9; and October 5, 1895, p. 9.]

Ireland, Rufus Johnson, Sr. (1874-1936)

Occupation(s):	industrialist - director, Gebo Coal Co.*;
	president, Owl Creek Coal Co.
	capitalist - president, Brunswick Home, Amityville;
	director, Westport Sanitarium, Westport, CT
	financier - director, Amityville Bond & Mortgage Co.;
	director, Bank of Amityville
Civic Activism:	commodore, Unqua Corinthian Yacht Club, Amityville; president, Bayview Gun Club
Marriage(s):	1897-1936 – Grace E. Myton (1873-1956)
	- Civic Activism: vice-president, Amityville Free Library
Address:	39 Ocean Avenue, Amityville
Name of estate:	
Year of construction:	1897
Style of architecture:	Victorian
Architect(s):	
Landscape architect(s):	
Builder:	Purdy & Ketcham
House extant: yes	
Historical notes:	

   The house was built by Rufus Johnson Ireland, Sr.

   The *Long Island Society Register, 1929* lists Rufus J. and Grace E. Myton Ireland [Sr.] as residing at 39 Ocean Avenue, Amityville.

   He was the son of John Edward and Ann Eliza Trembly Ireland of Amityville.

   Grace E. Myton Ireland's father William Sidney and Mary P. Sully Myton of Amityville was arrested for shooting an engineer surveying for the Long Island Rail Road.

   Rufus Johnson and Grace E. Myton Ireland, Sr.'s son Rufus Johnson Ireland, Jr. married Dorothy Haff and, later, Elizabeth Terrell, the daughter of Eugene Terrell of Manhattan.

   *In 1909, Ireland was charged with allegedly conspiring to defraud the federal government out of thousands of acres of coal lands in Wyoming. [*The New York Times* May 22, 1903, p. 16.]

front facade, 2005

Isbrandtsen, Hans Jeppesen (1891-1953)

Occupation(s):	capitalist - president, Western Operating Co. (largest American-owned whaling company); president, Pan-American Wharfage Co.; founder, Hans Isbrandtsen, Inc., NYC (managed terminal and warehouses)
	shipping* - founder and president, Isbrandtsen–Moller Co., Inc. (shipping line to Gulf, Pacific Coast, and Far Eastern Ports); president, Isbrandtsen Co., Inc. (steamship freighter firm)
	industrialist - founder, Isbrandtsen Company of Louisiana, Inc. (owned and operated oil and gas fields)
Civic Activism:	established Isbrandtsen Foundation
Marriage(s):	1921-1953 – Gertrude Mirus (1898-1959)
	- Civic Activism: president, Long Island College Hospital Guild; regent, Long Island College Hospital
Address:	South Country Road, West Bay Shore
Name of estate:	
Year of construction:	1895
Style of architecture:	Queen Anne
Architect(s):	Clarence K. Birdsall designed the house, 1899, barn, and 1899 golf course's clubhouse (for Richard Hyde)**
Landscape architect(s):	
Builder:	Brown and Howell
House extant: no**	
Historical notes:	

    The house was built by Richard Hyde. It was later owned by his son James Richard Hyde. In 1941, the 311-acre estate was purchased by Isbrandtsen. [*The Suffolk County News* March 14, 1941, p. 9.]

    He was the son of Jacob C. and Nicoline Jeppesen Isbrandtsen of Denmark.

    Gertrude Mirus Isbrandtsen was the daughter of Waldemar Mirus of Brooklyn.

    Hans Jeppesen and Gertrude Mirus Isbrandtsen's son Walter [Waldemar] married Evelyn Elizabeth Kelley, the daughter of The Reverend Harold H. Kelley of Manhattan and resided in Fair Haven, CT. Their daughter Niel married Albert E. Rising, Jr. of Kew Gardens, NY, and resided in Glen Cove. Their son Jacob married Patricia Cotten of Brooklyn and resided in Riverside, CT.

    *Known as the "lone wolf," Isbrandtsen, who was one of the largest independent ship owners in the country, staunchly believed in the freedom of the seas. He refused to participate in conferences that regulated shipping rates and imposed cargo rules. Rejecting government subsidies, Isbrandtsen was famous for undercutting the rates of his competitors. In 1950, several of his ships were damaged by gun fire while "running" the Nationalist Chinese blockage of Communist China. [*The New York Times* May 14, 1953, pp.6 and 29.]

    **The clubhouse for the estate's nine-hole golf course survives as a private residence.

front facade, 1903

Jackson, Charles Havemeyer, Sr. (1885-1971)
aka Charles Frederick Havemeyer Jackson

Occupation(s):	
Civic Activism:	secretary and treasurer, Central Island Forest Protective Association, 1929
Marriage(s):	1911-1971 – Emily deLoosey Potter (1889-1979)
Address:	St. Mark's Lane, Islip
Name of estate:	
Year of construction:	
Style of architecture:	
Architect(s):	
Landscape architect(s):	
House extant:	unconfirmed
Historical notes:	

The *Social Register Summer, 1915* list Charles H. and Emily deL. Potter Jackson [Sr.] as residing in Islip.

He was the son of Frederick Wendell and Sarah Louise Havemeyer Jackson.

Emily deLoosey Potter Jackson was the daughter of Edward Clarkson and Emily Blanche Havemeyer Potter of Glen Cove. [*See* Spinzia, *Long Island's Prominent North Shore Families, vol. II* – Potter entry.]

Charles Havemeyer and Emily deLoosey Potter Jackson, Sr.'s daughter Carlotta married Carlie Yachik and resided in Islip. Their daughter Emily married Henry Jackson Sillcocks, the son of Henry Sillcocks of Brooklyn and, later, Walter Lanning Worrall, Jr., the son of Walter Lanning and Los Wainwright Worrall, Sr., and resided in Providence, RI. Their son Charles Havemeyer Jackson, Jr. died in 1914 at the age of one.

By 1928 the Jacksons had relocated to *Honey Hollow Farm* which was located at the corner of Old Willets Path and Veterans Highway in Hauppauge.

At the time of Charles' death, they were residing on St. Mark's Lane is Islip.

Jacoby, James Ralph (1871-1971)

Occupation(s):	physician - neurologist, Lenox Hill Hospital, NYC
	capitalist - director, New York & Honduras Rosario Mining Co.,
	secretary, Clifford Park Co.
	writer - *Electricity of Medicine*, 1919
Civic Activism:	rear commodore, Babylon Yacht Club, 1906
	a founder and director, Babylon Town Hospital, 1921
Marriage(s):	1906-1971 – Ray Scull (1889-1975)
	- Civic Activism: president, Long Island Diocesan Woman's Auxiliary of the Protestant National Episcopalian Council of the District of New York
Address:	The Crescent and Sumpwams Avenue, Babylon
Name of estate:	
Year of construction:	1910
Style of architecture:	Modified Colonial Revival
Architect(s):	
Landscape architect(s):	
House extant:	yes
Historical notes:	

side facade

The house was built by Dr. James Ralph Jacoby. [*The Suffolk County News* October 15, 1909, p. 6.]

He was the son of Samuel R. and Rosalade Ralph Jacoby of Manhattan. James' brother Dr. George W. Jacoby was one of the physicians engaged by the mother of Harry K. Thaw to have Harry declared insane in his 1906 trial for murdering the noted architect Stanford White of *Box Hill* in Head of the Harbor, Long Island.

In 1920, James and George were indicted for defrauding an 82-year-old woman who was in the Bloomingdale Asylum by taking advantage of her dementia. [*The New York Tribune* March 21, 1920, p. 12, and *The Sun and New York Herald* March 21, 1920, p. 7.]

James Ralph and Ray Scull Jacoby's daughter Mary married Willard Brown.

Johnson, Aymar (1883-1942)

Occupation(s):	financier - partner, Johnson, Wood, and Rogers (stock brokerage firm) (later, Johnson and Wood); partner, Johnson and Wood (stock brokerage firm)
	intelligence agent - Naval Intelligence during World War II
Civic Activism:	trustee, Cathedral of St. John the Divine, NYC;
	chairman, Suffolk County Work Relief Committee during 1930s;
	lay manager, Seaman's Church Institute, NYC
Marriage(s):	1924-1942 – Marion Krumbhaar Hoffman (1901-1981)
Address:	Suffolk Lane, East Islip
Name of estate:	*Woodland*
Year of construction:	1909
Style of architecture:	Modified Neo-Federal
Architect(s):	Isaac Henry Green II designed the second 1909 house (for Bradish Johnson, Jr.)
Landscape architect(s):	Olmsted, 1915 (for Bradish Johnson, Jr.)
House extant:	first house on the site was destroyed by fire in 1905; second (1909) house was demolished; gatehouse is extant

Historical notes:

The first house on the site was built by James Boorman Johnston. In 1880, it was purchased from Johnston by Charles Thomas Harbeck. In 1882, Bradish Johnson, Jr. purchased the house from Harbeck and called it *Woodland*. After it was destroyed by fire, Johnson built a second house on the site, which he also called *Woodland*. It was later owned by his son Aymar who continued to call it *Woodland*.

Aymar was the son of Bradish and Amiee Elizabeth Gaillard Johnson.

Marion Krumbhaar Hoffman Johnson was the daughter of Charles Frederick and Zelia Krumbhaar Preston Hoffman of Manhattan, Newport, RI, and *Blicking Hall* in Norfolk, England.

Aymar and Marion Krumbhaar Hoffman Johnson's daughter Zelia married Eugene Minton Moore, the son of William Minton Moore.

[See following Johnson entries for additional family information.]

In 1946, Mrs. Aymar Johnson sold the estate to the Hewlett School of East Islip.

In 2006, the school sold the estate to a developer who demolished the house.

side / rear facade, 2005

Johnson, Bradish, Jr. (1851-1918)

Occupation(s):	capitalist - Bradish Johnson & Co. (Louisiana real estate holding company)
	industrialist - director, American Cotton Oil Co.
	financier - director, Commonwealth Insurance Co.;
	director, Equitable Trust Co.;
	director, Equitable Life Assurance Society of the United States;
	director, Greenwich Savings Bank;
	president, State Investing Co.;
	director, Lincoln Trust Co.
Civic Activism:	director, Bay Shore Horse Show Association, 1903
Marriage(s):	1877-1918 – Amiee Elizabeth Gaillard (1854-1929)
	- Civic Activism: vice-chair, Town of Islip chapter, American Red Cross, 1915
Address:	Suffolk Lane, East Islip
Name of estate:	*Woodland*
Year of construction:	1909
Style of architecture:	Modified Neo-Federal
Architect(s):	Isaac Henry Green II designed the second 1909 house (for Bradish Johnson, Jr.)
Landscape architect(s):	Olmsted, 1915 (for Bradish Johnson, Jr.)

House extant: first house on the site was destroyed by fire in 1905;
second (1909) house was demolished;
gatehouse is extant

Historical notes:

The first house on the site was built by James Boorman Johnston. In 1880, it was purchased from Johnston by Charles Thomas Harbeck. In 1882, Bradish Johnson, Jr. purchased the house from Harbeck and called it *Woodland*. After it was destroyed by fire, Johnson built a second house on the site, which he also called *Woodland*.

He was the son of Bradish and Louisa Anna Lawrance Johnson, Sr., who resided at *Sans Souci* in West Bay Shore.

Amiee Elizabeth Gaillard Johnson was the daughter of Joseph Gaillard.

Bradish and Amiee Elizabeth Gaillard Johnson, Jr.'s son Bradish Gaillard Johnson III married Emma Marie Grima and resided in Islip. Their son Enfin also resided in Islip. Their daughter Marie married William Hamilton Russell, Jr. and resided in Islip. She subsequently married Gordon Crother and resided at *La Casetta* in Islip. Their son Aymar, who married Marion Krumbhaar Hoffman, later owned *Woodland*.

[See other Johnson entries for additional family information.]

In 1946, Mrs. Aymar Johnson sold the estate to the Hewlett School of East Islip.

In 2006, the school sold the estate to a developer who demolished the house.

Woodland, gatehouse, 2005

Johnson, Bradish, Sr. (1811-1892)

Occupation(s):	attorney
	industrialist - partner, with his father William M. Johnson, William M. Johnson & Sons (later, Johnson and Lazarus) (distillery and sugar refinery);
	partner, Johnson and Lazarus (distillery and sugar refinery)
	capitalist - president, Bradish Johnson & Co. (Louisiana real estate holding company)*
	financier - director, Chemical National Bank
Marriage(s):	1836-1870 – Louisa Anna Lawrance (1817-1870)
Address:	South Country Road, West Bay Shore
Name of estate:	*Sans Souci*
Year of construction:	c. 1860
Style of architecture:	High Victorian Gothic
Architect(s):	
Landscape architect(s):	
House extant:	no
Historical notes:	

The house, originally named *Sans Souci*, was built by Bradish Johnson, Sr.

He was the son of William M. and Sarah Rich Johnson. William M. Johnson was a native of Nova Scotia, Canada, who relocated to Manhattan and made his fortune in the distilling industry and in real estate. The senior Johnson had extensive real estate holdings in New York City and in the New Orleans area of Louisiana. The latter included *Woodland Plantation*, where Bradish Johnson, Sr. was born. Bradish Johnson, Sr.'s brother John Dean Johnson married Helen Maria Wederstrandt and resided in Islip. His brother Edwin Augustus Johnson, Sr. married Ellen Woodruff and resided in East Islip and, later at *Deer Range Farm*, also in East Islip.

Louisa Anna Lawrance Johnson was the daughter of Thomas and Margaret Ireland Lawrance. Her sister Cornelia married George G. Wilmerding and resided in West Bay Shore. Her brother William married Mary Helen Crandell.

Bradish and Louisa Anna Lawrance Johnson, Sr.'s daughter Lucy married Dr. Alfred Ludlow Carroll and resided in Bay Shore. Their daughter Helena married Schuyler Livingston Parsons, Sr. and resided at *Whileaway* in Islip. Their son Effingham married Amy Rowan Scott and resided in Bay Shore. Their daughter Louisa married Robert Cooper Townsend. Their son Bradish Johnson, Jr. married Amiee Elizabeth Gaillard and resided at *Woodland* in East Islip. Their daughter Louise married Stephen Whitney. Their son Henry Meyer Johnson, who married Grace Baldwin, inherited *Sans Souci*.

[See other Johnson entries for additional family information.]

*According to the 1860 Federal Census, Bradish Johnson owned 214 slaves and 2,800 acres of land in Plaquemines Parish, LA. [Joseph Karl Menn, *The Large Slaveholders of Louisiana – 1860* (New Orleans: Pelican Publishing Co., 1964), pp. 310-311.] Both of Johnson's Louisiana plantations still exist. *Woodland* was restored in 1998 and is open to the public as a nine-room country inn. *Whitney Plantation* is privately owned and not open to the public. Johnson's New Orleans house at 2343 Prytania Street, in the Garden District of the city, became a college preparatory school for girls in 1912 and is still operated as Louise S. McGehee School. His Manhattan house, located at the corner of Fifth Avenue and Twenty-first Street, was purchased by the Lotos Club.

Prior to President Lincoln's proclamation to free slaves, Johnson offered to free his Louisiana slaves and pay for their return to Africa. The slaves refused, preferring to remain as his freed employees. During the Union Army's attack on New Orleans, Johnson raised the American flag on his *Woodland Plantation*. [*The New York Times* April 27, 1933, p. 17.]

front facade, c. 1903

Johnson, Bradish Gaillard, III (1878-1944)

Occupation(s):	capitalist - secretary and treasurer, Bradish Johnson & Co. (Louisiana real estate holding company)
Marriage(s):	1911-1944 – Emma Marie Grima (1887-1967) - Civic Activism: member of board, Coordinating Council for French Relief Societies
Address:	St. Mark's Lane, Islip
Name of estate:	*Enfin*
Year of construction:	
Style of architecture:	
Architect(s):	
Landscape architect(s):	
House extant: unconfirmed	
Historical notes:	

The *Social Register Summer, 1915* lists Bradish G. and Emma M. Grima Johnson [III] as residing at *Enfin* in Islip.

He was the son of Bradish and Amiee Elizabeth Gaillard Johnson, Jr., who resided at *Woodland* in East Islip.

Emma Marie Grima Johnson was the daughter of Louis Alfred and Emma Cameron Pugh Grima.

Bradish Gaillard and Emma Marie Grima Johnson III's son Alfred Grima Johnson, who was a member of the Office of Strategic Services during World War II and, later, its successor the Central Intelligence Agency, married Francine Buffet, the daughter of Andre and Simone Querenet Buffet of France. [*See* Raymond E. Spinzia "To Look in the Mirror and See Nothing: Long Islanders and the Office of Strategic Services and Its Successor, the Central Intelligence Agency." www.spinzialongislandestates.com] Their daughter Adelaide married Count Alain D'Eudeville, the son of Count Henri Eudes and Countess Marthe Thomas D'Eudeville of France. In 1937, their twenty-three-year-old son Bradish Gaillard Johnson IV, a war correspondent for *Spur* magazine, was killed covering the Spanish Civil War. [*The New York Times* January 1, 1938, p. 4.]

[See other Johnson entries for additional family information.]

Johnson, Edwin Augustus, Sr. (1824-1861)

Occupation(s):	capitalist - real estate developer in Town of Islip industrialist - partner, with his father and brother Bradish, William M. Johnson & Sons (distilling and sugar refining firm) (later, Johnson and Lazarus)
Marriage(s):	1847-1861 – Ellen A. Woodruff (1828-1872)
Address:	Suffolk Lane, East Islip
Name of estate:	
Year of construction:	c. 1840's
Style of architecture:	
Architect(s):	
Landscape architect(s):	
House extant: unconfirmed	
Historical notes:	

The house was built by Edwin Augustus Johnson, Sr. The Johnsons resided here from 1846 to 1851 prior to building *Deer Range Farm* which was also located in East Islip.

He was the son of William Martin and Sarah Rice Johnson.

Edwin Augustus and Ellen A. Woodruff Johnson, Sr.'s son Lee married Frances Augusta Nicoll, the daughter of William and Sarah Augusta Nicol Nicoll VII of *Grange* in East Islip, and resided in East Islip and Garden City. [*See* Spinzia, *Long Island's Prominent Families in the Town of Hempstead* – Johnson entry.] Their daughter Helen married Charles Fiske Bound and resided in Manhattan. Their son Edwin Augustus Johnson, Jr. remained a bachelor. Their daughter Estella married John Coats Seymour, the son of Walter M. and Eliza Martin Otto Seymour.

[See other Johnson entries for additional family information.]

Johnson, Edwin Augustus, Sr. (1824-1861)

Occupation(s): *[See previous entry.]*

Marriage(s): 1847-1861 – Ellen A. Woodruff (1828-1872)

Address: Heckscher Parkway, East Islip
Name of estate: *Deer Range Farm*
Year of construction: c. 1850s
Style of architecture: Eclectic
Architect(s):
Landscape architect(s):
Builder: Jabez Ephraim Van Orden built the
    house (for E. A. Johnson, Sr.)
Erastus Peterson, 1899 carriage
    house (for J. I Plumb)
House extant: no; demolished in 1909*
Historical notes:

    The house, originally named *Deer Range Farm*, was built by Edwin Augustus Johnson, Sr.
[See previous entry for additional family information.]
    In 1872, the estate was purchased by Sarah Caroline Ives Plumb. Upon her death, it was inherited by her husband James Neale Plumb and, subsequently, by their son James Ives Plumb. The Plumbs continued to call it *Deer Range Farm*.
    In 1884, alterations were made to the house by James Neale Plumb.
    In 1903, James Ives Plumb sold the estate to George Campbell Taylor and relocated to Islip.
    The estate remained in the Taylor / Pyne family corporation until 1924 when it was confiscated by Robert Moses and became part of Heckscher State Park. [Harry W. Havemeyer, *Along the Great South Bay From Oakdale to Babylon: The Story of a Summer Spa 1840 to 1940* (Mattituck, NY: Amereon House, 1996), p. 135.]
    *Portions of the house were salvaged, moved, and relocated into buildings in the Islip area.

Johnson, Effingham Lawrance (1860-1897)

Occupation(s):

Marriage(s): 1889-1897 – Amy Rowan Scott (1866-1953)

Address: South Country Road and Penataquit Avenue, Bay Shore
Name of estate: *The Evergreens*
Year of construction:
Style of architecture:
Architect(s):
Landscape architect(s):
House extant: unconfirmed
Historical notes:

    Effingham Lawrance Johnson was the son of Bradish and Louisa Anna Lawrance Johnson, Sr., who resided at *Sans Souci* in West Bay Shore.
    Johnson's fortune, at the time of his death, was valued at $10 million. [*The New York Times* April 14, 1897, p. 1.]
    Amy Rowan Scott Johnson was the daughter of James Rowan and Sarah Antoinette Tams Scott. Amy subsequently married General William Graves Bates, with whom she continued to reside at *The Evergreens*.
    Effingham Lawrance and Amy Rowan Scott Johnson's daughter Amy married Herbert Groesbeck, Jr. and resided in Manhattan.
[See other Johnson entries for additional family information.]

rear facade

Johnson, Enfin

Occupation(s):

Marriage(s):

Address: St. Mark's Lane, Islip
Name of estate:
Year of construction:
Style of architecture:
Architect(s):
Landscape architect(s):
House extant: unconfirmed
Historical notes:

Enfin Johnson was the son of Bradish and Amiee Elizabeth Gaillard Johnson, Jr., who resided at *Woodland* in East Islip.
[See other Johnson entries for additional family information.]
The house was purchased by Joseph Sears Lovering, Sr.

Johnson, Frederick Merle, Sr. (1899-1950)
aka Merle Johnson, Sr.

Occupation(s):	advertising executive - vice-president, motion picture department, General Motors Corp.
Marriage(s):	Edith D. *[unable to determine maiden name]* - entertainers and associated professions - actress
Address:	407 Middle Road, Bayport
Name of estate:	
Year of construction:	1915
Style of architecture:	Colonial Revival
Architect(s):	Isaac Henry Green II, 1915 alterations (for Rice) *[unconfirmed]*
Landscape architect(s):	
Builder:	Asby & Breckenridge, garage, greenhouse, and alterations to main residence, 1915 (for Rice)

House extant: yes
Historical notes:

Dr. George Edwin Rice remodeled Amelia E. Needham Waterman's (Mrs. Henry M. Waterman) residence into a six-bedroom, four-bath, 6,000-square-foot Colonial Revival residence which he called *Maywood*. [*The Suffolk County News* May 5, 1916, p. 4.] In 1943, Johnson purchased the house. [*The Suffolk County News* April 30, 1943, p. 5.]

He was the son of Mrs. T. C. Johnson of Quincy, IL.

Frederick Merle and Edith D. Johnson's daughter Eve married an animal trainer in Hollywood and resided in Nebraska. Their son Frederick Merle Johnson, Jr. (aka Merle Johnson, Jr.) was the noted actor Troy Donohue who married Suzanne Pleshette, Valerie Allen, Alma Sharpe, and Vicki Taylor.

In 1955, Mrs. Johnson sold the house to Richard Wolford Dodson. [*The Suffolk County News* August 5, 1955, p. 2.]

In 1986, Dodson sold the house to Mark Kleine. [*The Suffolk County News* June 11, 1998, p. 6.]

front facade

Johnson, Henry Meyer (1856-1907)

Occupation(s):	attorney - member, Platt and Bowers
	capitalist - managed his father's estate
Civic Activism:	a founder and trustee, Waverly Gun Club, Islip, 1890
Marriage(s):	M/1 – 1890-1902 – Sarah Kathleen Baldwin (d. 1902)
	M/2 – 1902-1907 – Grace Baldwin (1857-1930)
Address:	South Country Road, West Bay Shore
Name of estate:	*Sans Souci*
Year of construction:	c. 1860
Style of architecture:	High Victorian Gothic
Architect(s):	
Landscape architect(s):	
House extant: no	
Historical notes:	

The house, originally named *Sans Souci*, was built by Bradish Johnson, Sr. It was later owned by his son Henry Meyer Johnson, who continued to call it *Sans Souci*.

Both Sarah Kathleen Johnson and Grace Baldwin Johnson were the daughters of Harvey Baldwin, the first mayor of Syracuse, NY, and his wife Ann Sarah Dodge Baldwin. Their brother Townsend Burnet Baldwin married Mary Nesmith Dillon and resided at *Gable Hall* in Edgewater, NJ.

Sarah Kathleen Baldwin Johnson had previously been married to Cornelius W. Olliffee.

Henry Meyer and Sarah Kathleen Baldwin Johnson's daughter Louisa married Simon Vander Horst Waring.

The *Social Register Summer, 1915* lists Henry Meyer and Grace Baldwin Johnson as residing at *Sans Souci* in Bay Shore [West Bay Shore]

Grace Baldwin Johnson had previously been married to James Francis Ruggles with whom she resided at *The Rushes* in Southampton. Grace continue to reside at *The Rushes* with Henry. [*See* Spinzia, *Long Island's Prominent Families in the Town of Southampton* – Johnson and Ruggles entries.]

James Francis and Grace Baldwin Ruggles' daughter Grace married George Lane of Troy, NY. Their son Burnet Rathbone Ruggles married Natalie E. Smith and resided at *Ox Ridge Farm* in Darien, CT.

[See other Johnson entries for additional family information.]

Johnson, John Dean (1813-1861)

Occupation(s):	capitalist - owned Louisiana sugar plantation
Civic Activism:	delegate to Whig State Convention
Marriage(s):	Helen Maria Wederstrandt (1825-1888)
Address:	St. Mark's Lane, Islip
Name of estate:	
Year of construction:	c. 1840s
Style of architecture:	
Architect(s):	
Landscape architect(s):	
House extant: unconfirmed	
Historical notes:	

The house was built by John Dean Johnson.

He was the son of William M. and Sarah Rich Johnson.

Helen Maria Wederstrandt Johnson was the daughter of Philemon Charles and Helen Smith Wederstrandt of New Orleans, LA.

John Dean and Helen Maria Wederstrandt Johnson's son Bradish W. Johnson, who was known as the "Hog" and "A Great Wrecker" because of his zeal to be the first to reach the site of a shipwreck to claim the right of salvage, married Irene Bethel, the daughter of Charles Walter and Olivia Archer Bethel.

John Dean Johnson's yacht *Wanderer* was built in 1857 by Joseph Rowland of Setauket. After Johnson sold the yacht, it was used as a slave trade ship. It eventually ran aground on the eastern tip of Cuba.

[See other Johnson entries for additional family information.]

Wanderer

In 1886, the house was purchased by Henry Hutchinson Hollister, Sr., who remodeled and expanded it.

Johnson, Lee (1845-1895)

Occupation(s):	capitalist - subdivided property in the Town of Islip for development; built and rented houses in the Town of Islip
	industrialist - partner, William M. Johnson & Sons (distilling and sugar refining) (later, Johnson and Lazarus)
Marriage(s):	1874-1895 – Frances Augusta Nicoll (1849-1930)
Address:	Suffolk Lane, East Islip
Name of estate:	
Year of construction:	
Style of architecture:	Shingle
Architect(s):	
Landscape architect(s):	
House extant:	no; demolished in 1952*
Historical notes:	

front facade

Lee Johnson was the son of Edwin Augustus and Ellen A. Woodruff Johnson, Sr., who resided in East Islip and, later, at *Deer Range Farm*, also in East Islip.

Frances Augusta Nicoll Johnson was the daughter of William and Sarah Augusta Nicoll VII of *Grange* in East Islip. Her sister Sarah married Dr. Silias R. Corwith and resided in Bridgehampton. [*See* Spinzia, *Long Island's Prominent Families in the Town of Southampton* – Corwith entry.] Her sister Mary married Coryton Woodbury. Her brother Edward married Ella Lattling. Her brother William Greenly Nicoll, who married Phoebe Disbrow and, subsequently, Kate Cornwall, resided in Babylon. Her brother Henry married Augusta Mattby and resided in Virginia. Her sister Helen married Charles Fiske Bound and resided in Manhattan.

[See other Johnson entries for additional family information.]

In 1885, Johnson sold the house to Henry Rieman Duval and relocated to Garden City. [*See* Spinzia, *Long Island's Prominent Families in the Town of Hempstead* – Johnson entry.] Duval called it *Falmouth*.

*The house was severely damaged by fire during World War II.

Johnson, Parmenus, Sr. (1792-1874)

Occupation(s):	capitalist - extensive real estate and rental holdings in Brooklyn; director, New York Brooklyn Ferry Co.
Marriage(s):	c. 1822-1879 – Mary Joralemon (1795-1879)
Address:	St. Mark's Lane, Islip*
Name of estate:	
Year of construction:	
Style of architecture:	
Architect(s):	
Landscape architect(s):	
House extant:	yes
Historical notes:	

The house was built by Parmenus Johnson, Sr.

He was the son of William and Deborah Peterson Johnson.

Mary Joralemon Johnson was the daughter of Judge Teunis and Mrs. Jannetje Vredenburgh Losie Joralemon of Brooklyn.

Parmenus and Mary Joralemon Johnson, Sr.'s daughter Catharine married Cornelius B. Bergen of Brooklyn. Their daughter Jane married Edwin Kutesoph Scranton. Their son Isaac married Ruth Johnson.

In January 1880, the twenty-one-acre estate was purchased by C. A. Backett of New York. By June 1880 it was owned by E. B. Spaulding who enlarged and modernized the house [*The Brooklyn Daily Eagle* January 27, 1880, p. 4, and June 7, 1880, p. 1.] In 1886, the estate was purchased by Robert Cambridge Livingston III, who called it *Lakeside*. The estate was then owned by the Livingstons' daughter Maud who married Henry Worthington Bull. By the early 1940s it was owned by the Bulls' niece Phyllis Livingston Baker Astaire, who married the noted dancer/choreographer/actor Fred Astaire, Sr. (aka Frederick Austerlitz). In 2006, the house was owned by ____ Dowden.

In 2008, the seven thousand-square-foot, twenty-room house with seven bedrooms was for sale. The asking price was $1,499,990; the taxes were $16,089.

*The estate originally bordered on St. Marks Lane. With its subdivision, the house is currently located on Suellen Road.

Johnston, James Boorman (1822-1887)

Occupation(s):	capitalist - director, Metropolitan Railroad, NYC; commissioned Richard Morris Hunt to design artist studios in Greenwich Village section, NYC*
	financier - founder, J. Boorman and Co.; a founder, Northern Assurance Co., England; director, Queen Insurance Co., England; director, National Bank of the Republic
Marriage(s):	1853-1887 – Mary Hoppin Humphreys (1830-1916)
	- Civic Activism: vice-president, Colonial Dames of America, Paris chapter
Address:	Suffolk Lane, East Islip
Name of estate:	
Year of construction:	
Style of architecture:	
Architect(s):	Isaac Henry Green II designed the 1909 house (for Bradish Johnson, Jr.)
Landscape architect(s):	Olmsted, 1915 (for Bradish Johnson Jr.)
House extant:	first house on the site was destroyed by fire in 1905; second (1909) house was demolished; gatehouse is extant

Historical notes:

The first house on the site was built by James Boorman Johnston.

He was the son of John and Margaret Taylor Johnston of NYC. His father John was a wealthy Manhattan merchant who was a founder of New York University.

James Boorman and Mary Hoppin Humphreys Johnston's son John Humphreys Johnston, the noted artist, married Annie Lazarus.

*Johnston's building of the artist studio complex in Greenwich Village is credited with beginning the Greenwich Village art movement.

In 1880, the house was purchased from Johnston by Charles Thomas Harbeck. In 1882, Bradish Johnson, Jr. purchased the house from Harbeck and called it *Woodland*. After it was destroyed by fire, Johnson built a second house on the site, which he also called *Woodland*. The estate was later owned by his son Aymar Johnson, who continued to call it *Woodland*.

In 1946, Mrs. Aymar Johnson sold the estate to the Hewlett School of East Islip.

In 2006, the school sold the estate to a developer who demolished the house.

Jones, Frank Smith (1847-1927)

Occupation(s):	merchant - a founder and president, Jones Brothers Tea Co., Scranton, PA; president, Grand Union Tea Co. (Grand Union Supermarkets)
Civic Activism:	trustee, Wesleyan University, Middletown, CT; trustee, Brooklyn Institute of Arts and Sciences
Marriage(s):	1879-1927 – Mary Louise Granbery (1853-1927)
Address:	Handsome Avenue, Sayville
Name of estate:	*Beechwold*
Year of construction:	1903
Style of architecture:	Shingle
Architect(s):	Isaac Henry Green II designed the main residence, gatehouse, and 1905 playhouse. The latter included a bowling alley and billiard room (for F. S. Jones)
Landscape architect(s):	
Builder:	Ashley & Breckinridge, Bayport

House extant: no; destroyed by fire in 1957*
Historical notes:

The house, originally named *Beechwold*, was built by Frank Smith Jones.
He was the son of Isaac Smith and Frances Weed Jones of Stanford, CT.
Mary Louise Granbery Jones was the daughter of Henry Augustus Thaddeus and Prudence Nimmo Granbery of Norfolk, VA. Mary's sister Mabel married Roland Whitney Betts and resided at *Sunneholm* in Sayville. Mabel subsequently married Charles Edward Spratt.
Frank Smith and Mary Louise Granbery Jones' daughter Henrietta married William Robinson Simonds and resided at *Wyndemoor* in Sayville and *Williston House* in Southampton. [*See* Spinzia, *Long Island's Prominent Families in the Town of Southampton* – Simonds entry.] Their daughter Maude, who married Clarence Frederick Westin, Sr. and, subsequently, David J. Shea, later owned *Beechwold*. The Sheas resided in the estate's gatehouse.
In 1945, the house was purchased by Elwell Palmer, who, in 1949, sold it to Dr. Daniel McLaughlin who owned the house at the time of the fire.
*The gatehouse and playhouse are extant. The gatehouse is located at 254 Handsome Avenue and the playhouse is at 96 Benson Avenue.

Beechwold

Kalbfleisch, Sarah Pirnie Schenck (1848-1921)

Occupation(s):	
Marriage(s):	1867-1921 – Franklin H. Kalbfleisch (1846-1929)
	- industrialist - president and treasurer, Franklin H. Kalbfleisch Co. (chemical manufacturer with plants in Erie, PA, Waterbury, CT, Elizabeth, NJ, and Brooklyn, NY)
Address:	24 The Crescent, Babylon
Name of estate:	*Larklawn*
Year of construction:	1881
Style of architecture:	Modified Dutch Colonial
Architect(s):	
Landscape architect(s):	
Builder:	E. W. Howell, rose house, 1905
House extant: no	
Historical notes:	

The house was built by Sarah Pirnie Schenck Kalbfleisch.

The *Social Register Summer, 1915* lists Franklin H. and Sarah P. Schenck Kalbfleisch as residing at *Larklawn* in Babylon.

He was the son of Brooklyn mayor and congressman Martin Kalbfleisch and Mrs. Elizabeth Harvey Kalbfleisch.

Sarah Pirnie Schenck Kalbfleisch was the daughter of Cornelius C. and Mary Pirnie Schenck.

Franklin H. and Sarah Perine Schenck Kalbfleisch's daughter Augusta, who resided at *Blyenbeck* in Huntington, did not marry. Their son Gordon died in 1881 at the age of four. Their daughter Isabella died in 1881 at the age of two. Their son Martin died in 1874 at the age of four.

Keith, Minor Cooper (1848-1929)

Occupation(s):	engineer
	capitalist - president and chairman of board, International Railways of Central America;
	president, Guatemala and Salvador Railway;
	president, St. Andrew's Bay Lumber Co.;
	extensive property holdings in several states and foreign countries;
	president, Costa Rica Railway Co.;
	founder, Costa Rica's first large scale banana plantation, 1873;
	owner, coffee plantations and cattle ranches
	industrialist - a founder, with Andrew W. Preston, and vice-president, United Fruit Co.;
	president, Polochic Banana Co.;
	president, Abangarez Gold Fields, Costa Rica;
	vice-president, Premier Gold Mining Co., British Columbia, Canada;
	director, International Food Products Corp.;
	director, General Lead Batteries Co.
	financier - director, Empire Trust Co.
Civic Activism:	bequeathed his gold coin collection to the American Museum of Natural History, NYC
Marriage(s):	1883-1929 – Cristina Castro (1862-1944)
Address:	South Country Road, West Islip
Name of estate:	
Year of construction:	
Style of architecture:	Modified French Empire
Architect(s):	
Landscape architect(s):	
House extant: no; demolished c. 1937	
Historical notes:	

In 1913, Minor Cooper Keith purchased John Lloyd Stephen's estate *Lone Oak*. [*South Side Signal* January 10, 1913, p. 5.] The house was built over an old Native American burying ground. [*South Side Signal* August 25, 1888, p. 2.]

Keith, the son of Minor Hubbell and Emily Meiggs Keith of Brooklyn, was known as the "Banana King."

Cristina Castro Keith was the daughter of Jose Maria Castro, the President of the Republic of Costa Rica.

The Keiths did not have children.

After selling the house to William Pancoast Clyde, Sr., the Keiths relocated to Babylon. [Harry W. Havemeyer, *Along the Great South Bay From Oakdale to Babylon: The Story of a Summer Spa 1840 to 1940* (Mattituck, NY: Amereon House, 1996), p. 179 and *The New York Times* March 16, 1944, p. 19.]

*Minor Cooper Keith residence,
rear facade*

Keith, Minor Cooper R., II (b. 1899)

Occupation(s):

Marriage(s):   1923-separated 1925 – Clara Turnbull (d. 1939)

Address: South Country Road, West Islip
Name of estate:
Year of construction:
Style of architecture:
Architect(s):
Landscape architect(s):
House extant: unconfirmed
Historical notes:

   Minor Cooper R. Keith II was the grand-nephew of Minor Cooper Keith and an heir to Minor Cooper Keith's $22 million estate.
   Clara Turnbull Keith was the daughter of George R. and Clara Jenkins Turnbull, who resided at *The Pines* in West Islip. Clara bequeathed $50,000 for the care of her dogs and only $20,000 to her husband Minor. [*The New York Times* July 29, 1939, p. 20.]
   In 1932, Keith asked the court to annul his marriage charging Clara was forty-six and not thirty years old at the time of their marriage, that he had been coerced into the marriage, that she took advantage of his youth and lack of sophistication, that she held him prisoner in her home, and that he tried three times to escape on their wedding day but was captured by her. [*The Brooklyn Daily Eagle* July 14, 1933, pp. 1-3.] They separated in 1925. In 1930, Minor was charged with stealing an automobile. In 1931, he was convicted of passing a worthless check and sentenced to a year in Eastview Penitentiary. [*Daily News* August 15, 1932, p. 9.]

Kelly, James P.

Occupation(s):   financier - vice-president, West End Bank of Brooklyn
                      capitalist - president, Kingsway Realty Corp.

Marriage(s):   Cecelia Rafter (d. 1937)

Address: 117 Awixa Avenue, Bay Shore
Name of estate: *Awixaway*
Year of construction:
Style of architecture: Shingle
Architect(s):
Landscape architect(s):
House extant: no
Historical notes:

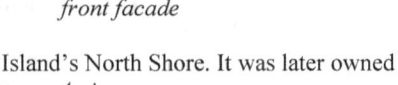
front facade

   The house was built by Rudolph Oelsner, who by 1906 had relocated to Long Island's North Shore. It was later owned by George Winthrop Hodges, Sr., who sold it to Kelly in 1923. Kelly called the house *Awixaway*.

Kempster, James H.

Occupation(s):	capitalist - president, James Kempster Printing Co., NYC
Civic Activism:	president, Olympic Club
Marriage(s):	
Address:	Saxon Avenue, Bay Shore
Name of estate:	*Westbeach*
Year of construction:	
Style of architecture:	Second Empire
Architect(s):	
Landscape architect(s):	
House extant: no	
Historical notes:	

front / side facade, c. 1903

Keppy, Dr. Frederick Beardsley (1864-1917)

Occupation(s):	physician - dentist
Marriage(s):	M/1 – 1889-1893 – Augusta Boughton (1867-1893)
	M/2 – 1903-1917 – Mary Herbert Cornwell (1858-1931)
Address:	West Main Street, Bayport
Name of estate:	
Year of construction:	
Style of architecture:	
Architect(s):	
Landscape architect(s):	
House extant: unconfirmed	
Historical notes:	

In 1908, Dr. Frederick Beardsley Keppy purchased Francis Melville, Sr.'s residence. In 1913, he joined it together with that of Vinal S. Terry. [*The Suffolk County News* March 13, 1908, p. 2; August 11, 1916, p. 4; and November 12, 1937, p. 8.]

He was the son of John and Linda M. Beardsley Keppy.

Augusta Boughton Keppy was the daughter of John A. and Imogene Augusta Weeks Boughton.

Dr. Frederick Beardsley and Mrs. Augusta Boughton Keppy's son Boughton Keppy died in 1911 at the age of twenty-one. Their daughter Alice married Harry Tompkins and resided in Brooklyn.

Mary Herbert Cornwell Keppy was the daughter of Timothy and Amelia Alvord Cornwell.

In 1937, the house was purchased by Frank Cahill of Brooklyn. [*The Brooklyn Daily Eagle* November 10, 1937, p. 1.]

King, Dr. George Suttie (1878-1966)

Occupation(s):	physician - surgeon, Metropolitan Hospital, 1899-1900; examining surgeon, Travelers Life Insurance Co.; physician, Foresters of America; physician, Modern Woodmen of America
	capitalist - founder, Dr. King's Hospital, 11 Maple Avenue, Bay Shore, 1918
	writer - *Doctor on a Bicycle*, 1958 (autobiography); *The Last Slaver**
Civic Activism:	**
Marriage(s):	M/1 – 1903-1941 – Elizabeth Marie Graham (1878-1941) M/2 – Ruth Kahler
Address:	32 Maple Avenue, Bay Shore
Name of estate:	
Year of construction:	
Style of architecture:	Victorian
Architect(s):	
Landscape architect(s):	
House extant: yes	
Historical notes:	

side / front facade, 2006

Dr. George Suttie King was the son of Elbert S. and Ellen Suttie Woodruff King of Patchogue. His sister Lotta married ___ Smith and resided in Patchogue. His sister Aida did not marry.

Dr. George Suttie and Mrs. Elizabeth Marie Graham King's daughter Elinor married Cornelius Furgueson III and resided in Brightwaters. Their daughter Virginia married Joseph Salkeld Rider and resided in Brightwaters.

In 1963, Dr. King's Hospital became the South Bay Manor Rest Home. It was demolished in c. 2005.

*King's book *The Last Slaver* was adapted into the 1937 motion picture "Slave Ship." The script was written by William Faulkner and the film starred Tay Garnett, Warner Baxter, Wallace Beery, Elizabeth Allan, Mickey Rooney, George Sanders, Jane Darwell, and Joseph Schildkraut.

**Known for his generosity to the poor, his hospital ledgers had the notation C. T. G., "Charge To God," next to many of his patients' names.

Bay Shore's Dr. George S. King Park is named in his honor.

Kingsland, George Lovett, Sr. (1827-1892)

Occupation(s):	capitalist - president, George Creek Railroad
	industrialist - director, George Creek and Cumberland Coal Co.
Civic Activism:	commodore, New York Yacht Club (1842-1911)
Marriage(s):	Helen Schermerhorn Welles (d. 1911)
Address:	South Country Road, Babylon
Name of estate:	
Year of construction:	
Style of architecture:	
Architect(s):	
Landscape architect(s):	
House extant: unconfirmed	
Historical notes:	

George Lovett Kingsland Sr. was the son of New York City Mayor Ambrose Cornelius Kingsland and Mrs. Mary Lovett Kingsland.

Helen Schermerhorn Welles Kingsland was the daughter of Benjamin Sumner and Catherine Elida Schermerhorn Welles, Sr. of Islip. Her brother Benjamin Sumner Welles, Jr. married Frances Swan and resided at *Welles House* in Islip. Her sister Harriet did not marry.

George Lovett and Helen Schermerhorn Welles Kingsland, Sr.'s daughter Ethel married Dr. Walter Palmer Anderton. Their son George Lovett Kingsland, Jr. married de Forest Cannon, the daughter of Harry Le Grand Cannon. Their daughter Helen married Newbold Morris, the son of Augustus Newbold and Eleanor Colford Jones Morris, Sr. Their son Augustus Newbold Morris II, who resided at *Wind Break* in Southampton, married Margaret Copley Thaw and, later, Constance Hand. [*See* Spinzia, *Long Island's Prominent Families in the Town of Southampton* – Morris entry.]

Kleinman, David E. (b. 1901)

Occupation(s): attorney

Marriage(s):

Address: South Country Road, Bay Shore
Name of estate:
Year of construction:
Style of architecture:
Architect(s):
Landscape architect(s):
House extant: unconfirmed
Historical notes:

In 1950, Kleinman purchased the house from Howard Drummond. [*The New York Times* September 24, 1950, p. R5.]
In 1959, Kleinman was charged with "ambulance chasing." [*The Long Island Traveler* July 16, 1959, p. 3.]

Knapp, Edward Spring, Sr. (1852-1895)

Occupation(s): capitalist - manager, Greenport Ferry Co.;
                              president, Thirty-Fourth Street Ferry
               financier -   president, Queens County Bank

Civic Activism: a founder and trustee, Waverly Gun Club, Islip, 1890

Marriage(s): 1878-1895 – Margaret Ireland Lawrance (1855-1934)

Address: 52 South Saxon Avenue, Bay Shore
Name of estate: *Awixa Lawn*
Year of construction: 1880
Style of architecture: Colonial Revival
Architect(s): Isaac Henry Green II designed
  the 1889 southwestern wing
  addition of a living room,
  and four bedrooms
  (for E. S. Knapp, Sr.)
Landscape architect(s):
House extant: yes
Historical notes:

The house, originally named *Awixa Lawn*, was built by Edward Spring Knapp, Sr.
He was the son of Gideon Lee and Augusta Murray Spring Knapp.
Margaret Ireland Lawrance Knapp was the daughter of William R. and Mary Helen Crandell Lawrance.
Edward Spring and Margaret Ireland Lawrance Knapp, Sr.'s son Edward Spring Knapp, Jr., who resided at *The Barn* in Roslyn, married Rosalie Moran, the daughter of Amedee Depau Moran of East Islip, and, later, Dorothee Dibblee, the daughter of Walter A. Dibblee of Glen Head. [*See* Spinzia, *Long Island's Prominent North Shore Families, vol. I* – Knapp entry.]. Their daughter Margaret married Dr. Lee Hollister Ferguson of New York and Delaware, OH. Their son Thomas married Jessie Danes and resided in Blue Point.
[See other Knapp entries for additional family information.]
In 1896, after Edward's death, Margaret decided to rent *Awixa Lawn* and build a second house in which to reside. The second house, which is presently located at 52 Saxon Avenue, was subsequently owned by Julius Oppenheimer.
In 1915, Mrs. Knapp sold *Awixa Lawn* to August Belmont III.
In 1923, Mrs. Belmont sold the estate, which at that time consisted of a twenty-five-room main residence on nine acres with six hundred feet of shoreline on Awixa Creek, stables, and a five-car garage to John Allen Dillon, Sr.

front facade, 2006

Knapp, Harry Kearsarge, II (1890-1943)

Occupation(s):	
Civic Activism:	treasurer, Westminster Kennel Club; treasurer, St. Mark's Episcopal Church, Islip
Marriage(s):	M/1 – 1911-div. 1920 – Phebe Schoonhoven Thorne (1891-1969)
	M/2 – 1921 – Elizabeth Marshall Mann (1888-1988)
Address:	Meadow Farm Road, East Islip
Name of estate:	*Creekside*
Year of construction:	1929
Style of architecture:	Neo-Federal
Architect(s):	William Hamilton Russell, Jr. designed the house (for H. K. Knapp II)
Landscape architect(s):	Charles Wellford Leavitt and Sons (for H. K. Knapp II)

House extant: yes
Historical notes:

The house, originally named *Creekside*, was built by Harry Kearsarge Knapp II.

He was the son of Harry Kearsarge and Caroline Burr Knapp, Sr., who resided at *Brookwood* in East Islip.

Phebe Schoonhoven Thorne Knapp was the daughter of Edwin and Phebe Ketchum Thorne II, who resided at *Okonok* in West Islip. She subsequently married John Tucker. Her brother Landon married Julia Atterbury Loomis and resided at *Thornham* in West Islip. Her brother Francis, who married Evelyn Brown and, subsequently, Hildegarde Kobbe, resided at *Brookwood* in East Islip. Her sister Anna married Robert Titus and resided in West Islip.

Elizabeth Marshall Mann Knapp was the daughter of Francis Norton Mann of Troy, NY. She subsequently married Walter Russell Herrick, the son of Frederick Chamberlin and Josephine C. Flanagan Herrick, and resided at *Ivy Cottage* in Watch Hill, RI.

Harry Kearsarge and Elizabeth Marshall Mann Knapp II's daughter Theodosia married Duer McLanahan, Jr. of *Windvale* in Watch Hill, RI; John B. Watkins of *Willow Farm* in North Salem, NY; and, subsequently, Richard K. Barnes with whom she resided in Mt. Kisco, NY. Their son Harry Kearsarge Knapp III married Louise Weidman and resided in Stonington, CT.

[See other Knapp entries for additional family information.]

In 1939, the house was purchased by William Hamilton Gregory, Jr., who continued to call it *Creekside*.

rear facade

Knapp, Harry Kearsarge, Sr. (1865-1926)

Occupation(s):	capitalist -	general manager, Union Ferry;
		director and vice-chairman of board, The Queens County Jockey Club (owned and operated Aqueduct Race Track)
	financier -	director, Corn Exchange Bank;
		director, Queens City Bank;
		director, Kings County Trust Co.;
		partner, Hyatt and Co. (stock brokerage firm);
		partner, Benedict, Drysdale, and Co. (stock brokerage firm)
Civic Activism:	president, Racquet and Tennis Club;	
	director, Saratoga Racing Association;	
	chairman of board, New York State Racing Commission, 1906	
Marriage(s):	1886-1926 – Caroline Burr (1860-1928)	
Address:	South Country Road, East Islip	
Name of estate:	*Brookwood*	
Year of construction:	1902	
Style of architecture:	Georgian Revival	
Architect(s):	Delano and Aldrich designed the house (for H. K. Knapp, Sr.]	
Landscape architect(s):		
House extant: yes		
Historical notes:		

The house, originally named *Brookwood*, was built by Harry Kearsarge Knapp, Sr.

He was the son of Gideon Lee and Augusta Murray Spring Knapp, Sr.

The *Long Island Society Register, 1929* lists Caroline Burr Knapp as residing at *Brookwood* in East Islip.

She was the daughter of Andrew E. and Ida Vandervoot Burr.

Harry Kearsarge and Caroline Burr Knapp, Sr.'s son Harry Kearsarge Knapp II, who married Phebe Schoonhoven Thorne and, subsequently, Elizabeth Marshall Mann, resided at *Creekside* in East Islip. Their daughter Caroline married Charles Kintzing Post, the son of Waldron Kintzing and Mary Lawrence Perkins Post of *Strandhome* in Bayport. Their son Theodore, who later owned *Brookwood*, married Gladys Quarre.

[See other Knapp entries for additional family information.]

In 1929, Theodore sold the estate to Francis Burritt Thorne, Sr.

In 1942, the house was owned by the Orphan Asylum Society of Brooklyn.

In 1965, the Society sold it to Alfred and Fred Wimmer, who sold the house to the Town of Islip in 1967. It is currently the site of The Islip Art Museum, a leading exhibit space for contemporary art.

The Empire State Carousel, now located in Binghamton, NY, was built in the carriage house of *Brookwood*.

front facade, 2005

Harry Kearsarge Knapp, Sr. estate, *Brookwood*

entrance hall

sitting room

side facade, 2005

Knapp Lake, c. 1939

carriage house, 2005

Knapp, Shepherd, II (1847-1902)

Occupation(s):	financier - director, Queens County Bank, Long Island City
Marriage(s):	Emma Benedict (d. 1907)
Address:	South Country Road, West Islip
Name of estate:	
Year of construction:	c. 1869
Style of architecture:	
Architect(s):	
Landscape architect(s):	
House extant:	unconfirmed
Historical notes:	

Shepherd Knapp, Sr. was the son of Gideon Lee and Augusta Murray Spring Knapp, Sr.

Emma Benedict Knapp was the daughter of Jessie W. Benedict.

Shepherd and Emma Benedict Knapp II's daughter Elsie married Manhattan attorney Wilson M. Powell, Jr. Their son Shepherd Knapp III, a bachelor, was a clergyman. Their daughter Kate married George A. Vondermuhll, Sr., the son of Alfred Vondermuhll.

[See other Knapp entries for additional family information.]

Knapp, Shepherd Fordyce, Sr. (1832-1886)

Occupation(s):	financier - member, Mechanic's Bank, NYC; receiver, Bowling Green Savings Bank, 1871 merchant - partner, with his brother Peter, leather business politician, New York City Street Commissioner
Civic Activism:	president, Wawayanda Fishing Club, Fire Island; a founder, New York Driving Club
Marriage(s):	M/1 – 1853-1876 – Catherine Floyd Smith (1835-1876) M/2 – 1881-1886 – Mary Helen Crandall (1830-1900)
Address:	*[unable to determine street address]*, Babylon
Name of estate:	
Year of construction:	
Style of architecture:	
Architect(s):	
Landscape architect(s):	
House extant:	unconfirmed
Historical notes:	

Shepherd Fordyce Knapp, Sr. was the son of Shepherd and Catherine Louisa Kumble Knapp I.

Catherine Floyd Smith Knapp was the daughter of John Holly and Judith Nicoll Smith.

Shepherd Fordyce and Catherine Floyd Smith Knapp, Sr.'s son William married Alice Margaret Davelin, the daughter of John E. and Lucy Stetson Develin. Their son Charles married Alice Develia Stetson, the daughter of Prince Redington and Rebecca Hiester Eckert Stetson. In 1884, their son Shepherd Fordyce, Jr. drowned in the North River at the age of four.

Knapp, Theodore Jackson (1892-1947)

Occupation(s):	financier - partner, Montgomery, Scott and Co. (stock brokerage firm)
	capitalist - president, The Queens County Jockey Club (owned and operated Aqueduct Race Track)
Civic Activism:	member, board of managers, New York Society for the Ruptured and Crippled;
	executive head, Long Island Hunt Club
Marriage(s):	1947-1947 – Gladys Quarre (1901-1989)
	- capitalist - thoroughbred horse breeder;
	an owner, Hotel IL Pellicano, Porto Ercole, Italy (5-star hotel);
	Civic Activism: drove ambulances from their Detroit factories to various destinations in the country during World War II;
	Hollywood Canteen worker during World War II;
	benefactor, Pepperdine University, Malibu, CA;
	benefactor, Scripps Clinic, La Jolla, CA;
	a founder, The American Museum, Bath, England
Address:	South Country Road, East Islip
Name of estate:	*Brookwood*
Year of construction:	1902
Style of architecture:	Georgian Revival
Architect(s):	
Landscape architect(s):	
House extant: yes	
Historical notes:	

The house, originally named *Brookwood*, was built by Harry Kearsarge Knapp, Sr. It was later owned by his son Theodore, who died of a self-inflicted wound from a twenty-eight-gauge shotgun in his three-room suite at the Southside Sportsman's Club in Oakdale. [*The New York Times* May 8, 1947, p. 52.]

Gladys Quarre Knapp, whose son David said she lived the life of the fictional character Auntie Mame and who had been a member of the Hollywood actor's community since the silent picture era, was the daughter of Emil and Carlotta Howard Jackson Quarre of San Francisco, CA. Gladys had previously been married to Frederick Griffith Peabody of Troy, NY, who was an heir to the Arrow Shirt and Jockey underwear fortune. After Theodore's death, she married Howard Bell.

[See other Knapp entries for additional family information.]

In 1929, Theodore sold the estate to Francis Burritt Thorne, Sr.

In 1942, the house was owned by the Orphan Asylum Society of Brooklyn.

In 1965, the Society sold it to Alfred and Fred Wimmer, who sold the house to the Town of Islip in 1967. It is currently the site of The Islip Art Museum, a leading exhibit space for contemporary art.

The Empire State Carousel, now located in Binghamton, NY, was built in the carriage house of *Brookwood*.

front facade

Knapp, William Kumbel (1827-1877)

Occupation(s):	capitalist - director, Greenport Ferry Co.
	merchant - partner, Melvin & Knapp (leather and hide firm)
Marriage(s):	Maria Meserole (1828-1904)
Address:	St. Mark's Lane, Islip
Name of estate:	*Winganhauppauge**
Year of construction:	c. 1850s
Style of architecture:	
Architect(s):	
Landscape architect(s):	
House extant: unconfirmed	
Historical notes:	

The house, originally named *Winganhauppauge*, was built by William Kumbel Knapp. It was the second house to be built on St. Mark's Lane; the first was that of Benjamin Sumner Welles, Sr.

William was the son of Shepherd and Catherine Louisa Kumble Knapp I.

William Kumbel and Maria Meserole Knapp's daughter Maria did not marry. Their daughter Evelina married Harry Bowly Hollins, Sr. and resided at *Meadow Farm* in East Islip. Their daughter Kate Louise died in 1879.

**Winganhauppauge* is Native American for Sweet Flowing River. [*Union Times* July 24, 1935, p. 6A.]

[See other Knapp entries for additional family information.]

Kobbe, George Christian (1852-1923)

Occupation(s):	attorney - partner, Roosevelt and Kobbe
	industrialist - a founder and director, Standard Beet Sugar Co.
	capitalist - director, Brooklyn Bridge Freezing & Cold Storage Co.;
	director, Harrison Street Cold Storage Co.
	financier - director, U. S. Casualty Co.
Marriage(s):	Alice Leavitt (1858-1933)
Address:	*[unable to determine street address]*, Bayport
Name of estate:	
Year of construction:	
Style of architecture:	
Architect(s):	
Landscape architect(s):	
House extant: no	
Historical notes:	

George Christian Kobbe was the son of the New York Consul General of the Duchy of Nassau, William Augustus Kobbe and Mrs. Sarah Lord Sistare Kobbe.

Alice Leavitt Kobbe was the daughter of Henry Sheldon and Martha Ann Young Leavitt of New York.

George Christian and Alice Leavitt Kobbe's daughter Louise married Peter Elting Farnum and, later, William M. Manning, the son of David F. Manning of Brooklyn. Their daughter Martha did not marry. Their son Walter married Florence Smith. Their son George Louis Kobbe married Lillian McConnell. Their daughter Alice married Curtis Gordon Rand. The Rands' son George Curtis Rand married Eleanor Close, the daughter of Edward Bennett and Marjorie Merriweather Post Close of *Hillwood* in Brookville. [*See* Spinzia, *Long Island's Prominent North Shore Families*, vol. II – M. M. Post entry.].

Kobbe, Gustav (1857-1918)

Occupation(s):	publisher - a founder, *Lotus* magazine, 1909
	journalist - music critic, *New York Herald;* editor, *Musical Review*
	writer - a novel and several reference books about music and the theater, including *The Complete Opera Book*, 1919
Marriage(s):	1892-1918 – Carolyn Wheeler (d. c. 1953)
Address:	Carll Avenue, Babylon
Name of estate:	
Year of construction:	
Style of architecture:	
Architect(s):	
Landscape architect(s):	
House extant:	no

Historical notes:

    Gustav Kobbe was a long-time renter of Cyrus Miller's residence. [*South Side Signal* April 19, 1912, p. 1.]

    He was the son of Carl Wilhelm Ludwig August and Sarah Lord Sistare Kobbe.

    Gustav was killed while sailing on the Great South Bay when the mast of his boat was struck by an airplane. [Harry W. Havemeyer, *Along the Great South Bay From Oakdale to Babylon: The Story of a Summer Spa 1840 to 1940* (Mattituck, NY: Amereon House, 1996), p. 322.]

    Carolyn Wheeler Kobbe was the daughter of George Minor Wheeler of Scarsdale, NY.

    Gustav and Carolyn Wheeler Kobbe's daughter Beatrice married Raymond Demarest Little, the son of Joseph J. Little, and resided in Babylon. Their daughter Hildegarde married Joseph Hutchins Stevenson, the son of Richard W. Stevenson of Cedarhurst, and, later, Francis Burritt Thorne, Sr., with whom she resided at *Brookwood* in East Islip. Their daughter Carol married Robert Woodward Morgan, Sr., the son of Charles Morgan and resided in East Islip. Carol subsequently married George Palen Snow, the son of Frederick Augustus and Mary Palen Snow of *Gardenside* in Southampton, and resided in Syosset. [*See* Spinzia, *Long Island's Prominent North Shore Families, vol. II* – Snow entry – and *Long Island's Prominent Families in the Town of Southampton* – Snow entry.] Their son George married Marjorie W. Goss, the daughter of Gustav Goss of Cincinnati, OH. Their daughter Virginia married Gerald Vanderbilt Hollins, Sr., with whom she resided at *The Hawks* in East Islip, and, subsequently, Henry Morgan.

    Shorty prior to Gustav's death, the Kobbes relocated to Garden City. [*See* Spinzia, *Long Island's Prominent Families in the Town of Hempstead* – Kobbe entry.]. After Gustav's death, Mrs. Kobbe's new residence was in East Islip.

Koehler, Robert H. (1880-1962)

Occupation(s):	attorney - member, Strong and Cadwalader; general counsel and director, Fifth Avenue Association; attorney for New York Furniture Exchange
	industrialist - director, Atlantic Carton Corp.
	financier - director, Roselle Park Building & Loan Association
	capitalist - president, Fenimore Building Corp.
Civic Activism:	director, Nassau County Bar Association; a founder, Sayville Yacht Club
Marriage(s):	M/1 – 1905-1927 – Harriet Bischoff (d. 1927)
	- Civic Activism: second vice-president, Bayport chapter, American Red Cross
	M/2 – 1929 – Ruth Allen Young
Address:	Ocean Avenue, Bayport
Name of estate:	
Year of construction:	1922
Style of architecture:	
Architect(s):	
Landscape architect(s):	
House extant:	unconfirmed

Historical notes:

    The house was built by Robert H. Koehler. [*The Suffolk County News* November 12, p. 12.]

    The *Long Island Society Register, 1929* lists Robert H. Koehler as residing in Brooklyn and Bayport.

    He was the son of Henry and Bertha Russell Koehler.

    At the time of death, Robert was residing at 158 Brixton Road, Garden City. [*See* Spinzia, *Long Island's Prominent Families in the Town of Hempstead* – Koehler entry.]

Lacombe, Charles Frederick (1867-1935)

Occupation(s):	civil engineer -	assayer and surveyor, silver mines in Utah;
		hired by New York City to fight the Gas and Electric Trust and relight the city, 1902;
		chief engineer, Power and Light, NYC;
		assistant assayist, Columbia School of Mines;
		director, Department of Economics and Statistics, Brooklyn Edison
	capitalist -	owned cattle ranch in the West;
		a founder and president, Contracting and Selling Co. (engineering firm)*;
		a founder, Mountain Engineering Co.

Marriage(s):　　　M/1 – 1890-1893 – Sara Laller Thayer (d. 1893)
　　　　　　　　　M/2 – 1900-1935 – Nancy E. Edrington

Address:　　　　　88 Douglas Avenue, Babylon
Name of estate:
Year of construction:
Style of architecture:
Architect(s):
Landscape architect(s):
House extant: no
Historical notes:

　The *Social Register Summer, 1915* lists Charles F. and Nancy E. Edrington Lacombe as residing at Argyle Park, Babylon.
　Charles was the son of James Pierre and Mary Catherine Burckle Lacombe. Charles fathered no children.
　*He was the builder of some of the first long distance electric power transmission plants in the United States.

Laidlaw, George Q., Sr. (1849-1932)

Occupation(s):　　　financer - 　bond and mortgage business
　　　　　　　　　　industrialist - 　officer, Mechanical Rubber Tire Co. (automobile tires)
Civic Activism:　　　member, Old Volunteers (Brooklyn Fire Department);
　　　　　　　　　　member, executive committee, Good Government Republican Club, 1912;
　　　　　　　　　　a founder, Bayport Republican Club, 1914;
　　　　　　　　　　member, road committee, Bayport Board of Trade, 1910

Marriage(s):　　　　1897-1932 – Mary Elizabeth Schmalix (1868-1954)

Address:　　　　　　Snedecor Avenue and Middle Road, Bayport
Name of estate:　　　*Bonnie Doon*
Year of construction:　1905
Style of architecture:　Modified Dutch Colonial Revival
Architect(s):
Landscape architect(s):
Builder:　　　　　　Joseph Harris, addition to barn, 1911;
　　　　　　　　　　addition to boathouse, 1912
House extant: no; destroyed by fire, 1976
Historical notes:

front facade

　The house, originally named *Bonnie Doon*, was built by George Q. Laidlaw, Sr.
　He was the son of John and Elisa Laidlaw of Brooklyn.
　George Q. and Mary Elizabeth Schmalix Laidlaw, Sr.'s daughter Margaret married Gilbert Clark and resided in Brightwaters. Their adopted daughter Victoria married Leander P. Wood and, later, John T. Strong, Jr. with whom she resided in Setauket. Their son George Q. Laidlaw, Jr. married Elizabeth Erhardt, the daughter of George Erhardt of Patchogue.
　In 1962, the United Methodist Church purchased the house for use as a Sunday School building.

Lawrance, Charles Lanier (1882-1950)

Occupation(s):	industrialist - a founder, president, and chief engineer, Lawrance Aero Engine Co. (formerly, S. S. Pierce Aeroplane; later, Wright Aeronautical Corp.);
	president, Wright Aeronautical Corp., Paterson, NJ;
	vice-president, Curtiss–Wright Corp.;
	chairman of board, Montreal Aircraft Industries, Ltd.
	capitalist - president, O–Co–Nee (Bay Shore land development company);
	president, C. L. Lawrance (Bay Shore land development company);
	president, Islip Airport;
	president, Plain Speaker Corp.;
	president, Voice of the Sky Corp.;
	director, Transcontinental Air Transport, Inc.;
	director, Fuel Air Motor Corp.;
	a founder and vice-president, National Air Transport (later, United Aircraft Corp.);
	a founder, president, and chairman of board, Lawrance Engineering & Research Corp., Linden, NJ;
	director, Lawrance Park Properties, Bronxville, NY
	inventor - Lanier–Lawrance airplane wing design*;
	Wright Whirlwind air-cooled airplane engine**
Civic Activism:	treasurer, Emergency Shelter Inc., NYC;
	director, Aeronautical Chamber of Commerce of America;
	director, Southside Hospital, Bay Shore (now, South Shore University Hospital)
Marriage(s):	1910-1950 – Emily Margaret Gordon Dix (1885-1973)
Address:	South Country Road, Bay Shore
Name of estate:	*Manatuck Farm*
Year of construction:	
Style of architecture:	
Architect(s):	Clarence K. Birdsall designed 1897 brick carriage house (for F. C. Lawrance, Sr.)
Landscape architect(s):	
House extant: unconfirmed	
Historical notes:	

    Charles Lanier Lawrance was the son of Francis Cooper and Sarah Eggleston Lanier Lawrance, Jr. of Bay Shore.
    He inherited the estate from his grandfather Francis Cooper Lawrance, Sr.
    Emily Margaret Gordon Dix Lawrance was the daughter of The Reverend Morgan Dix, the rector of Trinity Parish in Manhattan, and his wife Mrs. Emily Woolsey Soutter Dix.
    Charles Lanier and Emily Margaret Gordon Dix Lawrance's daughter Margaret married Drayton Cochran of Centre Island and, subsequently, Winston H. Frost. [*See* Spinzia, *Long Island's Prominent North Shore Families*, vol. *I* – Cochran entry.] The Lawrances' daughter Emily married Joseph Sherman Frelinghuysen, Jr. of New Jersey. Their son Francis Cooper Lawrance III, who resided in East Islip, married Priscilla C. Howe and, later, Anne Dudley.
    In 1925, the Lawrances relocated to East Islip.
    [See other Lawrance entries for additional family information.]
    *Lawrance's airplane wing design was used by Great Britain and Germany during World War I.
    **His air-cooled airplane engine was used by the New York Militia during World War I, by Admiral Richard Byrd on his North Pole and Antarctica expeditions, and by Charles Lindbergh in his solo flight across the Atlantic in the *Spirit of St. Louis*.
    [For information on the Southside Hospital, see Cooper entry.]

Lawrance, Charles Lanier (1882-1950)

Occupation(s):	*[See previous entry.]*
Marriage(s):	1910-1950 – Emily Margaret Gordon Dix (1885-1973)
Address:	Hollins Lane, East Islip
Name of estate:	
Year of construction:	c. 1880
Style of architecture:	Shingle
Architect(s):	
Landscape architect(s):	Olmsted (for H. B. Hollins, Sr.)

House extant: no; demolished 2003*
Historical notes:

front facade

In 1940, Charles Lanier Lawrance purchased Harry Bowly Hollins, Sr.'s estate *Meadow Farm*.

He was the son of Francis Cooper and Sarah Eggleston Lanier Lawrance, Jr. of Bay Shore.

[See other Lawrance entries for additional family information.]

*The estate's stables and clock tower survived and are currently a private residence at 37 Blackmore Lane. The farm house at 42 Blackmore Lane also survives. In the 1980s the carriage house was demolished.

Lawrance, Francis Cooper, Jr. (1857-1904)

Occupation(s):	attorney - never practiced
Marriage(s):	M/1 – Sarah Eggleston Lanier (1862-1893)
	M/2 – 1897-1904 – Susan Ridgeway Willing (1866-1933)
Address:	South Country Road, Bay Shore
Name of estate:	*Manatuck Farm*
Year of construction:	
Style of architecture:	
Architect(s):	Clarence K. Birdsall designed 1897 brick carriage house (for F.C. Lawrance, Sr.)

Landscape architect(s):
House extant: unconfirmed
Historical notes:

Francis Cooper Lawrance, Jr. was the son of Francis Cooper and Frances Adelaide Garner Lawrance, Sr., who also resided at *Manatuck Farm*.

Sarah Eggleston Lanier Lawrance was the daughter of Charles and Sarah Eggleston Lanier of New York.

Francis Cooper and Sarah Eggleston Lanier Lawrance, Jr.'s son Charles Lanier Lawrance, who married Emily Margaret Gordon Dix, later owned *Manatuck Farm*. In 1925, Charles relocated to East Islip. The Lawrances' daughter Katharine married William Averell Harriman, who resided in Sands Point and Old Westbury. Katharine later married Dr. Eugene Hillhouse Pool, with whom she resided in Lattingtown. [*See* Spinzia, *Long Island's Prominent North Shore Families, vol. I* – Harriman entries – and *Long Island's Prominent North Shore Families, vol. II* – Pool entry.]

Susan Ridgeway Willing Lawrance was the daughter of Edward S. Willing of Philadelphia, PA. Her sister Ava married John Jacob Astor IV.

Francis Cooper and Susan Ridgeway Willing Lawrance, Jr.'s daughter Frances married Prince Andre Poniatowski of Poland and resided in France.

[See other Lawrance entries for additional family information.]

Lawrance, Francis Cooper, Sr. (1829-1911)

Occupation(s): capitalist - Manhattan real estate

Marriage(s): Frances Adelaide Garner (1835-1908)

Address: South Country Road, Bay Shore
Name of estate: *Manatuck Farm*
Year of construction:
Style of architecture:
Architect(s): Clarence K. Birdsall designed
    1897 brick carriage house
    (for F. C. Lawrance, Sr.)

Landscape architect(s):
House extant: unconfirmed
Historical notes:

    Francis Cooper Lawrance, Sr. was the son of Thomas and Margaret Lawrence Ireland Lawrance and the grandson of John Busteed Ireland of West Islip. His sister Cornelia married George Gorman Wilmerding and resided in West Bay Shore.
    Frances Adelaide Garner Lawrance was the daughter of Thomas and Frances Mathilda Thorn Garner, Sr. of Bay Shore. Her brother Thomas Garner, Jr. married Harriet H. Amory and resided in Bay Shore. Her brother William married Macellite Thorn and also resided in Bay Shore. Her sister Annie did not marry.
    Francis Cooper and Frances Adelaide Garner Lawrance, Sr.'s daughter Fanny married George William Henry Veron, the Seventh Baron Veron of *Sudbury Hall* in Derbyshire, Great Britain. She was the first of the South Shore daughters to marry a member of the British nobility. [Harry W. Havemeyer, *Along the Great South Bay From Oakdale to Babylon: The Story of a Summer Spa 1840 to 1940* (Mattituck, NY: Amereon House, 1996), p. 208.] Their son Francis Cooper Lawrance, Jr., who married Sarah Eggleston Lanier, and, subsequently, Susan Ridgeway Willing, also resided at *Manatuck Farm*. Their son Thomas died in 1883 while a student at Yale University.
    [See other Lawrance entries for additional family information.]

Lawrence, Chester Bulkley, Sr. (1845-1918)

Occupation(s): capitalist - partner, Lawrence & Gerrish (Brooklyn warehouses)
    politician - Brooklyn Fire Commissioner (Schieren administration);
        member, executive committee, Brooklyn Young
        Republican Club, 1884-1894

Marriage(s): 1867-1918 – Catherine Covell (1845-1922)

Address: Ocean Avenue, Bay Shore
Name of estate:
Year of construction:
Style of architecture:
Architect(s):
Landscape architect(s):
House extant: unconfirmed
Historical notes:

    Chester Bulkley Lawrence, Sr. was the son of Effingham Nicoll and Margaret Clendenning Lawrence.
    Catherine Covell Lawrence was the daughter of George Covell.
    Chester Bulkley and Catherine Covell Lawrence, Sr.'s daughter Marion married Ernest M. Lawrence and resided in Bay Shore and, later, Staten Island, NY. Their son Chester Bulkley Lawrence, Jr. married Florence Beekman Bailey.
    Distraught over his wife's death, Chester committed suicide three hours later.

Lawrence, John Ireland (d. 1889)

Occupation(s):

Marriage(s): 1850-1889 – Anna Stanton (1830-1909)

Address: South Country Road, West Bay Shore
Name of estate:
Year of construction:
Style of architecture:
Architect(s):
Landscape architect(s):
House extant: unconfirmed
Historical notes:

John Ireland Lawrence was the son of Thomas and Margaret Ireland Lawrence, Jr.
Anna Stanton Lawrence was the daughter of George W. Stanton of Albany, NY.
John Ireland and Anna Stanton Lawrence's daughter Sara, who did not marry, inherited the house.
[See other Lawrance entries for additional family information.]

Lazare, Andrew (1880-1930)

Occupation(s): capitalist - founder, Lazare Employment Agency, NYC

Marriage(s):

Address: South Country Road, Islip
Name of estate:
Year of construction:
Style of architecture:
Architect(s):
Landscape architect(s):
House extant: unconfirmed
Historical notes:

In 1924, Lazare purchased the Joseph Byron Creamer, Sr. house and its twelve surrounding acres from Mrs. Creamer. Lazare later relocated to Woodmere.
His son George married Daphne Sangree, the daughter of Dr. T. Chalmers Sangree of Bayport.

Lemmerman, Frederick C. (1894-1947)

Occupation(s):   capitalist - partner, Gross & Lemmerman, Inc., Queens County, NY (construction firm)
politician - County Clerk of New York City; member, Triborough Bridge Authority, 1933
financier - vice-president, Ridgewood Savings Bank

Civic Activism: president, Queens County Chamber of Commerce;
trustee, Wyckoff Heights Hospital, Brooklyn;
member, Queens County War Ration Board during World War II;
director, Queens Borough Business Men's League, Inc.;
director, Queens Society for the Prevention of Cruelty to Children

Marriage(s):   Mabel *[unable to determine maiden name]*

Address: 32 Awixa Avenue, Bay Shore
Name of estate:
Year of construction: c. 1899
Style of architecture: Shingle
Architect(s):   Ernest George Washington Dietrich designed the house (for Wray)
Landscape architect(s):
House extant: yes
Historical notes:

The house, originally named *Whileaway*, was built by William Henry Wray, Sr. It was later owned by Lemmerman and, subsequently, by William Kemble Clarkson, Jr.
In 2003, the house was purchased by Dr. Mark Foehr.

front facade, c. 1903

Lentilhon, Eugene, II (1869-1932)

Occupation(s):
Civic Activism: charter member, Bay Shore Yacht Club, 1884;
rear commodore, Penataquit Corinthian Yacht Club, Bay Shore;
a founder, director, and president, Suffolk County Taxpayers Good Roads Association, 1908

Marriage(s):   M/1 – 1896-1898 – Rose Parran Buchanan (1873-1898)
M/2 – 1900 – Florence Bergh Brown (b. 1871)
   - Civic Activism: president, South Side Garden Club

Address: South Country Road and Saxon Avenue, Bay Shore
Name of estate: *Brookside Farm*
Year of construction:
Style of architecture:
Architect(s):
Landscape architect(s):
House extant: unconfirmed
Historical notes:

Eugene Lentilhon II was the son of Joseph and Zella Trelawney Detwold Lentilhon of New York.
Rosa Parran Buchanan Lentilhon was the daughter of James A. and Rosa Morgan Parran Buchanan of Philadelphia.
The *Social Register Summer, 1910* lists Eugene and Florence B. Brown Lentilhon [II] are residing at *Brookside Farm* in Bay Shore.
She was the daughter of Edwin Bergh and Agnes Pollock Brown. Florence's sister Jean married Walter Jennings and resided at *Burrwood* in Lloyd Harbor. [See Spinzia, *Long Island's Prominent North Shore Families, vol. I* – Jennings entry]

Lester, Joseph Huntington (1847-1918)

Occupation(s):	capitalist - tea importer financier - *
Civic Activism:	director, The Tea Association of New York (tea merchants); a founder and director, Bay Shore Protective Association
Marriage(s):	Henrietta Frances Maxwell (1848-1940)
Address:	South Country Road and Awixa Avenue, Bay Shore
Name of estate:	*Lestaley*
Year of construction:	1903
Style of architecture:	Colonial Revival
Architect(s):	
Landscape architect(s):	
Builder:	Jabez Ephraim Van Orden, house, carriage house, and stables, 1903 (for Lester)

House extant: no
Historical notes:

The house, originally named *Lestaley*, was built by Joseph Huntington Lester. [*Brooklyn Daily Eagle* November 22, 1902, p. 11.]

The *Long Island Society Register, 1929* lists Mrs. Joseph Lester as residing at *Lestaley* in Bay Shore.

She was the daughter of John and Caroline Elizabeth Brigham Maxwell. Henrietta's brother Henry William Maxwell also resided in Bay Shore. Her brother John Rogers Maxwell, Sr. married Marie Louise Washburn and resided at *Maxwelton* in Glen Cove. [*See* Spinzia, *Long Island's Prominent North Shore Families, vol. I* – Maxwell entry]

At the age of twenty-four, while married to Henrietta, Joseph Huntington Lester allegedly married a sixteen-year-old girl in a scandalous elopement. No charges were pressed; no punishment resulted. [*Brooklyn Daily Eagle* August 9, 1880, p.4.]

*Lester was part of a syndicate that purchased massive amounts of wheat on the commodities market in an attempt to "corner" the cereal market. [*Brooklyn Daily Eagle* December 19, 1897, p. 4.]

Joseph Huntington and Henrietta Frances Maxwell Lester's son Maxwell Lester, Sr. married Laura Norma Hegeman and resided at *Four Hedges* in Bay Shore.

[See other Lester and Maxwell entries for additional family information.]

Lester, Maxwell, Jr. (1903-1979)

Occupation(s):	financier - member, James H. Oliphant and Co. (later, Hornblower, Weekes, Spencer, and Trask) (stock brokerage firm) politician - councilman and mayor, Summit, NJ; commissioner, New Jersey State Turnpike Authority
Civic Activism:	director, Summit, NJ, Civil Defense, 1941-1977
Marriage(s):	M/1 – 1927 – S. Katharine Libby (d. 1957) M/2 – Emily Baldwin (d. 1973)
Address:	Main Street, Bay Shore
Name of estate:	
Year of construction:	
Style of architecture:	
Architect(s):	
Landscape architect(s):	

House extant: unconfirmed
Historical notes:

The *Long Island Society Register, 1929* lists the Lesters as residing in Bay Shore.

He was the son of Maxwell and Laura Norma Hegeman Lester, Sr., who resided at *Four Hedges* in Bay Shore.

S. Katharine Libby Maxwell was the daughter of Walter Gillette Libby of Summit, NJ, and Brooklyn. Her brother Walter Gillette Libby, Jr. resided in Urbanna, VA. Her sister Elizabeth married Paul Wiser and, subsequently, Ruford Davis Franklin of New York.

Maxwell and S. Katharine Libby Maxwell, Jr.'s son Maxwell Lester III married Mary Randolph Pennywitt, the daughter of John Pennywitt.

Emily Baldwin Lester had previously been married to ____ Reach.

[See other Lester and Maxwell entries for additional family information.]

Lester, Maxwell, Sr. (1876-1920)

Occupation(s):	industrialist - director, Atlas Portland Cement Co.
Civic Activism:	secretary, Long Island College Hospital, Brooklyn
Marriage(s):	1902-1920 – Laura Norma Hegeman (1879-1967) - Civic Activism: vice-president, Long Island College Hospital Guild, Brooklyn
Address:	*[unable to determine street address]*, Bay Shore
Name of estate:	*Four Hedges*
Year of construction:	
Style of architecture:	
Architect(s):	
Landscape architect(s):	
House extant:	unconfirmed
Historical notes:	

The *Long Island Society Register, 1929* lists only Mrs. Lester, Sr. as residing at *Four Hedges* in Bay Shore.

Maxwell Lester, Sr. was the son of Joseph Huntington and Henrietta Frances Maxwell Lester, who resided at *Lestaley* in Bay Shore.

Laura Norma Hegeman Lester was the daughter of Peter Augustus and Lavinia Edna Speir Hegeman of Brooklyn. Her sister Florence married John Fowler Pound.

Maxwell and Laura Norma Hegeman Lester, Sr.'s son Maxwell Lester, Jr., who married S. Katharine Libby and, subsequently, Emily Baldwin, resided in Bay Shore and Summit, NJ.

[See other Lester and Maxwell entries for additional family information.]

Liebmann, Julius (1867-1957)

Occupation(s):	industrialist - president and chairman of board, S. Liebmann and Sons Brewing Co., Brooklyn (brewer of Rheingold Beer; later, C. Schmidt & Sons of Philadelphia, PA) financier - director, Broadway Bank of Brooklyn; vice-president, Manufacturers Trust Co. of Brooklyn
Civic Activism:	vice-president, technical advisory committee, United Brewers Association; trustee, Federal Brewers Association
Marriage(s):	1894 – M. Antoniette Scharmann (b. 1872) - Civic Activism: trustee, Brooklyn Maternity Center Association
Address:	Suydam Lane, Bayport
Name of estate:	
Year of construction:	c. 1854
Style of architecture:	Italianate
Architect(s):	
Landscape architect(s):	
House extant:	no; demolished in 1987
Historical notes:	

front facade

John Richard Suydam, Sr. purchased the house in 1854 as a wedding present for this wife. They called it *Edgewater*. It was later owned by his son John Richard Suydam, Jr., who continued to call it *Edgewater*. In 1920, the house was purchased by Herbert and Grace Whiting Seaman, who immediately sold it to Liebmann.

He was the son of Charles and Sophia Bendix Liebmann of Brooklyn.

M. Antoniette Scharmann Liebmann was the daughter of Herman Balthazar and Frieda Stehlin Scharmann of Brooklyn.

Julius and M. Antoniette Scharmann Liebmann's daughter Catherine married Dr. Morris L. Rakieten of New Haven, CT. The Rakietens relocated to Bay Shore where Dr. Rakieten opened a medical clinic. Their son Dr. James Liebmann, who later owned his parents' Bayport house, married Winfred Bronson, the daughter of Miles Bronson of Yonkers, NY. James changed his surname to Leland. [Harry W. Havemeyer, *East on the Great South Bay: Sayville and Bayport 1860-1960* (Mattituck, NY: Amereon House, 2001), pp. 199-200.]

The estate was later owned by James' daughter Anne, who sold it to Ira Rubenstein in 1987. Rubenstein demolished the house and built a new one on the site, which he called *Cheap John's Estate*.

Lindsay, Lewin Seton (1879-1970)

Occupation(s):	financier - vice-president, New York Life Insurance Co.
Marriage(s):	M/1 – 1903-1932 – Gwendolyn Blackburn Chuwys Owen (1880-1932)
	- Civic Activism: chair, South Suffolk County chapter, American Red Cross, 1924
	M/2 – 1936 – Edith Louise Riley
	- Civic Activism: co-chair, national women's committee, United Seaman's Service, 1942
Address:	South Bay Avenue, Islip
Name of estate:	
Year of construction:	
Style of architecture:	
Architect(s):	
Landscape architect(s):	
House extant:	unconfirmed

Historical notes:

The *Social Register Summer, 1915* lists L. Seton and Gwendolyn Owen Lindsay as residing in Islip.

He was the son of Charles Seton and Mary Lewin Lindsay of New York.

Gwendolyn Blackburn Chuwys Owen Lindsay was the daughter of Welsh Owen of Richmond Surry, England.

Lewin Seton and Gwendolyn Blackburn Chuwys Owen Lindsay's son Owen married Nancy Hill of Los Angeles and resided in Bedford Hills, NY. Their daughter Mary, who was presented at Buckingham Palace, married A. Guy Hiddingh of the 14th-20th Hussars in the British Army who was killed in World War II.

Edith Louise Riley Lindsay had previously been married to G. Geranger Gaither of Westbury and Thomas H. Symington.

Litchfield, Electus Backus (1813-1889)

Occupation(s):	merchant - wholesale grocer, NYC, 1844-1854
	capitalist - builder, Fifth Avenue Street Railway, Brooklyn;
	builder, Coney Island Plank Road, Brooklyn;
	owner, Brooklyn, Bath and West End Railroad;
	owner, St. Paul and Pacific Railroad, 1862-1870;
	real estate - invested in Brooklyn real estate;
	owner, with his brothers Edwin Clark Litchfield and Erasmus Darwin Litchfield:
	Michigan Southern Railroad;
	Indiana Northern Railroad;
	Toledo and Cleveland Railroad;
	Toledo and Detroit Railroad;
	Toledo and Elkhart Railroad;
	Terre Haute and Alton Railroad
	co-owner, with August Belmont Sr., Argyle Hotel, Babylon, 1882
Marriage(s):	1838-1873 – Hannah Maria Breed (1818-1873)
Address:	South Country Road, Babylon
Name of estate:	*Blythebourne*
Year of construction:	1864
Style of architecture:	Colonial Revival
Architect(s):	
Landscape architect(s):	
House extant:	unconfirmed

Historical notes:

The house, originally named *Blythebourne*, was built by Electus Backus Litchfield.

He was the son of Elisha and P. Tiffany Litchfield of Delphi Falls, NY.

front facade

Hannah Maria Breed Litchfield was the daughter of Elias Breed of NYC.

Electus Backus and Hannah Maria Breed Litchfield's son William married Emily Pope and resided in Brooklyn. Their daughter Mary married Walter Colton. Their daughter Heloise married George Albert Allin of Brooklyn.

In 1881, Austin Corbin, Jr. purchased the fifteen-acre estate for $65,000. A portion of the estate's land was used for the site of the Argyle Hotel.

Little, Raymond Demarest (d. 1932)

Occupation(s):	industrialist - treasurer, Kingspoint Press Sales, NYC (book manufacturing firm)
Marriage(s):	M/1 – 1907-div. – Beatrice Kobbe (b. 1886)
	- Civic Activism: member, ladies auxiliary, Southside Hospital, Bay Shore (now, South Shore University Hospital)
	M/2 – 1925-1932 – Marion Mellon
Address:	South Country Road, Babylon
Name of estate:	
Year of construction:	
Style of architecture:	
Architect(s):	
Landscape architect(s):	
House extant: unconfirmed	
Historical notes:	

The *Social Register Summer, 1911* lists Raymond D. and Beatrice Kobbe Little as residing on South Country Road, Babylon.

He was the son of Joseph J. Little and a member of the American Davis Cup team at Wimbledon in 1906.

Beatrice Kobbe Little was the daughter of Gustav and Carolyn Wheeler Kobbe of Babylon.

Raymond Demarest and Beatrice Kobbe Little's daughter Elsie, who was a Power's model and lent her name to the wife of Bordon Milk's cow Elmer for milk commercials, married James Holmes Madden, the son of Jay Madden of Greenwich, CT, and, later, H. Adams Ashforth, Sr.

Little killed himself with a shotgun in the bathroom of his Park Avenue apartment.

[For information on the Southside Hospital, see Cooper entry.]

Livingston, Miss Frances Lewis (1886-1949)

Civic Activism:	chairman of board, American Red Cross Town and County Nursing Service, Islip, 1914;
	chair, nurses committee, Town of Islip chapter, American Red Cross;
	member, executive committee, Town of Islip chapter, American Red Cross, 1917;
	secretary, South Suffolk chapter, American Red Cross, 1928
Marriage(s):	
Address:	Bay View Avenue, East Islip
Name of estate:	
Year of construction:	1916
Style of architecture:	Basque-inspired Farmhouse
Architect(s):	Cross and Cross designed the house (for F. L. Livingston)
Landscape architect(s):	
House extant: no; demolished in 1960s	
Historical notes:	

The house was built by Frances Lewis Livingston.

She was the daughter of Henry Beckman and Frances Redmond Livingston, Jr. of Bay Shore. Her sister Lilias married Harry Bowly Hollins, Jr. and resided at *Crickholly* in East Islip. Her sister Mary died in 1898 at the age of fifteen.

At the time of her death, Frances was residing at *Johnny Cake Farm* in Cooperstown, NY.

front facade

Livingston, Henry, III (1837-1906)

Occupation(s):	publisher - *Times*, Armenia, NY; founder and editor, *South Side Signal*, 1869; *New York Business Mirror*
Civic Activism:	vice president, Suffolk County Press Association; first chief, Babylon Fire Department
Marriage(s):	1861-1884 – Augusta Carll (1839-1884)
Address:	Main Street, Babylon
Name of estate:	
Year of construction:	
Style of architecture:	French Empire
Architect(s):	
Landscape architect(s):	
House extant: unconfirmed	
Historical notes:	

front facade

Henry Livingston III was the son of Sidney Montgomery and Joanna Maria Holthuysen Livingston of Hyde Park-on-the-Hudson, NY, and a descendant of Philip Livingston, a signer of the Declaration of Independence.

Henry claimed that his grandfather Henry Livingston, Jr., not Clement Clarke Moore, was the author of the poem "Twas the Night Before Christmas."

Augusta Carll Livingston was the daughter of Elbert and Mary Ann Carll of Babylon.

Henry and Augusta Carll Livingston III's daughter Mabel died in 1872 at the age of four. Their daughter Julia and son Elbert did not marry.

Livingston, Henry Beekman, Jr. (1854-1931)

Occupation(s):	financier - partner, Maxwell and Co. (stock brokerage firm); member, Munds and Winslow (stock brokerage firm)
Civic Activism:	a founder and trustee, Waverly Gun Club, Islip, 1890
Marriage(s):	M/1 – 1876-1978 – Stephanie Jacqueline Fox (1853-1878) M/2 – 1881-1916 – Frances Redmond (1849-1916) M/3 – 1918 – Mrs. Leonie Dufard de la Claire
Address:	Saxon Avenue, Bay Shore
Name of estate:	
Year of construction:	1893
Style of architecture:	Shingle
Architect(s):	
Landscape architect(s):	
House extant: unconfirmed	
Historical notes:	

front facade, c. 1909

Henry Beekman Livingston, Jr. was the son of Henry Beekman and Mary Lawrence Livingston, Sr.

Stephanie Jacqueline Fox Livingston was the daughter of Samuel and Marie Adelaide Livingston Fox.

Henry Beekman and Stephanie Jacqueline Fox Livingston, Jr.'s daughter Angelica did not marry.

The *Social Register Summer, 1915* lists Henry B. and Frances Redmond Livingston [Jr.] as residing in Islip [Bay Shore].

She was the daughter of William and Sabrina Hoyt Redmond of Manhattan. Frances' brother Roland married Helen Clark Bulkley and rented a summer residence in Islip.

Henry Beekman and Frances Redmond Livingston, Jr.'s daughter Lilias married Harry Bowly Hollins, Jr. and resided at *Crickholly* in East Islip. Their daughter Frances Lewis Livingston, who did not marry, resided in East Islip. Their daughter Mary died in 1898 at the age of fifteen.

Livingston, Robert Cambridge, III (1847-1895)

Occupation(s): capitalist - treasurer, National Express Co.

Marriage(s): 1870-1895 – Maria Whitney (1851-1918)

Address: St. Mark's Lane, Islip*
Name of estate: *Lakeside*
Year of construction:
Style of architecture: Victorian Gothic
Architect(s):
Landscape architect(s):
House extant: yes
Historical notes:

    The house was built by Parmenus Johnson, Sr. In January 1880, the twenty-one-acre estate was purchased by C. A. Backett of New York. By June 1880 it was owned by E. B. Spaulding who enlarged and modernized the house [*The Brooklyn Daily Eagle* January 27, 1880, p. 4, and June 7, 1880, p. 1.] In 1886, the estate was purchased by Livingston, who called it *Lakeside*.
    The *Social Register Summer, 1915* lists Maria Whitney Livingston as residing at *Lakeside* in Islip.
    She was the daughter of Henry and Maria Lucy Fitch Whitney of New Haven, CT.
    Robert Cambridge Livingston III was the son of Robert Cambridge and Maria Bronson Murray Livingston II of Manhattan.
    Robert Cambridge and Maria Whitney Livingston III's daughter Eloise married James L. Kernochan. Their son John married Clara M. Dudley, the daughter of B. William and Maria Hunt Dudley, and resided in Lawrence. Their son Henry, who resided in Islip, remained a bachelor. Their son Johnston. who resided at *Still Pond* in Huntington, married Natalie Fellows Moss, the daughter of Courtland Dixon and Camilla Woodward Moss, Sr., and, subsequently, Ruth Helene Moller, the daughter of Charles George Moller, Jr. Ruth later relocated to East Hampton. [*See* Spinzia, *Long Island's Prominent North Shore Families*, vol. *I* and *Long Island's Prominent Families* in the Town of East Hampton – Livingston entries.] Their son Louis married Charlotte Atlee Black, the daughter of C. Irving Cunard Black of Chicago, IL, and, later, Catherine Murphy with whom he resided in Manhattan. Their daughter Caroline married Maxwell Stevenson of *The Lodge* in Hempstead and, later, ____ Male of Paris, France. [*See* Spinzia, *Long Island's Prominent Families* in the Town of Hempstead – Livingston and Stevenson entries.]
    The house was later owned by the Livingstons' daughter Maud who married Henry Worthington Bull.
    By the early 1940s it was owned by the Bulls' niece Phyllis Livingston Baker Astaire, who was married to the noted dancer/choreographer/actor Fred Astaire, Sr. [aka Frederick Austerlitz].
    In 2006, the house was owned by ____ Dowden.
    In 2008, the seven thousand-square-foot, twenty-room house with seven bedrooms was for sale. The asking price was $1,499,990; the taxes were $16,089.
    *The estate originally bordered on St. Marks Lane. With its subdivision, the house is currently located on Suellen Road.

Lorillard, George Lyndes (1843-1886)

Occupation(s): industrialist - president, Pierre and G. L. Lorillard (tobacco firm)
capitalist - partner, Monmouth Park Racetrack

Civic Activism: *

Marriage(s): 1882-1886 – Maria Louise La Farge (1850-1899)

Address: South Country Road, Great River
Name of estate: *Westbrook Farm*
Year of construction: c. 1860s
Style of architecture: Neo-Tudor
Architect(s):
Landscape architect(s):
House extant: no; demolished in c. 1900**
Historical notes:

The house, originally named *Westbrook Farm*, was built by Robert Lenox Maitland, Sr. In 1873, Mrs. Maitland sold it to Lorillard.

He was the son of Pierre and Catherine Anne Griswold Lorillard III.

Maria Louise La Farge Lorillard was the daughter of the noted artist John La Farge and his wife Margaret Mason Perry LaFarge, who was the granddaughter of Commodore Perry. Perry's daughter Caroline married August Belmont, Sr. and resided at *Nursery Stud Farm* in North Babylon. Maria had previously been married to Edward Whyte. After Lorillard's death, she married Count Casa de Agreda of Spain.

The Lorillards were childless.

The estate was later owned by Robert Fulton Cutting and, subsequently, by his brother William Bayard Cutting, Sr.

*Lorillard arranged to have boys from New York House of Refuge brought to Great River to be schooled at *Westbrook Farm* and to learn to ride horses. After a five-year apprenticeship, they were given the opportunity to become professional jockeys.

**After the Spanish American War the house was used by the federal government as a convalescent home for returning servicemen and then demolished. [Harry W. Havemeyer, *Along the Great South Bay From Oakdale to Babylon: The Story of a Summer Spa 1840 to 1940* (Mattituck, NY: Amereon House, 1996), p. 148.]

Westbrook Farm

Lovering, Joseph Sears, Sr. (1908-1962)

Occupation(s):

Marriage(s): M/1 – 1929 – Carol Stevenson (b. 1909)
M/2 – 1945-1962 – Anne Valentine (1911-1983)

Address: St. Mark's Lane, Islip
Name of estate:
Year of construction:
Style of architecture:
Architect(s):
Landscape architect(s):
House extant: unconfirmed
Historical notes:

Joseph Sears Lovering, Sr. purchased the Enfin Johnson house.

He was the son of Joseph Swain Lovering, Sr. of *Sunny Ridge* in Hewlett. His brother William was killed in World War II. His brother Charles married Margaret Murray, the daughter of Herman S. and Susanne E. Warren Murray, who resided at *Our House* in Woodmere. [*See* Spinzia, *Long Island's Prominent Families in the Town of Hempstead* – Lovering and Murray entries.]

Carol Stevenson Lovering was the daughter of Joseph Hutchinson and Hildegarde Kobbe Stevenson. Carol subsequently married Max Stuart Roesler of Cos Cob, CT. Her sister Hildegarde married Fredrick Bourne Hard of West Sayville.

Joseph Sears and Carol Stevenson Lovering, Sr.'s daughter Elsie married William Hamilton Gregory III, the son of William Hamilton and Edith A. Crowley Gregory, Jr. of *Creekside* in Islip, and, later, Eugene Morris Cheston, Jr. with whom she resided in Darien, CT. [*See* Spinzia, *Long Island's Prominent North Shore Families, vol. I* – Gregory entry.] Their son Joseph Sears Lovering, Jr. married Virginia Terrell Sydnor, the daughter of Thomas Austin Sydnor of Richmond, VA.

Ann Valentine Lovering was the daughter of Langdon Barrett and Louise Hollister Valentine of Islip.

Joseph Sears and Anne Valentine Lovering, Jr.'s daughter Alis married George M. Fern.

Low, Chauncey Edward, Sr. (1851-1890)

Occupation(s): merchant - member, A. A. Low & Brother (tea importer and merchant)
Civic Activism: director, Brooklyn Philharmonic Society;
a founder and president, South Side Field Club, Bay Shore, 1886

Marriage(s): Mary Thompson Frothingham (b. 1854)

Address: 87 South Penataquit Avenue, Bay Shore
Name of estate: *Seaward*
Year of construction: c. 1880
Style of architecture: Queen Anne
Architect(s):
Landscape architect(s):
House extant: yes
Historical notes:

Seaward, c. 1903

The house, originally named *Seaward*, was built by Chauncey Edward Low, Sr.

The *Brooklyn Blue Book and Long Island Society Register, 1918* lists Chauncey E. and Mary T. Frothingham Low as residing in Bay Shore.

He was the son of Josiah O. Low, Sr.

Mary Thompson Frothingham Low was the daughter of John Whipple and Mary Angeline Thompson Frothingham of Brooklyn. Her brother John Sewell Frothingham married Katharine Kent and resided in Bay Shore.

Chauncey Edward and Mary Thompson Frothingham Low's daughter Mary married The Reverend Roger Sawyer Forbes, the son of The Reverend John Perkin Forbes. Their son Josiah married Dorothy Lewis, the daughter of Theodore J. Lewis of Philadelphia, PA. Their daughter Nathalie married James McFarlan Baker and resided in Brooklyn. Their son Chauncey Edward Low, Jr. died in 1892 at eleven months of age.

The house was subsequently owned by Michael Quinn.

In 2018, the 6,000-square-foot, eight-bedroom, four-bath house sold for $849,000.

Ludlow, William Handy, Sr. (1821-1890)

Occupation(s):	politician - member, New York State Assembly; speaker of the house, New York State Assembly, 1853
	military - general in Civil War
	financier - president, American Tontine Life Insurance Co.
Marriage(s):	1841-1887 – Frances Louisa Nicoll (1822-1887)
Address:	South Country Road, Oakdale
Name of estate:	*Old Oak Farm*
Year of construction:	
Style of architecture:	
Architect(s):	
Landscape architect(s):	
House extant:	unconfirmed
Historical notes:	

William Handy Ludlow, Sr. was the son of Ezra and Rachel Seguine Ludlow.

Frances Louisa Nicoll Ludlow was the daughter of William and Sarah Greenly Nicoll.

William Handy and Frances Louisa Nicoll Ludlow, Sr.'s son Admiral Nicoll Ludlow married Frances Mary Thomas. Their son General William Handy Ludlow, Jr. married Almira Sprigg of St. Louis, MO.

The estate was purchased by Frederick Gilbert Bourne.

Lyon, Dr. Edward Crane (b. 1880)

Occupation(s):	physician - consulting physician, Woman's Hospital, NYC
	educator - instructor, Columbia University Medical School, NYC
Marriage(s):	Louise Carskaddon Little (1895-1972)
Address:	46 Carll Avenue, Babylon
Name of estate:	
Year of construction:	1914
Style of architecture:	Modified Shingle
Architect(s):	
Landscape architect(s):	
House extant:	yes
Historical notes:	

The *Long Island Society Register, 1929* lists Dr. Edward C. and Mrs. Louise C. Little Lyon as residing at 46 Carll Avenue, Babylon.

He was the son of Edward Canfield and Caroline Hannah Crane Lyon.

Louise Carskaddon Little Lyon was the daughter of Henry Lyman and Erbanda C. Carskaddon Little.

Dr. Edward Crane and Mrs. Louise Carskaddon Little Lyon's son Gordon resided in Westhampton Beach. Their daughter Louise married Donald J. Strait, the son of Fred G. Strait of Montclair, NJ, and resided in Babylon. Their daughter Patricia married Joseph Cecil Hearn, Jr. and resided in Charlottesville, VA.

In 2020, the house was for sale. The asking price was $594,000.

front facade, 2020

MacConnell, John B. (1829-1895)

Occupation(s):	financier - auditor, New York Life Insurance Co.
Marriage(s):	Margaret Macdonald (1832-1892)
Address:	Middle Road and McConnell Avenue, Bayport
Name of estate:	
Year of construction:	1873
Style of architecture:	Victorian Gothic
Architect(s):	
Landscape architect(s):	
House extant: yes	
Historical notes:	

front facade

The Middle Road house was built by John B. MacConnell.

John B. and Margaret Macdonald MacConnell's daughter Jennie married Francis Melville, Jr., the son of Francis and Mary Bamman Melville, Sr. of Bayville, and resided at *Sunwood* in Old Field. Their daughter Mary married Sir Pomeroy Burton. Their son Arthur resided in Virginia. Their daughter Jessie did not marry.

The house was inherited by his daughters who split the house in two and relocated it to 164 and 180 McConnell Avenue.

MacLeod, Thomas Woodward, Sr. (1899-1974)

Occupation(s):	merchant - president and chairman of board, Stern Brothers Department Store, 1950-58 (which merged into Allied Stores Corp., 1951; Allied Stores Corp. merged into Federated Department Stores in 1992);
	president, S. H. Kress & Co. ("five and dime" retail store chain);
	president, retail division, Cluett, Peabody & Co., Inc., Chicago (national department store chain originating in Troy, NY);
	merchandise manager, Best & Co.
	financier - member, advisory board, Fifth Avenue office, Manufacturers Trust Co.
Civic Activism:	president and chairman of board, New York City Convention and Visitors Center;
	director, New York Better Business Bureau;
	trustee, National Jewish Hospital, Denver, CO;
	president, press and promotion committee, New York Arthritis and Rheumatism Foundation, 1954-1955;
	chairman, employee fund raising committee, Greater New York Fund, 1954
Marriage(s):	M/1 – Henrietta Dobie (d. 1967)
	M/2 – Josephine E. McGraw (d. 1976)
Address:	Garner Lane, Bay Shore
Name of estate:	
Year of construction:	
Style of architecture:	
Architect(s):	
Landscape architect(s):	
House extant: unconfirmed	
Historical notes:	

Henrietta Dobie MacLeod subsequently married Trevett C. Chase and resided in Bayside.

Thomas Woodward and Henrietta Dobie MacLeod, Sr.'s son Donald married Marion Norton, the daughter of Thomas J. Norton of Provo, UT. Their son Thomas Woodward MacLeod, Jr. married Jeanne Carolyn Buss, the daughter of Henry C. Buss of Ridgewood, NJ.

Josephine E. McGraw MacLeod had previously been married to Leon A. Swirbul, who resided in Brightwaters and, later, Brookville.

Macy, George Henry (1858-1918)

Occupation(s):	capitalist - president, Carter, Macy & Co. (tea importer)*; president, George H. Macy & Co. (tea importer); director, St. Louis, Southwestern Railway; director, Union Pacific Tea Co.
	financier - vice-president, Seaman's Savings Bank, NYC; director, Atlantic Mutual Insurance Co.; director, Commonwealth Insurance Co.
	industrialist - Sterling Salt Co.
Marriage(s):	1880-1918 – Kate Louise Carter (1857-1921)
Address:	Penataquit Avenue, Bay Shore
Name of estate:	
Year of construction:	
Style of architecture:	
Architect(s):	
Landscape architect(s):	
House extant:	unconfirmed
Historical notes:	

George Henry Macy was the son of Silvanus Jenkins and Caroline Ridgeway Macy, Sr. of Manhattan. George's sister Margaret married Charles W. Pestalozzi, the son of W. Pestalozzi of Zurich, Switzerland.

George Henry and Kate Louise Carter Macy's son Oliver married Martha J. Law, the daughter of Walter W. Law of Scarborough, NY. Their son William Kingsland Macy, Sr. married Julia A. H. Dick and resided in Islip. Their son Thomas married Mary Louise Pugh, the daughter of A. and Mary Pugh. Their daughter Kathleen married James Anthony Finn and resided in Islip. Their daughter Helen married Irving Hall, the son of Joseph and Myra Garrison Hall and resided in Scituate, MA.

[See following entry for additional family information.]

[For Macy's residence *The Bungalow* in Lawrence, see Spinzia, *Long Island's Prominent Families in the Town of Hempstead* – Macy entry and picture below.]

*Carter, Macy and Company was one of the largest importers of tea in the country.

George Henry Macy residence, Lawrence,
The Bungalow

Macy, William Kingsland, Sr. (1889-1961)

Occupation(s):	financier - chairman of board, Franklin National Bank, Franklin Square, NY; trustee, Seaman's Bank for Savings, NYC; director, Norwich [England] Union Fire Insurance Society; partner, Abbott, Hoppin and Co. (stock brokerage firm)
	capitalist - chairman of board, Suffolk Broadcasting Corp.; chairman of board, Suffolk Consolidated Press Co.; director, Eagle Fire Co., NYC; chairman of board, Great River Realty Corp.
	politician - chairman, New York State Republican Committee, 1926-1951*; member, New York State Senate, 1944; member, United States Congress representing 1st Congressional District, 1946-1950; chairman, Town of Islip Planning Board, 1926-1951
Civic Activism:	member, New York State Board of Regents, 1940-1952; member, United States Food Administration during World War I; anti-suffragist; a founder, director, and first president, Great River Club, 1920 (later, Timber Point Club)
Marriage(s):	1912-1961 – Julia A. H. Dick (1891-1977)
Address:	385 Ocean Avenue, Islip
Name of estate:	
Year of construction:	
Style of architecture:	Modified Georgian Revival
Architect(s):	
Landscape architect(s):	
House extant: yes	
Historical notes:	

William Kingsland Macy, Sr. was the son of George Henry and Kate Louise Carter Macy of Bay Shore.

*Known as Suffolk County's "Little King," no political decision of any significance in the county was made without Macy's approval.

Julia A. H. Dick Macy was the daughter of John Henry and Julia Theodora Mollenhauer Dick, who resided at *Allen Winden Farm* in Islip. Her brother William, who married Madeline Talmadge Force and, subsequently, Virginia Montez Kenniston Conner, resided in Islip. Her sister Doris married Horace Havemeyer, Sr. and resided at *Olympic Point* in Bay Shore. Her brother Adolph remained a bachelor.

William Kingsland and Julia A. H. Dick Macy, Sr.'s son John Henry Dick Macy married Elizabeth B. Bacon, the daughter of William S. Bacon. Their daughter Julia married Wilson Cary Potter, the son of Alonzo and Elsie Methilde Nichols Potter II of *Westmoor* in Southampton; Charles Henschel Thieriot II, who resided in Matinecock; and, subsequently, William Thompson, with whom she resided in Tucson, AZ. [*See* Spinzia, *Long Island's Prominent Families in the Town of Southampton* – Potter entry – and *Long Island's Prominent North Shore Families, vol. II* – Thieriot entry.] Their son William Kingsland Macy, Jr. married Margarette Hanes Old, the daughter of William Thomas Old of Jamestown Crescent, VA.

[See previous entry for additional family information.]

The estate is currently the convent of the Daughters of Wisdom.

rear facade, 1992

Magoun, Francis Peabody, Sr. (1866-1929)

Occupation(s):	financier - partner, with his brother George, Magoun Brothers and Co. (stock brokerage firm)
	industrialist - director, Acme Ball Bearing Co.
Civic Activism:	a founder and trustee, Live Stock Society of America, 1895; director, South Shore Country Club, West Islip
Marriage(s):	1892-1929 - Jeanne Cassard Bartholow (1870-1958)
Address:	South Country Road, West Islip
Name of estate:	
Year of construction:	1880s
Style of architecture:	Neo-Federal
Architect(s):	
Landscape architect(s):	
Builder:	Rogers and Blydenburgh, 1896 alterations to house
House extant: yes	
Historical notes:	

rear facade

   Francis Peabody Magoun, Sr. was the son of George Calvin and Adelaide Louisa Tisdale Magoun.
   Jeanne Cassard Bartholow Magoun was the daughter of John Marshall and Anne Louise Cassard Bartholow of West Orange, NJ.
   Francis Peabody and Jeanne Cassard Bartholow Magoun, Sr.'s son, the noted Harvard scholar, Francis Peabody Magoun, Jr. married Margaret Boyden, the daughter of William Cowden Boyden, Sr. of Chicago, IL.
   In 1905, Francis was arrested for grand larceny after he allegedly failed to account for $20,000 worth of a client's stocks. [*The New York Times* March 25, 1905, p. 1.]
   [See following Magoun entries for additional family information.]
   In 1901, the house was purchased by Julien Townsend Davies, Sr., who called it *Casa Rosa*. It was later owned by the Wyckoff family.

Magoun, George Butler (1869-1902)

Occupation(s):	financier - partner, with his brother Francis, Magoun Brothers and Co. (stock brokerage firm)
	industrialist - director, American Sugar Refining Co.; director, Acme Ball Bearing Co.
	capitalist - secretary and treasurer, New York & New Jersey Bridge Co.
Civic Activism:	president, Oak Island Clay Pigeon Club, West Islip
Marriage(s):	1895-1902 – Katharine Trabue Jordan (1871-1961)
Address:	Eaton Lane, West Islip
Name of estate:	*The Meadows*
Year of construction:	1896
Style of architecture:	Colonial Revival
Architect(s):	Isaac Henry Green II designed the house (for G. B. Magoun)
Landscape architect(s):	
Builder:	Philip Ritch
House extant: unconfirmed	
Historical notes:	

   In 1880, Magoun purchased the Udall farm for use as his summer residence. [Harry W. Havemeyer, *Along the Great South Bay From Oakdale to Babylon: The Story of a Summer Spa 1840 to 1940* (Mattituck, NY: Amereon House, 1996), p. 179.] In 1896, he built a new residence in West Islip. [*South Side Signal* April 25, 1896, p. 3, and November 14, 1896, p. 3.]
   George Butler Magoun was the son of George Calvin and Adelaide Louise Tisdale Magoun.
   The *Social Register, 1907* lists Katharine Jordan Magoun as residing in Babylon [West Islip].
   She was the daughter of Isaac Alfred M. and Elizabeth Phelps Jordan of Cincinnati, OH.
   George Butler and Katharine Trabue Jordan Magoun's daughter Katharine married Fred Clute Wallace, Jr.
   [See other Magoun entries for additional family information.]

Magoun, Kinsley (1867-1898)

Occupation(s):	financier - partner, Baring, Magoun and Co. (stock brokerage firm)
Civic Activism:	a founder and trustee, Live Stock Society of America, 1895
Marriage(s):	1894-1898 – Jessie Norton Torrence (1875-1923)
Address:	South Country Road, West Islip
Name of estate:	
Year of construction:	
Style of architecture:	
Architect(s):	
Builder:	Elmer W. Howell, automobile garage, moved barns, stables, and gardener's cottage, 1906 (for Orr)
Landscape architect(s):	
House extant:	unconfirmed

Historical notes:

Kingsley Magoun was the son of George Calvin and Adelaide Louisa Tisdale Magoun.

While returning to his Old Westbury 175-acre estate *Oasis* from a polo game at the Rockaway Hunt Club, Kinsley was thrown from his carriage and killed when his head struck the macadam surface of the road. [*The New York Times* July 11, 1898, p. 7, and Spinzia, *Long Island's Prominent North Shore Families, vol. I* – Magoun entry.]

The *Social Register, 1907* lists Jessie Torrence Magoun as residing at *Oasis* in Westbury [Old Westbury].

She was the daughter of General Joseph Thacher and Mrs. Elizabeth Norton Torrence of Chicago, IL and *Oasis* in Old Westbury. [*See* Spinzia, *Long Island's Prominent North Shore Families, vol. II* – Torrence entry.]

In 1902, Jessie sued her brother-in-law George Butler Magoun for failure to provide account of her husband's estate, which George was administrating. [*The New York Times* April 26, 1902, p. 1.]

Jessie later married Henry Addison Alexander whom she divorced in 1909. Alexander was to receive a large portion of Jessie's fortune provided he took the Keeley cure and agreed not to remarry his former wife Grace Green whom he had married twice previously. [*The San Francisco Call* December 2, 1908.]

Jessie's step-daughter Eleanor Butler Alexander married Theodore Roosevelt, Jr., the son of President Theodore Roosevelt, and resided at *Old Orchard* in Cove Neck. [*See* Spinzia, *Long Island's Prominent North Shore Families, vol. II* – Roosevelt entries.]

Jessie subsequently married William Graham Blakiston of England.

[See other Magoun entries for additional family information.]

In 1905, the house was purchased by John Clifton Orr, Sr. [*South Side Signal* October 21, 1905, p. 3, and *The Brooklyn Daily Eagle* November 1, 1907, p. 3.]

Maitland, Robert Lenox, Sr. (1818-1870)

Occupation(s):	merchant - president, Robert L. Maitland & Co., NYC (tobacco merchant)
	financier - director, Merchants' National Bank
Marriage(s):	1842-1870 – Mary Currie (1813-1877)
Address:	South Country Road, Great River
Name of estate:	*Westbrook Farm*
Year of construction:	c. 1860s
Style of architecture:	Neo-Tudor
Architect(s):	
Landscape architect(s):	
House extant:	no; demolished in c. 1900*

Historical notes:

side facade

The house, originally named *Westbrook Farm*, was built by Robert Lenox Maitland, Sr.

Born in Edinburgh, Scotland, he was the son of Robert and Eliza Sprat Lenox Maitland.

John Lenox and Mary Currie Maitland, Sr.'s son Alexander married Mary Jane McCosh, the daughter of The Reverend James McCosh. Their son John Lenox Maitland, Jr. married Ellen M. Taylor, the daughter of The Reverend William MacKergo and Mrs. Jessie Steedman Taylor of NYC.

In 1873, Mrs. Maitland sold the estate to George Lyndes Lorillard.

It was later owned by Robert Fulton Cutting and, subsequently, by his brother William Bayard Cutting, Sr.

*After the Spanish American War the house was used by the federal government as a convalescent home for returning servicemen and then demolished. [Harry W. Havemeyer, *Along the Great South Bay From Oakdale to Babylon: The Story of a Summer Spa 1840 to 1940* (Mattituck, NY: Amereon House, 1996), p. 148.]

Major, Alfred Sarony (1973-1929)

Occupation(s): artist - internationally-known engraver
industrialist - vice-president, American Bank Note Co. (designed and manufactured bank notes, stamps, and securities)

Marriage(s): Minnie Josephine Cammeyer (d. 1949)

Address: 120 South Gillette Avenue, Bayport
Name of estate:
Year of construction: 1909
Style of architecture: Dutch Colonial Revival
Architect(s): Isaac Henry Green II designed the house (for Pollock)
Landscape architect(s):
Builder: Frederick D. Smith, house and garage, 1909 (for Pollock)
Clifford Munselll, alterations to main residence, 1928 (for Major)

House extant: yes
Historical notes:

The fourteen-room house with six bedrooms, three full bathrooms, and two half bathrooms was built by Walter B. Pollock. [*The Brooklyn Daily Eagle* April 4, 1909, p. 16, and *The Suffolk County News* February 12, 1909, p. 2.] In 1926, it was purchased by Major. [*The Suffolk County News* June 4, 1926, p. 2.]
   He was the son of Henry B. Major.
   Minnie Josephine Cammeyer Major was the daughter of Henry and Anne Matilda Davis Cammeyer.
   In 1935, Mrs. Major sold the house to James McClung of Brooklyn. [*The Suffolk County News* August 16, 1935, p. 8.]
   In 1955, it was purchased by John Busby of Hyde Park, NY. [*The Suffolk County News* September 2, 1955, p. 5.]
   In 2017, the house sold for $1.35 million.

side / rear facade, 2017

Manton, Martin Thomas (1880-1946)

Occupation(s):	attorney - judge, United States District Court for the Southern District of New York, 1916-1918; judge, United States Court of Appeals for the Second Circuit Court, 1918-1939*
Civic Activism:	trustee, Southside Hospital, Bay Shore (now, South Shore University Hospital); chairman, Bayport chapter and South Suffolk chapter, American Red Cross; Japan Relief Committee, 1923
Marriage(s):	1907 – Eva Marguerite Morier (1880-1966) - Civic Activism: committee member, Woman's Organization for National Prohibition Reform (for repeal of Prohibition laws)
Address:	Fairview Avenue, Bayport
Name of estate:	
Year of construction:	1888
Style of architecture:	
Architect(s):	Isaac Henry Green II designed the house (for C. F. Stoppani, Sr.)
Landscape architect(s):	
House extant: no**	
Historical notes:	

The house, originally named *Arcadia*, was built by Charles Francis Stoppani, Sr. It was later owned by his daughter Jennie, who married Stephen Perry Cox. The Coxes continued to call it *Arcadia*. In 1919, Cox sold the house to John J. O'Connor, who defaulted on its property taxes. The house was purchased by Manton at a sheriff's sale. Manton thus owned both Stoppani houses, *Liberty Hall* and *Arcadia*.

In 1939, Manton lost the house for failure to pay its property taxes.

He was the son of Michael and Catherine Mullen Manton of Bayside.

Eva Marguerite Morier Manton was the daughter of Edmund Louis and Selina Emma Underhill Morier.

*Manton, who had been mentioned as a possible United States Supreme Court candidate, was convicted in 1939 of accepting $186,000 in bribes from both sides in the cases brought before him. After his release from prison in 1941 "Preying Manton," as he was known, relocated to Fayetteville, NY, where he was residing at the time of his death. [*The New York Times* November 18, 1946, p. 21, and David Pietrusza, *Rothstein: The Life, Times and Murder of the Criminal Genius Who Fixed the 1919 World Series* (New York: Carroll & Graf Publishers, 2003), p. 370.]

**The gardener's house and carriage house are extant.

[For information on the Southside Hospital, see Cooper entry.]

Arcadia

Liberty Hall, front facade, 2005

Mason, John Hill Belcher (1858-1919)

Occupation(s): entertainers and associated professions -
- stage actor;
- director;
- producer;
- a founder, Mason–Manola Co. (touring company)

Marriage(s):
M/1 – 1891-div. 1900 – Marion Stevens (aka Marion Manola)
- entertainers and associated professions -   comic opera actor
M/2 – div. 1905 – Katherine Best (aka Katherine Grey (1873-1950)
- entertainers and associated professions -   Broadway actress

Address: 74 Snedecor Avenue, Bayport
Name of estate:
Year of construction: c. 1902
Style of architecture: Colonial Revival

Architect(s): Isaac Henry Green II designed the house (for R. H. Post)
Landscape architect(s):
Builder: Frederick D. Smith
House extant: unconfirmed
Historical notes:

The house was built by Regis Henri Post, Sr. as a rental. In 1912, he sold the house to Mason who was considered to be one of America's foremost actors. [*The Suffolk County News* November 22, 1912, p. 2.]
He was the son of Daniel Gregory and Susan W. Belcher Mason.
Marion Stevens Mason had previously been married to _____ Mould.
Katherine Best Mason had previously been married to Paul Arthur.
By 1946 the house was owned by agriculturalist Kurt Grundwald.

side facade

Maxwell, Henry William (1850-1902)

Occupation(s):	financier - partner, Maxwell and Graves (investment banking firm);
	director, American Exchange Bank;
	trustee, Caledonia Insurance Co. of Edinburgh, Scotland;
	trustee, Union Trust Co.;
	vice-president, Liberty National Bank;
	director, Hamilton Avenue Bank, Brooklyn;
	director, Brooklyn Trust Co.
	industrialist - vice-president, Ashcroft Manufacturing Co.;
	director, Atlas Portland Cement Co.*
	capitalist - director, Garwood Land and Improvement Co.;
	director, New York and Long Branch Railroad;
	director, Long Island Rail Road;
	director, Long Island Elevated Railroad;
	director, Jersey Central Railroad;
	director, Elmira, Cortland and Northern Railroad;
	vice-president, Lehigh Valley Railroad;
	director, Marine Railway Co.
Civic Activism:	director, Brooklyn Art Museum;
	director, Brooklyn Academy of Music;
	member, visiting committee, Bay Shore High School;
	member, Brooklyn Board of Education;
	president, board of regents, Long Island College Hospital, Brooklyn;
	donor, Maxwell House, Brooklyn, as memorial to his brother Eugene;
	donor, financed the donation of the Gertrude Lefferts Vanderbilt Industrial School, Brooklyn, to the Brooklyn Industrial Association;
	funded a dormitory building at Long Island College Hospital, Brooklyn;
	benefactor, Brooklyn Guild;
	established full scholarships at Adelphi College, Brooklyn, for 5 students per year;
	treasurer, Polhemus Clinic, Brooklyn;
	director, Brooklyn Free Kindergarten Society;
	paid the pharmaceutical bills of the poor at all drug stores in the vicinity of his Brooklyn home;
	reputed to have donated $300,000-per-year to charity
Marriage(s):	1883-1888 – Celia Gardner Alexander (d. 1888)
Address:	South Country Road, Bay Shore
Name of estate:	*Scrub Oaks*
Year of construction:	
Style of architecture:	Georgian Revival
Architect(s):	
Landscape architect(s):	
House extant: no	

Historical notes:

Henry William Maxwell was the son of John and Caroline Elizabeth Brigham Maxwell.

He was a business associate of Austin Corbin in the Long Island Rail Road, Long Island Elevated Railroad, Marine Railway Company, Lehigh Valley Railroad, and Marine Railway Company. Unlike Corbin, Maxwell's chief interest was not in the accumulation of wealth but rather philanthropy. [*Brooklyn Daily Eagle* May 12, 1902, p. 2, and *The New York Times* May 13, 1902, p. 9.]

On several occasions Maxwell had declined nominations for New York City Controller and the state's United States Senatorial and Congressional positions.

His sister Henrietta married Joseph Huntington Lester and resided at *Lestaley* in Bay Shore. His brother John Roger Maxwell, Sr. married Maria Louise Washburn and resided at *Maxwelton* in Glen Cove. [*See* Spinzia, *Long Island's Prominent North Shore Families, vol. I* – Maxwell entry.]

*The Atlas Portland Cement Company provided the cement for the Panama Canal.

front facade, c. 1903

McBurney, Dr. Malcolm (1884-1925)

Occupation(s):	physician
	financier - partner, Markoe, Morgan and Co. (stock brokerage firm)
Civic Activism:	a founder, Great River Club, 1920 (later, Timber Point Club)
Marriage(s):	1912-1925 – Helen Dorothy Moran (1889-1954)
Address:	Bayview Avenue, East Islip
Name of estate:	
Year of construction:	c. 1915
Style of architecture:	Neo-French Manorial
Architect(s):	Delano and Aldrich designed the house (for McBurney)

Landscape architect(s):
House extant: no; destroyed by fire in 1976
Historical notes:

The house was built by Dr. Malcolm McBurney.

The *Brooklyn Blue Book and Long Island Society Register, 1921* lists Dr. and Mrs. Malcolm McBurney as residing in East Islip.

He was the son of Dr. Charles Heber McBurney, who resided at *Cherry Hill* in Stockbridge, MA. His sister Alice married Dr. Austin Riggs and resided in Stockbridge, MA.

His father Dr. Charles Heber McBurney was the consulting physician who attended President William McKinley immediately after the president had been shot. He devised a muscle splitting surgical entry procedure employed in appendectomy. It is still known as the "McBurney's incision" but often called "gridiron."

[For other Long Island residents associated with McKinley's assassination, see Spinzia, *Long Island's Prominent North Shore Families, vol. I* – Cortelyou and Milburn entries – and *Long Island's Prominent Families in the Town of Southampton* – Dixon entry.]

Helen Dorothy Moran McBurney was the daughter of Amedee Depau and Helen Morgan Moran of East Islip. She subsequently married Daniel Raymond Noyes, with whom she continued to reside in the former McBurney East Islip house. Her brother Charles married Martha Adams. Her sister Rosalie married Edwin Chase Hoyt and resided in Brentwood.

Malcolm and Helen Dorothy Moran McBurney's daughter Bridget married Charles S. Sargent III, whose parents Charles S. and Dagmar Wetmore Sargent, Jr. resided in Lawrence. [*See* Spinzia, *Long Island's Prominent Families in the Town of Hempstead* – Sargent entry.] Distraught over her forthcoming divorce from Sargent, Bridget committed suicide in her Reno hotel. [*The Suffolk County News* September 11, 1942, p. 8.] Their daughter Nora married George F. Tooker, Jr. with whom she resided in West Islip, and, subsequently, ____ Kolczynski.

In 1949, the house was purchased by the Tesoro family.

rear facade

McClure, William (d. 1916)

Occupation(s): financier - chairman of board and secretary, New York Stock Exchange
Civic Activism: trustee, School District #1, Town of Islip;
a founder and director, South Shore Country Club, West Islip, 1895

Marriage(s): Ella Crane (d. 1921)

Address: Oak Neck Lane, West Islip
Name of estate: *Clurella*
Year of construction:
Style of architecture: Shingle
Architect(s):
Landscape architect(s):
House extant: no
Historical notes:

The *Social Register Summer, 1902* lists William and Ella Crane McClure as residing at *Clurella* in West Islip.

He was the son of Charles and Margaretta Gibson McClure of Carlisle, PA.

Ella Crane McClure was the daughter of Theodore Crane of NYC. The McClures did not have children.

Clurella, c. 1903

McCue, Alexander (1826-1889)

Occupation(s): attorney - solicitor, United States Treasury (Cleveland administration);
partner, McCue, Hall, and Cullen, Brooklyn;
judge, City of Brooklyn;
assistant district attorney, Kings County, NY
statesman - United States Assistant Secretary of the Treasury
capitalist - director, New York Bridge Co. (builder of the Brooklyn Bridge)
financier - trustee, Brooklyn Trust Co.;
director, Fulton Bank, Brooklyn;
director, Lafayette Fire Insurance Co.;
Civic Activism: a founder, Brooklyn Academy of Music;
donated property on Colt Avenue, Babylon, for construction of Roman Catholic Church

Marriage(s):

Address: South Country Road, Babylon
Name of estate:
Year of construction:
Style of architecture:
Architect(s):
Landscape architect(s):
House extant: no; destroyed by fire in 1901
Historical notes:

McCue's daughter Jennie married James Cornelius Bergen and resided in Babylon. His daughter Heloise married Francis Preston Blair Sands, the son of Rear Admiral Benjamin Franklyn and Mrs. Henrietta Maria French Sands, and resided in Babylon.

In 1885, the house was remodeled and enlarged. [*The Brooklyn Daily Eagle* April 12, 1885.]

McCurdy, Robert Henry, II (1859-1932)

Occupation(s):	financier -	general manager and trustee, Mutual Life Insurance Co;
		director, Astor National Bank;
		director, First National Bank of Morristown, NJ;
		director, Windsor Trust Co.;
		director, Commercial Trust Company of New Jersey;
		director, Metropolitan Trust Co;
		director, Casualty Company of America;
		director, National Safe Deposit Co.
		partner, Mc Curdy, Henderson, and Co. (investment banking firm)
	capitalist -	director, Central Realty Co.;
		director, O'Rourk Engineering Construction Co.;
		director, International Bell Telephone Co.;
		partial owner, Cornucopia Gold Mine, Oregon
Civic Activism:		president, board of managers, Southside Hospital, Bay Shore (now, South Shore University Hospital)
Marriage(s):		1898-1924 – Mary Suckley (1863-1924)
Address:		South Country Road, West Islip
Name of estate:		
Year of construction:		1879
Style of architecture:		French Empire
Architect(s):		
Landscape architect(s):		

House extant: no; demolished in 1950s
Historical notes:

The thirty-room house was built by Robert Henry McCurdy II.

The *Brooklyn Blue Book and Long Island Society Register, 1921* list Robert H. and Mary Suckley McCurdy [II] as residing on South Country Road, Babylon [West Islip].

He was the son of Richard Aldrich and Sarah Ellen Little McCurdy of Morristown, NJ.

Mary Suckley McCurdy was the daughter of John and Rosette Denning Morton Suckley.

The McCurdys did not have children.

McCurdy was distantly related to Long Island's Fortescue and Roosevelt families through his aunt Gertrude McCurdy's marriage to Gardiner Green Hubbard. [*See* Fortescue and Roosevelt entries in this volume; Spinzia, *Long Island's Prominent North Shore Families, vol. 1* – Roosevelt entries; and Raymond E. Spinzia, "Those Other Roosevelts: The Fortescues" *Freeholder*, 11 (Summer 2006) pp. 8-9, 16-22 – also available at www.spinzialongislandestates.com.]

The house was purchased with a bequest from Emily Bourne to create the Nurses Home where nurses from all over Long Island came to vacation and rest.

[For information on the Southside Hospital, see Cooper entry.]

front facade

McKee, Henry Sellers, II (1891-1978)

Occupation(s):	financier - partner, Phelps, Ellis, and McKee (stock brokerage firm)
Marriage(s):	1916-1970 – Alice Martin Davies (1897-1970)
Address:	9 Montrose Avenue, Babylon
Name of estate:	
Year of construction:	1885
Style of architecture:	
Architect(s):	
Landscape architect(s):	
House extant:	yes

Historical notes:

The *Long Island Society Register, 1929* lists Henry Sellers and Alice M. Davies McKee [II] as residing at 9 Montrose Avenue, Babylon.

He was the son of Thomas M. and Nellie Wood McKee.

Alice Martin Davies McKee was the daughter of Julien Townsend and Marie Rose de Garmendia Davies, Sr. of *Casa Rosa* in West Islip. Alice's sister Phebe married Walter J. Sutherland, Jr. Her brother Julien Townsend Davies, Jr., who resided in Flower Hill, married Faith de Moss Robinson, Marie O'Connor, and, subsequently, Ida Pasquali. [*See* Spinzia, *Long Island's Prominent North Shore Families, vol. I* – Davies entry.]

Henry Sellers and Alice Martin Davies McKee II's daughter Marie married Richard George Yates, Sr., the son of Herbert John and Petra Antonsen Yates, Sr. of *Onsufarm* in West Islip. Marie later married Joseph S. Bynum, the son of Samuel Bynum of Paducah, KY, and, subsequently, Ronald S. Correll, the son of Charles D. Correll. Their son Richard married Suzanne Eddy, the daughter of Harrison Prescott Eddy, Jr. of Cohasset, MA. Their son Julien married Helen Frances Busard and, later, Mary Van Rennselaer Robins, the daughter of Thomas and Louisa Winslow Cogswell Robins, Jr. of Hewlett. [*See* Spinzia, *Long Island's Prominent Families in the Town of Hempstead* – Robins entry.]

In 2005, the five-bedroom, four-bath, 4,500-square-foot house sold for $1.1 million.

McKee, John (1851-1915)

Occupation(s):	industrialist - president, McKee Refrigerator Co., Brooklyn (manufacturer of ice boxes)
	financier - director, Manufacturers–Citizens Trust Co.; trustee, Dime Savings Bank, Brooklyn
Civic Activism:	director, Williamsburgh Hospital, Brooklyn; president, Hanover Club
Marriage(s):	1874-1915 – Ida Belle Seaman (1851-1934)
Address:	Bayport Avenue, Bayport
Name of estate:	*Sans Souci*
Year of construction:	
Style of architecture:	Victorian
Architect(s):	
Landscape architect(s):	
House extant:	no

Historical notes:

In 1887, McKee purchased the Frank Seaman house.

Ida Belle Seaman McKee was the daughter of Edwin and Elizabeth Smith Seaman.

John and Ida Belle Seaman McKee's daughter Elsie married an heir to the American Chicle Company chewing gum fortune Garrison Barcalow Adams, the son of Thomas and Martha Dunbar Adams, Sr. of Brooklyn. Their daughter Josephine married J. Remsen Ditmars. Their son Percy married Edith Smith, the daughter of Wilson Randolph Smith of Bayport. Their son Frank married Marguerite Marie Creem, the daughter of Daniel James Creem of *The Maples* in Bellport.

The McKee family continued to reside at this address until the 1920s. [Harry W. Havemeyer, *East on the Great South Bay: Sayville and Bayport 1860-1960* (Mattituck, NY: Amereon House, 2001), p. 90.]

front facade, c. 1902

McKee, William L. (d. 1937)

Occupation(s):	financier - vice-president, National City Co.;
	assistant head, bond department, National City Bank;
	vice-president, Chase Securities Corp. (which merged with Harris, Forbes, & Co.);
	director, Harris, Forbes, & Co.
	industrialist - director, Idaho Copper Co.
Marriage(s):	Annie V. *[unable to determine maiden name]*
Address:	Oak Neck Road, West Islip
Name of estate:	
Year of construction:	
Style of architecture:	
Architect(s):	
Landscape architect(s):	
House extant:	unconfirmed
Historical notes:	

The *Long Island Society Register, 1929* lists Mr. and Mrs. William L. McKee as residing on Oak Neck Road, Babylon [West Islip].

Their daughter Valeria married Monroe Edwards Smith, the son of Floyd M. Smith of Omaha, NE. Their son William Francis McKee married June Harrah and, subsequently, Joan Armitage, the daughter of John Foster Armitage of Manhattan.

In 1932, John Suddueth, a thirty-two-year-old local resident, was arrested for sending William L. McKee a threatening note stating that McKee would be physically injured and his family scandalized if McKee didn't pay him $25,000. [*The New York Times* August 18, 1932, p. 15.]

McLaughlin, Dr. Daniel

Occupation(s):	physician
Marriage(s):	
Address:	Handsome Avenue, Sayville
Name of estate:	
Year of construction:	1903
Style of architecture:	Shingle
Architect(s):	Isaac Henry Green II designed the main residence, gatehouse, and 1905 playhouse. The latter included a bowling alley and billiard room (for F. S. Jones)
Landscape architect(s):	
House extant:	no; destroyed by fire in 1957*
Historical notes:	

The house, originally named *Beechwold*, was built by Frank Smith Jones. It was later owned by his daughter Maude and son-in-law David J. Shea. The Sheas chose to reside in the estate's gatehouse. In 1945, the main residence was purchased by Elwell Palmer, who, in 1949, sold it to McLaughlin.

McLaughin was the owner of the house at the time of the fire.

*The gatehouse and playhouse are extant. The gatehouse is located at 254 Handsome Avenue and the playhouse is at 96 Benson Avenue.

gatehouse, 2006

McNamee, John (1842-1914)

Occupation(s):	financier - trustee, Kings County Trust Co.;
	trustee, Brooklyn Trust Co.;
	trustee, Brevoort Savings Co.
	civil engineer
	capitalist - president, Eagle Warehouse and Storage Co., Brooklyn;
	director, a Manhattan sanitation company;
	president, Reliance Development Co.;
	trustee, National Water Meter Co.;
	partner, with Frederick L. and Walter Cranford, Cranford & McNamee*
Civic Activism:	chairman, building committee, Brooklyn Board of Education;
	member, Brooklyn Board of Education (21 years);
	member, New York State Prison Commission (3 years);
	director, Bay Shore Protective Association
Marriage(s):	1885-1914 – Mary Burnett (b. 1865)
Address:	South Country Road and Saxon Avenue, Bay Shore
Name of estate:	
Year of construction:	1903
Style of architecture:	
Architect(s):	
Landscape architect(s):	
House extant: unconfirmed	
Historical notes:	

The house was built by John McNamee. [*The Suffolk County News* December 19, 1902, p. 1.]

*McNamee, with a succession of partners, was involved in building the foundations of the elevated railroads in Brooklyn, Portsmouth and Suffolk Water Works in Virginia, the Montclair Water Works, part of Brooklyn's Interborough subway, and a section of the Centre Street subway loop in Brooklyn. [*The New York Times* April 9, 1914, p. 11.] He also owned water rights in Suffolk County.

Mary Burnett McNamee was the daughter of William Burnett, who was one of the original members of the New York Produce Exchange.

John and Mary Burnett McNamee's daughter Marie married Dr. Raymond Peter Sullivan, Sr. and lived in Bay Shore. Marie's twin sister Esther died at the age of ten.

Meeks, Edwin Bartlett (1841-1926)

Occupation(s):	financier - stockbroker
Marriage(s):	1866 – Emma A. Stellenwerf (1847-1912)
Address:	St. Mark's Lane and Maple Street, Islip
Name of estate:	
Year of construction:	1903
Style of architecture:	Colonial Revival
Architect(s):	
Landscape architect(s):	
House extant: no; destroyed by fire, 1907	
Historical notes:	

Edwin Bartlett Meeks was the son of Joseph William and Sophia Theresa Vidal Meeks, Sr. of Islip.

Emma A. Stellenwerf Meeks was the daughter of Amos Ryder and Jane Travis Stellenwerf, Sr. of Islip.

In 1901, Emma was severely injured when her carriage was struck by a team of run-away horses and their wagon. The hay hook on the wagon struck Mrs. Meeks in the back and suspended her on a pole between the horses.

Edwin Bartlett and Emma A. Stellenwerf Meek's daughter Edna married John Edward Carpenter of Nyack, NY. Their daughter Helena married John Ireland Tucker, the son of John Ayscough Tucker.

[See other Meeks entries for additional family information.]

Meeks, Joseph William, Jr. (1834-1897)

Occupation(s):	industrialist - manufacturer of "high end" furniture
Marriage(s):	Catherine Lillian *[unable to determine maiden name]* (1838-1916)
Address:	22 South Ocean Avenue, Bayport
Name of estate:	
Year of construction:	1881
Style of architecture:	Neo-Italianate
Architect(s):	
Landscape architect(s):	
House extant: yes	
Historical notes:	

The house was built by Joseph William Meeks, Jr.

He was the son of Joseph William and Sophia Vidal Meeks, Sr. of Islip.

While his grave stone lists his death as occurring in 1901, his obituary in *The Brooklyn Daily Eagle* April 28, 1897, p. 5, confirms the 1897 date although his name is incorrectly given as M. J. Meeks.

[See other Meeks entries for additional family information.]

In 1916, Mrs. Meeks sold the house to George Washington Dahl.

front / side facade, 2005

Meeks, Joseph William, Sr. (1805-1878)

Occupation(s):	capitalist - Big Cottonwood Mine (silver mine)
	industrialist - manufacturer of "high end" furniture
Marriage(s):	1828-1878 – Sophia Theresa Vidal (1808-1895)
Address:	Route 111 and South Country Road, Islip
Name of estate:	
Year of construction:	
Style of architecture:	Colonial Revival
Architect(s):	
Landscape architect(s):	
House extant: no	
Historical notes:	

In 1869, Meeks purchased *Champlin House* and renovated it into his country residence.

Joseph William Meeks, Sr. was the son of Joseph and Sarah Clark Van Dyke Meeks.

Joseph William and Sophia Theresa Vidal Meeks, Sr.'s daughter Sophie married Dexter Arnoll Hawkins. Their son Albert married Sara Anne Diehl. Their daughter Emma married Gustavis Henry Witthaus. Their son Edwin, who resided in Islip, married Emma A. Stellenwerf.

[See other Meeks entries for additional family information.]

The house was subsequently owned by James Ives Plumb, who remodeled it into a Colonial Revival style of architecture and called it *Shadowbrook*.

front facade, c. 1906

Melville, Francis, Jr. (1860-1935)
aka Frank Melville, Jr.

Occupation(s): merchant - founder and chairman of board, John Ward
(a twelve-store shoe chain);
founder and chairman of board, Rival Stores
(a seventeen-store shoe chain);
founder, president, and chairman of board, Melville Shoe
Corp. (holding company);
founder and chairman of board, Thom McAn Shoe Co.
(a 565-store shoe chain)
capitalist - president, Suffolk Improvement Co. (built residential
housing in Old Field);
president, R–W Realty Co.

Marriage(s): 1886-1935 – Jennie Florence MacConnell (1857-1939)

Address: West Main Street, Bayport
Name of estate:
Year of construction:
Style of architecture:
Architect(s):
Landscape architect(s):
House extant: unconfirmed
Historical notes:

By 1904 the Melvilles had relocated to Old Field. The *Brooklyn Blue Book and Long Island Society Register, 1921* lists Frank [Francis] and Jennie Florence MacConnell Melville, Jr. as residing at *Sunwood* in Setauket [Old Field].
He was the son of Francis and Mary Bamman Melville, Sr. of Bayport.
Jennie Florence MacConnell Melville was the daughter of John B. and Margaret Macdonald MacConnell, who resided in Bayport.
Francis and Jennie Florence MacConnell Melville, Jr.'s son Ward married Dorothy Bigelow and resided at *Wide Water* in Old Field.

Melville, Francis, Sr. (1832-1916)

Occupation(s): artist - etcher and watercolorist
educator - art teacher, New York Evening High School

Marriage(s): 1858-1907 – Mary Bamman (d. 1907)

Address: West Main Street, Bayport
Name of estate:
Year of construction:
Style of architecture:
Architect(s):
Landscape architect(s):
House extant: unconfirmed
Historical notes:

Francis and Mary Bamman Melville, Sr.'s daughter Maud died in 1891. Their daughter Anna married Wilfrid Gould Lay and resided in Manhasset and Amagansett. Their son Francis Melville, Jr., who resided in Bayport and at *Sunwood* in Old Field, married Jennie Florence MacConnell, the daughter of John B. and Margaret Macdonald MacConnell of Bayport.
In 1908, Melville sold the house to Dr. Frederick Beardsley Keppy who, in 1913 joined it together with that of Vinal S. Terry. [*The Suffolk County News* March 13, 1908, p. 2; August 11, 1916, p. 4; and November 12, 1937, p. 8.]
In 1937, the house was purchased by Frank Cahill of Brooklyn. [*The Brooklyn Daily Eagle* November 10, 1937, p. 1.]

Mildeberger, Elwood (1861-1943)

Occupation(s):	capitalist - Manhattan real estate
Marriage(s):	M/1 – 1891-1895 – Adelaide Louisa Lockwood (1861-1895) M/2 – Mollie Drumm
Address:	47 Awixa Avenue, Bay Shore
Name of estate:	*Oakelwood*
Year of construction:	1904
Style of architecture:	Shingle
Architect(s):	
Landscape architect(s):	
House extant:	yes
Historical notes:	

Oakelwood

The house, originally named *Oakelwood*, was built by Elwood Mildeberger.

He was the son of Thomas D. and Sarah Amelia Hawes Mildeberger.

Adelaide Louisa Lockwood Mildeberger was the daughter of Charles Augustus and Louisa C. Lockwood, Sr.

The *Long Island Society Register, 1928* lists Elwood and Mollie Drumm Mildeberger as residing at *Oakelwood* in Bay Shore.

Over the years the house has had numerous owners. In 1945, it was purchased by Robert L. Collier who, in 1946, sold the house to Reginald Beach. In 1949, it was owned by Reginald's daughter Barbara, Mrs. James Carr.

In 1963, the house was bought at auction by Joseph W. Koch who made extensive alterations.

In 1980, it was purchased by William J. Ferguson, Jr.

In 1981, the house was purchased by Storm Kheem who also made extensive alterations.

In 1995, it was repossessed by the Bank of Seoul.

In 1998, the house was purchased by John Choi who made extensive alterations.

In 2000, it was purchased by Paul Riley who called it *Awixa Castle*.

In 2020, the 10,992-square-foot, nine-bedroom, eight-bath house was for sale. The asking price was $1,999,999.

Moffitt, William Henry

Occupation(s):	capitalist - president, William H. Moffitt Realty Co. (builder and residential real estate developer, Towns of Islip and Hempstead, Staten Island, and New Jersey)* publisher - owner, *Bay Shore Independent* capitalist - founder and president, South Side Fair (fairgrounds); founder and president, Willow Brook Driving Park, Islip, 1908 (horse racing track)
Civic Activism:	president, New York State Realty Dealers Association; president, Islip Board of Trade; president, East Islip Board of Trade; commodore, Bay Shore Motor Club
Marriage(s):	Ellie F. *[unable to determine maiden name]* (d. 1921) capitalist - treasurer, William H. Moffit Realty Co., NY
Address:	South Country Road, Islip
Name of estate:	*Beautiful Shore*
Year of construction:	1910
Style of architecture:	Modified Mediterranean
Architect(s):	Palmer and Hornbostel designed the house (for Moffitt)
Landscape architect(s):	
House extant:	no
Historical notes:	

Beautiful Shore

The twenty-one-room house, originally named *Beautiful Shore*, was built by William Henry Moffitt.

William Henry and Ellie F. Moffitt's daughter Ellen married Joseph Byron Creamer, Sr., the son of Francis D. and Louise Murray Creamer, Sr. of Islip, and resided in Islip. Their son Charles married Mabel Slater of Montreal, Canada.

In 1915, the house was purchased by Walter George Oakman, Sr.

In 1918, Mrs. Oakman sold it to George Scott Graham of Philadelphia, PA. who renamed the estate *Lohgrame*. [*The New York Times* February 3, 1918, p. 32.]

*Moffitt relocated to San Jose, CA. While there, he was indicted by a New York Grand Jury for grand larceny in connection with his New York real estate transactions. [*The New York Times* February 3, 1918, p. 3.]

Mollenhauer, John (1827-1904)

Occupation(s):	industrialist - a founder, Mollenhauer Sugar Refining Co. (later, The National Sugar Refining Co.)
	financier - president, Dime Savings Bank of Williamsburg; director, Manufacturers Bank of Williamsburg
Marriage(s):	1854-1904 – Doris Siems (1830-1915)
Address:	60 Awixa Avenue, Bay Shore
Name of estate:	
Year of construction:	1893
Style of architecture:	Shingle
Architect(s):	Ernest George Washington Dietrich designed the house (for J. Mollenhauer)

Landscape architect(s):
House extant: yes
Historical notes:

The house was built by John Mollenhauer.
Doris Siems Mollenhauer was the daughter of Theodor and Julia Kaiser Siems.
John and Doris Siems Mollenhauer's son John Adolph married Anna Margaretta Dick and resided at *Homeport* in Bay Shore. Their son J. Eldred died before attaining adulthood. Their son Frederick married May Craig. Their daughter Julia married John Henry Dick and resided at *Allen Winden Farm* in Islip. Their son Henry married Sarah W. Howe.
[See other Mollenhauer entries for additional family information.]
The house was subsequently owned by Dr. Raymond Peter Sullivan, Sr.
In 2011, the house, which is on the National Register of Historic Places, was for sale. The asking price was $925,000.

front facade, c. 1903

Mollenhauer, John Adolph (1857-1926)

Occupation(s):	industrialist - vice-president, Mollenhauer Sugar Refining Co.;
	director, Cuban–American Sugar Co.;
	director, The National Sugar Refining Co.;
	director, St. Regis Paper Co.
	financier - trustee, Brooklyn Trust Co.;
	president, Allied Mutual Liability Insurance Co.;
	director, Manufacturers National Bank;
	trustee, German Savings Bank;
	trustee, Title Guarantee & Trust Co.
	shipping - director, Consolidated Shipping Corp.
Civic Activism:	director, Home of St. Giles the Cripple;
	donated land on Main Street in Bay Shore for Soldiers and Sailors Memorial Building;
	trustee, Brooklyn Bureau of Charities;
	trustee, Brooklyn Hospital & Dispensary;
	director, Brooklyn Academy of Music;
	director, Brooklyn Institute of Arts and Sciences;
	chairman, Bay Shore chapter, American Red Cross Japan Relief Committee, 1923;
	manager, Southside Hospital, Bay Shore (now, South Shore University Hospital);
	a founder and director, Bay Shore Protective Association;
	director, Bay Shore Horse Show;
	commodore, Penataquit Corinthian Yacht Club, Bay Shore
Marriage(s):	1882-1926 – Anna Margaretha Dick (1861-1935)
	- Civic Activism: chairman, Tiny Tim Society of the Home of St. Giles the Cripple;
	chairman, Visiting Nurse Association of Brooklyn;
	president, Suffolk County Y.W.C.A.;
	president, Brooklyn Y.W.C.A.;
	member, National Board of Y.W.C.A.;
	president, Moravian School for Girls, Bethlehem, PA;
	a founder and director, Hanover Club
Address:	Awixa Avenue, Bay Shore
Name of estate:	*Homeport*
Year of construction:	1898-1899
Style of architecture:	Modified Shingle
Architect(s):	Alfred Hopkins designed the farm complex, and farmer's cottage, 1913* (for J. A. Mollenhauer)
Landscape architect(s):	Nathan F. Barrett (for J. A. Mollenhauer)
Builder:	Jabez Ephraim Van Orden
House extant:	yes
Historical notes:	

The house, originally named *Homeport*, was built by John Adolph Mollenhauer.

He was the son of John and Doris Siems Mollenhauer of Bay Shore.

Anna Margaretha Dick Mollenhauer was the daughter of William and Anna Maria Vagts Dick, who resided at *Allen Winden Farm* in Islip.

John Adolph and Anna Margaretha Dick Mollenhauer did not have children.

The house was subsequently owned by their nephew Adolph Mollenhauer Dick, who sold it in 1936 without ever having resided at the estate. [Harry W. Havemeyer, *Along the Great South Bay From Oakdale to Babylon: The Story of a Summer Spa 1840 to 1940* (Mattituck, NY: Amereon House, 1996), p. 239.]

*The farmer's cottage is currently a private residence at 82 Awixa Avenue.

[For information on the Southside Hospital, see Cooper entry.]

*John Adolph Mollenhauer residence,
rear facade, c. 1903*

Montgomery, Richard Malcolm, Sr. (1854-1942)

Occupation(s):	capitalist - real estate builder and broker
	founder, Richard M. Montgomery and Co., NYC (real estate broker and auctioneer)
	merchant - partner, James and John Montgomery (tea brokerage and commission firm);
	founder and president, Montgomery Auction and Commission Co., 1890 (first tea auction firm in United States)
	financier - president, American Exchange National Bank, NY;
	trustee, Bay Shore Savings Bank
Civic Activism:	a founder, City Club of New York, 1892;
	a founder and president, Iowa Society of New York;
	superintendent and trustee, Church of the Pilgrims Sunday School, Brooklyn;
	president, First Congregational Church, Bay Shore;
	a founder, South Side Field Club, Bay Shore
Marriage(s):	M/1 – 1878-div.– Alice Stanley Coe (1852-1936)
	M/2 – 1903-1942 – Blanche Maud MacFarland (1873-1951)
Address:	116 South Penataquit Avenue, Bay Shore
Name of estate:	
Year of construction:	1883
Style of architecture:	Queen Anne
Architect(s):	
Landscape architect(s):	Hicks Nursery supplied plantings (for R. A. Pinkerton, Sr.)

House extant: yes
Historical notes:

   The house was built by Richard Malcolm Montgomery, Sr.
   He was the son of John Robb and Jane Malcolm Ball Montgomery.
   Alice Stanley Coe Montgomery was the daughter of George Simmons and Almira Stanley Coe.

   Richard Malcolm and Alice Stanley Coe Montgomery, Sr.'s son George was an infant at the time of his death in 1880. Their son Stanley was two years old at the time his death in 1886. Their son John married Arline McCanless and resided in Short Hill, NJ. Their son Richard Malcolm Montgomery, Jr. married Anna Hanford Conrow.

   The house was subsequently owned by Robert Allan Pinkerton, Sr., who called the estate *Dearwood*.

   In 2021, the eight-bedroom, four-bath, 5,000-square-foot house was for sale. The asking price was $1.2 million.

front facade

Moore, Dr. David Dodge (1899-1972)

Occupation(s):	physician - president, Southside Hospital, Bay Shore (now, South Shore University Hospital)
Civic Activism:	medical consultant, Central Islip State Hospital; medical consultant, Mental Health Board of Suffolk County; medical consultant, Planned Parenthood Association
Marriage(s):	1928-1972 – Margaret Leighton Hatch (1907-1981)
Address:	137 West Bayberry Road, Islip
Name of estate:	
Year of construction:	1899-1900
Style of architecture:	Moorish
Architect(s):	Grosvenor Atterbury designed the house (for H. O. Havemeyer)*
Landscape architect(s):	Nathan F. Barrett (for H. O. Havemeyer)**
Builder:	[See Jabez Epraim Van Order entry.]

House extant: yes; but substantially altered

front / side facade, 2006

Historical notes:
   The house, originally named *Bayberry Point*, was built by Henry Osborne Havemeyer as his own residence in his "Modern Venice" development. It was later owned by Frank Gulden, Sr. and, subsequently, by Moore.
   Moore's sister Carol married Adlai Stevenson Hardin, Sr., the son of The Reverend Martin David Hardin, pastor of the First Presbyterian Church of Ithaca, NY. His sister Amy married Dr. Anson Phelps Stokes Hoyt and resided in Pasadena, CA.
   Margaret Leighton Hatch Moore was the daughter of Harold Ames and Margaret Leighton Milliken Hatch of Manhattan and Sharon, CT. Margaret's sister Barbara married Dr. James T. Emert and resided in Manhattan.
   Dr. David Dodge and Mrs. Margaret Leighton Hatch Moore's daughter Barbara married Melville Ezra Ingalls IV of Babylon. Their daughter Joyce married John Bruce Maclay of Gettysburg, PA. Their daughter Margaret married John Gerard Dempsey, the son of Joseph Francis and May E. Dempsey, Sr. of *Estancia* in Great River.
   *The sales brochure for "Modern Venice" states that the Moorish-style architecture was suggested by Louis Comfort Tiffany.
   **The sales brochure also states that "Modern Venice" would be devoid of trees and vegetation and that Nathan F. Barrett was the landscape architect.
   [For information on the Southside Hospital, see Cooper entry.]

Moran, Amedee Depau (1853-1915)

Occupation(s):	financier - partner, Moran Brothers (investment banking firm)
	capitalist - director, Detroit & Mackinac Railway Co.; treasurer, Nevada, California & Oregon Railway
Marriage(s):	1878-1891 – Helen Morgan (1854-1891)
Address:	Suffolk Lane, East Islip
Name of estate:	
Year of construction:	
Style of architecture:	Italian Renaissance
Architect(s):	
Landscape architect(s):	

House extant: unconfirmed

rear facade

Historical notes:
   Amedee Depau Moran rented Lucius Kellogg Wilmerding, Sr.'s house *White Lodge* on a ten-year lease.
   He was the son of Charles A. and Arabella Jones Adams Moran of Manhattan.
   Amedee Depau and Helen Morgan Moran's daughter Helen, who resided in East Islip, married Dr. Malcolm McBurney and, subsequently, Daniel Raymond Noyes. Their daughter Rosalie married Edward Spring Knapp, Jr. and resided in Roslyn. [*See* Spinzia, *Long Island's Prominent North Shore Families, vol. I* – Knapp entry.] Their son Charles married Martha Adams. Their daughter Maria married Edwin Chase Hoyt, Sr. and resided in Brentwood.

Moran, Eugene Francis, Jr. (1903-1971)

Occupation:	shipping - vice-president, Moran Towing and Transportation Co.
Civic Activism:	president, Friendly Sons of St. Patrick; director, Brooklyn Chamber of Commerce
Marriage(s):	1936 – Marie Josephine Staudt
Address:	235 Lakeview Avenue West, Brightwaters
Name of estate:	*Shadow Lawn*
Year of construction:	
Style of architecture:	Shingle
Architect(s):	
Landscape architect(s):	
House extant: yes	
Historical notes:	

Eugene Francis Moran, Jr. was the son of Eugene Frances and Julia Claire Browne Moran, Sr. of Brooklyn and Quogue. [*See* Spinzia, *Long Island's Prominent Families in the Town of Southampton* – Moran entry.] His sister Helen married Harry Lee Warren and resided in Bay Shore. His sister Claire married Harold B. Epp and resided in Bay Shore. His sister Eugenia married Thomas S. Dwyer and resided in Pelham Manor, NY. His sister Marion married William Brendan Mattimore and resided in Brightwaters. His brother Joseph H. Moran II married Pauline Cotter, the daughter of Richard J. Cotter of Cambridge and Duxbury, MA.

Marie Josephine Staudt Moran was the daughter of John Staudt of Brightwaters. Marie's sister Christine married George Lane Maurer, the son of Edmund John Maurer, and, subsequently, Harry A. Fisher, with whom she resided in Manhattan.

Eugene Francis and Marie Josephine Staudt Moran, Jr.'s son Michael married Margaret Mary Stuberfield, the daughter of William Francis Stuberfield, and resided in Garden City. [*See* Spinzia, *Long Island's Prominent Families in the Town of Hempstead* – Moran entry.] Their daughter Marie Ann did not marry.

side / front facade, 2006

Morgan, Charles Jr. (1885-1937)

Occupation:	financier - member, W. H. Goadby and Co., NY (stock brokerage firm)
Civic Activism:	chairman, civilian relief committee, Islip chapter, American Red Cross, 1917; a founder and director, Great River Club, 1920 (later, Timber Point Club); governor, Racquet and Tennis Club
Marriage(s):	1910-1937 – Ethel Cowdin (1888-1966)
Address:	Ocean Avenue, Islip
Name of estate:	
Year of construction:	
Style of architecture:	
Architect(s):	
Landscape architect(s):	
House extant: unconfirmed	
Historical notes:	

In 1917, Morgan purchased Mary Boyce's residence and remodeled the house. [*The Brooklyn Daily Eagle* May 21, 1917, p. 4.]

The *Long Island Society Register, 1928* lists Charles and Ethel Cowdin Morgan [Jr.] as residing on Ocean Avenue, Islip.

He was the son of Charles and Clara Woodward Morgan, Sr. of Bayport.

Ethel Cowdin Morgan was the daughter of John Elliot and Gertrude Cheever Cowdin of Far Rockaway and Tuxedo Park, NY.

Charles and Ethel Cowdin Morgan, Jr.'s daughter Nancy married James Hopkins Smith, II, the son of James H. Smith. Their daughter Camilla married Remsen Ditmars Donald, the son of George Donald of New York.

Morgan, Charles, Sr. (1858-1908)

Occupation(s): industrialist - Morgan Mineral Water Co.*

Marriage(s): 1882-1908 – Clara Woodward (1856-1939)

Address: Morgan Lane, Bayport**
Name of estate:
Year of construction:
Style of architecture:
Architect(s):
Landscape architect(s):
House extant: yes
Historical notes:

Charles Morgan, Sr. was the son of John and Sarah Elizabeth Oakley Morgan, who resided at *Idle Hour* in Bayport. Clara Woodward Morgan was the daughter of Robert Thomas and Hetty Davis Woodward.

Charles and Clara Woodward Morgan, Sr.'s son Robert, who resided in East Islip, married Carol Kobbe, the daughter of Gustav and Carolyn Wheeler Kobbe of Babylon. Their son Henry married Carol's sister Virginia and resided at *The Stables* in East Islip. Their son Charles Morgan, Jr. married Ethel Cowdin, the daughter of John Elliot and Gertrude Cheever Cowdin of Far Rockaway and Tuxedo Park, NY, and resided in Islip.

[See John Morgan surname entry for additional family information.]

*After the Morgan family sold the Morgan Mineral Water Company, it became White Rock Soda.

**Morgan resided at the former John A. Hicks house. Originally located on Middle Road, the house was moved to its present location on the west side of Morgan Lane in 1946.

Morgan, Henry (1883-1942)

Occupation(s): financier - partner, Henry Morgan and Co. (stock brokerage firm)

Marriage(s): 1937-1943 – Virginia Kobbe (1891-1947)

Address: 37 Blackmore Lane, East Islip
Name of estate: *The Stables*
Year of construction:
Style of architecture:
Architect(s):
Landscape architect(s):
House extant: yes
Historical notes:

The house, originally named *The Stables*, was the stable of Harry Bowly Hollins, Sr.'s estate *Meadow Farm* which Morgan remodeled into his residence.

Born in Bordentown, NJ, and raised in Pau, France, Henry Morgan was the son of Charles and Clara Woodward Morgan, Sr. of Bayport.

Virginia Kobbe Morgan was the daughter of Gustav and Caroline Wheeler Kobbe of Bay Shore. She had previously been married to Gerald Vanderbilt Hollins, Sr., with whom she resided at *The Hawks* in East Islip. Her sister Hildegarde married Joseph Hutchinson Stevenson and, subsequently, Francis Burritt Thorne, Sr., with whom she resided at *Brookwood* in East Islip. Her sister Carol married Henry's brother Robert Woodward Morgan, Sr. and also resided in East Islip. Carol subsequently married George Palen Snow, the son of Frederick Augustus and Mary Palen Snow of *Gardenside* in Southampton, and resided in Syosset. [*See* Spinzia, *Long Island's Prominent Families in the Town of Southampton* and *Long Island's Prominent North Shore Families, vol. II* – Snow entries.]

Morgan, John (1837-1915)

Occupation(s):	industrialist - founder, Morgan Mineral Water Co.*
Marriage(s):	1861-1915 – Sarah Elizabeth Oakley (1843-1934)
Address:	78 South Ocean Avenue, Bayport
Name of estate:	*Idle Hour*
Year of construction:	c. 1879
Style of architecture:	Queen Anne
Architect(s):	Isaac Henry Green II designed the alterations (for John Morgan)
Landscape architect(s):	
House extant:	yes
Historical notes:	

The house, originally named *Idle Hour*, was built by John Morgan.

Sarah Elizabeth Oakley Morgan was the daughter of Henry Stannard Oakley.

John and Sarah Elizabeth Oakley Morgan's son Charles Morgan, Sr. married Clara Woodward, the daughter of Robert Thomas and Hetty Davis Woodward, and resided in Bayport. Their daughter Gertrude married James Sherwood. Their daughter Sarah did not marry. Their son Edward resided in Alaska.

[See Charles Morgan, Sr. surname entry for additional family information.]

*After the Morgan family sold the Morgan Mineral Water Company, it became White Rock Soda.

front facade, 2005

Morgan, Robert Woodward, Sr. (1888-1960)

Occupation(s):	financier - partner, Stillman, Maynard and Co. (stock brokerage firm); vice-president, Mohawk Valley Investing Co., Utica, NY
Marriage(s):	1921-1960 – Carol Kobbe (1893-1976)
Address:	Meadow Farm Road, East Islip
Name of estate:	
Year of construction:	1927
Style of architecture:	Colonial Revival
Architect(s):	Philip Cusak designed the house (for R. W. Morgan, Sr.)
Landscape architect(s):	
House extant:	yes
Historical notes:	

The house was built by Robert Woodward Morgan, Sr.

He was the son of Charles and Clara Woodward Morgan, Sr. of Bayport.

Carol Kobbe Morgan was the daughter of Gustav and Carolyn Wheeler Kobbe of Babylon. Carol subsequently married George Palen Snow, the son of Frederick Augustus and Mary Palen Snow of *Gardenside* in Southampton, and resided in Syosset. [*See* Spinzia, *Long Island's Prominent Families in the Town of Southampton* and *Long Island's Prominent North Shore Families, vol. II* – Snow entries.] Her sister Virginia married Gerald Vanderbilt Hollins, Sr., with whom she resided at *The Hawks* in East Islip, and, subsequently, Robert's brother Henry also of East Islip. Her brother George married Marjorie W. Goss. Her sister Hildegarde married Joseph Hutchinson Stevenson and, subsequently, Francis Burritt Thorne, Sr., with whom she resided at *Brookwood* in East Islip.

Robert Woodward and Carol Kobbe Morgan, Sr.'s son Matthew, who resided in Oyster Bay, married Rosetta Ghibrera and, subsequently, Rosalinda Rosales. Their son Robert Woodward Morgan, Jr. married Dorothea Alexander.

The house was later owned by Robert Allan Pinkerton II and, subsequently, by Robert William Entenmann, Sr.

Morris, Stuyvesant Fish, III (1902-1948)

Occupation(s): financier - member, New York Produce Exchange

Marriage(s): 1925-1948 – Madeleine White (1897-1977)

Address: 179 Fire Island Avenue, Babylon
Name of estate:
Year of construction: 1800s
Style of architecture: Colonial Revival
Architect(s):
Landscape architect(s):
House extant: yes
Historical notes:

front facade

The *Long Island Society Register, 1929* lists Stuyvesant Fish and Madeleine White Morris [III] as residing on Fire Island Avenue in Babylon.

He was the son of Stuyvesant Fish and Elizabeth Hilles Wynkoop Morris, Jr. of Hewlett and the great-grandson of President Martin Van Buren. His sister Hilles married Louis Gordon Hamersley, Sr., of *The Moorings* in Sands Point and *The Moorings* in Southampton. His brother Martin Van Buren Morris married Helen Sloan and resided at *Longacre* in Quogue. [*See* Spinzia, *Long Island's Prominent Families in the Town of Hempstead* and *Long Island's Prominent Families in the Town of Southampton* – Morris entries; *Long Island's Prominent North Shore Families, vol. I* – Hamersley entry.]

Madeleine White Morris was the daughter of William Towle White of Lowell, MA. She had previously been married to Spencer Kennard, Sr.

Stuyvesant Fish and Madeline White Morris III's son Peter married Audrey Watts McTigue, the daughter of Harold McTigue of Lawrence. Their son Livingston married Rosalie Ann Chapman, the daughter of William Richard Chapman III of Haverford, PA, and resided in Lawrence. Their son Stuyvesant Fish Morris IV married Katharine Renee Cossitt, the daughter of Harry Rene and Virginia Cossitt of LaGrange, IL.

Morrison, George Alexander (1867-1931)

Occupation(s): politician - Brooklyn alderman, prior to its incorporation into New York City
capitalist - real estate developer, specializing in the construction of apartment buildings;
owner, Cedarshore Hotel, Sayville*
financier - a founder and president, Greenport National Bank, Brooklyn

Marriage(s): 1893-1931 – Jessie Rae Dickson (1868-1941)

Address: Handsome Avenue, Sayville
Name of estate:
Year of construction: c. 1888
Style of architecture: Queen Anne
Architect(s):
Landscape architect(s):
House extant: no; destroyed by fire in 1916
Historical notes:

The house, originally named *Cedarshore*, was built by David Baisley Powell and his son Leander Treadwell Powell. The estate was later owned by Leander's wife Rebecca. In 1912, Rebecca Powell sold it to Morrison, who subdivided its property for a housing development and to build the Cedarshore Hotel.

The *Long Island Society Register, 1929* lists Mr. and Mrs. George A. Morrison as residing on Handsome Avenue in Sayville.

George Alexander and Jessie Rae Dickson Morrison's son George Elliot Morrison married Dorothy Nash and resided in Sayville.

*In 1917, the Cedarshore Hotel was destroyed by fire. In 1924, the hotel was rebuilt by Morrison.

In 1942, the hotel was purchased by the Herald Tribune Fresh Air Fund.

In 1959, after going through several ownerships, the hotel, renamed the Bayview Plaza, was destroyed by fire.

Morse, William Otis (1880-1967)

Occupation(s):	capitalist - Formosan tea importer
Marriage(s):	1907-1937 – Harriet Burr Harmon (1881-1937)
Address:	Fire Island Avenue, Babylon
Name of estate:	
Year of construction:	
Style of architecture:	
Architect(s):	
Landscape architect(s):	
House extant:	no
Historical notes:	

The *Long Island Society Register, 1929* lists Harriet Burr Harmon Morse as residing on Fire Island Avenue in Babylon.
She was the daughter of Frank Denham Harmon, a granddaughter of Aaron Burr, and a niece of William Havemeyer. Her sister Marie married Guernsey Curran, Sr. of *Farlands* in Upper Brookville and, subsequently, Walworth Pierce, with whom she resided in Boston, MA. [*See* Spinzia, *Long Island's Prominent North Shore Families, vol. 1* – Curran entry.]
William Otis Morse was the son of William Morse of Manhattan.
William Otis and Harriet Burr Harmon Morse's son Franklin married Victoria Sartori, the daughter of Mrs. Frederick Janssen Bloempot of Babylon. Their son William Harmon Morse married Louise Foster Dodd, the daughter of Frank N. Dodd of *Millfield* in Babylon.
Prior to its demolition, the house was used as a rest home.

Moses, Robert (1888-1981)

Occupation(s):	politician -	president, Long Island State Parks Commission, 1924-1963;
		chairman, New York State Council of Parks, 1924-1963;
		Commissioner of Parks, NYC, 1934-1960;
		chairman, New York State Power Authority, 1954-1963;
		chairman, Triborough Bridge and Tunnel Authority, 1954-1963;
		New York Secretary of State, 1927-1928;
		unsuccessful candidate for governor of New York State, 1934
	writer -	*Theory and Practice of Politics*, 1939;
		Tomorrow's Cars and Roads;
		articles in numerous periodicals
Marriage(s):		M/1 – 1915-1966 – Mary Louise Sims (1884-1966)
		M/2 – 1966-1981 – Mary Alicia Grady (1916-1993)
Address:		Thompson Avenue, Babylon
Name of estate:		
Year of construction:		
Style of architecture:		Victorian
Architect(s):		
Landscape architect(s):		
House extant:		destroyed by arson, 1967*
Historical notes:		

Robert Moses was the son of Emanuel and Bella Cohen Moses.
Between 1924 and 1964, Robert Moses, known as "New York State's master builder," supervised the construction of eleven bridges, 481 miles of highways, 658 playgrounds, and seventy-five state parks for a total cost to New York State of $27 billion.
Moses later rented houses at Oak Beach and Gilgo.
*The arsonist was a local youth.

front facade

Mowbray, Dr. Jarvis Rogers (1820-1886)

Occupation(s):	physician
	politician - supervisor, Town of Islip
Marriage(s):	1861-1886 – Ellen Mowbray Smith (1834-1911)
Address:	Mowbray Avenue, Bay Shore
Name of estate:	
Year of construction:	1858
Style of architecture:	Victorian
Architect(s):	
Landscape architect(s):	
House extant: yes	
Historical notes:	

Jarvis Rogers Mowbray was the son of Eliphalet and Aletta Monfort Mowbray.

Ellen Mowbray Smith Mowbray was the daughter of Joshua Brewster and Mary Rogers Smith of Hauppauge.

Dr. Jarvis Rogers and Mrs. Ellen Mowbray Smith Mowbray's daughter Helen was an infant at the time of her death. Their daughter Mary remained unmarried. Their daughter Aletta married Leander G. Homan and resided in Bay Shore. Their son Edward, who died at the age of twenty-nine of typhoid fever, married Louise Lovell Tilton of Laconia, NH. Their daughter Anna married Ezra A. Tuttle.

In 1945, the house was moved by Mowbray's grandson Walter Tuttle from Main Street to its present location on Mowbray Avenue.

front facade

Murdock, Uriel Atwood, II (1881-1927)

Occupation(s):	capitalist - president, Murdock Realty Co.
	financier - member, Belmont and Co. (investment banking firm)
Marriage(s):	1909-1927 – Rita Nicholas (1887-1930)
	- Civic Activism: chair, Babylon chapter and South Suffolk chapter, American Red Cross Japan Relief Committee, 1923
Address:	49 Robbins Avenue, Babylon
Name of estate:	
Year of construction:	
Style of architecture:	
Architect(s):	
Landscape architect(s):	
House extant: no; demolished	
Historical notes:	

The *New York Social Register, 1920* lists Uriel Atwood and Reta [sic] Nicholas Murdock [II] as residing in Babylon.

He was the son of Lewis Champlin and May M. Shiland Murdock and a descendant of Francis Lewis, a signer of the Declaration of Independence.

Rita Nicholas Murdock was the daughter of Harry Ingersoll and Alice McKim Hollins Nicholas, Sr. of *Virginia Farm* in Babylon. Rita's sister Evelyn married Alexander Duncan Cameron Arnold of West Islip, and, subsequently, Joseph Hutchinson Stevenson with whom she resided at *The Farm* in Hewlett Bay Park. Her brother Harry Ingersoll Nicholas II married Dorothy Snow and resided at *Rolling Farm* in Muttontown. Her sister Beatrice married Edward Nicholl Townsend, Jr. of Garden City. Her sister Daisy married Grosvenor Nichol and resided in Old Westbury. Her sister Elsie married Alonzo Potter II and resided at *Harbor House* in St. James and *Westmoor* in Southampton. Her sister Maud married George Casper Niles and resided at *Cross Cottage* in Bridgehampton. [See Spinzia, *Long Island's Prominent Families in the Town of Hempstead* – Stevenson and Townsend entries; *Long Island's Prominent North Shore Families, vol. II* – Nicholas entry; and *Long Island's Prominent Families in the Town of Southampton* – Potter and Niles entries.]

Uriel Atwood and Rita Nicholas Murdock II's daughter Frances married John F. T. Langley of Leicester, England. Their daughter Margaret married E. Cecil Hoar of Kent, England.

Myers, Nathaniel

Occupation(s):
Civic Activism: a founder and director, Bay Shore Protective Association
Marriage(s):
Address: Montgomery Avenue, Bay Shore
Name of estate:
Year of construction: 1899
Style of architecture: Neo-Dutch Colonial
Architect(s): Clarence K. Birdsall designed the house and 1905 farm cottage (for Meyers)
Landscape architect(s):
House extant: unconfirmed
Historical notes:

rear facade, 1932

The house was built by Nathaniel Myers.
It was subsequently owned by John Henry Eastwood.

Neville, Timothy Francis (1837-1898)

Occupation(s): attorney - partner, Neville and Neville, NYC
capitalist - a founder and director, Babylon Water Works Co., 1892
politician - member, New York State assembly
Civic Activism: vice president, Alumni Association, Fordham College, The Bronx
Marriage(s): 1862-1898 – Joanna Hodges Simons (1840-1922)
- Civic Activism: suffragist -
a founder and president, Babylon chapter, Equal Franchise Society, 1912;
vice-president, Equal Suffrage League, 1912;
president, Suffrage Study Club of Babylon, 1912

Address: South Country Road, Lindenhurst
Name of estate: *Warwick House*
Year of construction: 1871
Style of architecture: Victorian
Architect(s):
Landscape architect(s):
House extant: no; demolished in 1980s
Historical notes:

The house, originally named *Welwood Lane*, was built by Thomas Welwood. In 1887, it was purchased by Neville who renamed it *Warwick House* in honor of his ancestor the Earl of Warwick.

Timothy was the son of Michael and Ann Delaney Neville of Waterbury, CT.

Joanna Hodges Simons Neville was the daughter of Aaron and Abigail Brown Whipple Simons.

Timothy Francis and Joanna Hodges Simons Neville's daughters Eleanor and Augusta did not marry, nor did their sons Arthur and Francis. Their daughter Alexina eloped with Jesse M. Cadwallader. Their daughter Elizabeth married Harnett J. Wellstel and resided in Toledo, OH. Their son John eloped with Martha Riechert, the daughter of Carl Riechert of Lindenhurst. Their daughter Abbie died at the age of two. Their son William died at the age of twelve.

front facade

Nicholas, Alice McKim Hollins (1850-1917)

Marriage(s):	Harry Ingersoll Nicholas, Sr. (1846-1901)
	  - financier - member, New York Stock Exchange
	  capitalist - director, Mobile and Ohio Railroad Co.
	  Civic Activism: a founder, president, and director, South Shore
	                      Country Club, Islip, 1895

Address:	Deer Park Avenue, Babylon
Name of estate:	*Virginia Farm*
Year of construction:	c. 1856
Style of architecture:	
Architect(s):	
Landscape architect(s):	
House extant:	unconfirmed
Historical notes:	

The house had previously been owned by Eugene Return Durkee. In 1880, it was purchased by Alice McKim Hollins Nicholas who called it *Virginia Farm*.

The *Social Register Summer, 1915* lists Harry I. and Alice M. Hollins Nicholas as residing in Babylon.

He was the son of John Smith and Esther Goodwin Stevenson Nicholas.

Alice McKim Hollins Nicholas was the daughter of Francis and Elizabeth Coles Morris Hollins. Her brother Harry Bowly Hollins, Sr. married Evelina Meserole Knapp and resided at *Meadow Farm* in East Islip.

Harry Ingersoll and Alice McKim Hollins Nicholas, Sr.'s son Harry Ingersoll Nicholas II, who resided in Muttontown, married Dorothy Snow, the daughter of Frederick Augustus and Mary Palen Snow of *Gardenside* in Southampton. Their daughter Beatrice married Edward Nicoll Townsend, Jr. of Garden City. Their daughter Rita married Uriel Atwood Murdock II and resided in Babylon. Their daughter Daisy married Grosvenor Nicholas and resided in Old Westbury. Their daughter Elsie married Alonzo Potter II and resided at *Harbor House* in St. James and *Westmoor* in Southampton. Their daughter Evelyn married Alexander Duncan Cameron Arnold, Sr. of West Islip and, subsequently, Joseph Hutchinson Stevenson with whom she resided at *The Farm* in Hewlett Bay Park. Their daughter Maud married George Casper Niles and resided at *Cross Cottage* in Bridgehampton. [*See* Spinzia, *Long Island's Prominent Families in the Town of Southampton* – Niles, Potter, and Snow entries; *Long Island's Prominent Families in the Town of Hempstead* – Stevenson and Townsend entries; and *Long Island's Prominent North Shore Families, vol. II* – Nicholas entry.]

In 1896, the Nicholas family became incensed when the memorial chapel, which they had donated to Christ Episcopal Church in West Islip was rented by its rector, The Reverend Samuel Moran, to Mrs. James Duffin for use as a pickling and preserving establishment. [*The New York Times* July 4, 1896, p. 1.]

[See previous entry for additional family information.]

Nicholas, George Stevenson, Sr. (1840-1922)

Occupation(s):	capitalist - president, George S. Nicholas & Co., (wine, cigar, and liquor importers)
Marriage(s):	1869-1921 – Elizabeth Teackle Purdy (1844-1921)
Address:	South Country Road, West Islip
Name of estate:	*Effingham Park*
Year of construction:	
Style of architecture:	Colonial Revival
Architect(s):	
Landscape architect(s):	
House extant:	unconfirmed
Historical notes:	

The *Social Register Summer, 1915* lists George S. and Elizabeth T. Purdy Nicholas [Sr.] as residing at *Effingham Park*, Babylon [West Islip].

He was the son of John Smith and Esther Goodwin Stevenson Nicholas.

Elizabeth Teackle Purdy Nicholas was the daughter of John F. and Virginia Teackle Purdy.

George Stevenson and Elizabeth Teackle Purdy Nicholas, Sr.'s daughters Elizabeth and Virginia did not marry. Their son Ridgely married Irenie Mosier and resided in Big Horn, WY. Their son Grosvenor, who married Daisy Hollins Nicholas and resided in Old Westbury, was disinherited by his father's will because of Grosvenor's alleged "unfilial attitude." Grosvenor contested the will claiming that his father was mentally incompetent when he signed it. Grosvenor's position was upheld by the Grand Jury but overturned by the judge who stated that the Grand Jury's decision wasn't binding. [*The New York Times* January 16, 1924, p. 11, and February 26, 1924, p. 21.]

[See following entry for additional family information.]

Nicoll, William, VII (1820-1900)

Occupation(s):	politician - unsuccessful Republican candidate for the New York State Senate;
	Commissioner of Highways, Town of Islip, 1846;
	Suffolk County delegate to New York State Constitutional Convention, 1886;
	Overseer of Highways, Town of Islip, 1843, 1848, 1850-1859;
	supervisor, Town of Islip, 1852-1853
Civic Activism:	Suffolk School Commissioner, 1843-1860;
	Inspector of Schools, Town of Islip, 1841-1842;
	a founder, Emmanuel Episcopal Church, Great River;
	a founder, Suffolk County Historical Society, Riverhead
Marriage(s):	1844-1900 – Sarah Augusta Nicol (1823-1910)
Address:	now part of Heckscher State Park, East Islip
Name of estate:	*Grange*
Year of construction:	c. 1710
Style of architecture:	Colonial
Architect(s):	
Landscape architect(s):	
House extant:	no
Historical notes:	

The house, originally named *Grange*, was built by William Nicoll I. It remained the family for six succeeding generations.

William Nicoll VII, who was the last owner of *Grange*, was the son of William and Sarah Greenly Nicoll VI.

Sarah Augusta Nicol Nicoll was the daughter of Edward A. and Frances Burbank Shelton Nicol.

William and Sarah Augusta Nicol Nicoll VII's daughter Sarah married Dr. Silas R. Corwith, the son of Silas W. and Susan M. Corwith, and resided in Bridgehampton. [*See* Spinzia, *Long Island's Prominent Families in the Town of Southampton* – Corwith entry.] Their daughter Frances married Lee Johnson, the son of Edwin Augustus and Ellen Woodruff Johnson, Sr. of East Islip, and resided in Garden City. [*See* Spinzia, *Long Island's Prominent Families in the Town of Hempstead* – Johnson entry.] Their daughter Mary married Coryton Messenger Woodbury, the son of Daniel Phineas and Catharine Woodbury. Their son Edward married Ella Pearsall Latting, the daughter of Joseph and Sarah Frost Latting. Their son William Nicoll VIII was an infant when he died in 1844. Their son William Greenly Nicoll, who resided in Babylon, married Phoebe Disbrow, and, later, Katherine Maurice Cornwall.

Nicoll Homestead

Nicoll, William Greenly (1845-1919)

Occupation(s):	attorney - judge, Suffolk County bankruptcy referee for Suffolk County, 1899-1909 justice of the peace, Town of Babylon politician – supervisor, Town of Babylon, 1893-1896
Civic Activism:	trustee, Babylon School District; treasurer, Christ Episcopal Church, West Islip
Marriage(s):	M/1 – 1873-1874 – Phoebe Disbrow (d. 1874) M/2 – 1878-1919 – Katherine Maurice Cornwell (1849-1927)
Address:	Carll Avenue, Babylon
Name of estate:	
Year of construction:	
Style of architecture:	
Architect(s):	
Landscape architect(s):	
House extant: unconfirmed	
Historical notes:	

William Greenly Nicoll was the son of William and Sarah Augusta Nicol Nicoll VII of *Grange* in East Islip and a direct descendant of William Nicoll I, the patentee of Islip.

Phoebe Disbrow Nicoll was the daughter of Thomas and Susan Penfield Disbrow.

William Greenly and Phoebe Disbrow Nicoll's daughter Phoebe married George Dart Ashley of Camden, NY.

Katherine Maurice Cornwell Nicoll was the daughter of William Hartwick and Mary Spring Marsh Cornwell.

William Greenly and Katherine Maurice Cornwell Nicoll's daughter Katherine married William Bridgman Churchman, the son of William Brown and Katherine Miller Maison Churchman. Their daughter Dorothy married William Haight Hubert with whom she resided in Babylon and Bellport and, later, George Strong Baxter, Jr. with whom she resided in Westerly, RI.

Noyes, Daniel Raymond (1883-1940)

Occupation(s):	financier - member, Brown Brothers Harriman and Co. (investment banking firm); vice-president and director, Foreign Credit Corp., NYC
Marriage(s):	1929-1940 – Helen Dorothy Moran (1889-1954)
Address:	Bayview Avenue, East Islip
Name of estate:	
Year of construction:	c. 1925
Style of architecture:	Neo-French Manorial
Architect(s):	Delano and Aldrich designed the house (for McBurney)
Landscape architect(s):	
House extant: no; destroyed by fire in 1976	
Historical notes:	

front facade, 1918

The house was built by Dr. Malcolm McBurney. Helen Dorothy Moran Noyes had previously been married to McBurney. She continued to reside at the Bayview Avenue residence with Noyes.

Helen was the daughter of Amedee Depau Moran of East Islip.

Daniel Raymond Noyes was the son of Daniel Rogers and Helen Abia Gilman Noyes, Jr. His sister Helen married William Adams Brown, the son of John Crosby Brown. His sister Carol married Thatcher M. Brown, Sr. and resided in Red Bank, NJ. His sister Evelyn married Rollin S. Saltus and resided in Mount Kisco, NY.

In 1949, the house was purchased by the Tesoro family.

Oakman, Walter George, Sr. (1845-1922)

Occupation(s):	financier -	chairman of board, Guaranty Trust Co. of New York; Morristown Trust Co.; Mutual Trust Co. of Westchester County; director, National Bank of Commerce
	capitalist -	vice-president, Central Railroad of New Jersey; president, Richmond & Virginia & Georgia Railroad Co.; vice-president, Hudson & Manhattan Railroad Co.; director, Brooklyn Heights Railroad Co.; Brooklyn Rapid Transit Co.; Interborough Rapid Transit Co.; Long Island Rail Road; Buffalo, Rochester, Pittsburgh Railway Co.; Kings County & Fulton Elevated Railroad Co.; Reynoldsville & Falls Creek Railroad; director, Long Island Electrical Companies; director, Greeley Square Realty Co.; director, Hudson Companies; director, Hudson Improvement Co.; director, Interboro Metropolitan Co.; director, New York & Queens Co.; director, New Jersey Dock & Improvement Co.; director, Rapid Transit Subway Construction Co; director, Subway Realty Co.
	industrialist -	director, Jefferson & Clearfield Coal & Iron Co.; director, American Car & Foundry Co.; director, Rogers Locomotive Works; director, Sloss–Sheffield Steel & Iron Co.

Marriage(s): 1879-1922 – Elizabeth Cockburn Conkling (1856-1931)

Address: South Country Road, Islip
Name of estate:
Year of construction: 1910
Style of architecture: Modified Mediterranean
Architect(s): Palmer and Hornbostel designed the house (for Moffitt)
Landscape architect(s):
House extant: no
Historical notes:

The twenty-one-room house, originally named *Beautiful Shore*, was built by William Henry Moffitt. In 1915, the house was purchased by Oakman.

He was the son of John and Harriette S. Campbell Oakman of Philadelphia, PA.

Elizabeth Cockburn Conkling Oakman was the daughter of United States Senator and boss of New York's Republican party machine Roscoe Conkling and his wife Julia Catherine Seymour Conkling.

Walter George and Elizabeth Cockburn Conkling Oakman, Sr.'s daughter Helen married Buchan Liddell and resided at *Ashford* in Ludlow, England. Their son George Walter Oakman, Jr. was severely wounded during World War I while serving with Britain's Coldstream Guard. Their daughter Katharine married John Hammond.

In 1918, Mrs. Oakman sold their Islip residence to George Scott Graham of Philadelphia, PA, and relocated to a new estate in Roslyn, which they named *Oakdene*. Graham called the Islip estate *Lohgrame*.

The Oakmans also had a residence in Southampton. [*See* Spinzia, *Long Island's Prominent Families in the Town of Southampton and Long Island's Prominent North Shore Families, vol. II* – Oakman entries.]

rear facade

Ockers, Jacob (1847-1918)

Occupation(s): capitalist - president, Blue Point Oyster Co. [Bluepoint Oyster Co.], West Sayville;
director, Live Fish Co., Islip;
president, Jacob Ockers Oyster Co., Greenport and Glenwood Landing
financier - director, Oystermen's National Bank of Sayville;
trustee, Union Savings Bank, Patchogue

Marriage(s): Louise Annette Smith (1849-1939)

Address: South Country Road, Oakdale
Name of estate:
Year of construction:
Style of architecture: Colonial Revival
Architect(s):
Landscape architect(s):
House extant: yes
Historical notes:

Known as "The Oyster King," Ockers was reputedly the largest individual oyster grower and shipper in the country and the first United States exporter of oysters to Europe. His export business alone amounted to 30,000 barrels-a-year. [*The New York Times* December 5, 1918, p. 13.]

Louise Annette Smith Ockers was the daughter of William Francis and Elizabeth Manning Smith, Sr.

The Ockers' house, owned by the Town of Islip, formerly housed the Vanderbilt Historical Society until the house and the research library it contained were damaged by arson in 1991. Much of the society's collection, recovered from the fire, was relocated to the Southside Sportsmen's Club.

front facade, 2005

O'Donohue, Charles Alfred (1859-1935)

Occupation(s): merchant - partner, John O'Donohue's Sons
financier - director, Kings County Trust;
trustee, East River Savings Institution;
director, Long Island Safe Deposit Co.
capitalist - director, Union Ferry
industrialist - director, Analomink Paper Co.;
director, Knickerbocker Mills

Civic Activism: trustee, Brooklyn Central Dispensary;
a founder, Bay Shore Yacht Club

Marriage(s): 1891-1935 – Olive A. Scoville (1870-1951)

Address: Clinton Avenue, Bay Shore
Name of estate: *The Moorings*
Year of construction:
Style of architecture: Modified Shingle
Architect(s):
Landscape architect(s):
House extant: no
Historical notes:

front facade, c. 1903

The *Brooklyn Blue Book and Long Island Society Register, 1918* and *1921* list Charles A. and Olive A. Scoville O'Donohue as residing at *The Moorings* in Bay Shore. The *Long Island Society Register, 1929* lists the O'Donohues as residing on Shore Road in Huntington [Huntington Bay]. [*See* Spinzia, *Long Island's Prominent North Shore Families, vol. II –* O'Donohue entry.]

He was the son of Peter J. and Emma M. Bachus O'Donohue.

Olive A. Scoville O'Donohue was the daughter of Amasha H. and Sarah Louisa Quick Scoville.

Oelsner, Rudolph (1849-1925)

Occupation(s):	capitalist - beer importer
	restaurateur - president and secretary, Germania Catering Co. (a holding company for Café New York, NYC, which was formerly the Kaiserhof Restaurant); president, German Restaurant Co. (a holding company for Stadtkeller Restaurant)
Marriage(s):	Dorothea Ringer (1855-1946)
Address:	117 Awixa Avenue, Bay Shore
Name of estate:	
Year of construction:	
Style of architecture:	Shingle
Architect(s):	
Landscape architect(s):	
House extant:	no
Historical notes:	

front facade

The house was built by Rudolph Oelsner.
Rudolph and Dorothea Ringer Oelsner's foster daughter Martha did not marry.
By 1906 the Oelsners had relocated to Long Island's North Shore, having purchased the three-hundred-acre Thayer estate in the Roslyn area of the Island.
In 1918, Oelsner was indicted for allegedly hoarding in excess of five tons of sugar in violation of World War I rationing legislation. [*The New York Times* August 6, 1918, p. 11.]
His Bay Shore residence was later owned by George Winthrop Hodges, Sr.
In 1923, Hodges sold the house to James P. Kelly, who called it *Awixaway*.

Oppenheimer, Julius (1891-1937)

Occupation(s):	capitalist - partner, Rothfeld, Stern & Co. (importers of men's suit linings); director, Metal and Thermit Corp.; director, Hanseatic Corp.
Civic Activism:	trustee, Ethical Culture Society; trustee, Hudson Guild
Marriage(s):	1903-1931 – Ella Friedman (1869-1931) - artist; educator - art instructor, Barnard College, NYC
Address:	52 South Saxon Avenue, Bay Shore
Name of estate:	
Year of construction:	c. 1896
Style of architecture:	Colonial Revival
Architect(s):	
Landscape architect(s):	
House extant:	yes
Historical notes:	

front facade, 2006

The house was built by Mrs. Edward Spring Knapp, Sr.
Julius Oppenheimer purchased the house in 1916 from Mrs. Knapp.
He was the son of Benjamin Pinhas Oppenheimer of Hanau, Germany.
Both of Julius and Ella Friedman Oppenheimer's sons Julius Robert [aka Robert] and Frank were noted scientists, who worked on the Manhattan Project during World War II to develop the atomic bomb. Julius Robert, known as the "Father of the Atomic Bomb" was the director of the project while Frank worked at government installations at Berkeley, CA, Oak Ridge, TN, and Los Alamos, NM. Both Julius Robert and Frank were later accused of being Communist agents and stripped of their security clearance. While Julius Robert steadfastly denied his involvement with the Communist Party, Frank eventually admitted that he and his wife Jacquenette were members of the party prior to the war.

Orr, John Clifton, Sr. (1841-1906)

Occupation(s):	merchant - president, John C. Orr Co., Brooklyn (lumber merchant)
	capitalist - director, Union Ferry Co.
	financier - director, Corn Exchange Bank, Brooklyn;
	director, Manufacturers Trust Co., Brooklyn
Civic Activism:	governor, Babylon Yacht Club
Marriage(s):	M/1 – Mary Louise Steers (1845-1875)
	M/2 – Amelia Sophia Killian (1852-1907)
Address:	Main Street, Amityville
Name of estate:	
Year of construction:	1889
Style of architecture:	
Architect(s):	
Landscape architect(s):	
House extant: unconfirmed	
Historical notes:	

The house was built by John Clifton Orr, Sr.
He was the son of Joseph and Sarah Ann Orr.
John Clifton and Mary Louise Steers Orr, Sr.'s son Henry married Mary Killian and resided in Garden City. [*See* Spinzia, *Long Island's Prominent Families in the Town of Hempstead* – Orr entry.] Their son John Clifton Orr, Jr. was youth at the time of his death.
Amelia Sophia Killian Orr was the daughter of Andrew and Mary E. Kohler Killian.
John Clifton and Amelia Sophia Killian Orr, Sr.'s son Joseph married Marie Wade, the daughter of John Wade of Philadelphia, PA.
In 1905, Orr purchased Kinsley Magoun's residence and furnishings. [*South Side Signal* October 21, 1905, p. 3, and *The Brooklyn Daily Eagle* November 1, 1907, p. 3.]

Otto, Thomas Nelson (1873-1949)

Occupation(s):	merchant - president, T. N. Otto Coal & Oil Co.;
	owner, chain of meat markets along Suffolk County's South Shore
Marriage(s):	1899-1949 – Julia Edna Hait (1881-1950)
	- Civic Activism: a founder, District Nursing Association;
	chairman, National Defense Council of Sayville during World War II
Address:	72 Saxton Avenue, Sayville
Name of estate:	
Year of construction:	
Style of architecture:	Colonial Revival
Architect(s):	
Landscape architect(s):	
House extant: yes	
Historical notes:	

Thomas Nelson Otto was the son of John and Cornelia Hage Otto of West Sayville.
Thomas Nelson and Julia Edna Hait Otto's daughter Virginia married Jeweth Holt Smith and resided in Sayville. Their daughter Julia married ____ Wallace and resided in Amityville.

front facade, 2006

Owens, Joseph Eugene, Sr. (1859-1919)

Occupation(s):	attorney - partner, Owens, Gray, and Tomlin, Brooklyn; legal advisor to Bishop McDonnell
	financier - trustee, Brooklyn Trust Co.
Civic Activism:	chairman, Local Draft Board Number 48, Brooklyn; secretary, Penataquit Corinthian Yacht Club; secretary, Catholic Club
Marriage(s):	Mary T. Carey
Address:	Saxon Avenue, Bay Shore
Name of estate:	
Year of construction:	
Style of architecture:	
Architect(s):	
Landscape architect(s):	
House extant: unconfirmed	
Historical notes:	

Joseph Eugene Owens, Sr. was the son of John and Mary Dickson Owens.

Mary T. Carey Owens was the daughter of Dr. George F. and Mrs. Maria F. Carey of Brooklyn.

Joseph Eugene and Mary T. Carey Owens, Sr.'s son Joseph Eugene Owens, Jr. married Beatrice Cronin, the daughter of John L. Cronin of Manhattan, and resided in Brooklyn. Their daughter Edith did not marry. Their daughter Olive married Dr. Austin Kilbourn, the son of Dr. Joseph Austin Kilbourn, of Hartford, CT.

Packer, Frederick Little (1886-1956)

Occupation(s):	artist - member, art staff, *Los Angeles Examiner*, 1906; member, art staff, *San Francisco Call* (which became the *Call-Post*), 1907; art director, *Call-Post*, 1913-1918; cartoonist, *New York American*, 1932; editorial cartoonist, *New York Daily Mirror*, 1932-1956*; commercial artist; book and magazine illustrator
Civic Activism:	vice-president, Victory Builders (prepared war posters), 1941-1946**; a founder and first president, South Shore Arts Association of Long Island
Marriage(s):	M/1 – Ruth *[unable to determine maiden name]*
	M/2 – 1941-1956 – Lillian Pabst (1902-1985)
Address:	216 Lakeview Avenue East, Brightwaters
Name of estate:	
Year of construction:	
Style of architecture:	Mediterranean
Architect(s):	
Landscape architect(s):	
House extant: yes	
Historical notes:	

Frederick Little Packer was the son of Jacob W. and Elizabeth Little Packer of Los Angeles, CA.

Lillian Pabst Packer was the daughter of William and Grace Ross Pabst of NYC. Lillian had previously been married to William Paul Wilson of Paris, TX.

*In 1952, Packer won the Pulitzer Prize for his editorial cartoon that depicted President Harry S Truman addressing members of the press. The cartoon's caption read "Your Editors Ought to Have More Sense Than to Print What I Say!"

**He received citations from the Department of Treasury and the War Production Board for his World War II cartoons and war posters.

In 1956, he received the Newspaper Guild's award for watercolor. In 1957, he was the recipient of the Freedom Award by the Freedoms Foundation.

front facade, 2006

Frederick Little Packer's Pulitzer Prize-winning cartoon

Page, Walter Hines, Sr. (1855-1918)

Occupation(s):	journalist - editor, *Age*;
	editor, *Daily Gazette*, St. Louis, MO;
	literary editor, *New York World*;
	managing editor, *Forum*;
	editor, *Atlantic Monthly*
	writer - *The Autobiography of a Southerner* [under pseudonym Nicholas Worth]
	publisher - a founder, *State Chronicle*, Raleigh, NC;
	a founder, with Frank Nelson Doubleday, Doubleday, Page & Co., Garden City (which became Doubleday & Co., Inc.)
	diplomat - United States Ambassador to the Court of St. James in Wilson administration
Civic Activism:	trustee, Peabody Fund;
	member, Southern Education Board;
	member, General Education Board
Marriage(s):	1880-1918 – Willa Alice Wilson (1858-1942)
Address:	Ocean Avenue, Bay Shore
Name of estate:	
Year of construction:	
Style of architecture:	Shingle
Architect(s):	
Landscape architect(s):	
House extant:	unconfirmed
Historical notes:	

    Walter Hines Page, Sr. rented the Harry M. Brewster house prior to relocating to Garden City.
    He was the son of Allison Francis and Catherine Raboteau Page.
    Willa Alice Wilson Page was the daughter of Dr. William Wilson of Michigan.
    Walter Hines and Willa Alice Wilson Page, Sr.'s daughter Katherine married Charles G. Loring of Boston, MA. Both King George and Queen Mary of Great Britain attended their wedding. [*The New York Times* June 28, 1915, p. 9.] Their son Arthur married Mollie W. Hall and resided at *County Line Farm* in West Hills. [*See* Spinzia, *Long Island's Prominent North Shore Families, vol. II*– Page entry.]

Palmer, Elwell (1890-1963)

Occupation(s):	attorney - Sayville-based practice
	capitalist - owned large tracts of land in Town of Islip
Marriage(s):	M/1 – 1922-1951 – Marjorie Cleaveland (1888-1951)
	- educator - Brooklyn and Manhattan Public Schools
	M/2 – 1955-1963 – Jeanett Edina Morrison (1895-1970)
Address:	71 Benson Avenue, Sayville
Name of estate:	
Year of construction:	c. 1910
Style of architecture:	Modified Colonial Revival
Architect(s):	Isaac Henry Green II
	designed the house
	(for W. R. Simonds)
Landscape architect(s):	
House extant: yes	
Historical notes:	

   The house, originally named *Wyndemoor*, was built by Frank Smith Jones as a present for his daughter Henrietta and son-in-law William Robinson Simonds. The house was later owned by David J. Shea, who continued to call it *Wyndemoor*, and, subsequently, by Palmer, who moved it to Benson Avenue.

   Marjorie Cleaveland Palmer was the daughter of John and Grace M. Law Cleaveland.

   Elwell and Marjorie Cleaveland Palmer's son George married Mary Jane Dowd, the daughter of Benjamin S. Dowd of Rockville Centre. He subsequently married Althea Trochelman, the daughter of Everett Trochelman of Bayport. Althea had previously been married to George N. Henrich. She later married George C. Palmer. Their son James married Elizabeth Therese Lewis, the daughter of Oscar Mayo Lewis of Cincinnati, OH. Their daughter Nancy married Thomas Paton Knapp, Jr. of Blue Point.

   Jeanett Edina Morrison was the daughter of George Alexander and Jessie Rae Morrison of Sayville. She had previously been married to Walter Francis Livingston.

front facade, 2005

Palmer, Elwell (1890-1963)

Occupation(s): *[See previous entry.]*

Marriage(s): M/1 – 1922-1951 – Marjorie Cleaveland (1888-1951)
- educator - Brooklyn and Manhattan Public Schools
M/2 – 1955-1963 – Jeanett Edina Morrison (1895-1970)

Address: Handsome Avenue, Sayville
Name of estate:
Year of construction: 1903
Style of architecture: Shingle
Architect(s): Isaac Henry Green II designed the main residence, gatehouse, and 1905 playhouse. The latter included a bowling alley and billiard room (for F. S. Jones)
Landscape architect(s):
House extant: no; destroyed by fire in 1957*
Historical notes:

stables, c. 1912

    The house, originally named *Beechwold*, was built by Frank Smith Jones. It was later owned by his daughter Maude and son-in-law David J. Shea. The Sheas chose to reside in the estate's gatehouse. In 1945, the house was purchased by Palmer, who, in 1949, sold it to Dr. Daniel McLaughlin. McLaughlin owned the house at the time of the fire.
    [See previous entry for additional family information.]
*The gatehouse and playhouse are extant. The gatehouse is located at 254 Handsome Avenue and the playhouse is at 96 Benson Avenue.

**Palmer, Frederick Timothy
aka Timothy Palmer**

Occupation(s):

Marriage(s): M/1 – 1966 – Jacqueline Carling
- model
M/2 – *[unable to determine maiden name]*

Address: 72 Oak Road, Bayport
Name of estate:
Year of construction: 2015
Style of architecture: Modified Tudor
Architect(s):
Landscape architect(s):
House extant: yes
Historical notes:

    He was the son of Carlton Humphreys and Antoinette Johnson Palmer, Sr. of *Hearthstone* on Centre Island. [*See* Spinzia, *Long Island's Prominent North Shore Families, vol. II* – Palmer entry.]

front facade, 2007

Pardee, Dwight W. (1852-1920)

Occupation(s): capitalist - director and secretary, New York Central Railway Co.;
director, Raquette Lake Railway Co.;
director and secretary, New York and Harlem Railroad;
director, Syracuse, Geneva, and Corning Railroad;
secretary, Michigan Central Railroad;
director, Dunkirk, Allegheny Valley, and Pittsburgh Railroad;
secretary, New York Central Niagara River Railroad;
secretary, New York Central and Hudson River Railroad

Marriage(s): Mary Mumby (1855-1937)

Address: South Country Road, Brightwaters
Name of estate:
Year of construction:
Style of architecture:
Architect(s):
Landscape architect(s):
House extant: unconfirmed
Historical notes:

Dwight W. Pardee was the son of Royal Bruce and Eliza J. Stevens Jordan Pardee.
In 1910, Dwight W. and Mary Mumby Pardee's nineteen-year-old daughter Elsa eloped with their chauffeur Kenneth Lee Collins. Their son Roy resided in Islip. Their daughter Mabel died in 1883 at the age of two.
[See following entry for additional family information.]

Pardee, Roy Edmund, Sr. (1888-1969)

Occupation(s): capitalist - real estate speculator;
one of Long Island's largest breeders of ducks
politician - Town of Islip Clerk;
Islip Republican committeeman
financier - director, First National Bank of Islip

Marriage(s): M/1 – 1909-div. 1910 – Lillian H. Beasley
    - entertainer -   actress
M/2 – 1912-1918 – Clair Lozier (1886-1918)
M/3 – Ellen Meagh (1905-1948)
M/4 – Marie Neff

Address: 112 Grant Avenue, Islip
Name of estate:
Year of construction:
Style of architecture: Neo-Tudor
Architect(s):
House extant: yes
Historical notes:

Roy Edmund Pardee, Sr. was the son of Dwight W. and Mary Pardee of Brightwaters.
Roy Edmund and Ellen Meagh Pardee, Sr.'s daughter Maureen married Richard G. Saunders, the son of Charles C. Saunders of Sag Harbor. Their son Dwight resided in Greensboro, NC. Their son Roy Edmund Pardee, Jr. married Anne Braun.
[See previous entry for additional family information.]

side / rear facade

Parkhurst, The Reverend Charles Henry (1842-1933)

Occupation(s):	clergy - pastor, Lenox Congregational Church, Lenox, MA, 1874-1880; pastor, Madison Square Presbyterian Church, NYC, 1880-1918
	educator - teacher, Amherst High School, Amherst, MA; professor, Greek and Latin, Williston Seminary, Easthampton, MA, 1879-1871
	writer - *The Forms of the Latin Verb*, 1870; *The Blind Man's Creed and Other Sermons*, 1883; *The Pattern on the Mount and Other Sermons*, 1885; *Three Gates on a Side*, 1887; *My Forty Years in New York*, 1923 (autobiography)
Civic Activism:	president, Society for the Prevention of Crime*; director, Union Theological Seminary, NYC
Marriage(s):	M/1 – 1870-1921 – Ellen Bodman (1848-1921)
	- Civic Activism: a founder, Women's Municipal League; president, American McCall Association
	M/2 – 1927-1931 – Eleanor *[unable to determine maiden name]* (1858-1931)
Address:	*[unable to determine street address]*, Babylon
Name of estate:	
Year of construction:	
Style of architecture:	
Architect(s):	
Landscape architect(s):	
House extant:	unconfirmed

Historical notes:

The Reverend Charles Henry Parkhurst was the son of Charles F. W. and Mrs. Mary Goodale Parkhurst of Framingham, MA.

Ellen Bodman Parkhurst was the daughter of Luther Bodman of Northampton, MA, and one of Charles' students at Amherst High School.

Eleanor Parkhurst had previously been married to Simon Marx. She was Mrs. Parkhurst's companion and Charles' secretary prior to her marriage to Parkhurst.

*Parkhurst was a fervent social reformer who railed against what he considered the hypocrisy and collusion of the New York City government which tolerated prostitution, gambling, and drunkenness.

He died when he plunged from the porch roof while sleepwalking at the New Jersey home of his nephew.

Parkinson, Thomas Ignatius, Jr. (1914-2010)

Occupation(s):	attorney - partner, Milbank, Tweed, Hope, and Hadley, NYC
	capitalist - president and chairman of board, Breecom Corp. (project management firm)
Civic Activism:	vice-president, New York War Fund, 1944; director, Foreign Policy Association, 1951; vice-president, New York State Charities Aid Association; director, Milbank Fund
Marriage(s):	1937-2010 – Geralda Moore
Address:	Lakeview Avenue, Brightwaters
Name of estate:	
Year of construction:	
Style of architecture:	Colonial Revival
Architect(s):	
Landscape architect(s):	
House extant:	yes

Historical notes:

Thomas Ignatius Parkinson, Jr. was the son of Thomas Ignatius and Georgia Childs Weed Parkinson, Sr. of West Islip.

Geralda Moore Parkinson was the daughter of Edward C. Moore of Brooklyn.

Thomas Ignatius and Geralda Moore Parkinson, Jr.'s son Geoffrey married Elizabeth Shirley Pidgeon, the daughter of William Arthur Pidgeon of Greenwich, CT. Their daughter Cynthia married Francisco Zuniga Pena, the son of Manuel Zuniga Pena of Santander, Spain, and, later, Jan Noreke with whom she resided in Westport, CT. Their son Thomas Ignatius Parkinson III resided in Lansdale, PA.

[See following entry for additional family information.]

Parkinson, Thomas Ignatius, Sr. (1881-1959)

Occupation(s):	attorney	
	capitalist -	director, Long Island Rail Road Co.;
		director, American Telephone & Telegraph Co.
	educator -	professor of legislation, Columbia University Law School, NYC;
		dean, law school faculty, Columbia University Law School, NYC
	financier -	president and chairman of board, Equitable Life Assurance Society of the United States;
		trustee, Atlantic Mutual Insurance Co.;
		director, Niagara Fire Insurance Co.;
		director, Centennial Insurance Co.;
		director, Chase National Bank;
		trustee, Emigrant Industrial Savings Bank
Civic Activism:	trustee, general education board, Rockefeller Foundation;	
	trustee, Columbia University, NYC;	
	trustee, University of Pennsylvania, Philadelphia, PA;	
	president, New York State Chamber of Commerce;	
	chairman, Greater New York Fund campaign;	
	chairman, United Negro College Fund campaign;	
	trustee, Sailor's Snug Harbor, NYC;	
	legal counsel, Bureau of War Risks Insurance, 1919*;	
	legislative council, United States Senate Commissions, 1919-1920**	
Marriage(s):	1912-1959 – Georgia Childs Weed (d. 1962)	
Address:	South Country Road, West Islip	

Name of estate:
Year of construction:
Style of architecture:
Architect(s):
Landscape architect(s):
House extant: no
Historical notes:

The *Long Island Society Register, 1929* lists Thomas I. Parkinson [Sr.] as residing on South Country Road, Babylon [West Islip].

He was the son of John Henry and Rose Fleming Parkinson of Philadelphia, PA.

Georgia Childs Weed Parkinson was the daughter of Henry Bannister Weed of Philadelphia, PA.

Thomas Ignatius and Georgia Childs Weed Parkinson, Sr.'s son Thomas Ignatius Parkinson, Jr. married Geralda Moore, the daughter of Edward C. Moore of Brooklyn, and resided in Brightwaters.

[See previous entry for additional family information.]

*Parkinson assisted in drafting War Risks Insurance Act.
**He also assisted in drafting Railroad Transportation Act.

Schuyler Livingston Parsons Sr., estate, Whileaway

Parsons, Schuyler Livingston, Jr. (1892-1967)

Occupation(s):	financier - sugar broker
	writer - *Untold Friendships*, 1955
Civic Activism:	member, Voluntary Ambulance Service of the American Red Cross in France during World War I;
	a founder and director, Great River Club, 1920 (later, Timber Point Club)
Marriage(s):	1920-div. 1923 – Elizabeth Pierson
Address:	St. Mark's Lane, Islip
Name of estate:	*Pleasure Island*
Year of construction:	1924
Style of architecture:	Ranch
Architect(s):	
Landscape architect(s):	
House extant: no; demolished in the 1980s	
Historical notes:	

Pleasure Island, c. 1970

The house, originally named *Pleasure Island*, was built by Schuyler Livingston Parsons, Jr.

The *Long Island Society Register, 1929* lists Schuyler Livingston Parsons [Jr.] as residing at *Pleasure Island* on St. Mark's Lane in Islip.

He was the son of Schuyler Livingston and Helena Johnson Parsons, Sr., who resided at *Whileaway* in Islip.

Elizabeth Pierson Parsons was the daughter of J. Frederick Pierson, Jr. of Newport, RI.

Schuyler Livingston Parsons, Jr. relocated to Newport, RI, Aikens, SC, Palm Beach, FL, and, subsequently, to Torrington, CT.

The Islip house was then owned by Schuyler Livingston Parsons, Jr.'s niece Marion and her husband Gerard Hallock III, who enlarged the house after moving it to the mainland.

[See following entry for additional family information.]

Parsons, Schuyler Livingston, Sr. (1852-1917)

Occupation(s):	merchant - president, Parsons & Peter (wholesale chemical dealers)
Marriage(s):	1877-1897 – Helena Johnson (1856-1897)
Address:	St. Mark's Lane, Islip
Name of estate:	*Whileaway*
Year of construction:	c. 1881
Style of architecture:	Shingle
Architect(s):	
Landscape architect(s):	
House extant: no	
Historical notes:	

front facade

The twelve-bedroom house, originally named *Whileaway*, was built by Schuyler Livingston Parsons, Sr.

The *Social Register Summer, 1910* lists Schuyler Livingston Parsons [Sr.] as residing at *Whileaway* in Islip.

He was the son of William Barclay and Eliza Livingston Parsons, Sr. of Manhattan. His brother William married Anna D. Reed and resided in Manhattan.

Helena Johnson Parsons was the daughter of Bradish and Louisa Anna Lawrance Johnson, Sr. of *Sans Souci* in West Bay Shore.

[See Johnson entries for additional family information.]

Schuyler Livingston and Helena Johnson Parsons, Sr.'s daughter Evelyn married Amor Hollingsworth of Boston, MA. Their son Schuyler Livingston Parsons, Jr. married Elizabeth Pierson and resided at *Pleasure Island* in Islip. Their daughter Helena, who later owned *Whileaway*, married Richard Wharton.

[See previous entry for additional Parsons family information.]

Parsons, William Decatur (1855-1930)

Occupation(s):	attorney
	writer - *The Decatur Genealogy*, 1921
Civic Activism:	donated a Gilbert Stuart portrait of Commodore Stephen Decatur to the National Art Gallery, Washington, DC;
	donated Commodore Decatur's dress uniform sword to the United States Naval Academy, Annapolis, MD
Marriage(s):	1899-1930 – Christine Hilsendegen (1859-1948)
Address:	91 Ocean Avenue, Bay Shore
Name of estate:	*Restina Cottage*
Year of construction:	
Style of architecture:	Modified Colonial Revival
Architect(s):	
Landscape architect(s):	
House extant: yes	
Historical notes:	

The *Long Island Society Register, 1929* lists William Decatur and Christine Hilsendegen Parsons as residing at *Restina Cottage*, 91 Ocean Avenue, Bay Shore.

He was the son of William H. and Anna Pine Parsons and the great-grandnephew of Commodore Stephen Decatur.

Christine Hilsendegen Parsons was the daughter of Valentine Hilsendegen of Detroit, MI. She had previously been married to William J. Ullrich of Mount Clemons, MI.

front facade, 2006

Pasternack, Richard (1891-c. 1974)

Occupation(s):	scientist*
	educator - taught chemistry in Germany
Marriage(s):	Elsa *[unable to determine maiden name]* (b.1894)
Address:	77 St. Mark's Lane, Islip
Name of estate:	
Year of construction:	1941
Style of architecture:	Neo-French Manorial
Architect(s):	
Landscape architect(s):	
House extant: yes	
Historical notes:	

By 1941 the Pasternacks had relocated from Idle Hour Boulevard, Oakdale, to Islip.

The Pasternacks' son Justus married Elizabeth Rowe, the daughter of Edward Comstock Rowe of Hamilton, NY.

*Pasternack is responsible for refining penicillin for commercial use.

In 2014, the eleven room house with four bedrooms and two-and-a-half bathrooms was for sale. The asking price was $1.795 million.

front facade, 2014

Payne, Albert (1835-1909)

Occupation(s): capitalist - real estate developer and builder

Marriage(s): Phebe Anna *[unable to determine maiden name]* (1845-1913)

Address: 80 Seaman's Avenue, Bayport
Name of estate:
Year of construction: 1883
Style of architecture: Queen Anne
Architect(s): Howard Payne designed the house
    (for his father Albert Payne)
Landscape architect(s):
House extant: yes
Historical notes:

   The house was built by Albert Payne.
   In 1893, he sold it to Louis C. Behman, Sr. who made extensive alterations to the house and property.
   While removing a nail from a horse's hoof, the horse kicked and the protruding nail struck Payne in the head. He died a short time later of lockjaw.
   Albert and Phebe Anna Payne's son Ralph married Mrs. Lillian Crosson of Washington, DC.
   In 1915, the house was owned by John La Spina and then, in 2017, by Manhattan real estate broker M. L. Osk.

front facade, 2005

Peck, William L., Sr. (1830-1902)

Occupation(s): industrialist - manufacturer of fertilizer
   capitalist - large real estate holdings in Town of Islip
   merchant - partner, with his brother, William L. Peck, NYC (dealers
         in stable manure and importers of Canadian hard wood
         unleached ashes)

Marriage(s): Phebe *[unable to determine maiden name]* (d. 1899)

Address: Clinton Avenue, Bay Shore
Name of estate:
Year of construction:
Style of architecture: Shingle
Architect(s):
Landscape architect(s):
House extant: unconfirmed
Historical notes:

   William L. and Phebe Peck, Sr.'s son Benjamin resided at 21 South Clinton Avenue, Bay Shore.

front facade, 1903

Perkins, Richard Sturgis, Sr. (1910-2003)

Occupation(s):	capitalist -	trustee, Consolidated Edison, NYC (utility company); director, International Telephone & Telegraph Co.; director, Astor Hotel, Inc., NYC; director, Carlton House, NYC
	financier -	president and chairman of board, City Bank Farmers Trust Co. (later, First National City Bank); chairman of board, First National City Bank; partner, Harris Upham and Co. (investment banking firm); director, Prudential Insurance Company of Great Britain; director, Liverpool, London & Globe Insurance Co.; director, New York Life Insurance Co.; director, British & Foreign Marine Insurance Co.; director, Thames & Mersey Marine Insurance Co.
	industrialist -	director, Phelps Dodge Corp.; director, Allied Chemical Corp.

Civic Activism: trustee, Metropolitan Museum of Art, NYC; chairman, Y.M.C.A. of Greater New York; trustee, Boys' Club of America; president, New York State Bankers Association

Marriage(s): 1935-div. c. 1976 – Adaline Havemeyer (1913-1998)

Address: 126 East Bayberry Road, Islip
Name of estate:
Year of construction: 1899-1900
Style of architecture: Moorish
Architect(s): Grosvenor Atterbury
  designed the house
  (for H. O. Havemeyer)*
Landscape architect(s): Nathan F. Barrett
  (for H. O. Havemeyer)**

House extant: yes
Historical notes:

    The house was built by Henry Osborne Havemeyer as part of his "Modern Venice" development. It was purchased in 1936 by Perkins, who subsequently relocated to a 1948 Colonial Revival house which was built by Horace Havemeyer, Sr. on his *Olympic Point* estate.
    He was the son of James Handasyd Perkins of Boston, MA. His sister Eleanor married Franklin E. Parker, Jr. and resided in Greenwich, CT.
    Adaline Havemeyer Perkins was the daughter of Horace and Doris Anna Dick Havemeyer, Sr., who resided at *Olympic Point* in Bay Shore and the granddaughter of Henry Osborne Havemeyer. She subsequently married Laurance B. Rand of Southport, CT. Her sister Doris married Dr. Daniel Catlin, Sr. and resided in Bay Shore. Her brother Harry married Eugenie Aiguier, the daughter of Dr. James E. Aiguier, and resides on the *Olympic Point* property in Bay Shore. Her brother Horace Havemeyer, Jr. married Rosalind Everdell, the daughter of William and Rosalind Romeyn Everdell of Manhasset, and resided in Islip and Dix Hills. [*See* Spinzia, *Long Island's Prominent North Shore Families, vol. I* – Everdell and Havemeyer entries.]
    Richard Sturgis and Adaline Havemeyer Perkins, Sr.'s son Richard Sturgis Perkins, Jr. married Mildred Duer Baxter, the daughter of Richard Seabury and Katherine Duer Irving Baxter, Sr. of Southampton. [*See* Spinzia, *Long Island's Prominent Families in the Town of Southampton* – Baxter entry.] Their son Thomas married Bonnie Campbell, the daughter of James Gordon Campbell of Princeton, NJ. After his divorce, Thomas relocated to Solvang, CA. Their daughter Sarah married William Moir, the son of James Tweed Moir of Edinburgh, Scotland. After the Moirs' divorce, Sarah relocated to Concord, MA. Their daughter Judith also resides in Concord, MA.
    *The sales brochure for "Modern Venice" states that the Moorish-style architecture was suggested by Louis Comfort Tiffany.
    **The sales brochure also states that "Modern Venice" would be devoid of trees and vegetation and that Nathan F. Barrett was the landscape architect.
    The house was subsequently owned by Anson McCook Beard, Jr.
    In 2005, it sold for $1.85 million.

Peters, Harry Twyford, Sr. (1881-1948)

Occupation(s):	merchant - president, Williams and Peters (wholesale coal); director, Peabody Coal Co.
	writer - *Just Hunting*, 1935; *Currier and Ives: Printmakers To the American People*, 1929*; *Track and Road: The American Trotting Horse*; *California on Stone*; *America on Stone*
Civic Activism:	chairman, New York State Coal Conservation Committee during World War I; master of hounds, Meadow Brook Hounds; a founder and director, Great River Club (later, Timber Point Club)
Marriage(s):	1905-1948 – Natalie Wells (1882-1976)
	- Civic Activism: president, Garden Club of America, 1944-1947
Address:	St. Mark's Lane, Islip
Name of estate:	*Nearholme*
Year of construction:	1882
Style of architecture:	Modified Shingle
Architect(s):	
Landscape architect(s):	
House extant:	no
Historical notes:	

rear facade

The house, originally named *Nearholme*, was built by Harry Twyford Peters, Sr.

The *Social Register Summer, 1910* lists Harry T. and Natalie Wells Peters [Sr.] as residing at *Nearholme* in Islip.

He was the son of Samuel Twyford and Adaline Mapes Elder Peters, who resided at *Windholme Farm* in Islip.

Natalie Wells Peters was the daughter of William Storrs Wells of *Chetwode* in Newport, RI.

Harry Twyford and Natalie Wells Peters, Sr.'s daughter Natalie married Charles Drake Webster and resided at *Twyford* in Islip. Their son Harry Twyford Peters, Jr. remained a bachelor and resided at *Windholme Farm* in Orange, VA.

*Harry Twyford Peters, Sr. was a noted collector, author, and authority on Currier and Ives prints.

[See Samuel Twyford Peters entry for additional family information.]

Peters, Harry Twyford, Sr. (1881-1948)

Occupation(s):	*[See previous entry.]*
Civic Activism:	*[See previous entry.]*
Marriage(s):	1905-1948 – Natalie Wells (1882-1976)
	- Civic Activism: president, Garden Club of America, 1944-1947
Address:	St. Mark's Lane, Islip
Name of estate:	*Windholme Farm*
Year of construction:	1882
Style of architecture:	Shingle
Architect(s):	Alfred Hopkins designed the c. 1910 farm and garage complex (for S. T. Peters)*
Landscape architect(s):	Ellen Biddle Shipman (for H. T. Peters, Sr.)

House extant: no; demolished in c. 1950
Historical notes:

The house was built by John Dyneley Prince II. [*The New York Times* July 30, 1882, p. 5.] It was purchased by Samuel Twyford Peters, who enlarged the house and called it *Windholme Farm*.

The estate was subsequently owned by his son Harry Twyford Peters, Sr., who continued to call it *Windholme Farm*.

[See other Peters entries for additional family information.]

*The barn complex still exists. It was converted into a residence by Mrs. Harry Twyford Peters, Sr.

farm complex, 1912

Peters, Samuel Twyford (1854-1921)

Occupation(s):	merchant - partner, with Richard H. Williams, Williams and Peters (wholesale coal)
	financier - director, Hanover Bank
	capitalist - a founder, South Side Improvement Co., 1885 (accumulation of water to sprinkle roads)
Civic Activism:	trustee, Metropolitan Museum of Art, NYC*
Marriage(s):	c. 1879-1921 – Adaline Mapes Elder (1859-1943)
Address:	St. Mark's Lane, Islip
Name of estate:	*Windholme Farm*
Year of construction:	1882
Style of architecture:	Shingle
Architect(s):	Alfred Hopkins designed the c. 1910 farm and garage complex (for S. T. Peters)**
Landscape architect(s):	Ellen Biddle Shipman (for H. T. Peters, Sr.)

House extant: no; demolished in c. 1950
Historical notes:

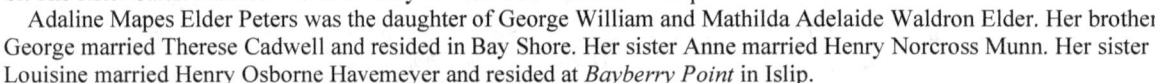

The house was built by John Dyneley Prince II. [*The New York Times* July 30, 1882, p. 5.] It was purchased by Peters, who enlarged the house and called it *Windholme Farm*.

He was the son of Samuel and Josephine Gemmel Peters, Sr. His sister Sarah married Richard Henry Williams and resided in Islip.

Windholme Farm

Adaline Mapes Elder Peters was the daughter of George William and Mathilda Adelaide Waldron Elder. Her brother George married Therese Cadwell and resided in Bay Shore. Her sister Anne married Henry Norcross Munn. Her sister Louisine married Henry Osborne Havemeyer and resided at *Bayberry Point* in Islip.

Samuel Twyford and Adaline Mapes Elder Peters' daughter Louisine married Harold Hathaway Weekes and resided in *Wereholme* in Islip. Louisine subsequently married Alexander Tcherepin and continued to reside at *Wereholme*. Their son Harry Twyford Peters, Sr., who married Natalie Wells and resided at *Nearholme* in Islip, later owned *Windholme Farm*.

[See other Peters entries for additional family information.]

*Samuel Twyford Peters donated over four hundred Oriental pieces of jade to the Metropolitan Museum of Art.

**The barn complex still exists. It was converted into a residence by Mrs. Harry Twyford Peters.

Phelps, Charles Egbert (1865-1918)

Occupation(s):	financier - treasurer, Equitable Life Assurance Society of the United States
Marriage(s):	M/1 – Emily Harriet Thompson (d. 1915)
	M/2 - Laura Wakefield
Address:	North Windsor Avenue, Brightwaters
Name of estate:	*Brightwaters*
Year of construction:	1902
Style of architecture:	Shingle
Architect(s):	Clarence K Birdsall designed the house (for Phelps)
Landscape architect(s):	
Builder:	Jabez Ephraim Van Orden

House extant: unconfirmed
Historical notes:

The twenty-three-room house was built by Charles Egbert Phelps.

Emily Harriet Thompson Phelps was the daughter of Abram Gardiner Thompson.

Charles Egbert and Emily Harriet Thompson Phelps' daughter Caroline married Samuel Ludlow Thompson. Their daughter Maude married Warren R. McVeigh.

Brightwaters

Phelps, Royal, Jr. (1809-1884)

Occupation(s):	financier - partner, Maitland, Phelps, and Co. (investment banking firm);
	director, Atlantic Mutual Insurance Co.;
	director, Royal Insurance Co.
	politician - member, New York State Assembly, District 14, 1862
Civic Activism:	vice-president, Chamber of Commerce;
	president, New York Eye and Ear Infirmary, NYC;
	trustee, Roosevelt Hospital, NYC
Marriage(s):	1831-1872 – Anita Maytin (1816-1872)
Address:	Phelps Lane, North Babylon
Name of estate:	
Year of construction:	
Style of architecture:	
Architect(s):	
Landscape architect(s):	
House extant: no	
Historical notes:	

The house was built by Royal Phelps, Jr.

He was the son of The Reverend Royal and Mrs. Hannah Spofford Phelps, Sr. of Sempronius, NY.

Royal and Anita Maytin Phelps, Jr.'s daughter Anita married the Governor of Maryland John Lee Caroll.

The house later became the headquarters of the Rod and Reel Club before it was purchased by John Montgomery Ward.

In 1941, it was sold to David Schnur who demolished the house and built a fourteen-room house on the site.

Robert Low Pierrepont residence,
side / front facade

Pierrepont, Robert Low (1876-1945)

Occupation(s):	financier - director, Home Life Insurance Co.; director, Lawyers Mortgage Co.; trustee, Brooklyn Trust Co.; director, Hanover Fire Insurance Co.; director, Fulton Fire Insurance Co.; director, South Brooklyn Savings Bank; director, Brooklyn City Safe Deposit Co. capitalist - director, Brooklyn Union Gas Co.; director, 580 Park Avenue, Inc. industrialist - director, Low–Moor Iron Co.
Civic Activism:	director, Greenwood Cemetery, Brooklyn; director, Church Charity Foundation; a founder and director, Bay Shore Protective Association
Marriage(s):	1900-1945 – Kathryn Isabel Reed (1879-1960) - Civic Activism: a founder, governor, and secretary, American Woman's Association
Address:	Saxon Avenue, Bay Shore
Name of estate:	
Year of construction:	
Style of architecture:	Shingle
Architect(s):	
Landscape architect(s):	

House extant: unconfirmed
Historical notes:

The *Social Register Summer, 1915* lists Robert Low and Kathryn I. Reed Pierrepont as residing on Saxon Avenue, Bay Shore.

He was the son of Henry Evelyn and Ellen Almir Low Pierrepont of Brooklyn; the great-great-grandson of Chief Justice of the United States Supreme Court John Jay; and a nephew of New York City Mayor Seth Low.

Kathryn Isabel Reed Pierrepont was the daughter of Josiah and Helen Marie Flanders Reed of South Weymouth, MA, and Brooklyn, NY.

Robert Low and Kathryn Isabel Reed Pierrepont's twin sons Henry and Samuel were one-day-old at the time of their deaths. Their son John married Mary Adelaide Scott, the daughter of Charles Herrington Scott of Montgomery, AL.

In 1915, Walter Ellwood Bedell purchased the house from Pierrepont. [*Suffolk County News* February 26, 1915, p. 2.]. In 1927, Beverley Montagu Eyre purchased it from Bedell. [*The New York Times* June 17, 1927, p. 41.]

Pinkerton, Allan, II (1876-1930)

Occupation(s):	capitalist - president, Pinkerton National Detective Agency; owner, Bay Shore Polo Field
Civic Activism:	director, Bay Shore Horse Show Association, 1903; governor, Penataquit Corinthian Yacht Club; chairman, Islip chapter, South Suffolk County chapter, American Red Cross Japan Relief Committee, 1923
Marriage(s):	1902-1930 – Franc Woolworth (d. 1945)
Address:	South Saxon Avenue, Bay Shore
Name of estate:	
Year of construction:	c. 1905
Style of architecture:	Colonial Revival
Architect(s):	
Landscape architect(s):	Hicks Nursery supplied plantings (for A. Pinkerton II)

House extant: no; demolished in c. 1950
Historical notes:

front facade

The *Long Island Society Register, 1929* lists Allan and Franc Woolworth Pinkerton [II] as residing on Saxon Avenue in Islip [Bay Shore].

He was the son of Robert Allan and Anna Elizabeth Hughes Pinkerton, Sr., who resided at *Dearwood* in Bay Shore.

Franc Woolworth Pinkerton was the daughter of Frank Herbert Woolworth.

Allan and Franc Woolworth Pinkerton II's son Robert Allan Pinkerton II married Louise Eliot Cutter and resided in the caretaker's cottage on his parents' estate, prior to relocating to East Islip.

[See other Pinkerton entries for additional family information.]

Pinkerton, Robert Allan, II (1904-1967)

Occupation(s):	capitalist - president and chairman of board, Pinkerton National Detective Agency
	financier - stockbroker
Civic Activism:	trustee, Southside Hospital, Bay Shore (now, South Shore University Hospital)
Marriage(s):	1930-1967 – Louise Eliot Cutter (d. 1983)
Address:	Meadow Farm Road, East Islip
Name of estate:	
Year of construction:	1927
Style of architecture:	Colonial Revival
Architect(s):	Philip Cusack designed the house (for R. W. Morgan, Sr.)
Landscape architect(s):	
House extant: yes	
Historical notes:	

The house was built by Robert Woodward Morgan, Sr. It was later owned by Pinkerton.
He was the son of Allan and Franc Woolworth Pinkerton II, who resided in Bay Shore.
Louise Eliot Cutter Pinkerton was the daughter of Eliot and Anna Louise McBride Cutter of *Minnebama* in Westhampton. [*See* Spinzia, *Long Island's Prominent Families in the Town of Southampton* – Cutter entry.]. Louise subsequently married John Hunt Marshall of Dedham, MA, with whom she resided in East Islip.
Robert Allan and Louise Eliot Cutter Pinkerton, II's daughter Ann did not marry.
The house was subsequently owned by Robert William Entenmann, Sr.
[See other Pinkerton entries for additional family information.]
[For information on the Southside Hospital, see Cooper entry.]

Pinkerton, Robert Allan, Sr. (1848-1907)

Occupation(s):	capitalist - president, Pinkerton National Detective Agency
Marriage(s):	1873-1907 – Anna Elizabeth Hughes (1850-1933)
Address:	116 South Penataquit Avenue, Bay Shore
Name of estate:	*Dearwood*
Year of construction:	1884
Style of architecture:	Queen Anne
Architect(s):	
Landscape architect(s):	Hicks Nursery supplied plantings (for R. A. Pinkerton, Sr.]
House extant: yes	
Historical notes:	

The house was built by Richard Malcolm Montgomery, Sr. In 1899, it was purchased by Pinkerton, who called it *Dearwood*.
He was the son of Allan and Joan Carfrae Pinkerton, Sr.
Robert Allan and Anna Elizabeth Hughes Pinkerton, Sr.'s daughter Mary married Jay Freeborn Carlisle, Sr. and resided at *Rosemary* in East Islip. Their daughter Anna married Lewis Mills Gibb, Sr. and resided at *Cedarholme* in Bay Shore. Their son Allan Pinkerton II married Franc Woolworth and resided in Bay Shore.
[See other Pinkerton entries for additional family information.]
In 2021, the eight-bedroom, four-bath, 5,000-square-foot house was for sale. The asking price was $1.2 million.

front facade

Placide, Henry (1799-1870)

Occupation(s): entertainers and associated professions - comic stage actor

Marriage(s): Margaret McBeth (1827-1895)

Address: Fire Island Avenue, Babylon
Name of estate:
Year of construction:
Style of architecture: Colonial Revival
Architect(s):
Landscape architect(s):
House extant: unconfirmed
Historical notes:

Henry Placide was the son of the French acrobat, dancer, actor, and manager Alexander Placide and his English wife Charlotte Sophia Wrighten Placide.

Henry made his stage appearance in Augusta, Georgia, at the age of nine. He would later be known as an expert in Gallic parts struggling between French and English speech.

front facade

Pless, John Anthony, Jr. (b. 1930)

Occupation(s): educator - teacher, Hewlett School of East Islip
Civic Activism: president, Suffolk Hearing and Speech Center, Bay Shore;
trustee, United Counseling;
member, advisory board, Southside Hospital, Bay Shore (now, South Shore University Hospital)

Marriage(s): 1966 – Helena Parsons Hallock (b. 1942)
 - Civic Activism: president, South Shore Garden Club

Address: St. Mark's Lane, Islip
Name of estate:
Year of construction:
Style of architecture: ranch
Architect(s):
Landscape architect(s):
House extant: no; demolished in 1980s
Historical notes:

John Anthony and Helena Parsons Hallock Pless, Jr. resided in the former chauffeur's cottage of the Parsons' estate *Whileaway*, which, in the 1970s, had been converted into a ranch-style house.

He was the son of John Anthony and Madeline Sichel Pless, Sr. of Holland and France.

Helena Parsons Hallock Pless was the daughter of Gerard and Marion Wharton Hallock III of Islip.

John Anthony and Helena Parsons Hallock Pless, Jr.'s daughter Elizabeth married Christopher Kirk of Darian, CT, and resided in Southwest Harbor, ME. Their daughter Katriena married Michael Devlin of Annapolis, MD, and resided in Darian, CT. Their son John Anthony Pless III married Lindley Tilghman of Greenwich, CT, and resided in Manhattan.

[For information on the Southside Hospital, see Cooper entry.]

Plumb, James Ives (1863-1937)

Occupation(s):

Marriage(s): 1885 – Frances Anna Parsons Burton (1866-1933)

Address: Heckscher Parkway, East Islip
Name of estate: *Deer Range Farm*
Year of construction: c. 1850s
Style of architecture: Eclectic
Architect(s):
Landscape architect(s):
Builder: Jabez Ephraim Van Orden,
    house (for E. A. Johnson, Sr.)
Erastus Peterson, 1899 carriage
    house (for J. I. Plumb)

House extant: no; demolished in 1909*
Historical notes:

Deer Range Farm

The house, originally named *Deer Range Farm*, was built by Edwin Augustus Johnson, Sr. on his 400-acre estate.
[For history of the estate, see Sarah Caroline Ives Plumb entry.]
    Frances Anna Parsons Burton Plumb was the daughter of Dr. Matthew H. Burton of Troy, NY.
    James Ives and Frances Anna Parsons Burton Plumb's son Burton married Marguerite de B. Taylor, the daughter of George W. Taylor of Norfolk, VA, and, subsequently, Louise Everett, the widow of Joseph de Tours Lentilhon of Tarrytown, NY.
[See other Plumb entries for additional family information.]
    In 1903, James Ives Plumb sold the estate to George Campbell Taylor and relocated to Islip.
*The demolition date of 1909 is given in *The Suffolk County News* November 19, 1909, p. 3.

Plumb, James Ives (1863-1937)

Occupation(s):

Marriage(s): 1885 – Frances Anna Parsons Burton (1866-1933)

Address: South Country Road, Islip
Name of estate: *Shadowbrook*
Year of construction:
Style of architecture: Colonial Revival
Architect(s):
Landscape architect(s):
House extant: no
Historical notes:

    In 1869, Joseph William Meeks, Sr. purchased *Champlin House* and renovated it into his country residence. In 1905, it was purchased by Plumb, who remodeled the house and called it *Shadowbrook*.
    The *Long Island Society Register, 1929* lists J. Ives and Anna Burton Plumb as residing at *Shadowbrook* on Main Street [South Country Road], Islip.
[See other Plumb entries for family information.]

front facade, c. 1906

Plumb, Sarah Caroline Ives (1840-1877)

Marriage(s):	1861-1877 – James Neale Plumb (1832-1899) - attorney capitalist - partner with James M. Plumb, J. M. & J. N. Plumb & Co. (importing firm)
Address:	Heckscher Parkway, East Islip
Name of estate:	*Deer Range Farm*
Year of construction:	c. 1850s
Style of architecture:	Eclectic
Architect(s):	
Landscape architect(s):	
Builder:	Jabez Ephraim Van Orden, house (for E. A. Johnson, Sr.) Erastus Peterson, 1899 carriage house (for J. I. Plumb)
House extant:	no; demolished in 1909
Historical notes:	

The house, originally named *Deer Range Farm*, was built by Edwin Augustus Johnson, Sr. on his 400-acre estate. In 1872, the estate was purchased by Sarah Caroline Ives Plumb. Over the years the estate acreage was increased to 700 acres by the Plumbs.

She was the daughter of Abram and Mary Merrill Ives of Waterbury, CT. Upon her death, the estate was inherited by her husband James Neale Plumb, who altered the house into the structure on the following page in 1884.

James Neale Plumb was the son of James Madison and Jeannette Frances Yale Plumb of San Francisco. His sister Grace married George H. Hughes and resided at 20 Fifth Avenue in Manhattan.

*After Sarah's death, the Plumbs' daughters Marie and Sarah Lenita sued James; Marie for an accounting of the expenses incurred by her mother's trust and Sarah Lenita, who was a minor at the time, to have him removed as her guardian. In 1899, Plumb murdered Alexander Masterton, the seventy-two-year-old trustee of his wife's trust. Plumb's animosity toward Masterton was long-standing, stemming, in part, from Masterton's opposition to Plumb's marriage to Sarah because of Plumb's gambling activities. As the years had passed, Plumb had come to blame Masterton for his alienation from his wife Sarah and their children. Further complicating matters was Plumb's opposition to the marriage of his son James to Frances Anna Parsons Burton; Marie's marriage to Ramsey Nares of Southampton, England, with whom she resided in Surrey, England; and the marriage of Sarah Lenita, who was a noted suffragist, to Jarvis R. Fairchild. While awaiting trial in New York City's Tombs, Plumb contracted erysipelas, a severe inflammatory condition caused by a hemolytic streptococcus infection. He was removed to Bellevue Hospital. His face and the underlying tissue of the head were initially affected and, despite warnings that the infection could reach the brain, Plumb refused all medication and died. [*The New York Times* June 27, 1895, p. 8; May 4, 1899, p. 1; May 7, 1899, p. 2; and June 6, 1899, p. 14.]

The estate was subsequently owned by the Plumbs' son James Ives Plumb, who continued to call it *Deer Range Farm*. *[See other Plumb entries for additional family information.]*

In 1903, James Ives Plumb sold the estate to George Campbell Taylor and relocated to Islip. Taylor merged *Deer Range Farm* into his adjoining estate which, with the addition of the Plumb estate, encompassed 1,500 acres. With Taylor's death in 1907, the combined estates passed to the Taylor / Pyne family corporation which, in 1909, demolished the Plumb mansion. Portions of the Plumb mansion were salvaged, moved, and incorporated into buildings in Great River and Bay Shore. The remaining Taylor mansion and estate acreage remained in the Taylor / Pyne family corporation until 1924 when it was confiscated by Robert Moses and became part of Heckscher State Park. [Harry W. Havemeyer, *Along the Great South Bay From Oakdale to Babylon: The Story of a Summer Spa 1840 to 1940* (Mattituck, NY: Amereon House, 1996), p. 135.] The Taylor house was demolished by Moses' Long Island State Park Commission.

August Heckscher, Sr. gave Moses the money to acquire the land, hence the name of the East Islip park and parkway. [*See* Spinzia, *Long Island's Prominent North Shore Families, vol. I* – Heckscher entries.]

Deer Range Farm

Deer Range Farm

Poillon, John Edward (1848-1927)

Occupation(s):	industrialist - partner, C. & R. Poillon Co. (Brooklyn shipyard which also operated under the names Poillon Brothers and C. & R. Poillon Steamboat Co.)*
Marriage(s):	
Address:	Clinton Avenue, Bay Shore
Name of estate:	
Year of construction:	
Style of architecture:	Queen Anne
Architect(s):	
Landscape architect(s):	
House extant: unconfirmed	
Historical notes:	

John Edward Poillon was the son of Cornelius Poillon, the co-founder of C. & R. Poillon Company.

John's daughter Gladys married Francis Guerrlich of Shippan Point, CT. His son Arthur married Winifred Robinson of Colorado Springs, CO.

*The company, formed in the early 19th century, was a major Brooklyn employer, employing, at one point, over three hundred workers in its two Brooklyn shipyards. Before its demise in c. 1904, its records note construction of over 175 yachts, steamships, transports, ferries, and Civil War gun boats. [Nannette Poillon. "C & R Poillon: 19th Century Brooklyn Shipbuilders." By-The-Sea: The On-Line Boating Magazine, 2002.] In 1867, C. & R. Poillon Co. built the *Sappho*. It was acquired by E. A. Lawrence who sold it in 1871 to William Proctor Douglas of *Overdune* in Southampton. In the same year Douglas defended the America's Cup by defeating the British challenger *Cambria*. In 1876, Douglas sold the *Sappho* to Prince Sciarra of Italy. [*See* Spinzia, *Long Island's Prominent Families in the Town of Southampton* – Douglas entry.]

front facade, c. 1903

Pollock, Walter B. (1857-1928)

Occupation(s):	capitalist -	auditor, New York Central Railroad; manager, marine department, New York Central Railroad; special representative to traffic department, New York Central Railroad; vice-president, Western Transit Co.
	financier -	vice-president, treasurer and president, New York Produce Exchange

Marriage(s): Helen *[unable to determine maiden name]*

Address:
Name of estate: 120 South Gillette Avenue, Bayport
Year of construction: 1909
Style of architecture: Dutch Colonial Revival
Architect(s): Isaac Henry Green II designed the house (for Pollock)
Landscape architect(s):
Builder: Frederick D. Smith, house and garage, 1909 (for Pollock)
Clifford Munsell, alterations to main residence, 1928 (for Major)

House extant: yes
Historical notes:

   The fourteen-room house with six bedrooms and three full and two half bathrooms, was built by Walter B. Pollock. [*The Brooklyn Daily Eagle* April 4, 1909, p. 16, and *The Suffolk County News* February 12, 1909, p. 2.]
   In 1926, it was purchased by Alfred Sarony Major. [*The Suffolk County News* June 4, 1926, p. 2.]
   In 1935, Mrs. Major sold the house to James McClung of Brooklyn. [*The Suffolk County News* August 16, 1935, p. 8.]
   In 1955, it was purchased by John Busby of Hyde Park, NY. [*The Suffolk County News* September 2, 1955, p. 5.]
   In 2017, the house sold for $1.35 million.

front facade

Post, Charles Alfred (1844-1921)

Occupation(s):	attorney
Civic Activism:	fellow, Royal Astronomical Society, Great Britain
Marriage(s):	1875-1921 – Marie Caroline de Trobriand (1845-1926) - writer - *The Life and Memoirs of General Count de Trobriand*; *The Post Family*, 1905
Address:	Ocean Avenue, Bayport
Name of estate:	*Strandhome*
Year of construction:	1880
Style of architecture:	Shingle
Architect(s):	Isaac Henry Green II designed the house (for W. R. Foster, Jr.) George Browne Post designed the alterations (for C. A. Post)
Landscape architect(s):	
House extant:	no; demolished in 1950s
Historical notes:	

Strandhome

The house, originally named *Strandhome*, was built by William Riley Foster, Jr.

In 1888, *Strandhome* was purchased at public auction by the Produce Exchange Gratuity Fund which sold it, in 1890, to Post. Post continued to call the estate *Strandhome*.

He was the son of Joel Browne Post of Manhattan. His brother, the noted architect George Browne Post, married Alice Stone. George Browne Post was on Ward McAllister's "Four Hundred" list, but Charles and Marie were omitted.

Marie Caroline de Trobriand Post was the daughter of Baron Philippe Regis Denis de Keredern and Mary Mason Jones de Trobriand. Marie had previously been married to Albert Kintzing Post.

Charles Alfred and Marie Caroline de Trobriand Post's daughter Beatrice married Duncan W. Candler, the son of Flamen Ball and Marie Lillian Welch Candler of Woodmere. [*See* Spinzia, *Long Island's Prominent Families in the Town of Hempstead* – Candler entry.] Their daughter Edith married Goelet Gallatin, the son of Frederick and Almy Goelet Gerry Gallatin of *Breezy Lawn* in East Hampton, and resided in Blue Point. [*See* Spinzia, *Long Island's Prominent Families in the Town of East Hampton* – Gallatin entry.]

[See other Post entries for additional family information.]

The estate was subsequently owned by Waldron Kintzing Post, who continued to call it *Strandhome*.

Bernard Mannes Baruch, Sr. rented the house during the summers of 1915 and 1916.

Post, Charles Kintzing (1897-1974)

Occupation(s):	military - lieutenant commander in command of a five-vessel task force in the Fourth Fleet intelligence agent - officer, Naval Intelligence during World War II
Marriage(s):	1919-div. 1926 – Caroline Burr Knapp (d. 1952)
Address:	Ocean Avenue, Bayport
Name of estate:	*Strandhome*
Year of construction:	1880
Style of architecture:	Shingle
Architect(s):	Isaac Henry Green II designed the house (for W. R. Foster, Jr.) George Browne Post designed the alterations (for C. A. Post)
Landscape architect(s):	
House extant:	no; demolished in 1950s
Historical notes:	

The house, originally named *Strandhome*, was built by William Riley Foster, Jr.

After World War II, Charles Kintzing Post returned to Bayport and resided with his father Waldron at *Strandhome*.

[See other Post entries for additional family information.]

Caroline Burr Knapp Post was the daughter of Harry Kearsarge and Caroline Burr Knapp, Sr., who resided at *Brookwood* in East Islip. Her brother Harry Kearsarge Knapp II, who resided at *Creekside* in East Islip, married Phebe Schoonhaven Thorne and, later, Elizabeth Marshall Mann. Her brother Theodore, who later owned *Brookwood*, married Gladys Quarre.

[See previous entry for additional estate information.]

Post, Edwin Main, Sr. (1870-1928)

Occupation(s):	financier - partner, Thomas and Post (investment banking firm)
	capitalist - director and secretary, Louisville, Henderson and St. Louis Railway;
	president, Coal Line Georgia Co.;
	president, Georgia Car Co.;
	director, Augusta Telephone and Electric Co.;
	director, Manhattan Car Trust Co.
Marriage(s):	M/1 – 1892-div. 1907 – Emily Bruce Price (1872-1960)
	- writer - *Flight of the Moth*, 1904;
	Purple and Fine Linen, 1906;
	Woven in the Tapestry, 1908;
	The Title Market, 1909;
	The Eagle Feather, 1910;
	By Car to the Golden Gate, 1916;
	Etiquette in Society, in Business, in Politics and at Home, 1922;
	Parade, 1925;
	How to Behave Though a Debutante, 1928;
	The Personality of a House, 1930;
	Children are People, 1940;
	The Emily Post Cook Book, 1949 (co-authored with her son Edwin);
	Motor Manners, 1950;
	The Blue Book of Social Usage (sold over one million copies in ten revisions)
	journalist - authored a syndicated column on etiquette in *McCall's* and in over 100 newspapers
	entertainers and associate professions - weekly radio show
	capitalist - founder, Emily Post Foundation (to handle her financial affairs)
	M/2 – 1911-1928 – Eleanor Malcolm (aka Nelly Malcolm)
	- entertainers and associate professions - actress
Address:	Post Place, Babylon
Name of estate:	
Year of construction:	
Style of architecture:	
Architect(s):	
Landscape architect(s):	
House extant:	unconfirmed
Historical notes:	

Edwin Main Post, Sr. was the son of Henry Albertson Van Zo and Caroline Burnet McLean Post of *Postholm* in Babylon.

Emily Bruce Price Post was the daughter of the noted architect Bruce Price and his wife Josephine Lee Price of Tuxedo Park, NY.

Edwin Main and Emily Bruce Price Post's son Bruce remained a bachelor. Their son Edwin Main Post, Jr., who married Barbara Baker Loew, the daughter of William Goadby and Florence Bellows Baker Loew of *Loewmoor* in Old Westbury, and, later, Marietta Szveteney, resided in Old Westbury and Westhampton Beach. [*See* Spinzia, *Long Island's Prominent North Shore Families, vol. I* – Loew entry; *Long Island's Prominent North Shore Families, vol. II* – Post entry; and *Long Island's Prominent Families in the Town of Southampton* – Post entry.]

Edwin Main and Eleanor Malcolm Post had three children, one of whom died in its infancy.

Edwin, who resided in Babylon after his divorce from Emily, drowned off Fire Island when the boat in which he was sailing capsized.

Post, Henry Albertson Van Zo (1832-1914)

Occupation(s):	industrialist - chief engineer, Novelty Iron Works (manufacturer of engines for steamships; director, American Equipment Co., NYC; partner, Perkins, Livingston, & Post (later, Post & Co.); partner, Post & Co., Cincinnati, OH (manufacturer of railroad supplies)
	financier - a founder, Clark, Post, and Martin (later, Post–Martin) (railroad bankers); partner, Post, Pomeroy, and Post, NYC (railroad bankers)
	capitalist - a founder, South Side Improvement Co., 1885 (accumulation of water to sprinkle roads)
Marriage(s):	M/1 – 1853-1860 – Maria Farquhar Taylor (1832-1860)
	M/2 – 1865-1914 – Caroline Burnet McLean (1844-1918)
Address:	East Main Street, Babylon
Name of estate:	*Postholm*
Year of construction:	1874
Style of architecture:	
Architect(s):	George Browne Post designed the alterations (for H. A. V. Post)
Landscape architect(s):	
House extant: unconfirmed	
Historical notes:	

The house was previously owned by James Harvey Carll.

The *Social Register Summer, 1915* lists Henry A. V. and Caroline B. McLean Post as residing at *Postholme* in Babylon. He was the son of Edwin and Lucretia Ann Main Post.

Henry Albertson Van Zo and Maria Farquhar Taylor Post's daughter Maria married John Christopher O'Connor. Their daughter Laura did not marry.

Caroline Burnet McLean Post was the daughter of Civil War General Nathaniel McLean and Mrs. Caroline T. Burnet McLean and the granddaughter of United States Supreme Court Justice John McLean. Through the Burnet side of the family Caroline was a direct descendant of Oliver Cromwell.

Henry Albertson Van Zo and Caroline Burnet McLean Post's daughter Caroline married Regis Henri Post, Sr. and resided at *Littlewood* in Bayport. Their son Henry R. Post died in 1914 at the age of twenty-nine. Their son Albertson married Meta L. Anderson, the daughter of Eli S. and Henrietta Anderson of Brooklyn. Their son Edwin Main Post, Sr. married Emily Bruce Price, the daughter of the noted architect Bruce Price and his wife Josephine Lee Price, and resided in Staten Island, NY, and, later, Eleanor Malcolm with whom he resided in Babylon. After Emily's divorce from Edwin, she went on to be one of the foremost authorities on etiquette.

Post, Regis Henri, Sr. (1870-1944)

Occupation(s):	capitalist - built and rented houses in Bayport area
	politician - member, New York State Assembly, 1899-1900; chairman, Suffolk County Progressive Party
	diplomat - auditor, Territory of Puerto Rico, 1903; secretary to the Governor of Puerto Rico, 1904; governor, Territory of Puerto Rico, 1907
	financier - director, Oystermans National Bank, Sayville
Civic Activism:	member, Volunteer American Ambulance Corp in France and Italy during World War I;
	secretary, American Society for Relief of French War Orphans, 1917-1918;
	chief, Bayport Fire Department, 1900-1903;
	president, Bayport School Board, 1898-1903;
	vice-commodore, Penataquit Corinthian Yacht Club, Bay Shore
Marriage(s):	M/1 – 1895-div. 1922 – Caroline Beatrice Post (1876-1961)
	M/2 – 1925-1931 – Leila Ellis (1882-1931)
	M/3 – 1933-1944 – Marguerite Denys de Largarde (1882-1963)
Address:	Gillette Avenue, Bayport
Name of estate:	*Littlewood*
Year of construction:	1896
Style of architecture:	Shingle
Architect(s):	George Browne Post designed the house (for R. H. Post, Sr.)
Landscape architect(s):	
House extant: yes	
Historical notes:	

The house, originally named *Littlewood*, was built by Regis Henri Post, Sr.

He was the son of Albert Kintzing and Marie Caroline de Trobriand Post.

Caroline Beatrice Post Post was the daughter of Henry Albertson Van Zo and Caroline Burnet McLean Post, who resided at *Postholme* in Babylon.

Regis Henri and Caroline Beatrice Post Post, Sr.'s son Regis Henri Post, Jr. married Julester H. Shrady, the daughter of Henry M. Shrady of Elmsford, NY.

Marguerite Denys de Lagarde Post was the daughter of Ludovic Eugene Denis and Mathilde Ignacia de la Caridad de Montalvo de Largarde. Marguerite had previously been married to Gilbert Sichel du Long.

[See other Post entries for additional family information.]

The house was subsequently owned by John Pierre Zerega, Sr., who continued to call it *Littlewood*.

Littlewood

Post, Regis Henri, Sr. (1870-1944)

Occupation(s): *[See previous entry.]*
Civic Activism: *[See previous entry.]*

Marriage(s): M/1 – 1895-div. 1922 – Caroline Beatrice Post (1876-1961)
M/2 – 1925-1931 – Leila Ellis (1882-1931)
M/3 – 1933-1944 – Marguerite Denys de Lagarde (1882-1963)

Address: Fairview Avenue, Bayport
Name of estate:
Year of construction: 1881
Style of architecture: Modified Second Empire
Architect(s):
Landscape architect(s):
House extant: no; destroyed by fire in 1940s
Historical notes:

The house, originally named *White House*, was built by Edward Edwards. In 1883, it was purchased by John R. Ely. Cyrus E. Staples purchased the house in 1890. In 1902, Staples lost the house in foreclosure proceedings. It was then owned by Waldron Kintzing Post and his brother Regis Henri Post, Sr., who, in turn, sold it to James Henry Snedecor in 1925.
[See previous entry and other Post entries for additional family information.]

front facade

Post, Regis Henri, Sr. (1870-1944)

Occupation(s): *[See first Regis Henri Post, Sr. entry.]*
Civic Activism: *[See first Regis Henri Post, Sr. entry.]*

Marriage(s): M/1 – 1895-div. 1922 – Caroline Beatrice Post (1876-1961)
M/2 – 1925-1931 – Leila Ellis (1882-1931)
M/3 – 1933-1944 – Marguerite Denys de Lagarde (1882-1963)

Address: 74 Snedecor Avenue, Bayport
Name of estate:
Year of construction: c. 1902
Style of architecture: Colonial Revival
Architect(s): Isaac Henry Green II designed the house (for R. H. Post)
Landscape architect(s):
Builder: Frederick D. Smith
House extant: unconfirmed
Historical notes:

The house was built by Post as a rental.
[See first Regis Henri Post, Sr. entry and other Post entries for additional family information.]
In 1912, he sold it to John Hill Belcher Mason. [*The Suffolk County News* November 22, 1912, p. 2.]
By 1946 the house was owned by agriculturalist Kurt Grundwald.

side facade

Post, Regis Henri, Sr. (1870-1944)

Occupation(s):	*[See first Regis Henri Post, Sr. entry.]*
Civic Activism:	*[See first Regis Henri Post, Sr. entry.]*
Marriage(s):	M/1 – 1895-div. 1922 – Caroline Beatrice Post (1876-1961)
	M/2 – 1925-1931 – Leila Ellis (1882-1931)
	M/3 – 1933-1944 – Marguerite Denys de Lagarde (1882-1963)
Address:	South Snedecor Avenue, Bayport
Name of estate:	
Year of construction:	c. 1902
Style of architecture:	Dutch Colonial Revival
Architect(s):	Isaac Henry Green II designed the house (for R. H. Post)
Landscape architect(s):	
House extant: unconfirmed	
Historical notes:	

The nine-bedroom house was built by Regis Henri Post, Sr. as a rental.

[See first Regis Henri Post, Sr. entry and other Post entries for additional family information.]

In 1912, he sold the house to the nationally acclaimed actress Effie Shannon.

side / front facade

Post, Regis Henri, Sr. (1870-1944)

Occupation(s):	*[See first Regis Henri Post, Sr. entry.]*
Civic Activism:	*[See first Regis Henri Post, Sr. entry.]*
Marriage(s):	M/1 – 1895-div. 1922 – Caroline Beatrice Post (1876-1961)
	M/2 – 1925-1931 – Leila Ellis (1882-1931)
	M/3 – 1933-1944 – Marguerite Denys de Lagarde (1882-1963)
Address:	South Snedecor Avenue, Bayport
Name of estate:	
Year of construction:	c. 1902
Style of architecture:	Elizabethan
Architect(s):	Isaac Henry Green II designed the house (for R. H. Post)
Landscape architect(s):	
House extant: unconfirmed	
Historical notes:	

The eight-bedroom house was built by Regis Henri Post, Sr. as a rental.

[See first Regis Henri Post, Sr. entry and other Post entries for additional family information.]

front facade

Post, Waldron Kintzing (1869-1955)

Occupation(s):	attorney - partner, Ward, Hayden, and Satterlee
	industrialist - director, Bigelow–Sanford Carpet Co.
	writer - *Harvard Stories*, 1893;
	Smith Brunt, 1899
Civic Activism:	a founder and president, Volunteer Fireman's Assoc. of Suffolk County;
	member, Bayport Fire Commission
Marriage(s):	1894-1939 – Mary Lawrence Perkins (1869-1939)
	- Civic Activism: chairman, Bayport chapter, American Red Cross;
	chairman, Suffolk County chapter, American Red Cross;
	secretary, Samaritan Home for the Aged
Address:	Ocean Avenue, Bayport
Name of estate:	*Strandhome*
Year of construction:	1880
Style of architecture:	Shingle
Architect(s):	Isaac Henry Green II designed the house (for W. R. Foster, Jr.)
	George Browne Post designed the alterations (for C. A. Post)

Landscape architect(s):
House extant: no; demolished in 1950s
Historical notes:

The house, originally named *Strandhome*, was built by William Riley Foster, Jr. In 1888, *Strandhome* was purchased at public auction by the Produce Exchange Gratuity Fund which, in 1890, sold it to Charles Alfred Post. Post continued to call the estate *Strandhome*. It was subsequently owned by his son Waldron, who also continued to call it *Strandhome*.

Waldron Kintzing Post was the son of Albert Kintzing and Marie Caroline de Trobriand Post.

Mary Lawrence Perkins Post was the daughter of Charles L. and Elizabeth W. Perkins of Summit, NJ.

Waldron Kintzing and Mary Lawrence Perkins Post's daughter Mary married Viscount Gerard Vernon Wallop of Portsmouth, England, and, subsequently, John Howe of London, England. Their daughter Elizabeth married Kiliaen M. Van Rensselaer II and resided in Hewlett Neck. [*See* Spinzia, *Long Island's Prominent Families in the Town of Hempstead* – Van Rensselaer entry.] Their son Charles married Caroline Knapp, the daughter of Harry Kearsarge and Caroline Burr Knapp, Sr., who resided at *Brookwood* in East Islip. Their son Robert married Margaret Lapsley of Pomfret, CT, and resided in Washington, DC. Their son Waldron, married Matilda Jellinghaus and resided in Westport, CT. Their son Landon married Janet Kirby and resided in Westport, CT. Their daughter Lina died at the age of twelve.

[See other Post entries for additional family information.]

Bernard Mannes Baruch, Sr. rented *Strandhome* during the summers of 1915 and 1916.

interior, c. 1950s

Post, Waldron Kintzing (1869-1955)

Occupation(s): *[See previous entry.]*

Marriage(s): 1894-1939 – Mary Lawrence Perkins (1869-1939)
- *[See previous entry.]*

Address: Fairview Avenue, Bayport
Name of estate:
Year of construction: 1881
Style of architecture: Modified Second Empire
Architect(s):
Landscape architect(s):
House extant: no; destroyed by fire in 1940s
Historical notes:

    The house, originally named *White House*, was built by Edward Edwards. In 1883, it was purchased by John R. Ely. Cyrus E. Staples purchased the house in 1890. In 1902, Staples lost the house in foreclosure proceedings. It was then owned by Waldron Kintzing Post and his brother Regis Henri Post, Sr., who, in turn, sold it to James Henry Snedecor in 1925.

Powell, David Baisley (1821-1904)

Occupation(s):
- financier - president, National City Bank of Brooklyn;
  - director, Phenix Insurance Company of Brooklyn;
  - director, National Bank Deposit, NYC;
  - trustee, Hamilton Trust Co.;
  - trustee, Washington Trust Co.
- merchant - partner, D. B. Powell & Brothers & Co. (wholesale shoe and boot firm);
  - partner, Powell & Campbell (wholesale shoe and boot firm)
- industrialist - director, Consolidated Fireworks, Co.;
  - director, Empire Sawmill Co.
- capitalist - director, New York and New Jersey Telephone Co.;
  - trustee, Brooklyn Warehouse and Dry Dock Co.

Marriage(s): Hester A. Treadwell (1825-1901)

Address: Handsome Avenue, Sayville
Name of estate: *Cedarshore*
Year of construction: c. 1888
Style of architecture: Queen Anne
Architect(s):
Landscape architect(s):
House extant: no; destroyed by fire in 1916
Historical notes:

Cedarshore

    The house, originally named *Cedarshore*, was built by David Baisley Powell and his son Leander Treadwell Powell. David was the son of Thomas and Sarah Cornwell Powell.
    He correctly predicted that he would die on the seventeenth, which was the date his wife had died. [*The New York Times* September 18, 1904, p. 7.]
    [See following entry for additional Powell family information.]
    The estate was later owned by Leander's wife Rebecca. In 1912, Rebecca Powell sold it to George Alexander Morrison, who subdivided its property for a housing development and to build the Cedarshore Hotel.
    *In 1917, the Cedarshore Hotel was destroyed by fire. In 1924, the hotel was rebuilt by Morrison.
    In 1942, the hotel was purchased by the Herald Tribune Fresh Air Fund.
    In 1959, after going through several ownerships, the hotel, renamed the Bayview Plaza, was destroyed by fire.

Powell, Leander Treadwell (1845-1894)

Occupation(s):	attorney - partner, Powell and Campbell
Civic Activism:	a founder and rear commodore, Great South Bay Yacht Club
Marriage(s):	Rebecca Francis (1850-1929)
Address:	Handsome Avenue, Sayville
Name of estate:	*Cedarshore*
Year of construction:	c. 1888
Style of architecture:	Queen Anne
Architect(s):	
Landscape architect(s):	
House extant: no; destroyed by fire in 1916	
Historical notes:	

The house, originally named *Cedarshore*, was built by David Baisley Powell and his son Leander Treadwell Powell.

Rebecca Francis was the daughter of millionaire furniture dealer John Francis of Brooklyn. She subsequently married Davis S. Harris.

Leander and Rebecca Francis Powell's daughter Isabella married Dr. Clarence Sumner Elebash of Manhattan. Their daughter Ethel married Charles Hall Delamater, Sr. and relocated to Long Island's North Shore.

[See previous entry for additional family information and a history of the estate's ownership.]

Pratt, Alexander Dallas Bache (1883-1947)

Occupation(s):	financier - stockbroker
Marriage(s):	M/1 – 1909-div. 1919 – Beatrice Mai Benjamin (1889-1956)
	- Civic Activism: suffragist - favored limited suffrage
	M/2 – 1921-div. 1923 – Katherine Harris (1890-1927)
	- entertainers and associated professions -
	stage and silent motion picture actress
	M/3 – Marie Julia Young (d. 1956)
Address:	Bayberry Point, Islip
Name of estate:	*Lands End*
Year of construction:	1899-1900
Style of architecture:	Moorish
Architect(s):	Grosvenor Atterbury designed the house (for H. O. Havemeyer)
Landscape architect(s):	Nathan F. Barett (for H. O. Havemeyer)
Builder:	
House extant: yes	
Historical notes:	

The *Social Register Summer, 1915* lists Alex [Alexander] Dallas Bache and Beatrice M. Benjamin Pratt as residing at *Lands End*, Bayberry Point, Islip. They appear to have been renting one of Henry Osborne Havemeyer's "Modern Venice" cottages.

He was the son of Dallas Bache and Mary Gordon Landon Pratt of Islip and *East Cottage* in Southampton. [*See* Spinzia, *Long Island's Prominent Families in the Town of Southampton* – Pratt entry.]

Beatrice Mai Benjamin Pratt was the daughter of William Evarts and Anne Engle Rogers Benjamin and the granddaughter of Henry H. Rogers of Standard Oil. Beatrice had previously been married to William Preston Gibson, the son of Confederate General Randell Lee Gibson and Mrs. Mary Elizabeth Montgomery Gibson. After her divorce from Alexander, Beatrice married Charles Aubrey Cartwright and, subsequently, Frederick J. McEvoy.

Alexander Dallas Bache and Beatrice Mai Benjamin Pratt's daughter Cynthia married William McKennon Laughlin, the son of Thomas and Lucy Hayes Laughlin. Their son Dr. Dallas Bache Pratt II resided in Manhattan.

Katherine Corri Harris Pratt was the daughter of Sidney and Katherine Maude Brady Harris. She had previously been married to the noted actor John Barrymore. After her divorce from Alexander, she married the secretary of the Polish legation Leon Orlowski.

Marie Julia Young Pratt was the daughter of Otto Christian and Ann Elizabeth Murphy Young of Chicago. Marie had previously been married to Louis Graverat Kaufman, the son of Samuel Robert and Juliet Adelaide Graverat Kaufman.

Pratt, Cleveland Forsyth, Sr. (1873-1932)

Occupation(s):
Civic Activism: financial secretary, New York Society for the Prevention of Vice;
president, Bayport School Board;
foreman and assistant chief, Bayport Fire Department Hose Co.;
a founder and treasurer, Suffolk County Council of Boy Scouts of
 America, 1919

Marriage(s): 1899-1927 – Sophia Jackson Briggs (1872-1927)
 - Civic Activism: secretary, Bayport branch, American Red Cross

Address: 102 South Ocean Avenue, Bayport
Name of estate: *Graytower*
Year of construction: 1885
Style of architecture: Queen Anne
Architect(s):
Landscape architect(s):
House extant: no; destroyed by fire c. 1995
Historical notes:

front facade

The *Social Register Summer, 1923* lists Cleveland F. and Sophia J. Briggs Pratt [Sr.] as residing at *Graytower* in Bayport.

He was the son of William Tudor and Clara Lyman Forsyth Pratt of Brooklyn.

Sophia Jackson Briggs Pratt was the daughter of James H. Briggs, Sr. of New York.

Cleveland Forsyth and Sophia Jackson Briggs Pratt, Sr.'s son James married Molly Edith Brett, the daughter of Augustine James Brett of Sayville. Their son Cleveland Forsyth Pratt, Jr. married Martha Newton of Charleston, SC, and resided in Freeport.

Pratt, Dallas Bache (1849-1929)

Occupation(s): financier - director, Bank of America, NYC;
 partner, Maitland, Phelps and Co. (later, Maitland, Coppell,
  and Co.) (investment banking firm);
 director, American Car & Foundry Securities Co.;
 trustee, Atlantic Mutual Insurance Co.;
 trustee, Central Savings Bank, NYC
industrialist - director, American Car & Foundry Co.;
 vice-president, Ohio Falls Car Manufacturing Co.,
  Jeffersonville, IN

Civic Activism: treasurer, Society for the Prevention of Cruelty to Children;
director, Metropolitan Hospital, NYC

Marriage(s): 1881 – Mary Gordon Landon (b. 1849)
 - Civic Activism: anti-suffragist

Address: *[unable to determine street address]*, Islip
Name of estate:
Year of construction:
Style of architecture:
Architect(s):
Landscape architect(s):
House extant: unconfirmed
Historical notes:

The *Social Register Summer, 1915* lists Dallas B. and Mary G. Landon Pratt as residing in Islip.

He was the son of Horace Logan Edgar and Kate Martin Pratt.

Mary Gordon Landon Pratt was the daughter of Charles Griswold Landon.

Dallas Bache and Mary Gordon Landon Pratt's daughter Katherine married Lycurgus Winchester, the son of John M. and Anne Gordon Price Winchester. Their daughter Constance married Walter Negley Stillman, the son of Joseph Frederick and Elizabeth McCannon Schley Stillman of *Ox Pasture* in Southampton.

By 1929 the Pratts has relocated to Southampton.

[*See* Spinzia, *Long Island's Prominent Families in the Town of Southampton* – Pratt and Stillman entries.]

Pratt, Horace A. (1841-1905)

Occupation(s):	industrialist - partner, Astral Oil Works, Brooklyn (whale oil illuminating firm) (merged into Standard Oil Co.); trustee, Standard Oil Co.; partner, with his brother Charles, Charles Pratt & Co.; partner, Atlantic Refining Co.
Marriage(s):	Josephine *[unable to determine maiden name]* (1858-1917)
Address:	South Country and Great East Neck Roads, West Babylon
Name of estate:	
Year of construction:	
Style of architecture:	
Architect(s):	
Landscape architect(s):	
Builder:	Boss Van Weelden, addition of veranda, 1895 (for H. A. Pratt)
House extant: unconfirmed	
Historical notes:	

In 1894, Horace A. Pratt purchased the original Charles M. Bergen residence. Bergen subsequently built a new residence in West Babylon. [*South Side Signal* September 15, 1894, p. 3.]

Horace was the son of Asa and Elizabeth Stone Pratt of Watertown, MA. Horace's brother Charles was a founder of Standard Oil Co. [For Pratt family estates on Long Island's North Shore, see Spinzia, *Long Island's Prominent North Shore Families*, vol. II – Pratt entries.]

Horace A. and Josephine Pratt's daughter Adele married Montgomery H. Loses, the son of Alanson F. Loses.

Pratt died of cerebro-spinal meningitis which was the result of an operation for an abscess in his ear. [*The Standard Union* September 28, 1905, p. 1.]

Prescott, William French (1893-1969)

Occupation(s):	financier - partner, Parr and Co. (stock brokerage firm); treasurer, New York Coffee & Sugar Exchange
Marriage(s):	M/1 – 1926-div. 1938 – Mary Agnes Worle (b. 1900) M/2 – 1939-1969 – Elizabeth Coe (1908-2002) - Civic Activism: president, South Side Garden Club
Address:	Blackmore Lane, East Islip
Name of estate:	*Still Pond*
Year of construction:	
Style of architecture:	
Architect(s):	
Landscape architect(s):	
House extant: unconfirmed	
Historical notes:	

The *Long Island Society Register, 1929* lists William F. and Mary A. Worle Prescott as residing on Park Row, Cedarhurst [Lawrence].

He was the son of The Reverend George Jarvis and Mrs. Lucille Campbell Prescott of Boston.

Mary Agnes Worle Prescott was the daughter of Charles and Catherine Donovan Worle. Mary subsequently married Douglass B. Simonson with whom she resided on Longwood Crossing, Lawrence.

The *Social Register New York, 1954* lists William F. and Elizabeth Coe Prescott as residing at *Still Pond* on Blackmore Lane, East Islip.

She was the daughter of Elmore Holloway and Elizabeth Wright Davie Coe of Hewlett. Elizabeth had previously been married to Daniel Aylesbury Finlayson, Jr. of Hewlett Bay Park. [*See* Spinzia, *Long Island's Prominent Families in the Town of Hempstead* – Coe, Finlayson, and Prescott entries.]

William French and Elizabeth Coe Prescott's son James was an infant at the time of his death in 1942.

Prince, John Dyneley, II (1844-1883)

Occupation(s):	financier - governor, New York Stock Exchange, 1871-1875; partner, Prince and Whiteley (stock brokerage firm)
Marriage(s):	Anna Maria Morris (1847-1904) - Civic Activism: member, board of governors, Trinity Sea Side Home, Great River (formerly, Sea Side Hospital for Sick Children)
Address:	St. Mark's Lane, Islip
Name of estate:	
Year of construction:	1882
Style of architecture:	Shingle
Architect(s):	Alfred Hopkins designed the c. 1910 farm and garage complex (for S. T. Peters, Sr.)*
Landscape architect(s):	Ellen Biddle Shipman (for H. T. Peters, Sr.)
House extant: no; demolished in c. 1950	
Historical notes:	

front facade

The house was built by John Dyneley Prince II. [*The New York Times* July 30, 1882, p. 5]
He was the son of John Dyneley and Mary Travers Prince, Sr.
Anna Maria Morris Prince was the daughter of Thomas H. and Mary Bowie Johnson Morris of Baltimore, MD.
John Dyneley and Anna Maria Morris Prince II's son John Dyneley Prince III, the noted linguist, diplomat, and politician, married Adeline Loomis, the daughter of Dr. Alfred Lebbeus and Sarah Jane Patterson Loomis of Manhattan. Their daughter Mary married Jacob Newton Beam.
The estate was purchased by Samuel Twyford Peters, who enlarged the house and called it *Windholm Farm*.
It was inherited by his son Harry Twyford Peters, Sr., who continued to call it *Windholm Farm*.
*The barn complex still exists. It was converted into a residence by Mrs. Harry Twyford Peters.

Proctor, Cecil Wykes (1881-1942)

Occupation(s):	politician - member, New York State Assembly, second assembly district merchant - wholesale coal firm
Civic Activism:	governor, Sayville Golf Club
Marriage(s):	Evelyn C. Plate (1895-1947)
Address:	240 Green Avenue, Sayville
Name of estate:	
Year of construction:	c. 1919
Style of architecture:	
Architect(s):	
Landscape architect(s):	
House extant: yes	
Historical notes:	

front facade, 2006

The *Long Island Society Register, 1929* lists Cecil W. Proctor as residing at 240 Green Avenue, Sayville.
He was the son of Samuel and Annie Proctor.
Evelyn C. Plate Proctor was the daughter of Frederick H. and Anna Albert Plate. Evelyn subsequently married John G. Gasteiger.
Cecil Wykes and Evelyn C. Plate Proctor's daughter Jane married George J. Schlehr, Jr. of Morrisville, NY.
The house was subsequently owned by the West Sayville automobile dealer P. J. Grady.

Purdy, Charles Robert, Sr. (1859-1922)

Occupation(s): capitalist - Manhattan real estate

Marriage(s): 1888-1922 – Abbie Wilkinson (1865-1954)

Address: Middle Road, Bayport
Name of estate: *Edgemere*
Year of construction: c. 1883
Style of architecture: Queen Anne
Architect(s):
Landscape architect(s):
Builder: Weeks and Ashby
House extant: yes*
Historical notes:

front facade

The house, originally named *Edgemere*, was built by Charles Robert Purdy, Sr.
He was the son of Isaac L. and Caroline Summers Purdy.
Abbie Wilkinson Purdy was the daughter of Dr. Wilkinson of Jersey City, NJ.
Charles Robert and Abbie Wilkinson Purdy, Sr.'s son Kenneth married Dorothy Cambern of Bayport. Their son Charles Robert Purdy, Jr. was an infant at the time of his death.
Abbie Wilkinson Purdy sold the house to Robert H. Koehler.
*Koehler subdivided the estate's property for a housing development and cut the main house in half. The two halves of the house survive as numbers 78 and 84 Connetquot Road, Bayport, to which they were moved by Koehler. The carriage house was also divided by Koehler and became private residences at 77 and 105 Connetquot Road.

Puzo, Mario (1920-1999)

Occupation(s): writer - *The Dark Arena*, 1955;
The Fortunate Pilgrim, 1965;
The Godfather, 1969*;
The Runaway Summer of Davie Shaw, 1966;
The Godfather Papers and Other Confessions, 1971;
The Sicilian, 1984;
The Last Don, 1996;
Omerta, 2000 (published posthumously)

Marriage(s): 1946-1978 – Erika Lina Broske (1921-1978)
Carol Gino

Address: 866 Manor Lane, West Bay Shore
Name of estate:
Year of construction: 1967
Style of architecture: Contemporary
Architect(s):
Landscape architect(s):
House extant: yes
Historical notes:

rear facade, 2020

Mario Puzo was born in New York City. His family lived above the railway yards in the area known as "Hell's Kitchen." He was the son of a railway trackman and one of six children born to the immigrant family. Mario moved to Bay Shore in 1968.
Mario and Erika Lina Broske Puzo had five children. Their daughter Dorothy Ann Puzo wrote and directed the 1987 film *Cold Steel*.
Mario died in Bay Shore, where he had continued to live with Carol, his companion of twenty years.
*He sold the motion picture rights for *The Godfather* to Paramount Pictures for $85,000. He and Francis Ford Coppola worked on the motion picture's script but, after a fifth rewrite, Puzo withdrew from the project because of differences of opinion with Coppola. Puzo and Coppola later collaborated on the motion picture scripts for *Godfather, Part II* and *Godfather, Part III*. Puzo was a collaborator on the scripts for *Earthquake*, *Superman I*, and, the sequel, *Superman II*.
In 2020, the 4,700-square-foot, eleven-room house, with four bedrooms and three-and-a-half bathrooms, was for sale. The asking price was $974,000; the annual taxes were $22,581.98.

Ranft, Richard Michael (1855-1925)

Occupation(s):	industrialist - partner, Richard Ranft (manufacturer of piano supplies)
Civic Activism:	vice-president, Bay Shore Protective Association, 1911, 1912
Marriage(s):	M/1 – 1883 – Mary M. Kapp (d. 1899)
	M/2 – 1900-1925 – Hermine T. Krieg (d. 1958)
	- Civic Activism: vice-chair, Bay Shore-Brightwaters chapter, American Red Cross, 1919
Address:	South Country Road and Penataquit Avenue, Bay Shore
Name of estate:	
Year of construction:	c. 1900
Style of architecture:	Mediterranean
Architect(s):	Henry F. Hornbostel designed the house (for Ranft)
Landscape architect(s):	
House extant: yes	
Historical notes:	

The twenty-room house was built by Richard Michael Ranft.

He was the son of Otto Richard and Elise Heep Ranft of Treben, Germany, and Manhattan. His sister Elizabeth married William Steinway, an heir to the Steinway piano fortune. His sister Martha married Major Canzler of the German Army.

Richard Michael and Hermine T. Krief Ranft's daughter Herma married Robert Frasse Whitlock and, subsequently, _____ Schuck. Their daughter Ella married Henrich Baumgartner.

In 2006, the house was converted into the Villa Promenade townhouse complex.

side / front facade, 2006

Redmond, Roland (1845-1894)

Occupation(s):	capitalist - William Redmond & Sons, NYC (importer of linens)
Civic Activism;	president, Southside Sportsmen's Club, Oakdale;
	a founder and trustee, Waverly Gun Club, Islip, 1890;
	member, Committee on People's Baths (financed the erection and maintenance of public bath-houses)
Marriage(s):	1880-1894 – Helen Clark Bulkley (1858-1935)
Address:	Ocean Avenue, Islip
Name of estate:	
Year of construction:	
Style of architecture:	
Architect(s):	
Landscape architect(s):	
House extant: unconfirmed	
Historical notes:	

Roland Redmond rented the James Harvey Doxsee house.

He was the son of William and Sabina Hoyt Redmond of Manhattan. His sister Frances married Henry Beekman Livingston, Jr. and resided in Bay Shore.

Helen Clark Bulkley Redmond was the daughter of Edward Henry and Catherine W. Clark Bulkley, Sr. of Manhattan. Helen's brother Edward H. Bulkley, Jr. married his nurse Margaret Stewart of St. Johns, New Brunswick, Canada. Her sister Katharine married Prescott Lawrence.

The Southside Sportsmen's Club donated the Redmond Tiffany stained-glass window to St. Mark's Episcopal Church in Islip. The reputed cost in 1896 was $1,800. [*The Corrector* March 28, 1896, p. 2.]

Reid, John Robert (1836-1902)

Occupation(s):	attorney -
	judge - Suffolk County
	publisher - *Suffolk Democrat*, Babylon
Civic Activism:	trustee, Babylon Common School;
	a founder and president of board, Babylon Union Free School District;
	a founder and member of board, State Normal School, Jamaica, NY
Marriage(s):	1856-1902 – Angeline Davis (1835-1916)
Address:	The Crescent, Babylon
Name of estate:	*The Towers*
Year of construction:	
Style of architecture:	Queen Anne
Architect(s):	
Landscape architect(s):	
House extant: no	
Historical notes:	

John Robert Reid was the son of James and Alma Hutchinson Reid of Middle Island.

Angeline Davis Reid was from Poughkeepsie, NY.

Judge John Robert and Mrs. Angeline Davis Reid's daughter M. Loreign Reid did not marry. Their son Willard married Ada Emeline Kitching.

[See following entry for additional family information.]

front facade, c. 1941

Reid, Willard Placide (1862-1925)

Occupation(s):	attorney - partner, with Jacob Neu, in Brooklyn law firm
	financier - president, New Terminal Bank;
	vice-president, Williamsburgh Trust Co.;
	second vice-president, Empire State Surety Co.
	industrialist - secretary, Edison Portland Cement Co., Orange, NJ;
	treasurer, Reid Ice Co.
	capitalist - director, Babylon & Oak Island Ferry Co.;
	director, Metropolitan Fire Proof and Storage Warehouse Co.;
	director, The Berry Realty Co.
	politician - Democratic state committeeman of his assembly district, 1896
Civic Activism:	trustee, Babylon Public Library
Marriage(s):	1891-1925 – Ada Emeline Kitching (1866-1954)
	- Civic Activism: secretary, Alliance of Women's Clubs of Brooklyn, 1938
Address:	The Crescent, Babylon
Name of estate:	*The Towers*
Year of construction:	
Style of architecture:	Queen Anne
Architect(s):	
Landscape architect(s):	
House extant: no	
Historical notes:	

The *Brooklyn Blue Book and Long Island Society Register, 1918* lists Willard Placide and Ada E. Kitching Reid as residing at *The Towers* on Crescent Avenue [The Crescent], Babylon.

He was the son of Judge John Robert and Mrs. Angeline Davis Reid, from whom he inherited the house.

Ada Emeline Kitching Reid was the daughter of Jamieson D. and Lucinda Jane Fursman Kitching of New York.

[See previous entry for additional family information.]

The Towers

Remsen, Annie Pearsall Hubbard (1848-1926)

Civic Activism:	anti-suffragist; a founder, South Shore Bridge Club, 1915; bequeathed $57,591.10 to Faith Home for Incurables
Marriage(s):	1868 – Jacob Remsen (b. 1840)
Address:	Little East Neck Road, Babylon
Name of estate:	*The Harbor*
Year of construction:	
Style of architecture:	
Architect(s):	
Landscape architect(s):	
House extant: unconfirmed	
Historical notes:	

 The house was built by Ernest H. Dodd. [*South Side Signal* September 25, 1914, p. 5.] It was later owned by Annie Pearsall Hubbard Remsen who called it Th*e Harbor.*
 The *Brooklyn Blue Book and Long Island Society Register, 1918* lists Annie P. Hubbard Remsen as residing at *The Harbor* in Babylon.
 She was the daughter of Asher Holmes and Catherine Amelia Pearsall Hubbard.
 Jacob Remsen was the son of Derick Richard and Elizabeth Suydam Remsen.
 In 1911, Jacob and Annie Pearsall Hubbard Remsen's son John Schenck Suydam Remsen, who was a commodore of the Babylon Yacht Club, died in London, England.

Remsen, Cornelius Wagstaff (1882-1920)

Occupation(s):	financier - member, Jones and Lamar; manager, bond department, Coggeshall and Hicks; a founder and partner, Struthers, Heath, and Remsen (bond brokerage firm)
Marriage(s):	1907-1920 – Ethel Folger White (1879-1938)
Address:	Argyle Avenue, Babylon
Name of estate:	*Tuloma*
Year of construction:	
Style of architecture:	
Architect(s):	
Landscape architect(s):	
House extant: unconfirmed	
Historical notes:	

 The *Social Register Summer, 1915* lists Cornelius Wagstaff and Ethel F. White Remsen as residing at *Tuloma* in Babylon. Their residence was located in the Argyle Park section of Babylon.
 Cornelius, who died of typhoid fever, was the son of Phoenix and Sarah Louisa Wagstaff Remsen, Sr. of West Islip.
 Ethel Folger White Remsen was the daughter of Benjamin Ogden and Susan Hubbard Meyers White and a descendant of Benjamin Franklin.
 The Remsens did not have children.
 In 1926, Ethel sued David Gardiner of Gardiner's Island in East Hampton for $400,000 in a breach of promise case. Gardiner agreed to settle out of court for $110,000. [*Daily News* October 23, 1926, p. 89.] [*See* Spinzia, *Long Island's Prominent Families in the Town of East Hampton* – Gardiner entries.]

Remsen, Phoenix, Sr. (1846-1922)

Occupation(s):	attorney
Civic Activism:	a founder and director, South Shore Country Club, 1895; donated a hose cart to the Babylon Fire Department
Marriage(s):	M/1 – 1870-1907 – Sarah Louisa Wagstaff (1847-1907)
	M/2 – 1908-1922 – Naomi Woodruff Bradford Clark (b. 1883)
Address:	South Country Road, West Islip
Name of estate:	
Year of construction:	late 1800s
Style of architecture:	French Empire
Architect(s):	
Landscape architect(s):	
Builder:	Smith & Van Weelden enlarged the carriage house, 1883 (for P. Remsen, Sr.)

House extant: no
Historical notes:

The house was built by Phoenix Remsen, Sr. on a portion of the Willetts farm. [James Brown Cooper. *Reminisces of Babylon and Its Vicinity.* privately printed, 1911.]

Phoenix Remsen, Sr., who was known as one of the best dressed men of the South Shore, was the son of Henry Rutgers and Elizabeth Waldron Phoenix Remsen.

Sarah Louisa Wagstaff Remsen was the daughter of Dr. Alfred and Mrs. Sarah Platt DuBois Wagstaff, Sr., who resided at *Tahlulah* in West Islip. Her brother Alfred Wagstaff, Jr. married Mary Anderson Barnard and resided at *Opekeeping* in West Islip. Her brother Cornelius married Amy Colt and also resided in West Islip. Her sister Mary married Henry Gribble.

Phoenix and Sarah Louisa Wagstaff Remsen, Sr.'s son Alfred married Frances Condit, the daughter of Goodhall Condit of Jersey City, NJ. Their son The Reverend Henry Rutgers Remsen II married Sarah Roberts Halter, the daughter of Richard Emanuel and Sarah Ann Halter, and resided in Huntington. Their daughter Helen married Woodruff Sutton, Jr. and resided at *Sunnycroft* in Babylon. Their son Cornelius married Ethel Folger White, the daughter of Benjamin Ogden and Susan Hubbard Meyers White, and resided at *Tuloma* in Babylon. Their son Phoenix Remsen, Jr. died in 1906.

Naomi Woodruff Bradford Clark Remsen was the daughter of Francis M. and Stella Louisa Victoria Cox Clark of St. Augustine, FL.

Phoenix and Naomi Woodruff Bradford Clark Remsen, Sr.'s son Du Bois married Anna Pell. In 1926, Du Bois was committed to the Eastern State Hospital for the Insane in Williamsburg, Virginia. He was later cleared of the insanity diagnosis.

In c. 1913, the house was purchased by Keitt Pinckney Walker (aka George Daniel Keitt Pinckney Walker) who called it *Villa Julia*. [*South Side Signal* March 14, 1913, p. 5.]

It was later owned by Julia Walton who sold it to James Hardenburgh. Hardenburgh called it *Villa Maria*.

side facade

Rice, Dr. George Edwin (1867-1938)

Occupation(s):	physician - dentist - partner, Rice & Partridge, NYC*
Civic Activism:	suffragist;
	president, Great South Bay Yacht Racing Association, 1909-1917;
	commander, United States Power Squadron, Inc.;
	member, executive board, American Power Boat Squadron
Marriage(s):	Mary Beresford (aka May Beresford) (1867-1938)
Address:	407 Middle Road, Bayport
Name of estate:	*Maywood*
Year of construction:	1915
Style of architecture:	Colonial Revival
Architect(s):	Isaac Henry Green II, 1915 alterations (for Rice) [unconfirmed]
Landscape architect(s):	
Builder:	Ashby & Breckenridge, garage, greenhouse, and alterations to main residence, 1915 (for Rice)
House extant: yes	
Historical notes:	

front facade

Dr. George Edwin Rice remodeled Amelia E. Needham Waterman's (Mrs. Henry M. Waterman) residence into a 6,000-square-foot, six-bedroom, four-bath Colonial Revival house he called *Maywood*. [*The Suffolk County News* May 5, 1916, p. 4.]

George Edwin and Mary Beresford Rice's daughter Ada married Thomas Marion Childs, the son of Thomas Childs of Manhattan. Their daughter Dorothy married Ralph T. Norton and resided in Sayville.

*Rice's dental practice treated Mark Twain, Serge Rachmaninoff, Mortimer Loeb Schiff of *Northwood* [I] in Oyster Bay, and Norman Mattoon Thomas, the six-time Socialist Party candidate for the Presidency of the United States of Cold Spring Harbor. [*See* Spinzia, *Long Island's Prominent North Shore Families, volume II* – Schiff and Thomas entries.]

In 1943, the house was purchased by Frederick Merle Johnson, Sr. [*The Suffolk County News* April 30, 1943, p. 5.]

In 1955, Mrs. Johnson sold the house to Richard Wolford Dodson. [*The Suffolk County News* August 5, 1955, p. 2.]

In 1986, Dodson sold the house to Mark Kleine. [*The Suffolk County News* June 11, 1998, p. 6.]

Richard, Alfred Joseph (1909-2004)

Occupation(s):	merchant - president and chairman of board, P. C. Richard & Son (fifty-store appliance and electronics chain, which now includes The Wiz*)
Marriage(s):	Victoria *[unable to determine maiden name]* (d. 1997)
Address:	181 Otis Lane, West Bay Shore
Name of estate:	
Year of construction:	
Style of architecture:	Condominium
Architect(s):	
Landscape architect(s):	
House extant: yes	
Historical notes:	

*P. C. Richard & Son was founded in 1909 by Alfred's father Peter Christiaan Richard, who immigrated from The Netherlands in 1889 the age of eighteen.

"A. J.," as Alfred was known, went to work in his father's Bensonhurst hardware store at the age of eight.

Richmond, Henry (1836-1894)

Occupation(s):	merchant - owned a drug store at the foot of Wall Street, NYC (supplied outgoing ships with medical supplies)
Civic Activism:	poet and historian, The Sayville Scientific Club, 1892
Marriage(s):	Caroline Emily Dougherty (1833-1908)
Address:	Middle Road, Bayport
Name of estate:	*Maplewood*
Year of construction:	
Style of architecture:	Victorian Italianate
Architect(s):	
Landscape architect(s):	
House extant: yes	
Historical notes:	

Henry and Caroline Emily Dougherty Richmond did not have children.

In 1909, John J. Asher purchased *Maplewood* from Mrs. Richmond for $18,000 and changed its architectural style from Victorian Italianate to Colonial Revival. [*The Brooklyn Daily Eagle* June 4, 1909, p. 7.]

front facade

Ridgeway, James W. (d. 1910)

Occupation(s):	attorney - Brooklyn District Attorney, 1884-1896
Marriage(s):	
Address:	Handsome Avenue, Sayville
Name of estate:	
Year of construction:	
Style of architecture:	Shingle
Architect(s):	
Landscape architect(s):	Isaac Henry Green II designed the house (for Ridgeway)
House extant: unconfirmed	
Historical notes:	

The house was built by James W. Ridgeway.

He was disqualified from being the Democratic candidate for governor because of his strong support of William Jennings Bryan and his free silver views.

In 1897, Ridgeway sold the house to Elward Smith, Sr.

front / side facade

Riggio, Frank Vincent (1906-1984)

Occupation(s):	industrialist - president, Riggio Tobacco Corp. (manufacturer of Regent cigarettes); director and vice-president, American Tobacco Co.
Civic Activism:	chairman, South Suffolk chapter, American Red Cross
Marriage(s):	1931-1984 – Margaret Boughton (1913-1988)
Address:	80 South Saxon Avenue, Bay Shore
Name of estate:	*Riggio House*
Year of construction:	1933
Style of architecture:	Neo-Tudor
Architect(s):	William Hamilton Russell, Jr. designed the house (for H. C. Sharp)
Landscape architect(s):	
House extant: yes	
Historical notes:	

The house, originally named *Millcreek / Mill Creek Farm*, was built by Hamlet Cecil Sharp. In 1944, it was purchased from Mrs. Sharp by Riggio, who renamed it *Riggio House*.

He was the son of Vincent and Antoinette Gallo Riggio, Sr. His sister Flavia married Montague Horace Hacket, Sr., the son of Horace Hacket of Brightwaters.

Margaret Boughton Riggio, who was still residing in the Bay Shore house when she died, was the daughter of H. Boughton of Manhattan.

Frank Vincent and Margaret Boughton Riggio's son Vincent Riggio II married Katherine Penelope Knowlton, the daughter of James A. F. Knowlton of Babylon.

In 2020, 9.68 acres and the 8,738-square-foot, nineteen-room house, with a seven-car garage, horse stables, guest cottage, and windmill, were for sale. The asking price was $4.999 million.

side facade, 2006

Robb, James (1871-1937)

Occupation(s):	industrialist - vice-president, American Telephone and Telegraph Co. military - general, New York National Guard
Civic Activism:	member, Emergency Relief Bureau, NYC (LaGuardia administration); trustee, Berkeley Institute; trustee, Veterans Association of 23rd Regiment
Marriage(s):	Elizabeth Donovan (d. 1940)
Address:	*[unable to determine street address]*, Sayville
Name of estate:	
Year of construction:	
Style of architecture:	
Architect(s):	
Landscape architect(s):	
House extant: unconfirmed	
Historical notes:	

The *Long Island Society Register, 1929* lists General James and Mrs. Elizabeth Donovan Robb as residing in Sayville.

His sisters, Mrs. Helen Crawford and Mrs. John Ross, both resided in Scotland.

James and Elizabeth Donovan Robb's daughter Helen married John Bernsee Catlin, Sr., the son of Rufus Olmstead and Caroline Bernsee Catlin of Brooklyn. John resided in Brooklyn and Sayville.

Robbins, John Clinton, Sr. (1861-1925)

Occupation(s):	capitalist - director and president, Sumpwams Water Works Co.; director, Long Island Home of Amityville
	financier - a founder and president, Bank of Babylon, 1913
	politician - Suffolk County Commissioner of Jurors; superintendent, Fire Island Park; supervisor, Town of Babylon
	merchant - partner, with Richard Higbie, Jr., Higbie and Robbins (general store)
Civic Activism:	president, Babylon Cemetery Association, 1916
Marriage(s):	Mary A. Buglar (1863-1927)
Address:	Carll Avenue and West Main Street, Babylon
Name of estate:	
Year of construction:	1891
Style of architecture:	
Architect(s):	
Landscape architect(s):	
House extant:	no

Historical notes:

The house was built by John Clinton Robbins, Sr.

He was the son of John and Selinda Smith Robbins.

Mary A. Buglar Robbins was the daughter of James Buglar.

John Clinton and Mary A. Buglar Robbins, Sr.'s son James married Mary Matilda Bishop and resided in Babylon. Their daughter Edna married Norton H. Morrison and resided in Seattle, WA. Their son John Clinton Robbins, Jr. married Mildred Hamilton Ross, the daughter of John Scott Ross of Brooklyn.

Robbins, Jeremiah (1863-1929)

Occupation(s):	capitalist - a founder, Sumpwams Water Works Co.
	merchant - partner, with Leopold Henry Fishel, Fishel and Robbins, Babylon (dry goods store)
	real estate agent - founder, Jeremiah Robbins Agency, Inc., Babylon
Civic Activism:	member, first division, Suffolk County Exemption Board; secretary, Babylon Cemetery Association, 1916
Marriage(s):	1888-1929 – Carrie Seaman Oakes (1864-1936)
	- Civic Activism: trustee, Babylon Library Association
Address:	29 South Carll Avenue, Babylon
Name of estate:	
Year of construction:	c. 1912
Style of architecture:	Colonial Revival
Architect(s):	Pickering & Walker designed the house (for Jeremiah Robbins)
Landscape architect(s):	
House extant:	unconfirmed

Historical notes:

The house was built by Jeremiah Robbins. [*The Brooklyn Daily Eagle* April 2, 1912, p. 17.]

The *Long Island Society Register, 1929* lists Jeremiah and Carrie Seaman Oakes Robbins as residing at 29 South Carll Avenue, Babylon.

He was the son of Walter Wilson and Cornelia Strong Robbins.

Carrie Seaman Oakes Robbins was the daughter of George Edward and Henrietta Seaman Oakes.

Jeremiah and Carrie Seaman Oakes Robbins daughter Cornelia married Ralph Harold Harry Honsberger.

front facade, 1912

Robbins, Josiah (1852-1918)

Occupation(s):	financier - trustee, Patchogue Savings Bank
	politician - unsuccessful Republican candidate for supervisor, Town of Islip
Civic Activism:	a founder, Bay Shore Protective Association;
	a founder, Great South Bay Yacht Club
Marriage(s):	Ella Blydenburgh (1854-1932)
Address:	South Country Road, Bay Shore
Name of estate:	
Year of construction:	
Style of architecture:	Modified Victorian
Architect(s):	
Landscape architect(s):	
House extant: no	
Historical notes:	

In 1915, Robbins was accused of allegedly destroying ballots in a congressional election. [*The New York Times* December 30, 1915, p. 6.]

Josiah and Ella Blydenburgh Robbins' son William married Martha Brewster and also resided in Bay Shore.

front facade, c. 1903

Robbins, William H., Sr. (1877-1943)

Occupation(s):	attorney - partner, Robbins, Wells, and Walser
	financier - a founder, president and chairman of board, First National Bank & Trust Co. of Bay Shore;
	director, Southside Bank of Bay Shore
Civic Activism:	trustee, Southside Hospital, Bay Shore (now, South Shore University Hospital);
	member, Bay Shore School Board;
	a founder and director, Bay Shore Protective Association
Marriage(s):	Marietta Brewster (1876-1937)
Address:	69 Lawrence Lane, Bay Shore
Name of estate:	
Year of construction:	1922
Style of architecture:	Neo-Tudor
Architect(s):	Hart and Shape designed the house (for W. H. Robbins, Sr.)
Landscape architect(s):	
House extant: yes	
Historical notes:	

The house was built by William H. Robbins, Sr.

He was the son of Josiah and Ella Blydenburgh Robbins of Bay Shore.

Marietta Brewster Robbins was the daughter of Henry Brewster.

William H. and Marietta Brewster Robbins, Sr.'s. daughter Eleanor married John A. Barringer.

The house was later owned by Charles Entenmann, Sr.

In 2020, the 7,000-square-foot, five-bedroom, nine-bath house was listed for sale. The asking price was $3.995 million.

[For information on the Southside Hospital, see Cooper entry.]

front facade, 2020

Robert, Christopher Rhinelander, Jr. (1831-1898)

Occupation(s):	capitalist - builder and owner La Rochelle, 57th Street, NYC (apartment building)
Marriage(s):	M/1 – Margaret McCrea (1833-1863)
	M/2 – Julia Remington (d. 1924)
Address:	south of Montauk Highway, Oakdale
Name of estate:	*Peperidge Hall*
Year of construction:	c. 1890
Style of architecture:	French Chateau
Architect(s):	H. Edward Ficken designed and reassembled the house (for C. R. Robert, Jr.)*

Landscape architect(s):
House extant: no; demolished in 1940
Historical notes:

The house, originally named *Peperidge Hall*, was built by Christopher Rhinelander Robert, Jr. who was on Ward McAllister's list of society's elite 400 people.

*The house's interior was from a chateau in Normandy, France, which Robert had brought to Long Island and had reassembled in his country house.

He was the son of Christopher Rhinelander and Anna Maria Shaw Robert, Sr. of Mastic.

Julia Remington Robert had previously been married to New England banker Charles Lee Morgan, Sr.

In 1896, Robert sold *Peperidge Hall* to William K. Aston, who unsuccessfully attempted to subdivide the estate's property for a housing development in 1907.

According to Julia, Robert's behavior in the last few days of his life was that of an "insane man." The circumstances surrounding his death, in the Roberts' La Rochelle apartment, were, to say the least, questionable. Julia testified that she was in the bathroom when she heard a shot and that she sent her maid to notify the apartment manager, who entered Robert's room and found him dead with a pistol shot in the temple and a pistol in his hand. The police were summoned with the statement that Mr. Robert had committed suicide. The coroner accepted it as a suicide even though there were no powder burns on Robert's temple, no autopsy was done, and there wasn't any record of Robert ever buying or owning a pistol. The authorities seemed to be unconcerned that Robert had just signed a will a few months before his death bequeathing his fortune to his wife. Robert's brother Frederick, who learned of Christopher's death in a newspaper article, publicly called for an in-depth and rigorous investigation. The police ignored Frederick's pleas and simply declared the death a suicide without ever performing an investigation. [*The New York Times* January 4, 1898, p. 4; January 29, 1898, p. 3; and January 30, 1898, p. 5.]

After Robert's death, Julia relocated to France, where she resided until her death.

front facade facing the Great South Bay

Peperidge Hall interior

Peperidge Hall interior

Rokenbaugh, Henry Scott (1852-1943)

Occupation(s):	attorney
Civic Activism:	member, auditing committee, Bay Shore Protective Association, 1911
Marriage(s):	Jeannette Elizabeth Eager (1866-1952)
Address:	Clinton Avenue, Bay Shore
Name of estate:	*Villa Avalon*
Year of construction:	1897
Style of architecture:	Neo-Tudor
Architect(s):	Clarence K. Birdsall designed the house (for Covell)
Landscape architect(s):	
Builder:	Jabez Ephraim Van Orden built the house
House extant:	yes
Historical notes:	

front facade

    The house, originally named *Villa Avalon*, was built by Charles Heber Covell, Sr. It was later owned by Rokenbaugh who continued to call it *Villa Avalon*.
    The *Social Register Summer, 1915* lists Henry S. and Jeannette E. Eager Rokenbaugh as residing at *Villa Avalon* in Bay Shore.
    He was the son of Samuel Rokenbaugh.
    Jeannette Elizabeth Eager Rokenbaugh had previously been married to ___ Taylor.

Rolston, Roswell, Graves (1832-1898)

Occupation(s): financier - president and chairman of board, Farmer's Loan and Trust Co.;
a founder, Fourth National Bank;
director, Queens Insurance Company of America;
director, National City Bank;
director, Commonwealth Insurance Company of New York
capitalist - director, Western Union Telegraph Co.;
member, board of managers, Delaware, Lackawanna, and Western Railroad;
trustee, Consolidated Gas Co.;
director, Northern Pacific Railroad
shipping - director, New Jersey Steamboat Co.

Civic Activism: trustee, American Museum of National History, NYC;
a founder and director, South Shore Country Club, West Islip, 1895;
a founder and vice-president, Citizens Law, Order and Improvement League, Babylon, 1892;
president, Olympic Club, Bay Shore

Marriage(s): Sarah Elizabeth Littell (1835-1914)

Address: Deer Park Avenue, North Babylon
Name of estate: *Armagh*
Year of construction:
Style of architecture:
Architect(s):
Landscape architect(s):
House extant: no
Historical notes:

The 100-acre estate was previously owned by John F. Cockerill. It was later owned by Rolston.
He was the son of William Henry and Jane Dow Rolston.
Sarah Elizabeth Littell Rolston was the daughter of Isaac William and Mary Crane Littell, Jr.
Roswell Graves and Sarah Elizabeth Littell Rolston's son Louis married Francis McAlpin Highet. Their son William married Mary Adele Highet. Their daughter Minnie married John Baxter Marston, the son of William Walker and Johanna Maxwell Marston.

*John Ellis Roosevelt residence, Meadow Croft,
front facade, 2005*

Roosevelt, John Ellis (1853-1939)

Occupation(s):	attorney - partner, Roosevelt and Henry; partner, Jones, Roosevelt, and Carley; partner, Roosevelt and Kobbe
	capitalist - director, Broadway Improvement Co.
Marriage(s):	M/1 – 1879-1912 – Nannie Mitchell Vance (1860-1912)
	M/2 – 1914-div. 1916* – Edith Hamersley (c. 1884-1943)
Address:	South Country Road, Sayville
Name of estate:	*Meadow Croft*
Year of Construction:	1891
Style of architecture:	Colonial Revival
Architect(s):	Isaac Henry Green II designed the c. 1891 alterations of the 19th century farmhouse (for J. E. Roosevelt)
Landscape architect(s):	
Builder:	Nelson Strong
House extant: yes	
Historical notes:	

living room

In 1890, John Ellis Roosevelt purchased the Woodward farm and combined its two farmhouses into one which became Roosevelt's country residence.

He was the son of Robert Barnwell and Elizabeth Thorn Ellis Roosevelt, Sr., who resided at *Lotos Lake*, Bayport.

Nannie Mitchell Vance Roosevelt was the daughter of New York City Acting-Mayor Samuel H. B. Vance. Nannie died of typhoid.

John Ellis and Nannie Mitchell Vance Roosevelt's daughter Anita, who was institutionalized for schizophrenia, never married. Their daughter Gladys, who died when her horse stumbled at a fence during a competition at the Meadow Brook Hunt Club, had been married to Fairman Rogers Dick and resided at *Apple Tree Hill* in Old Brookville. [*See* Spinzia, *Long Island's Prominent North Shore Families, volume I* – Dick entry.] Their daughter Jean married Philip James Roosevelt, Sr., the son of William Emlen and Christine Griffin Kean Roosevelt of *Yellowbanks* in Cove Neck, and resided at *Dolonar* in Cove Neck. Philip drowned when his dinghy capsized in Oyster Bay. Philip's wife Jean found his body on the beach near *Dolonar*. [*See* Spinzia, *Long Island's Prominent North Shore Families, volume II* – Roosevelt entries.]

Edith Hamersley Roosevelt was the daughter of Louis Randolph and Mary Palmer Hamersley, Sr. She had previously been married to United States Navy Paymaster Henry E. Biscoe. Her sister Lilie married Robert Barnwell Roosevelt, Jr. and, then, Rear Admiral Charles Edward Courtney.

*The notorious Roosevelt divorce trial was a very public affair. Edith was the first to file for divorce, alleging that John had, on several occasions, struck her, grabbed her about the neck, threatened her with violence, and used insulting epithets when referring to her. John unsuccessfully countered by filing for an annulment, claiming the marriage had never been consummated. Tearfully, John testified about his happy first marriage. He sobbed as he stated that he still loved Edith. John's brother Robert Barnwell Roosevelt, Jr. testified that John had told him that he was content with his marriage to Edith. Robert further testified that he was present during an occasion when John had verbally abused Edith. John countered by testifying that Robert's testimony about John's marriage to Edith was a lie, that Robert had a weak character, was under the domination of his strong-willed wife Lilie, and financially supported virtually the entire Hamersley family. John was exonerated by the court of all charges against him and won the divorce case. [*The Washington Post* October 31, 1915, p. 4; November 13, 1915, p. 3; February 16, 1916, p. 4; March 12, 1916, p. 5; and March 31, 1916, p. 4; *The New York Times* November 13, 1915, p. 14; March 12, 1916, p. 20; June 7, 1916, p. 9; June 8, 1916, p. 10; and June 27, 1916, p. 11.] Edith never remarried.

[See other Roosevelt entries for additional family information.]

The estate was later owned by Roosevelt's daughter Jean, who sold it to Suffolk County.

The house, which has been conscientiously restored by the county, Sayville Historical Society, and the Bayport Heritage Association, is on the National Register of Historic Places and is open to the public as the Sans Souci Lakes County Nature Preserve.

Roosevelt, Robert Barnwell, Jr. (1866-1929)

Occupation(s):	capitalist - owned a Sayville yacht basin and marine supply company*; extensive real estate investments
Civic Activism:	director, Suffolk County Taxpayers Good Roads Association, 1908
Marriage(s):	M/1 – 1890-1894 – Grace Guernsey Woodhouse (1867-1894)
	M/2 – 1898-1929 – Lilie Hamersley (1882-1958)
Address:	off South Country Road, Sayville
Name of estate:	*The Lilacs*
Year of construction:	c. 1899
Style of architecture:	Modified Shingle
Architect(s):	Isaac Henry Green II designed the house for (R. B. Roosevelt, Jr.)
Landscape architect(s):	
House extant:	no: demolished in c. 1954
Historical notes:	

The house, originally named *The Lilacs*, was built by Robert Barnwell Roosevelt, Jr.

He was the son of Robert Barnwell and Elizabeth Thorn Ellis Roosevelt, Sr., who resided at *Lotos Lake* in Bayport.

Grace Guernsey Woodhouse Roosevelt was the daughter of Lorenzo Guernsey and Emma Douglas Arrowsmith Woodhouse of *Greycroft* in East Hampton. [*See* Spinzia, *Long Island's Prominent Families in the Town of East Hampton* – Woodhouse entry.]

Robert Barnwell and Grace Guernsey Woodhouse Roosevelt, Jr.'s daughter Olga married Dr. Breckenridge Baye and, subsequently, Sidney Graves, with whom she resided in Washington, DC.

Lilie Hamersley Roosevelt was the daughter of Louis Randolph and Mary Palmer Hamersley, Sr. Lilie subsequently married Rear Admiral Charles Edward Courtney. Her brother Louis married May Harris, the daughter of Mrs. Stephen Perry Cox of Bayport. Her sister Edith married Henry E. Biscoe and, subsequently, John Ellis Roosevelt, with whom she resided at *Meadow Croft* in Sayville. Her sister May married Roland I. Curtin, and, subsequently, Thorwald A. Solberg.

Robert Barnwell and Lilie Hamersley Roosevelt, Jr.'s daughter Lilie eloped with James Lee, the son of James S. Lee of Boston, MA, and resided in Washington, DC. She later married Hugh O'Donnell and, subsequently, the first secretary of the British Embassy in Washington, DC, Christopher Bramwell, the son of Frederick Charles Bramwell, the Clerk of The Journals in the British House of Commons. Robert Barnwell and Lilie Hamersley Roosevelt, Jr.'s son Robert Barnwell Roosevelt III died at the age of twenty-two, when he was struck by a bus. He had married Virginia Lee Minor, the daughter of George A. and Jennie Prince Minor. Robert and Virginia's son Robert Barnwell Roosevelt IV was killed in 1944 when his plane crashed into the China Sea. Virginia subsequently married Arthur Percy Jones.

Robert Barnwell Roosevelt, Jr. was estranged from his brother John Ellis Roosevelt, despite the fact that they were married to sisters. A tall "spite" fence topped with jagged pieces of broken glass and barbed wire separated their adjoining estates. [Stephen Birmingham, *America's Secret Aristocracy* (Boston: Little Brown & Co., 1987), p 124.] The animosity between Robert and John stemmed from Robert's attempt to suppress a codicil in their father's will, which had been given to John on their father's deathbed. The relationship further deteriorated with the friction generated between Robert and John's first wife and John's testimony at Robert's divorce trial. [*The New York Times* February 16, 1916, p. 22, and March 12, 1916, p. 20.]

[*See other Roosevelt entries for additional family information.*]

In c. 1954, Mrs. Lillie Hamersley Roosevelt Courtney sold the estate to a real estate developer who demolished the house.

*Roosevelt's Sayville yacht basin and marine supply company was later owned by John Pierre Zerega, Sr. of Bayport. [*The New York Times* May 31, 1936, p. S5.]

front facade, c. 1954

Roosevelt, Robert Barnwell, Sr. (1829-1906)

Occupation(s):	attorney
	publisher - owner and editor, *New York Citizen* (a political newspaper)
	capitalist - trustee, Brooklyn Bridge
	politician - congressman from Manhattan, 1871-1873;
	a founder and president, New York Fisheries (which became New York State Department of Environmental Conservation)
	diplomat - United States Ambassador to The Netherlands (Cleveland and Benjamin Harrison administrations)
	writer - *Game Fish of the Northern States of America*, 1862;
	The Game Birds of the Coast and Lakes of the Northern States of America;
	The Striped Bass, Trout, and Black Bass of the Northern States, 1866;
	Superior Fishing, 1865;
	The South Bay of Long Island;
	Game Fish of the Northern States of America and the British Provinces;
	Love and Luck: The Story of a Summer's Loitering On The Great South Bay, 1887
Civic Activism:	president, New York Association for the Protection of Game;
	advocate, organic gardening;
	advocate, protection of wildlife;
	president, Founders and Patriots;
	president, Holland Society
Marriage(s):	M/1 – 1850-1887 – Elizabeth Thorn Ellis (1830-1887)
	M/2 – 1888-1902 – Marion Theresa O'Shea (1849-1902)
	(aka Mrs. Marion T. Fortescue)
Address:	McConnell Avenue, Bayport
Name of estate:	*Lotos Lake*
Year of construction:	c. 1873
Style of architecture:	Eclectic with Italianate elements
Architect(s):	
Landscape architect(s):	
House extant:	no destroyed by fire in 1958*
Historical notes:	

Lotos Lake, sketch by
Henry N. Betemann, 1958

In 1873, Robert Barnwell Roosevelt, Sr. purchased the two-hundred-acre farm of Daniel Lane and remodeled the farmhouse into his country residence *Lotos Lake*.

He was the son of Cornelius Van Schaack and Margaret Barnhill Roosevelt, Sr. of Manhattan. His brother Theodore, the father of President Theodore Roosevelt, married Martha Bullock and resided at *Tranquility* in Oyster Bay Cove. His brother Silas married Mary West. His brother James married Elizabeth Norris Emlen and resided at *Yellowbanks* in Cove Neck. [*See* Spinzia, *Long Island's Prominent North Shore Families, volume II* – Roosevelt entries.] His brother Cornelius Van Schaack Roosevelt, Jr. married Laura Horton Porter.

Elizabeth Thorn Ellis Roosevelt was the daughter of John French and Elizabeth Glen Thorn Ellis of Manhattan.

Robert Barnwell and Elizabeth Thorn Ellis Roosevelt, Sr.'s son Robert Barnwell Roosevelt, Jr., who resided at *The Lilacs* in Sayville, married Grace Guernsey Woodhouse and, subsequently, Lilie Hamersley. Their son John Ellis Roosevelt, who married Nannie Mitchell Vance and, subsequently, Edith Hamersley, resided at *Meadow Croft* in Sayville. Their daughter Margaret married August Van Horne Kimberly and resided in Chicago, IL.

[See Fortescue entry for information about Roosevelt's concurrent family.]

Roosevelt purchased garish green gloves for his numerous mistresses at A. T. Stewart Department Store in Manhattan. His friends made a point of looking for the gloves while strolling Fifth Avenue and Central Park.

The estate was subsequently owned by Roosevelt's illegitimate son Granville Roland Fortescue, who called it *Wildholme*.

In 1953, the house and its furnishings were severely vandalized.

*In 1954, it was sold to real estate developer Maurice Babash. While Babash was demolishing the house, it was destroyed by fire.

Rothschild, Simon Frank (1861-1936)

Occupation(s):	financier - member, F. and A. Rothschild (private investment banking firm founded by his father)
	merchant - a founder, president, and chairman of board, Abraham & Straus Department Store (which merged into Federated Department Stores, Inc.);
	president, Federated Department Stores, Inc.
Civic Activism:	director, Brooklyn Academy of Music;
	vice-president, Brooklyn Federation of Jewish Charities;
	a founder and chairman of board, Downtown Brooklyn Association;
	director, Better Business Bureau of Brooklyn;
	president, Hebrew Education Society;
	director, Hebrew Orphan Asylum of Brooklyn;
	director, Society for the Prevention of Cruelty to Children of Brooklyn;
	director, Bay Shore Horse Show Association, 1903;
	a founder and director, Bay Shore Protective Association;
	a founder and governor, Islip Polo Club, 1912;
	vice-president, Brooklyn chapter, Boy Scouts of America;
	director, Brooklyn Bureau of Charities;
	director, Brooklyn Jewish Hospital
Marriage(s):	1890-1927 – Lillian Isabelle Abraham (1869-1927)
Address:	Saxon Avenue, Bay Shore
Name of estate:	
Year of construction:	1903
Style of architecture:	Mediterranean
Architect(s):	
Landscape architect(s):	
House extant: no	
Historical notes:	

The house was built by Simon Frank Rothschild.

The *Brooklyn Blue Book and Long Island Society Register, 1918* lists Simon Frank and Lillian Abraham Rothschild as residing in Bay Shore. The *Brooklyn Blue Book and Long Island Society Register, 1921* lists the Rothschilds as residing at *The Hummocks* in Larchmont, NY.

He was the son of Frank and Amanda Blum Rothschild of Brooklyn.

Lillian Isabelle Abraham Rothschild was the daughter of Abraham Hyams Abraham. Her sister Edith married Percy S. Straus and resided in Red Bank, NJ. Her sister Florence married Edward Charles Blum and resided at *Shore Acres* in Bay Shore.

Simon Frank and Lillian Isabelle Abraham Rothschild's son Walter married Carola Therese Warburg, the daughter of Felix Moritz and Frieda Schiff Warburg of Manhattan. Carola's brother Gerald Felix Warburg resided at *Box Hill Farm* in Brookville. [*See* Spinzia, *Long Island's Prominent North Shore Families*, volume II – Warburg entry.] Their son Howard died at the age of nineteen.

front facade

Rubinstein, Ira

Occupation(s):	merchant - president, Cheap John's (a 25-store discount store chain)
Marriage(s):	Denise *[unable to determine maiden name]*
Address:	Suydam Lane, Bayport
Name of estate:	*Cheap John's Estate*
Year of construction:	1992
Style of architecture:	20th century Contemporary
Architect(s):	
Landscape architect(s):	
House extant: yes	
Historical notes:	

The house, originally named *Cheap John's Estate*, was built by Ira Rubinstein.

In 1987, Rubinstein purchased the former John Richard Suydam, Sr. estate *Edgewater*, demolished the house, and build a new house on the site.

In 1998, the nineteen-room, 13,000-square-foot house, with a pool house and three-car garage on 2.9 acres, was for sale. The asking price was $2 million; the annual taxes were $37,072.

Russell, William Hamilton, Jr. (1896-1958)

Occupation(s):	architect - partner, with George W. Clinton, Clinton and Russell *[See appendix for South Shore commissions.]*
Civic Activism:	president, Municipal Art Society of New York City, 1952
Marriage(s):	M/1 – 1918-div. – Marie Gaillard Johnson (1896-1977) M/2 – 1937 – Emma Muller (1892-1964)
Address:	off Maple Avenue, Islip
Name of estate:	*Le Rozel*
Year of construction:	1928
Style of architecture:	Modified Mediterranean
Architect(s):	William Hamilton Russell, Jr. designed his own house
Landscape architect(s):	
House extant: yes	
Historical notes:	

The house, originally named *Le Rozel*, was built by William Hamilton Russell, Jr.

The *Social Register Summer, 1932* lists William Hamilton and Marie G. Johnson Russell [Jr.] as residing at *Le Rozel* in Islip.

He was the son of William Hamilton and Florence Sands Russell, Sr.

Marie Gaillard Johnson Russell was the daughter of Bradish and Amiee Elizabeth Gaillard Johnson, Jr. of *Woodland* in East Islip. Her brother Aymar, who later owned *Woodland*, married Marion Krumbhaar Hoffman. Her brother Bradish Gaillard Johnson III married Emma Marie Grima and resided in Islip. Her brother Enfin also resided in Islip. Marie subsequently married Gordon Crothers, with whom she resided at *La Casetta* in Islip.

William Hamilton and Marie Gaillard Johnson Russell, Jr.'s daughter Amiee married Don Cino Tomaso Corsini, the eldest son of Don Emmanuele and Donna Maria Carolina Corsini of Florence, Italy. Their daughter Joan married Malcolm Scollary Low, the son of Benjamin R. C. Low of Manhattan. Their son The Reverend William Hamilton Russell III married Joan Schildhauer, the daughter of Clarence Henry Schildhauer of *White Oak* in Owings Mills, MD; Diane Sawyer Fenton; and, subsequently, Elizabeth Buck Truslow, the daughter of Francis Adams and Elizabeth Auchincloss Jennings Truslow of *The Point* in Laurel Hollow. [*See* Spinzia, *Long Island's Prominent North Shore Families, volume II* – Truslow entries.]

Emma Muller Russell had previously been married to ____ Wartman.

In 1954, William Hamilton and Emma Muller Russell, Jr. were residing at The Piping Rock Club in Lattingtown.

Ryan, John T.

Occupation(s):	capitalist - builder
	politician - unsuccessful Democratic candidate for New York State Assembly
Marriage(s):	1896 – Helen M. Oldner (b. 1876)
Address:	South Country Road, Bay Shore
Name of estate:	
Year of construction:	1899
Style of architecture:	Shingle
Architect(s):	
Landscape architect(s):	
House extant:	unconfirmed
Historical notes:	

The house was built by John T. Ryan.

He was the son of John F. Ryan of Bay Shore and Brooklyn.

Helen M. Oldner Ryan was the daughter of John George and Hellene M. Murray Oldner, Jr.

front facade, c. 1903

Sands, Francis Preston Blair (1842-1928)

Occupation(s):	attorney
	writer - *A Volunteer's Reminisces of Life in the North Atlantic Blockading Squadron, 1862-'5*, 1894
	The Last of the Blockade and the Fall of Fort Fisher, 1902;
	"Lest We Forget." Memories of Service Afloat from 1862-1865;
	The Brilliant Career of Lieutenant Roswell H. Lamson, U. S. Navy;
	The Loyal Legion and the Civil War;
	My Messmates and Shipmates Who Are Gone, 1862-1865;
	The Founders and Original Organizers of the Metropolitan Club, Washington, DC
Marriage(s):	M/1 – 1876-1884 – Emile Angelique Piquette (1848-1884)
	M/2 – 1887-1928 – Heloise McCue (1860-1933)
Address:	Little East Neck and South Country Roads, Babylon
Name of estate:	
Year of construction:	
Style of architecture:	
Architect(s):	
Landscape architect(s):	
House extant:	unconfirmed
Historical notes:	

Francis Preston Blair Sands was the son of Admiral Benjamin Franklin and Mrs. Henrietta Maria French Sands.

Emile Angelique Piquette Sands was the daughter of Jean Baptiste and Angelique Campau Piquette.

Francis Preston Blair and Emile Angelique Piquette Sands' daughter Henrietta married Richard T. Merrick. Their daughter Francis became a nun in Mount de Sales Monastery of the Visitation, Catonsville, MD. Their daughter Marie was a nun in the order of the Society of the Sacred Heart. She was among a group of nuns who were loaded aboard a ship in Baja, CA, that was smuggling Chinese and dumped at night near Monterey. As a result of the experience Marie suffered emotional problems.

Heloise McCue Sands was the daughter of Alexander McCue of Babylon. Her sister Jennie married James Cornelius Bergen and resided in Babylon.

Francis Preston Blair and Heloise McCue Sands' daughter Jane married Dr. Sylvanus Blanchard Newton, Sr., the son of Henry and Alice Kenney Newton.

Schieren, Charles Adolph, Sr. (1842-1915)

Occupation(s):	politician - mayor, Brooklyn, 1894-1895 (prior to its incorporation into NYC)
	industrialist - a founder and president, Charles A. Schieren & Co. (one of the country's largest leather tanneries/belting manufacturers);
	trustee, Holstein Extract Co.;
	trustee, Dixie Tanning Co.
	financier - a founder, Leather National Bank, Brooklyn;
	president, Germania Bank of Brooklyn;
	trustee, Nassau National Bank
Civic Activism:	president, Brooklyn Academy of Music;
	member, advisory board, Brooklyn Y. M. C. A.;
	trustee, Union for Christian Work;
	director, Society for the Prevention of Cruelty to Children;
	vice-president, Brooklyn Institute of Arts and Sciences;
	rear commodore, Penataquit Corinthian Yacht Club, Bay Shore
Marriage(s):	1865-1915 – Marie Louise Bramm (1839-1915)*
Address:	Ocean Avenue, Islip
Name of estate:	*Mapleton*
Year of construction:	c. 1890
Style of architecture:	Shingle
Architect(s):	Isaac Henry Green II designed the house (for C. A. Schieren, Sr.)
Landscape architect(s):	Olmstead

House extant: no; demolished in 1979**
Historical notes:

    The house, originally named *Mapleton*, was built by Charles Adolph Schieren, Sr.
    He was the son of Johann Niklaus and Catherine Wilhelmina Schieren.
    Marie Louise Bramm Schieren was the daughter of George Wilhelm and Louisa Wilhelmina Muller Bramm.
    Charles Adolph and Marie Louise Bramm Schieren, Sr.'s son Harrie married Alice Unkles and resided in Montclair, NJ. Their daughter married A. T. Mathews. Their son George married Blanche Mabelle Barker and resided at *Beachleigh* in Kings Point. [*See* Spinzia, *Long Island's Prominent North Shore Families, volume II* – Schieren entry.]
    *Mrs. Schieren was the principle beneficiary of her husband's will. Because she died one day after Charles, his bequest was subject to a second inheritance tax at her death. [*The New York Times* March 18, 1915, p. 20.]
    The house was purchased in 1926 by Kimball Chase Atwood, Jr., who continued to call it *Mapleton*.
    **The garage, stable, and caretaker's apartment are extant and are currently private residences. The estate's carriage house is also extant. It was moved to Frederic Lawrence Atwood's property.

west facade, c. 1908

Schnur, David (1882-1948)

Occupation(s):	industrialist - president, Reemtsma, Hamburg, Germany (cigarette manufacturing firm)
	capitalist - tobacco importer and cigarette exporter
	diplomat - Turkish Consul General, Berlin, Germany
Marriage(s):	Else *[unable to determine maiden name]* (d. 1966)
Address:	Phelps Lane, North Babylon
Name of estate:	
Year of construction:	c. 1941
Style of architecture:	Georgian Revival
Architect(s):	
Landscape architect(s):	
House extant: yes	
Historical notes:	

The fourteen-room house was built by David Schnur, who was reputed to be one of world's richest men with a fortune of nearly $100 million. He came to the United States to escape Nazi persecution. [*Daily News* March 17, 1948, p. 76.]

David and Else Schnur's daughter Gerda married ____ Hidalgo. Their daughter Alice married ____ Altman. Their daughter Anita married the Governor of Maryland John Lee Caroll.

The estate is currently the headquarters of the Town of Babylon Parks Department and a public park.

front facade

Schwenke, Oscar Louis, III (1883-1934)

Occupation(s):	capitalist - president, O. L. Land Investment Co., NYC; president, Althea Holding Co.
	merchant - secretary and treasurer, Nassau Auto Co.
Marriage(s):	1907 – Julia Wulfing
Address:	South Country Road, Bay Shore
Name of estate:	
Year of construction:	
Style of architecture:	
Architect(s):	Dwight James Baum designed alterations to the house, c. 1919 (for Schwenke)
Landscape architect(s):	
House extant: unconfirmed	
Historical notes:	

The *Long Island Society Register, 1929* lists Oscar L. Schwenke, Jr. [III] as residing on South Country Road, Bay Shore.

He was the son of Oscar Louis and Cecilia Sum Schwenke, Jr.

front facade, c. 1919

Scully, Charles Brewster (1896-1959)

Occupation(s):	capitalist - owner, camp for boys, East Otis, MA
Civic Activism:	chairman of recreation, Town of Islip; director, first aid, water safety, and accident prevention, New York chapter, American Red Cross; trustee, National Board of Campfire Girls
Marriage(s):	Adeline Hathaway Weekes (1925-1984) - Civic Activism: *
Address:	South Bay Avenue, Islip
Name of estate:	*Wereholme*
Year of construction:	c. 1917
Style of architecture:	Neo-French Manor
Architect(s):	Grosvenor Atterbury designed the house (for H. H. Weekes)
Landscape architect(s):	
House extant: yes	
Historical notes:	

rear facade, 1991

The house, originally named *Wereholme*, was built by Harold Hathaway Weekes. His wife, the former Louisine Peters, subsequently married Alexander Tcherepnin, with whom she continued to reside at *Wereholme*.

Harold Hathaway and Louisine Peters Weekes' daughter Adaline, who inherited *Wereholme*, married Charles Brewster Scully, the son of John Joseph and Mildred Louise Parker Scully, and resided at the estate. Adaline subsequently married Count Philip Orssich of Denkendorf bei Stuttgart, Germany.

*Mrs. Scully, who had divorced the count and reverted to the surname Scully, bequeathed the house to the National Audubon Society.

In 2004, the estate was purchased by Suffolk County and is now the county's Greenways Educational and Interpretive Nature Center.

Seaman, Frank (1855-1907)

Occupation(s):	industrialist - Brooklyn distiller
Marriage(s):	1886-1907 – Martina W. Beebe (1868-1926)
Address:	Bayport Avenue, Bayport
Name of estate:	
Year of construction:	
Style of architecture:	Victorian
Architect(s):	
Landscape architect(s):	
House extant: no	
Historical notes:	

In 1886, Seaman purchased the house. [*The Brooklyn Daily Eagle* May 23, 1886, p. 4.]

He was the son of Edwin Seaman.

Frank and Martina W. Beebe Seaman's daughter Minnie married Charles Edward Perry.

In 1887, Seaman sold the house to John McKee.

front facade

Searle, Charles (1850-1930)

Occupation(s):	capitalist - vice-president and director, Long Island Home of Amityville, 1921
	financier - cotton broker
Civic Activism:	a founder, governor, and commodore, Babylon Yacht Club; a founder and president, Oak Island Association, 1921; member of board, Babylon School District
Marriage(s):	Frances Barto (1855-1946)
Address:	90 Thompson Avenue, Babylon
Name of estate:	
Year of construction:	1910
Style of architecture:	Shingle
Architect(s):	
Landscape architect(s):	
House extant:	yes
Historical notes:	

front facade

The house was built by Charles Searle.

Frances Barto Searle was the daughter of Jared and Sarah Ann Wiggins Barto of Babylon and a descendant of the first white child born in New Netherlands.

Charles and Frances Barto Searle's daughter Frances did not marry. Their daughter Jessica married Edgar Harvey Monjo of NYC.

In 1999, the house sold for $800,000.

Shannon, Effie (1867-1954)

Occupation(s):	entertainers and associated professions - stage actress
Marriage(s):	1890-div. 1893 – Henry Guy Carleton (1851-1910)
	- journalist - editor, *Life*
	writer - playwright
Address:	South Snedecor Avenue, Bayport
Name of estate:	
Year of construction:	c. 1902
Style of architecture:	Dutch Colonial Revival
Architect(s):	Isaac Henry Green II designed the house (for R. H. Post, Sr.]
Landscape architect(s):	
House extant:	yes
Historical notes:	

side / front facade

The nine-bedroom house was built by Regis Henri Post, Sr. as a rental. In 1912, he sold the house to Shannon.

The *Long Island Society Register, 1928* lists Effie Shannon as residing on Snedecor Avenue [South] in Bayport.

She was the daughter of Robert and Ellen Ferren Shannon. Effie's sister Winona and brother-in-law Albert Garcia Andrews, both nationally acclaimed actors, also resided in the house.

Henry Guy Carleton, a noted humorist, was a descendant of General Guy Carleton who commanded British troops during the Revolutionary War.

In c. 1947, Shannon sold the house. [*The Suffolk County News* May 23, 1947, p. 6.]

Sharp, Hamlet Cecil (1894-1944)

Occupation(s):	capitalist - member, Automatic Electric Co.
Marriage(s):	1929-1944 – Ruth Lawrence Carroll (1892-1986)
Address:	80 South Saxon Avenue, Bay Shore
Name of estate:	*Millcreek / Mill Creek Farm*
Year of construction:	1933
Style of architecture:	Neo-Tudor
Architect(s):	William Hamilton Russell, Jr. designed the house (for H. C. Sharp)

Landscape architect(s):
House extant: yes
Historical notes:

Sharp demolished the Daniel Denice Conover house and built a new house on the site, which he called *Millcreek / Mill Creek Farm*.

The *Social Register, Summer 1937* lists H. Cecil and Ruth L. Carroll Sharp as residing at *Millcreek* in Islip [Bay Shore]. The *Social Register New York, 1933* lists the name of their estate as *Mill Creek Farm*.

He was the son of Hamlet Collier and Belle Green Sharp.

Ruth Lawrence Carroll Sharp was the daughter of Anson Livingston and Mabel W. Merritt Carroll. Ruth had previously been married to Eben Sumner Draper of Massachusetts. After Cecil's death, Mrs. Sharp relocated to Connecticut.

Hamlet Cecil and Ruth Lawrence Carroll Sharp's daughter Martha married Quentin Hugh Crewe, the son of Major Hugh Dodds Crewe and Lady Crewe of England.

In 1944, the house was purchased from Mrs. Sharp by Frank Vincent Riggio, who renamed it *Riggio House*.

In 2020, 9.68 acres and the 8,738-square-foot, nineteen-room house, with a seven-car garage, horse stables, guest cottage, and windmill, were for sale. The asking price was $4.999 million.

rear facade, 2020

Shea, David J.

Occupation(s):	industrialist - salesman for cash register company
Marriage(s):	1928 – Maude Virginia Jones (1885-1977)
Address:	71 Benson Avenue, Sayville
Name of estate:	*Wyndemoor*
Year of construction:	c. 1910
Style of architecture:	Modified Colonial Revival
Architect(s):	Isaac Henry Green II designed the main residence (for F. S. Jones)

Landscape architect(s):
House extant: yes
Historical notes:

The house, originally named *Wyndemoor*, was built by Frank Smith Jones for his daughter Henrietta and son-in-law William Robinson Simonds. Henrietta later sold the house to her sister Maude Virginia Jones Westin, who subsequently married Shea. The Sheas continued to call it *Wyndemoor*.

The house was then purchased by Elwell Palmer, who moved it to Benson Avenue.

front facade, 2005

Shea, David J.

Occupation(s):	industrialist - salesman for cash register company
Marriage(s):	1928 – Maude Virginia Jones (1885-1977)
Address:	Handsome Avenue, Sayville
Name of estate:	*Beechwold*
Year of construction:	1903
Style of architecture:	Shingle
Architect(s):	Isaac Henry Green II designed the main residence, gatehouse, and 1905 playhouse. The latter included a bowling alley and billiard room (for F. S. Jones)
Landscape architect(s):	
House extant:	no; destroyed by fire in 1957*
Historical notes:	

gatehouse, c. 1908

The house, originally named *Beechwold*, was built by Frank Smith Jones. It was later owned by his daughter Maude, who married Clarence Frederick Westin, Sr. and, subsequently, David J. Shea. The Sheas resided in the estate's gatehouse.

In 1945, the estate was purchased by Elwell Palmer, who sold it to Dr. Daniel McLaughlin in 1949. McLaughlin owned the house at the time of the fire.

*The gatehouse and playhouse are extant. The gatehouse is located at 254 Handsome Avenue and the playhouse is at 96 Benson Avenue.

Shea, Timothy Joseph, Sr. (1887-1933)

Occupation(s):	attorney -	New York State Assistant Attorney General, in charge of the state's Anti-Stock Fraud Bureau; member, Dykman, Oeland and Kuhn; member, Cullen and Dykman
	merchant -	chairman of board, National Bellas Hess & Co.* (mail order clothing firm which merged with National Coat and Suit Co.)
Marriage(s):	1911-1933 – Gertrude Scanlan (d. 1956)	
Address:	Garner Avenue, Bay Shore	
Name of estate:	*O'Conee*	
Year of construction:	c. 1930	
Style of architecture:	Neo-Tudor	
Architect(s):	Dwight James Baum designed the house (for T. J. Shea, Sr.)	
Landscape architect(s):		
House extant:	yes	
3Historical notes:		

The house, originally named *O'Conee*, was built by Timothy Joseph Shea, Sr.

*National Bellas Hess & Co. was founded by Harry Bellas Hess, who lived at *The Cedars* on New York Avenue, Huntington Station. Hess' firm was the third largest mail order company in the country.

front facade, c. 1931

Shortland, Thomas Francis (1859-1918)

Occupation(s):	shipping - partner, with his brother Stephen, and treasurer, Shortland Brothers (lighterage firm)
Civic Activism:	a founder, Babylon Yacht Club.
Marriage(s):	1883-1918 – Anita Rowland Ketcham (1860-1923)
Address:	55 The Crescent, Babylon
Name of estate:	
Year of construction	1904
Style of architecture:	Modified Queen Anne
Architect(s):	
Landscape architect(s):	
Builder:	E. W. Howell, residence and stable

House extant: yes
Historical notes:

The house was built by Thomas Francis Shortland.
He was the son of Thomas S. and Charlotte Ann Luff Shortland of Brooklyn. His sister Florence married Isaac Oliver Horton, Jr. of Brooklyn. His sister Maude married Albert H. Zugalla and resided in Brooklyn.
Anita Rowland Ketcham Shortland was the daughter of Edward Brush and Mary Caroline Ketcham of Babylon.
Thomas Francis and Anita Rowland Ketcham Shortland's daughter Hazel died at the age of twenty-eight.

front facade, 2006

Simonds, William Robinson (1878-1933)

Occupation(s): financier - member, Robert P. Marshall (stock brokerage firm);
partner, Blagden and Simonds (stock brokerage firm)
Civic Activism: a founder and director, Great River Club, 1920 (later, Timber Point Club);
governor, Southside Hospital, Bay Shore (now, South Shore University Hospital)

Marriage(s): 1903-1933 – Henrietta Louise Jones (1881-1936)

Address: 71 Benson Avenue, Sayville
Name of estate: *Wyndemoor*
Year of construction: c. 1910
Style of architecture: Modified Colonial Revival
Architect(s): Isaac Henry Green II designed the main residence, gatehouse, and 1905 playhouse. The latter included a bowling alley and billiard room (for F. S. Jones)
Landscape architect(s):
House extant: yes

Wyndemoor

Historical notes:

The house, originally named *Wyndemoor*, was built by Frank Smith Jones for his daughter Henrietta and son-in-law William Robinson Simonds.

William was the son of Henry Felt and Olivia Wealthy Elwell Simonds.

William Robinson and Henrietta Louise Jones Simonds' daughter Marjorie married William Mairs Duryea, Sr., the son of Walter B. Duryea of East Hampton. [*See* Spinzia, *Long Island's Prominent Families in the Town of East Hampton* – Duryea entry.] Their son Robinson married Mary Valentine Haskell, the daughter of George Dotson Haskell of Boston, MA, and, later, Jane Mellon, the daughter of Edward Purcell and Ethel Churchill Humphrey Mellon of *Villa Maria* in Southampton.

Henrietta later sold the house to her sister Maude Virginia Jones Westin, who subsequently married David J. Shea. The Sheas continued to call it *Wyndemoor*.

The house was then purchased by Elwell Palmer, who moved it to Benson Avenue.

The *Long Island Society Register, 1929* lists William Robinson and Henrietta Louise Jones Simonds as residing in Southampton.

[*See* Spinzia, *Long Island's Prominent Families in the Town of Southampton* – Mellon and Simonds entries.]
[*For information on the Southside Hospital, see Cooper entry.*]

Slote, Alonzo (1829-1901)

Occupation(s): merchant - partner, Tredwell & Slote (clothing firm)
financier - director, Firemen's Insurance Co.;
vice-president, Wallabout Bank;
trustee, People's Trust Co.;
director, Brooklyn Life Insurance Co.;
director, National Shoe and Leather Bank
capitalist - director, Brooklyn City Railroad
Civic Activism: a founder and member of executive committee, Great South Bay Yacht Club

Marriage(s):

Address: Saxon Avenue, Bay Shore
Name of estate:
Year of construction:
Style of architecture:
Architect(s):
Landscape architect(s):
House extant: unconfirmed
Historical notes:

Alonzo Slote was the son of Daniel and Ann Jane Slote, Sr. of Brooklyn and the first cousin of Duchess de Arcos. His brother Daniel also resided on Saxon Avenue.

[*See following entry for additional family information.*]

Slote, Daniel, Jr. (1828-1882)

Occupation(s):	publisher - president, Slote, Woodman & Co.;
	industrialist - president, Daniel Slote & Co. (blank book manufacturers)
Civic Activism:	member, New York City Board of Education;
	member, Old Volunteer Fire Department
Marriage(s):	1879-1882 – Sarah Baldwin Griffiths (1842-1925)
Address:	Saxon Avenue, Bay Shore
Name of estate:	
Year of construction:	
Style of architecture:	
Architect(s):	
Landscape architect(s):	
House extant: unconfirmed	
Historical notes:	

Daniel Slote, Jr. is reputed to have been the model for the character "Dan" in Mark Twain's *Innocents Abroad*. [*The New York Times* February 14, 1882, p. 5.]

He was the son of Daniel and Ann Jane Slote, Sr. of Brooklyn. His sister Sarah married John F. Wood and resided in Huntington.

Sarah Baldwin Griffiths Slote was the daughter of Alderman James Griffiths.

Daniel and Sarah Baldwin Griffiths Slote, Jr.'s daughter ____ married Albert Edward Angus.

[See previous entry for additional family information.]

Smedberg, Adolphus, Jr. (1871-1939)

Occupation(s):	industrialist - director, Electrical Securities Corp, NY (manufacturer of electrical, gas, water, and steam machinery)
	financier - member, Van Ingen and Co. (municipal bond firm)
Marriage(s):	1899-1939 – Marie Russ Corwin (1874-1941)
Address:	Fire Island Avenue, Babylon
Name of estate:	*Larkmeadow*
Year of construction:	
Style of architecture:	
Architect(s):	
Landscape architect(s):	
House extant: unconfirmed	
Historical notes:	

The *Social Register Summer, 1915* lists Adolphus and Marie R. R. Corwin Smedberg [Jr.] as residing at *Larkmeadow* in Babylon.

He was the son of Adolphus and Mary Ludlow Morton Smedberg, Sr. His sister Emily married Edwin Carnes Weeks, the son of James and Kezia Seabury Weeks, and resided in Babylon.

Adolphus and Marie Russ Corwin Smedberg, Jr.'s daughter Edith married Quentin F. Haig and resided in Larchmont, NY. Their daughter Mary married Monroe Bostwick Hall, the son of Benjamin Elihu Hall.

In 1923, the house was sold to Walter N. Dennis of Manhattan. [*The County Review* December 21, 1923, p. 18.]

Smith, Benjamin Franklin (1821-1871)

Occupation(s):

Marriage(s): 1848-1971 – Mary Anna Edwards (1829-1875)

Address: 473 Middle Road, Bayport
Name of estate:
Year of construction:
Style of architecture: Colonial Revival
Architect(s):
Landscape architect(s):
House extant: yes
Historical notes:

Lawrence Edwards built the house for his daughter Mary and son-in-law Benjamin Franklin Smith.

Benjamin was the son of William and Freelove Baldwin Smith.

Benjamin Franklin and Mary Anna Edwards Smith's daughter Annie married John Henry Hawkins. Their son Lawrence married Emily Jane Green. Their son Barnes married Margaret Jane Calhoun, the daughter of Irvin and Anna E. Calhoun.

front facade

Smith, Charles Robinson (1855-1930)

Occupation(s): attorney -   partner, Smith and Martin
industrialist - a founder and vice president, General Chemical Co.
         (later, Allied Chemical & Dye Co.);
       director, Pitnam Sewing Co.
capitalist - director, Wilhelms Realty Co.;
       director, Sackett & Wilhelms Lithographing & Printing Co.;
       director, Timmis Lithographing Co.;
       director, U. S. Aluminum Printing Plate Co.
writer - magazine articles on World War I and its aftermath

Civic Activism: director, Austin Fox Riggs Foundation (for treatment of psychoneurotic patients)

Marriage(s): 1879-1930 – Jeannie Porter Steele (d. 1945)

Address: 80 Montgomery Avenue, Bay Shore
Name of estate:
Year of construction: c. 1890
Style of architecture: Modified Shingle
Architect(s):
Landscape architect(s):
House extant: yes
Historical notes:

side / front facade, c. 1894

The house was built by Charles Robinson Smith. In 1892, Smith still owned a house on Montgomery Avenue. [*South Side Signal* April 23, 1892, p. 3.]

He was the son of Edwin and Jane Townsend Mather Smith.

Jennie Porter Steele Smith was the daughter of William Porter and Elizabeth Wadsworth Harris Steele of Manhattan.

Charles Robinson and Jennie Porter Steele Smith's daughter Gertrude did not marry. Their daughter Hilda married Lyman Beecher Stowe, the grandson of Harriet Beecher Stow. Another daughter died in childhood.

The house was subsequently owned by Edward Gordon.

The fifteen-room house, with nine bedrooms, six fireplaces, and five-and-a-half bathrooms, was for sale in 2006. The asking price was $1,490,000; the annual taxes were $18,055.

Smith, Elward, Jr. (1895-1947)

Occupation(s):	capitalist - real estate
Civic Activism:	member, Town of Islip Planning Board; commodore, South Side Yacht Club (later, Sayville Yacht Club); a founder and governor, Sayville Yacht Club
Marriage(s):	1928-1947 – Ella Katharine Bailey (1896-1957) - Civic Activism: charter member, Colonel Josiah Smith Chapter, Daughters of the American Revolution; charter member, Sayville Historical Society
Address:	308 Green Avenue, Sayville
Name of estate:	
Year of construction:	
Style of architecture:	
Architect(s):	
Landscape architect(s):	
House extant:	yes
Historical notes:	

Elward Smith Jr. was the son of Elward and Frances Cairns Smith, Sr. of Sayville.

Ella Katharine Bailey Smith was the daughter of Joseph Bailey and Lillian Belle Robinson of Patchogue.

[See following entry for additional family information.]

front facade

Smith, Elward, Sr. (1835-1900)

Occupation(s):	architect capitalist - builder politician - New York City Fire Commissioner
Marriage(s):	Frances Cairns (1855-1952)
Address:	Handsome Avenue, Sayville
Name of estate:	
Year of construction:	
Style of architecture:	Shingle
Architect(s):	Isaac Henry Green II designed the house (for Ridgeway)
Landscape architect(s):	
House extant:	unconfirmed
Historical notes:	

front facade

The house was built by James W. Ridgeway. In 1897, Smith purchased the house from Ridgeway.

Frances Cairns Smith subsequently married General Robert Gibson Smith.

Elward and Frances Cairns Smith, Sr.'s daughter Marjorie died at the age of twenty-one. In 1918, their son Irving died of the Spanish Flu. Their son Elward Smith, Jr. married Ella Katharine Bailey and resided in Sayville. Their son Jewett married Virginia Woodhull Otto and also resided in Sayville. Their daughter Frances married Admiral Harry Alexander Baldridge and resided in Sayville. Their daughter Laurie married Andrew Perry de Forest Allgood and also resided in Sayville.

Smith, Frederick D. (1866-1953)

Occupation(s):	capitalist - builder
	financier - director, Oysterman's National Bank of Sayville
	naval architect - designed Great South Bay scooters
Civic Activism:	chief, Bayport Volunteer Fire Department
Marriage(s):	Nettie May Berry (1872-1926)
	- vice-president, Ladies Aid Society;
	vice-president, Bayport chapter, American Red Cross
Address:	Fairview Avenue, Bayport

Name of estate:
Year of construction:
Style of architecture:
Architect(s):
Landscape architect(s):
House extant: unconfirmed
Historical notes:

    Frederick D. Smith was the son of Garrett J. and Matilda M. Smith.
    Nettie May Berry Smith was the daughter of James Hervey and Elizabeth Wright Berry of Islip.
    Frederick D. and Nettie May Berry Smith's son Hervey Garret Smith resided in Sayville.
    [See following entry for additional family information.]

Smith, Hervey Garret (1896-1979)

Occupation(s):	artist - marine subjects
	writer - *The Racing Sailor's Bible*, 1972;
	The Arts of the Sailor: Knotting, Splicing and Ropework,
	1953;
	Boat Carpentry, 1965;
	The Malinspike Sailor;
	The Small-Boat Sailor's Bible, 1964;
	How to Choose a Small Boat, 1969
Civic Activism:	a founder, Long Island Maritime Museum, West Sayville, 1966;
	a founder, Wet Pants Sailing Club, Sayville
Marriage(s):	1926 – Elsie Jeanette Beebe
Address:	76 Hampton Street, Sayville

Name of estate:
Year of construction:
Style of architecture:
Architect(s):
Landscape architect(s):
House extant: yes
Historical notes:

    Hervey Garret Smith was the son of Frederick D. and Nettie May Berry Smith of Bayport.
    Elsie Jeanette Beebe was the daughter of Ira and Josephine Newins Beebe of Sayville. Elsie's sister Marion married James Henry Snedecor and resided in Bayport.
    Hervey Garret and Elsie Jeanette Beebe Smith's daughter Betsey married Howard Nixon and resided in Naugatuck, CT.
    [See previous entry for additional family information.]

Smith, Jewett Holt (1898-1967)

Occupation(s):	capitalist - builder
	journalist - editor, *Suffolk Citizen*, Sayville
	financier - a founder and director, Community Trust Co., Sayville (later, Oystermen's Bank and Trust Co.)
Civic Activism:	treasurer, Sayville Yacht Club
Marriage(s):	1926 – Virginia Woodhull Otto (1900-1974)
	- Civic Activism: secretary, Episcopal Diocese of Long Island; a founder, Long Island Women's Organization of Democratic Party; a founder, president, and secretary, Sayville Historical Society
Address:	46 Saxton Avenue, Sayville
Name of estate:	
Year of construction:	1900
Style of architecture:	Colonial Revival
Architect(s):	
Landscape architect(s):	
House extant: yes	
Historical notes:	

front facade

Jewett Holt Smith, who committed suicide with a double-barreled shotgun, was the son of Elward and Frances Cairns Smith, Sr. of Sayville.

Virginia Woodhull Otto Smith was the daughter of Thomas Nelson and Julia Edna Hait Otto of Sayville.

[See Elward Smith, Sr. entry for additional family information.]

Smith, Selah Carll (1827-1884)

Occupation(s):	capitalist - proprietor, Watson House, Babylon (hotel); proprietor, American House, Babylon (hotel); acting superintendent of operations, Babylon Railroad Co.
Marriage(s):	1850-1884 – Hannah D. Jacobs (1828-1899)
Address:	109 Fire Island Avenue, Babylon
Name of estate:	*Smith Cottage*
Year of construction:	1874
Style of architecture:	Second Empire
Architect(s):	Hallock & Hait designed the house (for S. C. Smith)
Landscape architect(s):	
Builder:	under the direction of William L. Hallock of Hallock & Hait
House extant: yes	
Historical notes:	

The house, known as *Smith Cottage*, was built by Selah Carll Smith.

He was the son of Jonathan and Ann Elizabeth Wicks Smith.

Hannah D. Jacobs Smith was the daughter of Joseph and Margaret Seaman Jacobs.

Selah Carll and Hannah D. Jacobs Smith's son Edmund was a youth at the time of his death in 1869. In 1891, their son Jay, who resided in Babylon, was charged with cruelty to animals for setting his bull dog on the Newfoundland dog of S. B. Lang. [*The Brooklyn Daily Eagle* March 22, 1891, p. 2.] In 1892, their son Charles, who was a bachelor, committed suicide in his room in the Palace Hotel in San Francisco. Their son Augustus married Adeline Snedecor, the daughter of Obadiah and Adeline S. Snedecor of West Islip, and resided in West Islip. Their son Shephard married Estelle Louise Townsend, the daughter of Charles Townsend of Manhattan. In 1905, Shephard and his wife were charged with beating to death their five-year-old son Ralph with a razor strap. Estelle was sentenced to five years in jail. Shephard was exonerated of all charges. Ralph may have been Shephard's illegitimate son from a previous liaison. [*The Standard Union* August 22, 1902, p. 4; *The Evening World* April 29, 1905, p. 3; *The Republican – Journal* May 4, 1905, p. 6; and *The Brooklyn Daily Eagle* September 19, 1905, p. 10.]

The house was later owned by Crawford Blagden, Sr.

*Selah Carll Smith residence, Smith Cottage,
front / side facade, 2005*

Snedecor, Isaac Howard (1889-1970)

Occupation(s):	financier - director, Oystermen's Bank and Trust Co., Sayville
	merchant - partner, with his brother James Henry Snedecor, S. Snedecor's Sons, Bayport (later, Shands) (grocery store); president, Snedecor Coal & Fuel Co., Bayport
Marriage(s):	1916-1970 – Henrietta Emma Green (1885-1975)
Address:	508 Middle Road, Bayport
Name of estate:	
Year of construction:	1916
Style of architecture:	Colonial Revival
Architect(s):	Isaac Henry Green II designed the house (for I. H. Snedecor)
Landscape architect(s):	
House extant: yes	
Historical notes:	

front facade, 2020

The house was built by Isaac Howard Snedecor.
He was the son of Isaac Scudder and Sarah Elizabeth Homan Snedecor of Bayport.
Henrietta Emma Green Snedecor was the daughter of Isaac Henry and Emma Louise Hibbard Green II of *Brookside* in Sayville.
Isaac Howard and Henrietta Emma Green Snedecor's daughter Elizabeth married Wilber Prall and resided in Bayport. Their daughter Marjorie married Frank Leighton Tyson and resided in Bayport. Their daughter Jane married James William Herring, the son of H. Lewis and Edith Huntting Herring of Sayville, and resided in Gales Ferry, CT.
[See following entry for additional family information.]
In 2020, the five-bedroom, three-and-a-half-bath house was for sale. The asking price was $777,000; the annual taxes were $22,214.

Snedecor, James Henry (1887-1964)

Occupation(s):	merchant - partner, with his brother Isaac Howard Snedecor, S. Snedcor's Sons, Bayport (later, Shand's) (grocery store)
Civic Activism:	president, Bayport Board of Education; director, Bayport Republican Club; trustee and chief, Bayport Fire Department
Marriage(s):	1913-1964 – Florence Dawson Parker (1887-1966)
Address:	Fairview Avenue, Bayport
Name of estate:	
Year of construction:	1881
Style of architecture:	Modified Second Empire
Architect(s):	
Landscape architect(s):	
House extant:	no; destroyed by fire in 1940s
Historical notes:	

front facade

The house, originally named *White House*, was built by Edward Edwards. In 1883, it was purchased by John R. Ely. Cyrus E. Staples purchased the house in 1890. In 1902, Staples lost the house in foreclosure proceedings. It was later owned by Waldron Kintzing Post and his brother Regis Henri Post, Sr., who, in turn, sold it to Snedecor in 1925.

James Henry Snedecor was the son of Isaac Scudder and Sarah Elizabeth Homan Snedecor of Bayport.

Florence Dawson Parker Snedecor was the daughter of Charles Lamont and Mary L. Smith Parker of Syracuse, NY.

James Henry and Florence Dawson Parker Snedecor's daughter Marion married Warren Beebe, the son of Ira and Josephine Newins Beebe of Sayville. Their daughter Edith married William Spencer Beatty and resided in Hamburg, NY.

[See previous entry for additional family information.]

Snedeker, Charles Valentine (1895-1951)

Occupation(s):	financier - partner, Carreau and Snedeker (stock brokerage firm); president, Charles V. Snedeker and Co. (stock brokerage firm); partner, Snedeker and Bard (stock brokerage firm)
Civic Activism:	trustee, Village of Babylon; president, Babylon Village Economic Council
Marriage(s):	1924-1951 – Marion Olsen (1897-1968)
Address:	Little East Neck Road, Babylon
Name of estate:	*Wind's Will**
Year of construction:	
Style of architecture:	Colonial Revival
Architect(s):	
Landscape architect(s):	
House extant:	no; demolished, 1951
Historical notes:	

Charles Valentine Snedeker was the son of Alfred M. and Emma Gulden Snedeker of Manhattan.

Marion Olsen Snedeker was the daughter of Ole and Marie Swensen Olsen of Brooklyn.

Charles Valentine and Marion Olsen Snedeker's son John married Eve Kinloch, the daughter of Bohun Baker Kinloch of Charleston, SC. Their daughters Emma-Marie and Marianne did not marry.

Charles committed suicide in *Wind's Will* by shooting himself twice in the chest with a thirty-two caliber revolver.

*The estate's name *Wind's Will* was adopted from Henry Wadsworth Longfellow's poem "My Lost Youth." [John C Snedeker, *My Life on Long Island*.]

Snow, Frederick Billings (1870-1954)

Occupation(s):	capitalist - president, Jere Johnson, Jr., Co. (Brooklyn real estate, auctioneers, and appraisal firm)
Civic Activism:	chairman, auditing committee, Brooklyn Real Estate Board; a founder and secretary, Winona Social Club, Brooklyn, 1889
Marriage(s):	1897-1943 – Larissa G. Hough (1875-1943)
Address:	Garner Lane, Bay Shore
Name of estate:	
Year of construction:	
Style of architecture:	
Architect(s):	
Landscape architect(s):	
House extant:	unconfirmed
Historical notes:	

The *Long Island Society Register, 1929* lists Mr. and Mrs. Frederick B. Snow as residing on Garner Lane in Bay Shore.
He was the son of Augustine and Harriet Louisa Butler Snow of Albany, NY.
Larissa G. Hough Snow was the daughter of Edward Wade and Anna Maria Bosch Hough.
Frederick Billings and Larissa G. Hough Snow's daughter Anita married William Benedict Owen, Jr.

Spaulding, E. B.

Occupation(s):	capitalist - secretary, Wright Universal Electric Co., NYC
Marriage(s):	
Address:	St. Mark's Lane, Islip*
Name of estate:	
Year of construction:	
Style of architecture:	Victorian Gothic
Architect(s):	
Landscape architect(s):	
House extant:	yes
Historical notes:	

The house was built by Parmenus Johnson, Sr. In January 1880, the twenty-one-acre estate was purchased by C. A. Backett of New York. By June 1880 it was owned by Spaulding who enlarged and modernized the house [*The Brooklyn Daily Eagle* January 27, 1880, p. 4, and June 7, 1880, p. 1.]

In 1886, the estate was purchased by Robert Cambridge Livingston III, who called it *Lakeside*. The estate was then owned by the Livingstons' daughter Maud who married Henry Worthington Bull. By the early 1940s it was owned by the Bulls' niece Phyllis Livingston Baker Astaire, who married the noted dancer/choreographer/actor Fred Astaire, Sr. [aka Frederick Auterlitz].

In 2006, the house was owned by ____ Dowden.

In 2008, the seven thousand-square-foot, twenty-room house with seven bedrooms was for sale. The asking price was $1,499,990; the taxes were $16,089.

*The estate originally bordered on St. Marks Lane. With its subdivision, the house is currently located on Suellen Road.

Stanchfield, John Barry, Sr. (1855-1921)

Occupation(s):	attorney* - partner, Stanchfield and Levy; partner, Reynolds, Stanchfield, and Collins; partner, Hill and Stanchfield; district attorney, Chemung County, NY, 1880-1885 politician** - mayor, Elmira, NY, 1886-1888; member, New York State Assembly, 1895-1896; New York State Assembly Minority Leader, 1896
Civic Activism:	suffragist; a founder and director, Great River Club, 1920 (later, Timber Point Club)
Marriage(s):	1886-1921 – Clara Cornelia Spaulding (1860-1935)
Address:	Ocean Avenue, Islip
Name of estate:	*Afterglow*
Year of construction:	c. 1890
Style of architecture:	Shingle
Architect(s):	
Landscape architect(s):	
House extant:	no; demolished in c. 1950
Historical notes:	

The house, originally named *Afterglow*, was built by John Gibb. In 1909, it was purchased by Stanchfield.
He was the son of Dr. John K. and Mrs. Glovina S. Barry Stanchfield of Elmira, NY.
Clara Cornelia Spaulding Stanchfield was the daughter of Henry C. and Clara W. Spaulding of Elmira, NY.
John Barry and Clara Cornelia Spaulding Stanchfield, Sr.'s son Dr. John Barry Stanchfield, Jr., an endocrinologist, resided in Salt Lake City, UT. Their daughter Alice, who later owned the house, married Dr. Arthur Mullen Wright.
Both the Stanchfields and Wrights continued to call the estate *Afterglow*.
*Stanchfield established the right of non-incrimination based on the Fifth Amendment of the United States Constitution in the case of Forbes vs. Taylor. The 1894 case involved Cornell University sophomores who attempted to disrupt a freshman banquet by releasing chlorine gas. The gas caused the death of a college employee in the next room. Stanchfield advised his client Taylor not to answer any incriminating questions at the Grand Jury hearing which resulted in Taylor being charged with contempt of court. Stanchfield's position was upheld by the United States Supreme Court thus establishing a defendant's right to "Plead the Fifth." [*The National Cyclopaedia of American Biography* (Clifton, NJ: James T. White & Co., 1984), vol. 14, pp. 360-361.] In another famous court case, Stanchfield succeeded in having Harry K. Thaw, the murderer of architect Stanford White, released after Thaw had spent nine years as an inmate in the Matteawan Asylum. [*The New York Times* June 26, 1921, p. 23.]
**In the 1900 election for Governor of New York, Stanchfield, who was the Democratic candidate, lost. In 1901, he lost in the election for United States Senator from New York State.

Afterglow, c. 1901

Staples, Cyrus E. (1842-1903)

Occupation(s):	financier - investment banker (involved primarily in Brooklyn corporations)*; a founder, New York Mutual Title Insurance Co.
	shipping - president, New York, Maine and New Brunswick Steamship Co.
Marriage(s):	Anna *[unable to determine maiden name]*
Address:	Fairview Avenue, Bayport
Name of estate:	
Year of construction:	1881
Style of architecture:	Modified Second Empire
Architect(s):	
Landscape architect(s):	
House extant:	no; destroyed by fire in 1940s
Historical notes:	

The house, originally named *White House*, was built by Edward Edwards. In 1883 it was purchased by John R. Ely. Staples purchased the house in 1890.

Cyrus E. and Anna Staples' daughter Georgina married Edward H. Trecartin and, later, Archibald H. Mitford of London, England.

*As agent for the sale of the Long Island Water Supply Company to the City of Brooklyn, Staples became the center of a political scandal. The water company, a private corporation whose owners included former Senator Alfred Wagstaff, Jr. of West Islip and several other local and state politicians, supplied water to Brooklyn's Twenty-sixth Ward. Staples negotiated a contract whereby the company's $70-a-share stock was sold to the city at the inflated price of $800-a-share. Fortunately for the taxpayers, the sale was declared void by the courts. [*The New York Times* December 20, 1890, p. 9; December 29, 1890, p. 3; January 5, 1891, p. 1; January 31, 1891, p. 8; March 2, 1891, p. 1; May 29, 1891, p. 8; and May 31, 1892, p. 9.

In 1902, Staples lost the house in foreclosure proceedings. It was then owned by Waldron Kintzing Post and his brother Regis Henri Post, Sr., who, in turn, sold it to James Henry Snedecor in 1925.

front facade

Stephens, Benjamin, Jr. (1826-1907)

Occupation(s):	attorney
Civic Activism:	bequeathed over $100,000 to charity
Marriage(s):	
Address:	South Country Road, West Islip
Name of estate:	*Sunnymede*
Year of construction:	
Style of architecture:	
Architect(s):	
Landscape architect(s):	
House extant:	unconfirmed
Historical notes:	

The estate name was referenced in the *South Side Signal* August 25, 1888, p. 2.
He was the son of Benjamin and Hannah Maria Prall Stephens, Sr.
His estate, which was located on the south side of South Country Road, was opposite the residence of his brother John.

Stephens, John Lloyd (1838-1913)

Occupation(s):	attorney
Marriage(s):	1896-1913 – Julia B. True (1854-1936)
Address:	South Country Road, West Islip
Name of estate:	*Lone Oak*
Year of construction:	
Style of architecture:	Modified French Empire
Architect(s):	
Landscape architect(s):	

House extant: no; demolished, c. 1937
Historical notes:

front facade

The Society Register, 1907 lists John L. and Julia True Stephens as residing at *Lone Oak* in West Islip. The house was built over an old Native American burying ground. [*South Side Signal* August 25, 1888, p. 2.] It was located on the north side of South Country Road and was opposite the residence of his brother Benjamin.

He and Benjamin were the sons of Benjamin and Hannah Maria Prall Stephens, Sr.

In the years just prior to his marriage, John had been a virtual recluse at his estate with his dogs and books as his companions. [*The New York Times* April 11, 1896, p.5.] In the early 1890s, Stephens was severely injured in a railroad accident, which temporarily left him an invalid. [*The New York Times* February 14, 1896, p. 3.]

Julia B. True Stephens was the daughter of Benjamin Kimball and Martha Bunce True, Sr. of West Islip. Julia had previously been married to William J. Fowler.

[See previous entry for additional family information.]

In 1913, the estate was purchased by Minor Cooper Keith. [*South Side Signal* January 10, 1913, p. 5.]

Stewart, Anna May (1895-1961)
aka Anna Stuart

Occupation(s):	entertainers and associated professions - silent motion picture actress*; motion picture producer
	writer - *One;* *The Devil's Toy*
Marriage(s):	M/1 – 1917-div. 1928 – Rudolph Cameron Brennan (1894-1958) (aka Rudolph Cameron) - entertainers and associated professions – Vitagraph Film actor
	M/2 – 1929-div.1946 – George Peabody Converse - financier - banker
Address:	Windsor Avenue, Brightwaters**
Name of estate:	*Sweet Violet*
Year of construction:	1916
Style of architecture:	Modified Colonial Revival
Architect(s):	
Landscape architect(s):	

House extant: yes
Historical notes:

The house, originally named *Sweet Violet*, was built by Anna May Stewart.
She was the daughter of William and Marsha Stewart of Brooklyn.
*Anna's contribution to the motion picture industry has been recognized on Hollywood's Walk of Fame.
**The house was moved to its present site on Windsor Avenue.

Stewart, Dr. George David (1862-1933)

Occupation(s):	physician* - chief surgeon, Bellevue Hospital, NYC; president, medical board, St. Vincent's Hospital, NYC
	educator - professor of anatomy and surgery, Bellevue Hospital, NYC
	writer - poet
Civic Activism:	chairman, executive committee, Hospital Fund; a founder and president, American College of Surgeons; president, New York Academy of Medicine; president, Robert Burns Society
Marriage(s):	1890-1933 – Ida May Robb
Address:	Great River Road, Great River
Name of estate:	*Appin House*
Year of construction:	1899
Style of architecture:	Neo-Tudor
Architect(s):	Charles C. Thain designed the house (for R. S. White)

Landscape architect(s):
House extant: no

front facade

Historical notes:

The house was built by Raymond S. White. After White's death, it was owned by his wife Sarah, who married Francis Sessions Hutchins and continued to reside in the house which they called *Saramond*. It was later owned by Stewart, who called it *Appin House*.

The *Social Register Summer, 1915* lists George David and Ida May Robb Stewart as residing at *Appin House* in Great River.

He was the son of Daniel and Mary Jane MacCallum Stewart of Nova Scotia, Canada.

Ida May Robb Stewart was the daughter of James Finley Robb.

Dr. George David and Mrs. Ida May Robb Stewart's daughter Jean married Robert Vose White and resided at *Rohallion* in Rumson, NJ. Their daughter Margery married Porter Hoagland and resided at *Appin* in Rumson, NJ. Their daughter Dorothy married Edward Hope Coffey, Jr. Their daughter Mary did not marry.

*When New York City Mayor William Jay Gaynor, who resided at *Deepwells* in St. James, was shot in an assassination attempt, Stewart was a consulting physician. [*See* Spinzia, *Long Island: A Guide to New York's Suffolk and Nassau Counties* – *Deepwells Farm* – Estate of William Jay Gaynor – *Deepwells*, St. James.]

The house was subsequently owned by Joseph Francis Dempsey who renamed it *Estancia*.

Stillman, Benjamin D. (1805-1901)

Occupation(s):	attorney - district attorney, Eastern District
Civic Activism:	bequeathed $110,000 to Yale University, New Haven, CT; bequeathed $10,000 to Columbia University, NYC; member, Grant Monument Committee, NYC; vice-president, New York Bar Association; director, New England Society of Brooklyn; chairman, invitations committee, Committee of One Hundred Prominent Citizens of Brooklyn
Marriage(s):	
Address:	South Country Road, West Islip

Name of estate:
Year of construction:
Style of architecture:
Architect(s):
Landscape architect(s):
House extant: unconfirmed
Historical notes:

At the time of his death, Benjamin D. Stillman's total wealth was estimated at $1.5 million. [*Brooklyn Daily Eagle* January 29, 1901, p. 1.]

Stillman's sister Laura married ____ Blagden and resided in Washington, DC.

In 1902, the house was purchased by Stillman's niece Miss Caroline S. Taylor. [*Brooklyn Daily Eagle* July 30, 1902, p. 15.]

*Stillman's gift to Columbia University was for the establishment of the William Mitchell Fellowship.

Stoppani, Charles Francis, Jr. (1866-1941)

Occupation(s): financier - partner, Ennis and Stoppani (odd-lot brokers specializing in grain futures)*;
 member, McManamy and Co. (stock brokerage firm)

Marriage(s): Evalyn Henry

Address: *[unable to determine street address]*, Bayport
Name of estate:
Year of construction:
Style of architecture:
Architect(s):
Landscape architect(s):
House extant: unconfirmed
Historical notes:

Evalyn Henry Stoppani was the daughter of William Warner and Mary Merritt Henry of Berkeley, CA.

Charles Francis and Evalyn Henry Stoppani, Jr.'s daughter married Harding T. Mason and resided in Ridgefield, CT.

*As a result of alleged irregularities in their 1903, 1909, and 1916 stock transactions, arrest warrants were issued for Stoppani and his partner and fellow Bayport resident Thomas A. Ennis. The scandal caused the firm of Ennis and Stoppani to declare bankruptcy. [Harry W. Havemeyer, *East on the Great South Bay: Sayville and Bayport 1860-1960* (Mattituck, NY: Amereon House, 2001), p. 82, and *The New York Times* November 8, 1903, p. 20; April 14, 1909, p. 1; April 16, 1909, p. 5; April 22, 1909, p. 5; April 28, 1909, p. 18; May 5, 1909, p. 7; and May 22, 1909, p. 1.]

[See following Stoppani entries for additional family information.]

Stoppani, Charles Francis, Sr. (1832-1892)

Occupation(s):

Marriage(s): Eliza Jane Howe (1835-1910)

Address: Fairview Avenue, Bayport
Name of estate: *Arcadia*
Year of construction: 1888
Style of architecture:
Architect(s): Isaac Henry Green II
 designed the house
 (for C. F. Stoppani, Sr.)

Landscape architect(s):
House extant: no
Historical notes:

The house, originally named *Arcadia*, was built by Charles Francis Stoppani, Sr.

The *Brooklyn Blue Book and Long Island Society Register, 1918* lists Eliza J. Stoppani as residing in Manhattan.

Charles Francis and Eliza Jane Howe Stoppani, Sr.'s son Charles Francis Stoppani, Jr. married Evalyn Henry, the daughter of William Warner and Mary Merritt Henry of Berkeley, CA, and resided in Bayport. Their son Joseph married Ida Maloney and resided at *Liberty Hall* in Bayport. Their daughter Eliza, who later owned *Arcadia*, married ____ Harris and, later, Stephen Perry Cox.

The estate was later owned by Charles' daughter Jane, who married Stephen Perry Cox. The Coxes continued to call it *Arcadia*.

[See other Stoppani entries for additional family information.]

In 1919, Cox sold the house to John J. O'Connor, who defaulted on its property taxes.

The house was purchased by Judge Martin Thomas Manton at a sheriff's sale, thereby giving Manton ownership of both Stoppani houses, *Liberty Hall* and *Arcadia*. In 1939, Manton, who was convicted of accepting $186,000 in bribes, lost the house for failure to pay its property taxes.

Arcadia

Stoppani, Joseph H. (1870-1938)

Occupation(s):   capitalist -   president, Bayport Road Co.
                              financier -   Stoppani and Hotchkins (odd-lot brokers specializing in grain futures)*

Marriage(s):   1898- div. 1917 – Ida Maloney

Address: 133 South Ocean Avenue, Bayport
Name of estate: *Liberty Hall*
Year of construction: 1898
Style of architecture: Classic Revival
Architect(s):   Isaac Henry Green II designed the main house, carriage house, and gardener's cottage (for J. H. Stoppani)

Landscape architect(s):
House extant: yes*
Historical notes:

side / front facade, 2006

The house, originally named *Liberty Hall*, was built by Joseph H. Stoppani.

He was the son of Charles Francis and Eliza Jane Howe Stoppani, Sr., who resided at *Arcadia* in Bayport.

*Joseph and his brother Charles Francis Stoppani, Jr. were known locally as "the noodle kings of Bayport."

In 1916, Joseph's firm entered bankruptcy as a result of his overextension in grain speculation. Charged with alleged misappropriation of a client's funds, Joseph was convicted and received a four-year jail sentence in Sing Sing. After serving eighteen months, Stoppani was released from prison. [Harry W. Havemeyer, *East on the Great South Bay: Sayville and Bayport 1860-1960* (Mattituck, NY: Amereon House, 2001), pp. 81-3.]

After her divorce from Joseph, Ida resumed using her maiden name.

[See other Stoppani entries for additional family information.]

Liberty Hall was transferred to Joseph's brother-in-law Stephen Perry Cox to keep it out of bankruptcy proceedings. In 1916, Cox sold the estate to Judge Martin Thomas Manton, who lost it in 1939 for failure to pay its property tax.

*The gardener's house and the carriage house are extant.

Strong, James Henry (1821-1900)

Occupation(s):   capitalist -   real estate

Marriage(s):   1863-1900 – Georgiana Louisa Berryman (1834-1909)

Address: Montrose Avenue, Babylon
Name of estate:
Year of construction: c. 1884
Style of architecture:
Architect(s):
Landscape architect(s):
House extant: no
Historical notes:

The house was built by James Henry Strong.

The *Social Register Summer, 1895* lists James H. and Georgiana Berryman Strong as residing in Babylon.

He was the son of James and Alletta Remsen Strong.

Georgiana Louisa Berryman Strong was the daughter of Upschur Berryman.

James Henry and Georgiana Louisa Berryman Strong's daughter Silvie married Richard Bayley Post and, subsequently, Henry Chester Hepburn, with whom she resided in Babylon. Their daughter Henrietta married Daniel B. Fearing of Newport, RI. Their son James Henry Ward Strong, who resided in the Wyoming Territory, married Marion Landon Whipple, the daughter of Napoleon Dana Whipple of Flushing. They divorced soon after their honeymoon.

Strong, Theron George (1846-1924)

Occupation(s):	attorney*
	writer - *Landmarks of a Lawyer's Lifetime*, 1914;
	Joseph H. Choate: New Englander, New Yorker, Lawyer, Ambassador, 1917
Civic Activism:	trustee, New York Presbytery;
	president, Alumni Association, University of Rochester, Rochester, NY;
	director, New York Juvenile Asylum;
	director, Legal Aid Society of New York;
	director, New York Bible Society;
	president, South Side Field Club, Bay Shore
Marriage(s):	1878-1924 – Martha Howard Prentice (d. 1949)
Address:	Penataquit Avenue, Bay Shore
Name of estate:	
Year of construction:	1890
Style of architecture:	
Architect(s):	Romeyn and Stever designed the house (for Strong)
Landscape architect(s):	
House extant: no	
Historical notes:	

The house was built by Theron George Strong.

The *Brooklyn Blue Book and Long Island Society Register, 1918* and *1921* lists Theron George and Martha Howard Prentice Strong as residing at *The Dolphins* in East Hampton. [*See* Spinzia, *Long Island's Prominent Families in the Town of East Hampton* – Strong entry.]

He was the son of Judge Theron Rudd and Mrs. Cornelia Barnes Strong of Palmyra, NY.

Martha Howard Prentice Strong was the daughter of John H. Prentice of Brooklyn.

Theron George and Martha Howard Prentice Strong's son Theron Roundell Strong married Maude Robbins and resided at *Asher House* in Southampton. [*See* Spinzia, *Long Island's Prominent Families in the Town of Southampton* – Strong entry.] Their daughter Martha, who later owned *The Dolphins*, married Harold Turner.

*Strong was the author of the 1901 anti-policy provision in the New York State Penal Code.

The house was subsequently owned by John Healey.

Dr. Raymond Peter Sullivan, Sr. residence, front facade, 2006

Sullivan, Dr. Raymond Peter, Sr. (1882-1963)

Occupation(s):	physician - chief surgeon and surgical director, St. Vincent's Hospital, NYC; consultant in surgery, Brunswick General Hospital, Amityville; Kings Park State Hospital, Kings Park; Southside Hospital, Bay Shore (now, South Shore University Hospital); St. Vincent's Hospital, Staten Island; Hospital of the Holy Family, Brooklyn; Police Department of the City of New York; chief of surgery, division of Surgeon General's Office
	writer - numerous articles on cancer therapy; "Some Observations on Hyperthyroidism," 1912; "Perforated Ulcers of the Stomach and Duodenum," 1916; "Non-tubercular Kidney Infections," 1922; "Carcinoma of Stomach in Young People," 1924, 1927; "Tumors of Carotid Body," 1927
Civic Activism:	trustee, St. Patrick's Cathedral, NYC; trustee, Manhattan College, NYC
Marriage(s):	1911-1963 – Marie E. Mc Namee (1886-1972)
Address:	60 Awixa Avenue, Bay Shore
Name of estate:	
Year of construction:	1893
Style of architecture:	Shingle
Architect(s):	Ernest George Washington Dietrich designed the house (for J. Mollenhauer)
Landscape architect(s):	
House extant: yes	
Historical notes:	

The house was built by John Mollenhauer. It was subsequently owned by Sullivan.

The *Long Island Society Register, 1929* lists Dr. Raymond P. and Mrs. Marie E. Mc Namee Sullivan [Sr.] as residing in Bay Shore.

He was the son of Dr. D. and Mrs. Eleanor Sullivan.

Marie E. Mc Namee Sullivan was the daughter of John and Mary Burnett Mc Namee of Islip. Marie's twin sister Esther died at the age of ten.

Dr. Raymond Peter and Mrs. Marie E. Mc Namee Sullivan, Sr.'s daughter Marie did not marry. Their daughter Katherine married Joseph Ansbro Meehan, the son of Michael J. and Elizabeth Higgins Meehan, Sr. of Manhattan and resided in East Hampton and at *Adare* in Southampton. [*See* Spinzia, *Long Island's Prominent Families in the Town of Southampton* and *Long Island's Prominent Families in the Town of East Hampton* – Meehan entries.] Their son William married Jean Kay Simonson, the daughter of Henry James and Helen Myers Simonson, Jr. of Southampton. Their son John married Pauline Elaine Gerli, the daughter of Paolino Gerli of Manhattan and *Longford* in Ridgefield, CT. Their son Raymond Peter Sullivan, Jr., who resided in Southampton, married Catherine McDonnell, the daughter of James Francis and Anna Murray McDonnell, Sr. of *East Wickapogue Cottage* in Southampton. [*See* Spinzia, *Long Island's Prominent Families in the Town of Southampton* – McDonnell, Simonson, and Sullivan entries.] Catherine's sister Ann married Henry Ford II, the son of Edsel Bryant Ford.

In 2011, the house, which is on the National Register of Historic Places, was for sale. The asking price was $925,000.

[For information on the Southside Hospital, see Cooper entry.]

side facade, 2011

Sutton, Effingham Brown, Jr. (1853-1913))

Occupation(s):	capitalist - proprietor, Effingham Park, West Islip
	merchant - West Islip Greenhouses (retail flower sales on estate grounds)
	shipping - member, Cromwell Steamship Line
Civic Activism:	treasurer, Flushing Institute Association
Marriage(s):	
Address:	South Country Road, West Islip
Name of estate:	*Effingham Park*
Year of construction:	
Style of architecture:	Victorian
Architect(s):	
Landscape architect(s):	
Builder:	Harry Van Weelden, greenhouses, 1895 & 1896 (for E. B. Sutton, Jr.)
House extant:	no demolished, 1903

Effingham Park

Historical notes:

In c. 1870, Effingham Brown Sutton, Sr. moved *Skookwamp*, a c. 1819 house on the site, 200 feet further away from South Country Road and remodeled it into his residence which he called *Effingham Park*. It was later owned by Effingham Brown Sutton, Jr. In the late 1890s, Effingham sold the estate to Edwin Hawley who, in 1900, built an addition onto the house. [*Brooklyn Union Times* May 12, 1900, p. 22.] In 1903, Hawley sold the house to an Islip contractor named Brown who demolished it. [*The Suffolk County News* October 30, 1903, p. 1.]

In 1903, Sutton relocated to Flushing. [*The Sun* July 17, 1913, p. 7.]

[See other Sutton entries for additional family information.]

Sutton, Effingham Brown, Sr. (1817-1891)

Occupation(s):	shipping - a founder. Sutton Line, 1849 (clipper ships between New York City and California);
	a founder, Cromwell Steamship Line
	capitalist - proprietor, Effingham Park, West Islip
financier -	director, Shoe and Leather Bank
Marriage(s):	1840-1889 – Mary Lavinia Woodruff (1822-1889)
Address:	South Country Road, West Islip
Name of estate:	*Effingham Park**
Year of construction:	
Style of architecture:	Victorian
Architect(s):	
Landscape architect(s):	
Builder:	Harry Van Weelden, greenhouses, 1895 & 1896 (for E. B. Sutton, Jr.)
House extant:	no demolished, 1903

front facade

Historical notes:

In c. 1870, Effingham Brown Sutton, Sr. moved *Skookwamp*, a c. 1819 house on the site, 200 feet further away from South Country Road and remodeled it into his residence which he called *Effingham Park*. [*Brooklyn Times Union* July 26, 1887, p. 1.]

He was the son of David and Mary Ann Brown Sutton.

Mary Lavinia Woodruff Sutton was the daughter of Philetus H. and Susan Allen Woodruff.

Effingham Brown and Mary Lavinia Woodruff Sutton, Sr.'s son Frederick married Olive Brown, whose grandfather was mayor of New York City. The Suttons' nineteen-month-old daughter Pauline died of cholera. Their son Woodruff married Frances Steele and resided in West Islip. Their son James married Julia Gorham Marshall. Their son Theodore married Carrie Fleming. Their daughter Marie did not marry. Their daughter Carolyn married Edmund Eltinge, Jr., the son of Edmund and Magdaline DuBois Deyo Eltinge, Sr.

The house was later owned by Effingham Brown Sutton, Jr. who sold the estate to Edwin Hawley in the late 1890s. Hawley built an addition onto the house in 1900. [*Brooklyn Union Times* May 12, 1900, p. 22.] In 1903, he sold the house to an Islip contractor named Brown who demolished it. [*The Suffolk County News* October 30, 1903, p. 1.]

Sutton Place in New York City was named for Effingham Brown Sutton, Sr. [*The New York Times* February 18, 1957, p. 27.]

*Some sources reference Effingham Park as the name of Sutton's estate while others refer to him as the proprietor of the Effingham Park development.

[See other Sutton entries for additional family information.]

Sutton, Frank (1875-1957)

Occupation(s):	engineer
	shipping - president, Cromwell Steamship Line
	industrialist - a founder and director, Fire Island Manufacturing Co.
Civic Activism:	a founder, treasurer, secretary, and president, Southside Hospital, Babylon (now, South Shore University Hospital)*
Marriage(s):	Jane Louise Baumann (1888-1976)
Address:	Cameron and Argyle Avenues, Babylon
Name of estate:	*The Cloister*
Year of construction:	prior to 1910
Style of architecture:	
Architect(s):	
Landscape architect(s):	
House extant: unconfirmed	
Historical notes:	

The *Social Register Summer, 1910* lists Frank Sutton as residing at *The Cloister* in Babylon.

He was the son of Woodruff and Frances Steele Sutton, Sr., who resided at *Sutton Park / Woodruff Sutton Place* in West Islip.

Jane Louise Baumann Sutton was the daughter of Dr. Louis and Mrs. Letitia Cadwell Baumann. She had previously been married to William Tyson Hayward, Jr., with whom she resided in Babylon.
 [See other Sutton entries for additional family information.]
In 1938, the house was purchased by Martin and Harry Weinstein.

*The hospital was originally situated in the Babylon residence of James Brown Cooper, Sr. It was chartered in 1913 and, in 1923, relocated to a new site in Bay Shore.
 [For information on the Southside Hospital, see Cooper entry.]

Sutton, Frank (1875-1957)

Occupation(s):	*[See previous entry.]*
Civic Activism:	*[See previous entry.]*
Marriage(s):	Jane Louise Baumann (1888-1976)
Address:	94 Martha Court, North Babylon
Name of estate:	*North East Farm*
Year of construction:	1925
Style of architecture:	Neo-Tudor
Architect(s):	Bradley Delehanty designed the house (for F. Sutton) *[unconfirmed]*
Landscape architect(s):	
House extant: yes	
Historical notes:	

The house, originally named *North East Farm*, was built by Frank Sutton.

The *Long Island Society Register, 1929* lists Frank Sutton as residing at *North East Farm* in Babylon.
 [See other Sutton entries for additional family information.]
The house has been converted into an apartment complex.

rear facade, 1924

front facade, 1991

Sutton, Harold Falconer (1877-1917)

Occupation(s):	capitalist - partner, with Robert Colgate, Robert Colgate & Co. (later, Sutton and Benjamin) (Manhattan real estate firm)
Civic Activism:	a founder and governor, Southside Hospital, Babylon (now, South Shore University Hospital)*; director, Realty League, 1913; a founder and vice-president, Babylon Taxpayers Association, 1913
Marriage(s):	1908-1917 – Mary A. Anthony (1885-1925)
Address:	Cameron Avenue, Babylon
Name of estate:	
Year of construction:	
Style of architecture:	
Architect(s):	
Landscape architect(s):	
House extant:	unconfirmed
Historical notes:	

The *Social Register Summer, 1910* lists Harold F. and Mary A. Anthony Sutton as residing in Babylon.

He was the son of Woodruff and Frances Steele Sutton, Sr. of *Sutton Park/Woodruff Sutton Place* in West Islip.

Mary A. Anthony Sutton was the daughter of Alfred Rowan Anthony of *Shadow Lawn* in Montrose, PA.

Harold Falconer and Mary A. Anthony Sutton's son Allard married Augusta Myers, the daughter of John Hays and Amy Hull Myers of White Plains, NY.

[See other Sutton entries for additional family information.]

*The hospital was originally situated in the Babylon residence of James Brown Cooper, Sr. It was chartered in 1913 and, in 1923, relocated to a new site in Bay Shore.

[For additional information on the Southside Hospital, see Cooper entry.]

Sutton, Woodruff, Jr. (1869-1929)

Occupation(s):	industrialist - president, Science Coating Co.
Civic Activism:	a founder, secretary, and director, South Side Country Club, West Islip, 1895; president, Amateur Comedy Club
Marriage(s):	M/1 – 1895-1904 – Helen Rosalie Remsen (1874-1904) M/2 – 1913-1929 – Helen L. Anthles
Address:	Argyle Avenue, Babylon
Name of estate:	*Sunnycroft*
Year of construction:	
Style of architecture:	
Architect(s):	
Landscape architect(s):	
House extant:	unconfirmed
Historical notes:	

The house was built by Woodruff Sutton, Jr.

He was the son of Woodruff and Frances Steel Woodruff, Sr. of *Sutton Park/Woodruff Sutton Place* in West Islip.

Helen Rosalie Remsen Sutton was the daughter of Phoenix and Sarah Louisa Wagstaff Remsen, Sr. of West Islip.

The *Social Register Summer, 1915* lists Woodruff and Helen L. Anthles Sutton [Jr.] as residing at *Sunnycroft* in Babylon.

[See other Sutton entries for additional family information.]

Sutton, Woodruff, Sr. (1841-1896)

Occupation(s):	shipping - president, Cromwell Steamship Line; partner, Sutton & Co.
	capitalist - speculated in Colorado real estate
Civic Activism:	a founder and director, South Shore Country Club, West Islip, 1895;
	president, Oak Beach Association, Oak Island
Marriage(s):	Frances Steele (1842-1907)
Address:	South Country Road, West Islip
Name of estate:	*Sutton Park / Woodruff Sutton Place*
Year of construction:	
Style of architecture:	
Architect(s):	
Landscape architect(s):	
House extant: no	
Historical notes:	

Woodruff Sutton, Sr. was the son of Effingham Brown and Mary Lavinia Woodruff Sutton, Sr. of *Effingham Park* in West Islip.

Frances Steele Sutton was the daughter of Dr. William F. Steele of Manhattan.

Woodruff and Frances Steele Sutton, Sr.'s son Woodruff Sutton, Jr., who resided at *Sunnycroft* in Babylon, married Helen L. Remsen, the daughter of Phoenix and Sarah Louisa Wagstaff Remsen, Sr. of West Islip, and, subsequently, Helen Anthles. Their son Frank married Jane Louise Baumann and resided at *The Cloister* in Babylon and at *North East Farm* in North Babylon. Their son Harold married Mary Anthony, the daughter of Alfred Rowan Anthony of *Shadow Lawn* in Montrose, PA. Their son David married Mary A. Anthony's sister Lilly and, subsequently, Dorothy Magie, the widow of Robert B. Whittlesey, and resided in South Orange, NJ. Their son William married Muriel Winfred. Their son Richard, who resided in Smithtown, married Sarah Lawrence Smith, the daughter of Ethelbert Marshall and Emily L. Lawrence Smith of Smithtown. The Smiths were descendants of the founder of Smithtown Richard "Bull" Smith.

*The estate, which was located in Effingham Park, was known as *Sutton Park* and *Woodruff Sutton Place*. [*The New York Times* June 9, 1896, p. 5; *The Brooklyn Daily Eagle* October 24, 1897, p. 10; and *South Side Signal* June 13, 1896, p. 3.]

[See other Sutton entries for additional family information.]

The house was later owned by H. Muir who, in 1897, sold it to Edwin Hawley. [*The Brooklyn Daily Eagle* October 24, 1987, p. 10.]

Suydam, Charles (1818-1882)

Occupation(s):	merchant
Marriage(s):	1849-1882 – Ann White Schermerhorn (1818-1886)
Address:	*[unable to determine street address]*, Bayport
Name of estate:	
Year of construction:	
Style of architecture:	
Architect(s):	
Landscape architect(s):	
House extant: unconfirmed	
Historical notes:	

Charles Suydam was the son of Ferdinand and Eliza Underhill Suydam.

Ann White Schermerhorn Suydam was the daughter of Abraham and Helen Van Courtlandt White Schermerhorn of Manhattan. Her sister Catherine married Benjamin Sumner Welles, Sr. and resided in Islip. Her sister Caroline ["Mystic Rose"], who married William Blackhouse Astor, was the undisputed arbiter of society's elite "Four Hundred." Benjamin and Catherine Schermerhorn Welles, Sr. were on the elite "Four Hundred" list, that Ward McAllister compiled for Caroline Astor but Charles and Ann Schermerhorn Suydam were omitted.

Charles and Ann White Schermerhorn Suydam's daughter Helen married Robert Fulton Cutting and resided in Great River. Their son Walter married Jane Meiser Suydam, the daughter of John R. and Anna Middleton Lawrence Suydam, Sr. of Bayport and resided at *Manowtasquott Lodge* in Blue Point. In 1857, their son Augustus died at age of two.

Suydam, John Richard, Jr. (1858-1928)

Occupation(s): engineer
Civic Activism: governor, Penataquit Corinthian Yacht Club

Marriage(s): 1883-1927 – Harriet Penrose Cochran (1861-1927)

Address: Suydam Lane, Bayport
Name of estate: *Edgewater*
Year of construction: c. 1855
Style of architecture: Italianate
Architect(s):
Landscape architect(s):
House extant: no; demolished in 1987
Historical notes:

John Richard Suydam, Jr. inherited the house from his parents and continued to call it *Edgewater*.

Harriet Penrose Cochran Suydam was the daughter of William and Eliza Penrose Cochran of Philadelphia, PA.

John Richard and Harriet Penrose Cochran Suydam, Jr.'s son John Richard Suydam III married Margaret Thayer, the daughter of William Greenough Thayer of Southborough, MA. Their daughter Lisa married Paul Renshaw and resided in Manhattan.

[See other Suydam entries for additional family information.]

In 1920, the house was purchased from John Richard Suydam, Jr. by Herbert and Grace Whitney Seaman, who immediately sold it to Julius Liebmann.

The estate was later owned by Liebmann's son James, who had changed his surname to Leland.

The house was then owned by James Leland's daughter Anne.

In 1987, Anne sold it to Ira Rubenstein, who demolished the house the same year and built a new house on the site, which he called *Cheap John's Estate*.

Edgewater

Suydam, John Richard, Sr. (1807-1882)

Occupation(s): merchant - partner, Suydam & York (dry goods)

Marriage(s): 1854-1870 – Ann Middleton Lawrence (1823-1870)

Address: Suydam Lane, Bayport
Name of estate: *Edgewater*
Year of construction: c. 1855
Style of architecture: Italianate
Architect(s):
Landscape architect(s):
House extant: no; demolished in 1987
Historical notes:

John Richard Suydam, Sr. purchased the house in 1854 as a wedding present for his wife. They called it *Edgewater*. He was the son of John and Jane Mesier Suydam.

Ann Middleton Lawrence Suydam was the daughter of John L. and Sarah Augusta Smith Lawrence of Mastic.

[See other Suydam entries for additional family information.]

John Richard and Ann Middleton Lawrence Suydam, Sr.'s daughter Jane married her half, second cousin Walter L. Suydam. Their son John Richard Suydam, Jr. inherited the estate and continued to call it *Edgewater*.

[See previous entry for history of estate.]

John Richard Suydam, Sr. estate Edgewater, front facade

Swan, Alden Smith (1838-1917)

Occupation(s):	politician - Brooklyn alderman; tax collector, Brooklyn
	capitalist - trustee, Brooklyn Bridge; director, Salisbury and Albert Railroad
	financier - director, Market and Fulton National Bank
	merchant - director, Frederick Loeser & Co., Brooklyn
	industrialist - a founder and partner, Swan and Finch, 1892 (oil and grease firm); a founder, Alden S. Swan and Co. (oil and grease firm); president, Rubber Goods Manufacturing Co.; president, Menhaden Oil and Guano Co.; president Trilon Oil and Fertilizer Co.; president, Ulster Paint Works
Civic Activism:	a founder, Great South Bay Yacht Club
Marriage(s):	1863-1917 – Mary Althea Farwell (1841-1921)
Address:	Ocean Avenue, Islip
Name of estate:	*Orowoc*
Year of construction:	1887
Style of architecture:	Queen Anne
Architect(s):	
Landscape architect(s):	
House extant: unconfirmed	
Historical notes:	

The house, originally named *Orowoc*, was built by Alden Smith Swan. [*The Brooklyn Daily Eagle* September 10, 1886, p. 4.] He was the son of John H. and Mary Winchester Swan.

Mary Althea Farwell Swan was the daughter of James E. Farwell.

Alden Smith and Mary Althea Farwell Swan's daughter Florence married Walter Gibb and resided at *Old Orchard* in Glen Cove. [*See* Spinzia, *Long Island's Prominent North Shore Families, vol. I*– Gibb entry.]

Swirbul, Leon A. (1898-1960)

Occupation(s):	industrialist - a founder, general manager, and president, Grumman Aircraft Engineering Corp., Bethpage (now, Northrop–Grumman)*
	capitalist - director, Republic Pictures Corp.
Civic Activism:	president, Long Island Hospital Regional Planning Council;
	president, Long Island Industrial Hospital Commission;
	honorary vice-chairman, American Cancer Society;
	trustee, Nassau Hospital (now, Winthrop University Hospital), Mineola;
	member, New York State Racing Commission, 1949-1955;
	co-founder, Long Island Fund;
	chairman of board, Waldemar Clinic of Cancer Research Foundation, Port Washington;
	member, Greater Cornell Council;
	member, Aircraft Industry Advisory Committee of the Munitions Board;
	trustee, Adelphi College, Garden City, 1958-1960 (now, Adelphi University)**;
	trustee, Hofstra University, Hempstead
Marriage(s):	M/1 – div. – Josephine E. McGraw (d. 1976)
	M/2 – Estelle Stephens
Address:	Plymouth Avenue, Brightwaters

Name of estate:
Year of construction:
Style of architecture:
Architect(s):
Landscape architect(s):
House extant: unconfirmed
Historical notes:

Leon A. Swirbul was the son of Frederick and Lena Dannenberg Swirbul of Brooklyn and Sag Harbor.

Josephine E. McGraw Swirbul subsequently married Thomas Woodward MacLeod, Sr. and resided in Bay Shore.

Leon A. and Josephine E. McGraw Swirbul's son William married Thora Elizabeth Sullivan, the daughter of Marcus Henry Lewis Sullivan of Brightwaters. Their son Philip married Serene Dorothy Grey, the daughter of Mason W. Grey of Erie, PA, and resided in Bay Shore.

*In 1946, Swirbul was awarded the Medal of Merit by President Harry S Truman for Grumman's production and design excellence during World War II.

**The library at Adelphi University is named in honor of Swirbul.

The Swirbuls subsequently relocated to Brookville.

Tappin, Charles L. (1854-1941)

Occupation(s):	capitalist - partner, Borne Scrymser Co., NYC (later merged into Standard Oil)
Civic Activism:	president and treasurer, South Shore Country Club, West Islip
Marriage(s):	1914-1927 – Flora Cordelia Roberts (d. 1927)
Address:	South Country Road, Babylon
Name of estate:	*Twin Oaks*
Year of construction:	1893
Style of architecture:	Shingle
Architect(s):	Isaac Henry Green II designed the house (for C. L. Tappin)
Landscape architect(s):	
Builder:	Robert Nunns

House extant: no; destroyed by fire, 1950
Historical notes:

front facade, 1924

The house, originally named *Twin Oaks*, was built by Charles L. Tappin.

The *Social Register New York, 1916* lists Charles L. and Flora C. Roberts Tappin as residing at *Twin Oaks* in Babylon.

He was the son of John J. and Jane Lindsley Tappin of Manhattan.

Flora Cordelia Roberts Tappin was the daughter of Charles C. and Isabella Jacquette Murray Roberts of Philadelphia, PA. Flora had previously been married to Clarence Marshall Busch and ____ Lee.

[See following entry for additional family information.]

Tappin, John Crane (1851-1922)

Occupation(s):	financier - member, Stokes and Hedges Co. (stock brokerage firm); partner, Tappin and Stokes (stock brokerage firm); director, Manhattan Life Insurance Co.
Marriage(s):	1876-1922 – Helen Zaibee Spear (1857-1926)
Address:	St. Mark's Lane, Islip
Name of estate:	
Year of construction:	1888
Style of architecture:	Shingle with Dutch Revival Elements
Architect(s):	Isaac Henry Green II designed the house (for J. C. Tappin)
Landscape architect(s):	
House extant: no	
Historical notes:	

front facade

The house was built by John Crane Tappin.
He was the son of John J. and Jane Lindsley Tappin.
Helen Zaibee Spear Tappin was the daughter of Charles and Harriot Tryon Spear.
John Crane and Helen Zaibee Spear Tappin's son Lindsley, who resided at *Wayside* in Lawrence, married Elsie Huntington, the daughter of Charles R. Huntington. Elsie had previously been married to Leopold Francke.
[See previous entry for additional family information.]

Taylor, George Campbell (1835-1907)

Occupation(s):	diplomat - member, United States Embassy in Great Britain (Lincoln administration)
Marriage(s):	common-law-wife – Betsy Head (c. 1847-1907)
Address:	Heckscher Parkway, East Islip
Name of estate:	*Deer Range Farm*
Year of construction:	c. 1850s
Style of architecture:	Eclectic
Architect(s):	
Landscape architect(s):	
Builder:	Jabez Ephraim Van Orden
House extant: no; demolished in 1909*	
Historical notes:	

The house, originally named *Deer Range Farm*, was built by Edwin Augustus Johnson, Sr. on his 400-acre estate.
In 1872, the estate was purchased by Sarah Ives Plumb. Upon her death, it was inherited by her husband James Neale Plumb and, subsequently, by their son James Ives Plumb. The Plumbs continued to call the estate *Deer Range Farm*. Over the years the estate acreage was increased to 700 acres by the Plumbs.
In 1884, alterations were made to the house by James Neale Plumb.
In 1903, his son James Ives Plumb sold the estate to Taylor.
George Campbell Taylor was the son of Moses and Catharine A. Wilson Taylor of Manhattan from whom he had inherited an income from a $20 million trust his father had established. [*The New York Times* September 18, 1907, p. 9.] George's sister Albertina married Percy Rivington Pyne, Sr. and resided in Manhattan. His sister Catharine married Robert C. Winthrop and resided in Lenox, MA. His sister Mary married George Lewis, Jr. and resided in Manhattan. His brother Henry, who resided in Newport, RI, married ____ Fearing, the daughter of Daniel B. Fearing, and, later, Josephine Whitney Johnson, the daughter of Hezron A. Johnson of Manhattan.
Taylor met Betsy Head in England and engaged her as his housekeeper and private secretary. Betsy's eighteen-year-old daughter Lena married Taylor's gardener William Bodley, who was later employed as a foreman on William Kissam Vanderbilt, Jr.'s estate *Deepdale* in Lake Success. [*See* Spinzia, *Long Island's Prominent North Shore Families, vol. II* – Vanderbilt entry.] The Taylors became despondent over Lena's marriage and turned to alcohol. According to local lore, Taylor's alcoholism became so acute that he was unable to climb the stairs to his second-floor bedroom and resorted to drinking himself into a stupor in a log cabin on the estate. George and Betsey died in 1907 within three months of each other but not before disinheriting Lena.
*The estate was inherited by the Taylor / Pyne family corporation which, in 1909, demolished the house. The estate property remained in the Taylor / Pyne family corporation until 1924 when it was confiscated by Robert Moses and became part of Heckscher State Park. [Harry W. Havemeyer, *Along the Great South Bay From Oakdale to Babylon: The Story of a Summer Spa 1840 to 1940* (Mattituck, NY: Amereon House, 1996), p. 135.]

*George Campbell Taylor estate,
Deer Range Farm*

Taylor, George Campbell (1835-1907)

Occupation(s):	diplomat - member, United States Embassy in Great Britain (Lincoln administration)
Marriage(s):	common-law-wife – Betsy Head (c. 1847-1907)
Address:	Heckscher Parkway, East Islip
Name of estate:	
Year of construction:	1885
Style of architecture:	
Architect(s):	
Landscape architect(s):	
Builder:	Jabez Ephraim Van Orden
House extant:	no; demolished in 1933*
Historical notes:	

The house and approximately thirty service buildings were built by George Campbell Taylor.
[See previous entry for family information.]

In 1903, Taylor purchased the adjacent *Deer Range Farm* of James Ives Plumb, thus increasing his estate holdings to two main residences on approximately 1,500 acres. Taylor alternately resided at this house and the former Plumb house. [*Suffolk County News* June 5, 1903, p. 1.]

*The original Taylor house was demolished by Robert Moses' Long Island State Park Commission. The estate property is now part of Heckscher State Park. August Heckscher, Sr. gave Moses the money to acquire the land, hence the name of the East Islip park and parkway. [*See* Spinzia, *Long Island's Prominent North Shore Families*, vol. I – Heckscher entries.]

original 1885 house, front facade

front facade, c. 1924, after alterations

Tcherepnin, Alexander (1899-1977)

Occupation(s):	entertainers and associated professions - concert pianist; composer - *Ol, Ol*, 1934 (opera); Piano Sonata in A Minor; Ten Bagatelles; Arabesques; Scherzo in C Minor for Piano; Nocturne in G Sharp for Piano; Toccata in D Major for Piano
Marriage(s):	1926 – Louisine A. Peters (1886-1952)
Address:	South Bay Avenue, Islip
Name of estate:	*Wereholme*
Year of construction:	c. 1917
Style of architecture:	Neo-French Manor
Architect(s):	Grosvenor Atterbury designed the house (for H. H. Weekes)
Landscape architect(s):	
House extant:	yes
Historical notes:	

The house, originally named *Wereholme*, was built by Harold Hathaway Weekes.

His wife Louisine subsequently married Tcherepnin, with whom she continued to reside at *Wereholme*.

She was the daughter of Samuel Twyford and Adaline Mapes Elder Peters, Jr. of *Windholme Farm* in Islip. Her brother Harry Twyford Peters, Sr., who married Natalie Wells and resided at *Nearholme* in Islip, inherited *Windholme Farm*.

Alexander Tcherepnin was the son of the Russian composer Nikolai Tcherepnin.

Harold Hathaway and Louisine A. Peters Weekes' daughter Adaline, who married Charles B. Scully, inherited *Wereholme* and resided at the estate. Adaline subsequently married Count Philip Orssich of Denkendorf bei Stuttgart, Germany.

In 1984, Mrs. Scully, who had divorced the count and reverted to the surname Scully, bequeathed the house to the National Audubon Society.

In 2004, the estate was purchased by Suffolk County and is now the county's Greenways Educational and Interpretive Center.

Wereholme

Tenney, Charles Henry, Sr. (1911-1994)

Occupation(s): attorney - partner, Breed, Abbott, and Morgan;
judge, United States Federal Court, Southern District, 1964-1994
politician - deputy mayor, New York City, 1961-1964 (Robert F. Wagner administration)
intelligence agent - Naval intelligence during World War II

Marriage(s): 1938-1994 – Joan Penfold Lusk (d. 1996)

Address: Dover Court, Bay Shore
Name of estate:
Year of construction: 1903
Style of architecture: Shingle
Architect(s):
Landscape architect(s):
House extant: yes
Historical notes:

front facade, 2005

The house, originally named *Cedarholme*, was built by Lewis Mills Gibb, Sr. It was later owned by his son Lewis Mills Gibb, Jr., who continued to call it *Cedarholme*. It was subsequently owned by Tenney.

He was the son of Daniel Gleason and Marguerite Sedgwick Smith Tenney, Sr., who resided on Wheatley Road in Brookville. [*See* Spinzia, *Long Island's Prominent North Shore Families, vol. II* – Tenney entry.] Charles' brother Daniel Gleason Tenney, Jr. married Constance Lippincott Franchot, the daughter of Douglas Warner Franchot of Baltimore, MD. His sister Frances, who married G. Morgan Brown, Sr., and, subsequently, Laurent Oppenheim, Jr., resided in Manhattan.

Joan Penfold Lusk Tenney was the daughter of The Reverend William B. Lusk, Sr. of Ridgefield, CT.

Charles Henry and Joan Penfold Lusk Tenney, Sr.'s son Charles Henry Tenney, Jr. resided in Elizabethtown, NY. Their daughters Anne and Joan did not marry. Their daughter Marguerite married Talton R. Embry.

By 1950 the Tenneys had relocated to *Cedarsweep* at 65 Saxon Avenue, Bay Shore.

Terry, William Hazard (1827-1904)

Occupation(s):
Civic Activism: trustee, Long Island Chautauqua Assembly Association, Point O'Woods

Marriage(s): 1857-1904 – Mary Catherine Harned

Address: Foster Avenue, Sayville*
Name of estate:
Year of construction: 1886
Style of architecture: Queen Anne
Architect(s): Isaac Henry Green II designed the house (for Terry)

House extant: yes
Historical notes:

The house was built by William Hazard Terry.

He was the son of Joseph Hazard and Mary Wood Terry of Manhattan.

*The house was moved from Foster Avenue to Colton Avenue and Elm Street.

sketch of front facade, 1886

Thorn, Edward Floyd–Jones, Sr. (1890-1974)

Occupation(s): engineer - Bell Laboratories, NYC
Civic Activism: trustee, Amityville Public School District

Marriage(s): c. 1917-1969 – Marjorie Peirce (1892-1969)

Address: 106 Ocean Avenue, Amityville
Name of estate:
Year of construction:
Style of architecture: Long Island farmhouse
Architect(s):
Landscape architect(s):
House extant: yes
Historical notes:

front facade, 2006

The *Long Island Society Register, 1929* lists Edward F. J. and Marjorie Peirce Thorn [Sr.] as residing at 106 Ocean Avenue, Amityville.

He was the son of Conde Raguet and Louise Akerly Floyd–Jones Thorn of *Tryon Lodge* in Massapequa.

Edward Floyd–Jones and Marjorie Peirce Thorn, Sr.'s son William married Barbara Norton, the daughter of Algernon Sidney Norton of Manhattan. Their daughter Louisa married Paul Hyde Bonner, Jr., the son of Paul Hyde and Lilly Marguerite Stehli Bonner, Sr., who resided on Locust Valley–Bayville Road, Lattingtown. [*See* Spinzia, *Long Island's Prominent North Shore Families, vol. I* – Bonner entry.]

Thorne, Edwin, II (1861-1935)

Occupation(s): capitalist - director, New York Dock Co.
financier - trustee, Mutual Life Insurance Co.;
director, North American Trust Co.;
trustee, Central Hanover Bank & Trust Co.;
trustee, Bank of America
industrialist - director, Granby Consolidated Copper Co.;
director, Federal Terra Cotta Co.

Civic Activism: vice-president, New York Society for the Prevention of Cruelty to Children;
a founder and trustee, New York Zoological Society;
trustee, Northfield Schools;
a founder, Oak Island Clay Pigeon Club, 1899

Marriage(s): 1886-1931 – Phebe Ketchum (1865-1931)

Address: 75 Oak Neck Road, West Islip
Name of estate: *Okonok*
Year of construction: 1890
Style of architecture: Shingle
Architect(s):
Landscape architect(s):
House extant: yes
Historical notes:

front facade, 2006

The house, originally named *Okonok*, was built by Edwin Thorne II.

The *Long Island Society Register, 1929* lists Edwin and Phebe Ketchum Thorne [II] as residing at *Okonok* in Babylon [West Islip].

He was the son of Samuel and Phebe Smith Van Schoonhoven Thorne of Millbrook, NY.

Phebe Ketchum Thorne was the daughter of Landon and Ann Augusta Burritt Ketchum of Saugatuck, CT.

Edwin and Phebe Ketchum Thorne II's son Landon married Julia Atterbury Loomis, the daughter of Henry Patterson Loomis, and resided at *Thorneham* in West Bay Shore. Their son Francis, who married Evelyn Brown, and, subsequently, Hildegarde Kobbe, resided in East Islip. Their daughter Anna married Robert Titus and resided in West Islip. Their daughter Phebe, who married Harry Kearsarge Knapp II, the son of Harry Kearsarge and Caroline Burr Knapp, Sr., of *Brookwood* in East Islip, resided at *Creekside* in East Islip. Phebe later married John Tucker, the son of Russell Evans and Clara deRussy Tucker.

[See other Thorne entries for additional family information.]

The house was later called *Gracemore*.

Thorne, Edwin, III (1914-2002)

Occupation(s):	financier - vice-president, First National Bank of New York (now, Citibank);
	director, Vigilant Insurance Co.;
	director, Putnam Trust Co., Greenwich, CT;
	director, Federated Insurance Co.;
	director, First Boston Corp. (investment banking firm);
	chairman, Advanced Investors Corp. (closed-end investment firm)
	capitalist - director, Consumers Power Co.;
	director, Michigan Gas Storage Co.
Civic Activism:	trustee, American Museum of Natural History, NYC;
	trustee, Community Service Society of New York
Marriage(s):	1938-1986 – Helen Grand (1916-1986)
Address:	108 East Bayberry Road, Islip
Name of estate:	
Year of construction:	1899-1900
Style of architecture:	Moorish
Architect(s):	Grosvenor Atterbury designed the house (for H. O. Havemeyer)*
Landscape architect(s):	Nathan F. Barrett (for H. O. Havemeyer)**
Builder:	*[See Jabez Ephraim Van Orden entry.]*
House extant: yes	
Historical notes:	

The house was built by Henry Osborne Havemeyer as part of his "Modern Venice" development.

Edwin Thorne III was the son of Landon Ketchum and Julia Atterbury Loomis Thorne, Sr., who resided at *Thorneham* in West Bay Shore.

Helen Grand Thorne was the daughter of Gordon and Emma Dill Grand, Sr. of Millbrook, NY, and Greenwich, CT. Her brother Gordon Grand, Jr. married Ruth Young, the daughter of William Henry Young of Tuxedo Park, NY, and resided in Greenwich, CT.

Edwin and Helen Grand Thorne III's son Gordon married Lee Kellogg Ammidon, the daughter of Hoyt and Elizabeth Callaway Ammidon, Sr. of Glen Head. Their son Peter married Katherine Gross, the daughter of Sidney and Zenith Gross of New York. Their son Brinkley married Mary Ann Livingston Delafield Cox, the daughter of Howard Ellis and Ann Crane Delafield Finch Cox, Sr. of *Sunswyck Manor* in Westhampton Beach. [*See* Spinzia, *Long Island's Prominent Families in the Town of Southampton* – Cox entry.] Their son Edwin Thorne, Jr. [IV] married Laura Castleman Gary, the daughter of Theodore Sauvinet and Laura Brown Gary of Madeline Island, WI.

*The sales brochure for "Modern Venice" states that the Moorish-style architecture was suggested by Louis Comfort Tiffany.

**The sales brochure also states that "Modern Venice" would be devoid of trees and vegetation and that Nathan F. Barrett was the landscape architect.

The house was subsequently owned by Carleton Bell Howell.

front facade, 2006

Thorne, Francis Burritt, Jr. (1922-2017)

Occupation(s):	financier - stockbroker
	composer* - composed over one hundred pieces, including symphonies, concerti, string quartets, and choral music
Civic Activism:	a founder, president, and chairman of board, American Composers' Orchestra;
	president and treasurer, Thorne Music Fund;
	executive director, Naumburg Foundation;
	executive director, Music Theatre Group;
	executive director, American Composers Alliance;
	director, Composers Recording Inc.;
	director, American Music Center;
	director, Virgil Thomson Foundation
Marriage(s):	1942-2010 – Ann Chauncey Cobb (1922-2010)
	- artist
Address:	19 Lawrence Lane, Bay Shore
Name of estate:	
Year of construction:	
Style of architecture:	Modified Neo-Tudor
Architect(s):	
Landscape architect(s):	
House extant: yes	
Historical notes:	

The *Social Register, 1954* lists Francis B. and Ann C. Cobb Thorne [Jr.] as residing at 19 Lawrence Lane in Bay Shore. He was the son of Francis Burritt and Hildegarde Kobbe Thorne, Sr. of *Brookwood* in East Islip.

*Thorne studied music with Paul Hindemith at Yale University.

Ann Chauncey Cobb Thorne was the daughter of Boughton and Edith McKeever Cobb of Hewlett Bay Park. [*See* Spinzia, *Long Island's Prominent Families in the Town of Hempstead* – Cobb entry.]

Francis Burritt and Ann Chauncey Cobb Thorne, Jr.'s daughter Ann married William Freeman Niles, the son of Nicholas Niles of Menham, NJ. Their daughter Wendy married Willing H. Forsyth, Jr. of Salisbury, CT. Their daughter Candace married Anthony M. Canton, the son of Jess Canton of Poughquag, NY.

front facade, 2006

Thorne, Francis Burritt, Sr. (1892-1950)

Occupation(s):	financier - partner, Taylor and Thorne (stock brokerage firm); partner, Lindley and Co. (stock brokerage firm); partner, F. B. Thorne and Co. (stock brokerage firm) industrialist - chairman of board, North Central Texas Oil Co.
Civic Activism:	director, Society for the Prevention of Cruelty to Children, NYC
Marriage(s):	M/1 – 1915-1917 – Evelyn Brown (1894-1917) M/2 – 1920-1950 – Hildegarde Kobbe (1889-1959)
Address:	South Country Road, East Islip
Name of estate:	*Brookwood**
Year of construction:	1902
Style of architecture:	Georgian Revival
Architect(s):	
Landscape architect(s):	
House extant: yes	
Historical notes:	

The house, originally named *Brookwood*, was built by Harry Kearsarge Knapp, Sr. It was later owned by his son Theodore Jackson Knapp, who sold the estate to Thorne in 1929.

Francis Burritt Thorne, Sr. was the son of Edwin and Phebe Ketchum Thorne II of *Okonok* in West Islip.

Evelyn Brown Thorne was the daughter of James and Adele Quartley Brown of *Villa Vera* in Locust Valley. [*See* Spinzia, *Long Island's Prominent North Shore Families, vol. I* – Brown entry.] Evelyn's sister Adele married Robert Abercrombie Lovett, the son of Robert Scott and Lavinia Chilton Abercrombie Lovett of *Woodfold* in Lattingtown, and resided at *Green Arbors* in Lattingtown. Her sister Angelica married Peter Cooper Bryce, the son of Lloyd Stephens and Edith Cooper Bryce of *Bryce House* in Roslyn Harbor, and resided at *Villa Vera* in Locust Valley. [*See* Spinzia, *Long Island's Prominent North Shore Families, vol. I* – Bryce and Lovett entries.]

Hildegarde Kobbe Thorne was the daughter of Gustav and Carolyn Wheeler Kobbe, who resided in Babylon. She had previously been married to Joseph Hutchinson Stevenson. Joseph Hutchinson and Hildegarde Kobbe Stevenson's daughter Carol married Joseph Sears Lovering, Jr. of Islip. Hildegarde's sister Virginia married Gerald Vanderbilt Hollins, Sr. and resided at *The Hawks* in East Islip. Virginia subsequently married Henry Morgan, with whom she resided in East Islip. Hildegarde's sister Carol married Robert Woodward Morgan and also resided in East Islip. Carol subsequently married George Palen Snow of Syosset. [*See* Spinzia, *Long Island's Prominent North Shore Families, vol. II* – Snow entry.] Their sister Beatrice married Raymond E. Little.

Francis Burritt and Hildegarde Kobbe Thorne, Sr.'s son Francis Burritt Thorne, Jr. married Ann C. Cobb, the daughter of Boughton Cobb of Manhattan, and resided in Bay Shore. Their daughter Phebe married Joseph Francis Dempsey, Jr. of Great River and resided in Islip. Their daughter Julia married Dennis McCarty. Their son Oakleigh Thorne II, who resided at *Valley Ranch* in Cody, WY, married Peggy N. Schroll and, subsequently, Lisa L. Bellows.

[See other Thorne entries for additional family information.]

*According to Francis Burritt Thorne, Jr., the name of his parents' estate was *Brookwood* and that it was renamed *Brookwood Hall* by a subsequent owner.

In 1942, the house was owned by the Orphan Asylum Society of Brooklyn.

In 1965, the Society sold it to Alfred and Fred Wimmer, who sold the house to the Town of Islip in 1967. It is currently the site of The Islip Art Museum, a leading exhibit space for contemporary art.

The Empire State Carousel, now located in Binghamton, NY, was built in the carriage house of *Brookwood*.

front facade, 1992

Thorne, Landon Ketchum, Jr. (1913-1980)

Occupation(s):	publisher - *The Rome Daily American*, Rome, Italy
	financier - vice-president, Bankers Trust Co.;
	director, United Corp. (closed-ended investment firm);
	managing director, Bankers International Corp.;
	managing director, Bankers International Financing Co, Inc.
	industrialist - president, Vorac Co. (chemical coating manufacturer)
	diplomat - United States Economic Minister, Office of Foreign Operations, to Italy;
	United States Economic Minister, Office of Foreign Operations, to Belgium
Civic Activism:	chairman of board, American University, Cairo, Egypt;
	chairman of board, YMCA–YWCA Camping Services of Greater New York;
	trustee, New York Zoological Society;
	trustee, Pierpont Morgan Library, NYC;
	trustee, American Academy, Rome, Italy;
	assistant treasurer, New York Young Republican Club
Marriage(s):	M/1 – 1936-div.1941 – Charlotte Elgitha Veronica Boswell Elliot (1913-1981)
	M/2 – 1942 – Alice Hoadley Barry
	M/3 – 1969-1980 – Miriam A. Rose (1907-2003)
Address:	Admiral's Drive East, West Bay Shore
Name of estate:	*The Lodge*
Year of construction:	
Style of architecture:	Ranch
Architect(s):	
Landscape architect(s):	
House extant:	yes
Historical notes:	

living room

    Landon Ketchum Thorne, Jr. was the son of Landon Ketchum and Julia Atterbury Loomis Thorne, Sr., who resided at *Thorneham* in West Bay Shore. Before moving to West Bay Shore, he had resided on Split Rock Road in Syosset and on Lake Avenue in Greenwich, CT.
    Charlotte Elgitha Veronica Boswell Elliot Thorne was the daughter of Sir Gilbert and Lady Flournoy Hopkins Elliot of *Wolfelee* in Rorburghshire, Scotland, and a descendant of Samuel Johnson's biographer James Boswell.
    Alice Hoadley Barry Thorne was the daughter of David Sheldon and Alice Hoadley Smith Barry of Washington, DC. Her sister Frances married B. Gordon Dickey, the son of Robert B. Dickey of Tuxedo, NY.
    Landon Ketchum and Alice Hoadley Barry Thorne, Jr.'s daughter Julia married John Forbes Kerry at the Thorne's ancestral home *Thorneham* in West Bay Shore. Kerry was the United States Senator from Massachusetts and unsuccessful Democratic candidate for the presidency of the United States in 2004. Julia subsequently married Richard J. Charlesworth, with whom she resided in Bozeman, MT, until her death in 2006. The Thornes' son Landon Ketchum Thorne III married Sarah Ashton Nuese, the daughter of Robert E. Nuese of *Indian Lane Farm* in Cornwall, CT. Their son David married Rose O'Neil Geer, the daughter of Garrow Throop Geer of Manhattan.
    The *Social Register, Summer 1974* lists Landon K. and Miriam A. Rose Thorne [Jr.] as residing at *The Lodge* on South Country Road in Bay Shore [Admiral's Drive East, West Bay Shore].
    Miriam A. Rose Thorne had previously been married to Fulton Irving Cahners, the son of James Albert and Katherine Louise Epstein Cahners. Miriam subsequently married the Deputy Secretary of Defense Roswell Leavitt Gilpatric.

west facade

Thorne, Landon Ketchum, Sr. (1888-1964)

Occupation(s):	financier -	president and partner, with brother-in-law Alfred Lee Loomis, Sr., Bonbright and Co. (investment banking firm)*;
		president, Thorne, Loomis & Co. (holding company);
		president, American Superpower Corp. (investment banking firm);
		trustee, United Corp. (closed-ended investment firm)**;
		director, Bankers Trust Co.;
		director, First National Bank of New York (now, Citibank);
		director, Federal Insurance Co.;
		director, Vigilant Insurance Co.
	capitalist -	director, Commonwealth & Southern Corp.;
		director, New York United Corp.;
		director, Niagara Hudson Power Corp.;
		director, Public Service Corporation of New Jersey;
		director, Southern Pacific Co.
	politician -	commissioner, Long Island State Parks Commission
Civic Activism:		suffragist, member, Babylon Suffrage Club, 1914;
		trustee, New York Zoological Society;
		governor, New York Hospital, Inc.;
		member, executive committee, New York World Fair Corp., 1963-1964;
		founder, with Alfred L Loomis II, Thorne–Loomis Foundation (which became Thorne Foundation)
Marriage(s):		1911-1964 – Julia Atterbury Loomis (1890-1974)
Address:		South Country Road, West Bay Shore
Name of estate:		*Thorneham*
Year of construction:		1928
Style of architecture:		Neo-Tudor
Architect(s):		William F. Dominick designed the house and boat landing (for L. K. Thorne, Sr.)
Landscape architect(s):		Ferruccio Vitale (for L. K. Thorne, Sr.)
		Umberto Innocenti designed the gardens (for L. K. Thorne, Sr.)

House extant: no; demolished in 1976
Historical notes:

The house, originally named *Thorneham*, was built by Landon Ketchum Thorne, Sr.
He was the son of Edwin and Phebe Ketchum Thorne II of *Okonok* in West Islip.
Julia Atterbury Loomis Thorne was the daughter of Henry Patterson and Julie Josephine Stimson Loomis of Tuxedo Park, NY. Her brother Alfred, who resided in Tuxedo Park and in East Hampton, married Elizabeth Ellen Farnsworth and, later, Manette Seeldrayers. Alfred and Julia's first cousin Henry Lewis Stimson, the noted statesman, resided at *Highold* in West Hills. [*See* Spinzia, *Long Island's Prominent Families in the Town of East Hampton* – Loomis entry – and *Long Island's Prominent North Shore Families, vol. II* – Stimson entry.]

Landon Ketchum and Julia Atterbury Loomis Thorne, Sr.'s son Landon Ketchum Thorne, Jr., who resided at *The Lodge* in West Bay Shore, married Charlotte Elgitha Veronica Boswell Elliot, Alice Hoadley Barry, and Miriam A. Rose. Their son Edwin Thorne III married Helen Grand and resided in Islip prior to relocating to Greenwich, CT.

*Bonbright and Co. is credited with helping shape the country's electrical utility industry. It was known as one of Wall Street's "Big Six" investment banks.

**United Corporation controlled twenty-one percent of the country's electrical production.

front facade

Landon Ketchum Thorne, Sr. estate, *Thorneham*

Thorneham

sitting room

side facade, c 1929

garden

side facade

Thurber, Frederick Charles (1873-1943)

Occupation(s): capitalist - owner, Bellport Hotel, Bellport;
    owner, Five Mile Look Hotel, Blue Point;
    owner, Central Hotel, Patchogue

Civic Activism: commodore, Patchogue Scooter Club, 1910;
a founder and director, The Fur, Fins, and Feather Club, Patchogue, 1904 (preservation of wildlife)

Marriage(s): 1897-1943 – Carrie Burkhardt (1877-1945)

Address: Penataquit Avenue, Bay Shore
Name of estate:
Year of construction:
Style of architecture: Queen Anne
Architect(s): Henry G. Hardenburg designed the house (for Thurber)
Landscape architect(s):
House extant: no
Historical notes:

  The house was built by Frederick Charles Thurber. He was the son of Daniel Jarvis and Phebe A. Wood Thurber.
  Carrie Burkhart Thurber was from Sag Harbor.
  The house was subsequently owned by Harmanus Barkulo Hubbard, who called it *Oakhurst*.

front facade, c. 1897

Timmermann, Henry Gerhard (d. 1925)

Occupation(s): financier - partner, Timmermann, Moore, and Schuley (stock brokerage firm)

Marriage(s): Kate Fry (d. 1933)

Address: Ocean Avenue, Islip
Name of estate: *Breeze Lawn*
Year of construction: c. 1889
Style of architecture: Colonial Revival with Shingle elements
Architect(s):
Landscape architect(s):
House extant: no
Historical notes:

  The house was built by Leander Waterbury. In 1890, it was purchased by Howard Gibb, Sr. [*Brooklyn Times Union* May 10, 1890, p. 2.] In 1898, Timmermann purchased the house and named it *Breeze Lawn*. He enlarged it in c. 1905.
  The *Social Register Summer, 1915* lists Henry G. and Kate Fry Timmermann as residing at *Breeze Lawn* in Islip.
  The house was subsequently owned by Timmermann's daughter Grace, who had married Orville Hurd Tobey. Mrs. Tobey continued to call the estate *Breeze Lawn*.

rear facade

Titus, James Gulden, Sr. (1911-1991)

Occupation(s):	restaurateur - vice-president, Harry M. Stevens Inc., Cranberry, NJ (catering firm for Yankee Stadium, New York Mets' Shea Stadium, Boston Red Sox' Fenway Park, Brooklyn Dodgers' Ebbets Field, San Francisco Giants' Candlestick Park, Aqueduct Race Track, Belmont Park Racetrack, Saratoga Raceway, Gulfstream Park, Tropical Park, Roosevelt Raceway, Mineola, Yonkers Raceway, Hialeah Park Racetrack, New York Coliseum, and Madison Square Garden)*
	capitalist - part-owner, Boston Red Sox baseball team
	military - member, Squadron A, United States Cavalry Reserve, 1939-1942; second lieutenant, United States Army, 1942-1946
Civic Activism:	member, St. Nicholas Society
Marriage(s):	1942-1991 – Alice Muriel Stevens (d. 2002)
Address:	21 Beech Road, Islip
Name of estate:	
Year of construction:	
Style of architecture:	Ranch
Architect(s):	
Landscape architect(s):	
House extant: yes	
Historical note:	

The *Social Register, Summer 1969* lists James G. and Alice M. Stevens Titus [Sr.] as residing at 21 Beech Road, Islip. He was the son of Walter Livingston and Margaret Gulden Titus, Sr. of West Islip.

Alice Muriel Stevens Titus was the daughter of Frank M. and Gertrude Honhorst Stevens of Manhattan.

James Gulden and Alice Muriel Stevens Titus, Sr.'s daughter Stephanie married Dr. William Shain Schley, the son of Dr. Frank Schley, and resided in Manhattan. Their daughter Sandra married Michael McCoy McKinstry, the son of Richard E. McKinstry, and resided in Englewood, CO. Their son James Gulden Titus, Jr. died in 2000.

[See other Titus entries for additional family information.]

*Harry M. Stevens Inc. had concession rights to approximately fifty race and harness tracks in the country.

front facade, 2006

Titus, Walter Livingston, Jr. (1906-1969)

Occupation(s):	capitalist - director, Republic Pictures (which became Republic Corp.)
Civic Activism:	member, St. Nicholas Society
Marriage(s):	1933-1969 – Elsa Marcia Yates (1911-1994)
Address:	88 East Bayberry Road, Islip
Name of estate:	
Year of construction:	1899-1900
Style of architecture:	Moorish
Architect(s):	Grosvenor Atterbury designed the house (for H. O. Havemeyer)*
Landscape architect(s):	Nathan F. Barrett (for H. O. Havemeyer)**
House extant: yes	
Historical notes:	

   The house was built by Henry Osborne Havemeyer as part of his "Modern Venice" development. It was owned by Charles Gulden II and, subsequently, by Titus.
   He was the son of Walter Livingston and Margaret Gulden Titus, Sr. of West Islip.
   Elsa Marcia Yates Titus was the daughter of Herbert John and Petra Antonsen Yates, Sr. of *Onsrufarm* in West Islip.
   Walter Livingston and Elsa Marcia Yates Titus, Jr.'s son Peter married Jill Mennella of Islip. Their son David married Joan Purdy of Englewood, NJ. Their son Walter Livingston Titus III married Louise McCarthy of Bronxville, NY. Their daughter Marcia married Thomas Young of Bay Shore.
   [See other Titus entries for additional family information.]
   *The sales brochure for "Modern Venice" states that the Moorish-style architecture was suggested by Louis Comfort Tiffany.
   **The sales brochure also states that "Modern Venice" would be devoid of trees and vegetation and that Nathan F. Barrett was the landscape architect.
   In 1991, the house sold for $490,000.

Titus, Walter Livingston, Sr. (1875-1953)

Occupation(s):	merchant - general store manager, Lord & Taylor Department Store
	industrialist - director, Nedick's Orange Drink
Civic Activism:	member, St. Nicholas Society
Marriage(s):	Margaret Gulden (1881-1965)
Address:	Eaton's Lane, West Islip
Name of estate:	
Year of construction:	
Style of architecture:	
Architect(s):	
Landscape architect(s):	
House extant: no; demolished c. 1962	
Historical notes:	

   Walter Livingston Titus, Sr. was the son of James Livingston and Harriet Louisa Pratt Titus of Manhattan.
   Margaret Gulden Titus was the daughter of Charles and Margaret Williams Gulden, Sr. of *Netherbay* in Bay Shore.
   Walter Livingston and Margaret Gulden Titus, Sr.'s son Walter Livingston Titus, Jr. married Elsa Marcia Yates and resided in Islip. The Tituses' daughter Margaret married Elsa's brother Douglas Thomas Yates, Sr. and resided in Islip. Their son James Gulden Titus married Alice Muriel Stevens and also resided in Islip.
   [See other Titus entries for additional family information.]

Tobey, Orville Hurd (1878-1934)

Occupation(s):	financier - partner, Lawrence Turnure and Co., NYC (investment banking firm)
Marriage(s):	M/1 – 1907 – Grace Ethel Timmermann M/2 – Elizabeth Fry (1878-1934)
Address:	Ocean Avenue, Islip
Name of estate:	*Breeze Lawn*
Year of construction:	c. 1889
Style of architecture:	Colonial Revival with Shingle elements
Architect(s):	
Landscape architect(s):	
House extant:	no
Historical notes:	

front facade c. 1903

The house was built by Leander Waterbury. In 1890, it was purchased by Howard Gibb, Sr. [*Brooklyn Times Union* May 10, 1890, p. 2.] In 1898, Henry Gerhard and Kate Fry Timmermann purchased the house and named it *Breeze Lawn* and, in c. 1905, enlarged it. The house was subsequently owned by the Timmermanns' daughter Grace Ethel Timmermann Tobey. Mrs. Tobey continued to call the estate *Breeze Lawn*.

The *Social Register, Summer 1937* lists Mrs. Grace E. T. Tobey as residing at *Breeze Lawn* in Islip.

Orville Hurd Tobey was the son of Frank Hurd and Katherine Maria Knecht Tobey of Manhattan.

Todd, William Henry (1864-1932)

Occupation(s):	industrialist - president, Robbins Dry Dock and Repair Co., Brooklyn, NY; president, Todd Shipyards Corp. (ship building firm)*; president, White Fuel Oil Co.; president, Todd Oil Burners, Ltd, London, England
Civic Activism:	director, Brooklyn Chamber of Commerce
Marriage(s):	1889-1928 – Mary Emma Babcock (1865-1928)
Address:	Middle Road and Marina Court, Bayport
Name of estate:	*Lenapes Lodge*
Year of construction:	
Style of architecture:	Colonial Revival
Architect(s):	
Landscape architect(s):	
House extant:	yes
Historical notes:	

front / side facade, 2005

In 1911, William Henry Todd purchased the William Brown farm and converted the farm house into his country residence *Lenapes Lodge*.

He was the son of James and Sarah Elizabeth Moody Todd.

Mary Emma Babcock Todd was the daughter of Peter James Babcock of Wilmington, DE.

William Henry and Mary Emma Babcock Todd's son J. Herbert Todd married Dorothy D. Barker, the daughter of Albert S. and Georgianna Driggs Barker, and resided in Brooklyn and Pinehurst, NC. Their daughter Natalie married Thomas R. Lilly of Stamford, CT. Their daughter Margaret, who later owned *Lenapes Lodge*, married William Henry Smith of Brooklyn and, subsequently, Herbert Williams Richter, also of Brooklyn. Margaret sold *Lenapes Lodge* in the 1960s.

*During World War I, Todd Shipyard Corp. had seven different facilities and was a major contractor for construction of cruisers for the United States Navy.

Trenchard, Edward, II (1850-1922)

Occupation(s):	artist - painter, marine subjects
	architect - member, Henry P. Richardsons, NYC
Civic Activism:	vice-president and assistant secretary, Long Island Association of the Sons of the Revolution;
	a founder and assistant secretary general, Society of the Colonial Wars;
	assistant secretary, Society of the Sons of the Revolution, 1883-1895;
	vice-president, Society of the War of 1812;
	recorder, New York Commandery
Marriage(s):	1878-1922 – Mary Cornelia Stafford (1850-1942)
Address:	307 Little East Neck Road, Babylon
Name of estate:	
Year of construction:	1910
Style of architecture:	Georgian Revival
Architect(s):	Nelson and Van Wagenen designed the house (for Trenchard)
Landscape architect(s):	
Builder:	E. W. Howell
House extant: yes	
Historical notes:	

front facade, 2005

The house was built by Edward Trenchard II.

He was the son of Rear Admiral Stephen Decatur and Mrs. Anne O'Connor Barclay Trenchard.

Mary Cornelia Stafford Trenchard was the daughter of William Bacon and Harriet Stafford of Manhattan.

Edward and Mary Cornelia Stafford Trenchard II's daughter Edith married John Anthony Power of Manhattan, Edward William Cameron Arnold of *Oknoke* in West Islip, and, subsequently, Storer Goodwin Decatur, the son of Stephen and Mabel Storer Decatur of Portsmouth, NH, and resided in Kittery Point, ME. Their sons Edward and Stafford were infants at the time of their deaths in 1879.

The house was later owned by David P. Stewart and, then, by George Brownlie, who called it *Willow Close*.

It is currently the clubhouse of the Long Island Yacht Club.

True, Benjamin Kimball, Sr. (1812-1876)

Occupation(s):	attorney
	capitalist - secretary, Southside Railroad
Civic Activism:	a founder, Christ Episcopal Church, West Islip
Marriage(s):	M/1 – 1849-1849 – A. Celestina Robertson (1829-1949)
	M/2 – 1851-1876 – Martha Bunce (1820-1893)
Address:	Oak Neck Road, West Islip
Name of estate:	*The Homestead*
Year of construction:	
Style of architecture:	Colonial Revival
Architect(s):	
Landscape architect(s):	
House extant: unconfirmed	
Historical notes:	

front facade

The house, originally named *The Homestead*, was built by Benjamin Kimball True, Sr.

He was the son of Deacon Benjamin and Mary Clift Kimball True.

A. Celestina Robertson True was the daughter of John T. Robertson of Charleston, SC. She contracted erysipelas and died during their honeymoon.

Martha Bunce True was the daughter of Joel and Jane Hicks Bunce.

Benjamin Kimball and Martha Bunce True, Sr.'s daughter Julia married William J. Fowler and, subsequently, John Lloyd Stephens of *Lone Oak* in West Islip. Their daughter Martha married Edward W. Blake. Their thirty-six-year-old son Benjamin Kimball True, Jr. was a bachelor at the time of his death in 1891.

Truslow, Frederick Cumings (1864-1920)

Occupation(s):	industrialist - general manager, Williamsburgh Cork Works (a division of Armstrong Cork Co.)*; partner, Truslow and Co., Brooklyn (manufacturer of corks and whiting)
	inventor - machine for making hollow corks
	financier - Fidelity and Guaranty Co., NYC; director, Brooklyn Bank
Civic Activism:	second vice-president, Civitas Club, Brooklyn; director, Kosmos Club, Brooklyn
Marriage(s):	1889-1920 – Anne Gates Babcock (1866-1946) - Civic Activism: trustee, Adelphi Academy, Brooklyn; vice-president, Civitas Club, Brooklyn.

Address: Great River Road, Great River
Name of estate: *Questover Lodge*
Year of construction:
Style of architecture: Shingle
Architect(s):
Landscape architect(s):
House extant: no
Historical notes:

front facade

The house, originally named *Questover Lodge*, was built by Frederick Cumings Truslow.

The *Brooklyn Blue Book and Long Island Society Register, 1918* lists Frederick C. and Anne Gates Babcock Truslow as residing in Cranford, NJ.

He was the son of James Linklater and Cornelia Josephine Cumings Truslow, Sr. Frederick's sister Elizabeth married William Newton Adams and resided in Brooklyn. His sister Alice married Dr. Henry Conklin and resided in Brooklyn. His brother James Linklater Truslow, Jr. married Amelia Louise Adams.

Anne Gates Babcock Truslow was the daughter of James A. and Ida Gates Babcock of Brooklyn. Anne's brother Edwin married Addie Burgess Murr and resided in Brooklyn. Her brother Augustus married Lillian A. Sloan, the daughter of Augustus Kellogg and Mary Cromwell Sloan, Sr. of Brooklyn.

Frederick Cumings and Anne Gates Babcock Truslow's son Percival married Grace Rhodes. Their daughter Helen married Charles Roy Auster, the son of Charles Auster of Cranford, NJ.

*James L. Truslow's wholesale cork companies of Truslow, Nostrand & Co. and Truslow & Co. were merged into Armstrong Cork Co. [*Brooklyn Daily Eagle* June 27, 1901, p. 3.]

The estate was subsequently owned by James Stewart.

Truslow, Gilbert Potter (1864-1932)

Occupation(s):	real estate agent - founder and president, G. P. Truslow & Co., Brooklyn
Marriage(s):	1886-1932 – Annie Amelia Manning (1864-1944)

Address: Clinton Avenue, Bay Shore
Name of estate:
Year of construction:
Style of architecture: Queen Anne
Architect(s):
Landscape architect(s):
House extant: unconfirmed
Historical notes:

Gilbert Potter Truslow was the son of Thomas Truslow, Jr.

Gilbert Potter and Annie Amelia Manning Truslow's daughter Ethel married Joseph Knapp Major, the son of Henry C. and Lucie Avilla Woodhull Major, and resided in Wading River. Their son Harold married Mildred B. Shroyer. Their son Theodore married Florence M. Art.

front facade, 1903

Tucker, Charles A.

Occupation(s):	inventor - electric temperature regulator, 1885
Marriage(s):	
Address:	Ocean Avenue, Islip
Name of estate:	
Year of construction:	c. 1883
Style of architecture:	Victorian
Architect(s):	Isaac Henry Green II designed the c. 1889 alterations (for W. Dick)
	Alfred Hopkins designed the garage and stables (for John Henry Dick)
Landscape architect(s):	
Builder:	P. B. McEntyre (for C. A. Tucker)
	E. W. Howell, alterations (for W. Dick)

House extant: no; demolished in 1960s*
Historical notes:

front facade, c. 1903

    The house was built by Charles A. Tucker.
    His brother Clarence also resided in Islip.
    The Ocean Avenue home was purchased in 1889 by William Dick [*The Brooklyn Daily Eagle* March 31, 1889, p. 11.] It was later owned by his son John Henry Dick and, subsequently, by William Karl Dick, all of whom called in *Allen Winden Farm*.
    *Garage and stables are extant.

Turnbull, George R. (1842-1909)

Occupation(s):	financier -	director, East River National Bank, NYC;
		director, Market & Fulton National Bank;
		director, South Brooklyn Savings Institution;
		director, Guaranty Trust Co.
	capitalist -	director, Norfolk & Southern Railroad;
		director, Brooklyn Union Gas Co.;
		director, Kansas City Gas Co.;
		director, Galveston City Railroad Co.
	industrialist -	treasurer, Butler Hard Rubber Co.;
		director, Central Stamping Co.;
		director, American Type Founders Co.;
		trustee, Central Asphalt Co.
Marriage(s):	1873-1909 – Clara Jenkins (d. 1935)	
	- Civic Activism: director, Destitute Children's Institute of Brooklyn	
Address:	South Country Road, West Islip	
Name of estate:	*The Pines*	
Year of construction:	1889	
Style of architecture:	Shingle	
Architect(s):		
Landscape architect(s):		

House extant: no
Historical notes:

    The house, originally named *The Pines*, was built by George R. Turnbull.   *front facade, c. 1903*
    He was the son of John and Elizabeth Whitehead Turnbull.
    The *Long Island Society Register, 1929* lists Clara Jenkins Turnbull as residing at *The Pines* on Main Road [South Country Road] in Bay Shore [West Islip].
    She was the daughter of Edward Osland and Henrietta Hodges Jenkins.
    George R. and Clara Jenkins Turnbull's daughter Clara married Minor Cooper R. Keith II and resided in West Islip.

Turnbull, John Gourlay, Sr. (1855-1903)

Occupation(s):

Marriage(s): 1885-1903 – Josephine Sherwood

Address: Potter Boulevard, Brightwaters
Name of estate: *The Pines*
Year of construction:
Style of architecture:
Architect(s):
Landscape architect(s):
House extant: unconfirmed
Historical notes:

    The *Brooklyn Blue Book and Long Island Society Register, 1918* lists John Gourlay and Josephine Sherwood Turnbull [Sr.] as residing in Brightwaters.
    She was the daughter of Robert Sherwood of Baltimore, MD.
    John Gourlay and Josephine Sherwood Turnbull, Sr.'s son John Gourlay Turnbull, Jr. married Harriette Boden Hutchinson, the daughter of David Wallace Hutchinson, and resided on Nassau Boulevard in Garden City. Their daughter Marjorie married Wallace MacNab Waddell, Sr. and resided in Garden City. [*See* Spinzia, *Long Island's Prominent Families in the Town of Hempstead* – Turnbull and Waddell entries.] Their daughter Josephine married William Wilson Heinith of Philadelphia, PA. Their daughter Elizabeth married Dr. Harold M. Marvin of New Haven, CT.

Udall, Joseph Sanford (1837-1901)

Occupation(s): capitalist - builder

Marriage(s): Harriet Fleet (1834-1904)

Address: The Crescent, Babylon
Name of estate:
Year of construction: 1870
Style of architecture: Italianate
Architect(s):
Landscape architect(s):
House extant: yes
Historical notes:

    In 1884, Udall hired Moses Drake's Sons to move the house from Deer Park Avenue and Green Street to The Crescent. He was the son of Jonas Udall.
    Harriet Fleet Udall was the daughter of Jacob and Frances Sammis Fleet of Babylon.
    Joseph Sanford and Harriet Fleet Udall's daughters Ida and Minnie did not marry.
    In 2018, the 4,000-square-foot house sold for $955,000.

front facade, 2018

Underhill, Edward Beekman, Sr. (1835-1899)

Occupation(s):	financier - partner, Underhill and Buckingham (stock brokerage firm)
	capitalist - Manhattan and Bay Shore real estate
Marriage(s):	Lydia Fowler Kip (1837-1921)
Address:	Ocean Avenue, Bay Shore
Name of estate:	
Year of construction:	
Style of architecture:	Eclectic*
Architect(s):	
Landscape architect(s):	
House extant: unconfirmed	
Historical notes:	

*Edward Beekman Underhill, Sr.'s Bay Shore house was built in the style of a lighthouse. [*Brooklyn Daily Eagle* July 3, 1887, p. 4.]

He was the son of Charles and Elvira A. Beekman Underhill.

Lydia Fowler Kip Underhill was the daughter of Samuel and Nancy Havens Fowler Kip.

Edward Beekman and Lydia Fowler Kip Underhill, Sr.'s' son Rawson married Grace C. Crowley and resided in Albany, NY. Their son Jacob married Elizabeth Wyman Aldrich, the daughter of William Aldrich. Their son Edward Beekman Underhill, Jr. married Kate Caldwell Isaacson, the daughter of Alfred G. Isaacson of Montreal, Canada.

Valentine, Langdon Barrett (1873-1931)

Occupation(s):	industrialist - president, Valentine & Co. (manufacturer of paint and Varnish)
Civic Activism:	member, board of managers, Southside Hospital, Bay Shore (now, South Shore University Hospital);
	a founder and director, Great River Club, 1920 (later, Timber Point Club)
Marriage(s):	M/1 – 1900-1904 – May Harper (1874-1904)
	M/2 – 1909-1931 – Louise Hollister (1882-1946)
Address:	South Bay Avenue, Islip
Name of estate:	
Year of construction:	
Style of architecture:	
Architect(s):	
Landscape architect(s):	
House extant: unconfirmed	
Historical notes:	

The *Long Island Society Register, 1929* lists Langdon Barrett and Louise Hollister Valentine as residing on South Bay Avenue in Islip.

He was the son of Henry Chamberlain and Grace Cleveland Barrett Valentine.

May Harper Valentine was the daughter of Joseph Henry and Mary G. Hoe Harper of *Brightside* in Lawrence. [*See* Spinzia, *Long Island's Prominent Families in the Town of Hempstead* – Harper entry.]

Langdon Barrett and May Harper Valentine's daughter Urling married Campbell Roberts Coxe, the son of George S. Coxe.

Louise Hollister Valentine was the daughter of Henry Hutchinson and Sarah Louise Howell Hollister, Sr. of Islip. She had previously been married to Richard E. Forest of *Longwood* in Lawrence. [*See* Spinzia, *Long Island's Prominent Families in the Town of Hempstead* – Forest entry.] Her brother Buell Hollister, Sr. married Louise R. Knowlton and resided in Islip. Her brother Henry Hutchinson Hollister, Jr. married Hope Shepley.

Langdon Barrett and Louise Hollister Valentine's daughter Anne married Joseph Sears Lovering, Jr. of Islip.

[For information on the Southside Hospital, see Cooper entry.]

Van Anden, Frank (1876-1952)

Occupation(s):	inventor - designed pontoons used on amphibian airplanes into the 1950s; constructed one of the first wind tunnels to test airplane wing stresses
Marriage(s):	M/1 – c. 1897 – Ida Kessberg* M/2 – Edwina May Wilce (1885-1924) M/3 – 1948-1952 – Nellie Rowland (1888-1975)
Address:	Ocean Avenue, Islip
Name of estate:	
Year of construction:	
Style of architecture:	
Architect(s):	
Landscape architect(s):	
House extant: unconfirmed	
Historical notes:	

Frank Van Anden was the son of William M. and Alice Hannah Frost Van Anden of Islip.

*While in Berlin, Germany, to improve his German language skills, Van Anden secretly married Ida Kessberg. Upon returning to the United States, he convinced his parents to advertise for a tutor to help him with his German writing skills. Ida answered the advertisement and was engaged by the family to tutor Frank. The Van Andens learned of Frank and Ida's marriage when his father William was congratulated by a friend on the marriage of his son. [*The New York Times* September 26, 1897, p. 8.]

Frank and Edwina May Wilce Van Anden's daughter Evelyn married Cecil Birch Seay, Sr., the son of William M. and Frances B. Birch, and resided in Buffalo, NY. Their daughter Italia married James Kincade.

Nellie Rowland Van Anden was the daughter of Robert Smith and Annie Joe Cason Rowland. Nellie had previously been married to Jared Erwin Dunn, the son of Edward Warren Davis and Augusta Hardin Dunn.

[See following entry for additional family information.]

Van Anden, William M. (1842-1918)

Occupation(s):	capitalist - director, American District Telegraph Co.; president, Eagle Warehouse and Storage Co. financier - director, Long Island Safe Deposit Co.; director, Capital Surplus publisher - president, secretary, and treasurer, *Brooklyn Daily Eagle**
Civic Activism:	director, South Shore Country Club, West Islip
Marriage(s):	Alice Hannah Frost (1851-1933)
Address:	Ocean Avenue, Islip
Name of estate:	
Year of construction:	
Style of architecture:	
Architect(s):	
Landscape architect(s):	
House extant: unconfirmed	
Historical notes:	

The *Brooklyn Blue Book and Long Island Society Register, 1918* and *1921* list William M. and Alice Frost Van Anden as residing in Islip.

He was the son of William Van Anden of Brooklyn.

*William M. Van Anden's uncle Isaac Van Anden was a founder of *The Brooklyn Daily Eagle*.

Alice Hannah Frost Van Anden was the daughter of Jacob and Sarah Titus Frost. Her sister Louise married George R. Read of Manhattan. Her brother Newbury H. Frost, a bachelor, resided in Hempstead. [*See* Spinzia, *Long Island's Prominent Families in the Town of Hempstead* – Frost entry.]

William M. and Alice Hannah Frost Van Anden's daughter Louise married George S. Frank, the son of Emil Henry and Paula Nathalia Glahn Frank, Sr. of Bay Shore, and resided in New Canaan, CT. Their daughter Estelle married D. Rait Richardson and resided in Manhattan. Their son Frank also lived in Islip. *[See previous entry.]*

Van Bourgondien, Cornelius John, Sr. (1885-1970)
aka Cornelis Johannes Van Bourgondien

Occupation(s):	merchant - founder and president, C. J. Van Bourgondien, Inc., West Babylon (wholesale and retail flowers)
Marriage(s):	1915-1967 – Elizabeth Clara Keser (1891-1967)
Address:	Albin Avenue, West Babylon
Name of estate:	
Year of construction:	1929
Style of architecture:	Neo-Tudor
Architect(s):	
Landscape architect(s):	
House extant:	unconfirmed
Historical notes:	

The house was built by Cornelius John Van Bourgondien, Sr.

He was the son of Karel and Johanna Zeestraten Van Bourgondien of Hillegom, The Netherlands.

Elizabeth Clara Keser Van Bourgondien was the daughter of Otto A. Keser of Portland, CT.

Cornelius John and Elizabeth Clara Keser Van Bourgondien, Sr.'s daughter Joan married Robert Condit and resided in West Babylon and, later, Peconic. Their son Cornelius John Van Bourgondien, Jr. married Gretchen Benjamin, the daughter of Eugene Benjamin of Bay Shore, and resided in Bozman, MD. Their son Philip married Kathryn Marian Nelis, the daughter of Harry Nelis, Sr.

The house is currently owned by the Town of Babylon and is situated in the Town's Van Bourgondien Park. The Town of Babylon and the Town of Babylon Historical Society are currently restoring the house for use as the Van Bourgondien Farm House Museum.

front facade

Vanderbilt, William Kissam, Sr. (1849-1920)

Occupation(s):	capitalist - president, New York Central Railroad and its subsidiaries
Civic Activism:	built and endowed St. Mark's Episcopal Church, Islip
Marriage(s):	M/1 – 1875-div. 1895 – Alva Erskine Smith (1853-1933)

- writer -   *Melinda and Her Sisters* (suffragist opera/with Elsa Maxwell);
    One Month's Log of the Seminole, 1916;
    two unpublished autobiographies, 1917, 1933
  journalist - numerous newspaper and magazine articles*
  Civic Activism: woman's suffrage -
  - founder and president, Political Equality Assoc.;
  - first president, National Woman's Party**;
  - purchased building in Washington, DC, for National Woman's Party Headquarters [now, known as Sewall–Belmont House];
  - primary benefactor and president of board, Hempstead Hospital, Hempstead [not the present-day hospital also named Hempstead Hospital];
  - established, Brookholt School of Agriculture for Women at East Meadow estate *Brookholt*;
  - built and supported, Sea Side Hospital for Sick Children, a 200-bed hospital in Great River (later, Trinity Sea Side Home);
  - paid for rectory furnishings for St. Mark's Episcopal Church, Islip (the church was financed by her first husband William Kissam Vanderbilt, Sr.];
  - built mission church Our Lady of Loretto Roman Catholic Church, Hempstead, 1904

M/2 – 1903-1920 – Anne Harriman (1860-1940)
- Civic Activism: a founder, Franco–American War Museum;
  donated $1 million for the establishment of the East River Home and Hospital, NYC;
  a founder and director, American Woman's Association, NYC;
  ***

Address:	South County Road, Oakdale
Name of estate:	*Idlehour* [I]****
Year of construction:	1878
Style of architecture:	Shingle
Architect(s):	Richard Morris Hunt designed the 1878 main residence and gatehouse (for W. K. Vanderbilt, Sr.)
	Isaac Henry Green II designed the farm complex and tea house (for W. K. Vanderbilt, Sr.)
Landscape architect(s):	
House extant:	no; 1878 house destroyed by fire in 1899*****

Idlehour [I], c. 1895

Historical notes:

The one-hundred-room house, originally named *Idlehour* [I], was built by William Kissam Vanderbilt, Sr.

He was the son of William Henry and Maria Kissam Vanderbilt of Staten Island, NY.

Alva Erskine Smith Vanderbilt was the daughter of Murray Forbes and Phoebe Desha Smith of Mobile, AL, and Manhattan. Alva subsequently married Oliver Hazard Perry Belmont, with whom she resided at *Marble House* and *Belcourt* in Newport, RI, and *Brookholt* in East Meadow. After Oliver's death in 1908, Alva relocated to *Beacon Towers* in Sands Point and, subsequently, to France, where she was living at the time of her death.

William Kissam and Alva Erskine Smith Vanderbilt Sr.'s daughter Consuelo, a noted suffragist, married Charles Richard John Spencer–Churchill, the Ninth Duke of Marlborough and, subsequently, Louis Jacques Balsan, with whom she resided at *Old Fields* in East Norwich, *Gardenside* in Southampton, and in Palm Beach, FL. Their son Harold, who later owned the second *Idlehour* house, married Gertrude Lewis Conaway. Their son William Kissam Vanderbilt, Jr., who like his brother Harold was a financial benefactor of the suffrage movement, married Virginia Graham Fair and, subsequently, Rosamund Lancaster and resided at *Deepdale* in Lake Success and at *Eagle's Nest* in Centerport. After her divorce from William, Virginia resided in Brookville, Glen Cove, and at *Fairmont* in Manhasset. [*See* Spinzia, *Long Island's Prominent North Shore Families, vol. I* – Balsan entry; *Long Island's Prominent North Shore Families, vol. II* – Vanderbilt entries; and *Long Island's Prominent Families in the Town of Southampton* – Balsan entry.]

    Anne Harriman Vanderbilt was the daughter of Oliver and Laura Low Harriman. She had previously been married to Samuel Stevens Sands, Jr. and Lewis Morris Rutherfurd. Samuel Stevens and Anne Harriman Sands, Jr.'s son Samuel Stevens Sands III married Gertrude Sheldon, the daughter of George R. Sheldon of Manhattan. Their son George married Anne Aldridge Gibson, the daughter of John Aldridge Gibson of Leesburg, VA. Both George and his brother Samuel were killed in automobile accidents. Lewis Morris and Anne Harriman Rutherfurd's daughter Barbara married Cyril Hatch and, subsequently, Winfield J. Nichols. Their daughter Margaret married Frederick Leybourne Sprague.

    *Mrs. Belmont donated the proceeds from her newspaper and magazine articles to the suffrage movement.

    **Alva Belmont's Sands Point estate *Beacon Towers* was the site of the 1920 National Woman's Party Conference.

    ***Anne Harriman Vanderbilt was the first woman to receive a gold medal from the French Ministry of Foreign Affairs for her service to France.

    ****According to Vanderbilt's own stationery and the name painted on his private railroad car, *Idlehour* was one word.

    *****In 1899, while William Kissam Vanderbilt, Jr., and his wife Virginia Graham Fair were spending their honeymoon at *Idlehour* [I], the house was destroyed by fire.

[See following entry for history of 1900 house.]

Vanderbilt, William Kissam, Sr. (1849-1920)

Occupation(s):	*[See previous entry.]*
Marriage(s):	*[See previous entry.]*
Address:	South Country Road, Oakdale
Name of estate:	*Idlehour* [II]
Year of construction:	1900
Style of architecture:	Beaux Arts with Flemish elements
Architect(s):	Richard Howland Hunt designed the 1900 house (for W. K. Vanderbilt, Sr.)
	Warren and Wetmore designed the 1903 bachelor annex and indoor tennis court (for W. K. Vanderbilt, Sr.)

Landscape architect(s):
House extant: yes
Historical notes:

    With the destruction of the first *Idlehour* by fire, William Kissam Vanderbilt, Sr. built a second house on the site which he also called *Idlehour*.

    The estate, which was later owned by his son Harold, had several subsequent owners including the firm of Edmund G. and Charles F. Burke, Inc., which, in the 1920s, was unsuccessful in its attempt to subdivide the estate's property for a housing development. In 1937, the main residence and the carriage house were acquired by the Fraternity of Master Metaphysicians. In 1947, National Dairy Research Labs, Inc. purchased the main residence, carriage house, and twenty-three acres. In 1963, the National Dairy holdings were acquired by Adelphi University of Garden City for use as its Adelphi Suffolk campus. In 1968, the Oakdale campus became Dowling College. In 2016, the college declared bankruptcy and closed. Mercury International LLC currently owns the college's library, the mansion, and several of the estate's service buildings.

    In 1974, the main residence was the site of a devastating fire. The smoking lounge, main staircase, plaster friezes in the dining room [Hunt Room], woodwork and the ornate ceiling in the living room, and velvet tapestry wallcovering throughout the house were destroyed. Repairs to the fire-damaged main residence were financed by the Fortunoff family; historic elements were not restored. Karl Bitter's sculpture, "Diana, the Huntress," in the dining room, was restored by a member of the college's art department.

[See previous entry for family information and a history of the 1878 house.]

Idlehour [II], *1990*

William Kissam Vanderbilt Sr. estate, *Idlehour* [II]

living room, c. 1903

living room, 1990

section of friezes in Hunt Room (dining room)

front entrance foyer and main staircase, c. 1903

men's smoking lounge, c. 1903

William Kissam Vanderbilt Sr. estate, *Idlehour* [II]

main staircase, c. 1903

main staircase, 1990

wallpaper replacement of Hunt Room friezes, 1990

hallway outside men's smoking lounge, c. 1903

hallway outside men's smoking lounge, 1990

Vander Veer, Dr. Albert, Jr. (1879-1959)*

Occupation(s):	physician - assistant physician, New York Dispensary, 1908-1912;
	assistant physician, Lincoln Hospital, NYC, 1912-1916;
	allergist, Out-Patient Department, New York Hospital, 1920-1927;
	allergy consultant, Roosevelt Hospital, NYC, 1928-1947;
	co-founder and assistant chief, Allergy Clinic, New York Hospital, 1919
	educator - instructor of medicine, Fordham University Medical School
	writer - numerous articles in professional journals
Civic Activism:	president, American Academy of Allergy;
	donated The Memorial Study at The Church at Point O'Woods in memory of his wife Sylvia
Marriage(s):	M/1 – 1913-1944 – Sylvia Angela de Murias (1888-1944)
	M/2 – 1951-1959 – Margaret Maxwell Clark
Address:	#59 Point O'Woods, Fire Island
Name of estate:	*Gray Shingles*
Year of construction:	c. 1928
Style of architecture:	Beach Cottage
Architect(s):	
Landscape architect(s):	
House extant: yes	
Historical notes:	

The house, originally named *Gray Shingles*, was built by Dr. Albert Vander Veer, Jr.

The *Social Register Summer, 1932* lists Dr. Albert and Mrs. Sylvia A. de Murias Vander Veer [Jr.] as residing at *Grey* [sic] *Shingles* in Point O'Woods [Fire Island].

He was the son of Dr. Albert and Mrs. Margaret E. Snow Vander Veer, Sr. of Albany, NY.

Sylvia Angela de Murias Vander Veer was the daughter of Ramon and Clara Garden de Murias of Cuba and Manhattan. Sylvia's brother Fernando married Virginia Cornwall Bunce, the daughter of Frederick Sidney and Annie M. Towne Bunce, Sr. of Babylon, and resided in Babylon.

Dr. Albert and Mrs. Sylvia Angela de Murias Vander Veer, Jr.'s daughter Margaret married Charles B. Colmore, Jr. and resided in Glen Ridge, NJ. Their daughter Jean married Girardeau Leland, Jr. of McLellanville, SC.

The *Social Register, Summer 1954* lists Dr. Albert and Mrs. Margaret M. Clark Vander Veer, Jr. as residing at *Gray Shingles* in Point O'Woods.

Margaret Maxwell Clark Vander Veer was the daughter of John Kirkland and Margaret Holbrook Clark of Manhattan.

*Another branch of the family uses Vanderveer for the spelling of the family surname.

The house was purchased by Josie Cornell. It later owned by Kevin Morrisey.

*John Vanderveer residence, Sunnymead,
front facade, 1930s*

Vanderveer, John (1868-1941)*

Occupation(s):	
Civic Activism:	philanthropist**
Marriage(s):	1906-1941 – Gertrude Van Siclen Lott (1870-1945)
Address:	South Country Road, West Islip
Name of estate:	*Sunnymead*
Year of construction:	
Style of architecture:	Shingle
Architect(s):	
Landscape architect(s):	
House extant: no; demolished c. 1953***	
Historical notes:	

John Vanderveer purchased the house in 1904.

The *Long Island Society Register, 1929* lists John and Gertrude V. S. Lott Vanderveer as residing on South Country Road, Babylon [West Islip].

He was the son of John Williamson and Mary Lott Vanderveer.

Gertrude Van Siclen Lott Vanderveer was the daughter of Abraham Van Siclen and Cornelia Debevoise Lott.

John and Gertrude Van Siclen Lott Vanderveer's daughter Cornelia, who married John Joseph Gibson, inherited *Sunnymead*.

*Another branch of the family uses Vander Veer for the spelling of the family surname.

**Vanderveer was known for his generosity to those in need in the local community.

During the 1930s and 1940s a local nursery leased a portion of the estate's property for Dutch bulb cultivation. During World War II German prisoners-of-war were utilized to assist in the bulb cultivation. [Personal communication from John Vanderveer Gibson]

In 1958, the sixty-acre estate became the site of Good Samaritan Hospital.

***The gardener's cottage, at 175 Beach Drive, is currently the hospital's Office of Hospital Development.

Van Orden, Jabez Ephraim (1863-1917)

Occupation(s):	capitalist - builder*
	politician - Town of Islip Assessor; delegate to Republican County Convention, Riverhead, 1897
Civic Activism:	trustee, East Islip School District
Marriage(s):	1886-div. 1913 – Ann Duryea (1864-1946)
Address:	60 River Road, Great River
Name of estate:	
Year of construction:	1901
Style of architecture:	Shingle
Architect(s):	
Landscape architect(s):	
Builder:	Jabez Ephraim Van Orden
House extant: yes	
Historical notes:	

front facade

The house was built by Jabez Ephraim Van Orden. [*South Side Signal* January 26, 1901, p. 2.]

He was the son of Henry S. and Rachel Ann Smith Van Orden of Pennsylvania.

Ann Duryea Van Orden was the daughter of Ruluf and Christina Augusta Goldsworth Duryea of Great River.

Jabez Ephraim and Ann Duryea Van Orden's son James married Ethel Bogert and resided in East Islip and Shinnecock Hills. [*See* Spinzia, *Long Island's Prominent Families in the Town of Southampton* – Van Orden entry.]

In 1917, Jabez was found dead in Brooklyn from gas poisoning. [*The Suffolk County News* May 18, 1917, p. 2.]

Van Orden's River Road house is currently George Martin's Strip Steak Restaurant.

*We have been unable to determine who built Henry O. Havemeyer's "Modern Venice" houses. *The Brooklyn Daily Eagle* April 9, 1899, p. 10, states "H. O. Havemeyer has given the contract for the execution of the ten cottages on Bayberry Point at the foot of Ocean Avenue, Islip to the Sturgis and Hill Company of New York City. *The Suffolk County News* March 2, 1900, p. 1, states "Jabez E. Van Orden of Great River has been awarded the contract for building three more cottages on Bayberry Point, at the foot of Ocean Avenue, by H. O. Havemeyer." The *E. Belcher Hyde Atlas of the Ocean Shore of Suffolk County*, 1915 (western section) shows only nine residences as having been built.

Van Orden, James (1887-1960)

Occupation(s):	capitalist - founder and president, James Van Orden Co., East Islip (building contractor)
	financier - director, First National Bank of Islip
	politician - director, Suffolk County Veterans Service; director of schools, Town of Islip, 1945
Civic Activism:	chairman, Islip Draft Board #704, 1941;
	president, board of education, East Islip School District, 1940;
	commissioner, East Islip Fire Department, 1932;
	member, board of appeals, Town of Islip;
	president, Town of Islip School Board Association;
	member, Town of Islip Zoning Board
Marriage(s):	Ethel Bogert
Address:	37 First Avenue, East Islip
Name of estate:	
Year of construction:	1915
Style of architecture:	Colonial Revival
Architect(s):	
Landscape architect(s):	
House extant: yes	
Historical notes:	

front facade 2017

James Van Orden was the son of Jabez Ephraim and Ann Duryea Van Orden of Great River.
Ethel Bogert Van Orden was from Sayville.
In 2017, the 2,800-square-foot house, which is now a legal two-family residence, sold for $360,000.
[For the Van Ordens' Shinnecock Hills residence, *see* Spinzia, *Long Island's Prominent Families in the Town of Southampton* – Van Orden entry.]

Waddell, Charles Falkiner Morton (1886-1966)
aka Morton Wadell

Occupation(s):	financier - member, Frazier Jelke and Co. (stock brokerage firm); vice-president, International Germanic Trust Co.
Civic Activism:	member, Bay Shore School Board; treasurer, Montauk Commuters Association
Marriage(s):	1905-1965 – Coretta Jean Hagen (1882-1965)
Address:	Bay Shore Avenue, Bay Shore
Name of estate:	
Year of construction:	
Style of architecture:	
Architect(s):	
Landscape architect(s):	
House extant: unconfirmed	
Historical notes:	

Charles Falkiner Morton Waddell was the son of Henry Alexander and Maria Joselin Waddell.
Coretta Jean Hagen Waddell was the daughter of John W. and Sarah Jane Cooper Hagen.
Charles Falkiner Morton and Coretta Jean Hagen Waddell's daughter Marjorie married George Mitchell Gregory, the son of William Hamilton and Elizabeth Mitchell Gregory, Sr. of Bay Shore, and resided in Bay Shore. Their daughter Hildegarde married Douglas Wilcox Brewster, the son of Carleton Brewster of Bay Shore, and resided in Bay Shore. Their daughter Catherine married Richard Housel.
In 1940, the Waddells were residing at 78 Shore Lane, Islip.

Wagner, Robert Ferdinand, Jr. (1910-1991)

Occupation(s):	diplomat - United States Ambassador to Spain, 1968-1969
	politician - tax commissioner, NYC;
	commissioner of housing and building, NYC;
	chairman, planning commission, NYC;
	member, New York State Assembly, district 16, 1938-1942;
	Manhattan Borough President, 1950-1953;
	New York City Mayor, 1954-1965
Marriage(s):	M/1 – 1942-1964 – Susan Edwards (1909-1964)
	M/2 – 1965-annulled 1971 – Barbara Cavanagh (1908-1986)
	M/3 – 1975-1991 – Helen Brown Nichols (aka Phyllis Fraser) (1916-2006)
	- advertising executive - member, McCann, Erickson, NYC
	publisher - a founder, Beginner Books (children's books)
	journalist
	writer - *The ABC and Counting Book*
	entertainers and associated professions - motion picture actress
Address:	99 Ocean Avenue, Islip
Name of estate:	
Year of construction:	1910
Style of architecture:	Colonial Revival
Architect(s):	
Landscape architect(s):	
House extant: yes	
Historical notes:	

   The *Social Register Summer, 1955* lists Robert F. and Susan M. Edwards Wagner as residing at 99 Ocean Avenue, Islip.
   He was the son of Robert Ferdinand and Margaret Marie McTague Wagner, Sr. of New York.
   Susan Edwards was the daughter of Duncan and Susan Willets Edwards of Greenwich, CT.
   Robert Ferdinand and Susan Edwards Wagner, Jr.'s son died in 1993 from complications due to AIDS. In 1975, their son Duncan became engaged to Anita Carole Lembo, the daughter of Samuel Lembo of Queens Village.
   Barbara Cavanagh Wagner was the daughter of Edward Francis and Mae Masterson Cavanagh, Sr. Her brother Edward Francis Cavanagh, Jr. married Nancy Miller and resided at *Naghward* in Old Brookville. [*See* Spinzia, *Long Island's Prominent North Shore Families, vol. I* – Cavanagh entry.]
   Helen Brown Nichols Wagner had previously been married to the noted television personality and publisher Bennett Alfred Cerf, the son of Gustave and Fredericka Wise Cerf.
   In 2019, the 6,600-square-foot house with six bedrooms and five-and-a-half bathrooms sold for $985,000.

front facade, 2019

Wagstaff, Alfred, Jr. (1844-1921)

Occupation(s):	attorney - partner, North, Ward, and Wagstaff
	politician - member, New York State Assembly from Manhattan's 5th District, 1867-1873;
	member, New York State Senate, 1876-1878;
	clerk, Court of Common Pleas, 1892-1895;
	clerk, Appellate Division, New York State Supreme Court;
	president, Brooklyn Bridge Commission, 1890-1891
	capitalist - president Brooklyn Bridge Co.;
	president, Christopher & 10th Street Railroad;
	director, Central Crosstown Railroad
Civic Activism:	president, American Society for the Prevention of Cruelty to Animals, 1906;
	president, New York Association for the Protection of Game;
	trustee, Samaritan Home for the Aged;
	president of board, Southside Hospital, Bay Shore (now, South Shore University Hospital);
	vice-president, South Shore Country Club, West Islip;
	a founder and trustee, Waverly Gun Club, Islip, 1890
Marriage(s):	1880-1921 – Mary Anderson Barnard (1860-1938)
	- Civic Activism: president, West Islip Board of Education
Address:	South Country Road, West Islip
Name of estate:	*Opekeepsing**
Year of construction:	
Style of architecture:	Shingle
Architect(s):	
Landscape architect(s):	
Builder:	W. S. Velsor, 1888 addition
House extant: no	
Historical notes:	

The house, originally named *Opekeepsing*, was built by Alfred Wagstaff, Jr.

He was the son of Dr. Alfred and Mrs. Sarah Platt DuBois Wagstaff, Sr., who resided at *Tahlulah* in West Islip.

Mary Anderson Barnard Wagstaff was the daughter of New York Supreme Court Judge George C. and Mrs. Mary Anderson Barnard. [Judge Barnard was a member of New York City's infamous Tweed Ring.]

Alfred and Mary Anderson Barnard Wagstaff, Jr.'s daughter Margaret married John Fairchild Adams, the son of Horatio M. and Mary Hartwell Carter Adams of *Appledale* in Glen Cove. [*See* Spinzia, *Long Island's Prominent North Shore Families, vol. I* – Adams entry.] Margaret subsequently married ____ Singleton and resided in Babylon. Their son George, who married Mary Cutting Cumnock, Dorothy Whiting Frothingham, and, subsequently, Lillian Hyde, resided at *The Farm House* in West Islip and on Lawrance Lane in Bay Shore. Their son David married Isabelle Tilford and resided at *Ledgelands* in Tuxedo Park, NY. Their son Samuel, who resided in Syosset and at *Driftwood* in West Islip, married Pauline Le Roy French, the daughter of Amos Tucker and Olga May Piorkowski French, and, subsequently, Cornelia Walker Scranton. [*See* Spinzia, *Long Island's Prominent North Shore Families, vol. II* – Wagstaff entry.] Their son Alfred Wagstaff III married Blanch Shoemaker of Philadelphia, PA, and, later, Katherine H. Curtis.

[See other Wagstaff entries for additional family information.]

**Opekeepsing* means "safe harbor." [Harry W. Havemeyer, *Along the Great South Bay From Oakdale to Babylon: The Story of a Summer Spa 1840 to 1940* (Mattituck, NY: Amereon House, 1996), p. 252.]

After Wagstaff relinquished ownership of the house, it became an establishment known locally as The Hammerhead Inn.

[For information on the Southside Hospital, see Cooper entry.]

Opekeepsing

Wagstaff, Dr. Alfred, Sr. (1804-1878)

Occupation(s):	physician
	capitalist - owned real estate in Manhattan
Civic Activism:	a founder and donor of site of Christ Episcopal Church, West Islip
Marriage(s):	1843-1878 – Sarah Platt DuBois (1813-1897)
Address:	South Country Road, West Islip
Name of estate:	*Tahlulah*
Year of construction:	c. 1827
Style of architecture:	Italianate
Architect(s):	
Landscape architect(s):	
House extant:	no
Historical notes:	

In 1827, Dr. Alfred Wagstaff, Sr. purchased the Bergen farm and built *Tahlulah* as his country residence. [*The New York Times* June 16, 1938, p. 23.]

He was the son of Manhattan merchant David Wagstaff. Alfred's sister married William Lowerre. His sister Ann married Thomas Benjamin Davies Kortright Craig with whom she resided in Quogue. [*See* Spinzia, *Long Island's Prominent Families in the Town of Southampton* – Craig entry.] Another sister married Henry Maunsell Schieffelin, the son of Henry Hamilton Schieffelin.

Sarah Platt DuBois Wagstaff was the daughter of Cornelius DuBois.

Dr. Alfred and Mrs. Sarah Platt DuBois Wagstaff, Sr.'s son Alfred Wagstaff, Jr. married Mary Anderson Barnard and resided at *Opekeepsing* in West Islip. Their son Cornelius married Amy Colt and resided in West Islip. Their daughter Sarah married Phoenix Remsen, Sr. and also resided in West Islip. Their daughter Mary married Henry Gribble.

[See other Wagstaff entries for additional family information.]

In 1904, the estate was sold at public auction. [*Brooklyn Daily Eagle* April 29, 1900, p. 41, and May 10, 1900, p. 13.]

In 1925, it was purchased by Realty Associates of Brooklyn for conversion into a housing development through its subsidiary The Dover Land Corporation. [*The Brooklyn Daily Eagle* November 21, 1925, p. 2.]

side / front facade

Wagstaff, Cornelius DuBois (1845-1919)

Occupation(s):
Civic Activism: a founder and director, South Side Country Club, West Islip, 1895;
                  a founder, Christ Episcopal Church, West Islip;
                  vice-president, Westminster Kennel Club

Marriage(s):   1880-1919 – Amy Colt (1858-1934)

Address: South Country Road, West Islip
Name of estate: *Church Lawn*
Year of construction:
Style of architecture: Shingle
Architect(s):
Landscape architect(s):
House extant: no
Historical notes:

   The *Social Register Summer, 1915* lists C. DuBois and Amy Colt Wagstaff as residing at *Church Lawn* in Babylon [West Islip].
   He was the son of Dr. Alfred and Mrs. Sarah Platt DuBois Wagstaff, Sr. of *Tahlulah* in West Islip.
   Amy Colt Wagstaff was the daughter of Robert Oliver and Adelaide Heideberg Colt, who resided in West Bay Shore.
   In 1899, the Wagstaff's fourteen-year-old son Oliver accidently shot himself in the hip while hunting quail on the estate. While the wound was serious, he survived and passed away in 1973. [*The Suffolk County News* November 17, 1899, p. 2.] Their daughter May did not marry.
   [See other Wagstaff entries for additional family information.]

side / front facade

Wagstaff, George Barnard (1886-1964)

Occupation(s):	financier - partner, E. F. Hutton and Co. (investment banking firm)
Civic Activism:	member, New York Stock Exchange committee to aid refugees from The Netherlands during World War II
Marriage(s):	M/1 – 1914-div.– Mary Cutting Holland Cumnock (1895-1940)
	M/2 – 1921-div. – Dorothy Whiting Frothingham (1895-1986)
	M/3 – 1940-1964 – Lillian B. Hyde (1888-1974)
Address:	57 Lawrence Lane, Bay Shore
Name of estate:	
Year of construction:	
Style of architecture:	Modified Colonial Revival
Architect(s):	
Landscape architect(s):	
House extant:	yes
Historical notes:	

The Farm House, 1916

The *Social Register Summer, 1915* lists George B. and Mary C. Cumnock Wagstaff as residing at *The Farm House* in Babylon [West Islip].

He was the son of Alfred and Mary Anderson Barnard Wagstaff, Jr., who resided at *Opekeepsing* in West Islip.

Mary Cutting Holland Cumnock Wagstaff was the daughter of Arthur J. and Mary Pomeroy Cutting Cumnock of Manhattan.

George Barnard and Mary Cutting Holland Cummock Wagstaff's daughter Beatrice married David Wagstaff, Jr. of *Ledgeland* in Tuxedo Park, NY, and, subsequently, Henri A. Luebermann.

In 1926, Mary married The Honorable Arthur Lionel Ochoncar Forbes–Sempill, with whom she resided in London, England. The death of Lord Sempill, the 10th Baronet of Forbes of Rux, in 1965 initiated an unprecedented and bizarre succession situation which centered on whether Lord Sempill's brother Ewan was the legitimate heir to the baronetcy. A physician, who practiced medicine under the name Elizabeth Forbes–Sempill until the age of forty, Dr. Forbes–Sempill was registered at birth as female but changed her name to Ewan Forbes–Sempill and her birth registration from female to male in 1952. A three-year private court case ensued during which extensive medical evidence was presented. Based on the court proceedings, the Home Secretary declared Ewan the 11th Baronet. It was not until 1997 that court records, which allegedly declared Ewan a true hermaphrodite, but male, became available. [Dr. Angus Campbell, "The Forbes–Sempill Case." The 6th International Congress on Sex and Gender Diversity: Reflecting Gender. The School of Law, Manchester Metropolitan University September 10th to 12th, 2004; *The New York Times* December 31, 1963, pp. 3, 23, and December 3, 1968, p. 13.]

The *Social Register Summer, 1923* lists George B. and Dorothy W. Frothingham Wagstaff as residing in West Islip.

She was the daughter of Charles Frederick Frothingham, Sr. Dorothy had previously been married to Edward William Cameron Arnold of *Oknoke* in West Islip.

George Barnard and Dorothy Whiting Frothingham Wagstaff's daughter Dorothy married Louis Rose Ripley, the son of Baillie Ripley of Litchfield, CT.

The *Social Register Summer, 1962* lists George B. and Lillian B. Hyde Wagstaff as residing at 57 Lawrence Lane, Bay Shore.

She was the daughter of Richard and Mary Kellar Hyde of West Bay Shore. She had previously been married to Quentin Field Feitner, Sr., the son of Thomas L. and Mary C. Moore Feitner of Manhattan. Lillian's sister Lulu married Vincent Booth Hubbell, Sr. and, subsequently, Howard Drummond with whom she resided at *Little House* in Bay Shore. Her brother William married Grace M. Riopelle and resided at *White Cottage* in Bay Shore.

57 Lawrence Lane, Bay Shore, *front facade, 2006*

Wagstaff, Samuel Jones, Sr. (1885-1975)

Occupation(s):	attorney
	merchant - director, Partridge, Clark, & Kerrigan, NYC (automobile dealership)
Civic Activism:	trustee, West Islip School District, 1916
Marriage(s):	M/1 – 1908-div. 1920 – Pauline Le Roy French (1887-1964)
	M/2 – 1920-div. 1932 – Olga Mary Piorkowska (1894-1973)
	- artist - illustrator, *Harper's Bazaar* and *Vogue*
	M/3 – 1933-1975 – Cornelia Walker Scranton (1896-1976)
Address:	South Country Road and Higbie Lane, West Islip
Name of estate:	*Driftwood*
Year of construction:	1910
Style of architecture:	Colonial Revival
Architect(s):	
Landscape architect(s):	
Builder:	E. W. Howell, garage, 1910
House extant:	no
Historical notes:	

The house was built by Alfred Wagstaff, Jr. as a gift to his son Samuel.

The *Social Register Summer, 1915* lists Samuel J. and Pauline LeR. French Wagstaff as residing at *Driftwood* in West Islip.

He was the son of Alfred and Mary Anderson Barnard Wagstaff, Jr. of *Opekeepsing* in West Islip.

Pauline Le Roy French Wagstaff was the daughter of Amos Tuck and Pauline Stuyvesant French of Newport, RI. She subsequently married Donald Oliver MacRae, the son of Alexander K. MacRae of Pittsburgh, PA.

Olga May Piorkowska Wagstaff was the daughter of Emil Piorkowska. She had previously been married to Arthur Paul Thomas. After her divorce from Wagstaff, she married Donald V. Newhall.

Samuel Jones and Olga May Piorkowska Wagstaff, Sr.'s daughter Judith married Thomas Lewis Jefferson IV of Longmeadow, MA, and Louisville, KY, and resided in New York. Their son Samuel Jones Wagstaff, Jr., who remained a bachelor, was a noted art curator and critic. He had participated in the Normandy landing on Omaha Beach during World War II.

Cornelia Walker Scranton Wagstaff was the daughter of Walker and Mary Halsey Woodbridge Scranton. Cornelia had previously been married to Samuel Sedwick Swift.

In 1921, Wagstaff purchased James Watson Webb, Sr.'s estate *Woodbury House* with its furnishings and relocated to Syosset. [*The Suffolk County News* November 4, 1921, p. 6, and Spinzia, *Long Island's Prominent North Shore Families*, vol. II – Wagstaff and Webb entries.]

In 1923, Wagstaff sold the West Islip house to William James Hyde. [*The County Review* May 18, 1923, p. 9, and *The Brooklyn Daily Eagle* June 21, 1923, p. 3.]

front facade

Wainwright, Stuyvesant, Jr. (1891-1975)

Occupation(s):	attorney
	financier - member, Smithers and Co. (stock brokerage firm)
	member, Estabrook and Co. (stock brokerage firm)
Marriage(s):	1924-1975 – Louise Flinn (1901-1986)
Address:	38 South Montgomery Avenue, Bay Shore
Name of estate:	
Year of construction:	
Style of architecture:	
Architect(s):	
Landscape architect(s):	
House extant:	unconfirmed
Historical notes:	

The *Long Island Society Register, 1929* lists Stuyvesant and Louise Flinn Wainwright [Jr.] as residing in Bay Shore. The *Social Register Summer, 1932* lists their address as 38 Montgomery Avenue, Bay Shore.

He was the son of Stuyvesant and Caroline Smith Snowden Wainwright, Sr. of Rye, NY. Caroline subsequently married Dr. Carl F. Wolff and resided at *Shadowmere* in East Hampton. His brother Loudon married Eleanor Painter Sloan and resided in Hewlett Neck. [*See* Spinzia, *Long Island's Prominent Families in the Town of Hempstead* – Wainwright entries.] His brother Carroll married Edith G. Gould and resided at *Gullcrest* in East Hampton. His brother John married Aimee Andrews and resided in East Hampton.

Louise Flinn Wainwright was the daughter of George Hamilton and Sara Louise Negley Flinn, Sr. of East Hampton.

[For additional family information, *see* Spinzia, *Long Island's Prominent Families in the Town of East Hampton* – Flinn, Wainwright, and Wolff entries.]

Stuyvesant and Louise Flinn Wainwright, Jr.'s son Peter married Gerry Jordan and resided in Paradise Valley, AZ. Their daughter Patricia married Ricardo Bonicatti of Rome, Italy. Their daughter Mimi married Charles Payson Coleman, Sr. and resided at *Valentine Farm* in Old Brookville and at *Winhall* in Lawrence. [*See* Spinzia, *Long Island's Prominent North Shore Families*, vol. I – Coleman entry.]

[For information on the Wainwright's Hampton Bays' residence *Duckwood*, *see* Spinzia, *Long Island's Prominent Families in the Town of Southampton* – Wainwright entry.]

Walbridge, Ernest Augustus (1892-1940)

Occupation(s):	financier - member, Mackay and Co. (stock brokerage firm);
	insurance broker
Marriage(s):	1919-1940 – Blanche Gifford Wandel (1885-1971)
	- Civic Activism: member, local draft board during World War II
Address:	3 Reid Avenue, Babylon
Name of estate:	
Year of construction:	1883
Style of architecture:	Victorian farmhouse
Architect(s):	
Landscape architect(s):	
Builder:	Medad Smith
House extant:	yes
Historical notes:	

front / side facade, 2006

The *Long Island Society Register, 1929* lists Ernest A. Walbridge as residing at 3 Reid Avenue, Babylon.

He was the son of Augustus and Katherine C. Walbridge. His sister Helen, a physician who did not marry, resided in Babylon. His sister Anna married Eugene H. Peck and resided in Manhattan. His sister Ethel married Merritt Leon McCully and resided in Bronxville, NY.

Blanche Gifford Wandel Walbridge was the daughter of William S. and Blanche E. Gifford Wandel of Brooklyn.

Ernest Augustus and Blanche Gifford Wandel Walbridge's son John married Michelle Kelley, the daughter of Leon Kelley of Babylon, and resided in Babylon. Their daughter Dorothy married Benjamin Burford King, the son of Benjamin King of London, England, and resided in Great Falls, VA.

By 1940 the Walbridges were residing on The Crescent, Babylon.

[See following entry for additional family information.]

Walbridge, George Huntington (1879-1931)

Occupation(s):	civil engineer - George H. Walbridge Co. (civil engineering and surveying firm)
Marriage(s):	1912-1931 – Emma Robbins (1888-1966)
Address:	102 The Crescent, Babylon
Name of estate:	
Year of construction:	1910
Style of architecture:	
Architect(s):	
Landscape architect(s):	
House extant: yes	
Historical notes:	

George Huntington Walbridge was the son of Augustus and Katherine C. Walbridge.

Emma Robbins Walbridge was the daughter of John James and Susan Emma Rowland Robbins.

George Huntington and Emma Robbins Walbridge's daughter Suzanne married Bryan Lawrence, the son of Joseph W. Lawrence of Babylon, and resided in Babylon.

[See previous entry for additional family information.]

In 2004, the house sold for $899,000.

Walker, Harford Pinckney, Sr. (1876-1921)
aka Frederick Harford Pinckney Walker, Sr.

Occupation(s):	capitalist -	owned Manhattan apartments; secretary and director, Eight-twenty-three Park Ave. Co.; treasurer and director, Randolph–Walker Corp, NYC
	attorney -	assistant corporation counsel, New York City (Mitchel administration)
Marriage(s):	Jeanne Preston Frost (1882-1919)	
Address:	South Country Road and de Forest Avenue, West Islip	
Name of estate:		
Year of construction:	c. 1915	
Style of architecture:		
Architect(s):		
Landscape architect(s):		
House extant: unconfirmed		
Historical notes:		

In 1913, Harford Pinckney Walker, Sr. purchased James Goodrich de Forest, Sr.'s estate, subdivided its property into an area he called "The Venice of Babylon," and built a new house as his residence.

He was the son of George Rivers and Annie Isabel Keitt Walker of Charleston, SC.

Jeanne Preston Frost Walker was the daughter of Henry William and Susan Hampton Preston Frost.

Harford Pinckney and Jeanne Preston Frost Walker, Sr.'s son Henry married Mary Taft, the daughter of Augustus Robert and Mary Walter Taft of Charleston, SC. Their daughter Jeanne married Austin S. Iglehard, Jr. of Green Pond, SC. Their daughter Caroline married Elmer Miller Claiborne, the son of George and Margaret Miller Claiborne. Their son George married Mary Ross Seibels, the daughter of John Jacob Seibels of Columbia, SC. Their daughter Annie married Keating Lewis Simons. Their son Harford Pinckney Walker, Jr. was infant at the time of his death in 1905.

Walker, Keitt Pinckney (1874-1936)
aka George Daniel Keitt Pinckney Walker

Occupation(s):	architect
	capitalist - director, Douglas L. Elliman & Co., NYC; built and owned several apartment buildings in Manhattan; treasurer and director, Eight-twenty-three Park Ave. Co.; founder and vice-president, 580 Park Avenue (14-story cooperative apartment building)
Marriage(s):	M/1 – 1899-div. 1925 – Julia Irving Graham
	M/2 – 1925-1936 – Martha Pintard Irving
Address:	South Country Road, West Islip
Name of estate:	*Villa Julia*
Year of construction:	late 1800s
Style of architecture:	French Empire
Architect(s):	
Landscape architect(s):	
Builder:	Smith & Van Weelden enlarged the carriage house, 1883 (for P. Remsen, Sr.)
House extant:	no

side facade

Historical notes:

The house was built by Phoenix Remsen, Sr. on a portion of the Willetts farm. [James Brown Cooper. *Reminisces of Babylon and Its Vicinity.* privately printed, 1911.] In c. 1913, the house was purchased by Walker who called it *Villa Julia*. [*South Side Signal* March 14, 1913, p. 5.]

The *Social Register Summer, 1915* lists Keitt Pinckney and Julia I. Graham Walker as residing at *Villa Julia* in Babylon [West Islip].

He was the son of George Rivers and Annie Isabel Keitt Walker of Charleston, SC.

Julia Irving Graham Walker was the daughter of William and Helen Schieffelin Graham and was a descendant of Washington Irving.

The house was later owned by Julia Walton who sold it to James Hardenburgh. Hardenburgh renamed the house *Villa Maria*.

Ward, Edwin Carrington (1858-1915)

Occupation(s):	attorney
	writer - *A Book of 1,500 Legal Questions*; co-author, *1,500 Questions Answered*
Civic Activism:	director and secretary, Brooklyn Academy of Music; a founder and director, Bay Shore Protective Association
Marriage(s):	1895-1915 – Marion Louette Matson (1865-1915)
Address:	Penataquit Avenue, Bay Shore
Name of estate:	*Wake Robin*
Year of construction:	
Style of architecture:	
Architect(s):	
Landscape architect(s):	
House extant:	unconfirmed

Historical notes:

Edwin Carrington Ward was the son of Augustus and Susan Cowles Ward.

The *Brooklyn Blue Book and Long Island Society Register, 1918* lists Marion Louette Matson Ward as residing at *Wake Robin* in Bay Shore.

She was the daughter of The Reverend Lewis Emmons and Mrs. Helen Maria Flanders Matson.

Edwin Carrington and Marion Louette Matson Ward's son Kenneth married Barbara Wey, the daughter of H. F. G. Wey, who resided at *The Birches* in Rye, NY. Their daughter Winifred married Walter Talbot Spalding and resided in Bronxville, NY.

Ward, John Montgomery (1860-1925)

Occupation(s):	attorney
	professional baseball player:
	pitcher, Providence Grays, 1878 (National League);
	pitcher/center fielder, New York Gothams (renamed New York Giants);
	manager, New York Gothams, 1884;
	shortstop, New York Giants;
	player/manager, Brooklyn Grooms (National League)
	capitalist - president and owner, Boston Braves;
	a founder, Players League
Civic Activism:	a founder, Brotherhood of Professional Base Ball Players (first sports labor union);
	president, Long Island Gunners' and Fishermen's Association, Babylon branch, 1911;
	president, Long Island Golfers' Association
Marriage(s):	M/1 – Ida Louise Gibson
	M/2 – 1887-div. 1893 – Helen Dauvray (1859-1923)
	- entertainers and associated professions - actress; owned a theater
	M/3 – Katherine Waas
	- suffrage - participated in New York City suffrage parade, 1913;
	a founder and second vice-president, Babylon chapter, Equal Franchise Society, 1912;
	vice-chair, New York State Second Assembly District Suffrage Convention, 1917
Address:	Phelps Lane, North Babylon
Name of estate:	
Year of construction:	
Style of architecture:	
Architect(s):	
Landscape architect(s):	
House extant:	no
Historical notes:	

    The house was built by Royal Phelps, Jr. It became the headquarters of the Rod and Reel Club of North Babylon before it was later purchased by Ward.
    He was the son of James and Ruth Ward of Bellefonte, PA.
    After their divorce, Helen married Rear Admiral Albert Winterhalter.
    In 1964, Ward was elected into the Baseball Hall of Fame.
    In 1941, the estate was sold to David Schnur who demolished the house and built a fourteen-room house on the site.

Warren, Northam, Sr. (1878-1962)

Occupation(s):	industrialist - secretary to William M. Warren and, later, member, import export division, Parke, Davis & Co. (pharmaceutical manufacturing firm);
	founder, Northam Warren's Special Products Co. (later, Northam Warren Corp, NYC (manufacturer of Phoebe Snow, Cutex, Dr. J. Parker Pray's, Elcaya Face Creams, Glazo Polishes, Peggy Sage, and Odo-Ro-No lines of beauty and personal care items;
	sole supplier of electrical conductors for United States aircraft during World War II*;
	produced anodizing for aircraft during World War II;
	produced Sniff Kits to train personnel in the smell of dangerous chemicals during World War II
Civic Activism:	governor, South Side Yacht Club (later, Sayville Yacht Club);
	governor, Sayville Yacht Club;
	governor, Sayville Golf Club;
	Sayville chairman, Japan Relief Committee, South Suffolk chapter, American Red Cross, 1923
Marriage(s):	Edna Louise O'Brien (1882-1962)
	- Civic Activism: trustee, Sayville Garden Club
Address:	80 Brown's River Road, Sayville
Name of estate:	*Sandy Point*
Year of construction:	1923
Style of architecture:	
Architect(s):	
Landscape architect(s):	
Builder:	Henry F. Rogers, garage / boathouse, 1922 (for Warren)

House extant: yes
Historical notes:

The house, originally named *Sandy Point*, was built by Northam Warren, Sr.

He was the son of The Reverend Leroy and Mrs. Fannie Louise Wadsworth Warren of Kansas.

Edna Louise O'Brien Warren was the daughter of Edward O'Brien of Chicago, IL.

Northam and Edna Louise O'Brien Warren, Sr.'s daughter Agnes married Karl Wilhelm Illigen, the son of Wilhelm Illigen, and resided in Harrisburg, PA. Their son Northam Warren, Jr. married Dorothy Calwell of Lawton, OK, and resided in Connecticut.

*In 1960, Warren sold the Northam Warren Corporation to Chesebrough Pond's.

In 1937, the estate was sold to Emma Nesbitt Gelshenen (Mrs. William Henry Gelshenen). [*The Patchogue Advance* November 26, 1937, p. 8.]

In 1949, it was owned by Mrs. Kathryn Brendel. [*The Suffolk County News* March 4, 1949, p. 4.]

The house, which has been remodeled, is now Land's End Waterfront Catering.

front facade

Waterbury, Leander (1842-1889)

Occupation(s):	politician - Brooklyn Parks Commissioner (Low administration); New York State Quarantine Commissioner (Cleveland administration)
	shipping - partner, Waterbury & Force
Marriage(s):	1884-1889 – Jennie Bullard Adams
Address:	Ocean Avenue, Islip
Name of estate:	
Year of construction:	c. 1889
Style of architecture:	Colonial Revival with Shingle elements
Architect(s):	
Landscape architect(s):	
House extant: no	
Historical notes:	

rear facade

The house was built by Leander Waterbury.
He was the son of Stephen P. and Sarah A. Waterbury.
Jennie Bullard Adams Waterbury was the daughter of Coe Adams of Brooklyn.

In 1890, the house was purchased by Howard Gibb, Sr. [*Brooklyn Times Union* May 10, 1890, p. 2.] In 1898, it was purchased by Henry Gerhard Timmermann who enlarged it in c. 1905. The house was later owned by Timmermann's daughter Grace, who married Orville Hurd Tobey. Both the Timmermans and the Tobeys called the house *Breeze Lawn*.

Watson, Jane Painter Elder (1849-1929)

Marriage(s):	1905-1929 – Robert Campbell Watson, Sr. (1849-1906)
Address:	Main Street, Islip
Name of estate:	*The Maples*
Year of construction:	
Style of architecture:	Queen Anne
Architect(s):	
Landscape architect(s):	
House extant: unconfirmed	
Historical notes:	

The *Social Register Summer 1913* and *1915* list Jeannie [Jane] P. Elder Watson as residing at *The Maples* in Islip.
She was the daughter of George William and Hannah Eliza Riker Elder. Jane's sister Mary married Henry Osborne Havemeyer.

Robert Campbell Watson, Sr. was the son of William and Maria Campbell Watson.

Robert Campbell and Jane Painter Elder Watson, Sr.'s son Robert Campbell Watson, Jr. married Alice Marion Pepper, the daughter of William Platt Pepper of Bellport and Philadelphia, PA, and rented Havemeyer's cottage number two on Bayberry Point.

In 1920, the fourteen-room, three-bathroom house and twelve acres were for sale. The asking price was $60,000. [*The New York Times* April 11, 1920, p. RE11.]

The Maples, 1915

Webster, Charles Drake (1905-1998)

Occupation(s):

Civic Activism: member, medieval art department visiting committee, Metropolitan Museum of Art, NYC;
committee chairman, The Cloisters, NYC;
trustee, Society for the Preservation of Fire Island Lighthouse;
fellow, Old Westbury Gardens, Old Westbury;
ornithological field associate, New York Zoological Society;
chairman of board, Seatuck Environmental Association, Islip;
trustee, Bayard Cutting Arboretum, Great River;
director, National Wild Waterfowl Association, Jamestown, MD;
director, Caribbean Conservation Corporation, Tallahassee, FL

Marriage(s): 1936-1979 – Natalie Peters (1907-1979)
- Civic Activism: president, Garden Club of America, 1959-1962

Address: South Bay Avenue, Islip
Name of estate: *Twyford*
Year of construction: c. 1880s
Style of architecture: Modified Neo-Victorian
Architect(s):
Landscape architect(s):
House extant: no; demolished in 2002*
Historical notes:

The house was built by Dr. T. S. Ryder. It was purchased by Samuel Twyford Peters, who used it as a guest house on his estate *Windholm Farm*. The house was later owned by his son Harry Twyford Peters, Sr., who remodeled it and called it *Twyford*. It was subsequently owned by Harry Twyford Peters, Sr.'s daughter Natalie, who married Webster.

He was the son of Josiah C. Webster of Shenandoah, IA, and a direct descendant of Roger Sherman, a signer of the Declaration of Independence and the Constitution of the United States.

In 1968, the Websters donated the house, to be used for staff offices and as a wildlife study and teaching center, and the surrounding property to the Seatuck National Wildlife Refuge. [*Seatuck* in Algonquian is said to mean "little creek flowing into the sea."] The terms of the gift gave the Websters life tenancy but did not specifically require maintenance or preservation of the house by the Department of the Interior after their deaths.

*The house was demolished in 2002 by the federal government.

front facade

Weekes, Harold Hathaway (1880-1950)

Occupation(s):	financier - Thomas, Maclay and Co. (stock brokerage firm)
Marriage(s):	M/1 – 1906-div. 1926 – Louisine A. Peters (1886-1952)
	M/2 – 1933-1950 – Frances Stokes (1888-1967)
Address:	South Bay Avenue, Islip
Name of estate:	*Wereholme*
Year of construction:	c. 1917
Style of architecture:	Neo-French Manor
Architect(s):	Grosvenor Atterbury designed the house (for H. H. Weekes)
Landscape architect(s):	
House extant:	yes

front facade, 1991

Historical notes:

The house, originally named *Wereholme*, was built by Harold Hathaway Weekes.

The *Long Island Society Register, 1929* lists Harold H. Weekes as residing in Oyster Bay.

He was the son of Arthur Delano and Margaret Eliza Underhill Weekes, Sr., who resided at *The Anchorage* in Oyster Bay Cove. His brother Arthur Delano Weekes, Jr., who later owned *The Anchorage*, married Dorothy Lee Higginson. His sister Edith married John Slade, Sr. and resided at *Underhill House* in Upper Brookville and at *Berry Hill House* in Oyster Bay Cove. [*See* Spinzia, *Long Island's Prominent North Shore Families, vol. II* – Slade entry.]

Louisine A. Peters Weekes was the daughter of Samuel Twyford and Adaline Mapes Elder Peters, Jr. of *Windholme Farm* in Islip. Her brother Harry Twyford Peters, Sr., who married Natalie Wells and resided at *Nearholme* in Islip, later owned *Windholme Farm*. Louisine subsequently married Alexander Tcherepnin, and continued to reside at *Wereholme*.

Harold Hathaway and Louisine A. Peters Weekes' daughter Adaline, who later owned *Wereholme*, married Charles Brewster Scully, the son of John Joseph and Mildred Louise Parker Scully, and resided at the estate. Adaline subsequently married Count Philip Orssich of Denkendorf bei Stuttgart, Germany.

Harold Hathaway Weekes subsequently married Frances Stokes and resided at *Valentine Farm* in Old Brookville. [*See* Spinzia, *Long Island's Prominent North Shore Families, vol. II* – Weekes entry.]

Frances Stokes Weekes was the daughter of Thomas Pym Cope and Ellen Welsh Stoke. She had previously been married to Louis Crawford Clark II, with who she resided at *Valentine Farm* in Old Brookville. [*See* Spinzia, *Long Island's Prominent North Shore Families, vol. I* – Clark entry.]

*In 1984, Mrs. Scully, who had divorced the count and reverted to the surname Scully, bequeathed the house to the National Audubon Society.

In 2004, the estate was purchased by Suffolk County and is now the county's Greenways Educational and Interpretive Nature Center.

Weeks, Edwin Carnes (1864-1937)

Occupation(s):	financier - partner, Henderson and Co. (stock brokerage firm)
Marriage(s):	1890-1937 – Emily Smedberg (1869-1944)
Address:	213 Fire Island Avenue, Babylon
Name of estate:	
Year of construction:	
Style of architecture:	Queen Anne
Architect(s):	
Landscape architect(s):	
House extant:	yes

front facade

Historical notes:

The *Long Island Society Register, 1929* lists Edward Carnes and Emily Smedberg Weeks as residing in Babylon.

He was the son of James and Kezia Seabury Weeks.

Emily Smedberg Weeks was the daughter of Adolphus and Mary Ludlow Morton Smedberg, Sr. Her brother Adolphus Smedberg, Jr. married Marie Russ Corwin and resided at *Larkmeadow* in Babylon.

Edward Carnes and Emily Smedberg Weeks' daughter Mary married Beverley Eyre, the son of Maynard Campbell and Mary Eloise Clark Eyre of Staten Island, NY, and resided in Bay Shore. Their daughter Katharine married Alexander Duncan Cameron Arnold of West Islip. Their daughter Helen married Lloyd Kitchel and resided in Wilmington, DE. Their son Robert married Marjorie Klehr, the daughter of William Klehr of Forest Hills, NY, and resided in Babylon. Their daughter Emily married Henry Wolcott Thomas and, later, Bleeker Bradford.

In 1992, the 3,450-square-foot, six-bedroom, four-bath house sold for $205,000.

Weld, Philip Balch (1887-1964)

Occupation(s):	financier - president, New York Cotton Exchange; member, Kidder, Peabody and Co. (stock brokerage firm); partner, Stephen M. Weld and Co.; partner, Weld, Jackson, and Curtis
Marriage(s):	1912-1964 – Katharine Leverett Saltonstall (1891-1987)
Address:	80 South Saxon Avenue, Bay Shore
Name of estate:	
Year of construction:	c. 1880
Style of architecture:	Victorian
Architect(s):	
Landscape architect(s):	
House extant:	no; demolished in 1932*
Historical notes:	

    The house was built by Daniel Denice Conover and later owned by his son Augustus Whitlock Conover, Sr. In 1902, the house was purchased by John Lorimer Worden III. [*The Brooklyn Daily Eagle* May 3, 1902, p. 10.] It was purchased in 1912 by Franklyn Laws Hutton, who called it *Win Sum Lodge*. He later sold it to his brother Edward Francis Hutton. In 1921, the house was purchased from E. F. Hutton by Weld.
    He was the son of General Stephen Minot and Mrs. Eloise Rodman Weld of Dedham, MA.
    Katharine Leverett Saltonstall Weld was the daughter of Philip Leverett and Frances Anna Fitch Saltonstall of Boston, MA.
    Philip Balch and Katharine Leverett Saltonstall Weld's son Philip Saltonstall Weld married Anne Warren, the daughter of Samuel Dennis Warren of *Rockyhill Farm* in Essex, MA. Their daughter Rose married Ian Baldwin, the son of Joseph Clark Baldwin, Jr. of Mt. Kisco, NY, and resided in Mt. Kisco. Their daughter Adelaide married Robert Bacon Whitney, Sr. and resided in Old Westbury. Adelaide later married James Knott II, the son of David Hurst and Agnes Gibson Geekie Knott, Sr. of Glen Cove, with whom she continued to reside in Old Westbury, and, subsequently, William Bradner. [*See* Spinzia, *Long Island's Prominent North Shore Families, vol. I* – Knott entry – and *Long Island's Prominent North Shore Families, vol. II* – Whitney entry.] Their daughter Katherine married Benjamin Bacon.
    In 1930, the house was purchased from Weld by Hamlet Cecil Sharp, who demolished it and built a new house on the site.
    *The estate's barn complex, stables, and windmill are extant.

2020

Welles, Benjamin Sumner, Jr. (1857-1935)

Occupation(s):

Marriage(s): Frances Wyeth Swan (1863-1911)

Address: St. Mark's Lane, Islip
Name of estate: *Welles House*
Year of construction:
Style of architecture:
Architect(s):
Landscape architect(s):
House extant: unconfirmed
Historical notes:

The *Long Island Society Register, 1929* lists Benjamin [Sumner] Welles [Jr.] as residing at *Welles House* on St. Mark's Lane in Islip. His Manhattan residence was located at 110 East Fifty-fifth Street.

He was the son of Benjamin Sumner and Catherine Schermerhorn Welles, Sr.

Frances Wyeth Swan Welles was the daughter of Frederick G. and Emily Wyeth Swan of Oyster Bay.

Benjamin Sumner and Frances Wyeth Swan Welles, Jr.'s daughter Emily married Harry Pelham Robbins, the son of Henry Archer Robbins, and resided at *Pelham Farm* in Southampton. [*See* Spinzia, *Long Island's Prominent Families in the Town of Southampton* – Robbins entry.] Their son Benjamin Sumner Welles III [aka Sumner Welles] later owned the house. [See Raymond E. Spinzia, "Sumner Welles: Brilliance and Tragedy." *The Freeholder* 9 (Winter 2005):8-9, 22. Also available at www.spinzialongislandestates.com.]

Mrs. Welles died of a stroke at a sanatorium in Kerhonkson, NY, where she was being treated for a nervous disorder. [Benjamin Welles, *Sumner Welles: FDR's Global Strategist* (New York: St. Martin's Press, 1999), p. 18.]

[See other Welles entries for additional family information.]

Welles, Benjamin Sumner, Sr. (1823-1904)

Occupation(s): merchant - dry goods

Marriage(s): 1850-1858 – Catherine Elida Schermerhorn (1828-1858)

Address: St. Mark's Lane, Islip
Name of estate:
Year of construction: c. 1850s
Style of architecture:
Architect(s):
Landscape architect(s):
House extant: unconfirmed
Historical notes:

The house, which was the first house built on St. Mark's Lane, was built by Benjamin Sumner Welles, Sr. [*Times Union*, July 24, 1935, p. 6A.]

He was the son of Benjamin and Mehitable Stoddard Sumner Welles and a member of the Patriarchs, an organization of twenty-five men which had been created in 1872 by Ward McAllister to "establish and lead" New York society.

Catherine Elida Schermerhorn Welles was the daughter of Abraham Schermerhorn of Manhattan. Her sister Ann married Charles Suydam and resided in Bayport. Her sister Caroline ["Mystic Rose"], who married William Blackhouse Astor, was the undisputed arbiter of society's elite "Four Hundred."

Benjamin Sumner and Catherine Schermerhorn Welles, Sr. were members of society's 'Four Hundred." However, Catherine's sister Ann and brother-in-law Charles Suydam were omitted from the list.

Their son Benjamin Sumner Welles, Jr. married Frances Wyeth Swan and resided at *Welles House* in Islip. Their daughter Helen married George Lovett Kingsland, Sr. and rented a house in Babylon for their summer residence. Their daughter Harriet did not marry.

[See other Welles entries for additional family information.]

St. Mark's Lane, Islip, c. 1920

Welles, Benjamin Sumner, III (1892-1961)
aka Sumner Welles

Occupation(s):	diplomat - secretary, United Sates Embassy in Japan, 1917; United States Ambassador to Cuba, 1933; chief, Latin American Affairs Division, Department of State, 1920
	statesman* - Assistant Secretary of State, 1933; Under Secretary of State, 1937
	writer - *Naboth's Vineyard*, 1928; *The World of Four Freedoms*, 1943; *The Time of Decision*, 1944; *The Ciano Diaries 1939-1943* (introduction by Welles), 1946; *Where Are We Heading?* 1946; *We Need Not Fail*, 1948; *Seven Decisions That Shaped History*, 1950
Marriage(s):	M/1 – 1915-div. 1923 – Esther Slater (1892-1951)
	M/2 – 1925-1949 – Mathilde Scott Townsend (1888-1949)
	M/3 – 1952-1961 – Harriette Appleton Post (1894-1969)
Address:	St. Mark's Lane, Islip
Name of estate:	*Welles House*
Year of construction:	c. 1850s
Style of architecture:	
Architect(s):	
Landscape architect(s):	
House extant:	unconfirmed
Historical notes:	

    Benjamin Sumner Welles III was the son of Benjamin Sumner and Frances Wyeth Swan Wells, Jr. whose residence *Welles House* he later owned.

    Esther Slater Welles was the daughter of Horatio and Mabel Hunt Slater II. Esther's uncle was the noted architect William Morris Hunt. She subsequently married Joseph John Kerrigan and resided in Cove Neck. [*See* Spinzia, *Long Island's Prominent North Shore Families, vol. I* – Kerrigan entry]

    Benjamin Sumner and Esther Slater Welles III's son Benjamin Sumner Welles IV, who served in the Office of Strategic Services during World War II, married Cynthia Monteith. [See Raymond E. Spinzia, "To Look in the Mirror and See Nothing: Long Islanders and the Office of Strategic Services and Its Successor, the Central Intelligence Agency." 2017, revised 2021.www.spinzialongislandestates.com] Their son Arnold married Adele Harman, the daughter of Archer Harman of Edgartown, MA, and resided in Savannah, GA.

    Mathilde Scott Townsend Welles was the daughter of Richard Holmes and Mary Tracy Scott. Mathilde had previously been married to United States Senator Peter Goelet Gerry of Rhode Island.

    Harriette Appleton Post Welles was the daughter of George Browne and Julia Cotton Smith Post of Bernardsville, NJ, and granddaughter of the noted architect George Browne Post. She had previously been married to Richard Thornton Wilson, the son of Marshall Orme Wilson of Manhattan, and to the ardent Austro–Hungarian Nazi sympathizer Baron Emmerich von Jeszenzky.

    Benjamin Sumner Welles III's Washington, DC, residence, located at 2121 Massachusetts Avenue, NW, was purchased by the Cosmos Club. His 250-acre estate in Maryland was located at Oxon Hill.

    *For a discussion of the personal scandal that led to Welles' fall from political power, *see* Raymond E. Spinzia, "Sumner Welles: Brilliance and Tragedy." *The Freeholder* 9 (Winter 2005):8-9, 22. Also available at www.spinzialongislandestates.com.

Welwood, Thomas (1817-1892)

Occupation(s):	capitalist - established the German community of Breslau (modern-day Lindenhurst), 1873
	writer - *Breslau Statistics*, 1873
Civic Activism:	donated land for Breslau Cemetery, North Lindenhurst, 1875
Marriage(s):	1843-1892 – Abby Cornwall (1818-1903)
Address:	South Country Road, Lindenhurst
Name of estate:	*Welwood Lane*
Year of construction:	1871
Style of architecture:	Victorian
Architect(s):	
Landscape architect(s):	
House extant:	no; demolished in 1980s
Historical notes:	

The house, originally named *Welwood Lane*, was built by Thomas Welwood.

Thomas and Abby Cornwell Welwood's son William married Elizabeth L. Walsh. Their son The Reverend John Cornwell Welwood married Alba Elizabeth Wall, the daughter of Joseph and Helen Wall, and, later, Cora Dutton, the daughter of Benjamin Franklin and Harriet Meriam Conant Dutton. Their daughters Ada and Abby did not marry. Their son Thomas Arthur Welwood married Mary A. Royael, the daughter of Charles L. and Mary A. Royael of Brooklyn.

In 1887, the house was purchased by Timothy Francis Neville who renamed it *Warwick House*. [*The Brooklyn Daily Eagle* July 11, 1887, p. 2.]

*Welwood is considered to be the founding father of Lindenhurst.

front facade

Westin, Clarence Frederick, Sr. (d. 1927)

Occupation(s): merchant - president, Jones Brothers Tea Co., Scranton, PA; director, Grand Union Tea Co. (which became Grand Union Supermarket)
industrialist - director, Anchor Pottery Co.

Marriage(s): 1909-div. 1922 – Maude Virginia Jones (1886-1977)

Address: Handsome Avenue, Sayville
Name of estate: *Beechwold*
Year of construction: 1903
Style of architecture: Shingle
Architect(s): Isaac Henry Green II designed the main residence, gatehouse, and 1905 playhouse; the latter included a bowling alley and billiard room (for F. S. Jones)
Landscape architect(s):
House extant: no; destroyed by fire in 1957*
Historical notes:

The house, originally named *Beechwold*, was built by Frank Smith Jones.
Clarence Frederick Westin, Sr. was the son of Charles F. Westin of Brooklyn.
Maude Virginia Jones Westin, the daughter of Frank Smith and Mary Louise Granbery Jones, later owned *Beechwold*. Maude, who had married Clarence Frederick Westin, Sr., subsequently married David J. Shea. The Sheas resided in the estate's gatehouse. Her sister Henrietta married William Robinson Simonds and resided at *Wyndemoor* in Sayville. Maude later purchased *Wyndemoor* from her sister.
Clarence Frederick and Maude Virginia Jones Westin, Sr.'s son Gordon died at the age of eight in a horse riding accident. [Harry W. Havemeyer, *East on the Great South Bay: Sayville and Bayport 1860-1960* (Mattituck, NY: Amereon House, 2001), p.154.] Their son Charles married Flora Harris, the daughter of Dr. Raymond Victor Harris of Savannah, GA. Their son Douglas married Florence Saunders, the daughter of Dr. Samuel Saunders, Jr. of Binghamton, NY, and resided in Sayville.
In 1945, *Beechwold* was purchased by Elwell Palmer.
In 1949, Palmer sold it to Dr. Daniel McLaughlin, who owned it at the time of the fire.
*The gatehouse and playhouse are extant. The gatehouse is located at 254 Handsome Avenue and the playhouse is at 96 Benson Avenue.

Beechwold

Wharton, Percival Charles (1880-1937)

Occupation(s):

Marriage(s): Ada Louise Lousdale (1880-1937)

Address: Bayview Avenue, East Islip
Name of estate:
Year of construction:
Style of architecture:
Architect(s):
Landscape architect(s):
House extant: unconfirmed
Historical notes:

Percival Charles Wharton was the son of William Fishbourne and Frances Turner Fisher Wharton of Philadelphia, PA, who rented a summer residence in East Islip.

Despondent over his poor health and financial problems, Percival shot his wife to death then committed suicide at their Cranberry Lake, NY, cabin. [*The New York Times* October 18, 1937, p. 36.]

Louise Lousdale Wharton's sister married Richard Elkins, the son of Stephen B. Elkins, United States Senator from West Virginia.

[See other Wharton entries for additional family information.]

Wharton, Richard (1875-1933)

Occupation(s): financier - member, Childs and Co. (stock brokerage firm)

Marriage(s): 1906-1933 – Helena Johnson Parsons (1878-1936)

Address: St. Mark's Lane, Islip
Name of estate: *Whileaway*
Year of construction: c. 1881
Style of architecture: Shingle
Architect(s):
Landscape architect(s):
House extant: no
Historical notes:

The house, originally named *Whileaway*, was built by Schuyler Livingston Parsons, Sr. It was later owned by his daughter Helena, who had married Richard Wharton and, then, by the Wharton's son Richard T. Wharton, Sr. The Whartons continued to call it *Whileaway*.

The *Long Island Society Register, 1929* lists Richard and Helena Parsons Wharton as residing at *Whileaway* in Islip.

He was the son of William Fishbourne and Frances Turner Fisher Wharton of Philadelphia, PA, and East Islip. His brother Percival married Ada Louise Lousdale and resided in East Islip.

Helena Johnson Parsons Wharton's brother Schuyler Livingston Parsons, Jr. married Elizabeth Pierson and resided at *Pleasure Island* in Islip. Her sister Evelyn married Amor Hollingsworth of Boston, MA.

Richard and Helena Johnson Parsons Wharton's son Richard T. Wharton, Sr. married Mara Lucy di Zoppola, the daughter of Count Andrea Alexsandro Mario and Countess Edith Mortimer di Zoppola of Mill Neck, and resided at *Whileaway* in Newport, RI, and at *Whileaway* in Islip. [*See* Spinzia, *Long Island's Prominent North Shore Families, vol. I* – di Zoppola entry.] Their daughter Marion married Gerald Hallock III of Great Barrington, MA, and Brooklyn, NY.

[See other Wharton entries for additional family information.]

Wharton, Richard T., Sr. (1909-1995)

Occupation(s): financier - member, Abbott, Proctor and Paine (stock brokerage firm)

Marriage(s): 1945-1995 – Mara Lucy di Zoppola (1924-2007)

Address: St. Mark's Lane, Islip
Name of estate: *Whileaway*
Year of construction: c. 1881
Style of architecture: Shingle
Architect(s):
Landscape architect(s):
House extant: no
Historical notes:

The house, originally named *Whileaway*, was built by Schuyler Livingston Parsons, Sr. It was inherited by his daughter Helena, who married Richard Wharton, and, then, by the Whartons' son Richard T. Wharton, Sr. The Whartons continued to call it *Whileaway*.

Mara Lucy di Zoppola Wharton was the daughter of Count Andrea Alexsandro Mario and Countess Edith Mortimer di Zoppola of Mill Neck. [*See* Spinzia, *Long Island's Prominent North Shore Families, vol. I* – di Zoppola entry.]

The *Social Register, Summer 1949* lists Richard T. and Mara di Zoppola Wharton [Sr.] as residing at *Whileaway* in Newport, RI.

Richard T. and Mara Lucy di Zoppola Wharton, Sr.'s daughter Stephanie married Peter M. Holbrook and resided in San Francisco, CA. Their daughter Lucie and their son Richard T. Wharton, Jr. did not marry.

At the time of his death, Richard T. Wharton, Sr. was residing in Pound Ridge, NY.

[See other Wharton entries for additional family information.]

Wharton, William Fishbourne (1846-1917)

Occupation(s): capitalist - vice president and director, Madison Square Garden Co.
financier - member, New York Stock Exchange
Civic Activism: a founder and secretary, National Horse Show Association of America

Marriage(s): 1871-1917 – Frances Turner Fisher (1846-1929)

Address: Suffolk Lane, East Islip
Name of estate:
Year of construction:
Style of architecture: Shingle
Architect(s):
Landscape architect(s):
House extant: unconfirmed
Historical notes:

The *Social Register, 1890* lists William Fishbourne and Fanny T. Fisher Wharton as residing in Islip [East Islip]. They rented this house for use as their summer residence.

He was the son of George Mifflin and Maria Markoe Wharton of Philadelphia, PA.

Frances Turner Fisher Wharton was the daughter of William and Sarah Julia Palmer Fisher of Philadelphia, PA.

William Fishbourne and Francis Turner Fisher Wharton's son Richard married Helena Parsons and resided at *Whileaway* in Islip. Their son Percival married Ada Louise Lousdale and resided in East Islip.

[See other Wharton entries for additional family information.]

front facade, c. 1913

White, Raymond S. (1873-1903)

Occupation(s):	attorney - partner, Baldwin and White
	industrialist - director, Union Typewriter Co.; treasurer and director, National Addograph Co., Jersey City, NJ (typewriter and adding machine manufacturing firm); vice-president and director, D. O. Hayes and Co.
	capitalist - director, General Building & Construction Co.
	financier - director, McKickar Realty Trust Co., NYC (banking firm)
	merchant - vice-president and director, Richard Hudnuts Pharmacy; vice-president and director, D. O. Haynes & Co. (pharmacy)
Marriage(s):	Sarah H. Crane
Address:	Great River Road, Great River
Name of estate:	
Year of construction:	1899
Style of architecture:	Neo-Tudor
Architect(s):	Charles C. Thain designed the house (for R. S. White)

Landscape architect(s):
House extant: no; demolished, 1961
Historical notes:

The house was built by Raymond S. White.
He was the son of Andrew J. White.
Raymond S. and Sarah H. Crane White's daughter Katherine married Herbert Frederick Garrick, the son of Frederick C. and Gertrude S. Garrick and resided in Manhattan. Their daughter Margaret married Chauncey Shaffer Truax Sr. with whom she resided in Sharon, CT.
Raymond S. White died as a result of an automobile accident in Bay Shore. [*The New York Times* December 22, 1903, p. 9.]
Sarah subsequently married Francis Sessions Hutchins, with whom she continued to reside in the house which they called *Saramond*.
The house was later owned by Dr. George David Stewart, who called it *Appin House* and, subsequently, by Joseph Francis Dempsey who renamed in *Estancia*.

front facade, c. 1910

Whitney, William Collins (1841-1904)

Occupation(s):	attorney - corporate council for the City of New York
	industrialist - partner, Standard Oil Co. (which became Exxon Corp.)
	capitalist - Metropolitan Street Railroad Co.
	statesman - Secretary of the Navy in the Cleveland and Benjamin Harrison administrations
Marriage(s):	M/1 – 1869-1893 – Flora Payne (1842-1893)
	M/2 – 1896-1899 – Edith Sybil May (1854-1899)
Address:	St. Mark's Lane, Islip
Name of estate:	
Year of construction:	1882
Style of architecture:	
Architect(s):	
Landscape architect(s):	
House extant:	unconfirmed

Historical notes:

The house was built by William Collins Whitney. [*The New York Times* July 30, 1882, p. 5.]

He is reported to have been the largest property owner in the Commonwealth of Massachusetts. [Jerry E. Patterson, *The First Four Hundred: Mrs. Astor's New York in the Gilded Age* (New York: Rizzoli International Publ., Inc., 2000), p. 136.]

Born in Conway, MA, William Collins Whitney was the son of Brigadier General James Scollay and Laurenda Collins Whitney. His sister Lillian married Charles Tracy Barney and resided in Old Westbury and Southampton. [*See* Spinzia, *Long Island's Prominent North Shore Families, vol. I* and *Long Island's Prominent Families in the Town of Southampton* – Barney entries.]

Flora Payne Whitney was the daughter of Senator Henry B. Payne of Ohio.

William Collins and Flora Payne Whitney were on Ward McAllister's "Four Hundred" list.

Their daughter Dorothy married William Dickerman Straight and, then, Leonard Knight Elmhirst. She resided at *Elmhurst*, later called *Applegreen*, in Old Westbury. [*See* Spinzia, *Long Island's Prominent North Shore Families, vol. I* – Elmhirst entry – and *Long Island's Prominent North Shore Families, vol. II* – Whitney entry.] Their son Henry [aka Harry Payne Whitney] married Gertrude Vanderbilt, the daughter of Cornelius and Alice Claypoole Gwynne Vanderbilt and resided in Old Westbury. [*See* Spinzia, *Long Island's Prominent North Shore Families, vol. II* – Whitney entry.]

Whitney's second wife was the former Edith Sybil May Randolph, who, with her first husband English Captain Arthur Randolph, had resided in Douglaston, NY. Her husband had died when their daughter Adelaide was thirteen and their son Arthur, known as Bertie, was eleven. Edith's father Dr. J. Frederick May was the physician who identified the body of John Wilkes Booth.

In 1882, Clarence Tucker purchased the house from Whitney who, by 1902, had relocated to Old Westbury. [*See* Spinzia, *Long Island's Prominent North Shore Families, vol. II* – Whitney entry.] The Whitney's Old Westbury estate was later owned by Whitney's son Harry. It was to this estate that Gertrude brought Gloria Laura Vanderbilt ("Little Gloria"), the daughter of her brother Reginald Claypoole Vanderbilt and Gloria Laura Mercedes Morgan Vanderbilt, during the vicious and much-publicized trial for custody of Little Gloria.

In 1893, Whitney's Islip house was purchased by Mrs. Richard Henry Williams, Sr.

*Whitney's Old Westbury estate,
rear facade*

Wilbur, Edward Russell, Sr. (1828-1905)

Occupation(s):	industrialist - partner, William & Hastings (stationery manufacturer)
	publisher - a founder, secretary, and treasurer, *Forest and Stream*, 1873;
	a founder, *Audubon* magazine
Civic Activism:	a founder, president, and director, Blooming Grove Park, Pike County, PA;
	a founder, National Rod and Reel Association, 1882;
	a founder, The Audubon Society for the Protection of Birds, 1886
	(for mercantile use)
Marriage(s):	
Address:	Handsome Avenue, Sayville
Name of estate:	*Beach Grove*
Year of construction:	1876
Style of architecture:	
Architect(s):	
Landscape architect(s):	
House extant: no	
Historical notes:	

In 1875, Benny Wilbur purchased the Manly farm and converted the house into his summer residence.

His son Edward Russell Wilbur, Jr. married Lydia Whiteside of Ashville, NC, and resided in Scarsdale, NY.

The sale of Beach Grove to Frank Smith Jones was forestalled by a question of ownership. It appears that the title was in joint ownership with Wilbur's first wife who had been granted a New Jersey divorce on the grounds of desertion, a cause which New York State did not recognize as being legal. In 1902, the sale was finally consummated. Its provisions included the sale of *While-Away*, Jones' Handsome Avenue estate, to Wilbur. In 1905, Wilbur sold *While-Away* to William J. Benney of Brooklyn. In the interim, Wilbur had relocated to the estate of Granville Hamilton on West Boulevard in Oyster Bay which he had purchased in 1902. [*The Brooklyn Daily Eagle* October 2, 1902, p. 9, and December 19, 1902, p. 12, and *Brooklyn Life* June 21, 1902, p. 15, and July 1, 1905, p. 14.]

Williams, Percy Garnett (1857-1923)

Occupation(s):	entertainers and related professions - comedian
	capitalist - partner, with Thomas Adams, Jr., real estate development,
	Bergen Beach, Brooklyn;
	constructed and owned a casino in Brooklyn, 1896;
	manager, Brooklyn Music Hall, Brooklyn;
	owner, Novelty Theater, Brooklyn;
	builder and owner, Orpheum Theater, Brooklyn;
	owner, Circle Theater, NYC;
	owner, Colonial Theater, NYC
Civic Activism:	established Percy G. Williams Home, East Islip*
Marriage(s):	1885-1923 – Ida E. *[unable to determine maiden name]* (d. 1927)
Address:	Suffolk Lane, East Islip
Name of estate:	*Pine Acres*
Year of construction:	1911
Style of architecture:	Modified Shingle
Architect(s):	
Landscape architect(s):	
House extant: no; demolished in c. 1975	
Historical notes:	

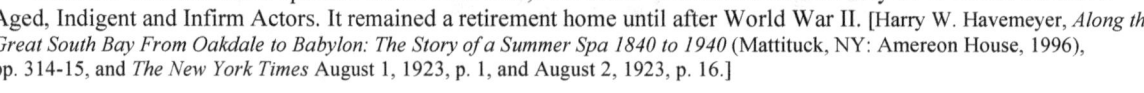

rear facade

The house, originally named *Pine Acres*, was built by Percy Garnett Williams.

The *Brooklyn Blue Book and Long Island Society Register, 1921* lists Percy G. Williams as residing in East Islip.

He was the son of Dr. John B. and Mrs. Sarah Williams.

Percy's wife Ida began to manifest signs of mental problems after the death of their son Victor.

*Williams' will stated that upon the death of his wife, *Pine Acres* would become the Percy G. Williams Home for Aged, Indigent and Infirm Actors. It remained a retirement home until after World War II. [Harry W. Havemeyer, *Along the Great South Bay From Oakdale to Babylon: The Story of a Summer Spa 1840 to 1940* (Mattituck, NY: Amereon House, 1996), pp. 314-15, and *The New York Times* August 1, 1923, p. 1, and August 2, 1923, p. 16.]

Williams, Sarah Welford Peters (1856-1929)

Marriage(s):	1879-1923 – Richard Henry Williams, Sr. (1854-1923) - merchant - partner, with Samuel Twyford Peters, Williams and Peters (wholesale coal)
Address:	St. Mark's Lane, Islip
Name of estate:	
Year of construction:	1882
Style of architecture:	
Architect(s):	
Landscape architect(s):	
House extant:	unconfirmed
Historical notes:	

   The house was built by William Collins Whitney. [*The New York Times* July 30, 1882, p. 5.] In 1882, Clarence Tucker purchased it from Whitney. In 1893, the house was purchased by Mrs. Richard Henry Williams, Sr.
   She was the daughter of Samuel T. and Josephine Gemmel Peters. Sarah's brother Samuel married Adaline Mapes Elder and resided at *Windholme Farm* in Islip.
   Richard Henry Williams, Sr. was the son of Charles and Theodora Amelia Hopkins Williams.
   Richard Henry and Sarah Welford Peters Williams, Sr.'s son Richard Henry Williams, Jr. married Julia Lorillard Edgar, the daughter of Newbold and Agnes Wood Strachan Edgar, and resided at *Brookrace* in Mendham, NJ. In 1896, their daughter Sally died at the age of four. Their daughter Josephine married William H. Dixon, the son of William Palmer and Evelina Babcock Dixon, Sr. [*See* Spinzia, *Long Island's Prominent Families in the Town of Hempstead* – Dixon entries.]

Wilmerding, George Gorman (1822-1889)

Occupation(s):	auctioneer - Wilmerding, Priest, & Mount
Civic Activism:	a founder and vice-president, Southside Sportsmen's Club
Marriage(s):	1851-1868 – Cornelia M. Lawrance (1830-1868)
Address:	South Country Road, West Bay Shore
Name of estate:	
Year of construction:	
Style of architecture:	
Architect(s):	
Landscape architect(s):	
House extant:	unconfirmed
Historical notes:	

   George Gorman Wilmerding was the son of William Edward and Johanna Mary Gosman Wilmerding. His brother Thomas married Anna Clinton.
   Cornelia M. Lawrance Wilmerding was the daughter of Thomas and Margaret Lawrence Ireland Lawrance. Her brother Francis married Frances Adelaide Garner and resided at *Manatuck Farm* in Bay Shore. Her brother Horatio married May Louise Romaine. Her sister Eleanor married William Edward Wilmerding, Jr. Her sister Julia married Horace Waldo, Jr. Her sister Louisa married Bradish Johnson, Sr. and resided at *Sans Souci* in Bay Shore.

Wilmerding, Lucius Kellogg, Sr. (1848-1922)

Occupation(s):	merchant - partner, Wilmerding & Huguet (dry goods importer and merchant); partner, Wilmerding & Bissett (dry goods importer and merchant)
	financier - partner, Gray and Wilmerding (stock brokerage firm); trustee, Greenwich Savings Bank
Civic Activism:	member, executive committee, Islip and East Islip Board of Trade, 1909
Marriage(s):	1876-1922 – Caroline Maria Murray (1853-1931)
	- Civic Activism: chair, Islip chapter, American Red Cross, 1915
Address:	Suffolk Lane, East Islip
Name of estate:	*White Lodge*
Year of construction:	
Style of architecture:	Italian Renaissance
Architect(s):	
Landscape architect(s):	
House extant: unconfirmed	
Historical notes:	

The *Social Register, Summer 1915* lists Lucius K. and Caroline Murray Wilmerding [Sr.] as residing at *White Lodge* in East Islip.

He was the son of Henry Augustus and Harriet Kellogg Wilmerding.

Lucius Kellogg and Caroline Maria Murray Wilmerding, Sr.'s son Lucius Kellogg Wilmerding, Jr. married Helen Suydam Cutting, the daughter of Robert Fulton and Helen Suydam Cutting of Great River, and resided in Far Hills, NJ. Their daughter Caroline married John Bond Trevor, Jr., the son of John Bond and Emily Norwood Trevor, Sr., and resided at *Trevallyn* in Paul Smiths, NY. In 1881, their daughter Edith died at the age of two.

The house was rented by Amedee Depau Moran under a ten-year lease agreement.

rear facade

Wood, Henry Duncan, Jr. (1880-1918)

Occupation(s):	financier - member, William M. Clarke (stock brokerage firm); member, Frederic H. Hatch and Co. (stock brokerage firm)
Marriage(s):	1904 – Effe J. Saunders
Address:	*[unable to determine street address]*, Bay Shore
Name of estate:	
Year of construction:	
Style of architecture:	
Architect(s):	
Landscape architect(s):	
House extant: unconfirmed	
Historical notes:	

The *Social Register, 1907* lists Henry Duncan and Effe J. Saunders Wood [Jr.] as residing in Bay Shore.

He was the son of Henry Duncan and Ellen Eliza Pulsifer Wood, Sr., who resided at *Ellenwood* in East Islip.

After being rejected several times for military service during World War I, he took a job at a munitions factory mixing chemicals. Henry was killed by an explosion at the age of thirty-seven.

Effie later married Augustus Heaton.

Henry Duncan and Effe J. Saunders Wood, Jr.'s son Henry Duncan Wood III married Gladys Howell Peters, the daughter of George Willis Peters.

[See following entry for additional family information.]

Wood, Henry Duncan, Sr. (1853-1915)

Occupation(s):	financier - a founder, with Harry Bowly Hollins, Sr., H. B. Hollins and Co. (stock brokerage firm)
	capitalist - director, Madison Square Garden Co.
Marriage(s):	1878-1915 – Ellen Eliza Pulsifer (1857-1926)
Address:	Islip Avenue, Islip
Name of estate:	*Ellenwood*
Year of construction:	1885

Style of architecture:
Architect(s):
Landscape architect(s):
House extant: unconfirmed
Historical notes:

In 1885, the original house on the site was destroyed by fire. Wood immediately built a new house on the site. [*The New York Times* April 9, 1885, p. 5.]

He was the son of William and Margaret Lawrence Wood.

Ellen Eliza Pulsifer Wood was the daughter of William Henry and Abby Williams Mayo Pulsifer.

Henry Duncan and Ellen Eliza Pulsifer Wood, Sr.'s son Henry Duncan Wood, Jr. married Effe J. Saunders and resided in Bay Shore. Their daughter Gertrude married Edward Bell, Jr., the son of Edward and Helen A. Wilmerding Bell, Sr. Their son William married Winifred M. Dobson, the daughter of T. T. Dobson of Manhattan.

[See previous entry for additional family information.]

Woolley, Dr. James Van Siclen, Sr. (1843-1919)

Occupation(s):	physician - assistant pathologist, Muhlenberg Hospital, NJ
Marriage(s):	1878-1919 – Emma Josephine Brinkerhoff (1847-1924)
Address:	Awixa Avenue, Bay Shore

Name of estate:
Year of construction:
Style of architecture:
Architect(s):
Landscape architect(s):
House extant: unconfirmed
Historical notes:

Dr. James Van Siclen Woolley, Sr. was the son of William Henry and Joanna Wyckoff Van Siclen Wooley.

Dr. James Van Siclen and Mrs. Emma Josephine Brinkerhoff Woolley, Sr.'s son Charles married Ethel Charlotte Genthner, the daughter of Dr. Philip J. Genthner. Their daughter Estelle married Edgar Bond Armstrong. Their son William married Florence Squarebriggs, the daughter of Daniel and Annie L. Ramsay Squarebriggs. Their daughter Emma married Henry Barker Fernald. Their son James Van Siclen Woolley, Jr. was an attorney and real estate speculator in Brooklyn and Queens.

front facade, c. 1903

Worden, John Lorimer, III (1874-1938)

Occupation(s):	financier - partner, Worden and Low (stock brokerage firm)
Marriage(s):	M/1 – 1901-div. 1920 – Angela Mills (1864-1956) - nobility
	M/2 – 1920-1938 – Edith Lounsberry (1887-1946)
Address:	80 South Saxon Avenue, Bay Shore
Name of estate:	
Year of construction:	c. 1880
Style of architecture:	Victorian
Architect(s):	
Landscape architect(s):	
House extant:	no; demolished in 1932*
Historical notes:	

The house was built by Daniel Denice Conover. It was later owned by his son Augustus Whitlock Conover, Sr. In 1902, Worden purchased the house. [*The Brooklyn Daily Eagle* May 3, 1902, p. 10.]

John Lorimer Worden III, who served as a private in Theodore Roosevelt's Rough Riders, was the grandson of John Lorimer Worden, Sr., the commander of the *Monitor* during its historic battle with the *Merrimac*. His sister Harriet married James Burnett Lowell and resided in Manhattan.

Angela Mills Worden had previously been married to Henry Mason Cutting. After her divorce from Worden, Angela married Russian Prince Boris Scherbatoff with whom she wintered at *Cherokee Grove* in Flagler County, FL. The Adirondack-style lodge is currently owned by Flagler County. The county has restored the residence and has opened, to the public, its surrounding 435 acres as The Princess Place Preserve.

By 1929, Angela had relocated to *Ivy Lodge* in Southampton. [*See* Spinzia, *Long Island's Prominent Families in the Town of Southampton* – Worden entry.]

The *Social Register Summer, 1937* lists J. Lorimer and Edith Lounsberry Worden [III] as residing at *Nethercliff* in Newport, RI.

She had previously been married to Henry Pierrepont Perry. The Perrys' son William married Gertrude Madison Wing, the daughter of Paul R. Wing of Beverly Hills, CA; Elizabeth Crofton of New York; Elizabeth Morris, the daughter of Lewis Gouverneur Morris of *Malbone* in Newport, RI; and, subsequently, Kathryn Von Stade, the daughter of Francis Skiddy and Kathryn N. Steel Von Stade, Sr. of Southampton and Old Westbury. [*See* Spinzia, *Long Island's Prominent North Shore Families, vol. II* and *Long Island's Prominent Families in the Town of Southampton* – Von Stade entries.]

Worden disappeared at sea while bound to Providence, RI, aboard the Colonial Line ship SS *Comet*. [*The New York Times* June 14, 1938, p. 3.]

The house was purchased in 1912 by Franklyn Laws Hutton, who called it *Win Sum Lodge*. He later sold it to his brother Edward Francis Hutton. In 1921, it was purchased from E. F. Hutton by Philip Balch Weld. In 1930, the house was purchased from Weld by Hamlet Cecil Sharp, who demolished it and built a new house on the site.

*The estate's barn complex, stables, and windmill are extant.

barn complex, 2020

Wray, William Henry, Sr. (1853-1929)

Occupation(s):	capitalist - owned commercial rental property, Brooklyn; builder, built houses in Town of Islip
Marriage(s):	M/1 – Charlotte Evelyn Osborn (d. 1878) M/2 – div. – Robina Marion Lees (1888-1987) M/3 – Clara Mills (1862-1916)
Address:	32 Awixa Avenue, Bay Shore
Name of estate:	*Whileaway*
Year of construction:	c. 1899
Style of architecture:	Shingle
Architect(s):	Ernest George Washington Dietrich designed the house (for Wray)
Landscape architect(s):	
House extant: yes	
Historical notes:	

front facade

The house, originally named *Whileaway*, was built by William Henry Wray Sr.

He was the son of Mark and Harriet Ann Irish Wray.

Charlotte Evelyn Osborn Wray was the daughter of Henry Fleet and Elizabeth Wagner Ruland Osborn.

William Henry and Charlotte Evelyn Osborn Wray, Sr.'s son Henry died in 1878 one day after his birth.

Robina Marion Lees Wray was the daughter of Raymond and Ann McPherson Lees. Robina had previously been married to John Francis Duffy.

William Henry and Robina Marion Lees Wray, Sr.'s daughter Dorothy married Everett Curtis Dearborn, the son of Roy Samuel and Florence Melissa Curtis Dearborn.

Clara Mills Wray, who disinherited her husband, was the daughter of Clark Wickham and Julia Sophia Coleman Mills.

William Henry and Clara Mills Wray, Sr.'s son Howard married Ada L. Schott, the daughter of Frederick Schott and, later, Martha Stoll, the daughter of Ferdinand and Martha Sauter Stoll. Their son William Henry Wray, Jr. married Ella Arline Hammer.

The house was later owned by Frederick C. Lemmerman and, then, by William Kemble Clarkson, Jr.

In 2003, the house was purchased by Dr. Mark Foehr.

Wright, Dr. Arthur Mullen (1879-1948)

Occupation(s):	physician - director of surgery, French Hospital, NYC; member, medical board, French Hospital; president, medical board, Bellevue Hospital, NYC
Marriage(s):	1912-1941 – Alice Spaulding Stanchfield (1887-1941)
Address:	Ocean Avenue, Islip
Name of estate:	*Afterglow*
Year of construction:	c. 1890
Style of architecture:	Shingle
Architect(s):	
Landscape architect(s):	
House extant: no; demolished in c. 1950	
Historical notes:	

The house, originally named *Afterglow*, was built by John Gibb. In 1909, it was purchased by John Barry Stanchfield, Sr. The house was later owned by his daughter Alice, who had married Dr. Arthur Mullen Wright. Both the Stanchfields and Wrights continued to call the estate *Afterglow*.

He was the son of Richard Brainard and Ella Agatha Mullen Wright.

Dr. Arthur Mullen and Mrs. Alice Spaulding Stanchfield Wright's son Richard, who married Adele Carlisle, the daughter of Floyd Leslie and Edna Rogers Carlisle, Sr. of Lattingtown, resided in Locust Valley prior to relocating to Ruxton, MD. [*See* Spinzia, *Long Island's Prominent North Shore Families*, vol. 1 – Carlisle entry.] Their son Stanchfield married Jeanne Riley, the daughter of Edward and Anna Riley, and resided in Earleville, MD.

Yates, Douglas Thomas, Sr. (1915-2014)

Occupation(s):	financier - partner, White, Weld, and Co. (investment banking firm); chairman of board, Seaboard Association (investment banking firm)
	capitalist - executive vice-president and director, Republic Pictures Corp., 1950-1978
	military - major, United States Army, 1941-1946
Civic Activism:	founding trustee, Episcopal School, NYC;
	trustee, General Theological Seminary;
	chairman of board, United Hospital Fund, NYC;
	chairman of board, Foreign Parishes of the Episcopal Church;
	trustee, Buckley School, NYC;
	trustee, Lenox Hill Hospital, NYC;
	trustee, Hospital Association of New York State
Marriage(s):	1941-2006 – Margaret Louise Titus (1918-2006)
	- Civic Activism: president, Altar Guild, St. James' Episcopal Church, NYC; a founder and tutor, East Harlem Neighborhood Study Group
Address:	69 West Bayberry Road, Islip
Name of estate:	
Year of construction:	1899-1900
Style of architecture:	Moorish
Architect(s):	Grosvenor Atterbury designed the house (for H. O. Havemeyer)*
Landscape architect(s):	Nathan F. Barrett (for H. O. Havemeyer)**
Builder:	*[see Jabez Ephraim Van Orden entry]*

House extant: yes
Historical notes:

The house was built by Henry Osborne Havemeyer as part of his "Modern Venice" development.

Douglas Thomas Yates, Sr. was the son of Herbert John and Petra Antonsen Yates, Sr., who resided at *Onsru Farm* in West Islip.

Margaret Louise Titus Yates was the daughter of Walter Livingston and Margaret Gulden Titus, Sr. of West Islip.

Douglas Thomas and Margaret Louise Titus Yates, Sr.'s son Douglas Thomas Yates, Jr. who married Doris Catlin, the daughter of Dr. Daniel and Mrs. Doris Havemeyer Catlin, Sr. of Bay Shore, and, later, Mary Caryl Vejvoda, resided in New Haven, CT. Their son Timothy, who resided in Rye, NY, married Dorinda Hoyte Le Maire, the daughter of Edward Le Maire, and, subsequently, Katherine Jurusik, the daughter of Eugene and Jean Jurusik of Elmira, NY. Their son Lawrance Randall Yates married Hope Starr Lloyd, the daughter of Morris Lloyd of Chestnut Hill, PA, and resided in Manhattan. Their daughter Margaret married Nathan Comstock Thorne, the son of Harold Wooster Thorne, Jr. of Oakland, CA, and also resided in Manhattan.

[See other Yates entries for additional family information.]

*The sales brochure for "Modern Venice" states that the Moorish-style architecture was suggested by Louis Comfort Tiffany.

**The sales brochure also states that "Modern Venice" would be devoid of trees and vegetation and that Nathan F. Barrett was the landscape architect.

front facade, 2006

Yates, Herbert John, Sr. (1880-1966)

Occupation(s):	capitalist - a founder, with his brother George, Republic Film Laboratories, Inc., NYC, 1917 (which became Consolidated Film Industries, Inc.);
	president and chairman of board, Consolidated Film Industries, Inc. (motion picture film developing laboratory and distributor, which became Republic Pictures Corp.);
	president and chairman of board, Republic Pictures Corp. (motion picture studio);
	director, Cinema Patents Co., Inc.
	financier - director, Liberty National Bank and Trust Co., NYC;
	director, Concord Casualty Insurance Co.
Civic Activism:	director, Motion Pictures Association of New York;
	director, St. Joseph Hospital, Burbank, CA
Marriage(s):	M/1 – 1910-1949 – Petra Antonsen (1882-1949)
	M/2 – 1952-1966 – Verra Hruba Ralston (1920-2003)
	- entertainers and associated professions - actress
Address:	South Country Road and Snedecor Avenue, West Islip
Name of estate:	*Onsrufarm*
Year of construction:	c. 1892
Style of architecture:	Colonial Revival
Architect(s):	
Landscape architect(s):	
House extant:	no; destroyed by fire, 1967*
Historical notes:	

Onsrufarm

Herbert John Yates, Sr. was the son of Charles Henry and Emma Worthington Yates of Brooklyn.

Petra Antonsen Yates was the daughter of Henry Antonsen of Oslo, Norway.

Herbert John and Petra Antonsen Yates, Sr.'s son Herbert John Yates, Jr. married Jean St. Amand and resided in Great Neck. Their son Douglas married Margaret Titus, the daughter of Walter Livingston and Margaret Gulden Titus, Sr. of West Islip, and resided in Islip. Their daughter Elsa married Walter Livingston Titus, Jr. and resided in Islip. Their son Richard, who resided in Brightwaters, married Marie Rose Mc Kee, the daughter of Henry Sellers and Alice Martin Davies Mc Kee II of Babylon, and, subsequently, Roberta Daniel, the daughter of Daniel M. Daniel.

[See other Yates entries for additional family information.]

*The tennis house is extant. It has been converted into a private residence.

front facade

Yates, Richard George, Sr. (1919-1992)

Occupation(s):	capitalist - vice-president and assistant sales director, Republic Pictures; motion picture producer, *What* [aka *Night is the Phantom*], 1965
	military - captain, United States Army, 1943-1947
Marriage(s):	M/1 – 1941-div. 1954 – Marie Rose McKee (b. 1921)
	- Civic Activism: established Marie Rose McKee Correll Fund
	M/2 – 1958-1992 – Roberta Daniel (1923-2008)
Address:	112 South Windsor Avenue, Brightwaters
Name of estate:	
Year of construction:	
Style of architecture:	Shingle with Victorian elements
Architect(s):	
Landscape architect(s):	
House extant: yes	
Historical notes:	

The *Social Register, New York 1948* lists Richard G. and Marie R. Mc Kee Yates [Sr.] as residing on South Country Road, West Islip. The *Social Register, 1952* lists them as residing at 112 Winsor [Windsor] Avenue, Brightwaters.

He was the son of Herbert John and Petra Antonsen Yates, Sr. of *Onsrufarm* in West Islip.

Marie Rose McKee Yates was the daughter of Henry Sellers and Alice Martin Davies McKee II of Babylon. Marie later married Joseph S. Bynum, the son of Samuel Bynum of Paducah, KY, and, subsequently, Ronald S. Correll, the son of Charles D. Correll.

Richard George and Marie Rose McKee Yates, Sr.'s son Jeffrey married Lauran Boakes. Their son Richard George Yates, Jr. married Linda Templeton.

Roberta Daniel Yates was the daughter of Daniel M. Daniel.

[See other Yates entries for additional family information.]

front facade, 2006

Young, Albert (1841-1895)

Occupation(s):	financier - stockbroker
Marriage(s):	1874-1895 – Minnie Edna Arents (d. 1931)
Address:	Awixa Avenue, Bay Shore
Name of estate:	*Awixaway*
Year of construction:	c. 1880
Style of architecture:	Queen Anne
Architect(s):	
Landscape architect(s):	
House extant: unconfirmed	
Historical notes:	

The house, originally named *Awixaway*, was built by Albert Young.

Minnie Edna Arents Young was an heir to the American Tobacco Company fortune. She subsequently married John Oldrin, an employee on her Darien, Connecticut, estate. John was twenty years her junior.

Albert and Minnie Edna Arents Young's son Albert M. Young died at the age of twenty-five. Their son Lewis married the actress Leona Anderson (aka Aronson). Their daughter Edna married the millionaire Alfred S. Dieterich, prior to eloping with Harry S. Brenchley, a trainer at Alfred Gwynne Vanderbilt, Sr.'s stables. [*The New York Times* February 17, 1909, p. 2.]

Zerega, John Pierre, Sr. (1865-1958)

Occupation(s):	capitalist - owned a Sayville yacht basin and marine supply company*; chairman of board, A. Zerega & Sons, Inc.; chairman of board, Alimentary Pastes, Fairlawn, NJ
Civic Activism:	governor, Sayville Golf Club, 1921
Marriage(s):	1901-1945 – Ethel Marie Hill (1879-1945)
Address:	Gillette Avenue, Bayport
Name of estate:	*Littlewood*
Year of construction:	1896
Style of architecture:	Shingle
Architect(s):	George Browne Post designed the house (for R. H. Post, Sr.)
Landscape architect(s):	
House extant:	yes
Historical notes:	

The house, originally named *Littlewood*, was built by Regis Henri Post, Sr. The house was subsequently owned by Zerega, who continued to call it *Littlewood*.

The *Long Island Society Register, 1929* lists John P. and Ethel Hill Zerega [Sr.] as residing at *Littlewood* on Gillette Avenue, Bayport.

He was the son of Antoine and Louise Bollinger Zerega.

John Pierre and Ethel Marie Hill Zerega, Sr.'s thirteen-year-old daughter Ethel died in 1918 of influenza during the Spanish Flu epidemic of 1918-1919. Their son John Pierre Zerega, Jr. married Kathryn Anne Hurst, the daughter of William H. Hurst of *Orchard Hill* in Monroe, CT. Their daughter Arlene married William Joseph Kent, Jr. of Brooklyn and South Norwalk, CT.

*The yacht basin and marine supply company had been previously owned by Robert Barnwell Roosevelt, Jr. [*The New York Times* May 31, 1936, p. 55.]

front facade

Frederick Gilbert Bourne estate, *Indian Neck Hall*

living room

main floor hall

APPENDICES

Elwood Mildeberger residence, *Oakelwood*

front facade prior to alterations

front facade after alterations

Table of Contents for Appendices

Architects	395
Civic Activism	403
Estate Names	409
Golf Courses on Former South Shore Estates	417
Landscape Architects	419
Maiden Names	423
Occupations	443
Rehabilitative Secondary Uses of Surviving Estate Houses	457
Statesmen and Diplomats Who Resided on Long Island's South Shore	459
Village Locations of Estates	461
America's First Age of Fortune: A Selected Bibliography	471
Selected Bibliographic References to Individual South Shore Estate Owners	479
Biographical Sources Consulted	501
Maps Consulted for Estate Locations	503
Illustration Credits	505
About the Authors	507

Dr. Malcolm McBurney residence

front facade

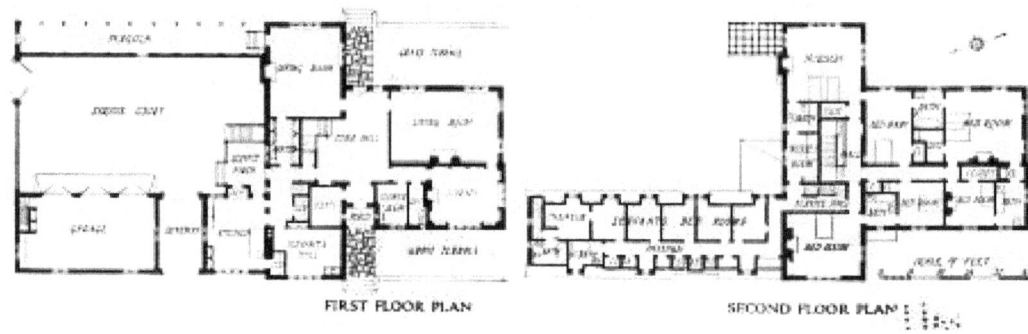

Architects

See the surname entry to ascertain if more than one architect was involved in designing the various buildings on an estate. This list reflects their South Shore commissions and includes the original and subsequent owners of the estates. When the owner who contracted with the architect is known, it is indicated by an asterisk.

Grosvenor Atterbury

	Baker, William Dunham		Islip
	Beard, Anson Mc Cook, Jr.		Islip
	Dempsey, Joseph Francis, Jr.		Islip
	Egly, Henry Harris		Islip
	Garben, Dr. Louis Francis, Sr.		Islip
	Gulden, Charles, III		Islip
	Gulden, Frank, Sr.		Islip
*	Havemeyer, Henry Osborne	*Bayberry Point*	Islip
	Havemeyer, Horace, Jr.		Islip
	Havemeyer, Horace, Sr.		Islip
	Howell, Carlton Bell		Islip
	Moore, Dr. David Dodge		Islip
	Perkins, Richard Sturgis, Sr.		Islip
	Scully, Charles Brewster	*Wereholme*	Islip
	Thorne, Edwin, III		Islip
	Titus, Walter Livingston, Jr.		Islip
*	Weekes, Harold Hathaway	*Wereholme*	Islip
	Yates, Douglas Thomas, Sr.		Islip

Dwight James Baum

*	Schwenke, Oscar Louis, III	(alterations, c. 1919)	Bay Shore
*	Shea, Timothy Joseph, Sr.	*O'Conee*	Bay Shore

Clarence K. Birdsall

*	Behman, Louis C., Sr.	*Lindenwalt* (1898 alterations)	Bayport
*	Burchell, George W.		Bay Shore
*	Covell, Charles Heber, Sr.		Bay Shore
	Eastwood, John Henry	(house & 1905 farm cottage)	Bay Shore
*	Ford, Malcolm Webster, Sr.	*My Fancy* (1894 alterations)	West Babylon
	Gilmore, William Guy, Sr.	*My Fancy* (1894 alterations)	West Babylon
*	Gulden, Charles, Sr.	*Netherbay* (1897 and 1901 alterations)	Bay Shore
*	Housman, Arthur Albert	(addition to main residence; stable and carriage house complex with living quarters for coachmen and grooms, harness rooms, cleaning rooms and offices; cattle barns and farmer's cottage, 1902)	West Islip
	Hyde, James Richard	(house, 1899 barn, & 1899 golf course clubhouse)	West Bay Shore
*	Hyde, Richard	(house, 1899 barn, & 1899 golf course clubhouse)	West Bay Shore

Architects

Clarence K. Birdsall (cont'd)

Ireland, John Busteed	(addition to main residence; stable and carriage house complex with living quarters for coachmen and grooms, harness rooms, cleaning rooms and offices; cattle barns and farmer's cottage, 1902)	West Islip
Isbrandtsen, Hans Jeppesen	(house, 1899 barn, & 1899 golf course clubhouse)	West Bay Shore
Lawrance, Charles Lanier	*Manatuck Farm* (designed 1897 brick carriage house)	Bay Shore
Lawrance, Francis Cooper, Jr.	*Manatuck Farm* (designed 1897 brick carriage house)	Bay Shore
* Lawrance, Francis Cooper, Sr.	*Manatuck Farm* (designed 1897 brick carriage house)	Bay Shore
* Myers, Nathaniel	(house & 1905 farm cottage)	Bay Shore
* Phelps, Charles Egbert	*Brightwaters*	
Rokenbaugh, Henry Scott	*Villa Avalon*	Bay Shore

Cross and Cross

* Hollins, Gerald Vanderbilt, Sr.	*The Hawks*	East Islip
* Hollins, Harry Bowly, Jr.	*Crickholly*	East Islip
* Hubbell, Lulu Hyde		Bay Shore
* Livingston, Miss Frances Lewis		East Islip

Philip Cusack

Entenmann, Robert William, Sr.		East Islip
* Morgan, Robert Woodward, Sr.		East Islip
Pinkerton, Robert Allan, II		East Islip

Delano and Aldrich

* McBurney, Dr. Malcolm		East Islip
Noyes, Daniel Raymond		East Islip

Bradley Delehanty

*Sutton, Frank	*North East Farm* [unconfirmed]	North Babylon

Adolph Mollenhauer Dick of Fuller and Dick

* Dick, Adolph Mollenhauer		Islip

Ernest George Washington Dietrich

Clarkson, William Kemble, Jr.		Bay Shore
Foehr, Dr. Mark [see Wray entry]		Bay Shore
Lemmerman, Frederick C.		Bay Shore
* Mollenhauer, John		Bay Shore
Sullivan, Dr. Raymond Peter, Sr.		Bay Shore
* Wray, William Henry, Sr.	*Whileaway*	Bay Shore

William F. Dominick

* Thorne, Landon Ketchum, Sr.	*Thornham* (house and boat landing)	West Islip

Architects

H. Edward Ficken

    Aston, William K.   *Peperidge Hall*   Oakdale
    (reassembled house)

* Robert, Christopher Rhinelander, Jr.   *Peperidge Hall*   Oakdale
    (reassembled house)

Ernest Flagg

* Bourne, Frederick Gilbert   *Indian Neck Hall*   Oakdale
(main house; alterations, 1907 and 1912; garage, c. 1909; original boathouse)

Charles Pierrepont Henry Gilbert

    Cameron, Miss Emma Cornelia
      aka Miss Emma Cornelia Sturges   *Effingham Towers*   West Islip

* Hawley, Edwin   *Effingham Towers*   West Islip

Isaac Henry Green II

* Allen, Theodore   (alterations)   Bayport

    Atwood, Kimball Chase, Jr.   Islip

* Ballard, F. E.   (greenhouse)   Bay Shore

    Baruch, Bernard Mannes, Sr.   *Strandhome*   Bayport

    Belmont, August, III   (alterations, 1889)   Bay Shore

* Bourne, Arthur Keeler, Sr.   *Lake House*   Oakdale

* Bourne, Frederick Gilbert   *Indian Neck Hall*   Oakdale
(gatehouse, c. 1904; boathouse, c. 1905; pumphouse, c. 1913; groundsman's house; superintendent's house; & barn)

    Busby, John   Bayport

* Childs, Eversley   Sayville

* Childs, William Hamlin   Sayville

    Cox, Stephen Perry   *Arcadia*   Bayport

* Cutting, William Bayard   *Westbrook Farm*   Great River
(1911 barns *[unconfirmed]*; staff houses *[unconfirmed]*; sheds *[unconfirmed]*; gatehouse *[confirmed]*)

    Dick, John Henry   *Allen Winden Farm*   Islip
(alterations, c. 1889)

* Dick, William   *Allen Winden Farm*   Islip
(alterations, c. 1889)

    Dick, William Karl   *Allen Winden Farm*   Islip
(alterations, c. 1889)

    Dillon, John Allen, Sr.   (alterations, 1899)   Bay Shore

    Dodson, Richard Wolford   (alterations, 1915)   Bayport
[unconfirmed]

    Edwards, Lawrence   (alterations)   Bayport

* Edwards, Lawrence Barnes   (alterations, 1886)   Bayport

* Foster, Andrew D.
      aka Andrew D. Forsslund   *Greycote*   Sayville

* Foster, William Riley, Jr.   *Strandhome*   Bayport

* Green, Isaac Henry, II   *Brookside*   Sayville

    Gunther, William Henry Jr.   (greenhouse)   Bay Shore

Architects

Isaac Henry Green II (cont'd)

	Harbeck, Charles Thomas	*The Pines* (1909 house)	East Islip
*	Hard, Anson, Wales, Jr.	*Meadow Edge* (main house, carriage house, barn, & gatehouse)	West Sayville
*	Hayward, Frank Earle, Sr.	*Joy Farm*	Sayville
*	Hayward, William Tyson, Sr.	*The Anchorage* (house & carriage house)	Sayville
	Helm, Gustave Adolph		Sayville
	Johnson, Aymar	*Woodland* (1909 house)	East Islip
*	Johnson, Bradish, Jr.	*Woodland* (1909 house)	East Islip
	Johnson, Frederick Merle, Sr. aka Merle Johnson, Sr.	(alterations, 1915) *[unconfirmed]*	Bayport
	Johnston, James Boorman	(1909 house)	East Islip
*	Jones, Frank Smith	*Beechwold* (main house, gatehouse, and 1905 playhouse)	Sayville
	Kleine, Mark [*see* Rice entry]	(alterations, 1915) *[unconfirmed]*	Bayport
*	Knapp, Edward Spring, Sr.	*Awixa Lawn* (alterations, 1889)	Bay Shore
*	Magoun, George Butler	*The Meadows*	West Islip
	Major, Alfred Sarony		Bayport
	Manton, Martin Thomas		Bayport
	Mason, John Hill Belcher		Bayport
	McClung, James [*see* Pollock entry)		Bayport
	McLaughlin, Dr. Daniel	(main house, gatehouse, and 1905 playhouse)	Bayport
*	Morgan, John	*Idle Hour* (alterations)	Bayport
	Palmer, Elwell		Sayville
	Palmer, Elwell	(main house, gatehouse, and 1905 playhouse)	Bayport
*	Pollock, Walter B.		Bayport
	Post, Charles Alfred	*Strandhome*	Bayport
	Post, Charles Kintzing	*Strandhome*	Bayport
*	Post, Regis Henri, Sr.	(three rentals)	Bayport
	Post, Waldron Kintzing	*Strandhome*	Bayport
*	Rice, Dr. George Edwin	*Maywood* (alterations, 1915) *[unconfirmed]*	Bayport
*	Ridgeway, James W.		Sayville
*	Roosevelt, John Ellis	*Meadow Croft* (alterations, c. 1891)	Sayville
*	Roosevelt, Robert Barnwell, Jr.	*The Lilacs*	Sayville
*	Schieren, Charles Adolph, Sr.	*Mapleton*	Islip

Architects

Isaac Henry Green II (cont'd)

	Shannon, Effie		Bayport
	Shea, David J.	*Beechwold* (main house, gatehouse, and 1905 playhouse)	Sayville
	Shea, David J.	*Wyndemoor*	Sayville
*	Simonds, William Robinson	*Wyndemoor*	Sayville
	Smith, Elward, Sr.		Sayville
*	Snedecor, Isaac Howard		Bayport
*	Stoppani, Charles Francis, Sr.	*Arcadia*	Bayport
*	Stoppani, Joseph H.	*Liberty Hall* (main house, carriage house, and gardener's cottage)	Bayport
*	Tappin, Charles L.	*Twin Oaks*	Babylon
*	Tappin, John Crane		Islip
*	Terry, William Hazard		Sayville
	Tucker, Charles A.	(alterations, c. 1889)	Islip
*	Vanderbilt, William Kissam, Sr.	*Idlehour* [I] (farm complex and tea house)	Oakdale
	Westin, Clarence Frederick, Sr.	*Beechwold* (main house, gatehouse, and 1905 playhouse)	Sayville

Rafael Guastavino, Jr.

*	Guastavino, Rafael, Jr.		Bay Shore
	Gulden, Frank, Jr.		Bay Shore
*	Gulden, Frank, Jr.		Islip

Charles Coolidge Haight

| * | Cutting, William Bayard, Sr. | *Westbrook Farm* (main house and east gate house) | Great River |

Hallock & Hait

| | Blagden, Crawford, Sr. | | Babylon |
| * | Smith, Selah Carll | *Smith Cottage* | Babylon |

Harry G. Hardenburg

| | Hubbard, Harmanus Barkulo | *Oakhurst* | Bay Shore |
| * | Thurber, Frederick Charles | | Bay Shore |

Hart and Shape

	Breese, William Laurence, Sr. aka William Lawrence Breese, Sr.	*Timber Point* (alterations)	Great River
	Davies, Julien Tappan	*Timber Point* (alterations)	Great River
	Entenmann, Charles, Sr.		Bay Shore
*	Robbins, William H., Sr.		Bay Shore

Architects

Alfred Hopkins

    * Bourne, Frederick Gilbert   *Indian Neck Hall*   Oakdale
        (farm complex, c. 1910)

    * Dick, John Henry   *Allen Winden Farm*   Islip
        (garage and stables)

    Dick, William   *Allen Winden Farm*   Islip
        (garage and stables)

    Dick, William Karl   *Allen Winden Farm*   Islip
        (garage and stables)

    * Havemeyer, Horace, Sr.   *Olympic Point*   Bay Shore
        (farm complex)

    * Mollenhauer, John Adolph   *Homeport*   Bay Shore
        (farm complex, 1913,
        and farmer's cottage)

    Peters, Harry Twyford, Sr.   *Windholme Farm*   Islip
        (c. 1910 garage and farm complex)

    * Peters, Samuel Twyford   *Windholme Farm*   Islip
        (c. 1910 garage and farm complex)

    Prince, John Dyneley, II   Islip

    Tucker, Charles A.   (garage and stables)   Islip

Henry F. Hornbostel

    * Ranft, Richard Michael   Bay Shore

Richard Howland Hunt

    * Vanderbilt, William Kissam, Sr.   *Idlehour* [II]   Oakdale
        (1900 house)

Richard Morris Hunt

    * Vanderbilt, William Kissam, Sr.   *Idlehour* [I]   Oakdale
        (1878 house)

Kirby, Petit and Green

    * Dodson, Robert Bowman   *Kanonsioni*   West Islip

Herbert W. Korber

    * Gibson, John Joseph   Bay Shore

Detlef Lienau

    Belmont, August, Jr.   *Nursery Stud Farm*   North Babylon

    * Belmont, August, Sr.   *Nursery Stud Farm*   North Babylon

    Belmont, Perry [legal address]   *Nursery Stud Farm*   North Babylon

Harrie T. Lindeberg

    * Havemeyer, Horace, Sr.   *Olympic Point*   Bay Shore

Nelson and Van Wagenen

    Brownlie, George   *Willow Close*   Babylon

    Stewart, David P.   Babylon
        [see Trenchard entry]

    * Trenchard, Edward, II   Babylon

Architects

Palmer and Hornbostel

    Graham, George Scott   *Lohgrame*   Islip

   * Moffitt, William Henry   *Beautiful Shore*   Islip

     Oakman, Walter George, Sr.   Islip

Howard Payne

   * Payne, Albert   Bay Shore

Pickering & Walker

   * Robbins, Jeremiah   Babylon

George Browne Post

     Baruch, Bernard Mannes, Sr.   *Strandhome*   Bayport
                                                   (alterations)

     Foster, William Riley, Jr.   *Strandhome*   Bayport
                                                   (alterations)

   * Post, Charles Alfred   *Strandhome*   Bayport
                                                   (alterations)

     Post, Charles Kintzing   *Strandhome*   Bayport
                                                   (alterations)

   * Post, Henry Albertson Van Zo   *Postholme*   Babylon
                                                   (alterations)

   * Post, Regis Henri   *Littlewood*   Bayport

     Post, Waldron Kintzing   *Strandhome*   Bayport
                                                   (alterations)

     Zerega, John Pierre, Sr.   *Littlewood*   Bayport

Francis Day Rogers of Rogers and Butler

   * Havemeyer, Harry Waldron   Bay Shore

Romeyn and Stever

   * Strong, Theron George   Bay Shore

William Hamilton Russell, Jr.

     Gregory, William Hamilton, Jr.   *Creekside*   East Islip

     Greve, William Marcus, Jr.   *Millcreek / Mill Creek Farm*   Bay Shore

   * Knapp, Harry Kearsarge, II   *Creekside*   East Islip

     Riggio, Frank Vincent   *Riggio House*   Bay Shore

   * Russell, William Hamilton, Jr.   *Le Rozel*   Islip

   * Sharp, Hamlet Cecil   *Millcreek / Mill Creek Farm*   Bay Shore

Prentice Sanger

   * Arnold, Edward William Cameron   *Oknoke*   West Islip

Charles C. Thain

     Dempsey, Joseph Francis, Sr.   *Estancia*   Great River

     Hutchins, Francis Sessions   *Saramond*   Great River

     Stewart, Dr. George David   *Appin House*   Great River

   * White, Raymond S.   Great River

Trowbridge and Ackerman

   * Carlisle, Jay Freeborn, Sr.   *Rosemary*   East Islip

Architects

Calvert Vaux
    Bossert, Louis   *The Oaks*   West Bay Shore
  * Hyde, Henry Baldwin, Sr.   *The Oaks*   West Bay Shore
    Hyde, James Hazen   *The Oaks*   West Bay Shore

Walker and Gillette
  * Blum, Edward Charles   *Shore Acres* (alterations)   Bay Shore

Warren and Wetmore
  * Vanderbilt, William Kissam, Sr.   *Idlehour* [II] (indoor tennis court and bachelor annex, 1903)   Oakdale

York and Sawyer
  * Foster, Jay Stanley   Babylon

William Henry Moffitt residence, *Beautiful Shore*

front facade

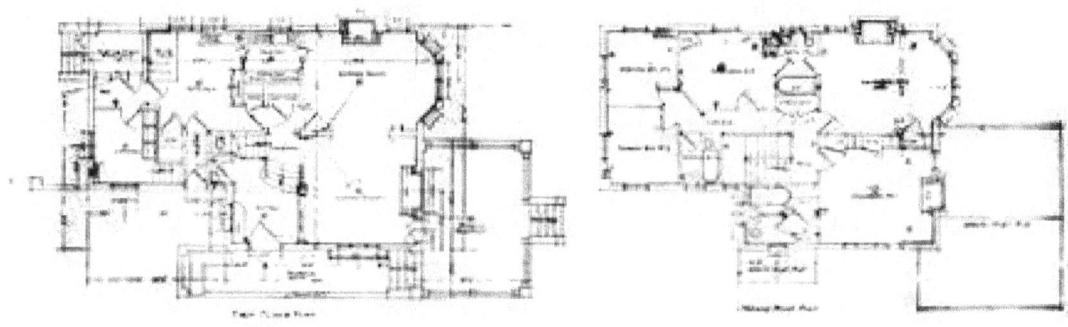

Civic Activism

See the surname entry to ascertain specific civic activism information.

Aldrich, Spencer
Allison, William Manwaring, Sr.
Andrews, Jane Elizabeth Crane
Andrews, William Loring
Arnold, Annie Stuart Cameron
Arnold, Edward William Cameron
Ash, Dr. Charles F.
Asten, Thomas B.
Atwood, Frederic Lawrence
Atwood, Kimball Chase, Jr.
Bachia, Richard Augustus, Jr.
Baker, George William, Sr.
Baruch, Bernard Mannes, Sr.
Bates, William Graves
Baxter, John Edward
Baxter, Katherine Byrne
Belmont, August, Jr.
Belmont, August, Sr.
Belmont, Eleanor Robson
Belmont, Perry
Benkard, James Gerald
Bergen, Charles M.
Bergen, James Cornelius
Betts, Mabel Granbery
Bigelow, Edward Hicks
Blagden, Crawford, Sr.
Blum, Edward Charles
Blum, Ethel Mildred Halsey
Blum, Florence May Abraham
Blum, Robert Edward
Bohack, Henry Christian
   aka Hinrich Christian Bohack
Bossert, Louis
Bourne, Alfred Severin, Sr.
Bourne, Arthur Keeler, Sr.
Bourne, Hattie Louise Barnes
Bruce–Brown, Ruth Arabella Loney
Bull, Henry Worthington
Bunce, Frederick Sidney, Sr.
Burchell, George W.
Burke, Charles Felix
Carlisle, Jay Freeborn, Sr.
Carlisle, Mary Pinkerton
Ceballos, Juan Manuel, Sr.
Ceballos, Louise Washington
Carroll, Dr. Alfred Ludlow
Childs, Eversley, Sr.
Childs, Nellie Spencer
Childs, William Hamlin

Clarkson, William Kemble, Jr.
Coleman, Leander Walter Townsend
Colt, Robert Oliver
Conover, Daniel Denice
Cooper, Gloriana S. Rice
Cooper, James Brown, Sr.
Cusachs, Philip Alain
Cutting, Olivia Peyton Murray
Cutting, Robert Fulton
Cutting, William Bayard, Sr.
Dahl, George Washington
Davies, Faith de Moss Robinson
Davies, Julien Tappan
Davies, Julien Townsend, Jr.
Davies, Julien Townsend, Sr.
de Goicouria, Albert Valentine
Delaney, Eleanor Gertrude Leary
Delaney, John Hanlon
del Garcia, Helen Margaret S. Graham
Dempsey, May E.
de Murias, Virginia Cornwall Bunce
Denby, Esther Jewell Strong
Denby, Thomas Garvin
   aka Garvin Denby
Dick, Adolph Mollenhauer
Dick, William Karl
Dodson, Mary Wells
Dodson, Robert Bowman
Doxsee, Almira S. Jennings
Dresser, Daniel LeRoy, Sr.
Duval, Henry Rieman
Eastwood, John Henry
Eaton, James Waterbury, Sr.
Ebinger, Walter D.
Edwards, Edward
Egly, Henry Harris
Ellis, George Augustus, Jr.
Entenmann, Charles, Sr.
Entenmann, Nancy Lee
Entenmann, Robert William, Sr.
Evers, Cecil Calvert
Evers, Violet Eleanor Vans Agnew
Fairchild, Julian Douglas
Field, Benjamin Prince, Jr.
Fishel, Leopold Henry
Fishel, Lillian H.
Flint, Margaret Olivia Slocum
Ford, Malcolm Webster, Sr.
Foster, Jay Stanley, II

Civic Activism

Foster, John Strong
Frank, Emil Henry, Sr.
Frothingham, John Sewell
Frothingham, Katharine Kent
Garben, Dr. Louis Francis
Gibb, John
Gibb, Anna Pinkerton
Gibson, Frederick E.
Gibson, John James
Gibson, John Joseph
Goodrich, Frances Wickes
Goodrich, William Winston
Graham, George Scott
Green, Isaac Henry, II
Gregory, William Hamilton, Jr.
Greve, William Marcus, Jr.
Guggenheim, Meyer Robert, Sr.
Gulden, Frank, Sr.
Gunther, William Henry, Jr.
Haff, Albert Douglas
Hallock, Gerard, III
Hallock, Marion Wharton
Harris, Alfred H.
Havemeyer, Eugenie Aiguier
Havemeyer, Harry Waldron
Havemeyer, Henry Osborne
Havemeyer, Horace, Jr.
Havemeyer, Horace, Sr.
Havemeyer, Louisine Waldron Elder
Hayward, Martha Eugenia Wemple
Hepburn, Henry Charles, Jr.
Hepburn, Henry Chester
Hepburn, Silvie Livingston Strong
Higbie, Richard
Hobbs, Charles Buxton
Hodges, George Winfield, Sr.
Hodges, Maitia Angus Marvin
Hollins, Gerald Vanderbilt, Sr.
Hollins, Harry Bowly, Jr.
Hollins, Harry Bowly, Sr.
Hollister, Buell, Sr.
Hollister, Henry Hutchinson, Sr.
Hoppin, Bayard Cushing
Howell, Elmer Brown, Sr.
Howell, Elmer Winfield
Howell, Frances C. Rogers
Howell, Jessie Dunseith
Howell, Kizze A.
Howell, Ralph DeWitt, Sr.
Hubbard, Harmanus Barkulo
Hubbard, Margaret Greenwood McKay
Huber, Harriet Louise Bossert
Hubert, Dorothy Nicoll

Hubert, William Haight
Hulse, The Reverend William Warren
Hutton, Edward Francis
Hutton, Marjorie Merriweather Post
Hyde, Helen Walker
Hyde, Henry Baldwin, II
Hyde, Henry Baldwin, Sr.
Hyde, James Hazen
Hyde, James Richard
Hyde, Marthe Dervaux
Hyde, Richard
Ireland, Rufus Johnson, Sr.
Isbrandtsen, Gertrude Mirus
Isbrandtsen, Hans Jeppesen
Jackson, Charles Havemeyer, Sr.
   aka Charles Frederick Havemeyer Jackson
Jacoby, Dr. James Ralph
Jacoby, Ray Scull
Johnson, Amiee Elizabeth Gaillard
Johnson, Aymar
Johnson, Bradish, Jr.
Johnson, Emma Marie Grima
Johnson, Henry Meyer
Johnson, John Dean
Johnston, Mary Hoppin
Jones, Frank Smith
Keith, Minor Cooper
Kempster, James H.
King, Dr. George Suttie
Kingsland, George Lovett, Sr.
Knapp, Edward Spring, Sr.
Knapp, Gladys Quarre
Knapp, Harry Kearsage, II
Knapp, Harry Kearsage, Sr.
Knapp, Shepherd Fordyce, Sr.
Knapp, Theodore Jackson
Koehler, Harriet Bischoff
Koehler, Robert H.
Laidlaw, George Q., Sr.
Lawrance, Charles Lanier
Lemmerman, Frederick C.
Lentilhon, Eugene, II
Lentilhon, Florence Bergh Brown
Lester, Joseph Huntington
Lester, L. Norma Hegeman
Lester, Maxwell, Jr.
Lester, Maxwell, Sr.
Liebmann, Julius
Liebmann, M. Antoniette Scharmann
Lindsay, Edith Louise Riley
Lindsay, Gwendolyn Blackburn Chuwys Owen
Little, Beatrice Kobbe
Livingston, Miss Frances Lewis

Civic Activism

Livingston, Henry, III
Livingston, Henry Beekman, Jr.
Lorillard, George Lyndes
Low, Chauncey Edward, Sr.
MacLeod, Thomas Woodward, Sr.
Macy, William Kingsland, Sr.
Magoun, Francis Peabody, Sr.
Magoun, George Butler
Magoun, Kinsley
Manton, Eva Morier
Manton, Martin Thomas
Maxwell, Henry William
McBurney, Dr. Malcolm
McClure, William
McCue, Alexander
McCurdy, Robert Henry, II
McKee, John
McNamee, John
Moffitt, William Henry
Mollenhauer, Anna Margaretha Dick
Mollenhauer, John Adolph
Montgomery, Richard Malcolm, Sr.
Moore, Dr. David Dodge
Moore, Eugene Francis, Jr.
Moran, Eugene Francis, Jr.
Morgan, Charles, Jr.
Murdock, Rita Nicholas
Myers, Nathaniel
Neville, Miss Augusta
　[*see* T. F. Neville entry]
Neville, Joanna Hodges Simons
Neville, Timothy Francis
Nicholas, Harry Ingersoll, Sr.
Nicoll, William, VII
Nicoll, William Greenly
O'Donohue, Charles Alfred
Oppenheimer, Julius
Orr, John Clifton, Sr.
Otto, Julia
Owens, Joseph Eugene, Sr.
Packer, Frederick Little
Page, Walter Hines, Sr.
Parkhurst, The Reverend Charles Henry
Parkinson, Thomas Ignatius, Jr.
Parkinson, Thomas Ignatius, Sr.
Parsons, Schuyler Livingston, Jr.
Parsons, William Decatur
Perkins, Richard Sturgis, Sr.
Peters, Harry Twyford, Sr.
Peters, Natalie Wells
Peters, Samuel Twyford
Phelps, Royal, Jr.
Pierrepont, Kathryn Isabel Reed

Pierrepont, Robert Low
Pinkerton, Allan, II
Pinkerton, Robert Allan, II
Pless, Helena Parsons Hallock
Pless, John Anthony, Jr.
Post, Charles Alfred
Post, Mary Lawrence Perkins
Post, Regis Henri, Sr.
Post, Waldron Kintzing
Powell, Leander Treadwell
Pratt, Beatrice Mai
Pratt, Cleveland Forsyth, Sr.
Pratt, Dallas Bache
Pratt, Mary Gordon Landon
Pratt, Sophia Jackson Briggs
Prince, Anna Maria Morris
Proctor, Cecil Wykes
Ranft, Hermine T. Krieg
Ranft, Richard Michael
Redmond, Roland
Reid, Ada Emeline Kitching
Reid, John Robert
Reid, Willard Placide
Remsen, Annie Pearsall Hubbard
Remsen, Phoenix, Sr.
Rice, Dr. George Edwin
Richmond, Henry
Riggio, Frank Vincent
Robbins, Carrie Seaman Oakes
Robbins, Jeremiah
Robbins, John Clinton, Sr.
Robbins, Josiah
Robbins, William H., Sr.
Rokenbaugh, Henry Scott
Rolston, Roswell Graves
Roosevelt, Robert Barnwell, Jr.
Roosevelt, Robert Barnwell, Sr.
Rothschild, Simon Frank
Russell, William Hamilton, Jr.
Schieren, Charles Adolph, Sr.
Scully, Adaline Hathaway Weekes
Scully, Charles Brewster
Searle, Charles
Shortland, Thomas Francis
Simonds, William Robinson
Slote, Alonzo
Slote, Daniel, Jr.
Smith, Charles Robinson
Smith, Ella Katharine Bailey
Smith, Elward, Jr.
Smith, Frederick D.
Smith, Hervey Garret
Smith, Jewett Holt

Civic Activism

Smith, Nettie Berry
Smith, Virginia Woodhull Otto
Snedecor, James Henry
Snedeker, Charles Valentine
Snow, Frederick Billings
Stanchfield, John Barry, Sr.
Stephens, Benjamin, Jr.
Stewart, Dr. George David
Stillman, Benjamin D.
Strong, Theron George
Sullivan, Dr. Raymond Peter, Sr.
Sutton, Effingham Brown, Jr.
Sutton, Effingham Brown, Sr.
Sutton, Frank
Sutton, Harold Falconer
Sutton, Woodruff, Jr.
Sutton, Woodruff, Sr.
Suydam, John Richard, Jr.
Swan, Alden Smith
Swirbul, Leon A.
Tappin, Charles L.
Terry, William Hazard
Thorn, Edward Floyd–Jones, Sr.
Thorne, Edwin, II
Thorne, Edwin, III
Thorne, Francis Burritt, Jr.
Thorne, Francis Burritt, Sr.
Thorne, Landon Ketchum, Jr.
Thorne, Landon Ketchum, Sr.
Thurber, Frederick Charles
Titus, James Gulden, Sr.
Titus, Walter Livingston, Jr.
Titus, Walter Livingston, Sr.
Todd, William Henry
Trenchard, Edward, II
True, Benjamin Kimball
Truslow, Anne Gates Babcock
Truslow, Frederick Cumings
Turnbull, Clara Jenkins

Valentine, Langdon Barrett
Van Anden, William M.
Vanderbilt, Alva Erskine Smith [*later*, Belmont]
Vanderbilt, Anne Harriman
Vanderbilt, William Kissam, Sr.
Vander Veer Dr. Albert, Jr.
Vanderveer, John
Van Orden, Jabez Ephraim
Van Orden, James
Waddell, Charles Falkiner Morton
   aka Morton Waddell
Wagstaff, Alfred, Jr.
Wagstaff, Dr. Alfred, Sr.
Wagstaff, Cornelius DeBois
Wagstaff, George Barnard
Wagstaff, Mary Anderson Barnard
Wagstaff, Mary Knight
Wagstaff, Samuel Jones, Sr.
Walbridge, Blanche Gifford Wandel
Ward, Edwin Carrington
Ward, John Montgomery
Ward, Katherine Waas
Warren, Edna Louise O'Brien
Warren Northam, Sr.
Webster, Charles Drake
Webster, Natalie Peters
Welwood, Thomas
Wilbur, Edward Russell, Sr.
Williams, Percy Garnett
Wilmerding, Caroline Maria Murray
Wilmerding, George Gorman
Wilmerding, Lucius Kellogg, Sr.
Yates, Douglas Thomas, Sr.
Yates, Herbert John, Sr.
Yates, Margaret Louise Titus
Yates, Marie Rose McKee
Zerega, John Pierre, Sr.

Brook Russell Astor,

chairman of the Astor Foundation and wife of William Vincent Astor,

quipped on the concept of *nobless oblige*:

Money is like manure; it should be spread around.

Civic Activism

*"Men who disapprove of Votes for Women
are divided into two classes,
those who are married to women who
lack intelligence and who are prone to
measure other women in the same bushel
with their wives, and those men whose wives
are so bright that the men are afraid to give
them a chance at the ballot."*

>Dr. George Edwin Rice, DDS
>*Maywood*, 407 Middle Road, Bayport
>[*The Suffolk County News* August 23, 1913, p. 4.]

1916

Anti – Suffragists:

Denby, Esther Jewell Strong
  99 Bennett Place, Amityville

Denby, Thomas Garvin
  aka Garvin Denby
  99 Bennett Place, Amityville

Howell, Frances C. Rogers
  (Mrs. Elmer Brown Howell, Sr.)
  Little East Neck Road, Babylon

Macy, William Kingsland, Sr.
  385 Ocean Avenue, Islip

Pratt, Mary Gordon Landon
  (Mrs. Dallas Bache Pratt)
  Islip;
  East Cottage, **James Street, Southampton**

Remsen, Annie Pearsall Hubbard
  (Mrs. Jacob Remsen)
  The Harbor, **Little East Neck Road, Babylon**

Ward, Justine Cutting
  (Mrs. George Cabot Ward)
  Westbrook Farm, **South Country Road,
    Great River**
  [*see* W. B. Cutting, Sr. entry]

Suffragists:

Balsan, Consuelo Vanderbilt
  (Mrs. Charles Richard John Spencer–Churchill;
   Mrs. Louis Jacques Balsan)
  Idlehour, **Idle Hour Boulevard, Oakdale**;
  Old Fields, **6601 Route 25A, East Norwich**;
  Gardenside, **77 Ox Pasture Road, Southampton**
  [*see* Vanderbilt entry]

  Baruch, Miss Isabelle
  (aka Belle Baruch)
  Strandhome, **Ocean Avenue, Bayport**
  [*see* B. M. Baruch, Sr. entry]

  Belmont, Alice Wall de Goicouria
  (Mrs. August Belmont III)
  52 South Saxon Avenue, Bay Shore

Belmont, Alva Erskine Smith
  (Mrs. William Kissam Vanderbilt, Sr.;
   Mrs. Oliver Perry Belmont)
  Idlehour [I], **Idle Hour Boulevard, Oakdale**;
  Brookholt, **Front Street, East Meadow**;
  Beacon Towers, **Sands Light Road, Sands Point**
  [*see* Vanderbilt entry]

Benkard, James Gerald
  57 Prospect Street, Babylon

Blum, Florence May Abraham
  (Mrs. Edward Charles Blum)
  Shore Acres, **Penataquit Avenue, Bay Shore**

Carlisle, Mary Pinkerton
  (Mrs. Jay Freeborn Carlisle, Sr.)
  Rosemary, **Suffolk Lane, East Islip**

Civic Activism

Fairchild, Sarah Lenita Plumb
(Mrs. Jarvis R. Fairchild)
Deer Range Farm, **Heckscher Parkway, East Islip**
[*see* S. C. Plumb entry]

Fishel, Lillian H.
(Mrs. Robert T. Oliver)
East Main Street, Babylon;
Magoun Road, **West Islip**

Gulden, Mary Catherine Kellers
(Mrs. Charles Gulden, Sr.)
Netherbay, **36 Clinton Avenue, Bay Shore**

Havemeyer, Louisine Waldron Elder
(Mrs. Henry Osborne Havemeyer)
Bayberry Point, **137 Bayberry Road, Islip**

Hepburn, Silvie Livingston Strong
(Mrs. Henry Chester Hepburn)
Bide a Wee, **44 Douglas Avenue, Babylon**

Hubert, Dorothy Nicoll
(Mrs. William Haight Hubert)
Carll Avenue, Babylon

Hubert, William Haight
Carll Avenue, Babylon

Hutton, Marjorie Merriweather Post
(Mrs. Edward Bennet Close;
Mrs. Edward Francis Hutton;
Mrs. Joseph Edward Davies;
Mrs. Herbert Arthur May)
80 South Saxon Avenue, Bay Shore;
Hillwood, **Route 25A, Brookville**

Hyde, James Richard
South Country Road, West Bay Shore

Neville, Miss Augusta
Warwick House, **South Country Road, Lindenhurst**
[*see* T. F. Neville entry]

Neville, Joanna Hodges Simons
(Mrs. Timothy Francis Neville)
Warwick House, **South Country Road, Lindenhurst**

Pratt, Beatrice Mai Benjamin
(Mrs. William Preston Gibson;
Mrs. Alexander Dallas Bache Pratt;
Mrs. Charles Aubrey Cartwright;
Mrs. Frederick J. McEvoy)
Lands End, **Bayberry Point, Islip**

Rice, Dr. George Edwin
Maywood, **407 Middle Road, Bayport**

Stanchfield, John Barry, Sr.
Afterglow, **Ocean Avenue, Islip**

Thorne, Landon Ketchum, Sr.
Thorneham, **South Country Road, West Bay Shore**

Vanderbilt, Harold Sterling
Idlehour [I and II], **Idle Hour Boulevard, Oakdale**

Vanderbilt, William, Kissam, Jr.
Idlehour [I and II], **Idle Hour Boulevard, Oakdale;**
Deepdale, **Westcliff Drive, Lake Success;**
Eagle's Nest, **Little Neck Road, Centerport**

Ward, Katherine Waas
(Mrs. John Montgomery Ward)
Phelps Lane, North Babylon

Suffragist parade, New York, City, 1916

Estate Names

When the owner who contracted with the architect is known, it is indicated by an asterisk. Multiple owners are listed in chronological order of ownership, not alphabetically by surname. Ownership of estates is listed only for those that used that particular estate name. See the surname entry to ascertain names used by other owners of the same estate.

Afterglow	* Gibb, John Stanchfield, John Barry, Sr. Wright, Dr. Arthur Mullen	Islip
Alkmaar Cottage	Vander Veer, Dr. Albert, Jr.	Fire Island
Allen Winden Farm	Dick, William Dick, John Henry Dick, William Karl	Islip
The Anchorage	* Hayward, William Tyson	Sayville
Appin House	Stewart, Dr. George David	Great River
Arcadia	* Stoppani, Charles Francis, Sr. Cox, Stephen Perry	Bayport
Ardmore	* Adams, Thomas, Jr. Ellis, George Augustus, Jr.	West Bay Shore
Armagh	Rolston, Roswell Graves	North Babylon
Armory	Havemeyer, Henry, Sr.	West Islip
Awixa Castle	Riley, Paul [*see* Mildeberger entry]	Bay Shore
Awixa Lawn	* Knapp, Edward Spring, Sr.	Bay Shore
Awixaway	* Young, Albert Kelly, James P.	Bay Shore
Azimuth	Dana, Richard Turner	East Islip
Bayberry Point	* Havemeyer, Henry Osborne	Islip
Beach Grove	* Wilbur, Edward Russell, Sr.	Sayville
Beautiful Shore	* Moffitt, William Henry	Islip
Beechwold	* Jones, Frank Smith Westin, Clarence Frederick, Sr. Shea, David J.	Sayville
Bide a Wee	Hepburn, Henry Chester	Babylon
Blythebourne	* Litchfield, Electus Backus	Babylon
Bonnie Doon	* Laidlaw, George Q., Sr.	Bayport
Breeze Lawn	Timmermann, Henry Gerhard Tobey, Orville Hurd	Islip
Brightwaters	* Phelps, Charles Egbert	Brightwaters
Bronhurst	* Bruce–Brown, Ruth Arabella Loney	Islip

Estate Names

Brookhurst Farm	Ceballos, Juan Manuel, Sr.	Bay Shore
Brookside	* Green, Isaac Henry, II	Sayville
Brookside Farm	Lentilhon, Eugene, II	Bay Shore
Brookwood	* Knapp, Harry Kearsarge, Sr. Knapp, Theodore Jackson Thorne, Francis Burritt, Sr.	East Islip
Casa Rosa	Davies, Julien Townsend, Sr.	West Islip
Cedarholme	* Gibb, Lewis Mills, Sr. Gibb, Lewis Mills, Jr.	Bay Shore
Cedarshore	* Powell, David Baisley * Powell, Leander Treadwell	Sayville
Cheap John's Estate	* Rubenstein, Ira	Bayport
Cherry Pool	Davies, Julien Townsend, Jr.	West Islip
Church Lawn	Wagstaff, Cornelius DuBois	West Islip
The Cloister	Sutton, Frank	Babylon
Clovelly	* Arnold, Annie Stuart Cameron	West Islip
Clurella	McClure, William	West Islip
Creekside	* Knapp, Harry Kearsarge, II Gregory, William Hamilton, Jr.	East Islip
The Crescent	* Arnold, Richard Arnold, William	West Islip
Crickholly	* Hollins, Harry Bowly, Jr.	East Islip
Dearwood	Pinkerton, Robert Allan, Sr.	Bay Shore
Deer Park Farm	* Corbin, Austin, Jr.	North Babylon
Deer Range Farm	* Johnston, Edwin Augustus, Sr. Plumb, Sarah Caroline Ives Plumb, James Ives Taylor, George Campbell	East Islip
Driftwood	Wagstaff, Samuel Jones, Sr.	West Islip
Edgemere	* Purdy, Charles Robert, Sr.	Bayport
Edgewater	Suydam, John Richard, Sr. Suydam, John Richard, Jr.	Bayport
Effingham Park	Sutton, Effingham Brown, Sr. Sutton, Effingham Brown, Jr.	West Islip
Effingham Towers	* Hawley, Edwin Cameron, Miss Emma Cornelia aka Miss Emma Cornelia Sturges	West Islip
Ellenwood	* Wood, Henry Duncan, Sr.	Islip

Estate Names

Elysian Views	Hulse, The Reverend William Warren	Bay Shore
Enfin	Johnson, Bradish Gaillard, III	Islip
Estancia	Dempsey, Joseph Francis, Sr.	Great River
The Evergreens	Johnson, Effingham Lawrence Bates, William Graves	Bay Shore
Evershade	Flint, Sherman	Islip
Fairlawn	Baker, George William, Sr.	Bay Shore
Falmouth	Duval, Henry Rieman	East Islip
The Farm House	Wagstaff, George Barnard	West Islip
Firenze Farm	Guggenheim, Meyer Robert, Sr.	North Babylon
The Firs	Hepburn, Henry Charles, Jr.	West Islip
Four Hedges	Lester, Maxwell, Sr.	Bay Shore
Grange	Nicoll, William, VII	East Islip
Graytower	Pratt, Cleveland Forsyth, Sr.	Bayport
Greycote	* Foster, Andrew D. aka Andrew D. Forsslund	Sayville
The Harbor	Remsen, Annie Pearsall Hubbard	Babylon
The Hawks	* Hollins, Gerald Vanderbilt, Sr.	East Islip
Homeport	* Mollenhauer, John Adolph	Bay Shore
The Homestead	* True, Benjamin Kimball, Sr.	West Islip
Idle Hour	* Morgan, John	Bayport
Idlehour [I and II]	* Vanderbilt, William Kissam, Sr.	Oakdale
Indian Neck Hall	* Bourne, Frederick Gilbert	Oakdale
Joy Farm	* Hayward, Frank Earl, Sr.	Sayville
Kanonsioni	* Dodson, Robert Bowman	West Islip
La Casetta	Crothers, Gordon	Islip
La Granja	del Garcia, Lester Mullen	East Islip
Lake House	* Bourne, Arthur Keeler, Sr.	Oakdale
Lakeside	Livingston, Robert Cambridge, III	Islip
Lands End	Pratt, Alexander Dallas Bache	Islip
Larklawn	* Kalbfleisch, Sarah Pirnie Schenck	Babylon
Larkmeadow	Smedberg, Adolphus, Jr.	Babylon

Estate Names

Lestaley	*	Lester, Joseph Huntington	Bay Shore
Lenapes Lodge	*	Todd, William Henry	Bayport
Le Rozel	*	Russell, William Hamilton, Jr.	Islip
Liberty Hall	*	Stoppani, Joseph H.	Bayport
The Lilacs	*	Roosevelt, Robert Barnwell, Jr.	Sayville
Lindenwalt		Behman, Louis C., Sr.	Bayport
Little House		Drummond, Howard	Bay Shore
Littlewood	*	Post, Regis Henri, Sr. Zerega, John Pierre, Sr.	Bayport
The Lodge		Thorne, Landon Ketchum, Jr.	West Bay Shore
Lohgrame		Graham, George Scott	Islip
Lone Oak		Stephens, John Lloyd	West Islip
Lotos Lake	*	Roosevelt, Robert Barnwell, Sr.	Bayport
Manatuck Farm		Lawrance, Francis Cooper, Sr. Lawrance, Francis Cooper, Jr. Lawrance, Charles Lanier	Bay Shore
The Maples		Dahl, George Washington	Bayport
The Maples		Watson, Jane Painter Elder	Islip
Mapleton	*	Schieren, Charles Adolph, Sr. Atwood, Kimball Chase, Jr.	Islip
Maplewood		Richmond, Henry	Bayport
Maywood	*	Rice, Dr. George Edwin	Bayport
Meadow Croft	*	Roosevelt, John Ellis	Sayville
Meadow Edge	*	Hard, Anson Wales, Jr.	West Sayville
Meadow Farm	*	Hollins, Harry Bowly, Sr.	East Islip
Meadow Road Farm		Morgan, Robert Woodward, Sr.	East Islip
The Meadows		Foster, William Riley, Sr. Foster, John Strong	Babylon
The Meadows	*	Magoun, George Butler	West Islip
Millcreek	*	Sharp, Hamlet Cecil	Bay Shore
Millcreek / Mill Creek Farm		Greve, William Marcus, Jr.	Bay Shore
The Moorings	*	Franklin, Emlen Pleasants	Brightwaters
The Moorings		O'Donohue, Charles Alfred	Bay Shore

Estate Names

My Fancy	Ford, Malcolm Webster, Sr. Gilmore, William Guy, Sr.	West Babylon
Nearholme	* Peters, Harry Twyford, Sr.	Islip
Netherbay	Gulden, Charles, Sr.	Bay Shore
North East Farm	* Sutton, Frank	North Babylon
Nursery Stud Farm	* Belmont, August, Sr. Belmont, August, Jr. Belmont, Perry [legal address]	North Babylon
Oakelwood	Mildeberger, Elwood	Bay Shore
Oakhurst	Hubbard, Harmanus Barkulo	Bay Shore
The Oaks	* Hyde, Henry Baldwin, Sr. Hyde, James Hazen Bossert, Louis	West Bay Shore
O'Conee	* Shea, Timothy Joseph, Sr.	Bay Shore
The following are two different houses:		
Oknoke	Arnold, Edward William Cameron	West Islip
Oknoke	* Thorne, Edwin, II	West Islip
Old Oak Farm	Ludlow, William Handy, Sr.	Sayville
Olympic Point	* Havemeyer, Horace, Sr.	Bay Shore
Onsrufarm	Yates, Herbert John, Sr.	West Islip
On-the-way	Hallowell, Thomas Jewett, Sr.	West Babylon
Opekeepsing	* Wagstaff, Alfred, Jr.	West Islip
Orowoc	* Swan, Alden Smith	Islip
Orowoc Point	Catlin, Dr. Daniel, Sr.	Bay Shore
Peperidge Hall	* Robert, Christopher Rhinelander, Jr. Aston, William K.	Oakdale
Pepperidges	Andrews, William Loring	West Islip
Pine Acres	* Williams, Percy Garnett	East Islip
The Pines	Harbeck, Charles Thomas	East Islip
The Pines	Turnbull, John Gourlay, Sr.	Brightwaters
The Pines	* Turnbull, George R.	West Islip
Pleasure Island	* Parsons, Schuyler Livingston, Jr.	Islip
The Poplars	Colt, Robert Oliver	West Bay Shore
Postholme	Post, Henry Albertson Van Zo	Babylon
Questover Lodge	* Truslow, Frederick Cumings	Great River

Estate Names

Restina Cottage	Parsons, William Decatur	Bay Shore
Riggio House	Riggio, Frank Vincent	Bay Shore
River Croft	* Hobbs, Charles Buxton	Great River
Rosemary	* Carlisle, Jay Freeborn, Sr.	East Islip
Sagtikos Manor	Gardiner, Robert David Lion	West Bay Shore
Sandy Point	* Warren, Northam, Sr.	Sayville
Sans Souci	* Johnson, Bradish, Sr. Johnson, Henry Meyer	West Bay Shore
Sans Souci	McKee, John	Bayport
Saramond	Hutchins, Francis Sessions	Great River
Scrub Oaks	Maxwell, Henry William	Bay Shore
Seaward	* Low, Chauncey Edward, Sr.	Bay Shore
Sequatogue Farm	* Havemeyer, Henry, Sr. Hubbs, Charles Francis	West Islip
Shadowbrook	Plumb, James Ives	Islip
Shadow Lawn	Moran, Eugene Francis, Jr.	Brightwaters
Shore Acres	* Blum, Edward Charles	Bay Shore
Skoookwamp	[*see* Sutton, Effingham Brown, Sr. entry]	West Islip
Smith Cottage	* Smith, Selah Carll	Babylon
South Country Lodge	Graham, James Varnum, Jr.	Babylon
The Stables	Morgan, Henry	East Islip
Still Pond	Prescott, William French	East Islip
Strandhome	* Foster, William Riley, Jr. Post, Charles Alfred Post, Waldron Kintzing Baruch, Bernard Mannes, Sr. [rented]	Bayport
Suanne	Bergen, James Cornelius	West Babylon
Sunneholm	Betts, Roland Whitney	Sayville
Sunnycroft	* Sutton, Woodruff, Jr.	Babylon
Sunnymead	Vanderveer, John Gibson, Cornelia Lott Vanderveer	West Islip
Sunnymede	Stephens, Benjamin, Jr.	West Islip
Sutton Park / Woodruff Sutton Place	Sutton, Woodruff, Sr.	West Islip
The Swamp	Corse, Israel Jr.	Sayville

Estate Names

Sweet Violet	* Stewart, Anna May aka Anna Stuart	Brightwaters
Tahlulah	* Wagstaff, Dr. Alfred, Sr.	West Islip
The Towers	Reid, John Robert Reid, Willard Placide	Babylon
Thorneham	* Thorne, Landon Ketchum, Sr.	West Bay Shore
Timber Point	* Breese, William Laurence, Sr. aka William Lawrence Breese, Sr. Davies, Julien Tappan	Great River
Tuloma	Remsen, Cornelius Wagstaff	Babylon
Twin Oaks	* Tappin, Charles L	Babylon
Twyford	Webster, Charles Drake	Islip
Villa Avalon	* Covell, Charles Heber, Sr. Rokenbaugh, Henry Scott	Bay Shore
Villa Julia	Walker, Keitt Pinckney aka George Daniel Keitt Pinckney Walker	West Islip
Villa Maria	Hardenburgh James [*see* P. Remsen, Sr. entry]	West Islip
Virginia Farm	Nicholas, Alice McKim Hollins	Babylon
Wake Robin	Ward. Edwin Carrington	Bay Shore
Warwick House	Neville, Timothy Francis	Lindenhurst
Welles House	Welles, Benjamin Sumner, Jr. Welles, Benjamin Sumner, III	Islip
Welwood Lane	* Welwood, Thomas	Lindenhurst
Wereholme	* Weekes, Harold Hathaway Scully, Charles Brewster	Islip
Westbeach	Kempster, James H.	Bay Shore
The following are two different houses:		
Westbrook Farm	* Maitland, Robert Lenox, Sr. (c. 1860's house) Lorillard, George Lyndes (c. 1860's house)	Great River
Westbrook Farm	* Cutting, William Bayard, Sr. (1886 house)	Great River
While-Away	Jones, Frank Smith [*see* Wilbur entry]	Sayville
Whileaway	* Parsons, Schuyler Livingston, Sr. Wharton, Richard Wharton, Richard T., Sr.	Islip
Whileaway	* Wray, William Henry, Sr.	Bay Shore

Estate Names

White Cottage	Hyde, William James	West Islip
White Lodge	Wilmerding, Lucius Kellogg, Sr.	East Islip
White House	* Edwards, Edward	Bayport
Wild Goose Farm	* Hawkins, William Elton	Copiague
Wildholme	Fortescue, Granville Roland	Bayport
Willow Close	Brownlie, George	Babylon
The Willows	deCoppet, Andre H.	Islip
Windermere	Aldrich, Spencer	Bay Shore
Windholme	Peters, Samuel Twyford, Sr. Peters, Harry Twyford, Sr.	Islip
Wind's Will	Snedeker, Charles Valentine	Babylon
Winganhauppauge	* Knapp, William Kumbel	Islip
Win Sum Lodge	Hutton, Franklin Laws	Bay Shore
Woodland	* Johnson, Bradish, Jr. Johnson, Aymar	East Islip
Woodlea	Adams, John Dunbar	Bay Shore
Wyndemoor	* Simonds, William Robinson Shea, David J.	Sayville

Frederick Gilbert Bourne estate, Indian Neck Farm,
farm complex

Golf Courses

South Shore estates that are presently golf courses are identified by the original owner. For subsequent estate owners, see surname entry.

Southward Ho Country Club, South Country Road, West Bay Shore
—located on the Henry Baldwin Hyde Sr. estate, *The Oaks*

Suffolk Country West Sayville Golf Course, South Country Road, West Sayville
—located on the Anson Wales Hard, Jr. estate, *Meadow Edge*

Timber Point Country Club, Great River Road, Great River
—located on the William Laurence Breese estate, *Timber Point*

The Oaks, main residence, c. 1900

*The Oaks, main residence, 2005,
after remodeling by the country club*

Jay Freeborn Carlisle, Sr. estate, Rosemary, steps below west lawn, 1921

Landscape Architects

When the date of landscaping is known, it has been included in brackets. Since, in some instances, more than one landscape architect worked on an estate and, in some rare instances, the architect who designed the house also designed the estate's grounds, the surname entry should be consulted to determine if anyone else was involved in designing the estate grounds. When the estate owner who contracted for landscaping is known, it is indicated by an asterisk. Original and subsequent estate owners are included in the list.

Nathan F. Barrett

	Baker, William Dunham		Islip
	Beard, Anson Mc Cook, Jr.		Islip
	Dempsey, Joseph Francis, Jr.		Islip
	Egly, Henry Harris		Islip
	Garben, Dr. Louis Francis, Sr.		Islip
	Gulden, Charles, III		Islip
	Gulden, Frank, Sr.		Islip
*	Havemeyer, Henry Osborne	*Bayberry Point*	Islip
	Havemeyer, Horace, Jr.		Islip
	Havemeyer, Horace, Sr.		Islip
	Howell, Carlton Bell		Islip
*	Mollenhauer, John Adolph	*Homeport*	Bay Shore
	Moore, Dr. David Dodge		Islip
	Perkins, Richard Sturgis, Sr.		Islip
	Thorne, Edwin, III		Islip
	Titus, Walter Livingston, Jr.		Islip
	Yates, Douglas Thomas, Sr.		Islip

Beatrix Jones Farrand

*	Cutting, William Bayard, Sr.	*Westbrook Farm* (animal cemetery)	Great River
*	Flint, Sherman	*Evershade* (landscape plan not executed)	Islip

Hicks Nursery

	Montgomery, Richard Malcolm	(supplied plantings)	Bay Shore
*	Pinkerton, Allan, II		Bay Shore
*	Pinkerton, Robert Allan, Sr.	*Dearwood* (supplied plantings)	Bay Shore

Martha Brooks Brown Hutcheson

*	Breese, William Laurence, Sr. aka William Lawrence Breese, Sr.	*Timber Point*	Great River
	Davies, Julien Tappan	*Timber Point*	Great River

Innocenti and Webel

*	Thorne, Landon Ketchum, Sr.	*Thornham* (gardens)	West Islip

Landscape Architects

William Roe Jones

Cameron, Miss Emma Cornelia aka Miss Emma Cornelia Sturges	*Effingham Towers* (1910 waterfall/dam complex)	West Islip
* Hawley, Edwin	*Effingham Towers* (1910 waterfall/dam complex)	West Islip

Charles Wellford Leavitt and Sons

Gregory, William Hamilton, Jr.	*Creekside*	East Islip
* Hard, Anson Wales, Jr.	*Meadow Edge*	West Sayville
* Knapp, Harry Kearsarge, II	*Creekside*	East Islip

Lewis and Valentine

* Arnold, Edward William Cameron	*Oknoke*	West Islip

W. C. McCallum & Son

*Ebinger, Walter D.	(1937)	Bay Shore

Olmsted

Atwood, Kimball Chase, Jr.	*Mapleton*	Islip
Bossert, Louis	*The Oaks* (designed landscaping, jointly with Jacob Weidenman)	West Bay Shore
* Bourne, Frederick Gilbert	*Indian Neck Hall*	Oakdale
* Cutting, William Bayard, Sr.	*Westbrook Farm* (1887-1894)	Great River
Harbeck, Charles Thomas	*The Pines* (1915)	East Islip
* Havemeyer, Horace, Sr.	*Olympic Point*	Bay Shore
* Hollins, Harry Bowly, Sr.	*Meadow Farm*	East Islip
* Hyde, Henry Baldwin, Sr.	*The Oaks* (designed landscaping, jointly with Jacob Weidenman)	West Bay Shore
Hyde, James Hazen	*The Oaks* (designed landscaping, jointly with Jacob Weidenman)	West Bay Shore
Johnson, Aymar	*Woodland* (1915)	East Islip
* Johnston, Bradish, Jr.	*Woodland* (1915)	East Islip
Johnston, James Boorman	(1915)	East Islip
Lawrence, Charles Lanier		East Islip
Schieren, Charles Adolph, Sr.	*Mapleton*	Islip

Harold Truesdel Patterson

* Dodson, Robert Bowman	*Kanonsioni*	West Islip

Ellen Biddle Shipman

Prince, John Dyneley, II		Islip
* Peters, Harry Twyford, Sr.	*Windholme Farm*	Islip
Peters, Samuel Twyford	*Windholme Farm*	Islip

Landscape Architects

Vitale, Brinkerhoff and Geiffert

    * Carlisle, Jay Freeborn, Sr.   *Rosemary*   East Islip

Ferruccio Vitale

    * Cutting, William Bayard, Sr   *Westbrook Farm*   Great River
    (designed entrance driveway)

    * Thorne, Landon Ketchum, Sr.   *Thornham*   West Islip

Jacob Weidenman

    Bossert, Louis   *The Oaks*   West Bay Shore
    (designed landscaping, jointly with Olmsted)

    * Hyde, Henry Baldwin, Sr.   *The Oaks*   West Bay Shore
    (designed landscaping, jointly with Olmsted)

    Hyde, James Hazen   *The Oaks*   West Bay Shore
    (designed landscaping, jointly with Olmsted

Landon Ketchum Thorne, Sr. estate,
Thorneham

Gladys Quarre Knapp
(Mrs. Theodore Jackson Knapp)

Jane Elizabeth Crane Andrews
(Mrs. William Loring Andrews)

Maiden Names

The following list of maiden names of women associated with Long Island South Shore estates was compiled from various biographical sources, social registers, and newspaper obituaries. It should be noted that women occasionally gave surnames from previous marriages to editors, without designating them as such. If there were multiple marriages, husbands are listed in chronological order. Please note that the women included in this list were either the homeowners or spouses of homeowners. Women of subsequent generations are not included unless they assumed ownership of the house.

Abraham, Florence May	*married*	**Blum**, Edward Charles
Abraham, Lillian		**Rothschild**, Simon Frank
Adams, Florence Vance		**Ellis**, George Augustus, Jr.
Adams, Jennie Bullard		**Waterbury**, Leander
Agnew, Violet Eleanor Vans		**Evers**, Cecil Calvert
Aiguier, Eugenie		**Havemeyer**, Harry Waldron
Alexander, Celia Gardner		**Maxwell**, Henry William
Alexandre, Helen Lispenard		**Hoppin**, Bayard Cushing
Alloway, Edna Woolman		**Chase**, Francis Dane
		Newton, Richard T.
Amory, Harriet H.		**Garner**, Thomas, Jr.
Anthles, Helen L.		**Sutton**, Woodruff, Jr.
Anthony, Mary A.		**Sutton**, Harold Falconer
Antonsen, Petra		**Yates**, Herbert John, Sr.
Arents, Minnie Edna		**Young**, Albert
Arnold, Marie Louise		**Cameron**, Edward Miller
Babcock, Ann Gates		**Truslow**, Frederick Cumings
Babcock, Mary Emma		**Todd**, William Henry
Bailey, Ella Katharine		**Smith**, Elward, Jr.
Bailey, Eunice		**Oakes**, William Pitt, II
		Gardiner, Robert David Lion
Baker, Phyllis Livingston		**Potter**, Eliphalet Nott, III
		Astaire, Fred, Sr.
		aka Frederick Austerlitz
Baldwin, Emily		**Reach**, ____
		Lester, Maxwell, Jr.
Baldwin, Grace		**Ruggles**, James F.
		Johnson, Henry Meyer
Baldwin, Marcia Walter		**Dresser**, Daniel LeRoy, Sr.
Baldwin, Sarah Kathleen		**Olliffee**, Cornelius W.
		Johnson, Henry Meyer
Balsdon, Harriet		**Gibb**, John
Bamman, Mary		**Melville**, Francis, Sr.
Barclay, Clara Wright		**Onativia**, Jose Victor, Jr.
		deCoppet, Andre H.
		Boatwright, John Lord
Barnard, Alice		**Childs**, Eversley, Sr.
Barnard, Mary Anderson		**Wagstaff**, Alfred, Jr.
Barnes, Hattie Louise		**Bourne**, Alfred Severin, Sr.

Maiden Names

Barry, Alice Hoadley — **Thorne,** Landon Ketchum, Jr.
Bartholow, Jeanne Cassard — **Magoun**, Francis Peabody, Sr.
Barto, Frances — **Searle**, Charles
Baumann, Jane Louise — **Hayward**, William Tyson, Jr.
   Sutton, Frank

Beasley, Lillian H. — **Pardee**, Roy Edmund
Beebe, Elise Jeanette — **Smith**, Hervey Garret
Beebe, Martina W. — **Seaman**, Frank
Beekman, Joanna N. — **Bergen**, Jacob M.
Bell, Grace Hubbard — **Fortescue**, Granville Roland
Bellotte, Leola — **Foster**, William Riley, Jr.
Benedict, Emma — **Knapp**, Shepherd, II
Benjamin, Beatrice Mai — **Gibson**, William Preston
   Pratt, Alexander Dallas Bache
   Cartwright, Charles Aubrey
   McEvoy, Frederick J.

Beresford, Mary — **Rice**, Dr. George Edwin
Bergen, Cornelia Udall — **Stuyvesant**, Frederic Schuchardt
   Hawkins, William Elton

Bernheimer, Grace Lilian — **Guggenheim**, Meyer Robert, Sr.
   Snellenberg, Morton E.

Berry, Nettie May — **Smith**, Frederick D.
Berryman, Georgiana Louisa — **Strong**, James Henry
Best, Katherine — **Arthur**, Paul
  aka Katherine Grey — **Mason**, John Hill Belcher
Bicar, Pauline — **Arnold**, Richard
Bischoff, Harriet — **Koehler**, Robert H.
Blum, Alice Isabel — **Bigelow**, Edwin Hicks
   Taliaferro, Eugene Sinclair
   Warfield, Ethelbert

Blydenburgh, Ella — **Robbins**, Josiah
Bodman, Ellen — **Parkhurst**, The Reverend Charles Henry
Bogert, Ethel — **Van Orden**, James
Bolmer, Georgiana Eleanor — **Arnold**, Richard
   Hartman, The Reverend Charles Harvey

Boscher, Margaret — **Heins**, John Lewis, Sr.
Bossert, Harriet Louise — **Huber**, Frederick Max, Sr.
Boughton, Augusta — **Keppy**, Dr. Frederick Beardsley
Boughton, Margaret — **Riggio**, Frank Vincent
Bourne, Florence — **Hard**, Anson Wales, Jr.
   Deans, Robert Barr, Sr.
   Thayer, Alexander Dallas

Bradley, Florence Irene — **Fairchild**, Julian Douglas
Bramm, Marie Louise — **Schieren**, Charles Adolph, Sr.
Breed, Hannah Maria — **Litchfield**, Electus Backus

Maiden Names

Brewster, Marietta — **Robbins**, William H., Sr.
Briggs, Sophia Jackson — **Pratt**, Cleveland Forsyth, Sr.
Brinckerhoff, Emma Josephine — **Woolley**, Dr. James Van Sicle
Broske, Erika Lina — **Puzo**, Mario
Bross, Elizabeth — **Eaton**, James Waterbury, Sr.
Brown, Ann Eliza — **Foster**, Andrew D. aka Andrew D. Forsslund

Brown, Evelyn — **Thorne**, Francis Burritt, Sr.
Brown, Florence Bergh — **Lentilhon**, Eugene, II
Brown, Kizze A. — **Howell**, Elmer Windfield
Brown, Mary Augusta — **Clarkson**, William Kemble, Jr.
Brumley, Josephine — **Bromell**, Alfred Henry
Buchanan, Rosa Parran — **Lentilhon**, Eugene, II
Buglar, Mary A. — **Robbins**, John Clinton, Sr.
Bulkley, Helen Clark — **Redmond**, Roland
Bulkley, Mary Faran — **Gulden**, Charles, III
Bunce, Martha — **True**, Benjamin Kimball, Sr.
Bunce, Virginia Cornwall — **de Murias**, Fernando, Enrique
Burchell, Susan — **Adams**, John Dunbar
Burgess, Sarah Jane — **Edwards**, Lawrence
Burnett, Mary — **McNamee**, John
Burkhardt, Carrie — **Thurber**, Frederick Charles
Burnham, Emma Louise — **Dresser**, Daniel LeRoy, Sr.
Burr, Caroline — **Knapp**, Harry Kearsarge, Sr.
Burr, Mary Louise — **Gibb**, Howard, Sr.
Vernet, ____

Burton, Frances Anna Parsons — **Plumb**, James Ives
Byrne, Katherine — **Baxter**, John Edward
Cadwell, Ellen Therese — **Elder**, George Waldron, Sr.
Cairns, Frances — **Smith**, Elward, Sr.
Smith, Robert Gibson

Cameron, Annie Stuart — **Arnold**, William
Cammeyer, Minnie Josephine — **Major**, Alfred Sarony
Carey, Mary T. — **Owens**, Joseph Eugene, Sr.
Carling, Jacqueline — **Palmer**, Frederick Timothy aka Timothy Palmer

Carll, Annie Snedecor — **Cameron**, Edward Miller
Carll, Augusta — **Livingston**, Henry, III
Carlton, Harriet — **Durkee**, Eugene Return
Carroll, Ruth Lawrence — **Draper**, Eben Sumner
Sharp, Hamlet Cecil

Carter, Kate Louise — **Macy**, George Henry

Maiden Names

Castro, Cristina — **Keith**, Minor Cooper
Cavanagh, Barbara — **Wagner**, Robert Ferdinand, Jr.
Child, Sophia — **Harbeck**, Charles Thomas
Clark, Helen M. — **Bergen**, Cornelius J., Sr.
Clark, Margaret Maxwell — **Vander Veer**, Dr. Albert, Jr.
Clark, Naomi Woodruff Bradford — **Remsen**, Phoenix, Sr.
Clarke, Pauline M. — **Graham**, George Scott
Cleaveland, Marjorie — **Palmer**, Elwell
Cobb, Ann Chauncey — **Thorne**, Francis Burritt, Jr.
Cochran, Harriet Penrose — **Suydam**, John Richard, Jr.
Cochran, Mary Jane — **Gilmore**, William Guy, Sr.
Coe, Alice Stanley — **Montgomery**, Richard Malcolm, Sr.
Coe, Elizabeth — **Finlayson**, Daniel Aylesbury, Jr.
    Prescott, William F.

Colt, Amy — **Wagstaff**, Cornelius DuBois
Conkling, Elizabeth Cockburn — **Oakman**, Walter George, Sr.
Conner, Virginia Montez Kenniston — **Dick**, William Karl
    Moseley, Frederick S., Jr.

Cook, Gladys — **Haight**, Gilbert Lawrence, Sr.
Cornwell, Katherine Maurice — **Nicoll**, William Greenly
Cornwell, Mary Herbert — **Keppy**, Dr. Frederick Beardsley
Corwin, Marie Russ — **Smedberg**, Adolphus, Jr.
Covell, Catherine — **Lawrence**, Chester Bulkley, Sr.
Cowdin, Ethel — **Morgan**, Charles, Jr.
Cowenhoven, Ellen — **Bergen**, Charles M.
Cox, Annabel Bancker — **Dahl**, George Washington
Crandall, Mary Helen — **Knapp**, Shepherd Fordyce, Sr.
Crane, Ella — **McClure**, William
Crane, Jane Elizabeth — **Andrews**, William Loring
Crane, Sarah H. — **White**, Raymond S.
    Hutchins, Francis Sessions

Crosby, Alice — **Allison**, William Manwaring, Sr.
Crowley, Edith A. — **Gregory**, William Hamilton, Jr.
Cumnock, Mary Cutting Holland — **Wagstaff**, George Barnard
    Forbes–Sempill, Honorable Arthur Lionel Ochoncar

Curley, Irene — **Bodde**, John R.
    Hutton, Franklyn Laws
    Moffett, James A.

Currie, Mary — **Maitland**, Robert Lenox, Sr.
Cushman, Lavonne Jeanette — **Gibson**, John James
Cutter, Louise Eliot — **Pinkerton**, Robert Allan, II
    Marshall, John Hunt

Dall, Hariette Holley — **Aldrich**, Spencer

Maiden Names

Daniel, Roberta — **Yates**, Richard George, Sr.
Dauvray, Helen — **Ward**, John Montgomery
  Winterhalter, Albert

Davies, Alice Martin — **McKee**, Henry Sellers, II
Davis, Angeline — **Reid**, John Robert
Dear, Dorothy — **Hutton**, Edward Francis
de Garmendia, Marie Rose — **Davies**, Julien Townsend, Sr.
de Goicouria, Alice Wall — **Belmont**, August, III
  Wing, John D.

de Lagarde, Marguerite Denys — **du Long**, Gilbert Sichel
  Post, Regis Henri, Sr.

de LaGrange, Marie — **Hyde**, Henry Baldwin, II
de Murias, Sylvia Angela — **Vander Veer**, Dr. Albert, Jr.
Dervaux, Marthe — **Thom**, ____
  Hyde, James Hazen

de Trobriand, Marie Caroline — **Post**, Albert Kintzing
  Post, Charles Alfred

Dick, Anna Margaretha — **Mollenhauer**, John Adolph
Dick, Doris Anna — **Havemeyer**, Horace, Sr.
Dick, Julia A. H. — **Macy**, William Kingsland, Sr.
Dickson, Jessie Rae — **Morrison**, George Alexander
Disbrow, Phoebe — **Nicoll**, William Greenly
Dix, Emily Margaret Gordon — **Lawrance**, Charles Lanier
di Zoppola, Mara Lucy — **Wharton**, Richard T., Sr.
Dobie, Henrietta — **MacLeod**, Thomas Woodward, Sr.
  Chase, C. Trevett

Dougherty, Caroline Emily — **Richmond**, Henry
Douglass, Margaret J. — **Edwards**, Edward
Drake, Nancy Lee — **Entenmann**, Charles, Sr.
Drumm, Mollie — **Mildeberger**, Elwood
DuBois, Sarah Platt — **Wagstaff**, Dr. Alfred, Sr.
Dunseith, Jessie — **Howell**, Ralph De Witt, Sr.
Durfey, Lucretia — **Ash**, Dr. Charles F.
Duryea, Ann — **Van Orden**, Jabez Ephraim
Eager, Jeannette Elizabeth — **Taylor**, ____
  Rokenbaugh, Henry Scott

Eaton, Elizabeth Bross — **Guggenheim**, Meyer Robert, Sr.
Edrington, Nancy E. — **Lacombe**, Charles Frederick
Edwards, Mary Anna — **Smith**, Benjamin Franklin
Edwards, Susan — **Wagner**, Robert Ferdinand, Jr.
Elder, Adeline Mapes — **Peters**, Samuel Twyford
Elder, Jane Painter — **Watson**, Robert Campbell, Sr.
Elder, Louisine Waldron — **Havemeyer**, Henry Osborne

Maiden Names

Elder, Mary Louise — **Havemeyer**, Henry Osborne

Elliot, Charlotte Elgitha Veronica Boswell — **Thorne**, Landon Ketchum, Jr.

Ellis, Elizabeth Thorn — **Roosevelt**, Robert Barnwell, Sr.

Ellis, Leila — **Post**, Regis Henri, Sr.

Epp, Carol Eugenia — **Gibson**, Gregory Martin

Ellis, Emma M. — **Graham**, George Scott

Everdell, Rosalind Anne — **Havemeyer**, Horace, Jr.

Eytinge, Elizabeth Sarah — **Hepburn**, Henry Charles, Jr.

Farrington, Josephine — **Hoff**, Albert Douglas

Farwell, Mary Althea — **Swan**, Alden Smith

Feitner, Mary Louise — **Gregory**, George Mitchell

Fisher, Frances Turner — **Wharton**, William Fishbourne

Fitch, Annie
 aka Annie Truesdell — **Hyde**, Henry Baldwin, Sr.

Fleet, Harriet — **Udall**, Joseph Sanford

Flinn, Louise — **Wainwright**, Stuyvesant, Jr.

Flood, Elizabeth — **Adams**, Thomas, Jr.

Force, Madeleine Talmadge — **Astor**, John Jacob, IV
Dick, William Karl
Fiermonte, Enzo

Fox, Stephanie Jacqueline — **Livingston**, Henry Beekman, Jr.

Francis, Rebecca — **Powell**, Leander Treadwell
Harris, David S.

French, Pauline Le Roy — **Wagstaff**, Samuel Jones, Sr.
MacRae, Donald Oliver

Friedman, Ella — **Oppenheimer**, Julius

Frost, Alice Hannah — **Van Anden**, William M.

Frost, Jeanne Preston — **Walker**, Harford Pinckney, Sr.
 aka Frederick Harford Pinckney Walker, Sr.

Frothingham, Dorothy Whiting — **Arnold**, Edward William Cameron
Wagstaff, George Barnard

Frothingham, Mary Thompson — **Low**, Chauncey Edward, Sr.

Fry, Elizabeth — **Tobey**, Orville Hurd

Fry, Kate — **Timmermann**, Henry Gerhard

Furgueson, Mary Buford — **Greve**, William Marcus, Jr.

Gaillard, Amiee Elizabeth — **Johnson**, Bradish, Jr.
Crother, Gordon

Garner, Frances Adelaide — **Lawrance**, Francis Cooper, Sr.

Geary, Evelyn J. — **Helm**, Gustave Adolph

Gibson, Ida Louise — **Ward**, John Montgomery

Gilbert, Kathleen — **Hayward**, Frank Earle, Sr.
McCullough, Richard Peter

Gino, Carol (common-law-wife) — **Puzo**, Mario

Girdner, Adela Overton — **Atwood**, Kimball Chase, Jr.

Maiden Names

Girdner, Mary Evelyn	**Atwood**, Kimball Chase, Jr.
Giusti, Jean	**Gibson**, Frederick E.
Glahn, Paula Nathalia	**Frank**, Emil Henry, Sr.
Grady, Mary Alicia	**Moses**, Robert
Graham, Elizabeth Marie	**King**, Dr. George Suttie
Graham, Helen Margaret S.	**del Garcia**, Lester Mullen
Graham, Julia Irving	**Walker**, Keitt Pinckney aka George Daniel Keitt Pinckney Walker
Granbery, Mabel	**Betts**, Roland Whitney **Spratt**, Charles Edward
Granbery, Mary Louise	**Jones**, Frank Smith
Grand, Helen	**Thorne**, Edwin, III
Graves, Jeanette Wilhelmina	**Ford**, Malcolm Webster, Sr.
Green, Henrietta Emma	**Snedecor**, Isaac Howard
Griffen, Annie	**Baruch**, Bernard Mannes, Sr.
Griffiths, Sarah Baldwin	**Slote**, Daniel, Jr.
Grima, Emma Marie	**Johnson**, Bradish Gaillard, III
Guastavino, Louise	**Gulden**, Frank, Jr.
Gulden, Margaret	**Titus**, Walter Livingston, Sr.
Hagen, Coretta Jean	**Waddell**, Charles Falkiner Morton aka Morton Waddell
Hait, Julia Edna	**Otto**, Thomas Nelson
Hallett, Julia T.	**de Forest**, James Goodrich, Sr.
Hallock, Helena Parsons	**Pless**, John Anthony, Jr.
Halsey, Ethel Mildred	**Blum**, Robert Edward
Hamersley, Edith	**Biscoe**, Henry E. **Roosevelt**, John Ellis
Hamersley, Lilie	**Roosevelt**, Robert Barnwell, Jr. **Courtney**, Charles Edward
Harmon, Harriet Burr	**Morse**, William Otis
Harned, Mary Catherine	**Terry**, William Hazard
Harper, May	**Valentine**, Langdon Barrett
Harriman, Anne	**Sands**, Samuel Stevens, Jr. **Rutherfurd**, Lewis Morris **Vanderbilt**, William Kissam, Sr.
Harris, Katherine Corri	**Barrymore**, John **Pratt**, Alexander Dallas Bache **Orlowski**, Leon
Hatch, Margaret Leighton	**Moore**, Dr. David Dodge
Hatch, Marie Louise	**Gunther**, William Henry, Jr.
Havemeyer, Adeline	**Perkins**, Richard Sturgis, Sr. **Rand**, Laurance B.
Havemeyer, Doris	**Catlin**, Dr. Daniel, Sr.
Haviland, Ellen Rushton	**Burchell**, George W.

Maiden Names

Hawkins, Marriette   **Edwards**, Lawrence Barnes
Head, Betsey (common-law-wife)   **Taylor**, George Campbell
Hegeman, Laura Norma   **Lester**, Maxwell, Sr.
Heideberg, Adelaide   **Colt**, Robert Oliver
Henes, Augusta   **Gulden**, Frank, Sr.
Henry, Evalyn   **Stoppani**, Charles Francis, Jr.
Hibbard, Emma Louise   **Green**, Isaac Henry, II
Hill, Emeline Field   **Clyde**, William Pancoast, Sr.
Hill, Ethel   **Zerega**, John Pierre, Sr.
Hilsendegen, Christine   **Ullrich**, William J.
                                                                                                                      Parsons, William Decatur

Hoar, Roseanne   **Beard**, Anson Mc Cook, Jr.
Hoffman, Marion Krumbhaar   **Johnson**, Aymar
Hollins, Alice McKim   **Nicholas**, Harry Ingersoll, Sr.
Hollins, Ethel L.   **Bourne**, Arthur Keeler, Sr.
Hollins, Faith   **Little**, Arthur W.
                                                                                                                      Gulden, Charles, III

Hollister, Louise   **Forest**, Richard E.
                                                                                                                      Valentine, Langdon Barrett

Hopkins, Mary   **Blagden**, Crawford, Sr.
Horton, Blanche   **Hutton**, Edward Francis
Hough, Larissa G.   **Snow**, Frederick Billings
Howe, Eliza Jane   **Stoppani**, Charles Francis, Sr.
Howe, Mary Richards   **Hubbs**, Charles Francis
Howell, Sarah Louise   **Hollister**, Henry Hutchinson, Sr.
Hubbard, Annie Pearsall   **Remson**, Jacob
Huber, Elizabeth   **Howell**, Carlton Bell
Huggins, Isabelle Caroline   **Baker**, George William, Sr.
Hughes, Anna Elizabeth   **Pinkerton**, Robert Allan, Sr.
Hughes, Greta   **Howell**, James Frederick, Sr.
                                                                                                                      Witherspoon, Herbert

Humphreys, Mary Hoppin   **Johnston**, James Boorman
Hyde, Lillian   **Feitner**, Quentin Field
                                                                                                                      Wagstaff, George Barnard

Hyde, Lulu   **Hubbell**, Vincent Booth, Sr.
                                                                                                                      Drummond, Howard

Irving, Martha Pintard   **Walker,** Keitt Pinckney
                                                                                                                      aka George Daniel Keitt Pinckney Walker

Isham, Samantha Gaynor   **Gulden**, Charles, III
Ives, Sarah Caroline   **Plumb**, James Neale
Jacobs, Hannah D.   **Smith**, Selah Carll
Jacoby, Agnes Ernestine   **Harris**, Alfred H.
Jenkins, Clara   **Turnbull**, George R.

Maiden Names

Jennings, Almira Smith — **Doxsee**, James Harvey, Sr.
Johnson, Edna Louise — **Cox**, George, Jr.
Johnson, Harriet W. — **Franklin**, Emlen Pleasants
Johnson, Helena — **Parsons**, Schuyler Livingston, Sr.
Johnson, Lucy Ann — **Carroll**, Dr. Alfred Ludlow
Johnson, Marie Gaillard — **Russell**, William Hamilton, Jr.
    Crothers, Gordon

Johnson, Muriel — **Belasco**, Raymond
    deCoppet, Andre H.
    Fitch, George Hopper

Johnston, Eileen — **deCoppet**, Andre H.
    Zu Wied, Prince Karl Viktor

Jones, Henrietta Louise — **Simonds**, William Robinson
Jones, Maude Virginia — **Westin**, Clarence Frederick, Sr.
    Shea, David J.

Jones, Nellie C. — **Hawkins**, William Elton
Joralemon, Mary — **Johnson**, Parmenus, Sr.
Jordan, Katharine Trabue — **Magoun**, George Butler
Kahler, Ruth — **King**, Dr. George Suttie
Kapp, Mary M. — **Ranft**, Richard Michael
Keeler, Elizabeth B. — **Ballard**, Frederick Edward, Sr.
Keeler, Emma Sparks — **Bourne**, Frederick Gilbert
Kellar, Mary — **Hyde**, Richard
Kellers, Mary Catherine — **Gulden**, Charles, Sr.
Kennedy, Laurette — **Brundage**, ____
    Hoppin, Bayard Cushing

Kent, Katharine — **Frothingham**, John Sewell
Keser, Elizabeth Clara — **Van Bourgondien**, Cornelius John, Sr.
    aka Cornelis Johannes Van Bourgondien

Kessberg, Ida — **Van Anden**, Frank
Ketcham, Anita — **Shortland**, Thomas Francis
Ketchum, Catherine — **Corse**, Israel, Jr.
Ketchum, Phebe — **Thorne**, Edwin, II
Ketchum, Sophia — **Edwards**, Edward
Killian, Amelia Sophia — **Orr**, John Clifton, Sr.
Kip, Lydia Fowler — **Underhill**, Edward Beekman, Sr.
Kitching, Ada Emeline — **Reid**, Willard Placide
Kloepfer, Bertha — **Entenmann**, William Charles, Sr.
  aka Bertha Goepfel

Knapp, Caroline Burr — **Post**, Charles Kintzing
Knapp, Evelina Meserole — **Hollins**, Harry Bowly, Sr.
Knight, Mary — **Arnold**, Edward William Cameron
Knowles, Estelle M. — **Bromell**, Alfred Henry
    Smith, Charles Arthur

Maiden Names

Knowlton, Louise R.	**Hollister**, Buell, Sr.
Kobbe, Beatrice	**Little**, Raymond Demarest
Kobbe, Carol	**Morgan**, Robert Woodward, Sr.
	Snow, George Palen
Kobbe, Hildegarde	**Stevenson**, Joseph H.
	Thorne, Francis Burritt, Sr.
Kobbe, Virginia	**Hollins**, Gerald Vanderbilt, Sr.
	Morgan, Henry
Krech, Helen Margaret	**Wing**, Louis Stuart, Jr.
	Cusachs, Philip Alain
Krieg, Hermine T.	**Ranft**, Richard Michael
Krippendorf, Philippine Louise	**Bossert**, Louis
Kronkright, Mary Lorena	**Aston**, William K.
La Farge, Maria Louise	**Whyte**, Edward
	Lorillard, George Lyndes
	de Agreda, Count Casa
Lake, Edith	**Benkard**, James Gerald
Landon, Mary Gordon	**Pratt**, Dallas Bache
Lane, Edith Violet	**Graham**, James Varnum, Jr.
Lanier, Sarah Eggleston	**Lawrance**, Francis Cooper, Jr.
Larsen, Alice	**Busby**, John
Lawrance, Cornelia M.	**Wilmerding**, George Gorman
Lawrance, Louisa Anna	**Johnson**, Bradish, Sr.
Lawrance, Margaret Ireland	**Knapp**, Edward Spring, Sr.
Lawrence, Anna Middleton	**Suydam**, John Richard, Sr.
Leary, Eleanor Gertrude	**Delaney**, John Hanlon
Leavitt, Alice	**Kobbe**, George Christian
Lees, Robina Marion	**Duffy**, John Francis
	Wray, William Henry, Sr.
Leishman, Marthe	**de Gontaut–Biron**, Count Louis
	Hyde, James Hazen
Levick, Virginia	**Hallock**, Gerald, III
Libby, S. Katharine	**Lester**, Maxwell, Jr.
Littell, Sarah Elizabeth	**Rolston**, Roswell Graves
Little, Louise Carskaddon	**Lyon**, Dr. Edward Crane
Livingston, Lilias	**Hollins**, Harry Bowly, Jr.
Livingston, Maude	**Bull**, Henry Worthington
Lockwood, Adelaide Louisa	**Mildeberger**, Elwood
Lockwood, Mary Shubrick	**Childs**, Eversley, Sr.
Loney, Ruth Arabella	**Bruce–Brown**, George
Loomis, Julia Atterbury	**Thorne**, Landon Ketchum, Sr.
Lott, Gertrude Van Siclen	**Vanderveer**, John

Maiden Names

Lounsberry, Edith
    Perry, Henry Pierrepont
    Worden, John Lorimer, III

Lousdale, Ada Louise
    Wharton, Percival Charles

Lozier, Clair
    Pardee, Roy Edmund, Sr.

Lusk, Joan Penfold
    Tenney, Charles Henry, Sr.

Lux, Emma
    Bunce, Frederick Sidney, Sr.

MacConnell, Jennie Florence
    Melville, Francis, Jr.
      aka Frank Melville, Jr.

Macdonald, Margaret
    MacConnell, John B.

MacFarland, Blanche Maud
    Montgomery, Richard Malcolm, Sr.

Mackay, Sarah D.
    Gibb, John

MacLeond, Mina E.
    Blagden, Crawford, Sr.

Malcolm, Eleanor
  aka Nelly Malcolm
    Post, Edwin Main, Sr.

Maloney, Ida
    Stoppani, Joseph H.

Mann, Elizabeth Marshall
    Knapp, Harry Kearsarge, II
    Herrick, Walter Russell

Manning, Annie Amelia
    Truslow, Gilbert Potter

Martin, Alice
    Davies, Julien Tappan

Marvin, Maita Angus
    Hodges, George Winthrop, Sr.

Matson, Marion Louette
    Ward, Edwin Carrington

Maxwell, Henrietta Frances
    Lester, Joseph Huntington

May, Edith Sybil
    Randolph, Arthur
    Whitney, William Collins

Maynard, Mary Abby
    Birdsall, Clarence K.

Mayton, Anita
    Phelps, Royal, Jr.

McBeth, Margaret
    Placide, Henry

McCrea, Margaret
    Robert, Christopher Rhinelander, Jr.

McCue, Heloise
    Sands, Francis Preston Blair

McCue, Jennie Adele
    Bergen, James Cornelius

McDermont, Rosalie Thurston
    Baldridge, Harry Alexander, Sr.

McGraw, Josephine E.
    Swirbul, Leon A.
    MacLeod, Thomas Woodward, Sr.

McKay, Margaret Greenwood
    Hubbard, Harmanus Barkulo

Mc Kee, Marie Rose
    Yates, Richard George, Sr.
    Bynum, Joseph S.
    Correll, Ronald S.

McKesson, Virginia Greenway
    Bruce–Brown, George

McLean, Caroline Burnet
    Post, Henry Albertson Van Zo

McNamee, Marie E.
    Sullivan, Dr. Raymond Peter, Sr.

Meagh, Ellen
    Pardee, Roy Edmund, Sr.

Mellon, Marion
    Little, Raymond Demarest

Meredith, Mary Rattoone
    Dana, Richard Turner

Meserole, Maria
    Knapp, William Kumbel

Maiden Names

Miller, Emily Boxley	**Bourne**, Arthur Keeler, Sr.
Mills, Angela	**Cutting**, Henry Mason
	Worden, John Lorimer, III
	Scherbatoff, Prince Boris
Mills, Clara	**Wray**, William Henry, Sr.
Mills, Emma	**Adams**, Thomas, Jr.
Minor, Mary E.	**Hobbs**, Charles Buxton
Mirus, Gertrude	**Isbrandtsen**, Hans Jeppesen
Mitchell, Elizabeth	**Gregory**, William Hamilton, Sr.
Moffit, Ellen Juliette	**Creamer**, Joseph Byron, Sr.
Mollenhauer, Julia Theodora	**Dick**, John Henry
Moller, Mary Jane	**Havemeyer**, Henry, Sr.
Moore, Geralda	**Parkinson**, Thomas Ignatius, Jr.
Moore, Sarita Clara	**Garben**, Dr. Louis Francis, Sr.
Moran, Helen Dorothy	**McBurney**, Dr. Malcolm
	Noyes, Daniel Raymond
Morgan, Elizabeth Hamilton	**Belmont**, August, Jr.
Morgan, Helen	**Moran**, Amedee Depau
Morgan, Jennie Rice	**Foster**, Jay Stanley
	Voekler, Edward
Morier, Eva Marguerite	**Manton**, Martin Thomas
Morris, Anna Maria	**Prince**, John Dyneley, II
Morrison, Jeanett Edina	**Livingston**, Walter Francis
	Palmer, Elwell
Morse, Elizabeth	**Atwood**, Frederic Lawrence, Sr.
Mumby, Mary	**Pardee**, Dwight W.
Murray, Caroline Maria	**Wilmerding**, Lucius Kellogg, Sr.
Murray, Louisa M.	**Creamer**, Francis D., Sr.
	aka Frank D. Creamer, Sr.
Murray, Olivia Peyton	**Cutting**, William Bayard, Sr.
Myton, Grace E.	**Ireland**, Rufus Johnson, Sr.
Neff, Marie	**Pardee**, Roy Edward, Sr.
Neger, Elizabeth	**Bossert**, Louis
Newall, Elizabeth	**Drummond**, Howard
Nicholas, Evelyn Hollins	**Arnold**, Alexander Duncan Cameron
	Stevenson, Joseph H.
Nicholas, Rita	**Murdock**, Uriel Atwood, II
Nichols, Helen Brown	**Cerf**, Bennett Alfred
aka Phyllis Fraser	**Wagner**, Robert Ferdinand, Jr.
Nicol, Sarah Augusta	**Nicoll**, William, VII
Nicoll, Dorothy	**Hubert**, William Haight
	Baxter, George Strong, Jr.
Nicoll, Frances Augusta	**Johnson**, Lee
Nicoll, Frances Louisa	**Ludlow**, William Handy, Sr.

Maiden Names

Noyes, Margaret Grace
Oakes, Carrie Seaman
Oakley, Caroline

Oakley, Sarah Elizabeth
O'Brien, Edna Louise
O'Connor, Marie

Oldner, Helen M.
Olsen, Marion
Osborn, Charlotte Evelyn
O'Shea, Marion Theresa
Ottens, Ann Katherine
Otto, Virginia Woodhull
Owen, Gwendolyn Blackburn Chuwys
Pabst, Lillian

Parker, Florence Dawson
Parsons, Helena Johnson
Parsons, Marie Louise

Pasfield, Matilda Anna
Pasquali, Ida
Payne, Flora
Pease, Martha Carroll
  aka Patty Carroll Pease
Peers, Harriet
Peirce, Marjorie
Peirce, Mary Buford

Pell, Adelia Duane
Perkins, Mary Lawrence
Perry, Caroline Slidell
Peters, Louisine A.

Peters, Natalie
Peters, Sarah Welford
Pierson, Elizabeth
Pinkerton, Anna Joan
Pinkerton, Mary
Piorkowska, Olga May

Hutchins, Francis Sessions
Robbins, Jeremiah
Thompson, ____
Foster, John Strong
Morgan, John
Warren, Northam, Sr.
Quinn, ____
Davies, Julien Townsend, Jr.
Ryan, John T.
Snedeker, Charles Valentine
Wray, William Henry, Sr.
Roosevelt, Robert Barnwell, Sr.
Ebinger, Walter D.
Smith, Jewett Holt
Lindsay, Lewin Seaton
Wilson, William Paul
Packer, Frederick Little
Snedecor, James Henry
Wharton, Richard
Breese, William Laurence, Sr.
  aka William Lawrence Breese, Sr.
Higgins, Henry Vincent
Egly, Henry Harris
Davies, Julien Townsend, Jr.
Whitney, William Collins
McKinney, Rigan
Gibb, Lewis Mills, Jr.
Foster, William Riley, Sr.
Thorn, Edward Floyd–Jones, Sr.
Kiser, John William, Jr.
Greve, William Marcus, Jr.
Ireland, John Busteed
Post, Waldron Kintzing
Belmont, August, Sr.
Weekes, Harold Hathaway
Tcherepnin, Alexander
Webster, Charles Drake
Williams, Richard Henry, Sr.
Parsons, Schuyler Livingston, Jr.
Gibb, Lewis Mills, Sr.
Carlisle, Jay Freeborn, Sr.
Thomas, Arthur Paul
Wagstaff, Samuel Jones, Sr.
Newhall, Donald V.

Maiden Names

Piquette, Emile Angelique — **Sands**, Francis Preston Blair

Plate, Evelyn C. — **Proctor**, Cecil Wykes
Gasteiger, John G.

Pollard, Rebecca — **Van Lennep**, William, Jr.
Guggenheim, Meyer Robert, Sr.
Logan, John A.

Post, Caroline Beatrice — **Post**, Regis Henri, Sr.

Post, Harriette Appleton — **Wilson**, Richard Thornton
Von Jeszenzky, Baron Emmerich
Welles, Benjamin Sumner, III

Post, Marjorie Merriweather — **Close**, Edward Bennett
Hutton, Edward Francis
Davies, Joseph Edward
May, Herbert Arthur

Potter, Emily deLoosey — **Jackson**, Charles Havemeyer, Sr.
   aka Charles Frederick Havemeyer Jackson

Potter, Katherine — **Avery**, Joseph W. Hemmersley
Hard, Anson Wales, Jr.
Wear, Joseph W.

Prentice, Martha Howard — **Strong**, Theron George

Price, Emily Bruce — **Post**, Edwin Main, Sr.

Prokoff, Elizabeth — **Piper**, Eugene Stanton
Hyde, Henry Baldwin, II

Pulsifer, Ellen Eliza — **Wood**, Henry Duncan, Sr.

Purchase, Mary Ann — **Field**, Benjamin Prince, Jr.

Purdy, Elizabeth Teackle — **Nicholas**, George Stevenson, Sr.

Putnam, Harriet Sheldon — **Coleman**, Leander Walter Townsend

Quarre, Gladys — **Peabody**, Frederick Griffith
Knapp, Theodore Jackson
Bell, Howard

Rafter, Cecelia — **Kelly**, James P.

Ralston, Verra Hruba — **Yates**, Herbert John, Sr.

Redmond, Frances — **Livingston**, Henry Beekman, Jr.

Reed, Kathryn Isabel — **Pierrepont**, Robert Low

Regan, Jean — **Gibb**, Lewis Mills, Jr.

Reilly, Emily F. — **Bachia**, Richard Augustus, Jr.

Remington, Julia — **Morgan**, Charles Lee, Sr.
Robert, Christopher Rhinelander, Jr.

Remsen, Helen Rosalie — **Sutton**, Woodruff, Jr.

Rice, Gloriana S. — **Cooper**, James Brown, Sr.

Rieliey, Mary Teresa — **Bachia**, Richard Augustus, Jr.

Riley, Edith Louise — **Gaither**, G. Granger
Symington, Thomas H.
Lindsay, Lewin Seton

Riley, Elizabeth L. — **Ennis**, Thomas A.

Ringer, Dorothea — **Oelaner**, Rudolph

Maiden Names

Riopelle, Grace M.   **Blakeley**, James M.
     Hyde, William J.
     Kiser, John William, Jr.

Robb, Helen Gordon   **Catlin**, John Bernsee, Sr.

Robb, Ida May   **Stewart**, Dr. George David

Robbins, Anna Smith   **Higbie**, Richard

Robbins, Emma   **Walbridge**, George Huntington

Robbins, Jessie A.   **Sloane**, Henry T.
     Belmont, Perry

Roberts, Flora Cordelia   **Busch**, Clarence Marshall
     Lee, ____
     Tappin, Charles L.

Robertson, A. Celestina   **True**, Benjamin Kimball, Sr.

Robinson, Faith de Moss   **Davies**, Julien Townsend, Jr.

Robinson, Mary Henrietta   **Conover**, Augustus Whitlock, Sr.

Robson, Eleanor   **Belmont**, August, Jr.

Rogers, Frances C.   **Howell**, Elmer Brown, Sr.

Rose, Miriam A.   **Cahners**, Fulton Irving
     Thorne, Landon Ketchum, Jr.
     Gilpatric, Roswell Leavitt

Rossiter, Elizabeth   **Gibb**, Howard, Sr.

Rowe, Adelaide Carlotta   **Hamilton**, A. C.
     Housman, Arthur Albert

Rowland, Nellie   **Dunn**, Jared Erwin
     Van Anden, Frank

Saltonstall, Katharine Leverett   **Weld**, Philip Balch

Saunders, Effe J.   **Wood**, Henry Duncan, Jr.
     Heaton, Augustus

Scanlan, Gertrude   **Shea**, Timothy Joseph, Sr.

Scharmann, M. Antoniette   **Liebmann**, Julius

Schenck, Natalie   **Cutting**, Robert Fulton

Schenck, Sarah Pirnie   **Kalbfleisch**, Franklin H.

Schermerhorn, Ann White   **Suydam**, Charles

Schermerhorn, Catherine Elida   **Welles**, Benjamin Sumner, Sr.

Schmalix, Mary Elizabeth   **Laidlaw**, George Q., Sr.

Schneider, Martha Clara   **Entenmann**, William Charles, Jr.

Schott, Theresa   **Fishel**, Leopold Henry

Scott, Amy Rowan   **Johnson**, Effingham Lawrence
     Bates, William Graves

Scott, Evelyn Phoebe   **Behman**, Louis C., Sr.

Scott, Margaret   **Behman**, Louis C., Sr.

Scoville, Olive A.   **O'Donohue**, Charles Alfred

Scranton, Cornelia Walker   **Swift**, Samuel Sedwick
     Wagstaff, Samuel Jones, Sr.

Seaman, Ida Belle   **McKee**, John

Maiden Names

Seidel, Elsie
    Guastavino, Rafael, Jr.
    Mann, Randolph

Shannon, Effie
    Carleton, Henry Guy

Sheibeler, Florence Elizabeth
    Howell, Elmer Winfield

Sherwood, Josephine
    Turnbull, John Gourlay, Sr.

Siems, Doris
    Mollenhauer, John

Simons, Joanna Hodges
    Neville, Timothy Francis

Simpson, Ximena Estelle
    Covell, Charles Heber, Sr.

Sims, Mary Louise
    Moses, Robert

Slater, Esther
    Welles, Benjamin Sumner, III
    Kerrigan, Joseph John

Slocum, Margaret Olivia
    Flint, Sherman

Slocum, Marion Ricketson
    Hallowell, Thomas Jewett, Sr.

Smedberg, Emily
    Weeks, Edwin Carnes

Smith, ____
    Allen, Theodore

Smith, Almira
    Doxsee, James Harvey, Sr.

Smith, Alva Erskine
    Vanderbilt, William Kissam, Sr.
    Belmont, Oliver Hazard

Smith, Catherine Floyd
    Knapp, Shepherd Fordyce, Sr.

Smith, Elizabeth
    Asten, Thomas B.

Smith, Ellen Mowbray
    Mowbray, Dr. Jarvis Rogers

Smith, Frances Elward
    Baldridge, Harry Alexander, Sr.

Smith, Laurie Elward
    Allgood, Andrew Perry de Forest

Smith, Louise Annette
    Ockers, Jacob

Spaulding, Clara Cornelia
    Stanchfield, John Barry, Sr.

Spear, Helen Zaibee
    Tappin, John Crane

Spence, Margaret
    Eastwood, John Henry

Spencer, Nellie White
    Childs, William Hamlin

Stafford, Mary Cornelia
    Trenchard, Edward, II

Stanchfield, Alice Spaulding
    Wright, Dr. Arthur Mullen

Stanton, Anna
    Lawrance, John Ireland

Staudt, Marie Josephine
    Moran, Eugene Francis, Jr.

Steele, Frances
    Sutton, Woodruff, Sr.

Steele, Jeannie Porter
    Smith, Charles Robinson

Steers, Mary Louise
    Orr, John Clifton, Sr.

Steffens, Emma Augusta
    Bohack, Henry Christian
        aka Hinrich Christian Bohack

Stellenwerf, Emma A.
    Meeks, Edwin Bartlett

Stephens, Estelle
    Swirbul, Leon A.

Stephenson, Anne Willard
    Hollister, Henry Hutchinson, Sr.

Stevens, Alice Muriel
    Titus, James Gulden, Sr.

Stevens, Marion
    aka Marion Manola
    Mould, ____
    Mason, John Hill Belcher

Maiden Names

Stevenson, Carol   **Lovering**, Joseph Sears, Sr.
     Roesler, Max Stuart

Stewart, Anna May   **Brennan**, Rudolph Cameron
  aka Anna Stuart   aka Rudolph Cameron
     Converse, George Peabody

Stokes, Frances   **Clark**, Louis Crawford, II
     Weekes, Harold Hathaway

Stoppani, Eliza Jane   **Harris**, ____
     Cox, Stephen Perry

Stout, Mary Ellen   **Dodson**, Richard Wolford

Strong, Esther Jewell   **Denby**, Thomas Gavin
       aka Garvin Denby

Strong, Silvie Livingston   **Post**, Richard Bayley
     Hepburn, Henry Chester

Suckley, Mary   **McCurdy**, Robert Henry, II

Suydam, Helen   **Cutting**, Robert Fulton

Swan, Frances Wyeth   **Welles**, Benjamin Sumner, Jr.

Taylor, Maria Farquhar   **Post**, Henry Albertson Van Zo

Taylor, Natalie L.   **Bossert**, Charles Volunteer

Thayer, Sara Laller   **Lacombe**, Charles Frederick

Thebaud, Emelia Isabelle   **Heckscher**, Charles Augustus, Jr.

Thomas, Anne Gordon   **Duval**, Henry Rieman

Thompson, Emily Harriet   **Phelps**, Charles Egbert

Thompson, Louise Ethel   **Baker**, William Dunham

Thorn, Frances Mathilda   **Garner**, Thomas, Sr.

Thorn, Macellite   **Garner**, William Thorn

Thorne, Phebe   **Dempsey**, Joseph Francis, Jr.

Thorne, Phebe Schoonhoven   **Knapp**, Harry Kearsarge, II
     Tucker, John

Tierney, Helen   **Harbeck**, Charles Thomas

Timmermann, Grace Ethel   **Tobey**, Orville Hurd

Tinley, Frances B.   **de Goicouria**, Albert Valentine

Titus, Margaret Louise   **Yates**, Douglas Thomas, Sr.

Torrence, Jessie Norton   **Magoun**, Kinsley
     Alexander, Henry Addison
     Blakiston, William Graham

Towne, Annie M.   **Bunce**, Frederick Sidney, Sr.

Townsend, Mathilde Scott   **Gerry**, Peter Goelet
     Welles, Benjamin Sumner, III

Treadwell, Hester A.   **Powell**, David Baisley

Trenchard, Edith Isabelle   **Power**, John Anthony
     Arnold, Edward William Cameron
     Decatur, Storer Goodwin

True, Julia B.   **Fowler**, William J.
     Stephens, John Lloyd

Turnbull, Clara   **Keith**, Minor Cooper R., II

Maiden Names

Vagts, Anna Maria — **Dick**, William
Valentine, Anne — **Lovering**, Joseph Sears, Sr.
Vance, Nannie Mitchell — **Roosevelt**, John Ellis
Vanderveer, Cornelia Lott — **Gibson**, John Joseph
Vans Agnew, Violet Eleanor — **Evers**, Cecil Calvert
Vidal, Sophia Theresa — **Meeks**, Joseph William, Sr.
Waas, Katherine — **Ward**, John Montgomery
Waddell, Marjorie Cooper — **Gregory**, George Mitchell
Wagstaff, Sarah Louisa — **Remsen**, Phoenix, Sr.
Wakefield, Laura — **Phelps**, Charles Egbert
Walker, Helen Ella — **Matuschka**, Baron Manfred
   Hyde, James Hazen
   Von Thur and Taxis, Prince Alexander

Wall, Mary Cecelia — **de Goicouria**, Albert Valentine
Wandel, Blanche Gifford — **Walbridge**, Ernest Augustus
Washington, Louisa — **Ceballos**, Juan Manuel, Sr.
Wederstrandt, Helen Maria — **Johnson**, John Dean
Weed, Georgia Childs — **Parkinson**, Thomas Ignatius, Sr.
Weekes, Adeline Hathaway — **Scully**, Charles Brewster
   Tcherepnin, Alexander
   Orssich, Count Philip

Weeks, Katharine — **Arnold**, Alexander Duncan Cameron
Weeks, Mary Ludlow Smedberg — **Eyre**, Beverley Montagu
Welles, Helen Schermerhorn — **Kingsland**, George Lovett, Sr.
Wells, Mary — **Dodson**, Robert Bowman
Wells, Natalie — **Peters**, Harry Twyford, Sr.
Wemple, Martha Eugenia — **Hayward**, William Tyson, Sr.
Weyher, Margaret Gibbs Miller — **Guggenheim**, Meyer Robert, Sr.
Wharton, Marion — **Hallock**, Gerard, III
Wheaton, Calla — **Esteva**, Manuel A., Sr.
Wheeler, Carolyn — **Kobbe**, Gustav
Wheeler, Hannah Maria — **Corbin**, Austin, Jr.
White, Ethel Folger — **Remsen**, Cornelius Wagstaff
White, Madeleine — **Kennard**, Spencer, Sr.
   Morris, Stuyvesant Fish, III

Whitlock, Catherine Eliza — **Conover**, Daniel Denice
Whitney, Maria — **Livingston**, Robert Cambridge, III
Wickes, Frances — **Goodrich**, William Winston
Widdifield, Adele Cornwell — **Howell**, James Frederick, Sr.
Wilce, Edwina May — **Van Anden**, Frank
Wilkinson, Abbie — **Purdy**, Charles Robert, Sr.
Williams, Margaret — **Gulden**, Charles, Sr.
Willing, Susan Ridgeway — **Lawrance**, Francis Cooper, Jr.

Maiden Names

Wilson, Willa Alice	**Page**, Walter Hines, Sr.
Winslow, Helen aka Cynthia Helen Winslow	**Durkee**, Eugene Return
Woodhouse, Grace Guernsey	**Roosevelt**, Robert Barnwell, Jr.
Woodrow, Lorena M.	**Burke**, Charles Felix
Woodruff, Ellen A.	**Johnson**, Edwin Augustus, Sr.
Woodruff, Mary Lavinia	**Sutton**, Effingham Brown, Sr.
Woodward, Clara	**Morgan**, Charles, Sr.
Woolworth, Edna	**Hutton**, Franklyn Laws
Woolworth, Franc	**Pinkerton**, Allan, II
Worle, Mary Agnes	**Prescott**, William French **Simonson**, Douglass B.
Worth, Josephine	**Hulse**, The Reverend William Warren
Wulfing, Julia	**Schwenke**, Oscar Louis, III
Yates, Elsa Marcia	**Titus**, Walter Livingston, Jr.
Young, Marie Julia	**Kaufman**, Louis Graverat **Pratt**, Alexander Dallas Bache
Young, Ruth Allen	**Koehler**, Robert H.
Zundt, Eliza Anna	**Heins**, John Lewis, Sr.

Emma Sparks Keeler Bourne
(Mrs. Frederick Gilbert Bourne)

Dorothy Whiting Frothingham Wagstaff
(Mrs. Edward William Cameron Arnold;
Mrs. George Barnard Wagstaff)

Mary Pinkerton and Jay Freeborn Carlisle, Sr.

*Florence Bourne and Anson Wales Hard, Jr.
with sons, Frederick and Anson*

Occupations

See the surname entry to ascertain if an individual is listed under several occupational headings.

ADVERTISING EXECUTIVES

Coffey, John Edward Develin, Sr.

Johnson, Frederick Merle, Sr.
  aka Merle Johnson, Sr.

Wagner, Helen Brown Nichols
  aka Phyllis Fraser

ARCHITECTS

Birdsall, Clarence K.

Cusachs, Philip Alain

Dick, Adolph Mollenhauer

Green, Isaac Henry, II

Russell, William Hamilton, Jr.

Smith, Elward, Sr.

Trenchard, Edward, II

Walker, Keitt Pinckney
  aka George Daniel Keitt Pinckney Walker

ARTISTS

Blum, Ethel Mildred Halsey

Major, Alfred Sarony

Melville, Francis, Sr.

Oppenheimer, Ella Friedman

Packer, Frederick Little

Smith, Hervey Garret

Thorne, Ann Chauncey Cobb

Trenchard, Edward, II

Wagstaff, Olga May Piorkowski

ATTORNEYS

Aldrich, Spencer

Aston, William K.

Atwood, Frederic Lawrence, Sr.

Bates, William Graves

Belmont, Perry

Bergen, James Cornelius

Cooper, James Brown, Sr.

Corbin, Austin, Jr.

Cutting, William Bayard, Sr.

Davies, Julien Tappan

Davies, Julien Townsend, Jr.

Davies, Julien Townsend, Sr.

Dempsey, Joseph Francis, Jr.

Dempsey, Joseph Francis, Sr.

Fortescue, Kenyon

Foster, Jay Stanley

Foster, William Riley, Jr.

Gibson, John Joseph

Goodrich, William Winston

Graham, George Scott

Haff, Albert Douglas

Hobbs, Charles Buxton

Hubbard, Harmanus Barkulo

Hutchins, Francis Sessions

Hyde, Henry Baldwin, II

Ireland, John Busteed

Johnson, Bradish, Sr.

Johnson, Henry Meyer

Kleinman, David E.

Kobbe, George Christian

Koehler, Robert H.

Lawrance, Francis Cooper, Jr.

Manton, Martin Thomas

McCue, Alexander

Neville, Timothy Francis

Nicoll, William Greenly

Owens, Joseph Eugene, Sr.

Palmer, Elwell

Parkinson, Thomas Ignatius, Jr.

Parkinson, Thomas Ignatius, Sr.

Parsons, William Decatur

Post, Charles Alfred

Post, Waldron Kintzing

Powell, Leander Treadwell

Reid, John Robert

Reid, Willard Placide

Remsen, Phoenix, Sr.

Ridgeway, James W.

Robbins, William H., Sr.

Occupations

ATTORNEYS (cont'd)

Rokenbaugh, Henry Scott
Roosevelt, John Ellis
Roosevelt, Robert Barnwell, Sr.
Sands, Francis Preston Blair
Shea, Timothy Joseph, Sr.
Smith, Charles Robinson
Stanchfield, John Barry, Sr.
Stephens, Benjamin, Jr.
Stephens, John Lloyd
Stillman, Benjamin D.
Strong, Theron George
Tenney, Charles Henry, Sr.
True, Benjamin Kimball, Sr.
Wagstaff, Alfred, Jr.
Wagstaff, Samuel Jones, Sr.
Wainwright, Stuyvesant, Jr.
Walker, Harford Pinckney
  aka Frederick Harford Pinckney Walker, Sr.
Ward, Edwin Carrington
Ward, John Montgomery
White, Raymond S.
Whitney, William Collins

CAPITALISTS

Aldrich, Spencer
Allison, William Manwaring, Sr.
Asher, John J.
Aston, William K.
Bedell, Walter Ellwood
Behman, Louis C., Sr.
Belmont, August, Jr.
Belmont, August, Sr.
Belmont, August, III
Bergen, Cornelius J., Sr.
Blum, Edward Charles
Bohack, Henry Christian
  aka Hinrich Christian Bohack
Bossert, Charles Volunteer
Bossert, Louis
Bourne, Arthur Keeler, Sr.
Bourne, Frederick Gilbert

Brownlie, George
Bunce, Frederick Sidney, Sr.
Burke, Charles Felix
Ceballos, Juan Manuel, Sr.
Childs, Eversley, Sr.
Childs, William Hamlin
Clarkson, William Kemble, Jr.
Clyde, William Pancoast, Sr.
Colt, Robert Oliver
Conover, Daniel D.
Corbin, Austin, Jr.
Creamer, Francis D., Sr.
  aka Frank D. Creamer, Sr.
Creamer, Joseph Byron, Sr.
Cutting, Robert Fulton
Cutting, William Bayard, Sr.
Davies, Julien Townsend, Sr.
deCoppet, Andre H.
Dempsey, Joseph Francis, Sr.
Dick, William Karl
Duval, Henry Rieman
Edwards, Edward
Edwards, Lawrence
Entenmann, Robert William, Sr.
Fairchild, Julian Douglas
Farrell, Frank J.
Fishel, Leopold Henry
Flint, Sherman
Ford, Malcolm Webster, Sr.
Foster, Andrew D.
  aka Andrew D. Forsslund
Foster, Jay Stanley
Foster, John Strong
Foster, William Riley, Sr.
Frothingham, John Sewell
Gardiner, Robert David Lion
Gibb, John
Gibb, Lewis Mills, Jr.
Gibb, Lewis Mills, Sr.
Gibson, Frederick E.
Gibson, Gregory Martin
Goodrich, William Winston

Occupations

CAPITALISTS (cont'd)

- Graham, George Scott
- Gregory, William Hamilton, Jr.
- Greve, William Marcus, Jr.
- Guastavino, Rafael, Jr.
- Hallowell, Thomas Jewett, Sr.
- Havemeyer, Henry, Sr.
- Havemeyer, Henry Osborne
- Havemeyer, Horace, Sr.
- Hawley, Edwin
- Heckscher, Charles Augustus, Jr.
- Heins, John Lewis, Sr.
- Higbie, Richard
- Hobbs, Charles Buxton
- Hollins, Harry Bowly, Sr.
- Hollister, Buell, Sr.
- Hollister, Henry Hutchinson, Sr.
- Hoppin, Bayard Cushing
- Housman, Arthur Albert
- Howell, Carlton Bell
- Howell, Elmer Brown, Sr.
- Howell, Elmer Winfield
- Howell, Ralph Dewitt, Sr.
- Hubbard, Harmanus Barkulo
- Hyde, Henry Baldwin, Sr.
- Hyde, James Hazen
- Hyde, James Richard
- Hyde, Richard
- Hyde, William James
- Ireland, John Busteed
- Ireland, Rufus Johnson, Sr.
- Isbrandtsen, Hans Jeppesen
- Jacoby, Dr. James Ralph
- Johnson, Bradish, Jr.
- Johnson, Bradish, Sr.
- Johnson, Bradish Gaillard, III
- Johnson, Edwin Augustus, Sr.
- Johnson, Henry Meyer
- Johnson, John Dean
- Johnson, Lee
- Johnson, Parmenus, Sr.
- Johnston, James Boorman
- Keith, Minor Cooper
- Kelly, James P.
- Kempster, James H.
- King, Dr. George Suttie
- Kingsland, George Lovett, Sr.
- Knapp, Edward Spring, Sr.
- Knapp, Gladys Quarre
- Knapp, Harry Kearsarge, Sr.
- Knapp, Theodore Jackson
- Kobbe, George Christian
- Koehler, Robert H.
- Lacombe, Charles Frederick
- Lawrance, Charles Lanier
- Lawrance, Francis Cooper, Sr.
- Lawrence, Chester Bulkley, Sr.
- Lazare, Andrew
- Lemmerman, Frederick C.
- Lester, Joseph Huntington
- Litchfield, Electus Backus
- Livingston, Robert Cambridge, III
- Lorillard, George Lyndes
- Macy, George Henry
- Macy, William Kingsland, Sr.
- Magoun, George Butler
- Maxwell, Henry William
- McCue, Alexander
- McCurdy, Robert Henry, II
- McNamee, John
- Meeks, Joseph William, Sr.
- Melville, Francis, Jr.
  aka Frank Melville, Jr.
- Mildeberger, Elwood
- Moffitt, Ellie F.
- Moffitt, William Henry
- Montgomery, Richard Malcolm, Sr.
- Moran, Amedee Depau
- Morrison, George Alexander
- Morse, William Otis
- Murdock, Uriel Atwood, II
- Neville, Timothy Francis

Occupations

CAPITALISTS (cont'd)

- Nicholas, George Stevenson, Sr.
- Nicholas, Harry Ingersoll, Sr.
- Oakman, Walter George, Sr.
- Ockers, Jacob
- O'Donohue, Charles Alfred
- Oelsner, Rudolph
- Oppenheimer, Julius
- Orr, John Clifton, Sr.
- Palmer, Elwell
- Pardee, Dwight W.
- Pardee, Roy Edmund, Sr.
- Parkinson, Thomas Ignatius, Jr.
- Parkinson, Thomas Ignatius, Sr.
- Payne, Albert
- Peck, William L., Sr.
- Perkins, Richard Sturgis, Sr.
- Peters, Samuel Twyford
- Pierrepont, Robert Low
- Pinkerton, Allan, II
- Pinkerton, Robert Allan, II
- Pinkerton, Robert Allan, Sr.
- Pollock, Walter B.
- Post, Edwin Main, Sr.
- Post, Emily Bruce Price
- Post, Henry Albertson Van Zo
- Post, Regis Henri, Sr.
- Powell, David Baisley
- Purdy, Charles Robert, Sr.
- Redmond, Roland
- Reid, Willard Placide
- Robbins, Jeremiah
- Robbins, John Clinton, Sr.
- Robert, Christopher Rhinelander, Jr.
- Rolston, Roswell Graves
- Roosevelt, John Ellis
- Roosevelt, Robert Barnwell, Jr.
- Roosevelt, Robert Barnwell, Sr.
- Ryan, John T.
- Schnur, David
- Schwenke, Oscar Louis, III
- Scully, Charles Brewster
- Searle, Charles
- Sharp, Hamlet Cecil
- Slote, Alonzo
- Smith, Charles Robinson
- Smith Elward, Jr.
- Smith Elward, Sr.
- Smith, Frederick D.
- Smith, Jewett Holt
- Smith, Selah Carll
- Smith, Virginia Woodhull Otto
- Snow, Frederick Billings
- Spaulding, E. B.
- Stoppani, Joseph H.
- Strong, James Henry
- Sutton, Effingham Brown, Jr.
- Sutton, Effingham Brown, Sr.
- Sutton, Harold Falconer
- Sutton, Woodruff, Sr.
- Swan, Alden Smith
- Swirbul, Leon A.
- Tappin, Charles L.
- Thorne, Edwin, II
- Thorne, Edwin, III
- Thorne, Landon Ketchum, Sr.
- Thurber, Frederick Charles
- Titus, James Gulden, Sr.
- Titus, Walter Livingston, Jr.
- True, Benjamin Kimball, Sr.
- Turnbull, George R.
- Udall, Joseph Sanford
- Underhill, Edward Beekman, Sr.
- Van Anden, William M.
- Vanderbilt, William Kissam, Sr.
- Van Orden, Jabez Ephraim
- Van Orden, James
- Wagstaff, Alfred, Jr.
- Wagstaff, Dr. Alfred, Sr.
- Walker, Harford Pinckney, Sr.
  aka Frederick Harford Pinckney, Sr.
- Walker, Keitt Pinckney
  aka George Daniel Keitt Pinckney Walker

Occupations

CAPITALISTS (cont'd)

Ward, Helen Dauvray
Ward, John Montgomery
Welwood, Thomas
Wharton, William Fishbourne
White, Raymond S.
Whitney, William Collins
Williams, Percy Garnett
Wood, Henry Duncan, Sr.
Wray, William Henry, Sr.
Yates, Douglas Thomas, Sr.
Yates, Herbert John, Sr.
Yates, Richard George, Sr.
Zerega, John Pierre, Sr.

CLERGY

Hulse, The Reverend William Warren
Parkhurst, The Reverend Charles Henry

COMPOSERS

Tcherepnin, Alexander
Thorne, Francis Burritt, Jr.

EDUCATORS

Cooper, Gloriana S. Rice
Dodson, Richard Wolford
Graham, George Scott
Lyon, Dr. Edward Crane
Melville, Francis, Sr.
Oppenheimer, Ella Friedman
Palmer, Marjorie Cleaveland
Parkhurst, The Reverend Charles Henry
Parkinson, Thomas Ignatius, Sr.
Pasternack, Richard
Pless, John Anthony, Jr.
Stewart, Dr. George David
Vander Veer, Dr. Albert, Jr.

ENTERTAINERS AND ASSOCIATED PROFESSIONS

Astaire, Fred
   aka Frederick Austerlitz
Behman, Margaret Scott
Belmont, Eleanor Robson
Brennan, Rudolph Cameron
   aka Rudolph Cameron
   [see Stewart entry]
Haight, Gilbert Lawrence, Sr.
Howell, Greta Hughes
Hyde, Grace M. Riopelle
Hyde, Richard
Johnson, Edith D.
Mason, John Hill Belcher
Mason, Katherine Best
   aka Katherine Grey
Mason, Marion Stevens
   aka Marion Manola
Pardee, Lillian H. Beasley
Placide, Henry
Post, Eleanor Malcolm
   aka Nelly Malcolm
Post, Emily Bruce Price
Pratt, Katherine Corrie Harris
Shannon, Effie
Stewart, Anna May
   aka Anna Stuart
Tcherepnin, Alexander
Wagner, Helen Brown Nichols
   aka Phyllis Frazer
Ward, Helen Dauvray
Williams, Percy Garnett
Yates, Vera Hruba Ralston

FINANCIERS

Andrews, William Loring
Atwood, Kimball Chase, Jr.
Bachia, Richard Augustus, Jr.
Baker, George William, Sr.
Ballard, Frederick Edward, Sr.
Baruch, Bernard Mannes, Sr.
Baxter, John Edward
Beard, Anson Mc Cook, Jr.
Bedell, Walter Ellwood
Belmont, August, Jr.
Belmont, August, Sr.

Occupations

FINANCIERS (cont'd)

Belmont, August, III
Benkard, James Gerald
Betts, Roland Whitney
Bigelow, Edwin Hicks
Blagden, Crawford, Sr.
Blum, Edward Charles
Blum, Robert Edward
Bohack, Henry Christian
   aka Hinrich Christian Bohack
Bossert, Louis
Bourne, Frederick Gilbert
Breese, William Laurence, Sr.
   aka William Lawrence Breese, Sr.
Bull, Henry Worthington
Burchell, George W.
Cameron, Edward Miller
Carlisle, Jay Freeborn, Sr.
Catlin, John Bernsee, Sr.
Ceballos, Juan Manuel, Sr.
Coleman, Leander Walter Townsend
Converse, George Peabody
   [*see* Stewart entry]
Cooper, James Brown, Sr.
Corbin, Austin, Jr.
Cox, George, Jr.
Cutting, Robert Fulton
Cutting, William Bayard, Sr.
Davies, Julien Tappan
deCoppet, Andre H.
de Forest, James Goodrich, Sr.
de Goicouria, Albert Valentine
del Garcia, Lester Mullen
Dempsey, Joseph Francis, Sr.
Denby, Thomas Garvin
   aka Garvin Denby
Dick, John Henry
Dick, William
Dick, William Karl
Dodson, Robert Bowman
Dresser, Daniel LeRoy, Sr.
Drummond, Howard

Duval, Henry Rieman
Eaton, James Waterbury, Sr.
Egly, Henry Harris
Ellis, George Augustus, Jr.
Ennis, Thomas A.
Entenmann, William Charles, III
Evers, Cecil Calvert
Eyre, Beverley Montagu
Fairchild, Julian Douglas
Field, Benjamin Prince, Jr.
Fishel, Leopold Henry
Flint, Sherman
Ford, Malcolm Webster, Sr.
Foster, Jay Stanley
Foster, John Strong
Foster, William Riley, Sr.
Frank, Emil Henry, Sr.
Frothingham, John Sewell
Gardiner, Robert David Lion
Gibb, John
Gibson, John James
Gibson, John Joseph
Gilmore, William Guy, Sr.
Goodrich, William Winston
Gordon, Edward
Graham, George Scott
Green, Isaac Henry, II
Gregory, George Mitchell
Gregory, William Hamilton, Jr.
Gregory, William Hamilton, Sr.
Greve, William Marcus, Jr.
Guggenheim, Meyer Robert, Sr.
Gulden, Charles, Sr.
Haff, Albert Douglas
Haight, Gilbert Lawrence, Sr.
Hallock, Gerard, III
Hallowell, Thomas Jewett, Sr.
Harbeck, Charles Thomas
Hard, Anson Wales, Jr.
Havemeyer, Henry Osborne
Havemeyer, Horace, Jr.

Occupations

FINANCIERS (cont'd)
Havemeyer, Horace, Sr.
Heins, John Lewis, Sr.
Helm, Gustave Adolph
Hepburn, Henry Charles, Jr.
Hepburn, Henry Chester
Higbie, Richard
Hodges, George Winthrop, Sr.
Hollins, Gerald Vanderbilt, Sr.
Hollins, Harry Bowly, Jr.
Hollins, Harry Bowly, Sr.
Hollister, Buell, Sr.
Hollister, Henry Hutchinson, Sr.
Hoppin, Bayard Cushing
Housman, Arthur Albert
Howell, Elmer Brown, Sr.
Howell, Elmer Winfield
Hubbard, Harmanus Barkulo
Hubbs, Charles Francis
Hutchins, Francis Session
Hutton, Edward Francis
Hutton, Franklyn Laws
Hyde, Henry Baldwin, Sr.
Hyde, James Hazen
Ireland, Rufus Johnson, Sr.
Johnson, Aymar
Johnson, Bradish, Jr.
Johnson, Bradish, Sr.
Johnston, James Boorman
Keith, Minor Cooper
Kelly, James P.
Knapp, Edward Spring, Sr.
Knapp, Harry Kearsarge, Sr.
Knapp, Shepherd, II
Knapp, Shepherd Fordyce, Sr.
Knapp, Theodore Jackson
Kobbe, George Christian
Koehler, Robert H.
Laidlaw, George Q., Sr.
Lemmerman, Frederick C.
Lester, Joseph Huntington

Lester, Maxwell, Jr.
Liebmann, Julius
Lindsay, Lewin Seton
Livingston, Harry Beekman, Jr.
Ludlow, William Handy, Sr.
MacConnell, John B.
MacLeod, Thomas Woodward, Sr.
Macy, George Henry
Macy, William Kingsland, Sr.
Magoun, Francis Peabody, Sr.
Magoun, George Butler
Magoun, Kinsley
Maitland, Robert Lenox, Sr.
Maxwell, Henry William
McBurney, Dr. Malcolm
McClure, William
McCue, Alexander
McCurdy, Robert Henry, II
McKee, Henry Sellers, II
McKee, John
McKee, William L.
McNamee, John
Meeks, Edwin Bartlett
Mollenhauer, John
Mollenhauer, John Adolph
Montgomery, Richard Malcom, Sr.
Moran, Amedee Depau
Morgan, Charles, Jr.
Morgan, Henry
Morgan, Robert Woodward, Sr.
Morris, Stuyvesant Fish, III
Morrison, George Alexander
Murdock, Uriel Atwood, II
Nicholas, Harry Ingersoll, Sr.
Noyes, Daniel Raymond
Oakman, Walter George, Sr.
Ockers, Jacob
O'Donohue, Charles Alfred
Orr, John Clifton, Sr.
Owens, Joseph Eugene, Sr.
Pardee, Roy Edmund, Sr.

Occupations

FINANCIERS (cont'd)

Parkinson, Thomas Ignatius, Sr.
Parsons, Schuyler Livingston, Jr.
Perkins, Richard Sturgis, Sr.
Peters, Samuel Twyford
Phelps, Charles Egbert
Phelps, Royal, Jr.
Pierrepont, Robert Low
Pinkerton, Robert Allan, II
Pollock, Walter B.
Post, Edwin Main, Sr.
Post, Henry Albertson Van Zo
Post, Regis Henri, Sr.
Potter, Eliphalet Nott, III
    [see Astaire entry]
Powell, David Baisley
Pratt, Alexander Dallas Bache
Pratt, Dallas Bache
Prescott, William French
Prince, John Dyneley, II
Reid, Willard Placide
Remsen, Cornelius Wagstaff
Robbins, John Clinton, Sr.
Robbins, Josiah
Robbins, William H., Sr.
Rolston, Roswell Graves
Rothschild, Simon Frank
Schieren, Charles Adolph, Sr.
Searle, Charles
Simonds, William Robinson
Slote, Alonzo
Smedberg, Adolphus, Jr.
Smith, Frederick D.
Smith, Jewett Holt
Snedecor, Isaac Howard
Snedeker, Charles Valentine
Staples, Cyrus E.
Stoppani, Charles Francis, Jr.
Stoppani, Joseph H.
Sutton, Effingham Brown, Sr.
Swan, Alden Smith

Tappin, John Crane
Thorne, Edwin, II
Thorne, Edwin, III
Thorne, Francis Burritt, Jr.
Thorne, Francis Burritt, Sr.
Thorne, Landon Ketchum, Jr.
Thorne, Landon Ketchum, Sr.
Timmermann, Henry Gerhard
Tobey, Orville Hurd
Truslow, Frederick Cumings
Turnbull, George R.
Underhill, Edward Beekman, Sr.
Van Anden, William M.
Van Orden, James
Wadell, Charles Falkiner Morton
    aka Morton Waddell
Wagstaff, George Barnard
Wainwright, Stuyvesant, Jr.
Walbridge, Ernest Augustus
Weekes, Harold Hathaway
Weeks, Edwin Carnes
Weld, Philip Balch
Wharton, Richard
Wharton, Richard T., Sr.
Wharton, William Fishbourne
White, Raymond S.
Wilmerding, Lucius Kellogg, Sr.
Wood, Henry Duncan, Jr.
Wood, Henry Duncan, Sr.
Worden, John Lorimer, III
Yates, Douglas Thomas, Sr.
Yates, Herbert John, Sr.
Young, Albert

INDUSTRIALISTS

Adams, John Dunbar
Adams, Thomas, Jr.
Andres, William Loring
Andrews, William Loring
Bachia, Richard Augustus, Jr.

Occupations

INDUSTRIALISTS (cont'd)

Baker, George William, Sr.
Baxter, John Edward
Bossert, Charles Volunteer
Bossert, Louis
Bourne, Arthur Keeler, Sr.
Bourne, Frederick Gilbert
Cameron, Edward Miller
Ceballos, Juan Manuel, Sr.
Childs, Eversley, Sr.
Childs, William Hamlin
Clarkson, William Kemble, Jr.
Corbin, Austin, Jr.
Crothers, Gordon
Dahl, George Washington
deCoppet, Andre H.
Delaney, John Hanlon
Dempsey, Joseph Francis, Sr.
Denby, Thomas Garvin
  aka Garvin Denby
Dick, John Henry
Dick, William
Dick, William Karl
Dillon, John Allen, Sr.
Doxsee, James Harvey, Sr.
Dresser, Daniel LeRoy, Sr.
Duval, Henry Rieman
Eastwood, John Henry
Eaton, James Waterbury, Sr.
Elder, George Waldron, Sr.
Ely, John R.
Entenmann, Charles, Sr.
Entenmann, Martha Clare Schneider
Entenmann, Robert William, Sr.
Entenmann, William Charles, Jr.
Entenmann, William Charles Sr.
Entenmann, William Charles, III
Fairchild, Julian Douglas
Franklin, Emlen Pleasants
Frothingham, John Sewell
Garner, Thomas, Jr.

Garner, Thomas, Sr.
Garner, William Thorn
Gibson, John Joseph
Gilmore, William Guy, Sr.
Graham, George Scott
Gregory, George Mitchell
Gregory, William Hamilton, Jr.
Greve, William Marcus, Jr.
Guggenheim, Meyer Robert, Sr.
Gulden, Charles, III
Gulden, Charles, Sr.
Gulden, Frank, Jr.
Gulden, Frank, Sr.
Hallowell, Thomas Jewett, Sr.
Havemeyer, Harry Waldron
Havemeyer, Henry, Sr.
Havemeyer, Henry Osborne
Havemeyer, Horace, Jr.
Havemeyer, Horace, Sr.
Hawkins, William Elton
Hayward, William Tyson, Jr.
Hayward, William Tyson, Sr.
Hobbs, Charles Buxton
Hollins, Harry Bowly, Jr.
Hollins, Harry Bowly, Sr.
Hollister, Buell, Sr.
Housman, Arthur Albert
Hubbs, Charles Francis
Huber, Frederick Max, Sr.
Hutton, Edward Francis
Hutton, Marjorie Merriweather Post
Ireland, Rufus Johnson, Sr.
Isbrandtsen, Hans Jeppeson
Johnson, Bradish, Jr.
Johnson, Bradish, Sr.
Johnson, Edwin Augustus, Sr.
Johnson, Lee
Kalbfleisch, Franklin H.
Keith, Minor Cooper
Kingsland, George Lovett, Sr.
Kobbe, George Christian

Occupations

INDUSTRIALISTS (cont'd)

Koehler, Robert H.
Laidlaw, George Q., Sr.
Lawrance, Charles Lanier
Lester, Maxwell, Sr.
Liebmann, Julius
Little, Raymond Demarest
Lorillard, George Lyndes
Macy, George Henry
Magoun, Francis Peabody, Sr.
Magoun, George Butler
Major, Alfred Sarony
Maxwell, Henry William
McKee, John
McKee, William L.
Meeks, Joseph William, Jr.
Meeks, Joseph William, Sr.
Mollenhauer, John
Mollenhauer, John Adolph
Morgan, Charles, Sr.
Morgan, John
Oakman, Walter George, Sr.
O'Donohue, Charles Alfred
Peck, William L., Sr.
Perkins, Richard Sturgis, Sr.
Pierrepont, Robert Low
Poillon, John Edward
Post, Henry Albertson Van Zo
Post, Waldron Kintzing
Powell, David Baisley
Pratt, Dallas Bache
Pratt, Horace A.
Ranft, Richard Michael
Reid, Willard Placide
Riggio, Frank Vincent
Schieren, Charles Adolph, Sr.
Schnur, David
Seaman, Frank
Shea, David J.
Slote, Daniel, Jr.
Smedberg, Adolphus, Jr.

Smith, Charles Robinson
Sutton, Frank
Sutton, Woodruff, Jr.
Swan, Alden Smith
Swirbul, Leon A.
Thorne, Edwin, II
Thorne, Francis Burritt, Sr.
Thorne, Landon Ketchum, Jr.
Titus, Walter Livingston, Sr.
Todd, William Henry
Truslow, Frederick Cumings
Turnbull, George R.
Valentine, Langdon Barrett
Warren, Northam, Sr.
Westin, Clarence Frederick, Sr.
White, Raymond S.
Whitney, William Collins
Wilbur, Edward Russell, Sr.

INTELLIGENCE AGENTS

Baldridge, Harry Alexander, Sr.
Gardiner, Robert David Lion
Hyde, Henry Baldwin, II
Johnson, Aymar
Johnson, Alfred Grima
   [*see* B. G. Johnson, III entry]
Post, Charles Kintzing
Tenney, Charles Henry, Sr.

INVENTORS

Dresser, Daniel LeRoy, Sr.
Field, Benjamin Prince, Jr.
Lawrance, Charles Lanier
Newton, Richard T.
   [*see* Chase entry]
Truslow, Frederick Cumings
Tucker, Charles A.
Van Anden, Frank

JOURNALISTS

Blum, Ethel Mildred Halsey

Occupations

JOURNALISTS (cont'd)

Carleton, Henry Guy
    [*see* Shannon entry]

Chase, Edna Woolman Alloway

Coffey, Clara Sebring
    aka Elizabeth Troy

Coffey, John Edward Develin, Sr.

Ford, Malcolm Webster, Sr.

Fortescue, Granville Roland

Hyde, Marie de LaGrange

Kobbe, Gustav

Page, Walter Hines, Sr.

Post, Emily Bruce Price

Smith, Jewett Holt

Vanderbilt, Alva Erskine Smith
    [*later*, Belmont]

Wagner, Helen Brown Nichols
    aka Phyllis Fraser

MERCHANTS

Arnold, Richard

Arnold, William

Baker, George William, Sr.

Bergen, Cornelius J., Sr.

Blum, Edward Charles

Blum, Robert Edward

Bohack, Henry Christian
    aka Hinrich Christian Bohack

Bunce, Frederick Sidney, Sr.

Busby, John

Conover, Augustus Whitlock, Sr.

Corse, Israel, Jr.

Covell, Charles Heber, Sr.

Creamer, Francis D., Sr.
    aka Frank D. Creamer, Sr.

Creamer, Joseph Byron, Sr.

Dresser, Daniel LeRoy, Sr.

Durkee, Eugene Return

Ebinger, Walter D.

Edwards, Edward

Fishel, Leopold Henry

Foster, William Riley, Sr.

Gibb, Howard, Sr.

Gibb, John

Gibb, Lewis Mills, Jr.

Gibb, Lewis Mills, Sr.

Gilmore, William Guy, Sr.

Gunther, William Henry, Jr.

Helm, Gustave Adolph

Jones, Frank Smith

Knapp, Shepherd Fordyce, Sr.

Knapp, William Kumbel

Litchfield, Electus Backus

Low, Chauncey Edward, Sr.

MacLeod, Thomas Woodward, Sr.

Maitland, Robert Lenox

Melville, Francis, Jr.
    aka Frank Melville, Jr.

Montgomery, Richard Malcolm, Sr.

O'Donohue, Charles Alfred

Orr, John Clifton, Sr.

Otto, Thomas Nelson

Parsons, Schuyler Livingston, Sr.

Peck, William L., Sr.

Peters, Harry Twyford, Sr.

Peters, Samuel Twyford

Powell, David Baisley

Proctor, Cecil Wykes

Richard, Alfred Joseph

Richmond, Henry

Robbins, Jeremiah

Robbins, John Clinton, Sr.

Rothschild, Simon Frank

Rubinstein, Ira

Schwenke, Oscar Louis, III

Shea, Timothy Joseph, Sr.

Slote, Alonzo

Snedecor, Isaac Howard

Snedecor, James Henry

Sutton, Effingham Brown, Jr.

Suydam, Charles

Suydam, John Richard, Sr.

Swan, Alden Smith

Titus, Walter Livingston, Sr.

Occupations

MERCHANTS (cont'd)

Van Bourgondien, Cornelius John, Sr.
   aka Cornelis Johannes Van Bourgondien

Wagstaff, Samuel Jones, Sr.

Welles, Benjamin Sumner, Sr.

Westin, Clarence Frederick, Sr.

White, Raymond S.

Williams, Richard Henry, Sr.

Wilmerding, Lucius Kellogg

MILITARY

Baldridge, Harry Alexander, Sr.

Bates, William Graves

Fortescue, Granville Roland

Ludlow, William Handy, Sr.

Post, Charles Kintzing

Titus, James Gulden, Sr.

Yates, Douglas Thomas, Sr.

Yates, Richard George, Sr.

NAVAL ARCHITECTS

Smith, Frederick D.

PHYSICIANS

Ash, Dr. Charles F.

Carroll, Dr. Alfred Ludlow

Catlin, Dr. Daniel, Sr.

Garben, Dr. Louis Francis, Sr.

Jacoby, Dr. James Ralph

Keppy, Dr. Frederick Beardsley

King, Dr. George Suttie

Lyon, Dr. Edward Crane

McBurney, Dr. Malcolm

McLaughlin, Dr. Daniel

Moore, Dr. David Dodge

Mowbray, Dr. Jarvis Rogers

Rice, Dr. George Edwin

Stewart, Dr. George David

Sullivan, Dr. Raymond Peter, Sr.

Vander Veer, Dr. Albert, Jr.

Wagstaff, Dr. Alfred, Sr.

Woolley, Dr. James Van Siclen, Sr.

Wright, Dr. Arthur Mullen

POLITICIANS

Allen, Theodore

Asten, Thomas B.

Baker, George William, Sr.

Belmont, August, Sr.

Belmont, Perry

Brownlie, George

Conover, Daniel D.

Cooper, James Brown, Sr.

Creamer, Francis D., Sr.
   aka Frank D. Creamer, Sr.

Delaney, John Hanlon

Fairchild, Julian Douglas

Foster, William Riley, Sr.

Gibson, Gregory Martin

Goodrich, William Winston

Graham, George Scott

Higbie, Richard

Howell, James Frederick, Sr.

Hulse, The Reverend William Warren

Knapp, Shepherd Fordyce, Sr.

Lawrence, Chester Bulkley, Sr.

Lemmerman, Frederick C.

Lester, Maxwell, Jr.

Ludlow, William Handy, Sr.

Macy, William Kingsland, Sr.

Morrison, George Alexander

Moses, Robert

Mowbray, Dr. Jarvis Rogers

Neville, Timothy Francis

Nicoll, William, VII

Nicoll, William Greenly

Pardee, Roy Edmund, Sr.

Phelps, Royal, Jr.

Post, Regis Henri, Sr.

Proctor, Cecil Wykes

Reid, Willard Placide

Robbins, John Clinton, Sr.

Occupations

POLITICIANS (cont'd)

Robbins, Josiah

Roosevelt, Robert Barnwell, Sr.

Ryan, John T.

Schieren, Charles Adolph, Sr.

Smith, Elward, Sr.

Stanchfield, John Barry, Sr.

Swan, Alden Smith

Tenney, Charles Henry, Sr.

Thorne, Landon Ketchum, Sr.

Van Orden, Jabez Ephraim

Van Orden, James

Wagner, Robert Ferdinand, Jr.

Wagstaff, Alfred, Jr.

Waterbury, Leander

PUBLISHERS

Cooper, James Brown, Sr.

Delaney, John Hanlon

Eaton, James Waterbury, Sr.

Howell, Elmer Winfield

Hutchins, Francis Sessions

Kobbe, Gustav

Livingston, Henry, III

Moffitt, William Henry

Page, Walter Hines, Sr.

Reid, John Robert

Roosevelt, Robert Barnwell, Sr.

Slote, Daniel, Jr.

Smith, Virginia Woodhull Otto

Thorne, Landon Ketchum, Jr.

Van Anden, William M.

Wagner, Helen Brown Nichols
  aka Phyllis Fraser

Wilbur, Edward Russell, Sr.

REAL ESTATE AGENTS

Edwards, Edward

Graham, Alfred Henry

Robbins, Jeremiah

Truslow, Gilbert

RESTAURATEURS

Denby, Esther Jewell Strong

Huber, Frederick Max, Sr.

Oelsner, Rudolph

Titus, James Gulden, Sr.

SCIENTISTS

Dodson, Richard Wolford

Pasternack, Richard

SHIPPING

Bromell, Alfred Henry

Ceballos, Juan Manuel, Sr.

Clyde, William Pancoast, Sr.

Havemeyer, Horace, Sr.

Hawley, Edwin

Isbrandtsen, Hans Jeppesen

Mollenhauer, John Adolph

Moran, Eugene Francis, Jr.

Rolston, Roswell Graves

Shortland, Thomas Francis

Staples, Cyrus E.

Sutton, Effingham Brown, Jr.

Sutton, Effingham Brown, Sr.

Sutton, Frank

Sutton, Woodruff, Sr.

Waterbury, Leander

WRITERS

Andrews, William Loring

Belmont, Eleanor Robson

Belmont, Perry

Carlton, Henry Guy
  [see Shannon entry]

Carroll, Dr. Alfred Ludlow

Chase, Edna Woolman Alloway

Coffey, Clara Sebring
  aka Elizabeth Troy

del Garcia, Lester Mullen

Eaton, James Waterbury, Sr.

Evers, Cecil Calvert

Field, Benjamin Prince, Jr.

Occupations

WRITERS (cont'd)

- Fortescue, Granville Roland
- Goodrich, William Winston
- Harbeck, Charles T.
- Havemeyer, Harry Waldron
- Havemeyer, Louisine Waldron
- Hyde, James Hazen
- Ireland, John Busteed
- Jacoby, Dr. James Ralph
- King, Dr. George Suttie
- Kobbe, Gustav
- Moses, Robert
- Page, Walter Hines, Sr.
- Parkhurst, The Reverend Charles Henry
- Parsons, Schuyler Livingston, Jr.
- Parson, William Decatur
- Peters, Harry Twyford, Sr.
- Post, Emily Bruce Price
- Post, Marie Caroline de Trobriand
- Post, Waldron Kintzing
- Puzo, Mario
- Roosevelt, Robert Barnwell, Sr.
- Sands, Francis Preston Blair
- Smith, Charles Robinson
- Smith, Hervey Garret
- Stewart, Anna May
  aka Anna Stuart
- Stewart, Dr. George David
- Strong, Theron George
- Sullivan, Dr. Raymond Peter, Sr.
- Vanderbilt, Alva Erskine Smith
  [*later*, Belmont]
- Vander Veer, Dr. Albert, Jr.
- Wagner, Helen Brown Nichols
  aka Phyllis Fraser
- Ward, Edwin Carrington
- Welles, Benjamin Sumner, III

*Jabez Ephraim Van Orden residence,
currently George Martin's Strip Steak Restaurant*

Rehabilitative Uses

Non-residential rehabilitative secondary uses of surviving estate houses listed are current as of 2021. Estates are identified by the original owner. For subsequent estate owners, see surname entry.

Amity Education Group	Arthur Keeler Bourne, Sr. estate, *Lake House*, Oakdale
	Frederick Gilbert Bourne estate, *Indian Neck Hall*, Oakdale
Bayard Cutting Arboretum	William Bayard Cutting, Sr. estate, *Westbrook Farm*, Great River
Daughters of Wisdom Convent	William Kingsland Macy, Sr. estate, Islip
Fairfield Arnold Manor (apartment complex)	Annie Stuart Cameron Arnold estate, *Clovelly*, West Islip
George Martin's Strip Steak Restaurant	Jabez Ephraim Van Orden residence, Great River
Greenways Educational and Interpretive Nature Center	Harold Hathaway Weekes estate, *Wereholme*, Islip
The Islip Art Museum	Harry Kearsarge Knapp, Sr. estate, *Brookwood*, East Islip
Land's End Waterfront Catering	Warren Northam, Sr. estate, *Sandy Point*, Sayville
Long Island Maritime Museum	Anson Wales Hard, Jr. estate, *Meadow Edge*, West Sayville
Long Island Yacht Club	Edward Trenchard II estate, Babylon
Mercury International, LLC	William Kissam Vanderbilt, Sr. estate, *Idlehour*, Oakdale
Office of Hospital Development, Good Samaritan Hospital	John Vanderveer estate, *Sunnymead*, West Islip (gardener's cottage)
The Open Gate Association Home for the Aged	Charles Gulden, Sr. estate, *Netherbay*, Bay Shore
Sagtikos Manor	Stephanus Van Cortlandt estate, *Sagtikos*, West Bay Shore
Southward Ho Country Club	Thomas Adams, Jr. estate, *Ardmore*, West Bay Shore
	Henry Baldwin Hyde, Sr. estate, *The Oaks*, West Bay Shore
South Shore Neurologic Associates	Francis D. Creamer estate, Islip
Timber Point Country Club	William Laurence Breese, Sr. estate, *Timber Point*, Great River
Town of Babylon Parks Department Headquarters	David Schnur estate, North Babylon
Van Bourgondien Farm House Museum	Cornelius John Van Bourgondien, Sr. estate, West Babylon
Villa Promenade (townhouse complex)	Richard Michael Ranft estate, Bay Shore
West Sayville Golf Course	Anson Wales Hard, Jr. estate, *Meadow Edge*, West Sayville

Rehabilitative Uses

Richard Michael Ranft residence during conversion into Villa Promenade townhouse complex

front facade, 2006

rear facade, 2006

Statesmen and Diplomats

Listed are only those statesmen and diplomats who resided in the Towns of Babylon and Islip.

Statesmen

Department of State –

Welles, Benjamin Sumner, III
– Assistant Secretary of State (Franklin Delano Roosevelt administration)
– Under Secretary of State (Franklin Delano Roosevelt administration)
Welles House, Islip

Department of Treasury –

McCue, Alexander
– Assistant Secretary of Treasury
Babylon

Department of Navy (became part of Department of Defense in 1947) –

Whitney, William Collins
– Secretary of Navy (Cleveland and Benjamin Harrison administrations)
Islip

Diplomats

Belmont, August, Sr.
– United States Charge d' affairs, The Netherlands
– United States Minister to The Netherlands
– Austrian Council General to the United States
Nursery Stud Farm, North Babylon

Belmont, Perry
– Minister to Spain, 1887-1888
Nursery Stud Farm, North Babylon

Esteva, Manuel A., Sr.
– Mexican Vice-Council to United States
– Council General of Mexico to United States
Brightwaters

Guggenheim, Meyer Robert, Sr.
– Ambassador to Portugal, 1953-1954
Firenze Farm, North Babylon

Page, Walter Hines, Sr.
– Ambassador to Court of St. James (Wilson administration)
Bay Shore

Post, Regis Henri, Sr.
– Governor, Territory of Puerto Rico, 1907
Littlewood, Bayport

Prince, John Dyneley, III
– Envoy Extraordinary and Minister Plenipotentiary to Denmark, 1921-1926
– Envoy Extraordinary and Minister Plenipotentiary to Kingdom of Serbs,
Croats, and Slovenes, 1926-1929
– Ambassador to Kingdom of Yugoslavia, 1929-1932
Islip

Statesmen and Diplomats

Diplomats (cont'd)

Roosevelt, Robert Barnwell, Sr.
– Ambassador to The Netherlands
Lotos Lake, Bayport

Schnur, David
– Turkish Consul General, Berlin, Germany
North Babylon

Taylor, George Campbell
– Member, United States Embassy at Court of St. James (Lincoln administration)
East Islip

Thorne, Landon Ketchum, Jr.
– Economic Minister, Office of Foreign Operations, Italy
– Economic Minister, Office of Foreign Operations, Belgium
The Lodge, West Bay Shore

Wagner, Robert Ferdinand, Jr.
– Ambassador to Spain, 1968-1969
Islip

Welles, Benjamin Sumner, III
– Chief, Latin American Affairs Division, Department of State, 1920
– Ambassador to Cuba, 1933
Welles House, Islip

Advisors and Personal Secretaries

Post, Regis Henri, Sr.
– Auditor, Territory of Puerto Rico, 1903
– Secretary to the Governor of Puerto Rico, 1904
Littlewood, Bayport

Welles, Benjamin Sumner, III
– Secretary, United States Embassy in Japan, 1917
Welles House, Islip

Villages

The village references used in this compilation are the current (2021) village or hamlet boundaries and should not be confused with zip code designations. When the owner who contracted for the original construction of the house is known, it is indicated by an asterisk.

AMITYVILLE

    Denby, Thomas Garvin
        aka Garvin Denby

    Gregory, Florence
        [*see* G. L. Haight, Sr.]

    Haight, Gilbert Lawrence, Jr.

    Haight, Gilbert Lawrence, Sr.

*   Ireland, Rufus Johnson, Sr.

*   Orr, John Clifton, Sr.

    Thorn, Edward Floyd–Jones

BABYLON

    Benkard, James Gerald

    Bergen, Jacob M.

    Blagden, Crawford, Sr.

    Bromell, Estelle M. Knowles

    Brownlie, George, *Willow Close*

    Bunce, Frederick Sidney, Sr.

    Carll, James Henry
        [*see* H. A. V. Post entry]

    Chase, Edna Woolman Alloway

    Coleman, Leander Walter Townsend

    Cooper, James Brown, Sr.

    Cox, George, Jr.

    de Murias, Fernando Enrique

    Dennis, Walter N.
        [*see* Smedberg entry]

    Dodd, Ernest H.
        [*see* Remsen entry]

    Dresser, Emma Louise Burnham

    Durkee, Eugene Return

    Evers, Cecil Calvert

    Field, Benjamin Prince, Jr.

    Fishel, Leopold Henry

*   Foster, Jay Stanley

    Foster, John Strong, *The Meadows*

    Foster, William Riley, Sr., *The Meadows*

    Graham, James Varnum, Jr.,
        South Country Lodge

    Haff, Albert Douglas

    Harris, Alfred H.

    Hayward, William Tyson, Jr.

    Hepburn, Henry Chester, *Bide a Wee*

    Howell, Elmer Brown, Sr.

    Howell, Elmer Winfield

    Howell, Ralph DeWitt, Sr.

    Hubert, William Haight

*   Jacoby, Dr. James Ralph

*   Kalbfleisch, Sarah Pirnie Schenck, *Larklawn*

    Kingsland, George Lovett, Sr.

    Knapp. Shepherd Fordyce, Sr.

    Kobbe, Gustav

    Lacombe, Charles Frederick

*   Litchfield, Electus Backus, *Blythebourne*

    Little, Raymond Demarest

    Livingston, Henry, III

    Lyon, Dr. Edward Crane

    McCue, Alexander

    McKee, Henry Sellers, II

    Morris, Stuyvesant Fish, III

    Morse, William Otis

    Moses, Robert

    Murdock, Uriel Atwood, II

    Nicholas, Alice McKim Hollins, *Virginia Farm*

    Nicholl, William Greenly

    Parkhurst, The Reverend Charles Henry

    Placide, Henry

    Post, Edwin Main, Sr.

    Post, Henry Albertson Van Zo, *Postholme*

    Reid, John Robert, *The Towers*

    Reid, Willard Placide, *The Towers*

    Remsen, Annie Pearsall Hubbard, *The Harbor*

    Remsen, Cornelius Wagstaff, *Tuloma*

*   Robbins, Jeremiah

    Robbins, John Clinton, Sr.

Villages

BABYLON (cont'd)

    Rogers, Kenneth
        [*see* de Murias entry]

    Sands, Francis Preston Blair

*   Searle, Charles

*   Shortland, Thomas Francis

    Smedberg, Adolphus, Jr., *Larkmeadow*

*   Smith, Selah Carll, *Smith Cottage*

    Snedeker, Charles Valentine, *Wind's Will*

    Stewart, David P.
        [*see* Trenchard entry]

*   Strong, James Henry

    Sutton, Frank, *The Cloisters*

    Sutton, Harold Falconer

*   Sutton, Woodruff, Jr., *Sunnycroft*

*   Tappin, Charles L., *Twin Oaks*

*   Trenchard, Edward, II

    Udall, Joseph Sanford

    Walbridge, Ernest Augustus

    Walbridge, George Huntington

    Weeks, Edwin Carnes

    Weinstein, Harry
        [*see* F. Sutton entry]

    Weinstein, Martin
        [*see* F. Sutton entry]

BAYPORT

    Allen, Theodore

    Asher, John J.

    Baruch, Bernard Mannes, Sr., *Strandhome*

    Behman, Louis C., Sr., *Lindenwalt*

    Busby, John

    Cahill, Frank
        [*see* Francis Melville, Sr. entry]

    Cox, Stephen Perry, *Arcadia*

    Dahl, George Washington, *The Maples*

*   Delancy, John Hanlon

    Dodson, Richard Wolford

*   Edwards, Edward, *White House*

    Edwards, Lawrence

    Edwards, Lawrence Barnes

    Ely, John R.

    Ennis, Thomas A

    Fortescue, Granville Roland, *Wildholme*

*   Foster, William Riley, Jr., *Strandhome*

    Grundwald, Kurt
        [*see* Mason entry]

    Johnson, Frederick Merle, Sr.
        aka Merle Johnson, Sr.

    Keppy, Dr. Frederick Beardsley

    Kleine, Mark
        [*see* Rice entry]

    Kobbe, George Christian

    Koehler, Robert H.

*   Laidlaw, George Q., Sr., *Bonnie Doon*

    La Spina, John
        [*see* Payne entry]

    Liebmann, Julius

*   MacConnell, John B.

    Major, Alfred Sarony

    Manton, Martin Thomas

    Mason, John Hill Belcher

    McClung, James
        [*see* Pollock entry]

    McKee, John, *Sans Souci*

*   Meeks, Joseph William, Jr.

    Melville, Francis, Jr.
        aka Frank Melville, Jr.

    Melville, Francis, Sr.

*   Morgan, Charles, Sr.

*   Morgan, John, *Idle Hour*

    Osk, M. L.
        [*see* Payne entry]

    Palmer, Frederick Timothy
        aka Timothy Palmer

*   Payne, Albert

*   Pollock, Walter B.

    Post, Charles Alfred, *Strandhome*

    Post, Charles Kintzing, *Strandhome*

*   Post, Regis Henri, Sr., *Littlewood*
        [Post owned five houses in Bayport.]

    Post, Waldron Kintzing, *Strandhome*

    Post, William Kintzing

    Pratt, Cleveland Forsyth, Sr., *Graytower*

*   Purdy, Charles Robert, Sr., *Edgemere*

*   Rice, Dr. George Edwin, *Maywood*

*   Roosevelt, Robert Barnwell, Sr., *Lotos Lake*

*   Rubinstein, Ira, *Cheap John's Estate*

Villages

BAYPORT (cont'd)

Seaman, Frank

Shannon, Effie

Smith, Benjamin Franklin

Smith, Frederick D.

* Snedecor, Isaac Howard

Snedecor, James Henry

Staples, Cyrus E.

Stoppani, Charles Francis, Jr.

* Stoppani, Charles Francis, Sr., *Arcadia*

* Stoppani, Joseph H., *Liberty Hall*

Suydam, Charles

Suydam, John Richard, Jr., *Edgewater*

Suydam, John Richard, Sr., *Edgewater*

* Todd, William Henry, *Lenapes Lodge*

Zerega, John Pierre, Sr., *Littlewood*

BAY SHORE

Adams, John Dunbar, *Woodlea*

Aldrich, Spencer, *Windermere*

Allison, William Manwaring, Sr.

Ash, Dr. Charles F.

* Asten, Thomas B.

Bachia, Richard Augustus, Jr.

Baker, George William, Sr., *Fairlawn*

Ballard, Frederick Edward, Sr.

Bates, William Graves, *The Evergreens*

Baxter, John Edward

Beach, Reginald
  [*see* Mildeberger entry]

Bedell, Walter Ellwood

Belmont, August, III

Birdsall, Clarence K.

* Blum, Edward Charles, *Shore Acres*

Blum, Robert Edward

* Burchell, George W.

Carr, Barbara (Mrs. James Carr)
  [*see* Mildeberger entry]

* Carroll, Dr. Alfred Ludlow

Catlin, Dr. Daniel, Sr., *Orowoc Point*

Ceballos, Juan Manuel, Sr., *Brookhurst Farm*

Choi, John
  [*see* Mildeberger entry]

Clarkson, William Kemble, Jr.

Collier, Robert L.
  [*see* Mildeberger entry]

Conover, Augustus Whitlock, Sr.

* Conover, Daniel D.

* Covell, Charles Heber, Sr., *Villa Avalon*

Dillon, John Allen, Sr.

Drummond, Howard, *Little House*

Eastwood, John Henry

* Ebinger, Walter D.

Elder, George Waldron, Sr.

Entenmann, Charles, Sr.

* Entenmann, William Charles, Jr.

Entenmann, William Charles, Sr.

Eyre, Beverley Montagu

Fairchild, Julian Douglas

* Farrell, Frank J.

Ferguson, William J.
  [*see* Mildeberger entry]

Foehr, Dr. Mark
  [*see* Wray entry]

* Frank, Emil Henry, Sr.

Frothingham, John Sewell

Garner, Thomas, Jr.

Garner, Thomas, Sr.

Garner, William Thorn

Gibb, Lewis Mills, Jr., *Cedarholme*

* Gibb, Lewis Mills, Sr., *Cedarholme*

Gibson, Frederick E.

Gibson, John James

* Gibson, John Joseph

Goodrich, William Winston

Gordon, Edward

Gregory, George Mitchell

Gregory, William Hamilton, Sr.

Greve, William Marcus, Jr.,
  Millcreek / Mill Creek Farm

* Guastavino, Rafael, Jr.

Gulden, Charles, Sr., *Netherbay*

Gulden, Frank, Jr.

Gunther, William Henry, Jr.

BAY SHORE (cont'd)

* * Havemeyer, Harry Waldron
* * Havemeyer, Horace, Sr., *Olympic Point*
* Hodges, George Winthrop, Sr.
* Howell, James Frederick, Sr.
* Hubbard, Harmanus Barkulo, *Oakhurst*
* * Hubbell, Lulu Hyde
* Huber, Frederick Max, Sr.
* Hulse, The Rev. William Warren, *Elysian Views*
* Hutton, Edward Francis
* Hutton, Franklyn Laws, *Win Sum Lodge*
* Johnson, Effingham Lawrance, *The Evergreens*
* Kelly, James P., *Awixaway*
* Kempster, James H., *Westbeach*
* Kheem, Storm [see Mildeberger entry]
* King, Dr. George Suttie
* Kleinman, David E.
* * Knapp, Edward Spring, Sr., *Awixa Lawn*
* Koch, Joseph W. [see Mildeberger entry]
* Lawrance, Charles Lanier, *Manatuck Farm*
* Lawrance, Francis Cooper, Jr., *Manatuck Farm*
* Lawrance, Francis Cooper, Sr., *Manatuck Farm*
* Lawrence, Chester Bulkley, Sr.
* Lemmerman, Frederick C.
* Lentilhon, Eugene, II, *Brookside Farm*
* * Lester, Joseph Huntington, *Lestaley*
* Lester, Maxwell, Jr.
* Lester, Maxwell, Sr., *Four Hedges*
* Livingston, Henry Beekman, Jr.
* * Low, Chauncey Edward, Sr., *Seaward*
* MacLeod, Thomas Woodward, Sr.
* Macy, George Henry
* Maxwell, Henry William, *Scrub Oaks*
* * McNamee, John
* Mildeberger, Elwood, *Oakelwood*
* * Mollenhauer, John
* * Mollenhauer, John Adolph, *Homeport*
* * Montgomery, Richard Malcolm, Sr.
* Mowbray, Dr. Jarvis Rogers
* Myers, Nathaniel
* O'Donohue, Charles Alfred, *The Moorings*
* * Oelsner, Rudolph
* Oppenheimer, Julius
* Owens, Joseph Eugene, Sr.
* Page, Walter Hines, Sr.
* Parsons, William Decatur, *Restina Cottage*
* Peck, William L.
* Pierrepont, Robert Low
* Pinkerton, Allan, II
* Pinkerton, Robert Allan, Sr., *Dearwood*
* Poillon, John Edward
* Quinn, Michael [see Low entry]
* * Ranft, Richard Michael
* Richmond, Henry, *Maplewood*
* Riggio, Frank Vincent, *Riggio House*
* Riley, Paul, *Awixa Castle* [see Mildeberger entry]
* Robbins, Josiah
* * Robbins, William H., Sr.
* Rokenbaugh, Henry Scott, *Villa Avalon*
* * Rothschild, Simon Frank
* Ryan, John T.
* Schwenke, Oscar Louis, III
* * Sharp, Hamlet Cecil, *Millcreek*
* * Shea, Timothy Joseph, Sr., *O'Conee*
* Slote, Alonzo
* Slote, Daniel, Jr.
* * Smith, Charles Robinson
* Snow, Frederick Billings
* * Strong, Theron George
* Sullivan, Dr. Raymond Peter, Sr.
* Tenney, Charles Henry, Sr.
* Thorne, Francis Burritt, Jr.
* * Thurber, Frederick Charles
* Truslow, Gilbert Potter
* Underhill, Edward Beekman, Sr.
* Waddell, Charles Falkiner Morton aka Morton Waddell
* Wagstaff, George Barnard
* Wainwright, Stuyvesant, Jr.

Villages

BAY SHORE (cont'd)

    Ward, Edwin Carrington, *Wake Robin*

    Weld, Philip Balch

    Wood, Henry Duncan, Jr.

    Woolley, Dr. James Van Siclen, Sr.

    Worden, John Lorimer, III

* Wray, William Henry, Sr., *Whileaway*

* Young, Albert, *Awixaway*

BRIGHTWATERS

* Esteva, Manuel A., Sr.

* Franklin, Emlen Pleasants, *The Moorings*

    Gibson, Gregory Martin

    Moran, Eugene Francis, Jr., *Shadow Lawn*

    Packer, Frederick Little

    Pardee, Dwight W.

    Parkinson, Thomas Ignatius, Jr.

* Phelps, Charles Egbert, *Brightwaters*

* Stewart, Anna May, *Sweet Violet*
    aka Anna Stuart

    Swirbul, Leon A.

    Turnbull, John Gourlay, Sr., *The Pines*

    Yates, Richard George, Sr.

COPIAGUE

* Hawkins, William Elton, *Wild Goose Farm*

EAST ISLIP

    Bigelow, Edwin Hicks

* Carlisle, Jay Freeborn, Sr., *Rosemary*

    Cusachs, Philip Alain

    Dana, Richard Turner, *Azimuth*

    del Garcia, Lester Mullen, *La Granja*

    Duval, Henry Rieman, *Falmouth*

    Entenmann, Robert William, Sr.

    Gregory, William Hamilton, Jr., *Creekside*

    Harbeck, Charles Thomas
    [Harbeck owned two houses in East Islip.]

* Hollins, Gerald Vanderbilt, Sr., *The Hawks*

* Hollins, Harry Bowly, Jr., *Crickholly*

* Hollins, Harry Bowly, Sr., *Meadow Farm*

    Hoppin, Bayard Cushing

    Johnson, Aymar, *Woodland*

* Johnson, Bradish, Jr., *Woodland*

* Johnson, Edwin Augustus, Sr.

* Johnson, Edwin Augustus, Sr.,
    Deer Range Farm
    [Johnson built two houses in East Islip.]

    Johnson, Lee

* Johnston, James Boorman

* Knapp, Harry Kearsarge, II, *Creekside*

* Knapp, Harry Kearsarge, Sr., *Brookwood*

    Knapp, Theodore Jackson, *Brookwood*

    Lawrance, Charles Lanier

* Livingston, Miss Frances Lewis

* McBurney, Dr. Malcolm

    Moran, Amedee Depau

    Morgan, Henry, *The Stables*

    Morgan, Robert Woodward, Sr.

    Nicoll, William, VII, *Grange*

    Noyes, Daniel Raymond

    Pinkerton, Robert Allan, II

    Plumb, James Ives, *Deer Range Farm*

    Plumb, Sara Caroline Ives, *Deer Range Farm*

    Prescott, William French, *Still Pond*

    Taylor, George Campbell, *Deer Range Farm*

* Taylor, George Campbell
    [Taylor built two houses in East Islip.]

    Thorne, Francis Burritt, Sr., *Brookwood*

    Van Orden, James

    Wharton, Percival Charles

    Wharton, William Fishbourne

* Williams, Percy Garnett, *Pine Acres*

    Wilmerding, Lucius Kellogg, Sr., *White Lodge*

FIRE ISLAND

    Hyde, Henry Baldwin, II

    Vander Veer, Dr. Albert, Jr., *Alkmaar Cottage*

GREAT RIVER

* Breese, William Laurence, Sr., *Timber Point*
    aka William Lawrence Breese, Sr.

    Cutting, Robert Fulton

* Cutting, William Bayard, Sr., *Westbrook Farm*

    Davies, Julien Tappan, *Timber Point*

Villages

GREAT RIVER (cont'd)

    Dempsey, Joseph Francis, Sr., *Estancia* *

    Hobbs, Charles Buxton, *River Croft*

    Hutchins, Francis Sessions, *Saramond*

    Lorillard, George Lyndes, *Westbrook Farm*

* Maitland, Robert Lenox, Sr., *Westbrook Farm*

    Stewart, Dr. George David, *Appin House*

    Stewart, James
        [*see* Truslow entry]

* Truslow, Frederick Cumings, *Questover Lodge*

* Van Orden, Jabez Ephraim

* White, Raymond S.

ISLIP

    Astaire, Phyllis Livingston Baker

* Atwood, Frederic Lawrence, Sr.

    Atwood, Kimball Chase, Jr., *Mapleton*

    Baker, William Dunham

    Beard, Anson Mc Cook, Jr.

* Bruce–Brown, Ruth Arabella Loney, *Bronhurst*

    Bull, Henry Worthington

    Creamer, Francis D., Sr.
        aka Frank D. Creamer, Sr.

    Creamer, Joseph Byron, Sr.

    Crothers, Gordon, *La Casetta*

    deCoppet, Andre H., *The Willows*

    de Goicouria, Albert Valentine

    Dempsey, Joseph Francis, Jr.

* Dick, Adolph Mollenhauer

    Dick, John Henry, *Allen Winden Farm*

    Dick, William, *Allen Winden Farm*

    Dick, William Karl, *Allen Winden Farm*

    Doxsee, James Harvey, Sr.

    Egly, Henry Harris

    Entenmann, William Charles, III

    Flint, Sherman, *Evershade*

    Garben, Dr. Louis Francis, Sr.

    Gibb, Howard, Sr.

* Gibb, John, *Afterglow*

    Graham, George Scott, *Lohgrame*

    Gulden, Charles, III

* Gulden, Frank, Jr.

    Gulden, Frank, Sr.
        [Gulden owned two houses in Islip.]

    Hallock, Gerard, III

* Havemeyer, Henry Osborne, *Bayberry Point*

    Havemeyer, Horace, Jr.

    Havemeyer, Horace, Sr.

    Heckscher, Charles Augustus, Jr.

    Hollister, Buell, Sr.

    Hollister, Henry Hutchinson, Sr.

    Howell, Carlton Bell

    Jackson, Charles Havemeyer, Sr.
        aka Charles Frederick Havemeyer Jackson

    Johnson, Bradish Gaillard, III, *Enfin*

    Johnson, Enfin

    Johnson, John Dean

    Johnson, Parmenus, Sr.

* Knapp, William Kumbel, *Winganhauppauge*

    Lazare, Andrew

    Lindsay, Lewin Seton

    Livingston, Robert Cambridge, III, *Lakeside*

    Lovering, Joseph Sears, Sr.

    Macy, William Kingsland, Sr.

    Meeks, Edwin Bartlett

    Meeks, Joseph William, Sr.

* Moffit, William Henry, *Beautiful Shore*

    Moore, Dr. David Dodge

    Morgan, Charles, Jr.

    Oakman, Walter George, Sr.

    Pardee, Roy Edmund, Sr.

* Parsons, Schuyler Livingston, Jr.,
    Pleasure Island

* Parsons, Schuyler Livingston, Sr., *Whileaway*

    Pasternack, Richard

    Perkins, Richard Sturgis, Sr.

* Peters, Harry Twyford, Sr., *Nearholme*

    Peters, Harry Twyford, Sr., *Windholme Farm*

    Peters, Samuel Twyford, *Windholme Farm*

    Pless, John Anthony, Jr.

    Plumb, James Ives, *Shadowbrook*

    Pratt, Alexander Dallas Bache, *Lands End*

    Pratt, Dallas Bache

Villages

ISLIP (cont'd)
* Prince, John Dyneley, II
  Redmond, Roland
* Russell, William Hamilton, Jr., *Le Rozel*
* Schieren, Charles Adolph, Sr., *Mapleton*
  Scully, Charles Brewster, *Wereholme*
  Spaulding, E. B.
  Stanchfield, John Barry, Sr., *Afterglow*
* Swan, Alden Smith, *Orowoc*
* Tappin, John Crane
  Tcherepnin, Alexander
  Thorne, Edwin, III
  Timmerman, Henry Gerhard, *Breeze Lawn*
  Titus, James Gulden, Sr.
  Titus, Walter Livingston, Jr.
  Tobey, Orville Hurd, *Breeze Lawn*
* Tucker, Charles A.
  Tucker, Clarence
    [see W. C. Whitney entry]
  Valentine, Langdon Barrett
  Van Anden, Frank
  Van Anden, William M.
  Wagner, Robert Ferdinand, Jr.
* Waterbury, Leander
  Watson, Jane Painter Elder
  Webster, Charles Drake, *Twyford*
* Weekes, Harold Hathaway, *Wereholme*
  Welles, Benjamin Sumner, Jr., *Welles House*
  Welles, Benjamin Sumner, Sr.
  Welles, Benjamin Sumner, III, *Welles House*
  Wharton, Richard, *Whileaway*
  Wharton, Richard T., Sr., *Whileaway*
* Whitney, William Collins
  Williams, Sarah Welford Peters
* Wood, Henry Duncan, Sr., *Ellenwood*
  Wright, Dr. Arthur Mullen, *Afterglow*
  Yates, Douglas Thomas, Sr.

LINDENHURST
  Neville, Timothy Francis, *Warwick House*
* Welwood, Thomas, *Welwood Lane*

NORTH BABYLON
  Belmont, August, Jr., *Nursery Stud Farm*
* Belmont, August, Sr., *Nursery Stud Farm*
  Belmont, Perry, *Nursery Stud Farm* [legal address]
  Cockerill, John
    [see Rolston entry]
* Corbin, Austin, Jr., *Deer Park Farm*
  Guggenheim, Meyer Robert, Sr., *Firenze Farm*
* Phelps, Royal, Jr.
  Rolston, Roswell, Graves, *Armagh*
  Ward, John Montgomery
* Schnur, David
* Sutton, Frank, *North East Farm*
  Ward, John Montgomery

OAKDALE
  Aston, William K.
  Bourne, Alfred Severin, Sr.
* Bourne, Arthur Keeler, Sr., *Lake House*
* Bourne, Frederick Gilbert, *Indian Neck Hall*
  Burke, Charles Felix
  Ludlow, William Handy, Sr., *Old Oak Farm*
  Ockers, Jacob
* Robert, Christopher Rhinelander, Jr., *Peperidge Hall*
* Vanderbilt, William Kissam, Sr., *Idlehour* [I and II]

SAYVILLE
  Allgood, Andrew Perry de Forest
  Baldridge, Harry Alexander, Sr.
  Betts, Roland Whitney, *Sunneholm*
  Bohack, Henry Christian
    aka Hinrich Christian Bohack
  Bossert, Charles Volunteer
  Brendel, Kathryn
    [see N. Warren, Sr. entry]
  Catlin, John Bernsee, Sr.
* Childs, Eversley, Sr.
* Childs, William Hamlin
  Corse, Israel, Jr., *The Swamp*
  Fortescue, Kenyon

467

Villages

SAYVILLE (cont'd)

* Foster, Andrew D., *Greycote*
  aka Andrew D. Forsslund

Gelshenen, Mrs. William Henry
[*see* N. Warren, Sr. entry]

* Green, Isaac Henry, II, *Brookside*
* Hayward, Frank Earle, Sr., *Joy Farm*
* Hayward, William Tyson, Sr., *The Anchorage*

Helm, Gustave Adolph

* Jones, Frank Smith, *Beechwold*

Jones, Frank Smith, *While-Away*
[*see* Wilbur entry]

McLaughlin, Dr. Daniel

Morrison, George Alexander

Otto, Thomas Nelson

Palmer, Elwell
[Palmer owned a second house in Sayville.]

* Powell, David Baisley, *Cedarshore*
* Powell, Leander Treadwell, *Cedarshore*

Proctor, Cecil Wykes

* Ridgeway, James W.
* Roosevelt, John Ellis, *Meadow Croft*
* Roosevelt, Robert Barnwell, Jr., *The Lilacs*

Shea, David J., *Beechwold*
[Shea owned *Wydemoor*, also in Sayville.]

* Simonds, William Robinson, *Wyndemoor*

Smith, Elward, Jr.

Smith, Elward., Sr.

Smith, Hervey Garret

Smith, Jewett Holt

* Terry, William Hazard
* Warren, Northam, Sr., *Sandy Point*

Westin, Clarence Frederick, Sr., *Beechwold*

* Wilbur, Edward Russell, Sr., *Beach Grove*

WEST BABYLON

* Bergen, Charles M.

Bergen, Cornelius J., Sr.

Bergen, James Cornelius, *Suanne*

Ford, Malcolm Webster, Sr., *My Fancy*

Gilmore, William Guy, Sr., *My Fancy*

Hallowell, Thomas Jewett, Sr., *On-the-Way*

Pratt, Horace A.

* Van Bourgondien, Cornelius John, Sr.
  aka Cronelis Johannes Van Bourgondien

WEST BAY SHORE

* Adams, Thomas, Jr., *Ardmore*

Bossert, Louis, *The Oaks*

Colt, Robert Oliver, *The Poplars*

Ellis, George Augustus, Jr., *Ardmore*

Gardiner, Robert David Lion, *Sagtikos Manor*

* Hyde, Henry Baldwin, Sr., *The Oaks*

Hyde, James Hazen, *The Oaks*

Hyde, James Richard

* Hyde, Richard

Isbrandtsen, Hans Jeppesen

* Johnson, Bradish, Sr., *Sans Souci*

Johnson, Henry Meyer, *Sans Souci*

Lawrance, John Ireland

Puzo, Mario

Richard, Alfred Joseph

Thorne, Landon Ketchum, Jr., *The Lodge*

Thorne, Landon Ketchum, Sr., *Thorneham*

Wilmerding, George Gorman

WEST ISLIP

Andrews, William Loring, *Pepperidges*

Arnold, Alexander Duncan Cameron

* Arnold, Annie Stewart Cameron, *Clovelly*

Arnold, Edward William Cameron, *Oknoke*

* Arnold, Richard, *The Crescent*

Arnold, William, *The Crescent*

Cameron, Edward Miller

Cameron, Miss Emma Cornelia, *Effingham Towers*
aka Miss Emma Cornelia Sturges

Clyde, William Pancoast, Sr.

Coffey, John Edward Develin, Sr.

Davies, Julien Townsend, Jr., *Cherry Pool*

Davies, Julien Townsend, Sr., *Casa Rosa*

de Forest, James Goodrich, Sr.

* Dodson, Robert Bowman, *Kanonsioni*

Eaton, James Waterbury, Sr.

Gibson, Cornelia Lott Vanderveer, *Sunnymead*

Villages

WEST ISLIP (cont'd)

  Grosser, Hans
    [*see* Andrews entry]

  Harbeck, Charles Thomas

  Hardenburgh, James, *Villa Maria*
    [*see* P. Remsen, Sr. entry]

  Havemeyer, Henry, Sr., *Armory*

  Havemeyer, Henry, Sr., *Sequatogue Farm*

* Hawley, Edwin, *Effingham Towers*

  Heins, John Lewis, Sr.

  Hepburn, Henry Chester, *The Firs*

  Higbie, Richard

  Housman, Arthur Albert

  Hubbs, Charles Francis, *Sequatogue Farm*

  Hyde, William James, *White Cottage*

  Ireland, John Busteed

  Keith, Minor Cooper

  Keith, Minor Cooper R., II

  Knapp, Shepherd, II

  Magoun, Francis Peabody, Sr.

* Magoun, George Butler, *The Meadows*

  Magoun, Kinsley

  McClure, William, *Clurella*

* McCurdy, Robert Henry, II

  McKee, William L.

  Muir, H.
    [*see* W. Sutton, Sr. entry]

  Nicholas, George Stevenson, Sr.

  Orr, John Clifton, Sr.

  Parkinson, Thomas, Ignatius, Sr.

  Remsen, Phoenix, Sr.

  Stephens, Benjamin, Jr., *Sunnymede*

  Stephens, John Lloyd, *Lone Oak*

  Stillman, Benjamin D.

  Sutton, Effingham Brown, Jr., *Effingham Park*

  Sutton, Effingham Brown, Sr., *Effingham Park*

  Sutton, Woodruff, Sr.,
    Sutton Park / Woodruff Sutton Place

* Thorne, Edwin, II, *Okonok*

  Titus, Walter Livingston, Sr.

* True, Benjamin Kimball, Sr., *The Homestead*

* Turnbull, George R., *The Pines*

  Vanderveer, John, *Sunnymead*

* Wagstaff, Alfred, Jr., *Opekeepsing*

* Wagstaff, Dr. Alfred, Sr., *Tahlulah*

  Wagstaff, Cornelius DuBois, *Church Lawn*

  Wagstaff, George Barnard, *The Farm House*

  Wagstaff, Samuel Jones, Sr., *Driftwood*

* Walker, Harford Pinckney, Sr.
    aka Frederick Harford Pinckney Walker, Sr.

  Walker, Keitt Pinckney, *Villa Julia*
    aka George Daniel Keitt Pinckney Walker

  Walton, Julia
    [*see* P. Remsen, Sr. entry]

  Yates, Herbert John, Sr., *Onsrufarm*

WEST SAYVILLE

* Hard, Anson Wales, Jr., *Meadow Edge*

*Walter D. Ebinger's Bay Shore residence,
rear facade, 2018*

Chauncey Edward Low, Sr.'s Bay Shore residence, *Seaward*

rear facade, 2018

hallway, 2018

General Bibliography

America's First Age of Fortune: A Selected Bibliography

Books listed in this section are, in most instances, different from the listings in the section entitled Selected Bibliographic References to Individual South Shore Estate Owners. Both sections should, therefore, be consulted.

AIA Architectural Guide to Nassau and Suffolk Counties, Long Island. New York: Dover Publications, Inc., 1992.
Aldrich, Nelson W., Jr. *Old Money: The Mythology of America's Upper Class.* New York: Alfred A. Knopf, 1988.
Aldrich, Nelson W., IV. "The Upper Class, Up for Grabs." *Wilson Quarterly* 17:3 (Summer 1993).
Allen, Michael Patrick. *The Founding Fortunes: A New Anatomy of the Super–Rich Families in America.* New York: E. P. Dutton, 1987.
Alsop, Joseph W. *"I've Seen the Best of It: Memoirs"* New York: W. W. Norton & Co., 1992.
Amory, Cleveland. *Celebrity Register: An Irreverent Compendium of American Quotable Notables.* New York: Harper & Row Publishers, 1959. [Published intermittently. Since 1973 it has been edited by Earl Blackwell.]
Amory, Cleveland. *The Last Resorts.* New York: Harper & Brothers, 1952.
Amory, Cleveland. *Who Killed Society?* New York: Harper & Brothers, 1960.
Armour, Lawrence A. *The Young Millionaires.* Chicago: Playboy Press, 1973.
Armstrong, Hamilton Fish. *Those Days.* New York: Harper & Brothers, 1963.
Armstrong, Margaret. *Five Generations.* New York: Harper & Brothers, 1930.
Ashburn, Frank D. *Peabody of Groton.* New York: Coward, McCann & Co., 1944.
Aslet, Clive. *The American Country Home.* New Haven: Yale University Press, 1990.
Auchincloss, Louis. *The Rector of Justin.* Boston: Houghton, Mifflin & Co., 1964.
Auchincloss, Louis. *The Vanderbilt Era: Profiles of a Gilded Age.* New York: The Macmillan Co., 1989.
Bailey, Paul. *Long Island: A History of Two Counties.* New York: Lewis Historical Publishing Co., 1949.
Baker, John C. *American Country Homes and Their Gardens.* Philadelphia: C. Winston, 1906.
Baker, Paul R. *Richard Morris Hunt.* New York: MIT Press, 1980.
Baldwin, Richard P. *Residents: Town of Islip 1720-1865.* Oakdale, NY: William K. Vanderbilt Historical Society of Dowling College, 1989.
Balmori, Diana, Diana McGuire Kostial, and Eleanor M. McPeck. *Beatrix Farrand's American Landscapes: Her Gardens and Campuses.* Sagaponack, NY: Sagapress, 1985.
Baltzel, E. Digby. *The Protestant Establishment: Aristocracy and Caste in America.* New York: Random House, 1964.
Baltzel, E. Digby. *The Protestant Establishment Revisited.* New Brunswick, NJ: New Jersey Transaction Publishers, 1991.
Baron, Stanley Wade. *Brewed in America.* Boston: Little, Brown & Co., 1962.
Barrett, Richmond. *Good Old Summer Days.* Boston: Houghton, Mifflin & Co., 1952.
Batterberry, Michael and Ariane Batterberry. *Mirror, Mirror.* New York: Holt, Rinehart & Winston, 1977.
Bayles, Richard M. *Bayles' Long Island Handbook.* Babylon, NY: privately printed, 1885.
Bayport Heritage Association. *Bayport Heritage.* Dover, NH: Arcadia Publishing Co., 1997.
Beach, Moses Yale. *Wealth and Biography of the Wealthy Citizens of New York City.* New York: The Sun Office, 1845.
Bedford, Stephen and Richard Guy Wilson. *The Long Island Country House, 1870–1930.* Southampton, NY: Parrish Art Museum, 1988.
Beebee, Lucius Morris. *The Big Spenders.* Garden City: Doubleday & Co., Inc., 1966.
Beebee, Lucius. *Mansion On Rails: The Folklore of the Private Railway Car.* Berkeley: Howell–North, 1959.
Beer, Thomas. *The Mauve Decade: American Life at the End of the 19th Century.* New York: Alfred A. Knopf, Inc., 1926.
"Behind the Gates of the Last Estates," *Newsday* September 25, 1986.
Bender, Marilyn. *The Beautiful People.* New York: Coward–McCann, Inc., 1967.
Bendix, Reinhard and Seymour Martin Lipset, ed. *Class, Status and Power.* New York: The Free Press, 1966.
Biddle, Francis. *A Casual Past.* Garden City: Doubleday & Co., Inc., 1961.
Biddle, Francis. *The Llanfear Pattern.* New York: Charles Scribner's Sons, 1927.
Bigelow, Poultney. *Seventy Summers: New York.* 2 vols. Longmans, Green & Co., 1925.
Birmingham, Stephen. *America's Secret Aristocracy.* Boston: Little, Brown & Co., 1987.
Birmingham, Stephen. *The Grandees: America's Sephardic Elite.* New York: Harper & Row Publishers, 1971.
Birmingham, Stephen. *The Grandes Dames.* New York: Simon & Schuster, Inc., 1982.
Birmingham, Stephen. *Our Crowd: The Great Jewish Families of New York.* New York: Harper & Row Publishers, 1967.
Birmingham, Stephen. *Real Lace: America's Irish Rich.* New York: Harper & Row Publishers, 1973.
Birmingham, Stephen. *The Right People: A Portrait of the American Social Establishment.* Boston: Little, Brown & Co., 1968.

General Bibliography

Birmingham, Stephen. *The Right Places for the Right People.* Boston: Little, Brown & Co., 1973.
Bloom, Murray Teigh. *Rogues To Riches: The Trouble With Wall Street.* New York: G. P. Putnam's Sons, 1971.
Bolton, Sarah. *Famous Givers and Their Gifts.* New York: T. Y. Crowell & Co., 1896.
Bradley, Hugh. *Such Was Saratoga.* Garden City: Doubleday, Doran & Co., 1940.
Brandon, Ruth. *The Dollar Princesses: Sagas of Upward Nobility, 1870–1914.* New York: Alfred A. Knopf, 1980.
Bremner, Robert H. *American Philanthropy.* Chicago: The University of Chicago Press, 1960.
Bremner, Robert H. *American Social History Since 1860.* New York, 1971.
Brooklyn Blue Book. Brooklyn, NY: Rugby Press, Inc., annual.
Brooklyn Blue Book and Long Island Society Register. Brooklyn, NY: Brooklyn Life Publishing Co., annual.
Brooklyn Blue Book and Long Island Society Register. Brooklyn, NY: Rugby Press, Inc., annual.
Brooks, John. *Once In Galconda. A True Drama of Wall Street 1920–1938.* New York: Harper & Row Publishers, 1969.
Brooks, John. *Showing Off in America.* Boston: Little, Brown & Co., 1981.
Browder, Clifford. *The Money Game In Old New York: Daniel Drew and His Times.* Lexington, KY: University Press of Kentucky, 1986.
Brown, Jane. *Beatrix: The Gardening Life of Beatrix Jones Farrand 1872–1959.* New York: Viking Penguin Books, 1995.
Browne, Irving. *Our Best Society.* New York: Samuel French, 1875.
Burr, Anna Robeson. *The Portrait of a Banker: James Stillman, 1850–1918.* New York: Duffield & Co., 1927.
Burt, Nathaniel. *First Families.* Boston: Little, Brown & Co., 1970.
Byrnes, Rev. Horace W. *Pictorial Bay Shore and Vicinity: A Souvenir.* Bay Shore, NY: privately printed, 1903.
Cable, Mary. *Top Drawer: American Society from Gilded Age to the Roaring Twenties.* New York: Atheneum, 1984.
Cantacuzene, Princess. *My Life Here and There.* New York: Charles Scribner's Sons, 1921.
Capen, Oliver Bronson. *Country Homes of Famous Americans.* Garden City: Doubleday, Page & Co., 1905.
Caro, Robert A. *The Power Broker: Robert Moses and the Fall of New York.* New York: Alfred A. Knopf, 1989.
Carson, Gerald. *The Polite Americans.* New York: William Morrow & Co., 1966.
Cascone, Mary. *Postcard History Series: Babylon Village.* Charleston, SC: Arcadia Publishing, 2017.
Chanler, Mrs. Winthrop [Margaret]. *Autumn in the Valley.* Boston: Little, Brown & Co., 1936.
Chanler, Mrs. Winthrop [Margaret]. *Roman Spring.* Boston: Little, Brown & Co., 1934.
Chase, Edna Woolman and Ilka Chase. *Always in Vogue.* Garden City: Doubleday & Co., Inc., 1954.
Churchill, Allen. *The Splendor Seekers: An Informal Glimpse of America's Multimillionaire Spenders – Members of the $50,000,000 Club.* New York: Grosset & Dunlop, 1974.
Churchill, Allen. *The Upper Crust: An Informal History of New York's Highest Society.* Englewood Cliffs, NJ: Prentice Hall, 1970.
Clark, Herma. *The Elegant Eighties.* Chicago: A. C. McClurg & Co., 1941.
Clews, Henry. *Fifty Years in Wall Street.* New York: Irving Publishing Co., 1908.
Close, Leslie Rose. *Portrait of an Era in Landscape Architecture: The Photographs of Mattie Edwards Hewitt.* The Bronx, NY: Wave Hill, 1983.
Collora, Christopher M. *Images of America: Long Island Historic Houses of the South Shore.* Charleston, SC: Arcadia Publishing, 2013.
Conant, Jennet. *Tuxedo Park: A Wall Street Tycoon and the Secret Palace of Science That Changed the Course of World War II.* New York: Simon & Schuster, 2002.
Crockett, Albert Stevens. *Peacocks On Parade.* New York: Sears Publishing, 1931.
Crofutt, William A. *The Leisure Class in America.* New York: Arno Press, 1975.
Curtis, George W. *Our Best Society.* New York: G. P. Putnam's Sons, 1899.
Curwen, Henry Darcey, ed. *Exeter Remembered.* Exeter, NH: Phillips–Exeter Academy, 1965.
Darby, Edwin. *The Fortune Builders.* Garden City: Doubleday & Co., Inc. 1986.
Dayton, Abram C. *The Last Days of Knickerbocker Life in New York.* New York: G. P. Putnam's Sons, 1897.
Delano & Aldrich. *Portraits of Ten Country Houses.* Garden City: Doubleday, Page & Co., 1924.
Depew, Chauncey M. *My Memories of Eighty Years.* New York: Charles Scribner's Sons, 1924.
Dickerson, Charles P. *A History of Sayville Community.* Sayville, NY: The Suffolk County News, 1975.
Directory of American Society New York State and the Metropolitan District, 1929. New York: Town Topics, 1928.
Directory of Directors in the City of New York and the Tri–State Area. Southport, CT: Directory of Directors Co., Inc., annual.
Domestic Architecture of H. T. Lindeberg. New York: William Helburn, Inc., 1940.
Domhoff, G. William. *The Bohemian Grove and Other Retreats.* New York: Harper & Row Publishers, 1974.
Domhoff, G. William. *Fat Cats and Democrats.* Englewood, NJ: Prentice–Hall, 1972.
Domhoff, G. William. *The Higher Circles: The Governing Class in America.* New York: Random House, 1970.
Domhoff, G. William. *The Powers That Be: Process of Ruling Class Domination in America.* New York: Random House, 1978.
Downey, Fairfax. *Portrait of an Era.* New York: Charles Scribner's Sons, 1936.
Drury, Roger W. *Drury and St. Paul's: The Scars of a Schoolmaster.* Boston: Little, Brown & Co., 1964.

General Bibliography

Eaton, James W. *Babylon Reminiscences*. Babylon, NY: Babylon Publishing Co., 1911.
Eliot, Elizabeth [Lady Elizabeth Kinnaird]. *Heiresses and Coronets*. New York: McDowell, Obolensky, 1959.
Ellet, Elizabeth. *The Queens of American Society*. Philadelphia: Porter & Coates, 1867.
Elliott, Maude Howe. *This Was My Newport*. Cambridge, MA: The Mythology Co., 1944.
Elliott, Maude Howe. *Three Generations*. Boston: Little, Brown & Co., 1923.
Elliott, Osborne. *Men at the Top*. New York: Harper & Brothers, 1959.
"Estates and Their Story," *Newsday* December 1, 1965.
Faucigny–Lucinge, Prince Jean–Louis de. *Legendary Parties 1922–1972*. New York: The Vendome Press, 1987.
Ferrell, Merri McIntyre. "Fox Hunting on Long Island." *The Nassau County Historical Society Journal* 54 (2001):1-10.
Ferry, John William. *A History of the Department Store*. New York: The Macmillan Co., 1960.
Ferree, Barr. *American Estates & Gardens*. New York: Munn & Co., 1904.
Fifth Avenue Art Galleries. *Estates of the Late Arthur A. Housman Banker and Member of NY Stock Exchange, by Order of Benjamin F. Feiner, Esq., Attorney for Executrix and George Rutledge Gibson by Order of Executors*. London: Forgotten Books, reprint 2018.
Fisher, Kenneth L. *100 Minds That Made the Market*. Woodside, CA: Business Classics, 1993.
Fiske, Stephen. *Offhand Portraits of Prominent New Yorkers*. New York: George Lockwood & Sons, 1884.
Fleming, Nancy. *Money, Manure & Maintenance: Ingredients for Successful Gardens of Marian Coffin, Pioneer Landscape Architect 1876–1957*. Weston, MA: Country Place Books, 1995.
Forbes, Malcolm and Jeffery Block. *What Happened to Their Children?* New York: Simon & Schuster, Inc., 1990.
Fowler, Marian. *In a Gilded Cage: From Heiress to Duchess*. New York: St. Martin's Press, 1993.
Frelinhuysen, Alice Cooning, et al. *Splendid Legacy: The Havemeyer Collection*. New York: The Metropolitan Museum of Art, 1993.
Fuller, Henry B. *The Cliff Dwellers*. New York: Harper & Brothers, 1893.
Garth, The Rev. William H. *Historical Sketch of St. Mark's: Islip, Long Island*. privately printed, 1928.
Gerard, James W. *My First Eighty–Three Years in America*. Garden City: Doubleday & Co., Inc., 1951.
Geus, Averill Dayton. *The Maidstone Club: The Second Fifty Years 1941 to 1991*. East Hampton, NY: Maidstone Club, 1991.
Gordon, Panmure. *Land of the Almighty Dollar*. London: Frederick Warne & Co., 1892.
Goulden, Joseph, C. *The Money Givers*. New York: Random House Publishers, 1971.
Gouverneur, Marion. *As I Remember: Recollections of American Society During the Nineteenth Century*. New York: D. Appleton & Co., 1911.
Graham, Sheila. *How to Marry Super Rich or Love, Money and the Morning After*. New York: Grosset & Dunlap Publishers, 1974.
Greene, Bert and Philip Stephen Schulz. *Pity the Poor Rich: It's a Losing Battle to Stay on Top But See How They Try*. Chicago: Contemporary Books, 1978.
Gregory, Alexis. *Families of Fortune: Life in the Gilded Age*. New York: Rizzoli International Publications, Inc., 1993.
Griswold, Mac K. and Eleanor Weller. *The Golden Age of American Gardens . Proud Owners . Private Estates . 1890–1940*. New York: Harry N. Abrams, Inc., Publishers, 1991.
Gross, Michael. *740 Park: The Story of the World's Richest Apartment Building*. New York: Broadway Books, 2005.
Gunther, Max. *The Very Rich and How They Got That Way*. New York: Playboy Press, 1972.
Halberstam, David. *The Powers That Be*. New York: Alfred A. Knopf, 1979.
Hall, Edward Tuck. *Saint Mark's School: A Centennial History*. Southborough, MA: Saint Mark's Alumni Association, 1967.
Hamm, Margherita Arlina. *Famous Families of New York*. New York: G. P. Putnam's Sons, 1901.
Harmond, Richard and Vincitorio Gaetano. "Working on the Great Estates." *Long Island Forum* Spring 1988.
Harriman, E. Roland. *I Reminisce*. Garden City: Doubleday & Co., Inc., 1975.
Harriman, Mrs. J. Borden. *From Pinafores to Politics*. New York: Henry Holt & Co., 1923.
Harriman, Margaret Chase. *The Vicious Circle*. New York: Rinehart & Co., 1951.
Harris, Leon. *Merchant Princes: An Intimate History of Jewish Families Who Built Great Department Stores*. New York: Harper & Row Publishers, 1979.
Harrison, Constance Cary. *Recollections Grave and Gay*. New York: Charles Scribner's Sons, 1911.
Harrison, Constance Cary. *The Well–Bred Girl in Society*. Garden City: Doubleday, Page & Co., 1904.
Havemeyer, Harry W. *Along the Great South Bay From Oakdale to Babylon, the Story of a Summer Spa, 1840 to 1940*. Mattituck, NY: Amereon House, 1996.
Havemeyer, Harry W. *East on the Great South Bay: Sayville and Bellport 1860-1960*. Mattituck, NY: Amereon House, 2001.
Havemeyer, Harry W. *Fire Island's Surf Hotel and Other Hostelries on Fire Island Beaches in the Nineteenth Century*. Mattituck, NY: Amereon Ltd., 2006.
Havemeyer, Harry W., "The Story of Saxton Avenue." *Long Island Forum* Winter, February 1, 1990 and Spring, May 1, 1990.

General Bibliography

Havemeyer, Harry W. *Merchants of Williamsburg: Frederick C. Havemeyer, Jr., William Dick, John Mollenhauer, Henry O. Havemeyer.* New York: privately printed, 1989.
Havemeyer, Louisine W. *Sixteen to Sixty: Memoirs of a Collector.* New York: Ursus Press, 1993.
Hersh, Burton. *The Old Boys: The American Elite and the Origins of the CIA.* New York: Charles Scribner's Sons, 1992.
Hess, Stephen. *America's Political Dynasties from Adams to Kennedy.* Garden City: Doubleday & Co., Inc., 1966.
Hewitt, Mark Alan. *The Architect & the Country House, 1890–1940.* New Haven: Yale University Press, 1990.
Hoff, Henry B., ed. *Long Island Source Records: From the New York Genealogical and Biographical Record.* Baltimore: Genealogical Publishing, 1987.
Holbrook, Stewart H. *The Age of Moguls.* London: Victor Gollancz, Ltd., 1954.
Holliday, Diane and Chris Kretz. *Images of America: Oakdale.* Charleston, SC: Arcadia Publishing, 2010.
Holloway, Laura C. *Famous American Fortunes and the Men Who Have Made Them.* New York: J. A. Hill, 1889.
Homberger, Eric. *Mrs. Astor's New York: Money and Social Power in a Gilded Age.* New Haven: Yale University Press, 2002.
Hoogenboom, Ari and Olive Hoogenboom, eds. *The Gilded Age.* Englewood, NJ: Prentice–Hall, 1967.
Hopkins, Alfred. *Modern Farm Buildings.* New York: McBride, Nast & Co., 1913.
Hopkins, Alfred. *Planning for Sunshine and Fresh Air.* New York: Architectural Book Publishing, 1931.
Howath, Susan. *The Rich Are Different.* New York: Simon & Schuster, Inc., 1977.
Howe, Samuel. *American Country Houses of To–Day.* New York: Architectural Book Publishing Co., 1915.
Howell, E. W. *Noted Long Island Homes.* Babylon, NY: E. W. Howell Co., 1933.
Hunt, Freeman. *Lives of the American Merchants.* New York: Hunts' Merchants' Magazine, 1895.
Hunter, Floyd. *The Big Rich and the Little Rich.* Garden City: Doubleday & Co., Inc., 1965.
Ingham, John. *Biographical Dictionary of American Business Leaders.* New York: Greenwood Press, 1983.
Ingham, John and Lynne B. Feldman. *Contemporary Business Leaders: A Biographical Dictionary.* New York: Greenwood Press, 1990.
International Celebrity Register. New York: Celebrity Register Ltd., annual.
Irwin, William Henry, et al. *A History of the Union League Club of New York City.* New York: Dodd, Mead & Co., 1952.
Jaeger, Anna and Mary Cascone. *Images of America: From Breslau to Lindenhurst 1870-1923.* Charleston, SC: Arcadia Publishing, 2018.
Jaher, Frederic Cople. *The Gilded Elite: American Multimillionaires, 1865 to the Present.* London: Croom Helm, 1980.
Jaher, Frederic Cople, ed. *The Rich, The Wellborn, and The Powerful: Elite and Upper Classes in History.* Secaucus: Citadel Press, 1975.
Jenkins, Alan. *The Rich Rich: The Story of the Big Spenders.* New York: G. P. Putnam's Sons, 1978.
Jennings, Walter Wilson. *20 Giants of American Business.* New York: Exposition Press, 1953.
Josephson, Matthew. *The Money Lords: The Great Finance Capitalists 1925–1950.* New York: Weybright & Talley Publishers, 1972.
Josephson, Matthew. *The Robber Barons..., 1861–1901.* New York: Harcourt, Brace, Jovanovich, Publishers, 1934.
Kahn, E. J., III. "The Brahmin Mystique." *Boston Magazine* 75 (May 1983):119–161.
Kaiser, Harvey. *Great Camps of the Adirondacks.* Boston: David R. Godine, Publisher, Inc., 1982.
Kamisher, Lawrence, ed. *One Hundred Years of Knickerbocker History.* Port Washington, NY: Knickerbocker Yacht Club, 1974.
Kavaler, Lucy. *The Private World of High Society: Its Rules and Rituals.* New York: David McKay Co., Inc., 1960.
Kent, Joan Gay. *Discovering Sands Point: Its History, Its People, Its Places.* Sands Point, NY: Village of Sands Point, 2000.
Kirstein, George G. *The Rich: Are They Different?* Boston: Houghton Mifflin & Co., 1968.
Klepper, Michael. *The Wealthy 100: From Benjamin Franklin to Bill Gates – A Ranking of the Richest Americans Past and Present.* Secaucus, NJ: The Citadel Press, 1996.
Knapp, Edward Spring, Jr. *We Knapps Thought It Was Nice.* New York: privately printed, 1940.
Knox, Thomas W. "Summer Clubs on the Great South Bay." *Harper's New Monthly Magazine* July 1880.
Konolige, Kit. *The Richest Women in the World.* New York: The Macmillan Co., 1985.
Konolige, Kit and Frederica Konolige. *The Power of Their Glory: America's Ruling Class: The Episcopalians.* New York: Wyden Books, 1978.
Kouwenhoven, John A. *Partners in Banking: An Historical Portrait of a Great Private Bank, Brown Brothers Harriman & Co., 1818–1968.* Garden City: Doubleday & Co., Inc., 1968.
Kowet, Don. *The Rich Who Own Sports.* New York: Random House, 1977.
Krieg, Joann P., ed. *Long Island Architecture.* Interlaken, NY: Heart of the Lakes Publishing, 1991.
Krieg, Joann P., ed. *Robert Moses: Single–Minded Genius.* Interlaken, NY: Heart of the Lakes Publishing, 1989.
Lamont, Kenneth Church. *The Moneymakers: The Great Big New Rich in America.* Boston: Little, Brown & Co., 1969.
Lampman, Robert J. *The Share of Top Wealth–Holders in National Wealth 1922–1956.* Princeton, NJ: Princeton University Press, 1962.
Lapham, Lewis. *Money and Class in America.* New York: Weidenfeld & Nicolson, 1988.
Lee, Henry J., ed. *The Long Island Almanac and Year Book.* New York: Eagle Library Publications, 1931, 1934.

General Bibliography

Lehr, Elizabeth Drexel. *"King Lehr" and the Gilded Age*. Philadelphia: J. B. Lippincott Co., 1935.
Lehr, Elizabeth Drexel. *Turn of the World*. Philadelphia: J. B. Lippincott Co., 1937.
Lewis & Valentine Nursery. New York: Lewis & Valentine Co., 1916.
Lewis, Arnold, et al. *The Opulent Interiors of the Golden Age*. New York: Dover Publications, Inc., 1987.
Libby, Valencia. "Marian Cruger Coffin, the Landscape Architect and the Lady." The House and Garden Exhibition Catalog. Roslyn, NY: Nassau County Museum of Fine Art, 1986.
Lindeman, Eduard C. *Wealth and Culture*. New York: Harcourt, Brace & Co., Inc., 1936.
Livingston, Bernard. *Their Turf: America's Horsey Set and Its Princely Dynasties*. New York: Arbor House Publishers, 1973.
Logan, Andy. *The Man Who Robbed the Robber Barons*. New York: W. W. Norton & Co., 1965.
Long Island Society Register 1929. Brooklyn, NY: Rugby Press, Inc., 1929.
Lowe, Corinne. *Confessions of a Social Secretary*. New York: Harper & Brothers, 1916.
Lucas, Nora. "The Historic Resource Survey for the Period 1900–1940 of the Unincorporated Sections of the Town of North Hempstead." Preservation Computer Services, 1991.
Lucie–Smith, Edward and Celestine Dars. *How the Rich Lived*. New York: Two Continents Publishing Group, 1976.
Lundberg, Ferdinand. *America's 60 Families*. New York: The Vanguard Press, 1937.
Lundberg, Ferdinand. *The Rich and the Super–Rich: A Study in the Power of Money Today*. New York: Lyle Stuart & Co., 1968.
Lundberg, Ferdinand. "Who Controls Industry? [pamphlet concerning Richard Whitney case], c. 1938.
Lynes, Russell. *The Domesticated Americans*. New York: Harper & Row Publishers, 1963.
MacColl, Gail and Carol McD. Wallace. *To Marry an English Lord*. New York: Workman Publishing, 1989.
Mackay, Robert B., Anthony K. Baker, and Carol A. Traynor. *Long Island Country Houses and Their Architects 1860–1940*. New York: W. W. Norton & Co., 1997.
Maher, James T. *The Twilight of Splendor: Chronicles of the Age of American Palaces*. Boston: Little Brown & Co., 1975.
Maher, Matthew. "A Study of the Effects of Accelerated Suburbanization [in Nassau–Suffolk] Upon the Social Structure." M. A. thesis, St. John's University, 1982.
Mahoney, Tom and Leonard Stone. *The Great Merchants: America's Foremost Retail Institutions and People Who Made Them Great*. New York: Harper & Row Publishers, 1974.
Marcus, George E. *Lives In Trust: The Fortunes of Dynastic Families in Late Twentieth–Century America*. Boulder, CO: Westview Press, 1992.
Martin, Frederick Townsend. *Things I Remember*. New York: John Lane Co., 1913.
Martin, Frederick Townsend. *The Passing of the Idle Rich*. Garden City: Doubleday, Page, & Co., 1911.
Maxwell, Elsa. *The Celebrity Circus*. London: Allen, 1964.
Maxwell, Elsa. *R. S. V. P.: Elsa Maxwell's Own Story*. Boston: Little, Brown & Co., 1954.
Mayer, Martin. *The Bankers*. New York: Weybright & Talley Publishers, 1974.
Mazzola, Anthony T. and Frank Zachary, ed. *The Best Families: The Town and Country Social Directory, 1846–1996*. New York: Harry N. Abrams, Inc., Publishers, 1996.
McAllister, Ward. *Society As I Have Found It*. New York: Cassell Publishing Co., 1890.
McCash, June Hall. *The Jekyll Island Cottage Colony*. Athens, GA: The University of Georgia Press, 1998.
McCash, William Barton and June Hall McCash. *The Jekyll Island Club: Southern Haven for America's Millionaires*. Athens, GA: The University of Georgia Press, 1989.
McCusker, John J. *How Much Is That in Real Money? A Historical Price Index for Use as a Deflator of Money Values in the Economy of the United States*. Worcester, MA: American Antiquarian Society, 1992.
McKim, Mead, & White. *A Monograph of the Work of McKim, Mead & White 1879–1915*. New York: DaCapo Press, 1985.
McVickar, Harry Whitney. *The Greatest Show on Earth: Society*. New York: Harper & Brothers, 1892.
Metcalf, Pauline C. and Libby Valencia. *The House and Garden*. Roslyn, NY: Nassau County Museum of Fine Art, 1986.
Miller, Frances [Breese]. *More About Tanty*. Southampton, NY: Sandbox Press, 1980.
Miller, Frances [Breese]. *Tanty: Encounter With the Past*. Southampton, NY: Sandbox Press, 1979.
Mills, C. Wright. *The Power Elite*. New York: Oxford University Press, 1956.
Milne, Gordon. *The Sense of Society*. Cranbury, NJ: Fairleigh Dickinson University Press, 1977.
Minnigerode, Meade. *Certain Rich Men*. New York: G. P. Putnam's Sons, 1927.
Mondore, Robert and Patty Mondore. *Images of America: Singer Castle Revisited*. Charleston, SC: Arcadia Publishing, 2010.
Montgomery, Maureen E. *Gilded Prostitution: Status, Money and Transatlantic Marriage 1870–1914*. London: Routledge Press, 1989.
Moody, John. *The Masters of Capital: A Chronicle of Wall Street*. New Haven: Yale University Press, 1919.
Morris, Lloyd. *Incredible New York: High Life and Low Life of the Last Hundred Years*. New York: Random House, 1951.
Moses, Robert. *Working For the People*. New York: Harper and Brothers, 1956.

General Bibliography

Mountfield, David. *The Railway Barons.* New York: W. W. Norton & Co., 1979.
Myers, Gustavus. *The Ending of Hereditary American Fortunes.* New York: Julian Messner, Inc., 1939.
Myers, Gustavus. *History of the Great American Fortunes.* New York: Random House, 1937.
Nichols, Charles Wilbur de Lyon. *The Ultra-Fashionable Peerage of America: An Official List of Those People Who Can Be Called Ultra-Fashionable in the United States.* New York: George Harjes, 1904.
Noyes, Dorothy McBurney. *The World Is So Full.* Islip, NY: privately printed, 1953.
Obolensky, Serge. *One Man in His Time: The Memoirs of Serge Obolensky.* New York: privately printed, 1958.
O'Connor, Harvey. *The Empire of Oil.* New York: Monthly Review Press, 1955.
O'Connor, Richard. *The Oil Barons: Men of Greed and Grandeur.* Boston: Little, Brown & Co., 1971.
Old Oakdale History, Volume I. Oakdale, NY: William K. Vanderbilt Historical Society of Dowling College, 1983.
The Old Oakdale History, Volume II: Era of Elegance, Part I. Oakdale, NY: William K. Vanderbilt Historical Society of Dowling College, 1993.
Ostrander, Susan A. *Women of the Upper Class.* Philadelphia: Temple University Press, 1984.
Packard, Vance. *The Status Seekers.* New York: David McKay Co., Inc., 1959.
Parsons, Schuyler Livingston. *Untold Friendships.* Boston: Houghton Mifflin Co., 1955.
Patterson, Augusta Owen. *American Homes of Today.* New York: The Macmillan Co., 1924.
Patterson, Jerry E. *Fifth Avenue: The Best Addresses.* New York: Rizzoli International Publications, Inc., 1998.
Patterson, Jerry E. *The First Four Hundred: Mrs. Astor's New York in the Gilded Age.* New York: Rizzoli International Publications, Inc., 2000.
Pearson, Hesketh. *The Marrying Americans.* New York: Coward McCann, Inc., 1961.
Pendrell, Nan and Ernest Pendrell. *How the Rich Live and Whom to Tax.* New York: Workers Library Publishers, Inc., May 1939.
Persons, Stow. *The Decline of American Gentility.* New York: Columbia University Press, 1973.
Phillips, David. *The Reign of Gilt.* New York: James Pott & Co., 1905.
Picturesque Babylon, Bay Shore and Islip. New York: Mercantile Illustrating Co., 1894.
Pless, Princess Mary. *Better Left Unsaid.* New York: E. P. Dutton & Co., 1931.
Pless, Princess Mary. *What I Left Unsaid.* New York: E. P. Dutton & Co., 1936.
Porzelt, Paul. *The Metropolitan Club of New York.* New York: Rizzoli International Publications, Inc., 1982.
Prominent Residents of Long Island and Their Clubs. New York: Edward C. Watson, c. 1916.
Pulitzer, Ralph. *New York Society on Parade.* New York: Harper & Brothers, 1910.
Pulling, Sister Anne Frances. *Images of America: Babylon By the Sea.* Charleston, SC: Arcadia Publishing, 1999.
Randall, Monica. *The Mansions of Long Island's Gold Coast.* New York: Rizzoli International Publications, Inc., 1987.
Rattray, Jeannette Edwards. *Fifty Years of the Maidstone Club: 1891–1941.* East Hampton, NY: privately printed, 1941.
Residences Designed by Bradley Delehanty. New York: Architectural Catalogue Co., Inc., 1939.
Rodgers, Cleveland. *Robert Moses, Builder of Democracy.* New York: Henry Holt and Co., 1952.
Roosevelt, Felicia Warburg. *Doers and Dowagers.* Garden City: Doubleday & Co., Inc., 1975.
Roosevelt, Robert Barnwell. *Love and Luck: The Story of a Summer's Loitering on the Great South Bay.* New York: Harper, 1886.
Sachs, Charles L. *The Blessed Isle: Hal B. Fullerton's Image of Long Island, 1827-1927.* Interlaken, NY: Heart of the Lakes Publishing, 1990.
Schlesinger, Arthur M., Jr. *A Life in the 20th Century: Innocent Beginnings, 1917-1950.* Boston: Houghton Mifflin, 2000.
Schnadelbach, R. Terry. *Ferruccio Vitale: Landscape Architect of the Country Place Era.* New York: Princeton Architectural Press, 2001.
Schrag, Peter. *The Decline of the Wasp.* New York: Simon & Schuster, Inc., 1970.
Sclare, Liisa and Donald Sclare. *Beaux–Arts Estates: A Guide to the Architecture of Long Island.* New York: The Viking Press, 1980.
Sedgwick, Henry Dwight. *In Praise of Gentlemen.* Boston: Little, Brown & Co., 1935.
Sedgwick, John. *Rich Kids.* New York: William Morrow & Co., 1985.
Shodell, Elly. *In The Service: Workers on the Grand Estates of Long Island 1890s – 1940s.* Port Washington, NY: Port Washington Public Library, 1991.
Shopsin, William C. and Grania Bolton Marcus. *Saving Large Estates: Conservation, Historic Preservation, Adaptive Re–Use.* Setauket, NY: Society for the Preservation of Long Island Antiquities, 1977.
Simon, Kate. *Fifth Avenue: A Very Social History.* New York: Harcourt, Brace, Jovanovich Publishers, 1978.
Slater, Philip. *Wealth Addiction.* New York: E. P. Dutton & Co., 1980.
Smith, Arthur D. Howden. *Men Who Run America.* New York: Bobbs–Merrill Co., 1936.
Soben, Dennis P. *Dynamics of Community Change; the Case of Long Island's Declining "Gold Coast."* Port Washington, NY: Ira J. Friedman, 1968.
Social Register. New York: The Social Register Association, annual.
Social Register New York. New York: Social Register Association, annual.
Social Register Summer. New York: Social Register Association, annual.

General Bibliography

Spinzia, Judith Ader. "Artistry In Glass: Louis Comfort Tiffany's Legacy In Nassau County." *The Nassau County Historical Society Journal,* 1991:8-17. Also available at www.spinzialongislandestates.com.

Spinzia, Judith Ader. "Artistry In Glass: The Queens Ecclesiastical Windows of Louis Comfort Tiffany." *Newsletter of the Queens Historical Society,* July/August 1989:8-10.

Spinzia, Judith Ader. "Artistry In Glass: The Undisputed Master, Our Oyster Bay Neighbor." *The Freeholder* 2 (Winter 1998):3-5; and 2 (Spring 1998):3-5, 24. Also available at www.spinzialongislandestates.com.

Spinzia, Judith Ader. "Women of Long Island: Clare Boothe Luce (1903-1987), The Long Island Connection." *The Freeholder* 14 (Summer 2009):3-5; 17-20. Also available at www.spinzialongislandestates.com.

Spinzia, Judith Ader. "Women of Long Island: Cornelia Bryce Pinchot, Feminist, Social-Activist – The Long Islander Who Became First Lady of Pennsylvania." www.spinzialongislandestates.com.

Spinzia, Judith Ader. "Women of Long Island: Mary Elizabeth Jones; Rosalie Gardiner Jones." *The Freeholder* 11 (Spring 2007):2-7. Also available at www.spinzialongislandestates.com.

Spinzia, Judith Ader. "Women of Long Island: Mary Williamson Averell Harriman; Her daughter Mary Harriman Rumsey." *The Freeholder,* 12 (Spring 2008):8-9, 16-20. Also available at www.spinzialongislandestates.com.

Spinzia, Raymond E. "Adultery, Drugs, Murder, Untimely Deaths, and Long Island's Prominent Families; A Tangled Web." www.spinzialongislandestates.com.

Spinzia, Raymond E. "Elliott Roosevelt, Sr. – A Spiral Into Darkness: The Influences." *The Freeholder* 12 (Fall 2007): 3-7, 15-17. Also available at www.spinzialongislandestates.com.

Spinzia, Raymond E. "In Her Wake: The Story of Alva Smith Vanderbilt." *The Long Island Historical Journal* 6 (Fall 1993):96-105. Also available at www.spinzialongislandestates.com.

Spinzia, Raymond E. "Michael Straight and the Cambridge Spy Ring." *The Freeholder* 5 (Winter 2001):3-5. Also available at www.spinzialongislandestates.com.

Spinzia, Raymond E. "Socialite Spies: The Grandchildren of Henry Baldwin Hyde, Sr." *East Islip Historical Society Newsletter* 16 (March 2008):1, 3. Also available at www.spinzialongislandestates.com.

Spinzia, Raymond E. "Society Chameleons: Long Island's Gentlemen Spies." *The Nassau County Historical Society Journal* 55 (2000):27-38. Also available at www.spinzialongislandestates.com.

Spinzia, Raymond E. "Sumner Welles: Brilliance and Tragedy." *The Freeholder* 9 (Winter 2005):8-9, 22. Also available at www.spinzialongislandestates.com.

Spinzia, Raymond E. "Those Other Roosevelts: The Fortescues." *The Freeholder* 11 (Summer 2006):8-9, 16-22. Also available at www.spinzialongislandestates.com.

Spinzia, Raymond E. and Judith A. Spinzia. "*Gatsby:* Myths and Realities of Long Island's North Shore Gold Coast." *The Nassau County Historical Society Journal* 52 (1997):16–26. Also available at www.spinzialongislandestates.com.

Spinzia, Raymond E. and Judith A. Spinzia. *Long Island's Prominent Families in the Town of East Hampton: Their Estates and Their Country Homes.* College Station, TX: VirtualBookworm, 2020.

Spinzia, Raymond E. and Judith A. Spinzia. *Long Island's Prominent Families in the Town of Hempstead: Their Estates and Their Country Homes.* College Station, TX: VirtualBookworm, 2010.

Spinzia, Raymond E. and Judith A. *Long Island's Prominent Families in the Town of Southampton: Their Estates and Their Country Homes.* College Station, TX: VirtualBookworm, 2010.

Spinzia, Raymond E. and Judith A. Spinzia. *Long Island's Prominent South Shore Families: Their Estates and Their Country Homes in the Towns of Babylon and Islip.* College Station, TX: VirtualBookworm, 2007; revised 2021.

Spinzia, Raymond E. and Judith A. Spinzia. "*Gatsby:* Myths and Realities of Long Island's North Shore Gold Coast." *The Nassau County Historical Society Journal* 52 (1997):16–26. Also available at www.spinzialongislandestates.com.

Spinzia, Raymond E. and Judith A. Spinzia. *Long Island's Prominent North Shore Families: Their Estates and Their Country Homes.* vols. I, II. College Station, TX: VirtualBookworm, 2006; revised, 2019.

Starace, Carl A. *Book One: Islip Town Records.* Islip, NY: Town of Islip, 1982.

Stevenson, Charles Goldsmith. *But As Yesterday: The Early Life and Times of St. Ann's Church, Sayville, Long Island, New York (1864-1888).* privately printed, 1967.

Stein, Susan R. *The Architecture of Richard Morris Hunt.* Chicago: University of Chicago, 1986.

Stephens, W. P. *The Seawanhaka Corinthian Yacht Club: Origins and Early History, 1871–1896.* New York: privately printed, 1963.

Swaine, Robert T. *The Cravath Firm and Its Predecessors, 1819–1948, vols. 1, 2.* New York: Ad Press, Ltd., 1946, 1948.

Talese, Gay. *The Kingdom and the Power.* New York: World Publishers, 1969.

Tankard, Judith B. *The Gardens of Ellen Biddle Shipman.* Sagaponack, NY: Sagapress, Inc., 1996.

Tarbell, Ida. *History of Standard Oil Company.* New York: The Macmillan Co., 1925.

Tebbel, John William. *The Inheritors: A Study of America's Great Fortunes and What Happened to Them.* New York: Putnam, 1962.

Teutonico, Jeanne Marie. "Marian Cruger Coffin: The Long Island Estates; a Study of the Early Work of a Pioneering Woman in American Landscape Architecture." M. S. thesis, Columbia University, 1983.

Thompson, Jacqueline. *The Very Rich Book: America's Supermillionaires and Their Money – Where They Got It, How They Spend It.* New York: William Morrow & Co., Inc., 1981.

Thorndike, Joseph J., Jr. *The Very Rich: A History of Wealth.* New York: American Heritage, 1976.

General Bibliography

Tishler, William, ed. *American Landscape Architecture: Designers and Places.* Washington, DC: Preservation Press, 1989.
Townsend, Reginald T. *God Pack My Picnic Basket: Reminiscences of the Golden Age of Newport and New York.* New York: Hastings House, 1970.
Townsend, Reginald T. *Mother of Clubs.* New York: Union Club, 1936.
Trachtenberg, Alan. *The Incorporation of America: Culture and Society in the Gilded Age.* New York: Hill and Wang, 1982.
Tuttle, Etta Anderson. *A Brief History of Bay Shore.* privately printed, 1962.
Ulman, Albert. *New Yorkers from Stuyvesant to Roosevelt.* Port Washington, NY: Ira J. Friedman, 1969.
Updike, D. P. *Hunt Clubs and Country Clubs in America.* Cambridge, MA: The Merrymount Press, 1928.
Vanderbilt, Cornelius, Jr. *Farewell to Fifth Avenue.* New York: Simon & Schuster, Inc., 1935.
Vanderbilt, Cornelius, Jr. *Man of the World: My Life on Five Continents.* New York: Crown Publishers, Inc., 1959.
Vanderbilt, Cornelius, Jr. *Palm Beach.* New York: Macaulay, 1931.
Vanderbilt, Cornelius, Jr. *Reno.* New York: Macaulay, 1929.
Vanderbilt, Cornelius, Jr. *Queen of the Golden Age: The Fabulous Story of Grace Wilson Vanderbilt.* New York: McGraw–Hill Book, Co., Inc., 1956.
Van Rensselaer, Mrs. John King. *Newport: Our Social Capital.* Philadelphia: J. B. Lippincott Co., 1905.
Van Rensselaer, Mrs. John King. *New Yorkers of the XIX Century.* New York: F. T. Neely, 1897.
Van Rensselaer, Mrs. John King and Frederic Van De Water. *The Social Ladder.* New York: Henry Holt & Co., 1924.
Van Rensselaer, Peter. *Rich Was Better.* New York: Wynwood Press, 1990.
VanWagner, Judith, et al. *Long Island Estate Gardens.* Greenvale, NY: Hillwood Art Gallery, 1985.
Van Wyck, Frederick. *Recollections of an Old New Yorker.* New York: Liveright, Inc., Publishers, 1932.
Veblen, Thorstein. *The Theory of the Leisure Class: An Economic Study of Institutions.* New York: New Modern Library, 1934.
Verga, Christopher and Neil Buffett. *Images of America: Bay Shore.* Charleston, SC: Arcadia Publishing, 2017.
Views From the Circle: Seventy–Five Years of Groton School. Groton, MA: The Trustees of Groton Schools, 1960.
Wall Street Journal, ed. *American Dynasties Today.* Homewood, IL, c. 1980.
Walker, Stanley. *Mrs. Astor's Horse.* New York: Frederick A. Stokes Co., 1935.
Wecter, Dixon. *The Saga of American Society: A Record of Social Aspiration, 1607–1937.* New York: Charles Scribner's Sons, 1937.
Weeks, George L., Jr. *Isle of Shells.* Islip, NY: Buys Brothers Inc., 1965.
Weigold, Marilyn. *The American Mediterranean: An Environmental, Economic, and Social History of Long Island Sound.* Port Washington, NY: Kennikat Press, 1974.
Weinhardt, Donald H. *Bayport: Fading Views.* Bayport, NY: Bayport Heritage Association, 1986.
Weitzenhoffer, Frances. *The Havemeyers: Impressionism Comes to America.* New York: Harry N. Abrams, Inc., Publishers, 1986.
Wells, Richard A. *Manners, Culture and Dress of the Best American Society.* Springfield, MA: King Richardson & Co., 1894.
White, Samuel G. *The Houses of McKim, Mead, and White.* New York: Rizzoli International Publications, Inc., 1998.
Who's Who In New York State. New York: Lewis Historical Publishing Co., annual.
Williamson, Ellen. *When We Went First Class.* Garden City: Doubleday & Co., Inc., 1977.
Woolson, Abba G. *Woman in American Society.* Cambridge, MA: Roberts Brothers, 1873.
Worden, Helen. *Society Circus: From Ring to Ring With a Large Cast.* New York: Covici, Friede, Publishers, 1936.
Zerbe, Jerome. *The Art of Social Climbing.* Garden City: Doubleday & Co., Inc., 1965.

Harry Bowly Hollins, Sr. estate, Meadow Farm

Individual Bibliographical References

Selected Bibliographic References to Individual South Shore Estate Owners

This portion of the bibliography contains references not only to the South Shore estate owners, but also to their families and their estates. Since books listed in this section are, in most instances, different from the listings in the general bibliography, America's First Age of Fortune: A Selected Bibliography, both sections should be consulted.

Adams, John Dunbar - Bay Shore - *Woodlea*
> Mackay, Robert B., Anthony K. Baker, and Carol A. Traynor. *Long Island Country Houses and Their Architects 1860-1940*. New York: W. W. Norton & Co., 1997.
> Spinzia, Raymond E. and Judith A. Spinzia. *Long Island's Prominent North Shore Families: Their Estates and Their Country Homes. vols. I, II.* College Station, TX: VirtualBookworm, 2006, revised 2019.

Spur October 1914.

Adams, Thomas, Jr. - West Bay Shore - *Ardmore*
> Havemeyer, Harry W. *Along the Great South Bay From Oakdale to Babylon, the Story of a Summer Spa, 1840 to 1940.* Mattituck, NY: Amereon House, 1996.
> Ruther, Frederick. *Long Island Today*. Hicksville, NY: privately printed, 1909.
> Spinzia, Raymond E. and Judith A. Spinzia. *Long Island's Prominent North Shore Families: Their Estates and Their Country Homes. vols. I, II.* College Station, TX: VirtualBookworm, 2006, revised 2019.

Andrews, William Loring - West Islip - *Pepperidges*
> Byrnes, Horace W. *Pictorial Bay Shore and Vicinity: A Souvenir.* privately printed, 1903.

Arnold, Annie Stewart Cameron - West Islip - *Clovelly*
The Town of Babylon, Office of Historic Services has photographs of the estate.

Aston, William K. - Oakdale - *Peperidge Hall*
Library of Congress, Washington, DC, has photographs of the estate.
The Nassau County Photo Archive Center has photographs of the estate.
> Havemeyer, Harry W. *Along the Great South Bay From Oakdale to Babylon, the Story of a Summer Spa, 1840 to 1940.* Mattituck, NY: Amereon House, 1996.
> *Long Island Forum* February 1948.
> *Long Island Forum* December 1957.
> *Long Island Forum* December 1978.
> Mackay, Robert B., Anthony K. Baker, and Carol A. Traynor. *Long Island Country Houses and Their Architects 1860-1940*. New York: W. W. Norton & Co., 1997.
> *The Old Oakdale History, Volume II: Era of Elegance, Part I.* Oakdale, NY: William K. Vanderbilt Historical Society of Dowling College, 1993.
> *Town and Country* December 1921.

Behman, Louis C., Sr. - Bayport - *Lindenwalt*
The Nassau County Photo Archive Center has photographs of the estate.
> Havemeyer, Harry W. *East on the Great South Bay: Sayville and Bayport 1860–1960.* Mattituck, NY: Amereon House, 2001.
> Mackay, Robert B., Anthony K. Baker, and Carol A. Traynor. *Long Island Country Houses and Their Architects 1860-1940*. New York: W. W. Norton & Co., 1997.

Belmont, August, Sr. - North Babylon - *Nursery Stud Farm*
Alterman Library, University of Virginia, Charlottesville, VA, has the Nursery Stud Farm records.
Library of Congress, Washington, DC, has a portion of August Belmont, Sr.'s papers.
Massachusetts Historical Society, Boston, MA, has a portion of August Belmont, Sr.'s papers.
New York Public Library, NYC, has a portion of August Belmont, Sr.'s papers.
Office of the Historian, Town of Babylon, has photographs of the estate.
The Town of Babylon, Office of Historic Services has photographs of the estate.
> Beard, Patricia. *After the Ball: Gilded Age Secrets, Boardroom Betrayals, and the Party That Ignited the Great Wall Street Scandal of 1905.* New York: Harper Collins, 2003.
> Birmingham, Stephen. *The Grandes Dames*. New York: Simon & Schuster, 1982.
> Black, David. *The King of Fifth Avenue: The Fortune of August Belmont.* New York: The Dial Press, 1981.
> Catalogue: Loan Exhibition 1893. National Academy of Design. New York: Knickerbocker Press, 1893.

Individual Bibliographic References

Belmont, August, Sr. - North Babylon - *Nursery Stud Farm* (cont'd)
    Douglas, Roy. "The Great Sale, The Auctioning of August Belmont's Thoroughbreds: 1890-1891." *Long Island Forum* 61 (Spring 1998):24-36.
    Douglas, Roy. "Where They First Saw the Light – August Belmont Nursery Farm and Stud in North Babylon, 1867-1890." *Long Island Forum* 60 (Fall 1997):23-35.
    Gottheil, Richard James Horatio. *Belmont–Belmonte Family: A Record of Four Hundred Years, Put Together From the Original Documents in the Archives and Libraries of Spain, Portugal, Holland, England and Germany*, 1917.
    Havemeyer, Harry W. *Along the Great South Bay From Oakdale to Babylon, the Story of a Summer Spa, 1840 to 1940*. Mattituck, NY: Amereon House, 1996.
    Katz, Irving. *August Belmont: A Political Biography*. New York: Columbia University Press, 1968.
    Spinzia, Raymond E. and Judith A. Spinzia. *Long Island's Prominent North Shore Families: Their Estates and Their Country Homes. vols. I, II.* College Station, TX: VirtualBookworm, 2006, revised 2019.

Belmont, Eleanor Robson - North Babylon - *Nursery Stud Farm*
[*see* A. Belmont, Jr. entry]
Rare Book and Manuscript Library, Columbia University, NYC, has Mrs. August Belmont, Jr.'s papers.

Belmont, Perry - North Babylon - *Nursery Stud Farm*
Alterman Library, University of Virginia, Charlottesville, VA, has the Nursery Stud Farm records.
Office of the Historian, Town of Babylon, has photographs of the estate.
    Belmont, Perry. *An American Democrat: The Recollections of Perry Belmont*. New York: Columbia University Press, 1940.
    Douglas, Roy. "The Great Sale, The Auctioning of August Belmont's Thoroughbreds: 1890-1891." *Long Island Forum* 61 (Spring 1998):24-36.
    Douglas, Roy. "Where They First Saw the Light – August Belmont Nursery Farm and Stud in North Babylon, 1867-1890." *Long Island Forum* 60 (Fall 1997):23-35.
    Gottheil, Richard James Horatio. *Belmont–Belmonte Family: A Record of Four Hundred Years, Put Together From the Original Documents in the Archives and Libraries of Spain, Portugal, Holland, England and Germany*, 1917.
    Spinzia, Raymond E. and Judith A. Spinzia. *Long Island's Prominent North Shore Families: Their Estates and Their Country Homes. vols. I, II.* College Station, TX: VirtualBookworm, 2006, revised 2019.

Bossert, Louis - West Bay Shore - *The Oaks*
Frederick Law Olmsted National Historic Site, Brookline, MA, has the records of Olmsted's landscape commissions.
    Beard, Patricia. *After the Ball: Gilded Age Secrets, Boardroom Betrayals, and the Party That Ignited the Great Wall Street Scandal of 1905*. New York: Harper Collins, 2003.
    Cooney, Barbara. *Hattie and the Wild Waves: A Story from Brooklyn*. New York: Viking Press, 1990. [children's book]
    Country Life in America July 1903.
    Havemeyer, Harry W. *Along the Great South Bay From Oakdale to Babylon, the Story of a Summer Spa, 1840 to 1940*. Mattituck, NY: Amereon House, 1996.
    Howell, Liz. *Continuity: Biography 1819-1934*. Sister Bay, WI: The Dragonsbreath Press, 1993.
    Mackay, Robert B., Anthony K. Baker, and Carol A. Traynor. *Long Island Country Houses and Their Architects 1860-1940*. New York: W. W. Norton & Co., 1997.
    Town and Country October 1903.
    Town and Country, 1923.

Bourne, Frederick Gilbert - Oakdale - *Indian Neck Hall*
Avery Architectural and Fine Arts Library, Columbia University, NYC, has the architectural records of Ernest Flagg.
Frederick Law Olmsted National Historic Site, Brookline, MA, has the records of Olmsted's landscape commissions.
The Nassau County Photo Archive Center has photographs of the estate.
  Aeolian organ.
    Architectural Forum, 1919.
    Bacon, Mardges. *Ernest Flagg: Beaux-Arts Architecture and Urban Reformer*. Cambridge, MA: MIT Press, 1986.
    Brandon, Ruth. *Capitalist Romance: Singer and the Sewing Machine*. Philadelphia: J. B. Lippincott Co., 1977.
    Desmond, H. W. "The Works of Ernest Flagg." *Architectural Record* 11 (April 1902):1-104.

Individual Bibliographic References

Bourne, Frederick Gilbert - Oakdale - *Indian Neck Hall* (cont'd)
"A Fine Residence." *Suffolk News* III (June 18, 1897):2.
Fordyce, James. "Frederick Bourne and Indian Neck Hall." *Long Island Forum* March and April 1987.
Havemeyer, Harry W. *Along the Great South Bay From Oakdale to Babylon, the Story of a Summer Spa, 1840 to 1940*. Mattituck, NY: Amereon House, 1996.
Hopkins, Alfred. *Modern Farm Buildings*. New York: McBride, Nast & Co., 1913.
Mackay, Robert B., Anthony K. Baker, and Carol A. Traynor. *Long Island Country Houses and Their Architects 1860-1940*. New York: W. W. Norton & Co., 1997.
The Old Oakdale History, Volume II: Era of Elegance, Part I. Oakdale, NY: William K. Vanderbilt Historical Society of Dowling College, 1993.
Spinzia, Raymond E. and Judith A. Spinzia. *Long Island's Prominent North Shore Families: Their Estates and Their Country Homes*. vols. I, II. College Station, TX: VirtualBookworm, 2006, revised 2019.

Breese, William Laurence, Sr. - Great River - *Timber Point*
[aka William Lawence Breese, Sr.]
Havemeyer, Harry W. *Along the Great South Bay From Oakdale to Babylon, the Story of a Summer Spa, 1840 to 1940*. Mattituck, NY: Amereon House, 1996.
Howell, E. W. *Noted Long Island Homes*. Babylon, NY: E. W. Howell Co., 1933.
Mackay, Robert B., Anthony K. Baker, and Carol A. Traynor. *Long Island Country Houses and Their Architects 1860-1940*. New York: W. W. Norton & Co., 1997.

Bromell, Alfred Henry - Babylon
Mackay, Robert B., Anthony K. Baker, and Carol A. Traynor. *Long Island Country Houses and Their Architects 1860-1940*. New York: W. W. Norton & Co., 1997.
Picturesque Babylon, Bay Shore and Islip. New York: Mercantile Illustrating Co., 1894.

Brownlie, George - Babylon - *Willow Close*
Country Life in America October 1913.
Mackay, Robert B., Anthony K. Baker, and Carol A. Traynor. *Long Island Country Houses and Their Architects 1860-1940*. New York: W. W. Norton & Co., 1997.

Carlisle, Jay Freeborn, Sr. - East Islip - *Rosemary*
East Islip Historical Society has photographs of the estate.
Frances Loeb Library, Graduate School of Design, Harvard University, Cambridge, MA, has photographs of the estate.
Art Property of the Late Mr. & Mrs. Jay F. Carlisle Comprising the Entire Contents of Their County Home "Rosemary" East Islip, Long Island, NY. New York: Parke-Bernet Galleries, Inc., 1938. auction catalog.
Havemeyer, Harry W. *Along the Great South Bay From Oakdale to Babylon, the Story of a Summer Spa, 1840 to 1940*. Mattituck, NY: Amereon House, 1996.
Howell, E. W. *Noted Long Island Homes*. Babylon, NY: E. W. Howell Co., 1933.
Mackay, Robert B., Anthony K. Baker, and Carol A. Traynor. *Long Island Country Houses and Their Architects 1860-1940*. New York: W. W. Norton & Co., 1997.

Ceballos, Juan Manuel, Sr. - Bay Shore - *Brookhurst Farm*
Byrnes, Horace W. *Pictorial Bay Shore and Vicinity: A Souvenir*. privately printed, 1903.
Havemeyer, Harry W. *Along the Great South Bay From Oakdale to Babylon, the Story of a Summer Spa, 1840 to 1940*. Mattituck, NY: Amereon House, 1996.
Spinzia, Raymond E. and Judith A. Spinzia. *Long Island's Prominent North Shore Families: Their Estates and Their Country Homes*. vols. I, II. College Station, TX: VirtualBookworm, 2006, revised 2019.

Clarkson, William Kemble - Bay Shore
Byrnes, Horace W. *Pictorial Bay Shore and Vicinity: A Souvenir*. privately printed, 1903.
Mackay, Robert B., Anthony K. Baker, and Carol A. Traynor. *Long Island Country Houses and Their Architects 1860-1940*. New York: W. W. Norton & Co., 1997.
Picturesque Babylon, Bay Shore and Islip. New York: Mercantile Illustrating Co., 1894.

Conover, Daniel Denice - Bay Shore
Byrnes, Horace W. *Pictorial Bay Shore and Vicinity: A Souvenir*. privately printed, 1903.
Havemeyer, Harry W. *Along the Great South Bay From Oakdale to Babylon, the Story of a Summer Spa, 1840 to 1940*. Mattituck, NY: Amereon House, 1996.

Individual Bibliographic References

Cutting, William Bayard, Sr. - Great River - *Westbrook Farm*
Department of Landscape Architecture Documents Collection, University of California, Berkeley, CA, has Beatrix Jones Farrand's landscape records.
East Islip Historical Society has photographs of the estate.
Frederick Law Olmsted National Historic Site, Brookline, MA, has the records of Olmsted's landscape commissions.
The Nassau County Photo Archive Center has photographs of the estate.
- *The Bayard Cutting Arboretum Near Heckscher State Park, Great River, Long Island.* Babylon, NY: Long Island State Park Commission, 1952.
- *Country Life in America* July 1934.
- Havemeyer, Harry W. *Along the Great South Bay From Oakdale to Babylon, the Story of a Summer Spa, 1840 to 1940.* Mattituck, NY: Amereon House, 1996.
- Mackay, Robert B., Anthony K. Baker, and Carol A. Traynor. *Long Island Country Houses and Their Architects 1860-1940.* New York: W. W. Norton & Co., 1997.
- Moreland, Caroline. *Iris Origo: Marchesa of Val d-Orcia.* Boston: David R. Godine, 2002.
- Origo, Iris. *Images and Shadows: Part of a Life.* New York: Harcourt, Brace, Jovanovich, Inc., 1970.
- Roussos, George. "A History and Description of William Bayard Cutting and his Country House *Westbrook*, Great River." Board of Trustees and the Long Island State Park and Recreation Commission, 1984.
- Sclare, Liisa and Donald. *Beaux-Arts Estates: A Guide to the Architecture of Long Island.* New York: The Viking Press, 1980.
- Spinzia, Raymond E. and Judith A. Spinzia. *Long Island's Prominent North Shore Families: Their Estates and Their Country Homes.* vols. I, II. College Station, TX: VirtualBookworm, 2006, revised 2019.

Dick, John Henry - Islip - *Allen Winden Farm*
The Nassau County Photo Archive Center has photographs of the estate.
- Havemeyer, Doris Dick. *Memoirs of a Lifetime, 1890-1976.* Unpublished manuscript in the possession of the family.
- Havemeyer, Harry W. *Along the Great South Bay From Oakdale to Babylon, the Story of a Summer Spa, 1840 to 1940.* Mattituck, NY: Amereon House, 1996.
- Havemeyer, Harry W. *Merchants of Williamsburg: Frederick C. Havemeyer, Jr., William Dick, John Mollenhauer, Henry O. Havemeyer.* privately printed, 1989.
- Hopkins, Alfred. *Modern Farm Buildings.* New York: McBride, Nast & Co., 1913.
- Howell, E. W. *Noted Long Island Homes.* Babylon, NY: E. W. Howell Co., 1933.
- Mackay, Robert B., Anthony K. Baker, and Carol A. Traynor. *Long Island Country Houses and Their Architects 1860-1940.* New York: W. W. Norton & Co., 1997.
- Rania, Mildred. *Irvin Dick – William Dick and Allied Families.* privately printed, 1966.

Dick, William - Islip - *Allen Winden Farm*
The Nassau County Photo Archive Center has photographs of the estate.
- Havemeyer, Doris Dick. *Memoirs of a Lifetime, 1890-1976.* Unpublished manuscript in the possession of the family.
- Havemeyer, Harry W. *Along the Great South Bay From Oakdale to Babylon, the Story of a Summer Spa, 1840 to 1940.* Mattituck, NY: Amereon House, 1996.
- Havemeyer, Harry W. *Merchants of Williamsburg: Frederick C. Havemeyer, Jr., William Dick, John Mollenhauer, Henry O. Havemeyer.* privately printed, 1989.
- Hopkins, Alfred. *Modern Farm Buildings.* New York: McBride, Nast & Co., 1913.
- Howell, E. W. *Noted Long Island Homes.* Babylon, NY: E. W. Howell Co., 1933.
- Mackay, Robert B., Anthony K. Baker, and Carol A. Traynor. *Long Island Country Houses and Their Architects 1860-1940.* New York: W. W. Norton & Co., 1997.
- Rania, Mildred. *Irvin Dick – William Dick and Allied Families.* privately printed, 1966.

Dick, William Karl - Islip - *Allen Winden Farm*
The Nassau County Photo Archive Center has photographs of the estate.
- Havemeyer, Doris Dick. *Memoirs of a Lifetime, 1890-1976.* Unpublished manuscript in the possession of the family.
- Havemeyer, Harry W. *Along the Great South Bay From Oakdale to Babylon, the Story of a Summer Spa, 1840 to 1940.* Mattituck, NY: Amereon House, 1996.
- Havemeyer, Harry W. *Merchants of Williamsburg: Frederick C. Havemeyer, Jr., William Dick, John Mollenhauer, Henry O. Havemeyer.* privately printed, 1989.
- Hopkins, Alfred. *Modern Farm Buildings.* New York: McBride, Nast & Co., 1913.
- Howell, E. W. *Noted Long Island Homes.* Babylon, NY: E. W. Howell Co., 1933.

Individual Bibliographic References

Dick, William Karl - Islip - *Allen Winden Farm* (cont'd)
    Mackay, Robert B., Anthony K. Baker, and Carol A. Traynor. *Long Island Country Houses and Their Architects 1860-1940.* New York: W. W. Norton & Co., 1997.
    Rania, Mildred. *Irvin Dick – William Dick and Allied Families.* privately printed, 1966.

Dodson, Richard Wolford - Bayport
The Donald F. and Mildred Topp Othmer Library of Chemical History, Philadelphia, PA, has his papers.

Dodson, Robert Bowman - West Islip - *Kanonsioni*
Babylon Village Museum, Village of Babylon Historical and Preservation Society, Babylon, NY, has Harold Truesdel Paterson's landscape plans for *Kanonsioni*.
    American Architect and Building News, 1906
    Mackay, Robert B., Anthony K. Baker, and Carol A. Traynor. *Long Island Country Houses and Their Architects 1860-1940.* New York: W. W. Norton & Co., 1997.

Eaton, James Waterbury, Sr. - West Islip
The New York Public Library, Archives and Manuscripts Division, has his papers.

Ebinger, Walter D. - Bay Shore
The Library of Congress has photographs of his residence.

Ellis, George Augustus, Jr. - West Bay Shore - *Ardmore*
    Havemeyer, Harry W. *Along the Great South Bay From Oakdale to Babylon, the Story of a Summer Spa, 1840 to 1940.* Mattituck, NY: Amereon House, 1996.
    Ruther, Frederick. *Long Island Today.* Hicksville, NY: privately printed, 1909.

Fairchild, Julian Douglas - Bay Shore
    Byrnes, Horace W. *Pictorial Bay Shore and Vicinity: A Souvenir.* privately printed, 1903.
    Havemeyer, Harry W. *Along the Great South Bay From Oakdale to Babylon, the Story of a Summer Spa, 1840 to 1940.* Mattituck, NY: Amereon House, 1996.
    Mackay, Robert B., Anthony K. Baker, and Carol A. Traynor. *Long Island Country Houses and Their Architects 1860-1940.* New York: W. W. Norton & Co., 1997.
    Spinzia, Raymond E. and Judith A. Spinzia. *Long Island's Prominent North Shore Families: Their Estates and Their Country Homes.* vols. I, II. College Station, TX: VirtualBookworm, 2006, revised 2019.

Flint, Sherman - Islip - *Evershade*
Department of Landscape Architecture Documents Collection, University of California, Berkeley, CA, has Beatrix Jones Farrand's landscape records.
    Spinzia, Raymond E. and Judith A. Spinzia. *Long Island's Prominent North Shore Families: Their Estates and Their Country Homes.* vols. I, II. College Station, TX: VirtualBookworm, 2006, revised 2019.

Ford, Malcolm Webster, Sr. - Babylon - *My Fancy*
    Spinzia, Raymond E. and Judith A. Spinzia. *Long Island's Prominent North Shore Families: Their Estates and Their Country Homes.* vols. I, II. College Station, TX: VirtualBookworm, 2006, revised 2019.

Fortescue, Granville Roland - Bayport - *Wildholme*
Arlington National Cemetery, Arlington, VA, has Fortescue's military records.
    Havemeyer, Harry W. *Along the Great South Bay From Oakdale to Babylon, the Story of a Summer Spa, 1840 to 1940.* Mattituck, NY: Amereon House, 1996.
    Spinzia, Raymond E. "Those Other Roosevelts: The Fortescues." *The Freeholder* 11 (Summer 2006): 8-9, 16-22 and spinzialongislandestate.com.
    Spinzia, Raymond E. and Judith A. Spinzia. *Long Island's Prominent North Shore Families: Their Estates and Their Country Homes.* vols. I, II. College Station, TX: VirtualBookworm, 2006, revised 2019.

Foster, Jay Stanley - Babylon
Babylon Village Museum, Village of Babylon Historical and Preservation Society, Babylon, NY, has photographs of the estate.
    Picturesque Babylon, Bay Shore and Islip. New York: Mercantile Illustrating Co., 1894.

Frank, Emil Henry, Sr. - Bay Shore
    Byrnes, Horace W. *Pictorial Bay Shore and Vicinity: A Souvenir.* privately printed, 1903.
    Mackay, Robert B., Anthony K. Baker, and Carol A. Traynor. *Long Island Country Houses and Their Architects 1860-1940.* New York: W. W. Norton & Co., 1997.

Individual Bibliographic References

Gibb, Howard, Sr. - Islip
The Nassau County Photo Archive Center has photographs of the estate.
> Byrnes, Horace W. *Pictorial Bay Shore and Vicinity: A Souvenir.* privately printed, 1903.
> Havemeyer, Harry W. *Along the Great South Bay From Oakdale to Babylon, the Story of a Summer Spa, 1840 to 1940.* Mattituck, NY: Amereon House, 1996.
> Spinzia, Raymond E. and Judith A. Spinzia. *Long Island's Prominent North Shore Families: Their Estates and Their Country Homes.* vols. I, II. College Station, TX: VirtualBookworm, 2006, revised 2019.

Gibb, John - Islip - *Afterglow*
The Nassau County Photo Archive Center has photographs of the estate.
> Byrnes, Horace W. *Pictorial Bay Shore and Vicinity: A Souvenir.* privately printed, 1903.
> Havemeyer, Harry W. *Along the Great South Bay From Oakdale to Babylon, the Story of a Summer Spa, 1840 to 1940.* Mattituck, NY: Amereon House, 1996.
> Mackay, Robert B., Anthony K. Baker, and Carol A. Traynor. *Long Island Country Houses and Their Architects 1860-1940.* New York: W. W. Norton & Co., 1997.
> Spinzia, Raymond E. and Judith A. Spinzia. *Long Island's Prominent North Shore Families: Their Estates and Their Country Homes.* vols. I, II. College Station, TX: VirtualBookworm, 2006, revised 2019.

Green, Isaac Henry, II - Sayville - *Brookside*
> Currie, Constance Gibson. "Isaac H. Green, Long Island Architect and his Brookside." *Long Island Forum* 63 (Summer 2000):5-15

Guggenheim, Meyer Robert, Sr. - North Babylon - *Firenze Farm*
Library of Congress, Washington, DC, has a portion of Meyer Robert Guggenheim, Sr.'s correspondence in its Harry Frank Guggenheim collection.
The Town of Babylon, Office of Historic Services has photographs of the estate.
> Davis, John Hagg. *The Guggenheims: An American Epic.* New York: William Morrow & Co., Inc.,1978.
> Hoyt, Edwin P. *The Guggenheims and the American Dream.* New York: Funk & Wagnalls, 1967.
> Lomask, Milton. *Seed Money: The Guggenheim Story.* New York: Farrar, Straus & Co., 1964.
> O'Connor, Richard. *The Guggenheims: The Making of an American Dynasty.* New York: Covici Friede Publishers, 1937.
> Spinzia, Raymond E. and Judith A. Spinzia. *Long Island's Prominent North Shore Families: Their Estates and Their Country Homes.* vols. I, II. College Station, TX: VirtualBookworm, 2006, revised 2019.
> Tebbel, John. *An American Dynasty: The Story of the McCormicks, Medills and Pattersons.* New York: Greenwood Press, 1968.
> Unger, Irwin and Debi Unger. *The Guggenheims: A Family.* New York: Harper Collins Publishers, 2005.

Gulden, Charles, Sr. - Bay Shore - *Netherbay*
> Byrnes, Horace W. *Pictorial Bay Shore and Vicinity: A Souvenir.* privately printed, 1903.
> Havemeyer, Harry W. *Along the Great South Bay From Oakdale to Babylon, the Story of a Summer Spa, 1840 to 1940.* Mattituck, NY: Amereon House, 1996.

Haight, Gilbert Lawrence, Jr. - Amityville
> Howell, E. W. *Noted Long Island Homes.* Babylon, NY: E. W. Howell Co., 1933.

Harbeck, Charles Thomas - East Islip
Frederick Law Olmsted National Historic Site, Brookline, MA, has the records of Olmsted's landscape commissions.
> Havemeyer, Harry W. *Along the Great South Bay From Oakdale to Babylon, the Story of a Summer Spa, 1840 to 1940.* Mattituck, NY: Amereon House, 1996.

Havemeyer, Henry, Sr. - West Islip - *Sequatogue Farm*
> Byrnes, Horace W. *Pictorial Bay Shore and Vicinity: A Souvenir.* privately printed, 1903.
> Havemeyer, Harry W. *Along the Great South Bay From Oakdale to Babylon, the Story of a Summer Spa, 1840 to 1940.* Mattituck, NY: Amereon House, 1996.

Havemeyer, Henry Osborne - Islip - *Bayberry Point*
The Nassau County Photo Archive Center has photographs of the estate.
New York Metropolitan Museum of Art, NYC, has a portion of the Havemeyer art collection.
University of Michigan, Museum of Art, Ann Arbor, MI, has a portion of the Havemeyer art collection.
> Burnett, Robert N. "Henry Osborne Havemeyer." *Cosmopolitan* 34 (April 1903):701-704.
> Frelinghuysen, Alice Cooney. *Splendid Legacy: The Havemeyer Collection.* New York: New York Metropolitan Museum of Art, 1993.

Individual Bibliographic References

Havemeyer, Henry Osborne - Islip - *Bayberry Point* (cont'd)
    "Furnishings and Decorations From the Estate of Mrs. H. O. Havemeyer." New York: American Art Association and the Anderson Galleries, Inc., 1930. auction catalog
    Havemeyer, Harry W. *Along the Great South Bay From Oakdale to Babylon, the Story of a Summer Spa, 1840 to 1940*. Mattituck, NY: Amereon House, 1996.
    Havemeyer, Harry W. *Merchants of Williamsburg: Frederick C. Havemeyer, Jr., William Dick, John Mollenhauer, Henry O. Havemeyer*. privately printed, 1989.
    Havemeyer, Harry W. "The Story of Saxton Avenue." *Long Island Forum* Winter, February 1, 1990 and Spring, May 1, 1990.
    "Henry O. Havemeyer – Venice." *The New York Times Sunday Supplement* May 23, 1897:14.
    "The H. O. Havemeyer Collection." New York: New York Metropolitan Museum of Art Annual Report, 1958.
    H. O. Havemeyer Collection of Paintings, Prints, Sculpture, and Objects of Art. New York: New York Metropolitan Museum of Art, 1931. auction catalog
    Mackay, Robert B., Anthony K. Baker, and Carol A. Traynor. *Long Island Country Houses and Their Architects 1860-1940*. New York: W. W. Norton & Co., 1997.
    Rania, Mildred. *Irvin Dick – William Dick and Allied Families*. privately printed, 1966.
    Sternstein, Jerome L. "Corruption in the Gilded Age: Nelson W. Aldrich and the Sugar Trust" in *Capital Studies* (vol. 6) William Maury, ed. Washington, DC: Capitol Historical Society, 1978.
    Weitzenhoffer, Frances. *The Havemeyers: Impressionism Comes to America*. New York: Harry N. Abrams, Inc., 1986.

Havemeyer, Horace, Sr. - Bay Shore - *Olympic Point*
Frederick Law Olmsted National Historic Site, Brookline, MA, has the records of Olmsted's landscape commissions.
    Catlin, Daniel, Jr. *Good Work Well Done: The Sugar Business Career of Horace Havemeyer, 1903-1956*. privately printed, 1988.
    Havemeyer, Doris Dick. *Memoirs of a Lifetime, 1890-1976*. Unpublished manuscript in the possession of the family.
    Havemeyer, Harry W. *Along the Great South Bay From Oakdale to Babylon, the Story of a Summer Spa, 1840 to 1940*. Mattituck, NY: Amereon House, 1996.
    Havemeyer, Harry W. "The Story of Saxton Avenue." *Long Island Forum* Winter, February 1, 1990 and Spring, May 1, 1990.
    Hopkins, Alfred. *Modern Farm Buildings*. New York: McBride, Nast & Co., 1913.
    Impressionist Paintings and Drawings From the Estate of Doris D. Havemeyer. New York: Sotheby Park Bernet, Inc., 1983. auction catalog
    Mackay, Robert B., Anthony K. Baker, and Carol A. Traynor. *Long Island Country Houses and Their Architects 1860-1940*. New York: W. W. Norton & Co., 1997.
    Rania, Mildred. *Irvin Dick – William Dick and Allied Families*. privately printed, 1966.
    Spinzia, Raymond E. and Judith A. Spinzia. *Long Island's Prominent North Shore Families: Their Estates and Their Country Homes*. vols. I, II. College Station, TX: VirtualBookworm, 2006, revised 2019.
    Weitzenhoffer, Frances. *The Havemeyers: Impressionism Comes to America*. New York: Harry N. Abrams, Inc., 1986.

Havemeyer, Louisine Waldron Elder - Islip - *Bayberry Point*
[*see* H. O. Havemeyer entry]
The Nassau County Photo Archive Center has photographs of the estate.
New York Metropolitan Museum of Art, NYC, has a portion of the Havemeyer art collection.
University of Michigan, Museum of Art, Ann Arbor, MI, has a portion of the Havemeyer art collection.
    Frelinghuysen, Alice Cooney. *Splendid Legacy: The Havemeyer Collection*. New York: New York Metropolitan Museum of Art, 1993.
    "Furnishings and Decorations From the Estate of Mrs. H. O. Havemeyer." New York: American Art Association and the Anderson Galleries, Inc., 1930. auction catalog
    Havemeyer, Harry W. *Along the Great South Bay From Oakdale to Babylon, the Story of a Summer Spa, 1840 to 1940*. Mattituck, NY: Amereon House, 1996.
    Havemeyer, Louisine W. "The Prison Special, Memories of a Militant." *Scribner's Magazine* 71 (June 1922):665.
    Havemeyer, Louisine W. "The Waking of Women." Typescript of speech by Louisine W. Havemeyer, 1924-1925. In possession of family.
    Havemeyer, Louisine W. *Sixteen to Sixty: Memoirs of a Collector*. New York: Ursus Press, 1993. [reprint]
    Havemeyer, Louisine W. "The Suffrage Torch, Memories of a Militant." *Scribner's Magazine* 71 (May 1922):528.
    Hourwich, Rebecca. "An Appreciation of Mrs. Havemeyer." *Equal Rights* 14 (February 2, 1929).

Individual Bibliographic References

Havemeyer, Louisine Waldron Elder - Islip - *Bayberry Point* (cont'd)
    Mackay, Robert B., Anthony K. Baker, and Carol A. Traynor. *Long Island Country Houses and Their Architects 1860-1940.* New York: W. W. Norton & Co., 1997.
    Rania, Mildred. *Irvin Dick – William Dick and Allied Families.* privately printed, 1966.
    Spinzia, Raymond E. and Judith A. Spinzia. *Long Island's Prominent North Shore Families: Their Estates and Their Country Homes.* vols. I, II. College Station, TX: VirtualBookworm, 2006, revised 2019.
    Weitzenhoffer, Frances. *The Havemeyers: Impressionism Comes to America.* New York: Harry N. Abrams, Inc., 1986.

Hawkins, William Elton - Copaigue - Wild Goose Farm
The Town of Babylon, Office of Historic Services has photographs of the estate.

Hollins, Harry Bowly, Sr. - East Islip - *Meadow Farm*
Frederick Law Olmsted National Historic Site, Brookline, MA, has the records of Olmsted's landscape commissions.
    Havemeyer, Harry W. *Along the Great South Bay From Oakdale to Babylon, the Story of a Summer Spa, 1840 to 1940.* Mattituck, NY: Amereon House, 1996.
    Mackay, Robert B., Anthony K. Baker, and Carol A. Traynor. *Long Island Country Houses and Their Architects 1860-1940.* New York: W. W. Norton & Co., 1997.
    Old Oakdale History, Volume I. Oakdale, NY: William K. Vanderbilt Historical Society of Dowling College, 1983.

Hoppin, Bayard Cushing - East Islip
    Havemeyer, Harry W. *Along the Great South Bay From Oakdale to Babylon, the Story of a Summer Spa, 1840 to 1940.* Mattituck, NY: Amereon House, 1996.
    Spinzia, Raymond E. and Judith A. Spinzia. *Long Island's Prominent North Shore Families: Their Estates and Their Country Homes.* vols. I, II. College Station, TX: VirtualBookworm, 2006, revised 2019.

Housman, Arthur Albert - North Babylon;
                                    West Islip
    Fifth Avenue Art Galleries. *Estates of the Late Arthur A. Housman Banker and Member of NY Stock Exchange, by Order of Benjamin F. Feiner, Esq., Attorney for Executrix and George Rutledge Gibson by Order of Executors.* London: Forgotten Books, reprint 2018.

Hubbard, Harmanus Barkulo - Bay Shore - *Oakhurst*
    Architectural Record, 1897.
    Mackay, Robert B., Anthony K. Baker, and Carol A. Traynor. *Long Island Country Houses and Their Architects 1860-1940.* New York: W. W. Norton & Co., 1997.

Hubbs, Charles Francis - West Islip - *Sequatogue Farm*
    Byrnes, Horace W. *Pictorial Bay Shore and Vicinity: A Souvenir.* privately printed, 1903.
    Spinzia, Raymond E. and Judith A. Spinzia. *Long Island's Prominent North Shore Families: Their Estates and Their Country Homes.* vols. I, II. College Station, TX: VirtualBookworm, 2006, revised 2019.

Huber, Frederick Max, Sr. - Bay Shore
    Havemeyer, Harry W. *Along the Great South Bay From Oakdale to Babylon, the Story of a Summer Spa, 1840 to 1940.* Mattituck, NY: Amereon House, 1996.
    Howell, Liz. *Continuity: Biography 1819-1934.* Sister Bay, WI: The Dragonsbreath Press, 1993.

Hulse, The Reverend William Warren - Bay Shore - *Elysian Views*
    Byrnes, Horace W. *Pictorial Bay Shore and Vicinity: A Souvenir.* privately printed, 1903.

Hutton, Edward Francis - Bay Shore
    Byrnes, Horace W. *Pictorial Bay Shore and Vicinity: A Souvenir.* privately printed, 1903.
    Catalogue of a Fine Collection of Calligraphic Books and Manuscripts: The Property of Mrs. E. F. Hutton of New York City. London: Southeby & Co., 1922. auction catalog
    Carpenter, Donna Sammons and John Feloni. *The Fall of the House of Hutton.* New York: Henry Holt & Co., 1989.
    Havemeyer, Harry W. *Along the Great South Bay From Oakdale to Babylon, the Story of a Summer Spa, 1840 to 1940.* Mattituck, NY: Amereon House, 1996.
    Spinzia, Raymond E. and Judith A. Spinzia. *Long Island's Prominent North Shore Families: Their Estates and Their Country Homes.* vols. I, II. College Station, TX: VirtualBookworm, 2006, revised 2019.

Individual Bibliographic References

Hutton, Edward Francis - Bay Shore (cont'd)
    Sterngold, James. *Burning Down the House: How Greed, Deceit, and Bitter Revenge Destroyed E. F. Hutton*. New York: Summit Books, 1990.
    Steven, Mark. *Sudden Death: The Rise and Fall of E. F. Hutton*. New York: New American Library, 1989.

Hutton, Franklyn Laws - Bay Shore
    Byrnes, Horace W. *Pictorial Bay Shore and Vicinity: A Souvenir.* privately printed, 1903.
    Carpenter, Donna Sammons and John Feloni. *The Fall of the House of Hutton*. New York: Henry Holt & Co., 1989.
    Eldridge, Mona. *In Search of a Prince: My Life With Barbara Hutton*. London: Sedgwick & Jackson, 1988.
    Havemeyer, Harry W. *Along the Great South Bay From Oakdale to Babylon, the Story of a Summer Spa, 1840 to 1940*. Mattituck, NY: Amereon House, 1996.
    Heyman, C. David. *Poor Little Rich Girl: The Life and Legend of Barbara Hutton*. Secaucus, NJ: Lyle Stuart, Inc., 1984.
    Spinzia, Raymond E. and Judith A. Spinzia. *Long Island's Prominent North Shore Families: Their Estates and Their Country Homes. vols. I, II*. College Station, TX: VirtualBookworm, 2006, revised 2019.
    Sterngold, James. *Burning Down the House: How Greed, Deceit, and Bitter Revenge Destroyed E. F. Hutton*. New York: Summit Books, 1990.
    Steven, Mark. *Sudden Death: The Rise and Fall of E. F. Hutton*. New York: New American Library, 1989.
    Van Rensselaer, Philip. *Million Dollar Baby: An Intimate Portrait of Barbara Hutton*. New York: G. P. Putnam's Sons, 1979.

Hyde, Henry Baldwin, II - Fire Island
National Archives and Records Administration, Washington, DC, John E. Taylor Collection, has information on Hyde's activities in the OSS.
    Beard, Patricia. *After the Ball: Gilded Age Secrets, Boardroom Betrayals, and the Party That Ignited the Great Wall Street Scandal of 1905*. New York: Harper Collins, 2003.
    Brown, Anthony Cave. *The Last Hero: Wild Bill Donovan*. New York: Time Books. 1980.
    Casey, William. *The Secret War Against Hitler*. Washington, DC: Regnery Gateway, 1988.
    Hyde, Henry Baldwin, II. Unpublished manuscript of his experiences as Chief of OSS in Algeria.
    Persico, Joseph E. Piercing the Reich. New York: The Viking Press, 1979.
    Spinzia, Raymond E. "Society Chameleons: Long Island's Gentlemen Spies." *The Nassau County Historical Society Journal* 55 (2000):27-38 and www.spinzialongislandestates.com

Hyde, Henry Baldwin, Sr. - West Bay Shore - *The Oaks*
Frederick Law Olmsted National Historic Site, Brookline, MA, has the records of Olmsted's landscape commissions.
    Alexander, William. *A Brief History of the Equitable Society: Seventy Years of Progress and Public Service*. New York: The Equitable Life Assurance Society of the United States, 1929.
    Bailey, Carlyle R. *The Equitable Life Assurance Society of the United States 1859-1964*. (2 vols.) New York: The Equitable Life Assurance Society of the United States, 1967.
    Beard, Patricia. *After the Ball: Gilded Age Secrets, Boardroom Betrayals, and the Party That Ignited the Great Wall Street Scandal of 1905*. New York: Harper Collins, 2003.
    Country Life in America July 1903.
    Havemeyer, Harry W. *Along the Great South Bay From Oakdale to Babylon, the Story of a Summer Spa, 1840 to 1940*. Mattituck, NY: Amereon House, 1996.
    Henry Baldwin Hyde: A Biographical Sketch. New York: The DeVinne Press, 1901.
    Mackay, Robert B., Anthony K. Baker, and Carol A. Traynor. *Long Island Country Houses and Their Architects 1860-1940*. New York: W. W. Norton & Co., 1997.
    Old Oakdale History, Volume I. Oakdale, NY: William K. Vanderbilt Historical Society of Dowling College, 1983.
    Parkinson, Thomas Ignatius. *"Equitable" of the U. S.; What Henry B. Hyde Started in 1859*. New York: Newcome Society in North America, 1950.
    Rousmaniere, John. *The Life and Times of the Equitable*. New York: The Stinehour Press, 1995.
    Town and Country October 1903
    Town and Country, 1923.

Hyde, James Hazen - West Bay Shore - *The Oaks*
Baker Library, Harvard University, Cambridge, MA, has a portion of Hyde's papers.
Cooper Union Museum, The Smithsonian National Museum of Design, NYC, has a portion of Hyde's art collection.
Frederick Law Olmsted National Historic Site, Brookline, MA, has the records of Olmsted's landscape commissions.
The Long Island Museum of American Art, History and Carriages in Stony Brook, has Hyde's coach.
New York Historical Society, NYC, has a portrait of Hyde, photographs, and a portion of his papers.

Individual Bibliographic References

Hyde, James Hazen - West Bay Shore - *The Oaks* (cont'd)
    Alexander, William. *A Brief History of the Equitable Society: Seventy Years of Progress and Public Service*. New York: The Equitable Life Assurance Society of the United States, 1929.
    Amory, Cleveland. *Who Killed Society?* New York: Harper Brothers, Publishers, 1960.
    Baker, Paul R. *Stanny: The Gilded Life of Stanford White*. New York: The Free Press, 1989.
    Bailey, Carlyle R. *The Equitable Life Assurance Society of the United States 1859-1964*. (2 vols.) New York: The Equitable Life Assurance Society of the United States, 1967.
    Beard, Patricia. *After the Ball: Gilded Age Secrets, Boardroom Betrayals, and the Party That Ignited the Great Wall Street Scandal of 1905*. New York: Harper Collins, 2003.
    Beebee, Lucius. *The Big Spenders*. Garden City: Doubleday & Co., Inc., 1966.
    Beebee, Lucius. *Mansions On Rails: The Folklore of the Private Railway Car*. Berkeley, CA: Howell-North, 1959.
    Birmingham, Stephen. *Our Crowd: The Great Jewish Families of New York*. New York: Harper & Row Publishers, 1967.
    Birmingham, Stephen. *Real Lace: America's Irish Rich*. New York: Harper & Row Publishers, 1973.
    Brough, James. *Princess Alice: A Biography of Alice Roosevelt Longworth*. Boston: Little, Brown & Co., 1975.
    Cooper Union for the Advancement of Science and Art, New York – Museum for the Arts Decoration. "Four Continents From the Collection of James Hazen Hyde." New York: Cooper Union Museum, 1961.
    Country Life in America July 1903.
    "Fine French Furniture and Objects of Art, Paintings, Tapestries, Rugs: Property of Patrice Hennasy, Mrs. Myron Schafer, Mrs. Eileen Allen, James Hazen Hyde and Other Owners." New York: Parke-Bernet Galleries, Inc., 1949. auction catalog
    Gerard, James W. *My First Eighty-Three Years in America: The Memoirs of James W. Gerard*. Garden City: Doubleday & Co., Inc., 1951.
    Gregory, Alexis. *Families of Fortune: Life in the Gilded Age*. New York: Rizzoli International Publications, 1993.
    Harvey, George. *Henry Clay Frick: The Man*. privately printed, 1936.
    Havemeyer, Harry W. *Along the Great South Bay From Oakdale to Babylon, the Story of a Summer Spa, 1840 to 1940*. Mattituck, NY: Amereon House, 1996.
    Howell, Liz. *Continuity: Biography 1819-1934*. Sister Bay, WI: The Dragonsbreath Press, 1993.
    Kennan, George. *E. H. Harriman: A Biography*. Boston: Houghton Mifflin, 1922.
    Lehr, Elizabeth Drexel. *"King Lehr" and the Gilded Age*. Philadelphia: J. B Lippincott Co., 1935.
    Logan, Andy. *The Man Who Robbed the Robber Barons*. New York: W. W. Norton & Co., Inc., 1965.
    Lundberg, Ferdinand. *America's 60 Families*. New York: The Vanguard Press, 1937.
    Mackay, Robert B., Anthony K. Baker, and Carol A. Traynor. *Long Island Country Houses and Their Architects 1860-1940*. New York: W. W. Norton & Co., 1997.
    Matz, Mary Jane. *The Many Lives of Otto Kahn*. New York: The Macmillan Company, 1963.
    Morris, Lloyd. *Incredible New York: High Life and Low Life of the Last Hundred Years*. New York: Random House, 1951.
    Myers, Gustavis. *The Ending of Hereditary American Fortune*. New York: Julian Messner, Inc., 1939.
    The New York Times July 27, 1959:25.
    Rousmaniere, John. *The Life and Times of the Equitable*. New York: The Stinehour Press, 1995.
    Swanberg, W. A. *Pulitzer*. New York: Charles Scribner's Sons, 1967.
    Town and County October 1903.
    Town and Country, 1923.
    Vanderbilt, Cornelius, Jr. *Queen of the Golden Age: The Fabulous Story of Grace Wilson Vanderbilt*. New York: McGraw-Hill Book Co., Inc., 1956.
    Weeks, George L., Jr. *Isle of Shells*. Islip, NY: Buys Brothers, Inc., 1965.

Hyde, Richard - West Bay Shore
    Byrnes, Horace W. *Pictorial Bay Shore and Vicinity: A Souvenir*. privately printed, 1903.
    Havemeyer, Harry W. *Along the Great South Bay From Oakdale to Babylon, the Story of a Summer Spa, 1840 to 1940*. Mattituck, NY: Amereon House, 1996.
    Mackay, Robert B., Anthony K. Baker, and Carol A. Traynor. *Long Island Country Houses and Their Architects 1860-1940*. New York: W. W. Norton & Co., 1997.

Johnson, Alfred Grima - *Enfin* - Islip
[*see* B. G. Johnson III entry]
Special Collections, Hill Memorial Library, Louisiana State University, Baton Rouge, Louisiana, has his family papers.

Individual Bibliographic References

Johnson, Aymar - East Islip - *Woodland*
East Islip Historical Society has photographs of the estate.
Frederick Law Olmsted National Historic Site, Brookline, MA, has the records of Olmsted's landscape commissions.
    Havemeyer, Harry W. *Along the Great South Bay From Oakdale to Babylon, the Story of a Summer Spa, 1840 to 1940.* Mattituck, NY: Amereon House, 1996.
    Mackay, Robert B., Anthony K. Baker, and Carol A. Traynor. *Long Island Country Houses and Their Architects 1860-1940.* New York: W. W. Norton & Co., 1997.

Johnson, Bradish, Jr. - East Islip - *Woodland*
East Islip Historical Society has photographs of the estate.
Frederick Law Olmsted National Historic Site, Brookline, MA, has the records of Olmsted's landscape commissions.
    Havemeyer, Harry W. *Along the Great South Bay From Oakdale to Babylon, the Story of Summer Spa, 1840 to 1940.* Mattituck, NY: Amereon House, 1996.
    Mackay, Robert B., Anthony K. Baker, and Carol A. Traynor. *Long Island Country Houses and Their Architects 1860-1940.* New York: W. W. Norton & Co., 1997.

Johnson, Bradish, Sr. - West Bay Shore - *Sans Souci*
Bradish Johnson Plantation Records 1819-1822 and Times Books for 1868 and 1880.
    Byrnes, Horace W. *Pictorial Bay Shore and Vicinity: A Souvenir.* privately printed, 1903.
    Gibson, Dennis A. *A Guide to the Microfilm Collection of Early Louisiana State Records, 1731-1903.* Lafayette, LA: The University of Southwestern Louisiana, 1970.
    Havemeyer, Harry W. *Along the Great South Bay From Oakdale to Babylon, the Story of a Summer Spa, 1840 to 1940.* Mattituck, NY: Amereon House, 1996.
    Lambert, Rick. "An Oral History of Whitney Plantation." Unpublished transcript of an oral interview of Anthony Tassis in March 1990. Louisiana Division of Historic Preservation.
    Mackay, Robert B., Anthony K. Baker, and Carol A. Traynor. *Long Island Country Houses and Their Architects 1860-1940.* New York: W. W. Norton & Co., 1997.
    Menn, Joseph Karl. *The Large Slaveholders of Louisiana – 1860.* New Orleans: Pelican Publishing Co., 1964.
    Picturesque Babylon, Bay Shore and Islip. New York: Mercantile Illustrating Co., 1894.

Johnson, Henry Meyer - West Bay Shore - *Sans Souci*
    Byrnes, Horace W. *Pictorial Bay Shore and Vicinity: A Souvenir.* privately printed, 1903.
    Havemeyer, Harry W. *Along the Great South Bay From Oakdale to Babylon, the Story of a Summer Spa, 1840 to 1940.* Mattituck, NY: Amereon House, 1996.
    Mackay, Robert B., Anthony K. Baker, and Carol A. Traynor. *Long Island Country Houses and Their Architects 1860-1940.* New York: W. W. Norton & Co., 1997.

Johnson, John Dean - Islip
Emory University Library, Atlanta, GA, Special Collections, has a log of the *Wanderer*.
Library of Congress, Washington, DC, has a file of material on the *Wanderer*.
National Archives, Washington, DC, has a register of the *Wanderer* dated June 1858.
    Calonius, Erik. *The Wanderer: The Last American Slave Ship and the Conspiracy That Set Its Sails.* New York: St Martin's Press, 2006.
    Wells, Gordon. *Port Jefferson: The Story of a Village.* Port Jefferson, NY: Historical Society of Greater Port Jefferson, 1985.
    Wells, Tom Henderson. *The Slave Ship Wanderer.* Athens, GA: University of Georgia Press, 1968.

Johnston, James Boorman - East Islip
Frederick Law Olmsted National Historic Site, Brookline, MA, has the records of Olmsted's landscape commissions.
    Havemeyer, Harry W. *Along the Great South Bay From Oakdale to Babylon, the Story of a Summer Spa, 1840 to 1940.* Mattituck, NY: Amereon House, 1996.

Jones, Frank Smith - Sayville - *Beechwold*
The Nassau County Photo Archive Center has photographs of the estate.
    Havemeyer, Harry W. *East on the Great South Bay: Sayville and Bayport 1860–1960.* Mattituck, NY: Amereon House, 2001.
    Mackay, Robert B., Anthony K. Baker, and Carol A. Traynor. *Long Island Country Houses and Their Architects 1860-1940.* New York: W. W. Norton & Co., 1997.

Knapp, Gladys Quarre - East Islip - *Brookwood*
[*see* T. J. Knapp entry]
    Knapp, David. *A Lady Undefined: From Carriage to Concorde.* Montgomery, AL: E-BookTime, LLC, 2009.

Individual Bibliographic References

Knapp, Harry Kearsarge, II - East Islip - *Creekside*
>Havemeyer, Harry W. *Along the Great South Bay From Oakdale to Babylon, the Story of a Summer Spa, 1840 to 1940.* Mattituck, NY: Amereon House, 1996.
>Howell, E. W. *Noted Long Island Homes.* Babylon, NY: E. W. Howell Co., 1933.
>Knapp, Edward Spring. *We Knapps Thought It Was Nice.* privately printed, 1940.
>Mackay, Robert B., Anthony K. Baker, and Carol A. Traynor. *Long Island Country Houses and Their Architects 1860-1940.* New York: W. W. Norton & Co., 1997.

Knapp, Harry Kearsarge, Sr. - East Islip - *Brookwood*
East Islip Historical Society has photographs of the estate.
The Nassau County Photo Archive Center has photographs of the estate.
>Havemeyer, Harry W. *Along the Great South Bay From Oakdale to Babylon, the Story of a Summer Spa, 1840 to 1940.* Mattituck, NY: Amereon House, 1996.
>Knapp, Edward Spring. *We Knapps Thought It Was Nice.* privately printed, 1940.
>Mackay, Robert B., Anthony K. Baker, and Carol A. Traynor. *Long Island Country Houses and Their Architects 1860-1940.* New York: W. W. Norton & Co., 1997.

Lemmerman, Fred C. - Bay Shore
>Byrnes, Horace W. *Pictorial Bay Shore and Vicinity: A Souvenir.* privately printed, 1903.
>Mackay, Robert B., Anthony K. Baker, and Carol A. Traynor. *Long Island Country Houses and Their Architects 1860-1940.* New York: W. W. Norton & Co., 1997.
>*Picturesque Babylon, Bay Shore and Islip.* New York: Mercantile Illustrating Co., 1894.

Litchfield, Electus Backus - Babylon - *Blythebourne*
The Town of Babylon, Office of Historic Services has photographs of the estate.

Lorillard, George Lyndes - Great River - *Westbrook Farm*
>Garland, John. "The Legacy and Fall of Westbrook Farms." M. S. thesis, Hofstra University, Hempstead, NY, 1994.
>Havemeyer, Harry W. *Along the Great South Bay From Oakdale to Babylon, the Story of a Summer Spa, 1840 to 1940.* Mattituck, NY: Amereon House, 1996.
>Mackay, Robert B., Anthony K. Baker, and Carol A. Traynor. *Long Island Country Houses and Their Architects 1860-1940.* New York: W. W. Norton & Co., 1997.
>Sclare, Liisa and Donald. *Beaux-Arts Estates: A Guide to the Architecture of Long Island.* New York: The Viking Press, 1980.
>Whittlock, Lavern A. "The Story of Westbrook." *Long Island Forum* September 1986.

McBurney, Dr. Malcolm - East Islip
Avery Architectural and Fine Arts Library, Columbia University, NYC has photographs of the estate.
East Islip Historical Society has photographs of the estate.
McIlwaine Collection, Avery Architectural and Fine Arts Library, Columbia University, NYC, has the architectural records of Delano and Aldrich.
>*Architectural Forum* 29 (August 1918).
>Havemeyer, Harry W. *Along the Great South Bay From Oakdale to Babylon, the Story of a Summer Spa, 1840 to 1940.* Mattituck, NY: Amereon House, 1996.
>Mackay, Robert B., Anthony K. Baker, and Carol A. Traynor. *Long Island Country Houses and Their Architects 1860-1940.* New York: W. W. Norton & Co., 1997.
>Noyes, Dorothy McBurney. *The World Is So Full of a Number of Things.* privately printed, 1956.

McClure, William - West Islip - *Clurella*
>Byrnes, Horace W. *Pictorial Bay Shore and Vicinity: A Souvenir.* privately printed, 1903.
>Havemeyer, Harry W. *Along the Great South Bay From Oakdale to Babylon, the Story of a Summer Spa, 1840 to 1940.* Mattituck, NY: Amereon House, 1996.

Moffitt, William Henry - Islip - *Beautiful Shore*
The Nassau County Photo Archive Center has photographs of the estate.
>Havemeyer, Harry W. *Along the Great South Bay From Oakdale to Babylon, the Story of a Summer Spa, 1840 to 1940.* Mattituck, NY: Amereon House, 1996.

Mollenhauer, John - Bay Shore
>Havemeyer, Harry W. *Along the Great South Bay From Oakdale to Babylon, the Story of a Summer Spa, 1840 to 1940.* Mattituck, NY: Amereon House, 1996.
>Havemeyer, Harry W. *Merchants of Williamsburg: Frederick C. Havemeyer, Jr., William Dick, John Mollenhauer, Henry O. Havemeyer.* privately printed, 1989.
>Rania, Mildred. *Irvin Dick – William Dick and Allied Families.* privately printed, 1966.

Individual Bibliographic References

Mollenhauer, John Adolph - Bay Shore - *Homeport*
    Havemeyer, Harry W. *Along the Great South Bay From Oakdale to Babylon, the Story of a Summer Spa, 1840 to 1940.* Mattituck, NY: Amereon House, 1996.
    Havemeyer, Harry W. *Merchants of Williamsburg: Frederick C. Havemeyer, Jr., William Dick, John Mollenhauer, Henry O. Havemeyer.* privately printed, 1989.
    Hopkins, Alfred. *Modern Farm Buildings.* New York: McBride, Nast & Co., 1913.
    Mackay, Robert B., Anthony K. Baker, and Carol A. Traynor. *Long Island Country Houses and Their Architects 1860-1940.* New York: W. W. Norton & Co., 1997.
    Picturesque Babylon, Bay Shore and Islip. New York: Mercantile Illustrating Co., 1894.
    Rania, Mildred. *Irvin Dick – William Dick and Allied Families.* privately printed, 1966.

Moses, Robert - Babylon
    Bard, Erwin W. *The Port of New York Authority.* New York: Columbia University Press, 1942.
    Caro, Robert A. *The Power Broker: Robert Moses and the Fall of New York.* New York: Alfred A. Knopf, Inc., 1974.
    Kieley, John B. *Moses on the Green.* Tuscaloosa, AL: University of Alabama Press, 1959.
    Krieg, Joann P., ed. *Robert Moses Single-Minded Genius.* Interlaken, NY: Heart of the Lakes Publishing, 1989.
    Lines, Jon J., Ellen L. Parker, and David C. Perry. *Building Twentieth Century Public Works Machine: Robert Moses and the Public Authority.* Chicago: The Institute of Public Works History, 1987.
    Mackay, Robert B., Anthony K. Baker, and Carol A. Traynor. *Long Island Country Houses and Their Architects 1860-1940.* New York: W. W. Norton & Co., 1997.
    Rodgers, Cleveland. *Robert Moses: Builder for Democracy.* New York: Henry Holt and Co., 1952.
    Spinzia, Raymond E. and Judith A. Spinzia. *Long Island's Prominent North Shore Families: Their Estates and Their Country Homes.* vols. I, II. College Station, TX: VirtualBookworm, 2006, revised 2019.

Myers, Nathaniel - Bay Shore
    Country Life in America, 1932.
    Mackay, Robert B., Anthony K. Baker, and Carol A. Traynor. *Long Island Country Houses and Their Architects 1860-1940.* New York: W. W. Norton & Co., 1997.

Nicholas, Harry Ingersoll, Sr. - North Babylon - *Virginia Farm*
    Havemeyer, Harry W. *Along the Great South Bay From Oakdale to Babylon, the Story of a Summer Spa, 1840 to 1940.* Mattituck, NY: Amereon House, 1996.
    Spinzia, Raymond E. and Judith A. Spinzia. *Long Island's Prominent North Shore Families: Their Estates and Their Country Homes.* vols. I, II. College Station, TX: VirtualBookworm, 2006, revised 2019.

Oakman, Walter George, Sr. - Islip
    Havemeyer, Harry W. *Along the Great South Bay From Oakdale to Babylon, the Story of a Summer Spa, 1840 to 1940.* Mattituck, NY: Amereon House, 1996.
    Mackay, Robert B., Anthony K. Baker, and Carol A. Traynor. *Long Island Country Houses and Their Architects 1860-1940.* New York: W. W. Norton & Co., 1997.
    Spinzia, Raymond E. and Judith A. Spinzia. *Long Island's Prominent North Shore Families: Their Estates and Their Country Homes.* vols. I, II. College Station, TX: VirtualBookworm, 2006, revised 2019.

O'Donohue, Charles Alfred - Bay Shore - *The Moorings*
    Byrnes, Horace W. *Pictorial Bay Shore and Vicinity: A Souvenir.* privately printed, 1903.
    Spinzia, Raymond E. and Judith A. Spinzia. *Long Island's Prominent North Shore Families: Their Estates and Their Country Homes.* vols. I, II. College Station, TX: VirtualBookworm, 2006, revised 2019.

Packer, Frederick Little - Brightwaters
Library of Congress, Washington, DC, has four of Packer's wartime posters.

Page, Walter Hines, Sr. - Bay Shore
    Byrnes, Horace W. *Pictorial Bay Shore and Vicinity: A Souvenir.* privately printed, 1903.
    Hendrick, Burton J. The *Life and Letters of Walter H. Page* (3 vols.). Garden City: Doubleday, Page & Company, 1925.
    Spinzia, Raymond E. and Judith A. Spinzia. *Long Island's Prominent North Shore Families: Their Estates and Their Country Homes.* vols. I, II. College Station, TX: VirtualBookworm, 2006, revised 2019.
    Spinzia, Raymond E. and Judith A. Spinzia. *Long Island's Prominent Families in the Town of Hempstead: Their Estates and Their Country Homes.* College Station, TX: VirtualBookworm, 2010.

Individual Bibliographic References

Parsons, Schuyler Livingston, Jr. - Islip - *Pleasure Island*
    Havemeyer, Harry W. *Along the Great South Bay From Oakdale to Babylon, the Story of a Summer Spa, 1840 to 1940*. Mattituck, NY: Amereon House, 1996.
    Parsons, Schuyler Livingston, Jr. *Untold Friendships*. Boston, MA: Houghton Mifflin Co., 1955.

Parsons, Schuyler Livingston, Sr. - Islip - *Whileaway*
The Nassau County Photo Archive Center has photographs of the estate.
    Havemeyer, Harry W. *Along the Great South Bay From Oakdale to Babylon, the Story of a Summer Spa, 1840 to 1940*. Mattituck, NY: Amereon House, 1996.
    Parsons, Schuyler Livingston, Jr. *Untold Friendships*. Boston, MA: Houghton Mifflin Co., 1955.

Peck, William L., Sr. - Bay Shore
    Byrnes, Horace W. *Pictorial Bay Shore and Vicinity: A Souvenir*. privately printed, 1903.

Peters, Harry Twyford, Sr. - Islip - *Windholme Farm*
Olin Library, Cornell University, Ithaca, NY, has Ellen Biddle Shipman's landscape records.
Shelburne Museum, Shelburne, VT, has items from the Peterses' home including: a trade sign with a three-dimensional horse with blanket; 1820 English mochaware pepper shakers and bowl; a brass teapot with tilt-top; 1829 English candle reflectors, inkstand, and candle stand; English Staffordshire decorated cow creamers; 1840 English Staffordshire rabbit.
    American Architect and Building News, 1916.
    Country Life In America, 1912.
    Havemeyer, Harry W. *Along the Great South Bay From Oakdale to Babylon, the Story of a Summer Spa, 1840 to 1940*. Mattituck, NY: Amereon House, 1996.
    Hopkins, Alfred. *Modern Farm Buildings*. New York: McBride, Nast & Co., 1913.
    Mackay, Robert B., Anthony K. Baker, and Carol A. Traynor. *Long Island Country Houses and Their Architects 1860-1940*. New York: W. W. Norton & Co., 1997.
    Peters, Harry Twyford. *American on Stone; The Other Printmakers to the American People; A Chronicle of American Lithography Other Than That of Currier and Ives, From Its Beginning Shortly Before 1820 to Years When Commercial Single-Stone Hand-Colored Lithography Disappeared From the American Scene*. Garden City: Doubleday, Doran & Co., Inc., 1931.
    Peters, Harry Twyford. *California on Stone*. Garden City: Doubleday, Doran & Co., 1935.
    Peters, Harry Twyford. *Currier and Ives: Printmakers to the American People*. Garden City: Doubleday, Doran & Co., Inc., 1942.
    Presentation of the New York Historical Society's Gold Medal for Achievement in History to Harry Twyford Peters, Dec. 8, 1947. New York: New York Historical Society, 1948.

Peters, Samuel Twyford - Islip - *Windholme Farm*
Olin Library, Cornell University, Ithaca, NY, has Ellen Biddle Shipman's landscape records.
    American Architect and Building News, 1916.
    Country Life in America, 1912.
    Havemeyer, Harry W. *Along the Great South Bay From Oakdale to Babylon, the Story of a Summer Spa, 1840 to 1940*. Mattituck, NY: Amereon House, 1996.
    Hopkins, Alfred. *Modern Farm Buildings*. New York: McBride, Nast & Co., 1913.
    Mackay, Robert B., Anthony K. Baker, and Carol A. Traynor. *Long Island Country Houses and Their Architects 1860-1940*. New York: W. W. Norton & Co., 1997.
    Spinzia, Raymond E. and Judith A. Spinzia. *Long Island's Prominent North Shore Families: Their Estates and Their Country Homes*. vols. I, II. College Station, TX: VirtualBookworm, 2006, revised 2019.

Pinkerton, Allan, II - Bay Shore
    Havemeyer, Harry W. *Along the Great South Bay From Oakdale to Babylon, the Story of a Summer Spa, 1840 to 1940*. Mattituck, NY: Amereon House, 1996.
    Horan, James D. *The Pinkertons: The Detective Dynasty That Made History*. New York: Crown Publishers, Inc., 1967.
    Mackay, Robert B., Anthony K. Baker, and Carol A. Traynor. *Long Island Country Houses and Their Architects 1860-1940*. New York: W. W. Norton & Co., 1997.
    Spinzia, Raymond E. and Judith A. Spinzia. *Long Island's Prominent North Shore Families: Their Estates and Their Country Homes*. vols. I, II. College Station, TX: VirtualBookworm, 2006, revised 2019.

Placide, Henry - Babylon
The Davis Library, University of California, Davis, CA, has seventeen signed working scripts of Placide.

Individual Bibliographic References

Plumb, James Ives - Islip - *Shadowbrook*
The Nassau County Photo Archive Center has photographs of the estate.

Prince, John Dyneley, II - Islip
Olin Library, Cornell University, Ithaca, NY, has Ellen Biddle Shipman's landscape records.
    American Architect and Building News, 1916.
    Hopkins, Alfred. *Modern Farm Buildings*. New York: McBride, Nast & Co., 1913.

Reid, John Robert - Babylon - *The Towers*
The Town of Babylon, Office of Historic Services has photographs of the estate.

Remsen, Phoenix, Sr. - West Islip
The Town of Babylon, Office of Historic Services has photographs of the estate.

Robert, Christopher Rhinelander, Jr. - Oakdale - *Peperidge Hall*
Library of Congress, Washington, DC, has photographs of the estate.
The Nassau County Photo Archive Center has photographs of the estate.
    Havemeyer, Harry W. *Along the Great South Bay From Oakdale to Babylon, the Story of a Summer Spa, 1840 to 1940*. Mattituck, NY: Amereon House, 1996.
    Long Island Forum February 1948.
    Long Island Forum December 1957.
    Long Island Forum December 1978.
    Mackay, Robert B., Anthony K. Baker, and Carol A. Traynor. *Long Island Country Houses and Their Architects 1860-1940*. New York: W. W. Norton & Co., 1997.
    The Old Oakdale History, Volume II: Era of Elegance, Part I. Oakdale, NY: William K. Vanderbilt Historical Society of Dowling College, 1993.
    Town and Country December 1921.

Roosevelt, John Ellis - Sayville - *Meadow Croft*
Office of Suffolk County Historian, Great River, NY, has photographs, a printed booklet, and historical specifications of the estate collected for historical designation.
Theodore Roosevelt Association, Oyster Bay, NY, has John Ellis Roosevelt's scrapbook.
    Harmond, Richard P. and Donald H. Weinhardt. "John Ellis Roosevelt of Meadow Croft." *Long Island Forum* 51 (Fall 1988).
    Havemeyer, Harry W. *East on the Great South Bay: Sayville and Bayport 1860–1960*. Mattituck, NY: Amereon House, 2001.
    Mackay, Robert B., Anthony K. Baker, and Carol A. Traynor. *Long Island Country Houses and Their Architects 1860-1940*. New York: W. W. Norton & Co., 1997.
    "Monograph on Meadow Croft, the Former John E. Roosevelt Estate, Sayville, Long Island." Suffolk County Parks Department, Division of Cultural and Historic Services, 1984. unpublished booklet.
    Spinzia, Raymond E. and Judith A. Spinzia. *Long Island's Prominent North Shore Families: Their Estates and Their Country Homes*. vols. I, II. College Station, TX: VirtualBookworm, 2006, revised 2019.

Roosevelt, Robert Barnwell, Jr. - Sayville - *The Lilacs*
Office of Suffolk County Historian, Great River, NY, has vertical file material and photographs of the estate.
    Havemeyer, Harry W. *East on the Great South Bay: Sayville and Bayport 1860–1960*. Mattituck, NY: Amereon House, 2001.
    Mackay, Robert B., Anthony K. Baker, and Carol A. Traynor. *Long Island Country Houses and Their Architects 1860-1940*. New York: W. W. Norton & Co., 1997.
    Spinzia, Raymond E. and Judith A. Spinzia. *Long Island's Prominent North Shore Families: Their Estates and Their Country Homes*. vols. I, II. College Station, TX: VirtualBookworm, 2006, revised 2019.

Roosevelt, Robert Barnwell, Sr. - Bayport - *Lotos Lake*
Office of Suffolk County Historian, Great River, NY, has vertical file material and photographs of the estate.
    Bleyer, Bill. "The Forgotten Roosevelt." *Newsday* October 6, 1985:10-12, 25.
    Harmond, Richard P. "Lost and Found." *Long Island Historical Journal* 7 (Fall 1994):125-9.
    Harmond, Richard P. "Robert Barnwell Roosevelt and the Early Conservation Movement." *Theodore Roosevelt Association Journal* 14 (2).
    Harmond, Richard P. and Donald W. Weinhardt. "Robert Barnwell Roosevelt on the Great South Bay." *Long Island Forum* 50 (August/September 1987):164-71.
    Havemeyer, Harry W. *East on the Great South Bay: Sayville and Bayport 1860–1960*. Mattituck, NY: Amereon House, 2001.

Individual Bibliographic References

Roosevelt, Robert Barnwell, Sr. - Bayport - *Lotos Lake* (cont'd)
    Spinzia, Raymond E. "Those Other Roosevelts: The Fortescues." *The Freeholder* 11 (Summer 2006):
        8-9, 16-22 and spinzialongislandislandestates.com.
    Spinzia, Raymond E. and Judith A. Spinzia. *Long Island's Prominent North Shore Families: Their*
        Estates and Their Country Homes. vols. I, II. College Station, TX: VirtualBookworm, 2006, revised
        2019.

Russell, William Hamilton, Jr. - Islip - *Le Rozel*
The Avery Architectural and Fine Arts Library, Columbia University, NYC, has his architectural drawings and papers.

Schwenke, Oscar Louis, III - Bay Shore
    The American Architect May 14, 1919, has photograph of his residence.

Shea, David J. - Sayville - *Wyndemoor*
The Nassau County Photo Archive Center has photographs of the estate.

Simonds, William Robinson - Sayville - *Wyndemoor*
The Nassau County Photo Archive Center has photographs of the estate.

Smith, Charles Robinson - Bay Shore
Manuscripts and Archive Repository, Yale University, New Haven, CT, has his papers.
    Mackay, Robert B., Anthony K. Baker, and Carol A. Traynor. *Long Island Country Houses and Their*
        Architects 1860-1940. New York: W. W. Norton & Co., 1997.
    Picturesque Babylon, Bay Shore and Islip. New York: Mercantile Illustrating Co., 1894.

Stanchfield, John Barry, Sr. - Islip - *Afterglow*
The Nassau County Photo Archive Center has photographs of the estate.
    Byrnes, Horace W. *Pictorial Bay Shore and Vicinity: A Souvenir.* privately printed, 1903.
    Mackay, Robert B., Anthony K. Baker, and Carol A. Traynor. *Long Island Country Houses and Their*
        Architects 1860-1940. New York: W. W. Norton & Co., 1997.
    Spinzia, Raymond E. and Judith A. Spinzia. *Long Island's Prominent North Shore Families: Their*
        Estates and Their Country Homes. vols. I, II. College Station, TX: VirtualBookworm, 2006, revised
        2019.

Stewart, James - Great River
[*see* Truslow entry]
The Nassau County Photo Archive Center has photographs of the estate.
    Mackay, Robert B., Anthony K. Baker, and Carol A. Traynor. *Long Island Country Houses and Their*
        Architects 1860-1940. New York: W. W. Norton & Co., 1997.

Swan, Alden Smith - Islip - *Orowoc*
    Frost, Josephine C. *Ancestors of Alden Smith Swan and His Wife Mary Althea Farwell.* The Hill Press, 1923.

Taylor, George Campbell - East Islip
East Islip Historical Society has photographs of the estate.
The Long Island State Parks Commission has photographs of the estate.
    Havemeyer, Harry W. *Along the Great South Bay From Oakdale to Babylon, the Story of a Summer Spa,*
        1840 to 1940. Mattituck, NY: Amereon House, 1996.
    Mackay, Robert B., Anthony K. Baker, and Carol A. Traynor. *Long Island Country Houses and Their*
        Architects 1860-1940. New York: W. W. Norton & Co., 1997.

Terry, William Hazard - Sayville
    Architecture and Building April 23, 1887, has a sketch of the house

Thorne, Landon Ketchum, Sr. - West Bay Shore - *Thorneham*
Frances Loeb Library, Graduate School of Design, Harvard University, Cambridge, MA, has photographs of the
  estate.
Innocenti and Webel landscape records are located at their office in Locust Valley.
Queensborough Public Library, Long Island Collection, Jamaica, NY, has Thorne family records including
  genealogical notes c. 1920-1929.
    Architectural Annual, 1929. New York: Architectural League of New York, 1929.
    Havemeyer, Harry W. *Along the Great South Bay From Oakdale to Babylon, the Story of a Summer Spa,*
        1840 to 1940. Mattituck, NY: Amereon House, 1996.
    Hilderbrand, Gary R. *Making a Landscape of Continuity: The Practice of Innocenti & Webel.* Cambridge,
        MA: Harvard University Graduate School of Design, 1997.
    Howell, E. W. *Noted Long Island Homes.* Babylon, NY: E. W. Howell Co., 1933.

Individual Bibliographic References

Thorne, Landon Ketchum, Sr. - West Bay Shore - *Thorneham* (cont'd)
    Mackay, Robert B., Anthony K. Baker, and Carol A. Traynor. *Long Island Country Houses and Their Architects 1860-1940.* New York: W. W. Norton & Co., 1997.
    Sclare, Liisa and Donald. *Beaux-Arts Estates: A Guide to the Architecture of Long Island.* New York: The Viking Press, 1980.

Thurber, Frederick Charles - Bay Shore
    Architectural Record, 1897.
    Mackay, Robert B., Anthony K. Baker, and Carol A. Traynor. *Long Island Country Houses and Their Architects 1860-1940.* New York: W. W. Norton & Co., 1997.

Timmermann, Henry Gerhard - Islip - *Breeze Lawn*
The Nassau County Photo Archive Center has photographs of the estate.
    Byrnes, Horace W. *Pictorial Bay Shore and Vicinity: A Souvenir.* privately printed, 1903.
    Mackay, Robert B., Anthony K. Baker, and Carol A. Traynor. *Long Island Country Houses and Their Architects 1860-1940.* New York: W. W. Norton & Co., 1997.

Truslow, Frederick Cuming - Great River - *Questover Lodge*
The Nassau County Photo Archive Center has photographs of the estate.
    Mackay, Robert B., Anthony K. Baker, and Carol A. Traynor. *Long Island Country Houses and Their Architects 1860-1940.* New York: W. W. Norton & Co., 1997.

Tucker, Charles A. - Islip
    Byrnes, Horace W. *Pictorial Bay Shore and Vicinity: A Souvenir.* privately printed, 1903.
    Havemeyer, Harry W. *Along the Great South Bay From Oakdale to Babylon, the Story of a Summer Spa, 1840 to 1940.* Mattituck, NY: Amereon House, 1996.
    Hopkins, Alfred. *Modern Farm Buildings.* New York: McBride, Nast & Co., 1913.

Turnbull, George R. - West Islip - *The Pines*
    Byrnes, Horace W. *Pictorial Bay Shore and Vicinity: A Souvenir.* privately printed, 1903.
    Mackay, Robert B., Anthony K. Baker, and Carol A. Traynor. *Long Island Country Houses and Their Architects 1860-1940.* New York: W. W. Norton & Co., 1997.

General References to Vanderbilt Family

[*see also* references to individual Vanderbilt family members]

Biltmore Estate, Asheville, NC, has material collected from all Vanderbilt families in their archives.
Melville Library, SUNY Stony Brook, LI, has the National Woman's Party papers on microfilm.
New York State Library, Albany, NY, has Cornelius Vanderbilt's six–volume will.
Newport Historical Society, Newport, RI, has material relating to Woman Suffrage events held in Newport by Alva Vanderbilt Belmont.
The Preservation Society of Newport County, Newport, RI, has Alva Vanderbilt's personal scrapbook of newspaper clippings about the March 26, 1883, Masque Ball held at 660 Fifth Avenue, New York City.
Queens College Library, Historical Collection, Flushing, NY, has Vanderbilt family records, including 1699 tax rolls and a deposit of 1790–1840 material.
Sewall–Belmont House [National Woman's Party Headquarters], Washington, DC, has scrapbooks pertaining to Alva Vanderbilt Belmont and photographs of the Vanderbilt family.
Suffolk County Vanderbilt Museum and Planetarium archives, Centerport, LI, has photographs of the Vanderbilt family and an album of photographs of Alva Vanderbilt Belmont's house *Beacon Towers*, taken by Samuel H. Gottscho. The Gottscho collection is also in the Avery Architectural and Fine Arts Library, Columbia University, NYC, and in the Library of Congress, Washington, DC. Also included in the collection at the Vanderbilt Museum is an album with Alva Vanderbilt Belmont's funeral photographs and newspaper clippings.
    Allen, Armin Brand. *The Cornelius Vanderbilts of the Breakers: A Family Retrospective May 27 – October 1, 1995.* Newport: The Preservation Society of Newport County, 1995.
    Andrews, Wayne. *The Vanderbilt Legend: The Story of the Vanderbilt Family, 1794–1940.* New York: Harcourt, Brace and Co., 1941.
    Auchincloss, Louis. *The Vanderbilt Era: Profile of a Gilded Age.* New York: Charles Scribner's Sons, 1989.
    Baker, Paul. *Richard Morris Hunt.* Cambridge: The MIT Press, 1980.
    Beebee, Lucius. *The Big Spenders.* Garden City: Doubleday & Co., Inc., 1966.
    Belmont, Alva Vanderbilt. "Are Women Really Citizens?" *Good Housekeeping* September 1931.
    Belmont, Alva Vanderbilt. "Belief in Women Is Belief in Women's Suffrage." *Women's Magazine* December, 1909.
    Belmont, Alva Vanderbilt. "How Can Woman Get the Suffrage?" *The Independent* 31 (March 1910).
    Belmont, Alva Vanderbilt. "Jewish Women in Public Affairs." *American Citizen* May 1913.

Individual Bibliographic References

General References to Vanderbilt Family (cont'd)

Belmont Alva Vanderbilt. "The Liberation of a Sex." *Hearst's Magazine* April 1913.

Belmont Alva Vanderbilt. "New Standards for Business Women." *Business Woman's Magazine* January 1915.

Belmont, Alva Vanderbilt. *One Month's Log of the Seminole*. New York: privately printed, 1916.

Belmont, Alva Vanderbilt. Foreword to article by Christable Pankhurst, "Story of the Woman's War." *Good Housekeeping* November 1913.

Belmont, Alva Vanderbilt. "Unpublished 1917 Autobiography of Alva Vanderbilt Belmont." In Wood Collection, Huntington Library, San Marino, California.

Belmont, Alva Vanderbilt. "Unpublished 1933 Autobiography of Alva Vanderbilt Belmont." In Matilda Young Papers, Special Collections Department, William R. Perkins Library, Duke University, Durham, North Carolina.

Belmont, Alva Vanderbilt. "What the Woman's Party Wants." *Collier's* 23 (December 1922).

Belmont, Alva Vanderbilt. "Why I Am a Suffragist." *The World To–Day* October 1911.

Belmont, Alva Vanderbilt. "Woman's Right to Govern Herself." *North American Review* 190 (November 1909).

Belmont, Alva Vanderbilt. "Woman Suffrage as It Looks To–Day." *The Forum* March 1910.

Belmont, Alva Vanderbilt. "Women as Dictators." *Ladies Home Journal* September 1922.

"Belmont to Sell Belcourt." *New York Herald Tribune* December 30, 1908. [Newport estate]

"Brookholt on the Market." *The New York Times* January 6, 1909:1. [Uniondale estate]

Burden, Shirley. *The Vanderbilts in My Life: A Personal Memoir*. New Haven: Ticknor & Fields, 1981.

"Buys Chateau in France: Mrs. O. H. P. Belmont Plans to Live Abroad, Newport Hears." *The New York Times* September 4, 1926:5.

Field, Frederick Vanderbilt. *From Right to Left: An Autobiography*. Westport, CT: L. Hill, 1983.

Foreman, John and Robbe Pierce Stimson. *The Vanderbilts and the Gilded Age: Architectural Aspirations, 1879–1901*. New York: St. Martin's Press, 1991.

Fowler, Marian. *In a Gilded Cage: From Heiress to Duchess*. New York: St. Martin's Press, 1994.

Gavan, Terrence. *The Newport Barons*. Newport: Pineapple Publications, 1988.

Geidel, Peter. "Alva E. Belmont: A Forgotten Feminist." Ph.D. dissertation, Columbia University, 1993.

Goldsmith, Barbara. *Little Gloria . . . Happy At Last*. New York: Alfred A. Knopf, 1980.

Kaiser, Harvey H. *Great Camps of the Adirondacks*. Boston: David R. Godine, 1982.

Keeler, Rebecca T. "Alva Belmont: Exacting Benefactor for Women's Rights." Ph.D. dissertation, University of South Alabama, 1987.

King, Robert B. *The Vanderbilt Homes*. New York: Rizzoli International Publications, Inc., 1989.

Lane, Wheaton. *Commodore Vanderbilt: An Epic of the Steam Age*. New York: Alfred A. Knopf, 1942.

MacColl, Gail and Carol McD. Wallace. *To Marry an English Lord: Or, How Anglomania Really Got Started*. New York: Workman Publishing, 1989.

MacDowell, Dorothy K. *Commodore Vanderbilt and His Family: A Biographical Account of the Descendants of Cornelius and Sophia Johnson Vanderbilt*. privately printed by Dorothy K. MacDowell, 1700 Fifth Avenue W., Hendersonville, NC., 1989.

"Mrs. Belmont's Funeral." *The New York Times* January 27, 1933.

"Mrs. O. H. P. Belmont Buys a Lighthouse." *The New York Times* February 1, 1924:19.

"Mrs. O. H. P. Belmont Dies at Paris Home." *The New York Times* January 26, 1933.

The Old Oakdale History, Volume I. Oakdale, NY: William K. Vanderbilt Historical Society of Dowling College, 1983.

The Old Oakdale History, Volume II: Era of Elegance, Part I. Oakdale, NY: William K. Vanderbilt Historical Society of Dowling College, 1993.

Patterson, Jerry E. *The Vanderbilts*. New York: Harry N. Abrams, Inc., Publishers, 1989.

Rector, Margaret Hayden. *Alva, That Vanderbilt–Belmont Woman*. Wickford, RI: The Dutch Island Press, 1992.

Sloane, Florence Adele. *Maverick In Mauve*. Garden City: Doubleday & Co., Inc., 1983.

Smith, Arthur D. *Commodore Vanderbilt: An Epic of American Achievement*. New York: Robert M. McBride & Co., 1927.

Spinzia, Raymond E. "In Her Wake: The Story of Alva Smith Vanderbilt Belmont." *The Long Island Historical Journal* 6 (Fall 1993):96–105 and www.spinzialongislandestates.com.

Spinzia, Raymond E. and Judith A. Spinzia. *Long Island's Prominent North Shore Families: Their Estates and Their Country Homes. vols. I, II*. College Station, TX: VirtualBookworm, 2006, revised 2019.

Stasz, Clarice. *The Vanderbilt Women: Dynasty of Wealth, Glamour and Tragedy*. New York: St. Martin's Press, 1991.

Stein, Susan R. *The Architecture of Richard Morris Hunt*. Chicago: The University of Chicago Press, 1986.

Individual Bibliographic References

General References to Vanderbilt Family (cont'd)

Swanberg, W. A. *Whitney Father, Whitney Heiress.* New York: Charles Scribner's Sons, 1980.

"To Build Belmont Hospital: Mrs. O. H. P. Belmont the Sponsor for One as a Memorial." *The New York Times* September 17, 1909:1.

Vanderbilt, Arthur T. *Fortune's Children: The Fall of the House of Vanderbilt.* New York: William Morrow & Co., Inc., 1989.

Vanderbilt, Cornelius, Jr. *Farewell to Fifth Avenue.* New York: Simon & Schuster, Inc., 1935.

Vanderbilt, Cornelius, Jr. *Man of the World: My Life on Five Continents.* New York: Crown Publishers, Inc., 1959.

Vanderbilt, Cornelius, Jr. *Queen of the Golden Age: The Fabulous Story of Grace Wilson Vanderbilt.* New York: McGraw–Hill Book Co., Inc., 1956.

Vanderbilt, Gloria. *Black Knight, White Knight.* New York: Alfred A. Knopf, 1987.

Vanderbilt, Gloria. *Once Upon a Time.* New York: Alfred A. Knopf, 1985.

Vanderbilt, Gloria Morgan and Lady Thelma Furness. *Double Exposure: A Twin Autobiography.* New York: David McKay Co., Inc., 1958.

Vanderbilt, Gloria Morgan. *Without Prejudice.* New York: E. P. Dutton, 1936.

Van Rensselaer, Philip. *The Vanderbilt Women.* Chicago: Playboy Press, 1978.

Vichers, Hugo. *Gladys: Duchess of Marlborough.* New York: Holt, Rinehart & Winston, 1979.

"Belmont to Sell Belcourt." *New York Herald Tribune* December 30, 1908. [Newport estate]

"Want Wall Removed: Hempstead Board Denies Mrs. Belmont's Right to Fence Beach." *The New York Times* September 20, 1918:15.

Vanderbilt, William Kissam, Sr. - Oakdale - *Idlehour*

American Institute of Architects, Washington, DC, has architectural sketches of *Idlehour*.

Biltmore Estate, Ashville, NC, has material collected from all Vanderbilt families in their archives.

Culver Pictures, Hollywood, CA, has photographs of *Idlehour*.

Dowling College Library, Historical Collection, Oakdale, NY, has a photographic archive of the estate and family.

Library of Congress, Manuscript Division, Washington, DC, has a portion of Marlborough Papers.

The Long Island Museum of American Art, History and Carriages in Stony Brook has Vanderbilt's Chariot D'Orsay carriage.

The New York Historical Society, NYC, has the log of Vanderbilt's yacht *Valiant*.

Octagon Museum of American Architectural Foundation, Prints and Drawings Collection, Washington. DC, has photographs of the original *Idlehour*.

Queens College Library, Historical Collection, Flushing, NY, has Vanderbilt family records, including 1699 tax rolls and a deposit of 1790-1840 material.

Suffolk County Vanderbilt Museum and Planetarium archives, Centerport, LI, has photographs of the Vanderbilt family and an album of photographs of Alva Vanderbilt Belmont's house *Beacon Towers,* taken by Samuel H. Gottscho. The Gottscho collection is also in the Avery Architectural and Fine Arts Library, Columbia University, NYC, and in the Library of Congress, Washington, DC. Also included in the collection at the Vanderbilt Museum is an album with Alva Vanderbilt Belmont's funeral photographs and newspaper clippings.

"The Alva." *Historic Preservation* August 6, 1892.

Architectural Record October–December 1895.

Balsan, Consuelo Vanderbilt. *The Glitter and the Gold.* New York: Harper & Brothers, 1952.

Beard, Patricia. *After the Ball: Gilded Age Secrets, Boardroom Betrayals, and the Party That Ignited the Great Wall Street Scandal of 1905.* New York: Harper Collins, 2003.

Belmont, Alva Vanderbilt. One Month's Log of the Seminole. New York: privately printed, 1916.

Belmont, Alva Vanderbilt. "Unpublished 1917 Autobiography of Alva Vanderbilt Belmont" In Wood Collection. Huntington Library, San Marino, CA.

Belmont, Alva Vanderbilt. "Unpublished 1933 Autobiography of Alva Vanderbilt Belmont" In Matilda Young Papers, Special Collections Department, William R. Perkins Library, Duke University, Durham, NC.

Brough, James. *Consuelo: Portrait of an American Heiress.* New York: Coward, McCann & Geoghegan, Inc., 1979.

"Burial in Britain for Mrs. Balsan." *New York Times* December 12, 1964.

Havemeyer, Harry W. *East on the Great South Bay: Sayville and Bayport 1860–1960.* Mattituck, NY: Amereon House, 2001.

"*Idle Hour* [*Idlehour*]." *Locust Valley Leader* May 25, 1979.

"*Idle Hour* [*Idlehour*] Art Sale Yields $132,962.50." *New York Herald Tribune* May 1, 1926.

"*Idle Hour* [*Idlehour*] Art to Be Sold." *New York Herald Tribune* March 18, 1926.

"*Idle Hour* [*Idlehour*] Bought by Realty Operators." *New York Herald Tribune* January 7, 1926.

Individual Bibliographic References

Vanderbilt, William Kissam, Sr. - Oakdale - *Idlehour* (cont'd)
"Idle Hour [*Idlehour*] Development Brochure," exclusive sales agents E. A. White Organization, 225 West 34th Street, NYC, for Edmund G. and Charles F. Burke, Inc., owners, 146 Pierrepont St., Brooklyn, NY.
"*Idle Hour* [*Idlehour*]: The Estate of William K. Vanderbilt." *Architectural Record* 13 (May 1903).
"*Idle Hour* [*Idlehour*]: The Estate of William K. Vanderbilt." *Architectural Record* June 1903.
"*Idle Hour* [*Idlehour*] Treasures Bring $34,290 at Sale." *New York Herald* Tribune April 30, 1926.
"*Idle Hour* [*Idlehour*]: The William K. Vanderbilt, Sr. Estate." *Gold Coast* June 1981.
Indiana Limestone Company. "The W. K. Vanderbilt Home: An Example of Exquisitely Carved Gray Indiana Limestone." Bedford, IN: Indiana Limestone Co., 1929. [refers to New York City house]
Kahn, E. J. "A Reporter at Large: A Place to Think (Peace Haven)." *New Yorker* March 16, 1940.
Mackay, Robert B., Anthony K. Baker, and Carol A. Traynor. *Long Island Country Houses and Their Architects 1860-1940*. New York: W. W. Norton & Co., 1997.
Marlborough, Duchess of [Consuelo Vanderbilt Balsan]. "Hostels for Women." *The Nineteenth Century and After* 1911:858–66.
Marlborough, Duchess of [Consuelo Vanderbilt Balsan]. "The Position of Woman," Parts 2, 3, 10. *North American Review* 89 (1909):180–93, 351–59, 11–24.
Marlborough, Duchess of [Consuelo Vanderbilt Balsan]. "Saving the Children." Lady Priestly Memorial Lecture, National Health Society, June 29, 1916.
Marilyn Estates, Inc. "*Idle Hour* [*Idlehour*] Mansion Built by W. K. Vanderbilt: Located at Oakdale, Long Island, Offered for Immediate Sale or Lease." New York: Marilyn Estates, Inc., 1936.
Maxwell, Elsa. *R.S.V.P.: Elsa Maxwell's Own Story*. Boston: Little Brown and Co., 1954.
Oakdale Club: A Residential Club Located at Oakdale Long Island. privately printed, nd.
Old Oakdale History, Volume I. Oakdale, NY: William K. Vanderbilt Historical Society of Dowling College, 1983.
Old Oakdale History, Volume II: Era of Elegance, Part I. Oakdale, NY: William K. Vanderbilt Historical Society of Dowling College, 1993.
Prost, L. H. "*Collection de Madame et du Colonel Balsan* (Paris: c. 1930). Sale Catalogue of the Estate of Lady Sarah Consuelo Spencer–Churchill." Doyle, New York, 2001.
Rector, Margaret Hayden. *Alva, That Vanderbilt Woman: Her Story as She Might Have Told It*. Wickford, RI: The Dutch Island Press, 1991.
Sclare, Liisa and Donald Sclare. *Beaux-Arts Estates: A Guide to the Architecture of Long Island*. New York: The Viking Press, 1980.
Spinzia, Raymond E. "In Her Wake: The Story of Alva Smith Vanderbilt Belmont." *The Long Island Historical Journal* 6 (Fall 1993):96–105 and www.spinzialongislandestates.com.
Spinzia, Raymond E., Judith A. Spinzia, and Kathryn E. Spinzia. *A Guide to New York's Suffolk and Nassau Counties*. New York: Hippocrene Books, 1991 (revised).
Spinzia, Raymond E. and Judith A. Spinzia. *Long Island's Prominent North Shore Families: Their Estates and Their Country Homes*. vols. I, II. College Station, TX: VirtualBookworm, 2006, revised 2019.
Stuart, Amanda Mackenzie. *Consuelo and Alva Vanderbilt: The Story of a Daughter and a Mother in the Gilded Age*. New York: Harper Collins Publishers, 2005.
"Vanderbilt Sues *Idle Hour* [*Idlehour*] Buyers." *New York Herald Tribune* December 12, 1923.
Van Pelt, John V. "A Monograph of the William K. Vanderbilt House, Richard Morris Hunt Architect," *Architectural Record* September 1925. [discusses New York City house]
"When *Idle Hour* [*Idlehour*] was Peace Haven." *Long Island Forum* October and November 1980.

Wagstaff, Dr. Alfred, Sr. - West Islip - *Tahlulah*
Queensborough Public Library, Long Island Collection, Jamaica, NY, has records for Christ Episcopal Church [known locally as the "Wagstaff Church"], West Islip.
Havemeyer, Harry W. *Along the Great South Bay From Oakdale to Babylon, the Story of a Summer Spa, 1840 to 1940*. Mattituck, NY: Amereon House, 1996.
"Hanging Out: Stereographic Prints From the Collection of Samuel Wagstaff, Jr., at the J. Paul Getty Museum, October 13 through November 11, 1984." Providence, RI: Bell Gallery, List Art Center, Brown University, 1984.

Wagstaff, Samuel Jones, Jr. - West Islip
[*see* S. J. Wagstaff entry]
The Archives of American Art, Smithsonian Institution, Washington, DC, has his personal papers.
The J. Paul Getty Museum, Los Angeles, CA, has his photography collection.

Weekes, Harold Hathaway - Islip - *Wereholme*
Office of the Suffolk County Historian has photographs of the estate.
Original architects' model of *Wereholme* is currently located in the house.

Individual Bibliographic References

Weekes, Harold Hathaway - Islip - *Wereholme* (cont'd)
 Havemeyer, Harry W. *Along the Great South Bay From Oakdale to Babylon, the Story of a Summer Spa, 1840 to 1940*. Mattituck, NY: Amereon House, 1996.
 Mackay, Robert B., Anthony K. Baker, and Carol A. Traynor. *Long Island Country Houses and Their Architects 1860-1940*. New York: W. W. Norton & Co., 1997.
 Spinzia, Raymond E. and Judith A. Spinzia. *Long Island's Prominent North Shore Families: Their Estates and Their Country Homes*. vols. I, II. College Station, TX: VirtualBookworm, 2006, revised 2019.

Weld, Philip Balch - Bay Shore
 Byrnes, Horace W. *Pictorial Bay Shore and Vicinity: A Souvenir*. privately printed, 1903.
 Spinzia, Raymond E. and Judith A. Spinzia. *Long Island's Prominent North Shore Families: Their Estates and Their Country Homes*. vols. I, II. College Station, TX: VirtualBookworm, 2006, revised 2019.

Welles, Benjamin Sumner, III - Islip - *Welles House*
Franklin Delano Roosevelt Library, Hyde Park, NY, has a portion of Benjamin Sumner Welles III's papers.
 Gellman, Irwin F. *Secret Affairs: FDR, Cordell Hull, and Sumner Welles*. New York: Enigma Books, 2002.
 Spinzia, Raymond E. "Sumner Welles: Brilliance and Tragedy." *The Freeholder* 9 (Winter 2005):8-9, 22 and www.spinzialongislandestates.com.
 Spinzia, Raymond E. and Judith A. Spinzia. *Long Island's Prominent North Shore Families: Their Estates and Their Country Homes*. vols. I, II. College Station, TX: VirtualBookworm, 2006, revised 2019.
 Welles, Benjamin. *Sumner Welles: FDR's Global Strategist*. New York: St. Martin's Press, 1997.

Whitney, William Collins - Islip
Library of Congress, Washington, DC, has William Collins Whitney's papers.
The Nassau County Photo Archive Center has photographs of his Westbury estate.
 "The Fabled Past: The Whitneys of Westbury." *The North Shore Journal* 13 (May 27, 1982) n.p.
 "Furniture & Works of Art – Architectural Elements of the Residence of the Late Helen Hay Whitney, 972 Fifth Avenue, New York." New York: Parke–Bernet Galleries, Inc., 1946. auction catalog [New York City house]
 Hirsh, Mark D. *William C. Whitney: Modern Warwick*. New York: Dodd, Mead & Co., 1948.
 Hoyt, Edwin P. *The Whitneys: An Informal Portrait, 1635–1975*. New York: Weybright & Talley Publishers, 1976.
 Klepper, Michael. *The Wealthy 100: From Benjamin Franklin to Bill Gates – A Ranking of the Richest Americans Past and Present*. Secaucus, NJ: The Citadel Press, 1996.
 McKim, Mead & White. *A Monograph of the Work of McKim, Mead & White 1879–1915*. New York: DaCapo Press, 1985. [New York City house]
 Spinzia, Raymond E. and Judith A. Spinzia. *Long Island's Prominent North Shore Families: Their Estates and Their Country Homes*. vols. I, II. College Station, TX: VirtualBookworm, 2006, revised 2019.
 Swanberg, W. A. *Whitney Father, Whitney Heiress*. New York: Charles Scribner's Sons, 1980.

Wray, William Henry - Bay Shore - *Whileaway*
 Byrnes, Horace W. *Pictorial Bay Shore and Vicinity: A Souvenir*. privately printed, 1903.
 Mackay, Robert B., Anthony K. Baker, and Carol A. Traynor. *Long Island Country Houses and Their Architects 1860-1940*. New York: W. W. Norton & Co., 1997.
 Picturesque Babylon, Bay Shore and Islip. New York: Mercantile Illustrating Co., 1894.

Wright, Dr. Arthur Mullen - Islip - *Afterglow*
The Nassau County Photo Archive Center has photographs of the estate.
 Byrnes, Horace W. *Pictorial Bay Shore and Vicinity: A Souvenir*. privately printed, 1903.
 Mackay, Robert B., Anthony K. Baker, and Carol A. Traynor. *Long Island Country Houses and Their Architects 1860-1940*. New York: W. W. Norton & Co., 1997.
 Spinzia, Raymond E. and Judith A. Spinzia. *Long Island's Prominent North Shore Families: Their Estates and Their Country Homes*. vols. I, II. College Station, TX: VirtualBookworm, 2006, revised 2019.

*Aymar Johnson estate, Woodland,
hallway*

*Frederick Gilbert Bourne estate, Indian Neck Hall,
1907 Aeolian pipe organ*

Biographical Sources Consulted

Biographical Dictionaries Master Index 1975–1976. Detroit: Gale Research Co., 1975.

Biography and Genealogy Master Index 1981–1985. Detroit: Gale Research Co., 1985.

Biography and Genealogy Master Index 1986–1990. Detroit: Gale Research Co., 1990.

Biography and Genealogy Master Index 1991–1995. Detroit: Gale Research Co., 1995.

Brooklyn Daily Eagle Online 1841-1902, Internet.

Current Biography Yearbook. New York: The H. W. Wilson Co. [selected volumes]

Dow Jones News Internet Retrieval.

The Eagle and Brooklyn: The Record of the Progress of the Brooklyn Daily Eagle. 2 vols. Brooklyn, NY: The Brooklyn Eagle, 1893.

Levy, Felice, ed. *Obituaries on File.* New York: Facts on File, 1979.

Lexis Nexis Academic Universe, Internet.

Malone, Dumas, ed. *Dictionary of American Biography.* NY: Charles Scribner's Sons, 1935.

The National Cyclopaedia of American Biography. Clifton, NJ: James T. White & Co., 1984.

Newsday Internet Retrieval.

New York State's Prominent and Progressive Men. 2 vols. New York: New York Tribune, 1900.

The New York Times Index. New York: The New York Times. [annual obituaries from 1979–1997]

The New York Times Obituaries Index, vol. 1, 1858–1968. New York: The New York Times, 1970.

The New York Times Obituaries Index, vol. 2, 1969–1978. New York: The New York Times, 1980.

Prominent Families of New York. New York: The Historical Co., 1898.

Standard and Poor's Register of Corporations, Directors and Executives. Charlottesville, VA: Standard and Poors, Inc. [selected volumes]

Who's Who in America. Chicago: Marquis Who's Who, Inc. [selected volumes]

Who's Who in Finance and Industry. Chicago: Marquis Who's Who, Inc. [selected volumes]

Who's Who in New York. New York: Lewis Historical Publishing Co. [selected volumes]

Who's Who in New York City and State. New York: L. R. Hamersly Co., 1904–1960. [selected volumes]

Who's Who in the East. Chicago: Marquis Who's Who, Inc. [selected volumes]

Who's Who of American Women. Chicago: Marquis Who's Who, Inc. [selected volumes]

Who Was Who in America with World Notables. New Providence, NJ: Marquis Who's Who, Inc. [selected volumes]

Maps Consulted

George Lyndes Lorillard estate, *Westbrook Farm*

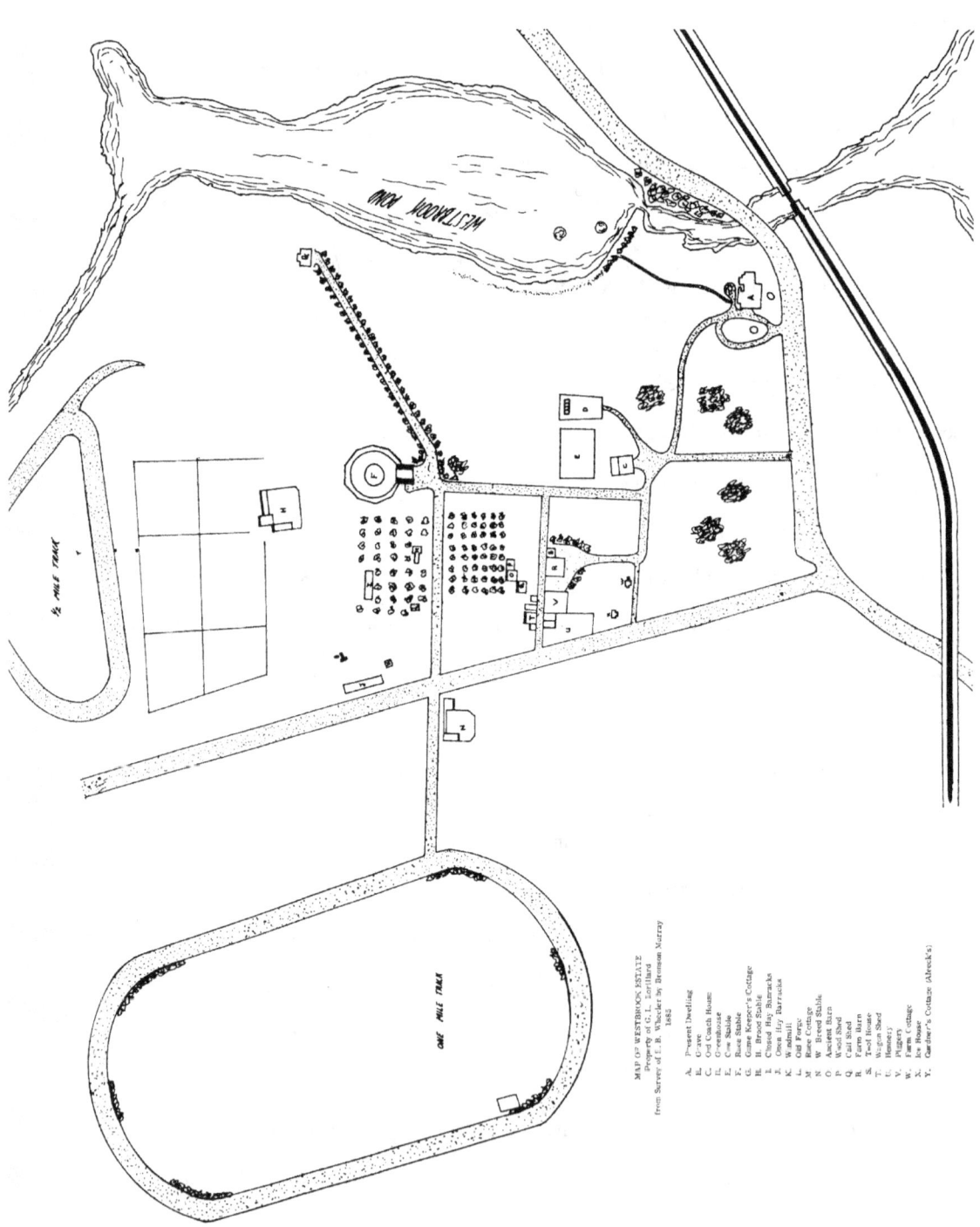

Maps Consulted

Atlas of Babylon, Bay Shore and Islip. Wendelken and Co., 1888.

Atlas of the Ocean Shore of Suffolk County. E. Belcher Hyde, Inc., 1915.

Dolph's Street, Road and Land Ownership Map of Suffolk County. New York: Dolph & Stewart, 1929.

Hagstrom Map of Western Suffolk County. Maspeth, NY: Hagstrom Map Co., Inc., 1996.

Hagstrom's Street, Road and Landownership Atlas of Suffolk County, Long Island, Western Half. New York: Hagstrom Co., Inc., 1944.

Real Estate Reference Map of a Part of Suffolk County, Long Island, N.Y.: Comprising of the Townships [Towns] of Huntington, Smithtown, Babylon and Islip. New York: E. Belcher Hyde, Inc. Engineers Publishers, 1931.

William Kissam Vanderbilt, Sr. estate, *Idlehour*

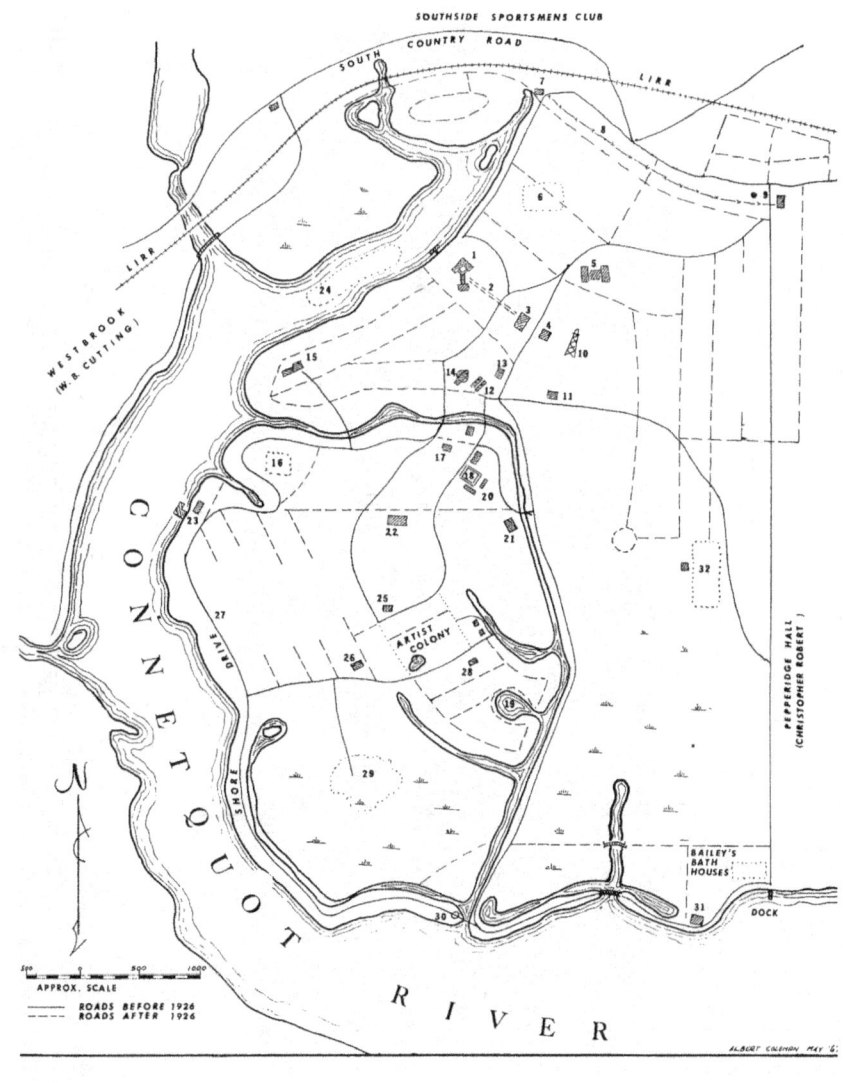

1. MANSION	9. EAST GATE LODGE & WELL	17. GUEST LIVERY QUARTERS	25. HAY SCALE
2. TUNNEL ("SUBWAY")	10. WATER TOWER	18. WALLED GARDEN	26. ORCHARD HOUSE
3. POWER HOUSE	11. ICE HOUSE	19. TURN AROUND BASIN	27. SHORE DRIVE
4. ENGINEER'S HOUSE	12. FLORAL GREENHOUSES	20. GARDEN GREEN HOUSES	28. EAGLE HOUSE
5. COACH HOUSE	13. ENGINEER'S TOOL HOUSE	21. COAL PACKETS	29. ASH PIT
6. CEMETERY	14. PALM HOUSE	22. LAUNDRY	30. TURN BRIDGE
7. WEST GATE LODGE	15. BOWLING ALLEY	23. DOCK & BOAT HOUSE	31. TEA HOUSE
8. FENCE	16. MAZE	24. BASS HOLE	32. GAME PEN

Christopher Rhinelander Robert, Jr. estate, *Peperidge Hall*

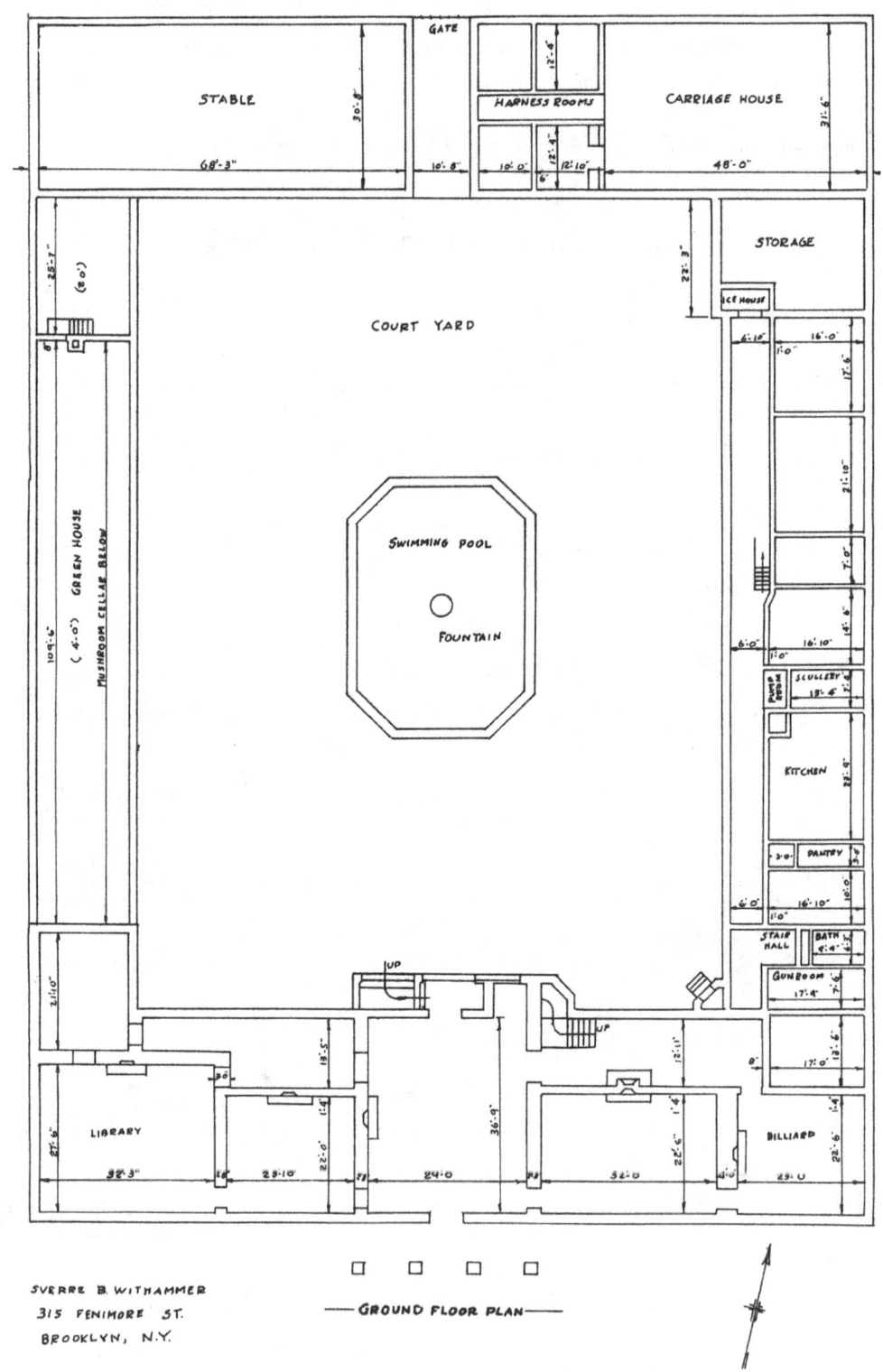

Illustration Credits

American Architect and Building News, 79, 298, 328, 331 bottom

Amityville Historical Society, 141 bottom right

Architectural Forum, 217, 239, 394 top and bottom

Architectural League of New York, 418

Architectural Record, 156 bottom, 338 middle, 339 top, 350, 352 top left, bottom right and bottom left, 353 top and bottom left

Bayport–Blue Point Heritage Association, 3, 10, 17 top, 44 bottom, 61 top, 66 top, 78 bottom, 83 bottom, 84, 85 top, 87, 98, 102, 176, 193, 208, 214 top, 215, 220, 265, 266, 270 top and bottom, 271 top and bottom, 272, 275, 278 top, 283, 284 top, 291, 292, 293, 299 bottom, 300 bottom, 306 top, 311, 314, 317, 325

Bay Shore Historical Society, 14, 48, 58, 175, 256 top, 277 top

The Brooklyn Daily Eagle, 29, 130, 153 top, 167, 286, 368 bottom

Marjorie Wilson Candiano, 245

Country Life in America, 82, 164, 236 top, 255 bottom

Elena de Murias, 73 top and bottom

Barry Dlouhy, 235

East Islip Historical Society, 47 top, middle left and bottom, 64, 108, 148, 150, 178, 190, 195, 202, 205, 212, 261 top, 263 top and bottom, 329 all, 337, 338 top right, bottom left and right, 355, 359 top, 372, 380, 442 top, 500 top

John Vanderveer Gibson, 114 top, 354

Samuel Gottscho, 421

Kate Hafels, 182 top

Harry Waldron Havemeyer, 139, 140 all

Charles F. Hayward, 144

Hicks Nursery, 258

Historic Services Suffolk County Parks Department, 117

Elizabeth Huber Howell, 158

Kingsway Realty, 182 bottom, 242 top

David Knapp, 422 top

Gary Lawrance, 379

Library of Congress, 83 top, 288, 289 top and middle, 302 bottom, 336 top and bottom, 408

Lindenhurst Historical Society, 236 bottom, 374

Philip B. Linker, 200, 326

Long Island Maritime Museum, 390 top and bottom, 416, 442 bottom, 500 bottom

Long Island Rail Road, 59, 153 bottom

Long Island Today, 86

Macy family, 209

Metropolitan Museum of Art, 422 bottom

Richard A. Milligan, 125 top, 165 top, 269, 369, 389

Multiple Listing Service, 9 top, 56, 88, 90, 94, 112, 118 bottom, 119, 149 bottom, 160, 161, 207, 213, 233, 252 bottom, 278 bottom, 287 bottom, 301 top, 309, 310 bottom, 320, 346, 356, 357, 371, 384, 469, 470 top and bottom

Illustration Credits

Museum of the City of New York, 36 top right and left

Nassau County Photo Archive Center, 20 bottom, 186, 188 top right and left, 304

National Woman Suffrage Publishing Company, 407

Noted Long Island Homes, 39, 67, 77, 128, 338 top left

Pictorial Bay Shore and Vicinity: A Souvenir, 5, 17, 50, 57, 60, 109, 110 bottom, 123 top, 131, 135, 157, 159 top, 169, 173, 183, 198, 206, 216, 218, 226, 228 top, 241 bottom, 253 bottom, 264, 287 top, 296, 342 top, 344 bottom, 345 top, 383

Picturesque Babylon, Bay Shore and Islip, 54 top, 93, 306 bottom, 385

Helena Parsons Hallock Pless, 129, 250, 251 top and bottom

Sayville Public Library, 143 top, 180, 247 top, 273, 307 bottom, 375

South Side Signal, 26, 40 top

Raymond E. Spinzia, 1, 2, 4, 6, 7 bottom, 12 top and bottom, 13, 15, 18, 22, 23, 28, 32, 33, 34, 36 middle and bottom right and left, 40, 41, 43, 44 top, 46 bottom, 47 middle right, 49, 51, 53, 61 bottom, 62, 65, 66 bottom, 68, 71, 74, 75, 76, 78 top, 81, 85 bottom, 91, 92, 99, 100, 103, 105, 106, 110 top, 111, 113, 114 bottom, 116, 118 top, 120, 121, 123 bottom, 124, 125 bottom, 126, 132, 134, 136, 137, 138, 143 bottom, 145 bottom, 146, 149 top, 154, 156 top, 165 bottom, 168, 171, 172, 177, 184, 185, 187, 188 middle and bottom right and left, 203 bottom, 210, 211, 214 bottom, 221, 223 top and bottom, 225 top and bottom, 229 top and bottom, 230, 232, 240, 241 top, 242 bottom, 243, 244, 246, 247 bottom, 248, 252 top, 253 top, 255 top, 257, 259, 261 bottom, 277 bottom, 279, 284 bottom, 285, 290, 294, 297, 299 top, 301 bottom, 302 top, 303, 307 top, 310 top, 313, 318, 319, 322 bottom, 330, 331 top, 332 top and bottom, 333, 334, 335, 339 bottom, 340, 342 bottom, 343 top, 344 top, 349, 351, 352 top right, 353 top right, middle and bottom right, 361 bottom, 363, 367, 370 top and bottom, 377, 382, 386, 388, 392 top and bottom, 402 top and bottom, 417 top and bottom, 441 both, 456, 458 top and bottom

Suffolk County Historical Society Museum, 238

Peter Titus, 387 top

Town and Country, 163

Town of Babylon Office of Historic Services, 7 top, 8, 21, 24, 95 bottom, 97, 122, 141 top and bottom right, 201, 260, 280 bottom, 282, 298 top, 321 top and bottom, 365

Vanderbilt Historical Society, 11, 37 top and bottom, 38 top and bottom, 72, 159 bottom, 162, 228 bottom, 316, 345 bottom, 352 middle, 368 top, 378, 478, 502, 503, 504

Van Orden Collection, Town of Islip, 147, 256 bottom, 289 bottom

Village of Babylon Historical and Preservation Society, 25, 45, 95 top, 96, 101, 115, 133, 142, 145 top, 170, 203 top, 219, 234, 280 top, 300 top, 322 top, 327, 343 bottom, 360

West Islip Historical Society, 54 bottom, 166, 315 top, 361 top, 362

Douglas Thomas Yates, Sr., 387 bottom

Bill Zantz, 46 top, 359 bottom

About the Authors

Judith Ader Spinzia is the former president of the Long Island Studies Council. She and her husband Raymond now reside in Central Pennsylvania. Their first book, *Long Island: A Guide to New York's Suffolk and Nassau Counties* (New York: Hippocrene Books, 1988; 1991, revised; 2007 revised), is a standard reference book which has been used as a textbook for teaching Long Island history and can still be found in almost all public libraries and schools on Long Island.

The Spinzias write and speak, jointly and separately, on a variety of Long Island-related subjects including the North and South Shore estates, Tiffany stained-glass windows, and the Vanderbilts of Long Island. On several occasions their lectures have been chosen by the radio station of *The New York Times*, WQXR, as the cultural event of the day in the New York Metropolitan area. Additionally, they have been featured on local television and radio programs and in articles published by *The New York Times, Newsday*, and other regional newspapers.

The Spinzias served as Long Island history consultants for a local cable television channel that, in an effort to encourage local interest, aired material from their guidebook twice daily. They also were consultants for a Japanese television network for a documentary on Louis Comfort Tiffany and contributed material to the Arts and Entertainment Network's "Biography" series for its presentations on the Vanderbilt and Tiffany families.

Their six-volume estate era series now encompasses, in addition to this South Shore book; *Long Island's Prominent North Shore Families: Their Estates and Their Country Homes*, a two-volume work published in 2006, which was updated and expanded in 2019; *Long Island's Prominent Families in the Town of Hempstead, Their Estates and Their Country Homes*, published in 2010; *Long Island's Prominent Families in the Town of Southampton, Their Estates and Their Country Homes*, published in 2010; and *Long Island's Prominent Families in the Town of East Hampton, Their Estates and Their Country Homes*, published in 2020.

Ordering information and sample pages for their books can be found by visiting the Spinzias' website www.**spinzialongislandestates.com.**

www.ingramcontent.com/pod-product-compliance
Lightning Source LLC
Chambersburg PA
CBHW080923020526
44114CB00043B/2440